PEARSON CUSTOM LIBRARY

Selections from Anthropology

Anthropology 201
Cultural Anthropology
California Polytechnic State University

PEARSON

Cover Art: Art Wolfe, "Karo Tribesman and Child" Courtesy of Corbis Photography/Veer Incorporated. "Tattooed Man Holding Baby" Courtesy of Art Wolfe/Veer Incorporated. "Cheering Fans" Courtesy of Corbis Photography/Veer Incorporated. "Alaska Native Eskimo Woman in Fur Parka" Courtesy of Canopy Photography/Veer Incorporated. "Portrait of an Asian woman holding up the palm of her hand which has henna patterns on it." Courtesy of Alloy Photography/Veer Incorporated. J. Rufenach, "Close up of man's face with lip ring" Courtesy of J. Rufenach/Veer Incorporated. Malcolm S. Kirk, "Mendi woman, New Guinea" Courtesy of Malcolm S. Kirk/Veer Incorporated. Grant Faint, "Karo tribe woman, portrait, close up" Courtesy of Grant Faint/Getty Images, Inc. Evolution of Man, Courtesy of James W. Porter/Corbis. Doctor treating boy in Ghana, Courtesy of Mika/Corbis. Tunichil Muknai, Belize (photo of skull), courtesy of Steven Alvarez/Getty Images. Girl with chimpanzee, portrait, Courtesy of Megan Lorenz/Getty Images. Additional images courtesy of Photodisc/Getty Images and Nova Development Corporation.

Attention Bookstores: For permission to return any unsold stock, contact *us at pe-uscustomreturns@pearson.com.*

Pearson Learning Solutions, 501 Boylston Street, Suite 900, Boston, MA 02116
A Pearson Education Company
www.pearsoned.com

Printed in the United States of America
V0UD

ISBN 10: 1-256-58670-6
ISBN 13: 978-1-256-58670-8

Table of Contents

What is Anthropology?

PREVIEW

- What are the core concepts of anthropology?
- How does anthropology overlap with other fields?
- What two perspectives do anthropologists use to study cultures?
- What is globalization? How can the concepts of culture contact and culture change help us understand globalization?
- What are the four subfields of anthropology? How is the study of culture integrated into each subfield?
- How is cultural relativism different from ethical relativism?
- What is applied anthropology? What contributions can applied anthropologists offer other fields?

Gallup Inter Tribal Indian Ceremonial; Gallup New Mexico Every August Gallup plays host to Native Americans from across the United States in a massive Inter-tribal ceremonial. *Chuck Place/Alamy*

Listen to the Chapter Audio on myanthrolab.com

Read on myanthrolab.com

There were villagers at the Middle Place and a girl had her home there . . . where she kept a flock of turkeys.

At the Middle Place they were having a Yaaya Dance . . . and during the first day this girl . . . stayed with her turkeys taking care of them. . . . [I]t seems she didn't go to the dance on the first day, that day she fed her turkeys . . . and so the dance went on and she could hear the drum.

When she spoke to her turkeys about this, they said, "If you went it wouldn't turn out well: who would take care of us?" That's what her turkeys told her.

She listened to them and they slept through the night.

Then it was the second day of the dance and . . . with the Yaaya Dance half over she spoke to her big tom turkey:

"My father-child, if they're going to do it again tomorrow why can't I go?" she said. "Well if you went, it wouldn't turn out well." That's what he told her. "Well then I mustn't go."

. . . The next day was a nice warm day, and again she heard the drum over there.

Then she went around feeding her turkeys, and when it was the middle of the day, she asked again, right at noon. "If you went, it wouldn't turn out well . . . our lives depend on your thoughtfulness," that's what the turkeys told her.

"Well then, that's the way it will be," she said, and she listened to them.

But around sunset the drum could be heard, and she was getting more anxious to go. . . .

She went up on her roof and she could see the crowd of people. It was the third day of the dance.

That night she asked the same one she asked before and he told her, "Well, if you must go, then you must dress well. . . .

"You must think of us, for if you stay all afternoon, until sunset, then it won't turn out well for you," he told her. . . .

The next day the sun was shining, and she went among her turkeys and . . . when she had fed them she said, "My fathers, my children, I'm going to the Middle Place. I'm going to the dance," she said. "Be on your way, but think of us. . . ." That's what her children told her.

She went to where the place was, and when she entered the plaza . . . , she went down and danced, and she didn't think about her children.

Finally it was mid-day, and . . . she was just dancing away until it was late, the time when the shadows are very long.

The turkeys said, "Our mother, our child doesn't know what's right."

"Well then, I must go and I'll just warn her and come right back and whether she hears me or not, we'll leave before she gets here," that's what the turkey said, and he flew . . . along until he came to where they were dancing, and there he glided down to the place and . . . sang,

"Kyana tok tok Kyana tok tok."

The one who was dancing heard him.

He flew back to the place where they were penned, and the girl ran all the way back. When she got to the place where they were penned, they sang again, they sang and flew away. . . .

When she came near they all went away and she couldn't catch up to them.

Long ago, this was lived. . . .

"The Girl Who Took Care of the Turkeys" is a Zuni narrative. A Native American people who live in what is now New Mexico, Zunis traditionally supported themselves by farming. They also kept domesticated turkeys, whose feathers they used to make ceremonial gear. In the story, the young girl uses kin terms when addressing the turkeys to indicate her close bonds with them.

You may have noticed similarities between this Zuni story and the European story of Cinderella. In both, the central character is a young woman who wants to go to a dance but is at first dissuaded or, in Cinderella's case, prevented from doing so. Eventually, she does attend, but is warned that she must be sure to return home early. In both stories, the girl stays past the appointed time because she is enjoying herself. The Zuni and European stories, however, differ in both outcomes and details.

The European folk-tale *Cinderella* has been retold countless times. In this musical version by Rodgers and Hammerstein, the cast includes Brandy, Whitney Houston, and Whoopi Goldberg. Everett Collection/Walt Disney Television/Everett Collection

The similarities and differences between these stories are no coincidence. Zunis first learned the Cinderella story from white settlers in the 1880s and transformed the tale to fit their circumstances, values, and way of life. This is an example of *selective borrowing* that takes place when members of different cultures meet, share experiences, and learn from one another. Global influences have accelerated borrowing over the last five centuries.

The Zunis reverse the ethical standing of the story's characters. Cinderella, who yearns to go to the ball, is a virtuous and long-suffering servant to her wicked family. The Zuni girl is also a caretaker for her family, the flock of turkeys (whom she significantly addresses as "father" and "child"), but she is not a figure of virtue. On the contrary, to go to the dance, she has to neglect her duties, threatening the turkeys' well-being, as they say to her, "You must think of us."

And what happens? Cinderella marries the prince and emerges triumphant, but disaster befalls the Zuni girl. The European story of individual virtue and fortitude rewarded has become a Zuni story of moral failing and irresponsibility to one's relatives and dependents.

The differences between Europeans and Zunis fit into a constellation of features that define Zuni and European culture—the languages they speak, how they feed and shelter themselves, what they wear, the material goods they value, how they make those goods and distribute them among themselves, how they form families, households, and alliances, and how they worship the deities they believe in. This concept—culture—is central to the discipline of anthropology in general and to cultural anthropology.

THE STUDY OF HUMANITY

Anthropology, broadly defined, is the study of humanity, from its evolutionary origins millions of years ago to its present worldwide diversity. Many other disciplines, of course, also focus on one aspect or another of humanity. Like sociology, economics, political science, psychology, and other behavioral and social sciences, anthropology is concerned with how people organize their lives and relate to one another in interacting, interconnected groups—**societies**—that share basic beliefs and practices. Like economists, anthropologists are interested in society's material foundations—how people produce and distribute food and other goods. Like sociologists, anthropologists are interested in how people structure their relations in society—in families, at work, in institutions. Like political scientists, anthropologists are interested in power and authority: who has them and how they are allocated. And, like psychologists, anthropologists are interested in individual development and the interaction between society and individual people.

Also, anthropologists share an interest in human evolution and human anatomy with those in the biological sciences. They share an interest in the past of peoples and communities with historians. As the discussion of the Zuni story that opens this chapter suggests, they share an interest in how people express themselves with students of literature, art, and music. And they are interested in the diversity of human philosophical systems, ethical systems, and religious beliefs.

anthropology
The study of humanity, from its evolutionary origins millions of years ago to its current worldwide diversity.

societies
Populations of people living in organized groups with social institutions and expectations of behavior.

Cultural anthropologists seek to explain people's thoughts and behaviors in terms of their culture or way of life. Jane Goodall Research Center USC Los Angeles/Craig Stanford/Jane Goodall Research Center

Although anthropology shares many interests with other disciplines, the following key features distinguish it as a separate area of study:

- A focus on the concept of culture
- A holistic perspective
- A comparative perspective

These features are the source of anthropology's insights into both common humanity and the diversity with which that humanity is expressed.

The Concept of Culture

Anthropology is unique in its focus on the role of **culture** in shaping human behavior. We can define culture as the learned values, beliefs, and rules of conduct shared to some extent by the members of a society and that govern their behavior with one another and how they think about themselves and the world. Culture can be broadly divided into **symbolic culture**—people's ideas and means of communicating those ideas—and **material culture**—the tools, utensils, clothing, housing, and other objects that people make or use.

culture
The learned values, beliefs, and rules of conduct that are shared to some extent by the members of a society, and that govern their behavior with one another.

symbolic culture
The ideas people have about themselves, others, and the world, and the ways that people express these ideas.

material culture
The tools people make and use, the clothing and ornaments they wear, the buildings they live in, and the household utensils they use.

holistic perspective
A perspective in anthropology that views culture as an integrated whole, no part of which can be completely understood without considering the whole.

A Holistic Perspective

Unlike other behavioral and social sciences, anthropology views cultures from a **holistic perspective**—as an integrated whole, no part of which can be completely understood in isolation. How people arrange rooms in their homes, for example, is related to their marriage and family patterns, which in turn are related to how they earn a living. Thus, the single-family home with individual bedrooms that became the norm in America's suburbs in the twentieth century reflects the value Americans place on individualism and the nuclear family—husband, wife, and their children. These values, in turn, are consistent with an economy in which families are dependent on wage earners acting individually and competitively to find employment. Thus, a holistic perspective that considers the interconnections among factors that contribute to people's behavior helps us understand the kinds of homes in which they live.

Anthropologists, then, attempt to understand all aspects of human culture, past and present. They are interested in people's economic lives and in learning about the food they eat, how they obtain their food, and how they organize their work. They also study people's political lives to know how they organize their communities, select their leaders, and make group decisions. And they investigate people's social lives to understand how they organize their families—whom they marry and live with, and to whom they consider themselves related. Anthropologists also study people's religious lives to learn about the kinds of deities they worship, their beliefs about the spirit world, and the ceremonies they perform.

Anthropologists understand that cultural norms and values guide but do not dictate people's behavior. They also know that people often idealize their own practices, projecting beliefs about what they do even though their actual behavior may differ from those ideals. For example, when workers are asked about their job responsibilities, they may talk about official procedures and regulations even though their daily work is more flexible and unpredictable.

The ubiquity of electronic music developed in Japan and Korea is an example of global cultural exchange. AP Photos/Aijaz Rahi/AP Images

A Comparative Perspective

The juxtaposition of the Cinderella story and the Zuni narrative of "The Girl Who Took Care of the Turkeys" is a small example of anthropology's comparative perspective at work. Comparing the two stories opens a window onto the contrasting values of Zuni and European cultures and increases our understanding of each.

Anthropology is fundamentally comparative, basing its findings on cultural data drawn from societies throughout the world and from throughout human history. Anthropologists collect data about behavior and beliefs in many societies to document the diversity of human culture and to understand common patterns in how people adapt to their environments, adjust to their neighbors, and develop unique cultural institutions. This **comparative perspective** can challenge common assumptions about human nature based solely on European or North American culture. For example, marriage and family take many different forms worldwide. Only through systematic comparison can we hope to determine what aspects of marriage and family—or any other aspect of culture, for that matter—might be universal (found in all human societies) and which aspects vary from society to society.

comparative perspective
An approach in anthropology that uses data about the behaviors and beliefs in many societies to document both cultural universals and cultural diversity.

culture change
Changes in people's ways of life over time through both internal and external forces.

globalization
The spread of economic, political, and cultural influences throughout a very large geographic area or through a great number of different societies. Through globalization, many countries and local communities are enmeshed in networks of power and influence far beyond their borders, exchanging goods and services, forms of entertainment, and information technologies.

The Comparative Perspective and Culture Change. The comparative, or "cross-cultural," perspective also helps people reexamine their own culture. Cultures are not static. They change in response to internal and external pressures. Anthropology's comparative perspective is a powerful tool for understanding **culture change**. Because this concept is so important, each subsequent chapter of this textbook contains a special feature on culture change.

The Comparative Perspective and Globalization. The comparative perspective also allows anthropologists to evaluate the impact of globalization. **Globalization** is the spread of economic, political, and cultural influences across a large geographic area or many different societies. Through globalization, many countries and communities are enmeshed in networks of power and influence that extend far beyond their borders, exchanging goods and services, forms of entertainment, and information technologies. Although all countries can contribute to globalization in principle, dominant countries have more control over the flow of goods and services and exert more influence over other societies in practice. However, no one country or region of the world currently controls the process of globalizing. Rather, many powerful countries contribute to globalization.

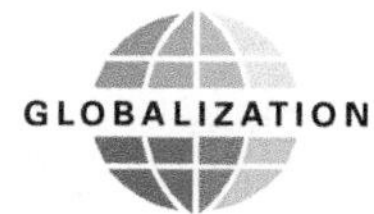

Culture contact and culture change, such as occurred between the Europeans and Zuni, underlie the phenomenon of globalization.

Globalization has occurred in the past when states and empires expanded their influence far beyond their borders. However, one of the distinctions of globalization today is the speed with which it is transforming local cultures as they participate in a worldwide system of interconnected economies and polities. These influences are also changing other aspects of culture, including family structures, religious practices, and aesthetic forms. Along with the export of products and technologies, rapid communications and information systems also spread attitudes and values throughout the world, including capitalist cultural practices, consumerism, cultural icons, and media and entertainment. Finally, globalization is uneven, both in the degree to which goods and services are exchanged in different places and in the way it creates inequalities as well as similarities.

Culture change is not, however, a recent phenomenon. Cultures are not and never were static systems. Indeed, changes in beliefs and practices help to strengthen societies and to endow them with the resilience to survive. Therefore, change and stability are not opposite processes. They depend on one another.

What signs of globalization do you see in your immediate surroundings—for example, in your clothes, cars, and information or communications technologies?

Anthropology focuses on the study of all aspects of being human. It has many concepts and subjects in common with other behavioral and social sciences, and with biological sciences. Core concepts include culture, culture change, and globalization. Three characteristics differentiate anthropology from other fields: the concept of culture, the holistic perspective, and the comparative perspective.

THE FOUR SUBFIELDS OF ANTHROPOLOGY

Almost since it emerged as an academic discipline in the late nineteenth century, anthropology in North America has encompassed four subfields, each with its own focus, methodologies, and theories: cultural anthropology, linguistic anthropology, archaeology, and

FIGURE 1
Subfields of Anthropology

Watch the **Animation:** *The Fields of Anthropology* on **myanthrolab.com**

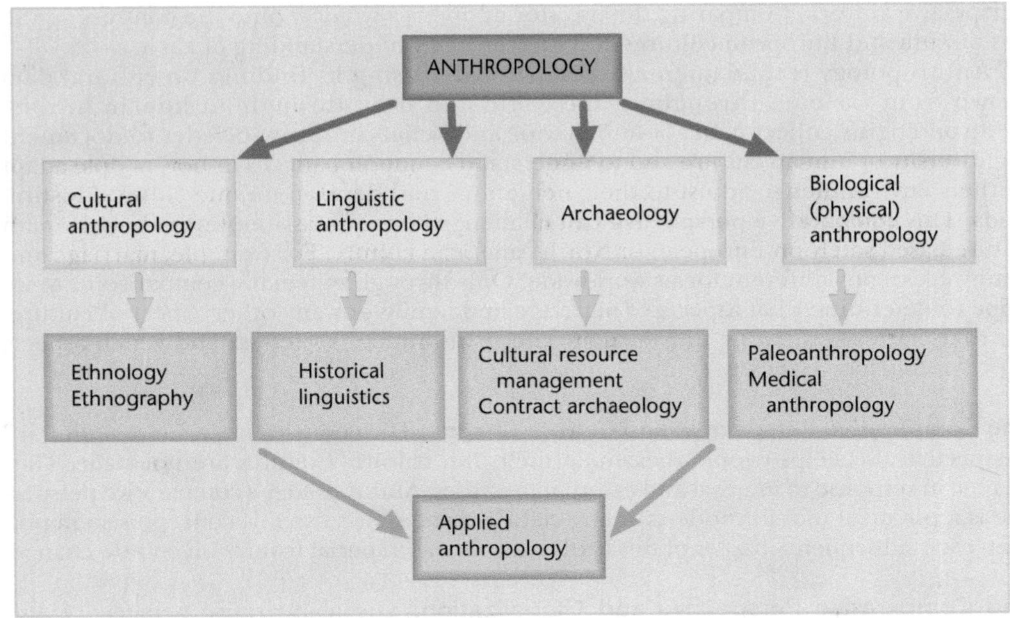

biological (or physical) anthropology. Each subfield also has branches or interest areas (see Figure 1). Table 1 identifies some of the many kinds of work anthropologists perform.

Cultural Anthropology

Cultural anthropology is, as the term implies, the study of culture—that is, the study of cultural behavior, attitudes, values, and conceptions of the world. The work of cultural anthropologists centers on **ethnology,** developing theories to explain cultural processes based on the comparative study of societies throughout the world. The method they use to gather these data is called **ethnography,** a holistic, intensive study of groups through observation, interview, participation, and analysis.

cultural anthropology
The study of cultural behavior, especially the comparative study of living and recent human cultures.

ethnology
Aspect of cultural anthropology involved with building theories about cultural behaviors and forms.

ethnography
Aspect of cultural anthropology involved with observing and documenting peoples' ways of life.

indigenous societies
Peoples who are now minority groups in state societies but who were formerly independent and have occupied their territories for a long time.

To conduct ethnographic research, anthropologists do "fieldwork"; that is, they live among the people they are studying to compile a full record of their activities. They learn about people's behaviors, beliefs, and attitudes. They study how they make their living, obtain their food, and supply themselves with tools, equipment, and other products. They study how families and communities are organized, and how people form clubs or associations, discuss common interests, make group decisions, and resolve disputes. And they investigate the relationship between the people and larger social institutions—the nations they are part of and their place in the local, regional, and global economies.

Collecting ethnographic information is a significant part of the preservation of indigenous cultures. It contributes to the fund of comparative data cultural anthropologists use to address questions about human cultural diversity.

In anthropology's early years, cultural anthropologists primarily studied non-Western societies, particularly traditional, **indigenous societies**—peoples who were once independent and have occupied their territories for a long time but are now usually minority groups in larger states. These early researchers favored societies in regions of the world that the West's expanding influence had left relatively unaffected or, like the native societies of southern Africa or North and South America, had been overwhelmed and transformed by conquest. The idea was that a small, comparatively homogeneous society could serve as a kind of laboratory for understanding humanity. Over the years, cultural anthropologists have challenged this view, however, and globalization has all but ended cultural isolation. Today, cultural anthropologists are likely to do an ethnographic study of, say, a small town in the American Midwest,

TABLE 1 CAREER OPPORTUNITIES IN THE FOUR SUBFIELDS OF ANTHROPOLOGY

Field	Definition	Examples
Cultural Anthropology	The study of human culture	Ethnographer Ethnologist Museum curator University or college professor International business consultant Cross-cultural researcher
Linguistic Anthropology	The study of language	International business consultant Diplomatic communications worker Administrator Ethnographer Domestic communications worker University or college professor
Archaeology	The study of past cultures	Cultural resource management worker Museum curator University or college professor State archaeologist Historical archaeologist Zoo archaeologist Environmental consultant
Biological (Physical) Anthropology	The study of human origins and biological diversity	Primatologist Geneticist University or college professor Medical researcher Genetic counselor Forensic specialist Government investigator Human rights investigator Biomedical anthropologist

Somali refugees adapting to life in Minnesota, Americans participating in a hospice program, changing political systems in Afghanistan, or life in a prison.

Two important concepts—ethnocentrism and cultural relativism—influence the anthropological approach to ethnography and cross-cultural research. **Ethnocentrism** refers to the tendency for people to see themselves metaphorically as being at the center of the universe. They perceive their own culture's way of doing things (making a living, raising children, governing, worshipping) as normal and natural and that of others as strange and possibly inferior or even unnatural or inhuman. Of course, it seems like common sense to acknowledge that people feel more comfortable in their own social and cultural milieu, engaging in familiar and routine activities. Ethnocentrism is only dangerous when it is used to justify either verbal or physical attacks against other people. Governments, for example, often ethnocentrically justify their economic and military dominance over other peoples by claiming the natural superiority of their culture. The ancient Romans, Chinese, Aztecs, Incas, and others similarly held themselves superior to the people they conquered. This tendency to view one's

ethnocentrism
The widespread human tendency to perceive the ways of doing things in one's own culture as normal and natural and that of others as strange, inferior, and possibly even unnatural or inhuman.

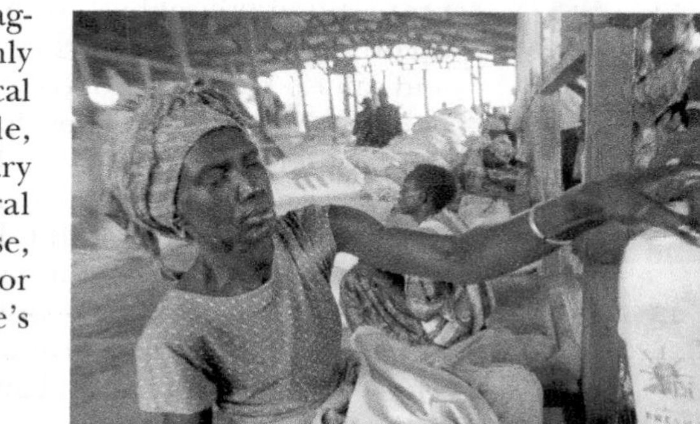

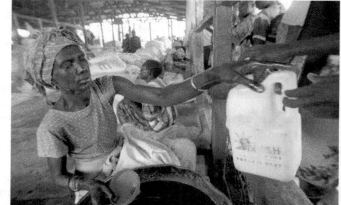

Cultural anthropologists study how refugees like these Somali Bantu adapt to American life and how American communities adapt to refugees. Zuma Press/David Waters/ZUMA Press

CONTROVERSIES

What Are the Limits of Cultural Relativism?

The controversial practice of female genital mutilation (FGM) or female circumcision, prevalent in twenty-eight countries in Africa and found in other regions as well, illustrates the uneasy relationship between cultural relativism and concern for individual human rights. FGM removes part or all of the external genitals of prepubescent girls. The procedure varies but usually entails the removal of the clitoris. In some areas, particularly in southern Egypt, Sudan, Somalia, Ethiopia, and Mali, it also includes *infibulation*—the stitching closed—of the vagina, leaving only a tiny opening for the passage of urine and menstrual blood. The United Nations Division for the Advancement of Women suggests that at least 100 million women living today have been subjected to FGM, whereas the World Health Organization (WHO) puts the number at more than 132 million women and girls in Africa alone, estimating also that about 2 million procedures are performed annually (Ras-Work 2006; Almroth et al. 2005). Although FGM is now sometimes performed in hospitals, local midwives usually perform the procedure, working with crude tools and without anesthesia on girls who are typically between 5 and 11 years old.

The two most common names by which the practice is known—female genital mutilation and female circumcision—reflect opposing attitudes toward it. Calling the practice *female circumcision* equates it with male circumcision, which is also debated but more widely accepted. The term *female genital mutilation* was introduced by the United Nations Inter-African Committee (IAC) on Traditional Practices Affecting the Health of Women and Children, a group established to help end the practice. This term reflects "the cruel and radical operation so many young girls are forced to undergo" involving "the removal of healthy organs" (Armstrong 1991, 42).

Although its exact origin is unknown, FGM predates both Christianity and Islam, and occurs among peoples of both faiths and among followers of traditional African religions. It is most common, however, in predominantly Islamic regions of Africa and is associated with strongly patriarchal cultures—that is, cultures that stress the subordination of women to male authority.

Medical risks for girls undergoing the procedure reportedly include pain, shock, loss of bladder and bowel control, and potentially fatal infections and hemorrhaging (Gruenbaum 1993). Infibulation in particular can have serious, painful, long-term consequences. Defenders of the procedure claim that there is no reliable evidence of its increasing a girl's risk of death or of excessive rates of medical complication. Opponents claim that FGM reduces a woman's capacity for sexual pleasure and that infibulation makes sexual intercourse and childbirth painful.

Groups who practice FGM defend it on cultural grounds. In their view, infibulation helps ensure a woman's premarital chastity and her sexual fidelity to her husband while increasing his sexual pleasure. Some prominent African women, such as Fuambai Ahmadu, an anthropologist from Sierra Leone, defend the practice. On the basis of her research, Ahmadu (2000, 304–05) views it as an emotionally positive validation of womanhood. In her interviews, African women reported that the practice did not diminish their sexual drive, inhibit sexual activity, or prevent sexual satisfaction, and that it did not adversely affect their health or birthing. The women looked forward to carrying on the tradition and initiating their younger female relatives into the pride of womanhood. Other local observers, such as Olayinka Koso-Thomas (1992),

---

own cultural norms as superior to others was also prevalent in European colonialism in modern-day imperialist ventures.

Watch the **Video:** *Relativity* on **myanthrolab.com**

In the nineteenth and early twentieth centuries, many Europeans assumed they represented the highest form of civilization, and ranked other societies beneath them according to how closely they approached middle-class European appearance, practices, and values. Early anthropologists, hardly immune to this pervasive ethnocentrism, developed evolutionary schemes that ranked people on a scale of progress from "savagery" to "civilization," with middle- and upper-class Europeans at the top.

cultural relativism
An approach in anthropology that stresses the importance of analyzing cultures in each culture's own terms rather than in terms of the culture of the anthropologist. This does not mean, however, that all cultural behavior must be condoned.

To counter the influence of ethnocentrism, cultural anthropologists try to approach cultures from the viewpoint of **cultural relativism.** That is, they try to analyze a culture in terms of that culture, rather than in terms of the anthropologist's culture. This principle is central to cultural anthropology. For example, in the nineteenth century, native peoples of the Pacific Northwest of North America engaged in rituals, called potlatches, which included feasting and giveaways of large amounts of food and personal and ceremonial property. Missionaries and officials in the United States and Canada considered these activities harmful, wasteful, and illogical because they contradicted Euro-American values that stress the importance of accumulating and saving wealth rather than giving away or destroying wealth. But anthropologists came to understand the economic and social a physician from Sierra Leone, oppose the practice for its brutality, its dangerous consequences, and its role in perpetuating the subordination of women.

Some anthropologists, citing cultural relativism and the ideal of objectivity, do not support outside organizations that pressure African, Middle Eastern, and Indonesian governments to abolish FGM. Although they don't condone the procedure, they prefer to hope for change from within. Other anthropologists point out that, although cultural relativism may help us understand a culture on its own terms, it can also help us understand how cultural beliefs reinforce inequalities by convincing people to accept practices that may be harmful and demeaning as natural.

Recent medical studies indicate multiple harmful effects of FGM. Research carried out by the World Health Organization (WHO) in six African countries concluded that, compared to women who have not had FGM, ". . . deliveries to women who have undergone FGM are significantly more likely to be complicated by cesarean section, postpartum hemorrhage, tearing of the vaginal wall, extended maternal hospital stay, and inpatient perinatal death [infant mortality]" (WHO 2006, 1835). The study was conducted in hospitals, and outcomes for women who give birth at home might be even more negative because emergency medical treatment would not be available. Another medical study of women in Sudan reported that women who had undergone the most extensive types of FGM were the most likely to be infertile (Almroth et al. 2005, 390). Because fertility in women is highly valued, particularly in patriarchal cultures, the finding that FGM is a significant cause of infertility might be an effective argument against the procedure.

Many anthropologists, together with health workers, women's rights advocates, and human rights organizations, oppose FGM and are working to end it, with some success. In 1995, a United Nations–sponsored Conference on the Status of Women declared FGM to be a violation of human rights. In 1996, the U.S. Board of Immigration Appeals, ruling that FGM is a form of persecution, granted political asylum to a young woman from Togo who feared returning to her native country because she would be forced to undergo the procedure as a prelude to her arranged marriage (Dugger 1996, A1, B2).

In response to campaigns against FGM, sixteen African governments have outlawed it, and others have taken steps to limit its severity and improve the conditions under which it is performed (Ras-Work 2006, 10). These initiatives have not eradicated FGM. Still, recent reports indicate that some women who specialize in the procedure have decided not to continue performing it. For example, a grassroots organization called Womankind Kenya has persuaded influential practitioners to join their cause. Among the arguments they use are teachings from the Koran that some imams interpret as opposing FGM (Lacey 2004). The Inter-African Committee of the United Nations is also organizing around the issues of religion, sponsoring conferences of Muslim and Christian religious leaders to speak out against FGM (Ras-Work 2006). Outreach programs are also training practitioners in other work, and are promoting messages about women's worthiness and the value of their bodies.

CRITICAL THINKING QUESTIONS

Are there universal human rights? Who defines those rights? What are the benefits and risks of intervening in other people's ways of life?

significance of potlatches to the native peoples. Potlatches effectively redistributed food and other goods to all members of a community. These displays of generosity also raised the social standing of the hosts because generosity, not accumulation, was a valued trait.

Although cultural anthropologists usually take for granted the need to embrace cultural relativism in their work, there is debate about the extent to which it is possible to apply the principle. Anthropologists, like everyone else, are products of their own society. No matter how objective they try to be, their own cultural experience inevitably colors how they analyze and interpret the behavior of people in other cultures. Anthropologists need to acknowledge the potential effect of their own attitudes and values on the kinds of research problems they formulate and how they interpret other people's behavior.

Globalization has included the spread of Western beliefs and values codified as laws on human rights.

Although cultural relativism requires anthropologists to try to understand other cultures on each culture's terms, it does not require them to abandon their own ethical standards or to condone oppressive practices. Cultural relativism, in other words, is not the same as **ethical relativism,** the acceptance of all ethical systems as equivalent to each other. Nevertheless, anthropologists have different views on the applicability of cultural and ethical relativism, as the Controversies feature illustrates. This is, and no doubt will continue to be, a topic of disagreement and controversy within the field.

ethical relativism
The belief that all rights and wrongs are relative to time, place, and culture, such that no moral judgments of behavior can be made.

With the spread of English and other languages of business, globalization has endangered native languages as well as the ways of life those languages express.

Do you use words among friends that you would never use in a job interview, in class, or with children? What does your use of language reveal about your relationships to the people you address?

historical linguistics
The study of changes in language and communication over time and between peoples in contact.

linguistic anthropology
The study of language and communication, and the relationship between language and other aspects of culture and society.

Linguistic Anthropology

Linguistics, the study of language, is a separate academic discipline independent of anthropology. However, language is a key concern of anthropology. Not only is it a defining feature of all cultures, language is also the primary means by which we express culture and transmit it from one generation to the next.

Linguistic anthropology shares with linguistics an interest in the nature of language itself, but with an added focus on the interconnections among language, culture, and society. To gain insight into social categories, for example, linguistic anthropologists might investigate how people use language in different social contexts. Do people use a formal style of speech in one situation and an informal style in another? Do they vary words, pronunciation, and grammar in different social contexts? Do they speak differently to relatives and nonrelatives, friends and strangers, males and females, children and adults?

Some linguistic anthropologists study the languages of indigenous peoples to document their grammars and vocabularies. This is critical work because increasing globalization has led to the worldwide advancement of English and other languages of business, often to the detriment of local languages. In their attempts to keep pace with the new world order, and under pressure from globalizing economic and political forces, native peoples are losing their traditions, and their languages are becoming extinct.

Many indigenous peoples are under pressure to abandon their own languages and adopt the official languages of the countries in which they find themselves. For example, in the United States and Canada, many indigenous languages have only a few speakers because of the intense pressures on native peoples to use English or French in place of their own languages. These social and political factors began under European colonialism, but they have continued in Canada and the United States. However, dozens of programs run by indigenous Americans and Canadians, and assisted by linguists, are now documenting and teaching indigenous languages so that they can be maintained and revitalized.

Linguistic anthropologists also document how language changes over time within a culture. And they are witnesses to how the expanding influence of a few globally spoken languages has reduced the number of indigenous languages spoken in the world. Endangered languages include Western languages as well, such as Gaelic (in both Scotland and Ireland), Breton (spoken in France), and Yiddish.

Other linguistic anthropologists specialize in **historical linguistics.** Their work is based on the premise that people who speak related languages are culturally and historically related, descended from a common ancestral people. By looking at the relationships among languages in a large area, historical linguists can help determine how people have migrated to arrive in the territories they now occupy. For example, the Apaches in New Mexico, the Navajos in Arizona, and the Hupas of northern California all speak related languages, which are, in turn, related to a family of languages known as Athabascan. Most Athabascan speakers occupy a large area of western Canada and Alaska. These linguistic ties suggest that the Hupas, Navajos and Apaches are all descended from Athabascan groups that migrated south from Canada.

By studying how people have borrowed words and grammatical patterns from other languages, historical linguists can also gain insight into how groups have interacted over time. Combined with archaeological evidence, these kinds of analyses can produce a rich picture of the historical relationship among peoples who otherwise left no written records, contributing to our understanding of the processes of culture change.

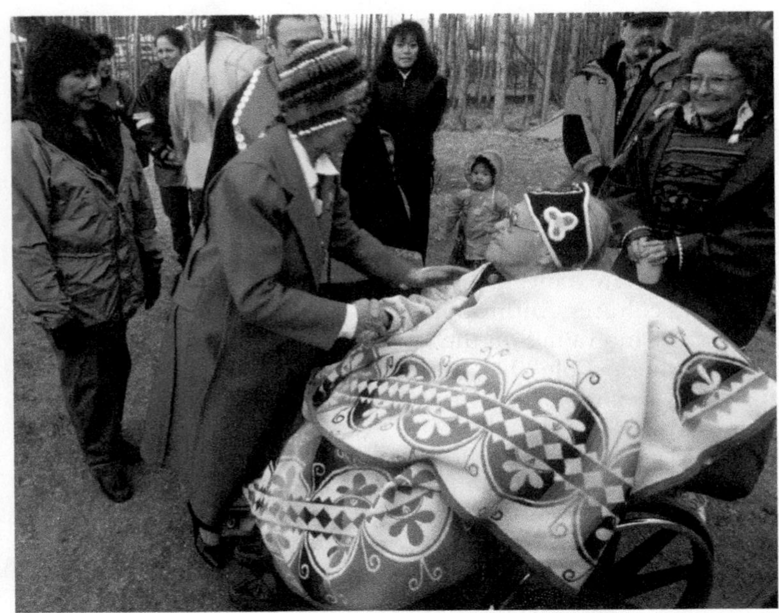

When she died in 2008, Marie Smith Jones was the last speaker of Eyak, a Na-Dene language of Alaska. Newscom/Erik Hill/MCT/Newscom

In Their Own VOICES

Why Save Our Languages

In this excerpt, Richard Littlebear describes some of the reasons that his Native Cheyenne language is threatened with loss and suggests some ways to keep it from dying. Littlebear is a member of the Cheyenne nation and a teacher of the Cheyenne language.

Why save our languages, since they now seem to have no political, economic, or global relevance? That is exactly the reason why we should save our languages, because it is the spiritual relevance deeply embedded in our languages that makes them relevant to us as American Indians today.

If we just spoke them, all of our languages would be healthier; but that is not what's happening. We do not speak our languages, and our languages are dying. We are also confronted with a voracious language, English, that gobbles up everything in its way.

The Cheyenne people began making the change to a different type of culture and to a written language about a century ago. Those of us who speak the Cheyenne language are quite possibly the last generation able to joke in our own language.

A second idea is that language is the basis of sovereignty. We have all the attributes that constitute sovereign nations: a governance structure, law and order, jurisprudence, literature, a land base, spiritual and sacred practices, and that one attribute that holds all of these others together—our languages.

A third idea is that of protocol in the language used in ceremonies. The dilemma is that the people who have the right to use that vocabulary and language, and who have done the rituals, are dying. The loss of this specialized language will become a major obstacle in retaining the full richness of our languages and cultures.

We need to make our children see our languages and cultures as viable and just as valuable as anything they see on television, in movies, or on videos.

In closing, I want to relate an experience I had in Alaska. I met Marie Smith, the last Native speaker of the Eyak language. It was truly a profoundly moving experience for me. I felt that I was sitting in the presence of a whole universe of knowledge that could be gone in one last breath. That's how fragile that linguistic universe seemed. It was really difficult for me to stop talking to her, because I wanted to remember every moment of our encounter.

I do not want any more of our languages to have that experience of having one last speaker. I want all of our languages to last forever, to always be around to nurture our children, to bolster their identities, to perpetuate our cultures.

The Cheyenne language is my language. English is also my language. Yet it is Cheyenne that I want to use when my time is completed here on this earth and journey on to the spirit world.

(Source: Just Speak Your Language, Richard Littlebear, in Native American Voices: A Reader, third edition (eds. Susan Lobo, Steve Talbot, Traci Morris), Prentice-Hall, pp. 90–92. 2010.

CRITICAL THINKING QUESTION

How does Dune Lankard's story illustrate the perspectives that cultural anthropology can bring to the study of people and their ways of life?

Archaeology

Archaeology is the study of material culture. Its methods apply to both historic cultures, those with written records, and prehistoric cultures, those that predate the invention of writing. Archaeologists have also applied their methods to living societies, a subfield called ethnoarchaeology, with sometimes surprising results.

Unlike cultural anthropologists, who can interact with and talk to living people, archaeologists rely mostly on evidence from material culture and the sites where people lived. Such evidence includes, among many other things, the tools that people made and used, the clothing and ornaments they wore, the buildings they lived and worked in, the remains of the plants and animals they relied on, and how they buried their dead.

This kind of evidence can reveal how people lived in the past. The remains of small, temporary encampments, for example, might indicate that the people who used them foraged their food. If the encampment had a lot of stone debris, it was likely used as a workshop for making stone tools. A settlement with permanent dwellings near farmable land and irrigation canals would have been inhabited by agriculturalists.

Judging from the density of settlements and household refuse like fragments of pots, archaeologists can estimate the population of a region at a particular time. The size and distribution of dwellings in a settlement or region can reveal aspects of a

archaeology
The study of past cultures, both historic cultures with written records and prehistoric cultures that predate the invention of writing.

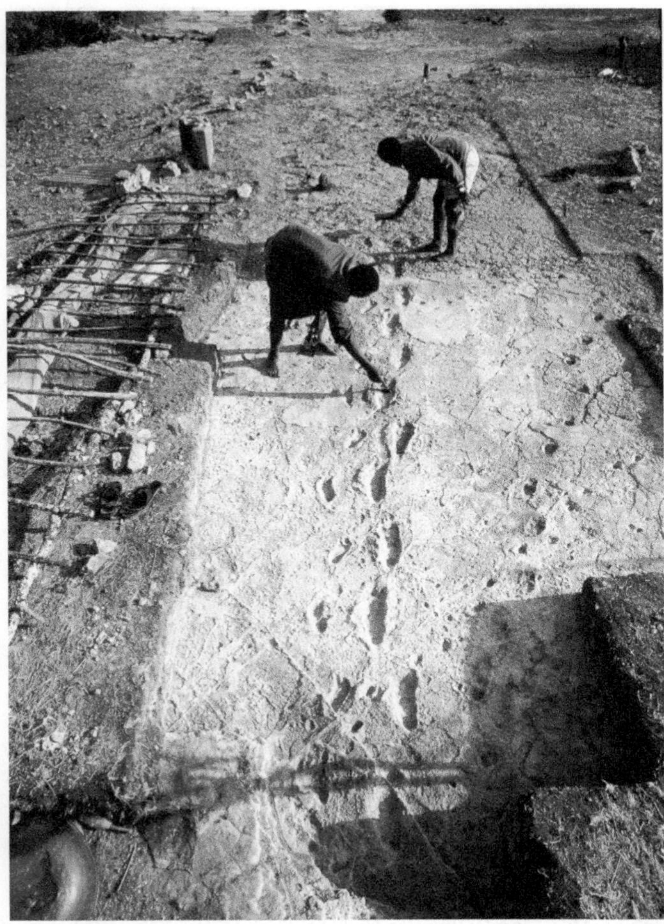

These 3.6-million-year-old tracks of hominids walking through an ashfall from a distant volcanic eruption in Tanzania are the first evidence of fully bipedal locomotion in ancient humans.
Photo Researchers/John Reader/Photo Researchers, Inc.

society's social structure. If a few of the houses in a settlement are much larger than most others, if they contain many more objects than other dwellings, especially luxury items, archaeologists can conclude that some people were wealthier than others. In contrast, if all of the houses are more or less the same size and contain similar types and amounts of possessions, archaeologists can infer that all of the people lived in more or less the same fashion and were probably of equal status.

Skeletal remains can provide similar clues to social structure. Archaeologists working at a site in Peru called Chavín de Huántar, which flourished from around 800 B.C. to 200 B.C., found evidence from skeletons that the people living close to the site's center ate better than those who lived on its margins. This evidence, combined with similar findings from other sites, suggests that Chavín society was becoming more stratified—that is, divided into classes (Burger 1992a; 1992b).

Archaeologists can also tell us about people's relationships with members of other communities. In much of the world, indigenous trading networks supplied people with goods and products not found in their own territories. Archaeologists can reconstruct these trading networks by studying the distribution of trade goods in relation to their place of origin. Similar evidence also can trace migrations, warfare, and conquest.

Written records add enormously to our understanding of the past, but they do not replace the need for archaeology. Archaeology provides a richer understanding of how people lived and worked than do documents alone. People write and keep records about what is important to them. Because the elite members of a society are usually those who are literate, the historical record is more likely to reflect their interests and points of view than that of poor and marginal people. Archaeology can help correct those biases. In 1991, construction in lower Manhattan in New York City uncovered the five-acre African Burial Ground containing the remains of 10,000 to 20,000 enslaved and free African Americans. Archaeologists were able to determine the diets, health, and causes of death of many of the people buried there, documenting the role slavery played in New York City in the early eighteenth century, a feature of urban life previously not well known (Encyclopedia of New York State 2008).

Watch the **Video:** *Being an Archaeologist* on **myanthrolab.com**

What might an analysis of refuse reveal about life in a dormitory?

Archaeological methods can help address important issues in contemporary societies. In the 1970s, the archaeologist William Rathje founded the Arizona Garbage Project to study what Americans throw away and what happens to this refuse. Rathje defined archaeology as the discipline that learns from garbage (Rathje and Murphy, 1992). Among the surprising findings, fast-food packaging actually makes up less than 1 percent of the volume of American landfills, contrary to popular opinion and the estimates of experts. Compacted paper takes up the most space.

Archaeology's great chronological depth—from humanity's origins millions of years ago to twenty-first-century landfills—makes it particularly suited to the study of culture change. Theories of culture change are one of the discipline's main concerns. For example, many archaeologists are interested in the processes that led to the first cities thousands of years ago, and with them the first states—societies with centralized governments, administrative bureaucracies, and inequalities of wealth and power.

The global spread of humans was made possible by the evolution of the capacity for culture and the development and spread of the first tool traditions.

Biological Anthropology

Biological, or **physical, anthropology** is the study of human origins and contemporary biological diversity. In the popular imagination, the study of human origins, or **paleoanthropology,** is probably the most visible face of biological anthropology.

Paleoanthropologists seek to decipher the fossil record—the usually fragmentary remains of human forebears and related animals—to understand human evolution. Paleoanthropologists have also turned to the science of genetics and the study of DNA for clues to human origins.

biological, or physical, anthropology
The study of human origins and contemporary biological diversity.

paleoanthropology
The study of the fossil record, especially skeletal remains, to understand the process and products of human evolution.

Humans are primates; we belong, in other words, to the same order of animals that includes monkeys and apes. DNA evidence indicates that we share a common ancestry with gorillas and chimpanzees—our closest living relatives—and that our evolutionary line separated from theirs in Africa between 5 million and 8 million years ago. Working from fossil evidence, paleoanthropologists are reconstructing the complex course of human evolution. They study changes in the environment in which our ancestors emerged millions of years ago to understand the adaptive benefits of the physical changes they underwent. They study the size and structure of teeth to learn about our ancestors' diets. And they study the distribution of fossils worldwide to learn how and when our ancestors migrated out of Africa and populated most of Earth.

Once humans began to create clothes, shelters, and tools appropriate for environments from the Arctic to the tropics, they no longer depended exclusively on their physical characteristics for survival. With language and more complex social organization, they could enhance group survival. Thus, paleoanthropologists are particularly interested in clues to the emergence of human culture. Here their interests and methods overlap with those of archaeologists as they excavate sites looking for evidence of early toolmaking in association with fossils.

Some physical anthropologists study nonhuman primates to gain insight into the nature of our own species. The primatologist Jane Goodall, for example, spent years observing the behavior of chimpanzees in the wild, and her discoveries about their social behavior have a bearing on the origins of our own social behavior. Goodall also found that chimpanzees can make and use rudimentary tools.

medical anthropology
A discipline that bridges cultural and biological anthropology, focusing on health and disease in human populations.

In addition to human origins and primate social behavior, physical anthropologists also study the interaction of biology, culture, and environment to understand humanity's current biological diversity. For example, the Inuit, an indigenous people of Arctic Canada, have developed ways to clothe and shelter themselves to survive in their harsh environment, but they also appear to have a greater rate of blood flow to their bodily extremities in response to cold than other people do (Itoh 1980; McElroy and Townsend 1989, 26–29). Indigenous inhabitants of the Andes Mountains in South America have a greater than average lung capacity, which is an adaptation to the low oxygen of their high-altitude environment. And people from regions rich in dairy products are genetically adapted to digest milk easily, whereas adults from regions where milk is not a traditional part of the diet are not. These lactase-deficient adults have digestive problems when they drink milk. Skin color also is in part an adaptation to climatic conditions and exposure to sun, as darker skin has a higher content of melanin, a substance that protects against overabsorption of the sun's harmful ultraviolet rays (Rensberger 2001, 83).

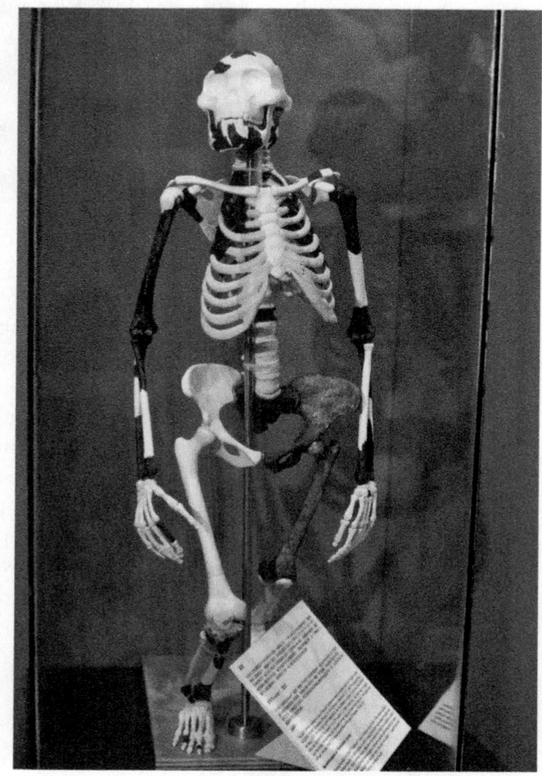

A reconstruction of "Lucy," an early hominid living some 3.2 million years ago. Newscom/ZUMA Press/Newscom

The subfield of **medical anthropology** focuses on health and disease in human populations. Medical anthropologists investigate the susceptibilities or resistances of populations to specific diseases. They also trace the spread of diseases within a population and from one population to another. Before the arrival of the first Europeans and Africans in South and North America in the sixteenth and seventeenth centuries, for example, smallpox, measles, and other infectious diseases were unknown. As a result, Native Americans, unlike the newcomers, had no natural immunity to the diseases. The results were catastrophic; once exposed to the diseases, millions of Native Americans died.

In contrast to the vulnerabilities of indigenous peoples of the Americas, some populations have advantageous resistances to diseases endemic in their areas, as the following Case Study investigates.

CASE STUDY

Environment, Adaptation, and Disease: Malaria and Sickle-Cell Anemia in Africa and the United States

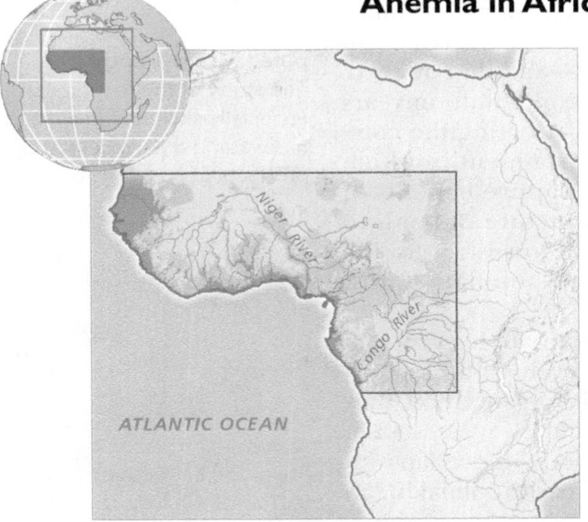

Study of the incidence of two diseases, malaria and sickle-cell anemia, demonstrates how the processes of biological adaptation and culture change can interact to affect human health.

Sickle-cell anemia is a genetic disease that causes red blood cells to have a sickle shape rather than their normal disk shape. Sickled cells cannot hold and transport oxygen normally. Because the disease can be fatal in those who have inherited the recessive gene from both parents, one might expect that the sickle-cell trait would naturally die out in a population. However, individuals who carry one dominant and one recessive copy of the gene survive and also happen to have immunity from another disease—malaria. Malaria is an infectious disease spread by the *Anopheles* mosquito. Both diseases are extremely debilitating and potentially fatal. And both are endemic to West Africa, the ancestral homeland of most African Americans.

What does this analysis of sickle-cell anemia and malaria suggest about the relationships between biological and cultural factors in human health?

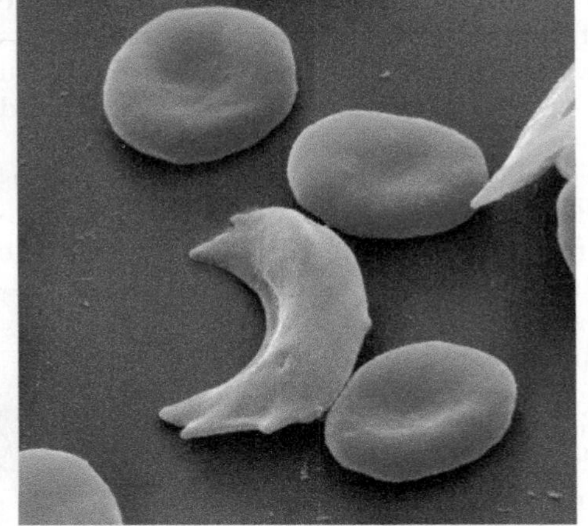

By not transporting oxygen properly and clogging organs, sickled red blood cells cause lifelong, potentially life-threatening health problems for people with this genetic disorder. Photo Researchers/Eye of Science/Photo Researchers, Inc.

The genetic trait that causes sickle-cell anemia probably evolved in human populations in West Africa about 2,400 years ago (Edelstein 1986). At the time, dense forests covered much of West Africa. The inhabitants had lived for millennia by hunting and collecting wild plants. The *Anopheles* mosquito was present; however, because it breeds in unshaded pools of standing water, the mostly shady conditions of the forest kept its numbers in check.

Around 2,000 years ago, however, farming peoples from East Africa began to filter into West Africa, displacing the indigenous population and clearing forestlands for their fields. This created the open areas with standing pools of water in which the *Anopheles* mosquito thrives (Foster and Anderson 1978). As farming spread, so did malaria. As the human population and its cattle herds increased, so did the mosquito population and malaria.

Those who inherit the sickle-cell gene from one parent gain some resistance to malaria, which lessens the severity of the infection. As a result, the sickle-cell gene has spread in malaria-stricken areas. An estimated 30 percent of West African farmers carry the gene. The lowest incidence of the gene is among those who live in still-forested peripheral areas of West Africa, where the *Anopheles* mosquito and malaria are also less prevalent.

The adaptive advantage of the sickle-cell trait, then, is high in populations that live in areas where malaria is prevalent but is less for those who live where the disease is less common. In the United States, where malaria is rare, people of West African descent have higher rates of the sickle-cell gene than do non-Africans, but their rates are much lower than among West Africans today.

If the cultural practice of farming helped spread malaria in West Africa, diet may contribute to the adaptive advantage of the sickle-cell gene. Common crops grown in Africa and the West Indies, including cassava (manioc), yams, sorghum, millet, sugarcane, and lima beans, reduce the severity of the symptoms of sickle-cell anemia because they contain chemical compounds that interfere with the sickling of the red blood cells. This may explain why a lower percentage of Africans suffer from sickle-cell anemia than do African Americans, even though more West Africans have the sickle-cell gene. A study revealed that Jamaicans with sickle-cell anemia had relatively mild symptoms when they lived in Jamaica and ate a Jamaican diet, but experienced more severe symptoms when they migrated to the United States or Britain and changed their eating habits (Frisancho 1981). **Read** the **Document** on **myanthrolab.com**

View the **Map:** *Distribution of Sickle Cell Trait* on **myanthrolab.com**

Anthropology has four subfields: cultural anthropology, linguistic anthropology, archaeology, and biological (or physical) anthropology. Because we all are prone to be ethnocentric, cultural anthropologists adopt the method of ethnography and the perspective of cultural relativism to avoid being judgmental of other cultures. The work of linguistic anthropologists and archaeologists sheds light on culture change, and subdisciplines such as medical anthropology combine biological and cultural anthropology.

APPLIED ANTHROPOLOGY

Applied anthropology intersects with and draws from the four major subfields. Indeed, many anthropologists regard applied anthropology as a fifth subfield of anthropology. Applied anthropologists employ anthropological understandings and perspectives to work outside traditional academic settings. For example, some biological anthropologists work as **forensic anthropologists,** applying their knowledge of human anatomy to help solve crimes. Working for police departments, the Federal Bureau of Investigation (FBI), and other law enforcement agencies, forensic anthropologists can help determine the cause of death by examining a victim's remains and the physical evidence found at a crime scene. Forensic anthropologists' knowledge of skeletal anatomy, blood types, and biochemical markers in the blood can also help identify a victim and provide leads to suspects. Forensic anthropologists have also been asked to study human remains for evidence of human rights abuses that occur during wars and civil conflicts.

Many government agencies, such as the FBI's behavioral science unit Violent Criminal Apprehension Program (ViCAP), employ forensic anthropologists. Forensic anthropologists and archaeologists also work for the Central Identification Laboratory—Hawaii (CILHI). Members of CILHI have traveled to Vietnam and Korea to find the remains of downed airplanes in attempts to identify people missing in action (MIAs) from the Vietnam and Korean wars. Forensic anthropologists also helped identify remains of victims of the terrorist attacks on the World Trade Center in New York City.

Applied archaeology has grown with federal and state laws that protect archaeological sites and materials, which has led to the creation of the field of **cultural resource management (CRM).** Laws now require archaeological surveys in advance of many highway and other construction projects to assess their impact on archaeological sites. The need for these assessments has given rise to **contract archaeology,** in which archaeologists are hired to do this kind of research.

Archaeologists' findings about the past can also be used to solve contemporary problems. Archaeologists working around Lake Titicaca in the Andes of South America, for example, discovered an ancient and productive method of cultivation that had fallen into disuse. They helped reintroduce this method to local farmers, which substantially increased their yields.

Some linguistic anthropologists apply their skills to preserve indigenous languages. They may work with native speakers to prepare dictionaries, grammars, and other aids for use in language classes and schools. Their work helps indigenous communities counter the rapid decline in the number of people who speak local languages. Collecting data from speakers of endangered languages is a fieldwork priority for linguistic anthropologists.

Cultural anthropologists complete applied anthropology work in nonacademic settings, such as government agencies, nongovernment organizations, charitable foundations, and private companies. Some help shape the policies of city, state, and federal agencies that deliver services to local communities; for example, they may advise on the best ways to

applied anthropology
An area of anthropology that applies the techniques and theories of the field to problem solving outside of traditional academic settings.

forensic anthropologists
Biological anthropologists who analyze human remains in the service of criminal justice and families of disaster victims.

cultural resource management (CRM)
The application of archaeology to preserve and protect historic structures and prehistoric sites.

contract archaeology
The application of archaeology to assess the potential impact of construction on archaeological sites and to salvage archaeological evidence.

Anthropology-based advocacy centers on protecting and preserving the native cultures of small-scale societies that share these goals from the impacts of globalization.

ANTHROPOLOGY APPLIED

Cultural Survival

Cultural anthropologists sometimes help indigenous communities improve their economic conditions, adapt to change, and preserve their traditions. They help communities find ways to use their resources productively while protecting their environment and cultural heritage. Some anthropologists have also helped protect indigenous peoples' rights to land and resources and their rights to continue cultural practices.

Cultural Survival is an organization founded by anthropologists that promotes the rights, voices, and visions of indigenous peoples around the world. The organization deals with conflict and migration, cultural preservation, improvement of health care, indigenous economic enterprises, law and self-determination, and the preservation of natural resources. Its initiatives include publications to publicize issues and share news, indigenous curricula, fair trade stores and exchanges such as the Coffee Alliance, legal defense, and an indigenous action network.

Not all applied anthropology concerns native peoples and their cultural survival, however. Some cultural anthropologists advise government agencies and private companies on how to overcome resistance from indigenous and rural communities to policies and projects that benefit national governments and private concerns but threaten indigenous rights and resources.

CRITICAL THINKING QUESTION

How can anthropological research affect public policy, private enterprise, and advocacy for indigenous peoples?

Corbis/Richard T. Nowitz/Corbis

Cultural Survival, Inc./Cultural Survival, Inc.

Shutterstock/pcruciatti/Shutterstock

contact different populations in a community to deliver services. These may be health care services, such as vaccinations, legal aid services, or preschool and other educational opportunities for children. Cultural anthropologists work in research firms and think tanks to solve social problems. They also help communities, companies, and organizations to resolve management disputes and conflicts. They help resolve labor and workplace issues and work for courts to develop and implement alternative sentencing programs for offenders.

Anthropologists may act as advocates and testify in courts to support native claims to land or other benefits or rights, and may help indigenous people present their history and culture from a native perspective. Cultural Survival, for example, helps native peoples in Ecuador, Peru, and Brazil protect their interests in the face of globalization.

Medical anthropologists may help preserve traditional medical practices and pharmaceuticals, and encourage practitioners of both traditional and Western medicine to understand the physical and psychological benefits of both medical models for developing treatment procedures that combine both forms of medicine.

How might Western pharmaceutical companies employ the services of anthropologists?

Anthropologists who work for industries and corporations analyze workplace interactions to suggest improvements in the working environment and worker productivity. Anthropologists may provide sensitivity training for American businesspeople planning to meet overseas with their foreign counterparts. Anthropologists even study consumer habits to help companies increase sales or develop new products and services. For example, Canon employed a team of anthropologists to study the kinds of pictures and notes that families create and affix to their walls and refrigerators. The company used the findings to develop Canon Creative software, which allows families to make their own greeting cards, posters, and T-shirts, and thus increased printer sales (Hafner 1999).

Watch the **Video:** *Career Videos* on **myanthrolab.com**

REVIEW

Applied anthropology is the practical use of all four subfields of anthropology outside academia. Applied anthropology includes forensic anthropologists, workers in cultural resource management, contract archaeologists, and linguistic and cultural anthropologists. All applied anthropologists use their training in other fields of anthropology.

Study and **Review** on **myanthrolab.com**

CHAPTER SUMMARY

The Study of Humanity

- Anthropology is the study of humanity, from its evolutionary origins millions of years ago to today's worldwide diversity of peoples and cultures.
- Three features distinguish anthropology from other social sciences: a focus on the concept of culture, a holistic perspective, and a comparative perspective.
- Culture is the constellation of learned values, beliefs, and rules of conduct that members of a society share. Culture change and globalization are important subjects of anthropological research.
- Anthropology's holistic perspective focuses on culture as an integrated whole, the various features and patterns of which can only be understood in relation to one another.
- Anthropology's comparative perspective is based on cultural data drawn from societies throughout the world and from throughout human history, documenting the diversity of human culture in an attempt to understand common patterns in people's adaptations to their environments and their unique cultural institutions.

The Four Subfields of Anthropology

- Cultural anthropology is the comparative study of living and recent cultures. Cultural anthropologists use ethnographic fieldwork and the perspective of cultural relativism.
- Linguistic anthropology is the study of language in its cultural and historical context. It includes the study of languages of indigenous peoples, language change, and the relationships between language and other aspects of culture, thought, and belief.
- Archaeology is the study of past cultures. Archaeologists study historic cultures with written records and prehistoric cultures whose lives can be inferred from material artifacts, settlement patterns, and remains of foods and tools.

- Biological anthropology is the study of human origins, using the fossil record to understand human evolution. Some biological anthropologists study the biological diversity of contemporary human populations.

Applied Anthropology

- Applied anthropology intersects with and draws from all of the major subdisciplines in anthropology to study and help solve contemporary problems in communities, government, and businesses.

REVIEW QUESTIONS

1. What features distinguish anthropology from other social and behavioral sciences? Why are the concepts of culture and culture change important in anthropology?
2. Why is globalization a major concern in anthropology today? How does culture change relate to globalization?
3. Why does anthropology use the holistic and comparative perspectives?
4. How does each of the four subfields of anthropology seek to fulfill anthropology's mission?
5. How do cultural anthropologists conduct research? What are some of the goals they try to achieve?
6. Why is cultural relativism important in studying other cultures? How does cultural relativism differ from ethical relativism?
7. What can linguistic anthropologists and archaeologists learn about symbolic and material culture?
8. How do diseases like sickle-cell anemia and malaria highlight the relationship between biology and culture?
9. How can research in each of the subfields of anthropology help solve problems and make policy?

MyAnthroLab Connections

Watch. Listen. View. Explore. Read. MyAnthroLab is designed just for you. Dynamic visual activities, videos, and readings found in the multimedia library will enhance your learning experience.

Resources from this chapter:

Watch on **myanthrolab.com**

- *The Fields of Anthropology*
- *Relativity*
- *Being an Archaeologist*
- *Career Videos*

View on **myanthrolab.com**

- *Distribution of Sickle Cell Trait*

Explore on **myanthrolab.com** In MySearchLab, enter the Anthropology database to find relevant and recent scholarly and popular press publications. For this chapter, enter the following keywords: ethnography, linguistic anthropology, ethnocentrism, medical anthropology

Read on **myanthrolab.com**

- *Are Ethnographies "Just-So" Stories?* by Paul Durrenberger
- *The Research Process* by Susan C. Weller
- *A Shaman to Organizations* by Andrew W. Miracle

Ethnography and Culture

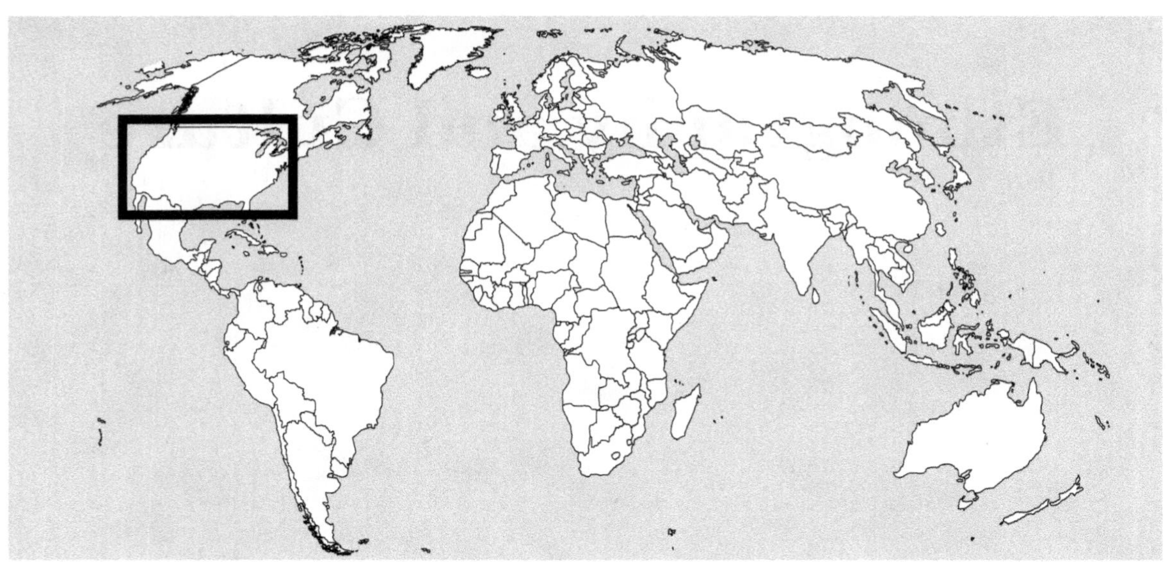

Ethnography and Culture

James P. Spradley

*Most Americans associate science with detached observation; we learn to observe whatever we wish to understand, introduce our own classification of what is going on, and explain what we see in our own terms. In this selection, James Spradley argues that cultural anthropologists work differently. Ethnography is the work of discovering and describing a particular culture; culture is the learned, shared knowledge that people use to generate behavior and interpret experience. To get at culture, ethnographers must learn the meanings of action and experience from the insider's or informant's point of view. Many of the examples used by Spradley also show the relevance of anthropology to the study of culture in the United States.**

Listen to the **Chapter Audio** on **myanthrolab.com**

Ethnographic fieldwork is the hallmark of cultural anthropology. Whether in a jungle village in Peru or on the streets of New York, the anthropologist goes to where people live and "does fieldwork." This means participating in activities, asking questions, eating strange foods, learning a new language, watching ceremonies, taking field notes, washing clothes, writing letters home, tracing out genealogies, observing play, interviewing informants, and hundreds of other things. This vast range of activities often obscures the nature of the most fundamental task of all fieldwork: doing ethnography.

Ethnography is the work of describing a culture. The central aim of ethnography is to understand another way of life from the native point of view. The goal of ethnography, as Malinowski put it, is "to grasp the native's point of view, his relation to life, to realize *his* vision of *his* world."[1] Fieldwork, then, involves the disciplined study of what the world is like to people who have learned to see, hear, speak, think, and act in ways that are different. Rather than *studying people,* ethnography means *learning from people.* Consider the following illustration.

George Hicks set out, in 1965, to learn about another way of life, that of the mountain people in an Appalachian valley.[2] His goal was to discover their culture, to learn to see the world from their perspective. With his family he moved into Little Laurel Valley, his daughter attended the local school, and his wife became one of the local Girl Scout leaders. Hicks soon discovered that stores and storekeepers were at the center of the valley's communication system, providing the most important social arena for the entire valley. He learned this by watching what other people did, by following their example, and slowly becoming part of the groups that congregated daily in the stores. He writes:

> At least once each day I would visit several stores in the valley, and sit in on the groups of gossiping men or, if the storekeeper happened to be alone, perhaps attempt to clear up puzzling points about kinship obligations. I found these hours, particularly those spent in the presence of the two or three excellent storytellers in the Little Laurel, thoroughly enjoyable. . . . At other times, I helped a number of local men gather corn or hay, build sheds, cut trees, pull and pack galax, and search for rich stands of huckleberries. When I needed aid in, for example, repairing frozen water pipes, it was readily and cheerfully provided.[3]

In order to discover the hidden principles of another way of life, the researcher must become a *student.* Storekeepers and storytellers and local farmers become *teachers.* Instead of studying the "climate," the "flora," and the "fauna" that made up the environment of this Appalachian valley, Hicks tried to discover how these mountain people defined and evaluated trees and galax and huckleberries. He did not attempt to describe social life in terms of what most Americans know about "marriage," "family," and "friendship"; instead he sought to discover how these mountain people identified relatives and friends. He tried to learn the obligations they felt toward kinsmen and discover how they felt about friends. Discovering the *insider's view* is a different species of knowledge from one that rests mainly on the outsider's view, even when the outsider is a trained social scientist.

Consider another example, this time from the perspective of a non-Western ethnographer. Imagine an Inuit woman setting out to learn the culture of Macalester College. What would she, so well schooled in the rich heritage of Inuit culture, have to do

[1]Bronislaw Malinowski, *Argonauts of the Western Pacific* (London: Routledge, 1922), p. 22.

[2]George Hicks, *Appalachian Valley* (New York: Holt, Rinehart, and Winston, 1976).

[3]Hicks, p. 3.

in order to understand the culture of Macalester College students, faculty, and staff? How would she discover the patterns that made up their lives? How would she avoid imposing Inuit ideas, categories, and values on everything she saw?

First, and perhaps most difficult, she would have to set aside her belief in *naive realism,* the almost universal belief that all people define the *real* world of objects, events, and living creatures in pretty much the same way. Human languages may differ from one society to the next, but behind the strange words and sentences, all people are talking about the same things. The naive realist assumes that love, snow, marriage, worship, animals, death, food, and hundreds of other things have essentially the same meaning to all human beings. Although few of us would admit to such ethnocentrism, the assumption may unconsciously influence our research. Ethnography starts with a conscious attitude of almost complete ignorance: "I don't know how the people at Macalester College understand their world. That remains to be discovered."

This Inuit woman would have to begin by learning the language spoken by students, faculty, and staff. She could stroll the campus paths, sit in classes, and attend special events, but only if she consciously tried to see things from the native point of view would she grasp their perspective. She would need to observe and listen to first-year students during their week-long orientation program. She would have to stand in line during registration, listen to students discuss the classes they hoped to get, and visit departments to watch faculty advising students on course selection. She would want to observe secretaries typing, janitors sweeping, and maintenance personnel plowing snow from walks. She would watch the more than 1,600 students crowd into the post office area to open their tiny mailboxes, and she would listen to their comments about junk mail and letters from home or no mail at all. She would attend faculty meetings to watch what went on, recording what professors and administrators said and how they behaved. She would sample various courses, attend "keggers" on weekends, read the *Mac Weekly,* and listen by the hour to students discussing things like their "relationships," the "football team," and "work study." She would want to learn the *meanings* of all these things. She would have to listen to the members of this college community, watch what they did, and participate in their activities to learn such meanings.

The essential core of ethnography is this concern with the meaning of actions and events to the people we seek to understand. Some of these meanings are directly expressed in language; many are taken for granted and communicated only indirectly through word and action. But in every society people make constant use of these complex meaning systems to organize their behavior, to understand themselves and others, and to make sense out of the world in which they live. These systems of meaning constitute their culture; ethnography always implies a theory of culture.

Culture

When ethnographers study other cultures, they must deal with three fundamental aspects of human experience: what people do, what people know, and the things people make and use. When each of these is learned and shared by members of some group, we speak of them as *cultural behavior, cultural knowledge,* and *cultural artifacts.* Whenever you do ethnographic fieldwork, you will want to distinguish among these three, although in most situations they are usually mixed together. Let's try to unravel them.

Recently I took a commuter train from a western suburb to downtown Chicago. It was late in the day, and when I boarded the train, only a handful of people were scattered about the car. Each was engaged in a common form of *cultural behavior: reading.* Across the aisle a man held the *Chicago Tribune* out in front of him, looking intently at the small print and every now and then turning the pages noisily. In front of him a young woman held a paperback book about twelve inches from her face. I could see her head shift slightly as her eyes moved from the bottom of one page to the top of the next. Near the front of the car a student was reading a large textbook and using a pen to underline words and sentences. Directly in front of me I noticed a man looking at the ticket he had purchased and reading it. It took me an instant to survey this scene, and then I settled back, looked out the window, and read a billboard advertisement for a plumbing service proclaiming it would open any plugged drains. All of us were engaged in the same kind of cultural behavior: reading.

This common activity depended on a great many *cultural artifacts,* the things people shape or make from natural resources. I could see artifacts like books and tickets and newspapers and billboards, all of which contained tiny black marks arranged into intricate patterns called "letters." And these tiny artifacts were arranged into larger patterns of words, sentences, and paragraphs. Those of us on that commuter train could read, in part, because of still other artifacts: the bark of trees made into paper; steel made into printing presses; dyes of various colors made into ink; glue used to hold book pages together; large wooden frames to hold billboards. If an ethnographer wanted to understand the full cultural meaning in our society, it would involve a careful study of these and many other cultural artifacts.

Although we can easily see behavior and artifacts, they represent only the thin surface of a deep lake. Beneath the surface, hidden from view, lies a vast reservoir of *cultural knowledge.* Think for a moment what the people on that train needed to know in order to read. First, they had to know the grammatical rules for at least one language. Then they had to learn what the little marks on paper represented. They also had to know the meaning of space and lines and pages. They had learned cultural rules like "move your eyes from left to right, from the top of the page to the bottom." They had to know that a sentence at the bottom of a page continues on the top of the next page. The man reading a newspaper had to know a great deal about columns and the spaces between columns and what headlines mean. All of us needed to know what kinds of messages were intended by whoever wrote what we read. If a person cannot distinguish the importance of a message on a billboard from one that comes in a letter from a spouse or child, problems would develop. I knew how to recognize when other people were reading. We all knew it was impolite to read aloud on a train. We all knew how to feel when reading things like jokes or calamitous news in the paper. Our culture has a large body of shared knowledge that people learn and use to engage in this behavior called *reading* and make proper use of the artifacts connected with it.

Although cultural knowledge is hidden from view, it is of fundamental importance because we all use it constantly to generate behavior and interpret our experience. Cultural knowledge is so important that I will frequently use the broader term *culture* when speaking about it. Indeed, I will define culture as *the acquired knowledge people use to interpret experience and generate behavior.* Let's consider another example to see how people use their culture to interpret experience and do things.

One afternoon in 1973 I came across the following news item in the *Minneapolis Tribune:*

> ***Crowd Mistakes Rescue Attempt, Attacks Police***
> *Nov. 23, 1973. Hartford, Connecticut.* Three policemen giving a heart massage and oxygen to a heart attack victim Friday were attacked by a crowd of 75 to 100 persons who apparently did not realize what the policemen were doing.
>
> Other policemen fended off the crowd of mostly Spanish-speaking residents until an ambulance arrived. Police said they tried to explain to the crowd what they were doing, but the crowd apparently thought they were beating the woman.
>
> Despite the policemen's efforts the victim, Evangelica Echevacria, 59, died.

Here we see people using their culture. Members of two different groups observed the same event, but their *interpretations* were drastically different. The crowd used their cultural knowledge (a) to interpret the behavior of the policemen as cruel and (b) to act on the woman's behalf to put a stop to what they perceived as brutality. They had acquired the cultural principles for acting and interpreting things in this way through a particular shared experience.

The policemen, on the other hand, used their cultural knowledge (a) to interpret the woman's condition as heart failure and their own behavior as a life-saving effort and (b) to give her cardiac massage and oxygen. They used artifacts like an oxygen mask and an ambulance. Furthermore, they interpreted the actions of the crowd in an entirely different manner from how the crowd saw their own behavior. The two groups of people each had elaborate cultural rules for interpreting their experience and for acting in emergency situations, and the conflict arose, at least in part, because these cultural rules were so different.

We can now diagram this definition of culture and see more clearly the relationships among knowledge, behavior, and artifacts (Figure 1). By identifying cultural knowledge as fundamental, we have merely shifted the emphasis from behavior and artifacts to their *meaning*. The ethnographer observes behavior but goes beyond it to inquire about the meaning of that behavior. The ethnographer sees artifacts and natural objects but goes beyond them to discover what meanings people assign to these objects. The ethnographer observes and records emotional states but goes beyond them to discover the meaning of fear, anxiety, anger, and other feelings.

As represented in Figure 1, cultural knowledge exists at two levels of consciousness. *Explicit culture* makes up part of what we know, a level of knowledge people can communicate about with relative ease. When George Hicks asked storekeepers and others in Little Laurel Valley about their relatives, he discovered that any adult over fifty could tell him the genealogical connections among large numbers of people. They knew how to trace kin relationships and the cultural rules for appropriate behavior among kins. All of us have acquired large areas of cultural knowledge such as this, which we can talk about and make explicit.

At the same time, a large portion of our cultural knowledge remains *tacit,* outside our awareness. Edward Hall has done much to elucidate the nature of tacit cultural knowledge in his books *The Silent Language* and *The Hidden Dimension.*[4] The way each culture defines space often occurs at the level of tacit knowledge. Hall points out that all of us have acquired thousands of spatial cues about how close to

[4]Edward T. Hall, *The Silent Language* (Garden City, NY: Doubleday, 1959); *The Hidden Dimension* (Garden City, NY: Doubleday, 1966).

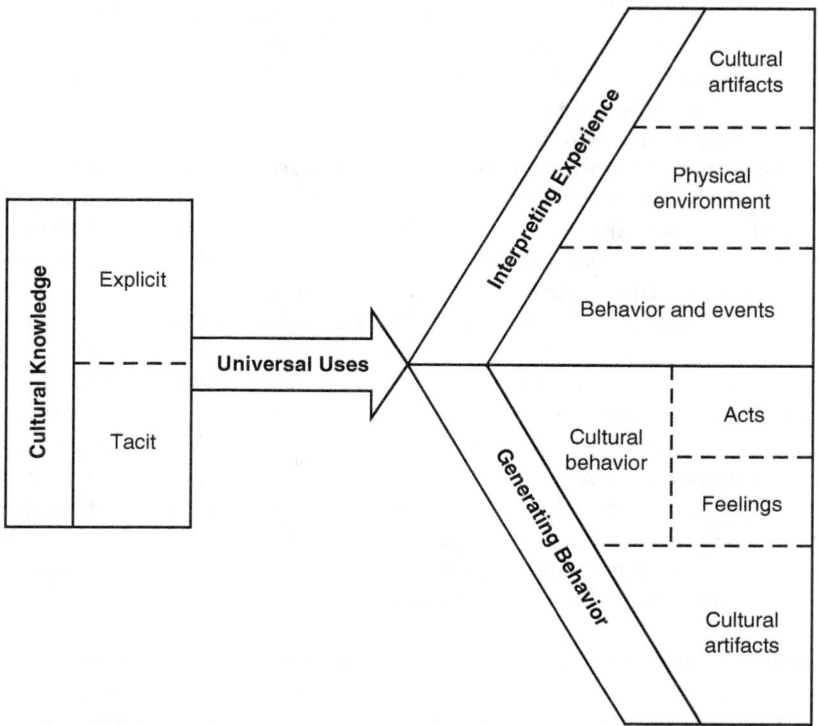

FIGURE 1

stand to others, how to arrange furniture, when to touch others, and when to feel cramped inside a room. Without realizing that our tacit culture is operating, we begin to feel uneasy when someone from another culture stands too close, breathes on us when talking, touches us, or when we find furniture arranged in the center of the room rather than around the edges. Ethnography is the study of both explicit and tacit cultural knowledge. . . .

The concept of culture as acquired knowledge has much in common with symbolic interactionism, a theory that seeks to explain human behavior in terms of meanings. Symbolic interactionism has its roots in the work of sociologists like Cooley, Mead, and Thomas. Blumer has identified three premises on which this theory rests.

The first premise is that "human beings act toward things on the basis of the meanings that the things have for them."[5] The policemen and the crowd in our earlier example interacted on the basis of the meanings things had for them. The geographic location, the types of people, the police car, the policemen's movements, the sick woman's behavior, and the activities of the onlookers—all were *symbols* with special meanings. People did not act toward the things themselves, but to their meanings.

The second premise underlying symbolic interactionism is that the "meaning of such things is derived from, or arises out of, the social interaction that one has with one's fellows."[6] Culture, as a shared system of meanings, is learned, revised, maintained, and defined in the context of people interacting. The crowd came to

[5]Herbert Blumer, *Symbolic Interactionism* (Englewood Cliffs, NJ: Prentice-Hall, 1969), p. 2.

[6]Blumer, p. 2.

share their definitions of police behavior through interacting with one another and through past associations with the police. The police officers acquired the cultural meanings they used through interacting with other officers and members of the community. The culture of each group was inextricably bound up with the social life of their particular communities.

The third premise of symbolic interactionism is that "meanings are handled in, and modified through, an interpretive process used by the person dealing with the things he encounters."[7] Neither the crowd nor the policemen were automatons, driven by their culture to act in the way they did. Rather, they used their cultural knowledge to interpret and evaluate the situation. At any moment, a member of the crowd might have interpreted the behavior of the policemen in a slightly different way, leading to a different reaction.

We may see this interpretive aspect more clearly if we think of culture as a cognitive map. In the recurrent activities that make up everyday life, we refer to this map. It serves as a guide for acting and for interpreting our experience; it does not compel us to follow a particular course. Like this brief drama between the policemen, a dying woman, and the crowd, much of life is a series of unanticipated social occasions. Although our culture may not include a detailed map for such occasions, it does provide principles for interpreting and responding to them. Rather than a rigid map that people must follow, culture is best thought of as

> a set of principles for creating dramas, for writing script, and of course, for recruiting players and audiences. . . . Culture is not simply a cognitive map that people acquire, in whole or in part, more or less accurately, and then learn to read. People are not just map-readers; they are map-makers. People are cast out into imperfectly charted, continually revised sketch maps. Culture does not provide a cognitive map, but rather a set of principles for map making and navigation. Different cultures are like different schools of navigation to cope with different terrains and seas.[8]

If we take *meaning* seriously, as symbolic interactionists argue we must, it becomes necessary to study meaning carefully. We need a theory of meaning and a specific methodology designed for the investigation of it.

Study and **Review** on **myanthrolab.com**

Review Questions

1. What is the definition of *culture?* How is this definition related to the way anthropologists do ethnographic fieldwork?
2. What is the relationship among cultural behavior, cultural artifacts, and cultural knowledge?
3. What is the difference between tacit and explicit culture? How can anthropologists discover these two kinds of culture?
4. What are some examples of naive realism in the way Americans think about people in other societies?

[7]Blumer, p. 2.

[8]Charles O. Frake, "Plying Frames Can Be Dangerous: Some Reflections on Methodology in Cognitive Anthropology," *Quarterly Newsletter of the Institute for Comparative Human Development* 3 (1977): 6–7.

The Nature of Culture

PREVIEW

- What is culture? What features are usually included in definitions of culture?
- What elements of culture are regarded as universal, and why?
- How can members of a society both share and not share culture?
- How is culture learned and transmitted?
- How can culture be both adaptive and maladaptive?
- What are some forces of cultural integration?
- How is culture based on symbols?
- How do cultures change from within and through contact?
- What are the dynamics of global culture change today?

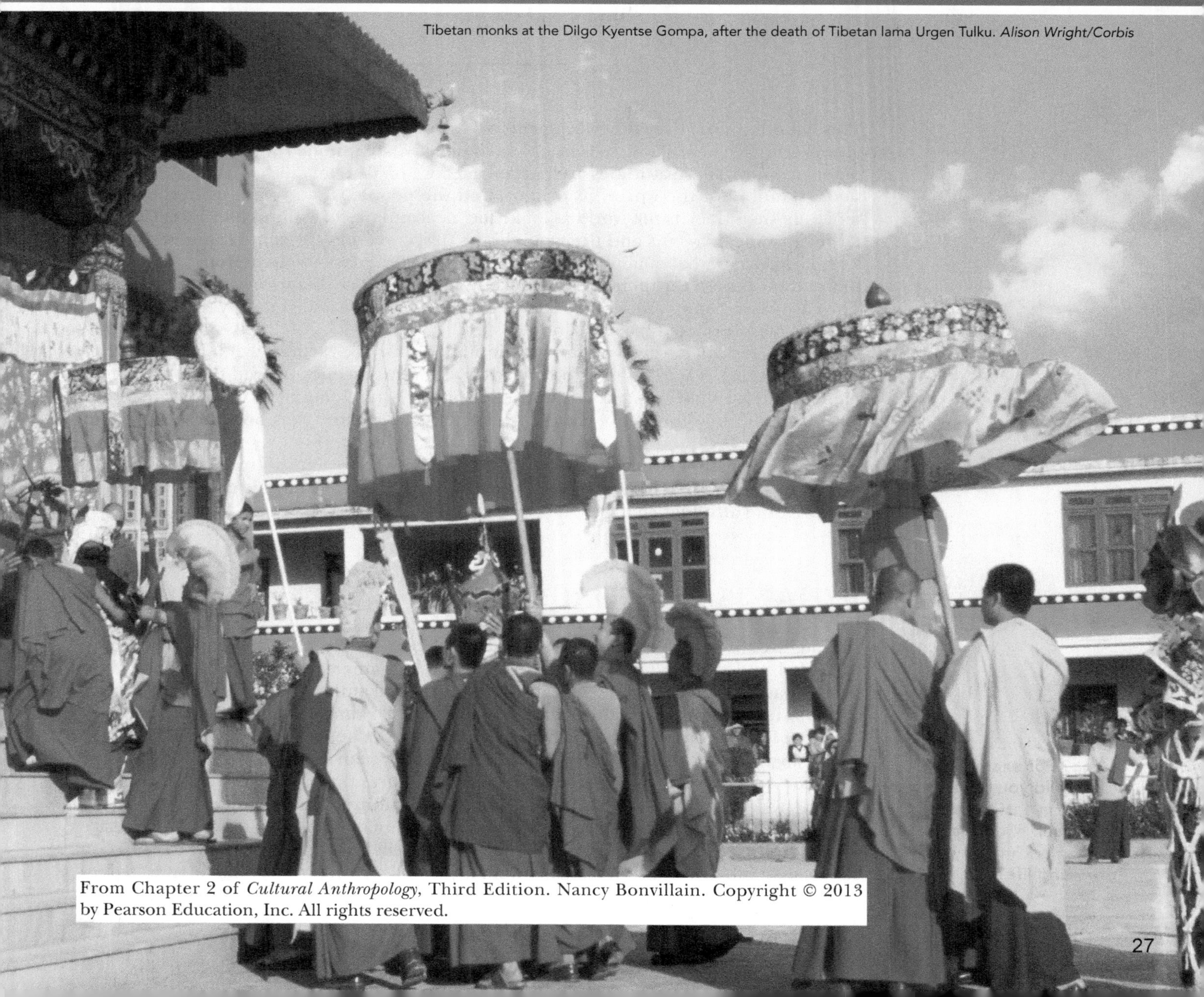

Tibetan monks at the Dilgo Kyentse Gompa, after the death of Tibetan lama Urgen Tulku. *Alison Wright/Corbis*

Listen to the Chapter Audio on myanthrolab.com

Read on myanthrolab.com

At the beginning there was on the earth only a single man; he had neither house nor tent, for at that time the winter was not cold, and the summer was not hot; the wind did not blow so violently, and there fell neither snow nor rain; the tea grew of itself on the mountains, and the flocks had nothing to fear from beasts of prey. This man had three children, who lived a long time with him, nourishing themselves on milk and fruits. After having attained to a great age, this man died. The three children deliberated what they should do with the body of their father, and they could not agree about it; one wished to put him in a coffin, the other wanted to burn him, the third thought it would be best to expose the body on the summit of a mountain. They resolved then to divide it into three parts. The eldest had the body and arms; he was the ancestor of the great Chinese family, and that is why his descendants have become celebrated in arts and industry, and are remarkable for their tricks and stratagems. The second son had the breast; he was the father of the Tibetan family, and they are full of heart and courage, and do not fear death. From the third, who had inferior parts of the body, are descended the Tartars, who are simple and timid, without head or heart, and who know nothing but how to keep themselves firm in their saddles.

This Tibetan narrative, describing the origin of the Tibetan people and two ethnic groups who live near them, tells us much about Tibetan attitudes toward themselves and other peoples. These attitudes are part of the core of Tibetan culture, that is, Tibetans' understanding of the world, its origins, and the people who inhabit it. In the beginning, the story depicts the world as an idyllic, peaceful place, without harsh weather and hardship. The Tibetans and their neighbors descend from the same founder. But the story also tells us what qualities the Tibetans believe differentiate them from others. They praise the Chinese for their arts and accomplishments but disapprove of their trickery. They are disparaging and condescending toward the Tartars. And they think of themselves as people of courage and kindness.

The narrative also gives us information about burial practices. Each brother advocated a method of burial that is practiced in different societies around the world: interment in the ground, cremation, and exposure to the elements. These practices are aspects of culture, how people organize their lives. The story thus provides insight into features of Tibetan culture. We learn about how Tibetans view themselves and their neighbors, how they think about their relationships with other groups, and some practices they engage in. In this chapter, we will explore what culture is and how cultural practices and attitudes change.

WHAT IS CULTURE?

Although defining what culture is may sound like a simple task, anthropologists have struggled to define and specify culture since the late nineteenth century, when anthropology was established as a discipline. The British social anthropologist Edward Tylor was the first to attempt a formal definition. Writing in *Primitive Culture* in 1871, he stated, "Culture is that complex whole which includes knowledge, belief, art, morals, law, custom, and any other capabilities and habits acquired by man as a member of society."

To what extent is culture shared? For example, what could you say about "American" attitudes toward self and others and "American" ways of organizing life?

Tylor's definition captures several significant features that most definitions of culture include today. It focuses on the holistic quality of culture ("that complex whole") and embraces all the activities, attitudes, and beliefs of human beings. Significantly, these are traits people "acquire." That is, people's attitudes, beliefs, and ways of acting are learned rather than inherited, instinctual, or automatic. Finally, Tylor stressed that people acquire culture "as a member of society." People live and interact with other people, learning skills and attitudes from them, and in turn transmitting their knowledge and beliefs to others.

Since Tylor, anthropologists have expanded on and refined the definition of culture innumerable times. By the 1950s, Alfred Kroeber and Clyde Kluckhohn had collected more than one hundred definitions, and all differ according to their focus and the theoretical orientation that underlies them (Kroeber and Kluckhohn 1952). Nevertheless, all the definitions include statements about human behavior and activities in families, groups, and communities, and about people's selectively shared knowledge, attitudes, values, and beliefs.

The cultural knowledge of these Sami includes everything there is to know about reindeer, living in the Arctic, and coping with citizenship in the modern state society of Norway. The Image Works/ Topham/The Image Works

As we shall see, anthropologists use the term "culture" in two distinct senses (Sewall 2008, 42). In one meaning, "culture" refers to a set of beliefs and practices that are analyzed and abstracted from people's actual lived experiences. The second meaning of "culture" refers to a particular identifiable group of people (a "society") who, to varying degrees, share or participate in social life.

Cultural knowledge refers to the information people have that enables them to function in their social and physical environments. Some of this information is practical—how to make a living, what kinds of clothes to wear and shelters to build, and so on. Other cultural knowledge is less obvious—for example, people share knowledge about the world, why people do the things they do, what a person can expect from others, and so on. This kind of cultural knowledge is expressed in people's attitudes, values, and beliefs, including ethical values about what is right and wrong and what is proper and improper behavior. Cultural knowledge thus includes religious beliefs and scientific theories about the past, the world, people and their origins, and people's relationships to plants, animals, and the natural world.

cultural knowledge Information that enables people to function in their society and contributes to the survival of the society as a whole.

In addition to cultural knowledge, social and cultural skills are included in the definition of culture, such as the activities and practices that people engage in to obtain their food, clothe and shelter themselves, and make or procure goods needed for their households. Cultural behaviors include the ways that people organize themselves to provide leadership, make decisions, and carry out communal activities. In all societies, people need to develop modes of subsistence and economic exchange, methods of social control and conflict resolution, and principles of leadership and governance. They need to organize families and provide for child care and socialization. Other aspects of culture, such as religion and artistic expression, are also part of the human experience. People share similar basic societal needs with members of other societies, but the strategies and institutions they develop to satisfy or cope with those needs vary.

Thus, people in all societies have their own specific thoughts (cultural knowledge) and behaviors (cultural skills) that vary from group to group. Although each society is unique, they all share similarities with others. In today's world, cultural influences are spreading in the context of global processes that include ways of organizing economies, purchasing goods and services, and communicating through the arts, travel, and the Internet. Elements of this global culture emanate from many parts of the world. Although Europe and the United States provide powerful centers for this global culture, economic, political, and artistic influences also come from Asia, Africa, and Latin America as well.

What is global culture? This question is widely debated among social scientists. What thoughts, behaviors, tools, and skills do you identify as making up today's global culture?

Culture includes cultural knowledge (people's ideas, attitudes, beliefs, and values) and cultural skills (people's activities and behaviors for living and organizing their lives). People's thoughts and behaviors are mutually reinforcing. Some aspects of culture deal with concrete knowledge, such as what food to eat, how to build a shelter, and what clothes to wear. Other aspects of culture deal with abstract ideas, such as how people are expected to behave, what attitudes are appropriate in given situations, and value systems. Concrete and abstract components of culture and their behavioral analogs are present in all human societies. At the same time that each culture is unique, a developing and expanding global culture also spreads economic, political, and aesthetic influences throughout the world.

cultural models
Shared assumptions that people have about the world and about the ideal culture.

norms
Sets of expectations and attitudes that people have about appropriate behavior.

CHARACTERISTICS OF CULTURE

Although each society is unique, a number of characteristics in their organization and functioning are universal. To begin, any culture is a product of a group of people who share and transmit some basic attitudes and assumptions about the world. In addition, aspects of culture tend to interrelate and function together with some consistency to form a coherent system of behaviors and beliefs. Through their cultures, people adapt to their life situations and to changes in their social and physical environments. Anthropologists often state that culture is shared, learned, adaptive, and integrated. And although these general principles make sense, as we shall see, they are not entirely unproblematic. Perhaps we can also state that cultures consist of a constellation of shared meanings and that these meanings are reflected in and reinforced by the behaviors in which people engage. Furthermore, meaning is both produced and interpreted by members in their interactions with one another. That is, culture is both meaning and practice.

Culture Is Shared

Humans are by nature social creatures; that is, we do not live as individuals alone. Rather, we live with other people in families, households, and communities of various sizes and relationships. The way we behave, our attitudes about right and wrong, our ideas about the world we live in are all formed through our interactions with others. We do not act alone, and we do not have ideas all to ourselves. Together with these other people, we are societies. A society is a group of people who live within an acknowledged territory, who could potentially interact with one another, and who share certain practices and values. Societies are held together by social structures that organize family life, means of making a living, and ways of arriving at decisions and establishing methods of leadership.

However, to say that culture is shared is not to say that all members of a particular society have exactly the same attitudes and do exactly the same things in the same way. Rather, the general principles of culture may be shared but there may be many differences in how people experience and think about their lives. For example, not all Americans vote or believe that voting is efficacious, but most would staunchly defend everyone's right to vote. Thus, voting is included in the broad cultural conception of legitimate governance in the United States.

Societies can function as groups to minimize conflicts because their members agree about the basic parameters of living. If this were not so, people would not be able to coordinate their activities or agree on what to do next. And even though they might speak the same language, they would not be able to accurately interpret each other's meanings and intentions if they did not share basic cultural assumptions about the world. These shared assumptions, or **cultural models,** form a background ideology in terms of which behavior becomes relatively coherent and consistent.

Despite cultural models, there are disagreements and conflicts within any community. In all communities, some people are more fully committed to general societal norms than others. Societal **norms** are sets of commonly held expectations and attitudes that people have about appropriate behavior. Although these norms are generally held to be valid within each culture, not everyone acts in accordance with them.

This young woman was photographed in traditional Burkina Faso garb with her aunt. The Image Works/Imapress/Charreire/The Image Works

Deviance from expected and appropriate behavior occurs in every community. Some types of deviance are tolerated whereas others are not. In fact, behavior that may be considered deviant within a community as a whole may be a marker of identity for a particular group. For example, body piercings or tattooing might violate adult conceptions of beauty, but teenagers may engage in these physical alterations to conform to youthful standards. Violent behavior such as assault and murder are deviant acts that are not tolerated in most societies. Other kinds of violence that occur within the family, though, such as spousal abuse, may be tolerated, even if not condoned.

People occupying different social roles and statuses may hold opposing views about the existing social order and prevailing cultural norms. For example, age may be a factor in the way people organize their lives and in the kinds of attitudes that they hold. Younger and older people have different experiences and different frames of reference. Opposing activities and norms for older and younger people may be relatively stable, though; that is, as younger people age, they adopt the lifestyles and norms of their elders. Differences between the young and the old may also signal ongoing social and culture change, if young people introduce new ways of living as they replace their elders through the normal aging process.

In the diverse society of Bolivia, this peasant woman of the Andes does not fully share the same culture as her counterpart in La Paz, the capital. The Image Works/Kike Calvo/V&W/ The Image Works

Gender differences are another common source of distinctions in people's activities and attitudes. Gender is a complex cultural concept through which people assign particular roles and convey particular attitudes. Gender as a social construct differs from sex, which is a biological attribute. In most societies, women and men usually have certain specific tasks that they fulfill in their homes and communities. The relationships between men and women in the family and in the public sphere influence the ways they experience their lives. For example, men and women are likely to have different ideas about their rights and responsibilities, depending on which gender is the dominant decision maker and authority in the household. Women who have the major share of the household and child-rearing responsibilities may feel burdened and restricted, or they may feel challenged and fulfilled. In societies that sanction violence against women and permit men to abuse their wives, women's experience of household life certainly contrasts sharply with men's.

Like differences in age and gender, other status differences in society result in incomplete sharing of culture. Such differences also may be a source of social tension and cultural disagreement. For example, members of elite groups may reap greater economic and social benefits from the way in which society is structured than do members of marginalized or oppressed groups. Although differences of experiences, attitudes, and opinions vary within all societies, such differences are likely to be sharper in complex, heterogeneous societies than in small, relatively homogeneous ones where people interact more personally with one another. Class, race, or ethnicity may segment large societies, creating group cultural distinctions in how people organize their lives. In addition, people who belong to different religions may apply different philosophical orientations and moral principles to their daily lives.

subculture
A group whose members and others think of their way of life as different in some significant way from that of other people in the larger society.

Thus, members of different groups in stratified societies may have different attitudes and values. For example, when economists and politicians in the United States tell us that the economy is booming, this does not mean that everyone is doing well. The wealthy and those who own shares on the stock market experience an economic boom very differently from workers whose factories have been relocated abroad, or from people on welfare. Thus, a culture is not fully shared in a diverse society.

Differences in social groups and in the ways that members of distinct groups live may remain relatively stable for long periods of time. However, tensions and struggles over cultural norms and values may lead to significant societal changes.

In addition to differences derived from distinct social roles and statuses, some societies contain groups that participate in identifiable subcultures. A **subculture** is a group of people who think of themselves, and are thought of by others, as different in a significant way from the majority of people living in the society. Members of subcultures interact more frequently among themselves than with "outsiders," and share attitudes and practices that distinguish them from other groups.

Hasidic families are an American urban subculture among many in New York City. Their subculture is distinguished through ethnic background and religious beliefs and practices. Corbis/Alain Keler/Sygma/Corbis

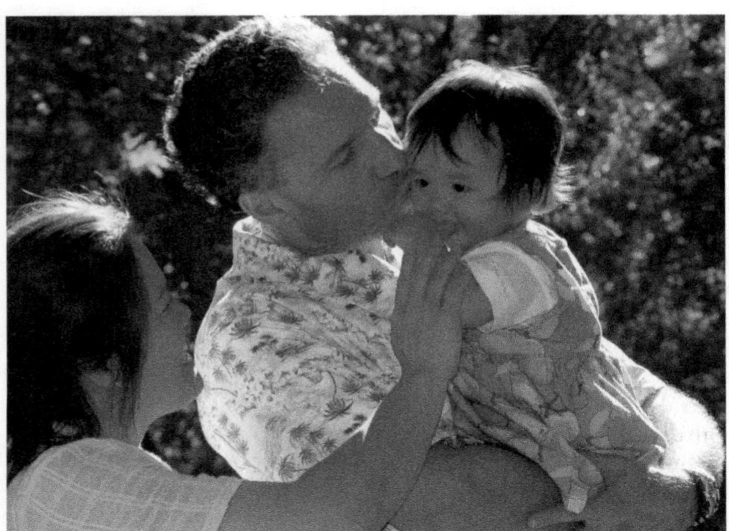
People can acquire any culture if they are raised in it, just as people can learn any language. Dreamstime LLC/Lyoung403b/Dreamstime

In complex, multiethnic societies, including American society, ethnic groups may comprise subcultures, especially if members retain allegiance to their native country, use their native language, and observe ethnic food, preferences, and family relations. Some occupational groups may also function as subcultures. For example, police officers may work and socialize together, have shared vocabulary, and share expectations of life patterns, cooperation, and mutual aid.

All of these sources of difference modify our understanding of culture as a constellation of shared behaviors and beliefs. Still, when people interact within the same society, they must share some basic premises about social order and social values. If they did not, community cohesion would disintegrate, and the groups within the society would separate.

Culture Is Learned

enculturation
Process of learning one's culture through informal observation and formal instruction.

Watch the Video: *Anthropology of Childhood* on **myanthrolab.com**

Culture is transmitted from generation to generation and is learned mainly in childhood and during maturation. We learn not only our behavior but also our attitudes and values. The ability to acquire culture in this way makes humans highly adaptable to different cultural environments. Humans are born with a potential to learn whatever knowledge and skills are practiced in their communities. They do this through the process of **enculturation**—learning one's culture through informal observation and formal instruction, beginning in earliest childhood. Children learn the culture that they are exposed to, as the Case Study "Daughter from Danang" illustrates. We all can acquire any culture if we are raised in it, just as most people can learn any language. Through these processes of exposure and learning, people acquire their culture and transmit it to others.

CASE STUDY

Daughter from Danang

Mai Thi Hiep was born in Danang, Vietnam, in 1968. She was the daughter of a Vietnamese mother and an American soldier who had abandoned Hiep's mother when she became pregnant. In 1975, her Vietnamese mother, troubled by the chaos of war, participated in "Operation Babylift," an American government program that placed racially mixed children from Vietnam for adoption in the United States, wanting to protect her child and expecting her to be returned later. Hiep's mother also feared reprisals from Vietnamese angered by the U.S. intervention in Vietnam.

At age seven, Hiep was sent to the United States, where a single woman adopted her. Hiep became Heidi and grew up in the small town of Pulaski, Tennessee. Heidi recalls that her adoptive mother advised her not to tell people that she was Vietnamese because of the racial climate in Pulaski. Heidi learned to think of herself as American. She forgot her native language quickly because she had no other Vietnamese people to speak with, and acquired all of the tastes and attitudes of American teenagers. By 1997, Heidi had married an American serviceman and became the mother of two young daughters.

Heidi longed to reconnect to her birth mother and to her Vietnamese family. By an odd coincidence, Heidi and her mother were contacting various agencies at about the same time, trying to find one another. Heidi located her mother and arranged for Heidi to visit her family in Danang. Before the trip, Heidi spoke of "going home."

It was ". . . going to be so healing for us. It would make all those bad memories [of war and separation] go away."

Reuniting with her Vietnamese family was deeply moving, but Heidi found the sights and sounds of Vietnam strange. She was shocked by the poverty of people on the streets and of her own family. At the first dinner, she did not know the etiquette of how to eat (dipping food from common plates into sauces rather than the American custom of placing a quantity of food on one's own plate), and was not used to the spiciness of the cooking. Within a few days, more problems surfaced. Heidi's mother never left her alone, holding her hand as they walked through the streets, touching and hugging her whenever she could. Although Heidi began to ". . . feel a little smothered," she was also a little "jealous" of the "love and unity" characteristic of Vietnamese kinship ties.

Her mother asked Heidi to help a sister who was extremely poor. Heidi gave her money, but when her sister asked for more, Heidi felt "insulted . . . I didn't come here to be anybody's salvation, I came here to be reunited." This was not what she had imagined. She wanted to "escape back to the world I feel comfortable in." For Heidi, love and asking for financial support were incompatible needs, but to her Vietnamese kin, asking for money didn't lessen the integrity of their love.

Before Heidi's departure, their final meeting revealed the stark contrasts between Heidi's expectations and those of her family. Her brother began to talk about their mother's advancing age and her need for material and emotional support. He said that, for twenty-two years, ". . . we, your siblings, have been taking care of our mother. We hope that now you will assume your filial responsibility toward her," meaning to send money monthly. Again, Heidi was shocked, but her mother understood her negative reaction to this direct request for financial help: "What does she know about the Vietnamese notion of love and emotion? She's used to living in a different way." Heidi's brother added, "We are trying to understand your situation and we hope you'll try to understand ours. . . . As a Vietnamese, I thought what I said was normal." Although saddened by her family's situation, Heidi could not respond the way they expected. "It's not how I wanted it to be."

From a cultural perspective, the complex, conflicting expectations of both Heidi and her Vietnamese relatives were understandable and appropriate, given the cultural contexts in which each lived and the attitudes and values that they had learned. Although Heidi was born Vietnamese, she had become an American. Because her family remembered her as the child known as Hiep, they expected her to conform to their own system of values. Heidi interpreted her family's expectations through the lens of American culture because most of her socialization had been in the United States.

This story demonstrates how cultural learning molds people to regard their society's practices and values as normal and natural. Understanding other people's reactions from their own perspective requires insight and empathy.

From *Daughter from Danang*, PBS American Experience. Directed by Gail Dolgin and Vicente Franco. © 2003 PBS.

Read the **Document** on **myanthrolab.com**

Although most human cultural behavior is the result of learning, this behavior is also influenced by inherited drives as well as acquired needs. People must fulfill important physical and survival needs, just like all living creatures. People need to eat, drink, sleep, eliminate body wastes, and engage in sexual activity. And, like other primates, people also need to interact with one another to obtain food and protection. Culture intervenes and influences the ways in which people satisfy these needs.

taboos
Norms specifying behaviors that are prohibited in a culture.

For example, each culture has attitudes about what kinds of foods are edible and suitable for human consumption. People do not eat everything that is edible in their environment; they select some foods and reject others, expressing these choices as preferences and prohibitions, or **taboos.** In the United States and Canada, most people consider eating insects distasteful, but many peoples of Australia, Asia, Mexico, and Africa consider insects a delicacy. The Maasai of Kenya and northern Tanzania drink the blood of their cattle. Koreans farm puppies for meat. Religion-based taboos forbidding Hindus to eat beef and forbidding Muslims and Jews to eat pork further illustrate the mediation of survival needs through culture. Further, people also have norms about how many meals to have, when to eat them, and which kinds of foods to eat at each meal.

How many meals do you eat in a day, and at what times? What kinds of foods do you eat at each meal? If you ate eggs at different mealtimes, how might you prepare them differently for each meal, and why? What do your answers to these questions reveal about your cultural norms and values?

cultural core
Practices by which people organize their work and produce food and other goods necessary for their survival.

Although all people need to sleep, they normally do so at a culturally prescribed time and place. No matter how tired you are at work, it would probably be inappropriate to lie down on the floor or your desk to sleep. People follow culturally prescribed rules about where and when to eliminate body wastes. Most people are taught not to urinate or defecate in public under any circumstances, for example. In fact, doing so may be a criminal offense. All cultures also have norms about when and how to satisfy sexual urges appropriately. These norms include strong taboos that prohibit sexual relations between parents and their children and between siblings.

Societies enculturate children in culturally specific ways. In many societies, children are expected to learn skills informally by observation and imitation. That is, they watch and observe their parents or other elders and learn by trying to do the same thing. Adults may offer guidance, but, for the most part, the child learns by doing and is an active participant in the process. This type of learning takes place in all communities in some contexts, but training and education also take place in formal settings such as schools in some societies.

Casual observation of others as they interact informally also plays a role in enculturation. Through observation, children learn attitudes: They hear what people have to say about themselves and others, and what they think of other people's behavior. They listen to people express their beliefs about the world. Through these conversations and interactions, children learn what is valued and what is criticized by members of the community. In these contexts, they thus gain a sense of personal identity as well as a sense of the world and their place in it.

Culture Is Adaptive

When anthropologists say that culture is adaptive, they are usually referring to behaviors and beliefs that respond to environmental constraints and opportunities that ensure a community's survival. People must adapt to their environment, and culture is their chief mechanism of adaptation. Because of their capacity for adaptation, humans can survive in nearly any environment. Further, people can modify their environments and create artificial ones to enhance survival. Cultural adaptations often involve technological innovation and the elaboration of material culture. For example, people living on islands or along coasts construct rafts, canoes, and boats to cross rivers, bays, and oceans, and people everywhere make a vast array of tools and equipment to help them obtain food and perform other kinds of subsistence tasks. The tools and practices that enable people to satisfy their survival and adaptation needs make up what is called a **cultural core**.

Although adaptation through culture is a fundamental and universal process, not all cultural practices are adaptive. Some practices may be maladaptive or have unintended negative consequences as circumstances change. Sometimes solving one problem may lead to new, unforeseen problems.

The Image Works/Jack K. Clark/The Image Works

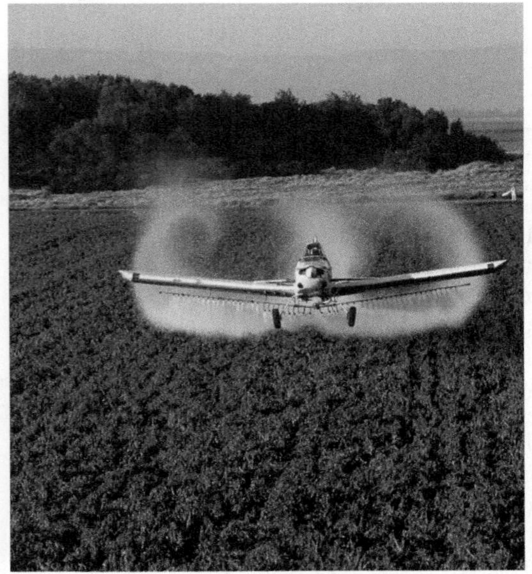

This cropduster's payload is carefully regulated because chemical fertilizers may contaminate food and deplete land productivity in the long term.

The archaeological record gives us some clues about how agricultural techniques that turned out to have unforeseen negative consequences contributed to the decline of several large and prosperous ancient cultures in both the Eastern and Western Hemispheres. For example, Sumer in ancient Mesopotamia (what is now southern Iraq) had developed large city-states by 3000 B.C. The Sumerian economy was based on intensive farming, made possible by extensive irrigation systems that channeled water from the Tigris and Euphrates rivers to fields. Sumerian farmers produced a greater yield of crops than farmers in the region produce today (Sasson 1995).

Over time, crop yields declined. One reason for the eventual fall of Sumerian civilization was that intensive irrigation increased salinization, or salt content, in the soil. As the land deteriorated, Sumer was no longer able to support large populations without a decline in living standards (Peregrine 2003).

The Industrial Revolution provides a more recent example of unintended negative consequences. Industry's ability to supply millions of people with an ever-increasing amount and variety of products has led to pollution, contamination, and overexploitation of natural resources and nonrenewable energy resources. Many practices, like the heavy reliance on chemical fertilizers and pesticides commonly used in industrial agriculture, are maladaptive in the long run, although they may increase productivity in the short term.

Thus, the idea that culture is adaptive needs to be considered in context. That is, a particular practice may be adaptive in one situation but not in another. For instance, farming techniques used in temperate climates to increase crop yields may be counterproductive in the Amazon rain forest because the topsoil there is too thin and relatively infertile to sustain them. This is exactly what is happening in parts of the Amazon today, where environmentally inappropriate farming techniques are harming the long-term viability of the soil (Schmink and Wood 1992).

CASE STUDY

Maladaptive Adaptations: Kuru and Mad Cow

In 1910, a new disease appeared among the South Fore (pronounced For'ray), a farming people of New Guinea. This progressive disease, called *kuru* (meaning "trembling" or "fear" in the Fore language), affects the central nervous system and slowly leads to complete physical incapacitation and death. Victims gradually become unable to sit or walk unaided, focus their eyes, speak clearly, or even swallow. Death usually occurs six to twelve months after the onset of symptoms, although some people may survive as long as two years.

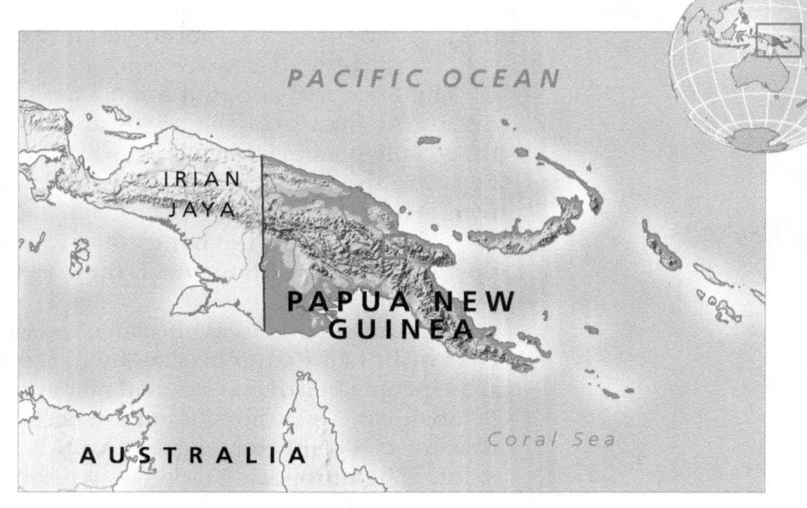

Investigation of the spread of kuru during the 1950s led to suspicion that it correlated with ritual cannibalism by women. In Fore society, as elsewhere in New Guinea, women are the primary farmers, growing sweet potatoes, yams, and other vegetables. They also care for the domesticated pigs each household keeps. Men clear the fields and hunt, but do little farm labor. Women live in small huts with their children and pigs, and men reside communally in a "men's house," eating and sleeping away from their families. Fore culture emphasizes concepts of pollution and danger, against which rituals serve as antidotes. This includes the belief that women pose a threat to male strength and vitality. Men and women also participate in different social and ceremonial activities.

In the early 1900s, South Fore women began practicing cannibalism as part of their mourning ceremonies when a female relative died. This ritual involved eating the brains and body parts of the deceased kin. According to anthropologist Shirley Lindenbaum (1979), this practice had some adaptive value because it provided needed protein, particularly for women. As the population increased and more land came under cultivation, sources of animal protein had declined. In addition, men had access to more high-quality protein than women because they claimed greater rights to the pigs. They believed that other sources of protein, such as insects, frogs, and small mammals, were not only unfit for men but might threaten their health and vigor. Thus, women may have turned to cannibalism to secure more protein.

When a South Fore woman died, her female relatives dismembered her body and ate it. Some of the meat was given to children of either sex, but adult men rarely ate it because of the belief that contact with women (and, logically, eating their flesh) was dangerous and polluting. The Fore did not associate cannibalism with kuru, but they were alarmed by the high incidence of the disease, particularly among women. They attributed kuru to sorcery, a common cause of illness and death in their belief system. When someone died of kuru, kinspeople tried to identify the evildoer, usually accusing someone who might have had reason to wish the victim harm.

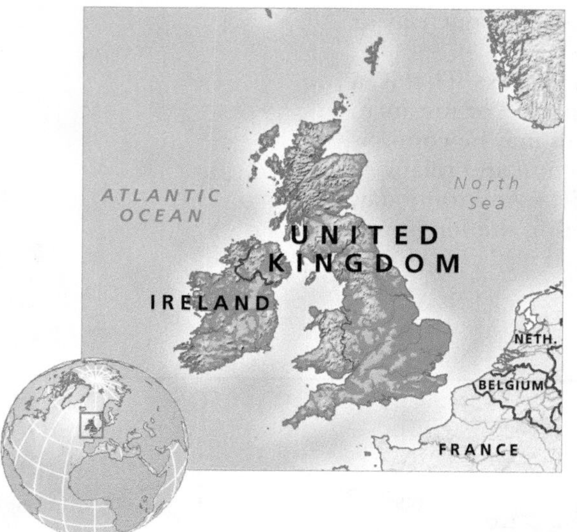

Between 1957 and 1968, when the disease was at its height, about 1,000 people died in the South Fore population of 8,000. The fact that nearly all the deaths were of adult women added to the social and economic burden, because women produced the crops, tended the pigs, and gave birth. In some villages, nearly half of the adult female deaths and nearly all of the deaths of children between ages 5 and 16 were due to kuru (Foster and Anderson 1978).

The riddle of kuru was not solved until the late 1960s, when the anthropologist-virologist Carlton Gajdusek discovered that the disease was transmitted by a prion, the same kind of agent responsible for mad cow disease. Prions, slow-acting proteins that attack and destroy brain tissue, remain dormant for years after they are ingested but eventually cause progressive damage to the brain. Thus, when South Fore women and children ate the brains of their female relatives, they unknowingly ingested the cause of their own deaths. The incidence of kuru began to decline after the Australian colonial administration in New Guinea persuaded the Fore to give up ritual cannibalism.

The Fore had adopted a maladaptive practice. Similarly, the spread of mad cow disease in Britain in the 1980s and 1990s resulted from a procedure that seemed financially beneficial in the short term but ultimately proved disastrous. Companies began to use bonemeal derived from sheep brains as cheap protein filler for cattle feed. However, some of the bonemeal was infected with a disease called scrapie, caused by agents of the family of prions similar to those that caused kuru. When cattle ate the infected bonemeal, they developed symptoms similar to those manifested by the Fore.

Once mad cow disease became known and its source identified, more than 140,000 cows in Britain had to be slaughtered to prevent the disease from spreading. In 1996, some people in Britain who died of a prion-caused disease now identified as Creutzfeldt-Jakob disease were thought to have become sick after eating beef infected with mad cow disease. As a consequence, more British cattle were slaughtered to stem a potential epidemic. The European Union banned the export of British beef from 1996 to 1999, and nearly half of the country's 11 million cattle were destroyed. Some British cattle imported into Canada and the United States also were destroyed.

The U.S. Department of Agriculture now bars importation of cattle and many cattle by-products from Britain and most other European nations. The Food and Drug Administration has also banned the use of beef proteins or hormonal extracts from cattle organs in medicines, dietary supplements, and cosmetics. The economic loss to the European and Canadian cattle industry has been disastrous. Using cheap sheep brains to fatten cattle ended up costing millions of dollars and many lives.

What are some other examples of "maladaptive" adaptations in today's world?

Mad cow disease, like kuru among the Fore, demonstrates that people sometimes engage in practices that seem to make sense when first introduced but have consequences in the long term that are maladaptive and even life-threatening. These two syndromes are vastly different in their cultural causes, one stemming from religious beliefs and the other driven by the economic motive to cut costs. However, they share a similar process, namely, that seemingly sensible behavior often has unforeseen and dangerous consequences. **Read** the **Document** on **myanthrolab.com**

Culture Is Integrated

cultural integration
Tendency for people's practices and beliefs to form a relatively coherent and consistent system.

Cultural integration refers to the observation that people's practices and beliefs form a relatively coherent and consistent system. Cultures are not simply random collections of activities but, instead, are patterned and interrelated in systematic ways. For example, behaviors that take place in one domain, such as political organization, tend to be compatible with and support behaviors taking place in other domains, such as family organization. Anthropologists recognize that terms such as *economy, social organization, family organization,* and *government* are not discrete, separable units of activity but are closely intertwined. For example, economic activities are usually integrated with, affect, and are affected by other kinds of activities. The work of obtaining food and other goods and services is often performed by people who occupy particular social roles and statuses. Gender roles may assign men and women different kinds of work in contributing to their household economies. Also, social norms or, in complex societies, laws enacted by legislators and policies formulated by political agencies tend to be consistent with particular economic consequences and to reinforce particular economic goals.

The shared ways that people organize their lives are major integrating factors. In some societies, religious beliefs permeate and guide all aspects of daily life. Religion then becomes an overarching, integrative system of beliefs and practices. People in societies integrated by religion might perform daily rituals to bless and safeguard themselves and their families; they may recite prayers when hunting or planting crops to ensure success; and they may ask for spirit protection when engaging in any dangerous activity. People in these societies believe that the human and spiritual realms are not separable but that spiritual forces are omnipresent and continually affect their lives.

Naturally, not all aspects of cultural behavior and belief are internally consistent or integrated with all others. Thus, the concept of cultural integration needs to be understood loosely, as a process of adjustment and change, not as static and rigid. Humans and their experiences are not so neat and tidy. Nevertheless, cultural systems as wholes tend toward consistency. A consequence of this consistency and integration is that change in one societal domain causes change in others (see the Case Study "Women and Work in the United States," for example). Societies are not bounded units (either of people or ideas); rather, external influences from other peoples or internal tensions and innovations lead to changes in practices and attitudes.

CASE STUDY

Consequences of Cultural Integration: Women and Work in the United States

In the United States, changes in women's participation in paid employment have affected both their roles in other spheres of life and the prevailing attitudes about men and women (Fox and Hesse-Biber 1984). Women's rates of employment began to rise significantly during World War II, as a consequence of the nation's military and economic policies. As millions of men entered the armed forces, millions of jobs necessary to support the economy and the war effort were left vacant. Public policy encouraged women to do their patriotic duty by working in factories and offices, where they had previously met resistance and discrimination. The banner of women's rights, which had won American women the right to vote in 1920, was raised again.

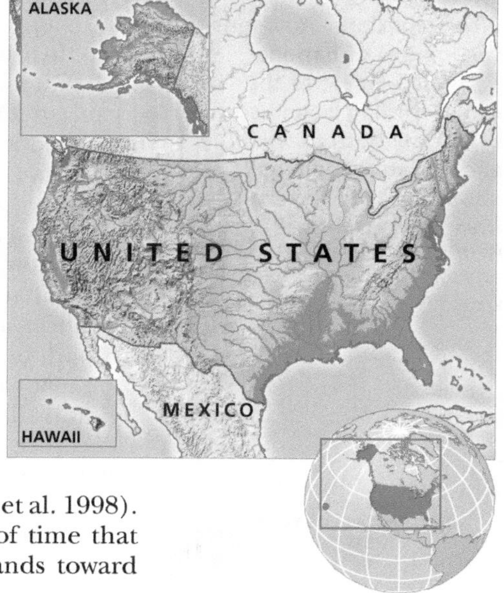

After the war, many women returned to exclusively domestic roles, but others remained in the work force, partly for personal reasons and partly to improve their family's standard of living. Also, work outside the home gave women a degree of financial equality with their husbands. Women's economic gains contributed to rising rates of divorce because wives could sometimes afford to leave unhappy marriages, and husbands could leave if they felt that their ex-wives could be at least partially self-supporting (Costello et al. 1998). In intact families, greater financial equality as well as the greater amount of time that women spent outside the home contributed to shifting the roles of husbands toward some household and child-care responsibilities.

By the late twentieth century, the percentage of marriages that ended in divorce had risen, and the social stigma formerly associated with divorce had all but disappeared. Also, women's paid employment and opportunities to make prominent contributions in public arenas had expanded. Today, more legislators, governors, and heads of government agencies are women. Women's leadership roles in religion have also

View the **Slideshow:** *Gender* on **myanthrolab.com**

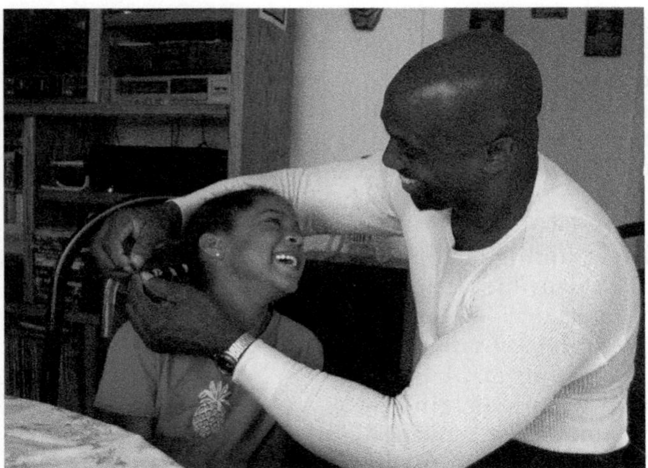

Changes in the roles and status of women in American society have affected men's lives as well as the society as a whole.
The Image Works/Geri Engberg/The Image Works

broadened; many Protestant and Jewish denominations ordain women ministers and rabbis. More women have advanced educational degrees and are more accepted in formerly male-dominated occupations and professions, such as law and law enforcement, the military, and the building trades.

Changes in women's roles have also affected how men think about themselves and their work. Husbands now expect their wives to contribute to household incomes. And work roles for men have become more flexible. A father could be a stay-at-home Dad if his wife's work brought in more money than his or if he simply preferred that role. And society has become more accepting of men working in certain jobs traditionally associated with women, such as nursing and elementary school teaching.

Thus, within a mere fifty years, changes in one societal sphere in the United States led to changes both in other spheres and in people's thoughts and behaviors. These multiple and interrelating effects illustrate how cultural integration can lead to cultural transformation.

Read the **Document** on **myanthrolab.com**

Culture Is Based on Symbols

symbol
A word, image, or object that stands for cultural ideas or sentiments.

People's behaviors and understanding of the world are based on meanings expressed through symbols. A **symbol** is a word or object that represents or stands for an idea, event, meaning, or sentiment. Language is a pervasive and powerful symbol system. Words in any language are just sequences of sounds, but each sequence is a symbol of or represents something other than the sounds themselves. The collection of sounds in each word in this sentence, for instance, stands for some arbitrarily assigned meaning.

Symbols permeate human culture in ways other than language. Objects, art, and artistic performances may represent powerful cultural ideas and attitudes. The colors and designs of national flags, for instance, come to be associated with complex levels of meaning. People can understand those meanings by examining the contexts of flag use, the way people talk about their national colors, and the way people react to them. Flags are used to symbolically represent a country, a territorial and cultural unit differentiated from all other similarly organized territorial and cultural units. Flags take on additional associations, demonstrated by the emotional reactions they can trigger in observers. People may use their country's flag in ways that show their attitudes and political beliefs. For example, in the United States, after the al Qaeda attack on 9/11, flag pins became necessities for many political figures and represented a show of support for the "war on terror" that the United States undertook.

What emotional reactions can images of national flags stir? How has the American flag been used to display both positive and negative feelings about the U.S. government or its policies?

Religion, too, is a domain filled with symbolic meanings. Believers invest tremendous importance in objects considered to have religious significance. Ordinary objects and substances used in rituals take on sacred properties. Books, cups, images, pieces of cloth or wood, or foodstuffs can be symbols of beliefs and can evoke powerful emotions and dramatize sacred actions. Symbolic culture thus includes both sacred and secular meanings and all the ways in which those meanings are communicated.

Culture often is expressed in symbolic interaction between individuals using verbal and nonverbal language. Thus, language can also be used to challenge basic assumptions encoded in ordinary speech. For example, a dialect of Caribbean immigrants and their descendants in Great Britain, called Afro-Lingua, focuses on the ways that standard English transmits common cultural assumptions about race in the uses and meanings that associate *white* with "good" and *black* with "bad." For example, in common English expressions, "a black day" means a day when things go drastically wrong, and "a black sheep" means an outcast family member (Bones 1986, 46). Afro-Lingua speakers might refer to "a white day" and "a white sheep" in equivalent contexts. In addition, Afro-Lingua also changes syllables in some English words to highlight cultural and political meanings: The word *politics* is transformed into *politricks,* and *oppression* becomes *downpression* (Wong 1986, 119).

Afro-Lingua is a language that was created to symbolically challenge the basic assumptions encoded in the ordinary speech of European colonizers of the Caribbean.

Humor is another form of symbolic cultural communication. For example, Western Apache communities in New Mexico have a repertoire of joke routines that ridicule Anglos by imitating and exaggerating their intrusive, domineering communicative styles (Basso 1979). Apaches find these Anglo communication styles insensitive at best or even offensive. Scorned behaviors include making direct eye contact with or staring at interlocutors, touching another person while talking to him or her, calling casual acquaintances "friend," and asking intrusive, personal questions. Through their informal comic routines, Apaches share the opposite norms and values.

Both the changes in English expressions used by speakers of Afro-Lingua and the joking routines of Western Apaches demonstrate the ways that symbolic behavior can be used to challenge dominant values. Through symbolic practices, people can forge their unity with others and can simultaneously develop and transmit messages of resistance. Afro-Lingua speakers defy commonplace notions of race and power; Western Apaches resist communicative norms imposed on them by dominant Anglo society.

What would you learn about cultural communication from studying in your workplace or dorm?

naturalized concepts
Ideas and behaviors so deeply embedded in a culture that they are regarded as universally normal or natural.

Culture Organizes the Way People Think about the World

Through exposure to cultural symbols, enculturation, and the acquisition of shared cultural concepts, people develop ways of thinking about themselves, their lives, other people, and the world. Culture, therefore, consists of systems of meaning produced and interpreted by members. Underlying shared concepts and meanings become so ingrained that they are taken for granted, assumed to be true. People understand them as natural and commonsense. These are **naturalized concepts,** ideas thought to be essential and to exist in nature. Since people understand these naturalized concepts to be part of the "natural" world, they are unaware of their cultural origins and do not question their legitimacy. Indeed, they don't think about them at all. And these taken-for-granted suppositions have all the more influence on people because they are not consciously thought about.

All societies have a core of naturalized ideas, based on societal norms. For example, in most capitalist societies, it is taken for granted that people want to own property and obtain wealth. It is assumed that people are naturally competitive and want to continually acquire more property, own larger and more expensive houses, and have unlimited access to possessions. Yet people in these societies generally may not understand that their attitudes and values about property and wealth stem from the kind of economic system they live in. Models of gender are also deeply naturalized in people's behaviors and attitudes. We come to believe that men's and women's roles and value are derived from qualities, feelings, and needs inherent in women and men rather than understanding that these gender models are largely derived from culture. In other words, people who lack an anthropological perspective think that their attitudes and values are natural and universal rather than products of their culture. Thus, naturalized concepts orient people's thinking about themselves and the world, forming a background ideology that gives meaning to people's behaviors and attitudes. To the extent that they shape the way we view other cultures, they are also a source of ethnocentrism.

Although all cultures have fundamental organizing concepts, these principles may be challenged from within the society. In all societies, members of different subcultures or

What are some examples of culture wars in U.S. society today? What are some examples of countercultures in U.S. history?

These Chinese and American children are forming group identities based on symbiotic culture. Getty Images/Hulton Archive/Getty Images; PhotoEdit/Michael Ventura/PhotoEdit, Inc.

culture wars
Internal disagreements in a society about cultural models or about how society or the world should be organized.

counterculture
An alternative cultural model within a society that expresses different views about the way that society should be organized.

worldview
A culture-based, often ethnocentric way that people see the world and other peoples.

subgroups hold alternative and conflicting values. Alternative views may be discussed and debated in the context of mutual respect or they may erupt in more contentious challenges, in what some observers refer to as **culture wars.** Expressions of antipathy between conservatives and liberals over many social policy issues in the United States, such as gun control, abortion rights, gay rights, and immigration policy, are examples of so-called culture wars.

On the other hand, individuals and groups engaging in practices with underlying meanings that conflict with prevailing assumptions and norms may be participants in a **counterculture**—an alternative culture model. Members of a counterculture view themselves as being in active opposition to dominant cultural themes and values. For example, the hippies of the 1960s openly rejected prevailing puritanical attitudes toward sex, the materialism of contemporary society, and the militaristic policies of the government as it escalated the war in Vietnam.

Challenges to widely recognized assumptions often come from members of groups that are marginalized or oppressed, or who hold different **worldviews** than those of the dominant groups or elites. For example, apartheid, South Africa's dominant racist cultural ideology until the 1990s, was imposed by a powerful white minority that had inherited power through colonial rule. That rule was challenged by the majority of black South Africans, who eventually overturned that ideology and rebelled against the government that oppressed them. Black South Africans asserted not only their political rights but also their right to replace the cultural model of white supremacy with one of racial equality. Thus, many political movements seek more than a reordering of social and political forces. They also seek the institutionalization of new cultural models as organizing principles in their society.

Similarly, through symbolic culture, some segments of a society might resist the official culture or offer an alternative cultural model. In the Middle East and North Africa, women's challenges to the ideology of male dominance often take the form of poetry and song, a low-risk context for expressing discontent. Bedouin women, for example, recite poetry and compose songs expressing their longings for love and respect. Song lyrics express passion and joy in attentions they receive from clandestine lovers (Abu-Lughod 1986; 1990). Artistic genres thus permit women to verbalize private feelings that run contrary to accepted norms of female deference and modesty.

Watch the **Animation:** *Characteristics of Culture* on **myanthrolab.com**

Table 1 summarizes the characteristics of culture as it is defined in this chapter. This section then closes with a story in the In Their Own Voices section

TABLE 1 CHARACTERISTICS OF CULTURE

Culture Is Shared	Behavior, attitudes, and ideas are formed through interaction with others. **Norms:** Sets of expectations and attitudes that people have about appropriate behavior. **Subculture:** A group whose members interact more frequently among themselves and share attitudes and practices that are distinct from others.
Culture Is Learned	Culture is acquired rather than inherited. **Enculturation:** The learning of one's cultural behaviors, attitudes, and values.
Culture Is Adaptive	Aspects of behavior and belief are responses to environmental constraints and the need to ensure a community's survival. **Cultural core:** Basic practices that function to satisfy people's adaptive needs.
Culture Is Integrated	Practices and beliefs that form a relatively coherent and consistent system. **Cultural model:** Comprehensive shared ideas about the ideal culture.
Culture Is Based on Symbols	People's behavior and understanding of the world are based on meanings expressed through language, art, and symbolic objects. **Symbols:** Words, images, or objects that stand for cultural ideas or sentiments.
Culture Organizes the Way People Think about the World	**Naturalized concepts:** Ideas and behaviors so deeply embedded in a culture that they are regarded as universally normal or natural. **Worldview:** The culture-based way that people see the world and other peoples. **Counterculture:** Alternative cultural model within a society that expresses opposition to dominant social and political views.

about an anthropologist's field experience that highlights the challenges of understanding cultures as unique collections of symbols and meanings.

Characteristics of culture include the fact that it is shared. Individuals who belong to a culture share assumptions about the world and develop cultural models and societal norms and taboos that define how one should and should not behave. Members of different subcultures in a society share culture differently. Culture is also learned through enculturation. We are enculturated both formally and informally through social interactions with other members of society. Culture is adaptive in that people change their culture when needed or when influenced to change. The knowledge, skills, and tools people use to survive and adapt are referred to as the cultural core. Culture is integrated—that is, aspects of culture are interconnected and mutually reinforcing. Thus, cultural integration means that change in one aspect of culture leads to changes in other aspects. The existence of culture wars and countercultures within a society illustrates, however, that cultures are not fully shared or rigidly integrated, that alternative cultural models coexist. Culture is based on symbols, and language is the most important symbol system people use. Symbolic objects and symbolic communication are used in diverse contexts, such as religion and humor. Culture influences the way people organize their experience and their worldview. They use naturalized concepts to apply their cultural assumptions to their own and other people's ways of life.

CULTURE CHANGE

Culture contact, a major force in the process of globalization, leads to several strategies and consequences of culture change, including acculturation, assimilation, and reactive adaptation.

Cultures are dynamic systems that respond to societal and historical changes from numerous sources. The view of "traditional" or indigenous societies as static and timeless is untenable. All societies experience innovation from within and influences from outside origins. Some sources of culture change are internal, emerging from new practices and attitudes, technological innovations, or adaptations to the consequences of earlier practices. Other sources of culture change emerge as people borrow ideas or artifacts from their neighbors or from people with whom they interact through migration, trade, or other contacts. Some borrowings take place in friendly interactions during **culture contact,** but others are forced on people, as in conquest or foreign intervention.

Although it may be possible to identify original sources of change as internal or external, in practice these are interconnected processes. For instance, cultural changes stimulated by external sources then typically undergo further change through internal processes. People usually adapt outside cultural borrowings to their own cultures. They may borrow only parts of a cultural item, whether a story or a way of organizing economic activity, and combine those parts with items that already exist in their cultural repertoire. For example, in the realm of religion, people often combine elements of their traditional beliefs with those that they learn from external sources as a consequence of culture contact. This process, called **syncretism,** is seen in religions such as Santería, which combines traditional Afro-Caribbean beliefs in magic and witchcraft with Roman Catholicism. Spanish colonizers in the Caribbean derisively called this religion of the Yoruba—and other Bantu slaves from Nigeria, Senegal, and the Guinea Coast—Santería, "Way of the Saints."

Anthropologists have other terms to describe the kinds of internal change that take place following culture contact, depending on the power relations between peoples and the extent of change. **Assimilation** occurs when a less numerous and less powerful group changes its ways to blend in with the dominant culture. In assimilating, people abandon or modify their prior beliefs and practices and adopt the cultural repertoire of the dominant population. For example, immigrants may voluntarily change their national and cultural identities by assimilating the language and culture of their new country. Assimilation is also sometimes forced on people by a dominant culture, especially in the context of conquest and colonization.

A group's adjustment to living within another, more dominant, culture while at the same time maintaining its original cultural identity is called **acculturation.** For example, many Native Americans in the United States and Canada adopt many features of dominant American culture such as the economic and political systems, but maintain their own languages, family systems, and religious beliefs. The term **cultural pluralism** describes

culture contact
Direct interaction between peoples of different cultures through migration, trade, invasion, or conquest.

syncretism
Process by which a cultural product is created when people adapt a cultural item selectively borrowed from another culture to fit their existing culture.

assimilation
Process by which a less numerous and less powerful cultural group changes its ways and cultural identity to blend in with the dominant culture.

acculturation
Process by which a group adjusts to living within a dominant culture while at the same time maintaining its original cultural identity.

cultural pluralism
Condition in a stratified society in which many diverse cultural groups ideally live together equally and harmoniously without losing their cultural identities and diversity.

In Their Own VOICES

Hamlet and the Tiv

An anthropologist's effort to explain Shakespeare's Hamlet to Tiv villagers in central Nigeria illustrates how far both the anthropologist and the Tiv culture shape the way they think about the world. When Laura Bohannan lived among the Tiv, they were a farming people living in small villages. Village life centered on groups of families related through men, with fathers, sons, and brothers forming the core of households. After marriage, women moved from their families to live with their husband's relatives. Men prepared fields for planting, but women planted seeds, weeded the plants, and harvested crops. In addition to their families, men depended on their age-mates—other men of the same age group—for help in times of trouble.

Bohannan was prompted to tell the story of Hamlet because she thought it had a universal meaning that people everywhere would understand in the same way. The Tiv elders also thought the story had universal meaning—but a different one. To both Bohannan and the elders, their particular understanding seemed obvious, showing how powerful cultural assumptions can be. If you need to refresh your memory on what Hamlet is about, read the summary at http://shakespeare.palomar.edu/lambtales/LTHAMLET.HTM. To read the rest of Bohannan's amusing and insightful article, search the Internet for "Shakespeare in the Bush."

The following excerpt expresses the views of both Bohannan and Tiv villagers on the meaning of the play.

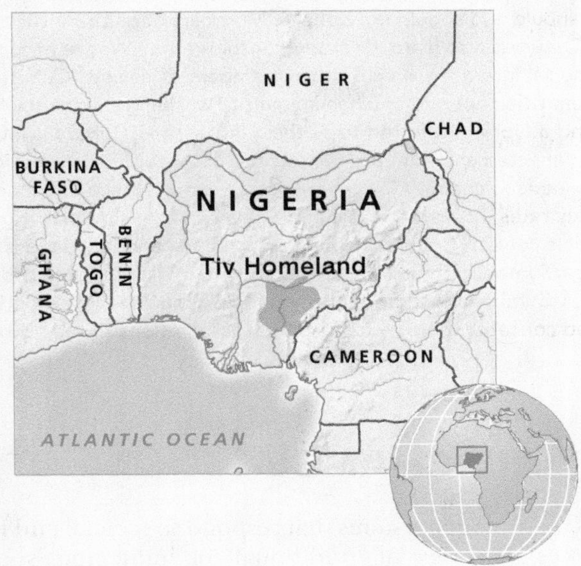

I began in the proper style, "Not yesterday, not yesterday, but long ago, a thing occurred. One night three men were keeping watch outside the homestead of the great chief, when suddenly they saw the former chief approach them."

"Why was he no longer their chief?"

"He was dead," I explained. "That is why they were troubled and afraid when they saw him."

"Impossible," began one of the elders. "Of course it wasn't the dead chief. It was an omen sent by a witch. . . ."

Slightly shaken, I continued. "One of these three was a man who knew things"—the closest translation for *scholar,* but unfortunately it also meant *witch.* "So he spoke to the dead chief saying, "Tell us what we must do so you may rest in your grave," but the dead chief did not answer. . . .

There was a general shaking of heads round the circle. "Had the dead chief no living brothers? Or was this son the chief?" . . .

"He had one living brother who became the chief when the elder brother died. In our country the son is next to the father. The dead chief's younger brother had become the great chief. He had also married his elder brother's widow only about a month after the funeral." . . .

"He did well," the old man beamed and announced to the others. "I told you that if we knew more about Europeans, we could find they really were very like us. In our country also," he added to me, "the younger brother marries the elder brother's widow and becomes the father of his children. Now, if your uncle, who married your widowed mother, is your father's full brother, then he will be a real father to you. Did Hamlet's father and uncle have one mother?"

His question barely penetrated my mind; I was too upset and thrown too far off balance by having one of the most important

modernization
Complex culture change, both internal and external, based on industrialism and a transnational market economy.

cultural evolution
Belief of early anthropologists that cultures evolve through various stages from a simpler and more primitive state to a complex and more culturally advanced state.

a stratified society that contains many diverse cultural groups who ideally live together equally and harmoniously. Other complex changes that occur through combinations of external and internal processes include economic transformations, such as **modernization,** based on industrialism and a market economy.

Internal Culture Change

Early anthropologists, such as Edward B. Tylor, believed that cultures evolve through various stages, from a simpler and more primitive state to a complex and more culturally advanced state. To Tylor and his nineteenth-century contemporaries, middle-class Euro-American culture represented the pinnacle of this **cultural evolution,** which other elements of Hamlet knocked straight out of the picture. Rather uncertainly I said that I thought they had the same mother, but I wasn't sure—the story didn't say. The old man told me severely that these genealogical details made all the difference and that when I got home I must ask the elders about it. . . .

Determined to save what I could of the mother motif, I took a deep breath and began again. "The son Hamlet was very sad because his mother had married again so quickly. There was no need for her to do so, and it is our custom for a widow not to go to her next husband until she has mourned for two years."

"Two years is too long," objected the elder's wife. "Who will hoe your farms for you while you have no husband?"

I gave up. . . .

"That night . . . the dead chief again appeared, and . . . Hamlet followed his dead father off to one side. When they were alone, Hamlet's dead father spoke."

"Omens can't talk!" The old man was emphatic. . . .

"It was Hamlet's dead father. It was a thing we call a *ghost*." I had to use the English word, for unlike many of the neighboring tribes, these people didn't believe in the survival after death of any individuating part of the personality. . . .

"Dead men can't walk," protested my audience as one man.

I was quite willing to compromise. "A ghost is the dead man's shadow."

But again they objected. "Dead men cast no shadows."

"They do in my country," I snapped. . . .

"Anyhow," I resumed, "Hamlet's dead father said that his own brother, the one who became chief, had poisoned him. He wanted Hamlet to avenge him. Hamlet believed this in his heart, for he did not like his father's brother." . . .

"Now Hamlet's age-mates," I continued, "had brought with them a famous storyteller. Hamlet decided to have this man tell the chief and all his homestead a story about a man who had poisoned his brother because he desired his brother's wife and wished to be chief himself. Hamlet was sure the great chief could not hear the story without making a sign if he was indeed guilty, and then he would discover whether his dead father had told him the truth. . . . It was true, for when the storyteller was telling his tale before all the homestead, the great chief rose in fear. Afraid that Hamlet knew his secret he planned to have him killed." . . .

This time I had shocked my audience seriously. "For a man to raise his hand against his father's brother and the one who has become his father—that is a terrible thing. The elders ought to let such a man be bewitched." . . .

I then pointed out that after all the man had killed Hamlet's father.

"No," pronounced the old man, speaking less to me than to the young men sitting behind the elders. "If your father's brother has killed your father, you must appeal to your father's age-mates; they may avenge him. No man may use violence against his senior relatives. . . . But if his father's brother had indeed been wicked enough to bewitch Hamlet and make him mad that would be a good story indeed, for it would be his fault that Hamlet, being mad, no longer had any sense and thus was ready to kill his father's brother."

There was a murmur of applause. Hamlet was again a good story to them, but it no longer seemed quite the same story to me. . . .

The old man made soothing noises. "You tell the story well, and we are listening. But it is clear that the elders of your country have never told you what the story really means. No, don't interrupt! We believe you when you say your marriage customs are different, or your clothes and weapons. But people are the same everywhere; therefore, there are always witches and it is we, the elders, who know how witches work. We told you it was the great chief who wished to kill Hamlet, and now your own words have proved us right. . . .

"Sometime," concluded the old man, "you must tell us some more stories of your country. We, who are elders, will instruct you in their true meaning, so that when you return to your own land your elders will see that you have not been sitting in the bush, but among those who know things and who have taught you wisdom."

From Laura Bohannan, "Shakespeare in the Bush," *Natural History* (August/September 1966).

CRITICAL THINKING QUESTION

What Tiv cultural assumptions and values caused them to interpret the story of *Hamlet* differently?

cultures could naturally and eventually achieve. Others treated the concept of cultural evolution as analogous to biological evolution, claiming that some cultures were naturally superior to others, modeled on the concepts of competition and the survival of the fittest. This faulty reasoning, known as **social Darwinism,** claimed that the wealth and power of Western societies were due to their natural and cultural superiority rather than to the consequences of historical processes. Social Darwinists saw competition between societies as based on similar processes as biological evolution. However, they failed to recognize that particular events and developments in fact contributed to the ability of some societies to dominate others. They also used models of efficiency and progress, analogous to biological processes, in their analyses of cultural development and change.

social Darwinism
Early belief that cultures compete for survival of the fittest, as in the process of natural selection in biological evolution.

Aboriginal star singer Archie Roach, shown here with Ruby Hunter, was a member of Australia's "Stolen Generation." Roach was put into a Salvation Army home at age three and then fostered out to three different white families. Corbis/John Van Hasselt/Sygma/Corbis

Today, however, evolutionary biologists study the adaptive value of social behavior, cognitive skills, and the capacity for both material and symbolic culture, all of which have contributed to the evolutionary success of the primates, and which all living human groups possess equally. Thus, **culture history** may be a more apt term than cultural evolution for ongoing culture change in which people respond and adapt to their environment and experiences. In adapting, people make themselves. That is, people develop, define, and direct their own cultural and ethnic identities, a process called **ethnogenesis** (Hill 1992). This concept of culture change views human beings as agents in their own history, continually creating and re-creating the conditions of their lives.

Some changes in societies are not intentional, like ethnogenesis, but result from gradual shifting of public norms and private sentiments. For example, in art and public performance, certain behaviors and language use that were unacceptable in the past have become standard, although not without arousing conflict among some sectors of the population.

What are some problems with applying principles of biological evolution to explanations of culture change?

Since the 1960s, the content of American films has changed considerably. In previous periods, violence generally was shown only from a distance, and its effects on the human body were not made explicit. Today, the depiction of explicit violence and its effects is commonplace. Nudity and sexual activity also have become routine in American films and videos, and language is not censored as it was in the past. These changes reflect changes in attitudes and values rather than in technology. And these changes are embedded in the wider social and political contexts of the times. The Motion Picture Production Code of the 1930s, which imposed strict limits on language, subject matter, and sexual representation, has been replaced by a rating system identifying film content. Publicized ratings warn potential viewers who do not want themselves or their children exposed to particular content.

Another source of internal culture change is the adaptations that people make by inventing new technologies and skills to better adjust to existing conditions or to deal with new problems. **Inventions** usually are based on previous tools, knowledge, and skills in a process called **innovation.** New environmental challenges and opportunities stimulate innovation and the invention of new adaptive strategies. Some technology-based cultural transformations are so sweeping that they are referred to as revolutions, such as the economic and technological changes termed the "Industrial Revolution." Political forms of **revolution,** in which people try to overturn the social and political order and replace it with new forms of society and culture, are another widespread form of internal culture change that has been a part of the history of many state societies.

culture history
Ongoing culture change in which people respond and adapt to their environment.

ethnogenesis
Ongoing process in which people develop, define, and direct their own cultural and ethnic identities.

inventions
New technologies and systems of knowledge.

innovation
Process by which new technologies and systems of knowledge are based on or built from previous tools, knowledge, and skills.

revolution
Process by which people try to change their culture or overturn the social order and replace it with a new, ideal society and culture.

diffusion
Spread of ideas, material objects, and cultural practices from one society to another through direct and indirect culture contact.

External Culture Change

Culture change also occurs through contact with other peoples as individuals migrate, trade, invade, intermarry, or interact in other ways. People learn ideas and skills and borrow tools, foods, clothing, and luxury items from other people with whom they have direct or indirect contact. This process, called **diffusion,** is responsible for the spread of material objects and cultural practices from one place to another.

Diffusion may be local, such as the spread of the invention of blow darts and the use of poisons among some native peoples of South America. Diffusion also can be widespread, even global within geographic constraints, such as the invention of agriculture, which spread east and west along certain latitudes over thousands of years, based on the cultivation of diverse kinds of grain. In addition to diffusion, independent invention may account for the appearance of similar cultural traits in different parts of the world. An example is the invention of writing systems, which likely occurred more than once in prehistory among different peoples in the ancient Middle East, Mexico, and China.

What do these television and movie scenes suggest about changes in American social and cultural norms over the past 60 years? Photofest/Photofest

Alamy Limited/AF archive/Alamy

Invasion and conquest also are common causes of external culture change. Most early state societies probably developed partly through the process of expanding into neighboring territories and incorporating the peoples living there (Carniero 1970). Colonization or conquest not only forced indigenous peoples to accept foreign goods and practices but also compelled them to alter many of their cultural practices to conform to their conquerors' ways. The attitudes and values of subject peoples eventually transformed as well to be more consistent with the changes in their behavior. However, subjects of colonial or conquered states are not passive pawns in national and global policies and processes. Rather, indigenous peoples make choices and engage in actions that, in their views, best achieve their goals of maintaining their communities while adapting to their changing conditions. Some of these strategies accommodate to dominant norms, but other processes may overtly or covertly express subversion and resistance.

Today, as in the past, diffusion is a major force in the process of globalization, as concepts, technologies, languages, and symbols spread from one culture to another, aided in part by past conquests and the history of colonization.

The imposition of British colonial rule on the Luo of Kenya in the nineteenth century, for example, led to many interrelated changes in the economic, social, and political systems of that tribal society. The Luo (speakers of the Luo language, today known mainly as the Karivongo) settled in Kenya and Tanzania in the fifteenth or sixteenth century, migrating south from the Sudan. In the Sudan, their economy had been centered on cattle herding but shifted gradually to farming after they arrived in Kenya. This change affected gender relations because men had been primarily responsible for herding the cattle and women were the farmers. Following Luo custom, land was owned communally by groups of relatives headed by men, but women actually controlled the production and distribution of crops resulting from their labor. In the colonial and postcolonial periods, however, women's rights to the land and their economic independence were undermined by British land reforms.

In 1899, the British colonial government imposed policies aimed at consolidating individual holdings that were intentionally scattered in different locations. Traditional Luo patterns of landholding gave individuals use rights in scattered parcels so that they could obtain food resources in different ecological zones. People thus could plant a variety of crops suited to each zone. British authorities did not understand this custom, however; in their view, the traditional system was inefficient. In keeping with European ideals, the British combined landholdings into single parcels, which were registered in the names of male heads of households.

In addition, British colonial authorities imposed hut taxes that had to be paid in cash. To obtain cash for taxes, Luo men as heads of households often had to find wage work

Culture change can result from either internal or external forces, which usually are mutually reinforcing. Internal culture changes can come about from technological inventions or innovations within a society or can be introduced through culture contact and spread through borrowing, or diffusion. In syncretism, people modify and adapt borrowed items of religious belief and practice to fit their own culture. Culture history and ethnogenesis describe change processes within a society that are self-defining as well as adaptive to both internal and external stimuli. Although the capacity for culture is an important adaptation in human evolution, culture change does not involve cultural evolution, an outdated idea based on beliefs in human progress, racial superiority, and social Darwinism. Outcomes of culture contact include, among others, assimilation and acculturation. Cultural pluralism describes culturally diverse societies in which groups have equal status under the law. Reactive adaptation is an outcome based on unrelieved stresses, often expressed through either violence or spiritual revitalization movements. Sweeping social and culture changes involving both internal and external factors stem from economic and political changes, such as the processes of modernization and revolution.

reactive adaptation
Coping response to loss and deprivation of captive, conquered, or oppressed peoples.

revitalization movement
Type of nonviolent reactive adaptation in which people try to resurrect their culture heroes and restore their traditional way of life.

global culture
A constellation of technologies, practices, attitudes, values, and symbols that spread internationally and enmesh nations and communities throughout the world in networks of power and influence.

away from their local communities. At the same time that taxation was a financial burden, men benefited from colonial policies. Participating in the cash economy gave them access to valuable manufactured goods, and their official status as individual landowners gave them greater power and authority. To raise more cash, Luo men turned land production over from home use to cash crops for export, making families more dependent on more expensive imported food to sustain themselves. The Kenyan government continued these land policies after independence in 1960.

Colonized or conquered peoples have responded to external sources of culture change in diverse ways, including assimilation and acculturation, discussed earlier in the chapter. Another kind of outcome is **reactive adaptation,** in which people react against loss, deprivation, and oppression through passive resistance or violence. Traditional religious leaders and beliefs may play a role in social movements aimed at restoring or revitalizing the traditional culture. A classic example of a **revitalization movement** is the Ghost Dance movement of the North American Plains Indians (Wallace 1956; Mooney 1965). This arose in 1889, at a time when native peoples had been forcibly confined to reservations after brutal military campaigns. Most of their land had been taken from them, and measles and smallpox had decimated their communities. Reduced to poverty and dependence on rations meagerly handed out by the U.S. government, a spiritual reawakening took place.

Begun by a northern Paiute prophet named Wovoka, the Ghost Dance movement predicted an imminent end to the world during a cataclysmic earthquake, to be followed by the reappearance of Native Americans who had died and the disappearance of white people. Although Wovoka taught the necessity of establishing peace, harmony, and good moral principles, his message was distorted by frightened settlers and government officials who feared an armed uprising of impoverished and beleaguered native people. Performances of the Ghost Dance were banned, and participants were threatened with imprisonment.

Watch the **Video:** *Ghost Dance Movement* on **myanthrolab.com**

Finally, after outlawing the dances and harassing participants, government officials in charge of the Lakota reservations in South Dakota sent Army units to arrest Ghost Dance adherents. The units entrapped more than 300 Lakotas and massacred them at Wounded Knee Creek on December 29, 1890. This final tragedy put an end to Ghost Dance performances. Since then, the message of the Ghost Dance has changed from foretelling the end of American control to focusing on personal improvement and spirituality (Kehoe 1989). Nevertheless, Wounded Knee continues as a potent symbol of U.S. government policies that crushed native peoples and their indigenous cultures.

GLOBAL CULTURE

It is commonplace to hear people say that cultures throughout the world are becoming more similar, that a kind of **global culture** is spreading to all corners of the earth. Global culture "clubs" are springing up on the Internet for people who want to participate actively in this ongoing trend. The term *globalization* can apply to many historical periods when developing states expanded their boundaries, incorporating and transforming neighboring societies. In addition, the spread of proselytizing religions (Christianity, Buddhism, Islam) contributed to fundamental changes in the societies they affected, beyond the domain of religion itself but including social relations, economic and political systems, and aesthetic and ethical values. Today's globalization stems from economic and political processes that have expanded from their original centers in Europe and the United States, as the major capitalist industrialized regions, to many other countries. These processes have affected national governments, urban centers, and the cultures of traditional and indigenous peoples everywhere.

Today's globalization stems from economic and political processes that spread their influence through consumerism, the mass media, and information technologies. How should we evaluate the consequences of this globalization?

Globalization has multiple and complex cultural consequences, summed up by three concepts: homogenization, polarization, and hybridization (Holton 2000). Proponents of the homogenization theory claim that contemporary globalization is creating a homogenized world culture dominated by similar values and practices. They stress the influence of Euro-American economic and political forces, associated with cultural values and norms. Multinational companies stimulate consumer buying throughout the world, and Hollywood images create and transmit an idealized version of American society. Homogenization also stems from the internationalization of elite classes and interests. In this view, elites from disparate countries identify more with each other than they do with their own compatriots, participating in and promulgating similar values. However, although Western influence is of course significant, homogenization theorists may overstate the global role of Euro-American culture and may understate processes of resistance.

The concept of polarization emerges in part as a reaction to homogenization. That is, the pressure toward homogenization creates antagonisms because members of other societies with different values and practices react against the influence of Euro-American culture and assert their own national and cultural identities. Discussions of polarization tend to focus on a dichotomy of West and non-West, especially centered in the Islamic, Afrocentric, and Confucian worlds (Holton 2000, 147). Resistance to homogenization may be motivated by authentic antiglobalization forces, particularly among indigenous communities, or by the desire to assert alternative globalizing influences.

Finally, the third concept, hybridization, stresses the development of ever-greater variety and vitality through new cross-cultural combinations of cultural elements that result from the worldwide exchange of products, technologies, information, and artistic expression. Hybridization can be fostered by travel, migration, and intermarriage. It also results from exposure to media, especially music and film that promote familiarity with aesthetic forms from other societies. In addition, many migrants are in fact transnational people, going back and forth between their country of origin and their country of settlement for visits to family and friends. These migrants are often active carriers of new forms of cultural expressions from their multiple life contexts. Hybridization is not uniform and allows for local differences in the mixture of cultural forms.

Although culture change is a continual and universal feature of societies, it occurs both locally and globally in the context of "friction" (Tsing 2005, 1) between various societies. And although global interactions have the potential to develop similarities throughout the world, globalizing processes have specific effects on the local level, leading to distinctions in access to products, services, and technologies, and resulting in inequalities in consumption.

Globalizing tendencies are as old as contacts among societies, but the scale and tempo of change has increased dramatically in the last century. The historical origin of contemporary globalization can be traced to European mercantile and colonial expansion of the fifteenth and sixteenth centuries. For hundreds of years, globalization was centered in Europe, especially in Great Britain, France, Portugal, and Spain. In the late nineteenth century, the United States began to influence other regions, particularly Latin America and the Pacific, competing with the European powers. In the mid-twentieth century, after World War II, the centers of world power were concentrated in the United States and the Soviet Union, seen as representing opposing views of economic, political, and cultural orders. After the early 1990s and the dismantling of the Soviet Union, world power centered in the United States, although several countries in Asia, especially China, Japan, South Korea, and India, as well as the European Union, now exert substantial economic and diplomatic influence. Due in part to the speed of transportation, communication, and information technologies, the influence of capitalist economics and

As governments, corporations, and the media spread their political, economic, and cultural influences, the traditional ways of life of indigenous peoples like this Tarahumara woman are increasingly threatened.
The Image Works/Zuidema Bzdak/The Image Works

political interests intensified and accelerated throughout the world. However, the cultural and political domination of the West is not uncontested and is countered by Asian economic giants. In addition, cultural influences flow from non-Western countries as Asian and African music, comics, video games, and other items of popular culture are adopted worldwide.

Principal agents of globalization are multinational corporations, which control much of the world's industry and commerce, and the mass media. A global network of finance, manufacture, export, and import has developed, incorporating every nation and many local communities. The prices that farmers receive for their crops are affected by worldwide economic forces through linkages from local to regional, and from national to international networks. Wages received in the manufacturing sector are also connected to worldwide patterns of labor and job availability. National and multinational consumer outlets sell their products in nearly every country. Companies such as McDonald's, Coca-Cola, Sony, and Nintendo are icons of global consumerism. Companies and their advertisers create demand for consumer goods through mass communication systems, such as radio, television, the cinema, and the Internet. Although the spread of products, technologies, and information systems seems relentless, these processes are not inevitable but rather are themselves affected by both global and local patterns of consumption and resistance.

taboos
Norms specifying behaviors that are prohibited in a culture.

Participation remains a challenge, however. Powerful state societies tend to sanction world domination through globalization on the assumptions that technological advances, industrialism, capitalism, environmental exploitation, and democracy are naturally necessary and superior, and that global progress toward those goals is good. Worldwide climate change can be seen as a maladaptive consequence of some of these attitudes. The loss or destruction of other ways of life is seen as sometimes unfortunate but nevertheless inevitable and unavoidable. However, the destruction of indigenous cultures may only be inevitable because the majority of people in the world accept it as such. This too may be a concept that has become naturalized, consistent with profit-oriented notions of progress and development.

Do you think the assumptions used to justify globalization are warranted? Why or why not?

REVIEW

Globalization is a process that historically has had many centers of power as states and empires have expanded their borders and have widened their economic and political influence. However, what is usually referred to today as globalization started in the fifteenth and sixteenth centuries with the development of European mercantile capitalism and state expansion affecting African, North and South American, and Asian peoples and nations. Now there are many centers of globalization, carried by a global economy instituted by multinational corporations. Economic and political forces as well as a global culture disseminated by the mass media and information technologies help create similarities in practices and attitudes, but also threaten the loss of traditional ways of life of indigenous societies and cultural diversity among the world's peoples.

ANTHROPOLOGY APPLIED

Development Anthropology

Development anthropology is a comparatively new branch of cultural anthropology in which anthropologists use their knowledge and skills to help developing countries maneuver through the processes of culture change. Many developing countries want and need help, for example, to balance their economic growth and industrialization with the maintenance of a sustainable environment. Countries also may need help in dealing with the impacts of economic growth and industrialization on their traditional social institutions and systems of social relationships.

The mission statement of the Institute for Development Anthropology (IDA) reflects the goals of developmental anthropologists. The IDA is "an independent, nonpartisan, non-profit, nongovernmental organization with a mission to promote environmentally sustainable development through poverty elimination, equitable economic growth, respect for human rights, gender equity, and cultural pluralism." This is done by applying the comparative and holistic theories and methods of anthropology to "empowering low-income majorities in developing countries." The IDA seeks to enhance the rights of low-income populations to land, natural resources, food, shelter, health, education, income, employment, and participation in democratic and transparent polities. Its activities relate directly to policies involving management and access to productive resources (land, water, forests), credit, employment and enterprise generation, marketing, rural cooperatives, extension programs, resettlement, river-basin development, social forestry, health delivery systems, and education (http://www.developmentanthropology.org/).

As an example of the work that organizations like the IDA do, consider Senegal's decision to permit flooding of the Senegal River valley to sustain traditional riverine economies rather than rely exclusively on damming and irrigation, which would have prevented water from reaching crops and pastures in small landholdings in valleys. The researchers showed that traditional flooding actually made the land more productive than did irrigation. The floodplain could support five to ten times more livestock than irrigated rangeland, and also would sustain the Senegal valley's yield of fish, an important subsistence resource for the people living there.

In 2002, the IDA was awarded a five-year Women in Development research contract, which encompasses projects in women's legal rights; antitrafficking of women and children and antidomestic violence activities; studies on the gender dimensions of population, health, and nutrition; and studies on the gender dimensions of democracy, governance, and the environment. Included under this grant are studies of rural women in central Bolivia; the interplay of ethnicity, gender, class, and caste in Pakistan; the gender dimensions of desertification (the spread of deserts) among pastoralists; and the gender dimensions of water use and water management in central Tunisia.

Getty Images/DESMOND KWANDE/AFP/Getty Images

Corbis/Yann Arthus-Bertrand/Corbis

Friedrich Stark/Friedrich Stark

CRITICAL THINKING QUESTION

Based on these examples, how might you define the role of development anthropologists in relation to the forces of globalization at work in the world today?

Study and Review on myanthrolab.com

CHAPTER SUMMARY

What Is Culture?

- Anthropologists use the term *culture* to refer to all of the customs, attitudes, values, and beliefs of members of a society. People acquire these elements of culture in the context of their interactions with others. As members of families, social groups, and communities, people learn what kinds of behaviors are considered appropriate and inappropriate.

Characteristics of Culture

- Several characteristics of culture are fundamental to the way all societies function. Culture consists of behaviors and beliefs that are "shared" by members of the group. If this were not the case, people could not achieve common goals. However, social status, age, gender, race, and ethnicity may create differences in how people's lives are organized and in the attitudes and values they hold.
- Culture is learned. That is, people's behavior is the result of learning, and not instinct. Even when human beings must fulfill critical physical and survival needs, their cultures influence how they satisfy those needs. Many of our attitudes and actions seem natural because our enculturation is so strong.
- Culture is adaptive. That is, people adapt to their environments through cultural means. Human beings can survive in nearly any climate and environment because of the inventions and cultural practices that they develop. However, some practices may become maladaptive over time or not be adaptive in a different context.
- Culture is integrated, forming a relatively coherent and consistent system. Change in one aspect of culture usually leads to changes in other aspects. When cultural traits are borrowed from other peoples, they usually are altered and adapted to fit more closely with the borrower's norms and expectations.
- Culture is symbolic. People's behavior and understandings of the world are based on meanings expressed through symbols. Language is the most obvious and powerful symbolic system, but human beings also use objects and rituals to represent deeply held cultural ideas and attitudes.
- Culture organizes how people think about the world. Through learning and interacting with others, members of a society absorb an array of underlying, taken-for-granted assumptions that help to integrate their activities and beliefs. These concepts become naturalized, so they feel innate and commonsensical rather than acquired. Because not all people accept the dominant cultural models of their society, these underlying assumptions can be the source of contention, which may, in turn, lead to change.

Culture Change

- Cultures are dynamic systems that change because of internal and external forces. Internal change may take place over time through invention and innovation, leading to new adaptive strategies, customs, technologies, and ideas. Culture history describes the selective record of change in a society, but cultures do not evolve in the same way as species. People define themselves through a process of ethnogenesis. Broad culture changes, such as modernization or revolution, are internal changes that usually are strongly influenced by external forces.
- Culture change also occurs through culture contact. People may borrow traits from other groups. In the process of syncretism, items borrowed through diffusion are modified to fit the existing culture. Culture changes also may be imposed on a society by another society through invasion and conquest. Colonized people are forced to adopt practices and beliefs consistent with those of their rulers.
- When a cultural group is in close contact with a dominant culture, the people may become assimilated or acculturated. Cultural pluralism describes a society with diverse cultural groups who retain their distinctiveness but live side by side on more or less equal terms. In contrast, conquered and oppressed peoples may undergo reactive adaptation to cope with deprivation and loss.

Global Culture

- A global culture, characterized by consumer spending and fueled by advertising by multinational corporations, is spreading to all parts of the world. Although globalization has helped to unify different peoples in a global economy, it may also lead to a loss of cultural and linguistic diversity.

REVIEW QUESTIONS

1. How is culture shared? How is it not shared?
2. How does the story of Mai Thi Hiep/Heidi Neville illustrate the point that culture is learned?
3. What differences with Western culture did the Tiv's reaction to Shakespeare's *Hamlet* illustrate? Why were the Tiv not surprised that Hamlet's mother married his uncle?
4. Why is culture a functionally integrated system? How does the history of women's entry into the labor force in the United States illustrate cultural integration?
5. What are internal and external culture changes?
6. Why do you think anthropologists are concerned by the loss of a language? In what other ways is culture symbolic?
7. How can culture be both adaptive and maladaptive?
8. What are the characteristics and implications of a global culture?

MyAnthroLab Connections

Watch. Listen. View. Explore. Read. MyAnthroLab is designed just for you. Dynamic visual activities, videos, and readings found in the multimedia library will enhance your learning experience.

Resources from this chapter:

Watch on **myanthrolab.com**
- *Anthropology of Childhood*
- *Characteristics of Culture*
- *Ghost Dance Movement*

View on **myanthrolab.com**
- *Gender*

Explore on **myanthrolab.com** In MySearchLab, enter the Anthropology database to find relevant and recent scholarly and popular press publications. For this chapter, enter the following keywords: enculturation, taboos, adaptation, norms

Read on **myanthrolab.com**
- *Family and Household: Who Lives Where, Why Does It Vary, and Why Is It Important?* by Burton Pasternak
- *Malaysia and "Original People": A Case Study of the Impact of Development on Indigenous Peoples* by Robert Knox Dentan, Kirk Endicott, Alberto G. Gomes, and M. B. Hooker

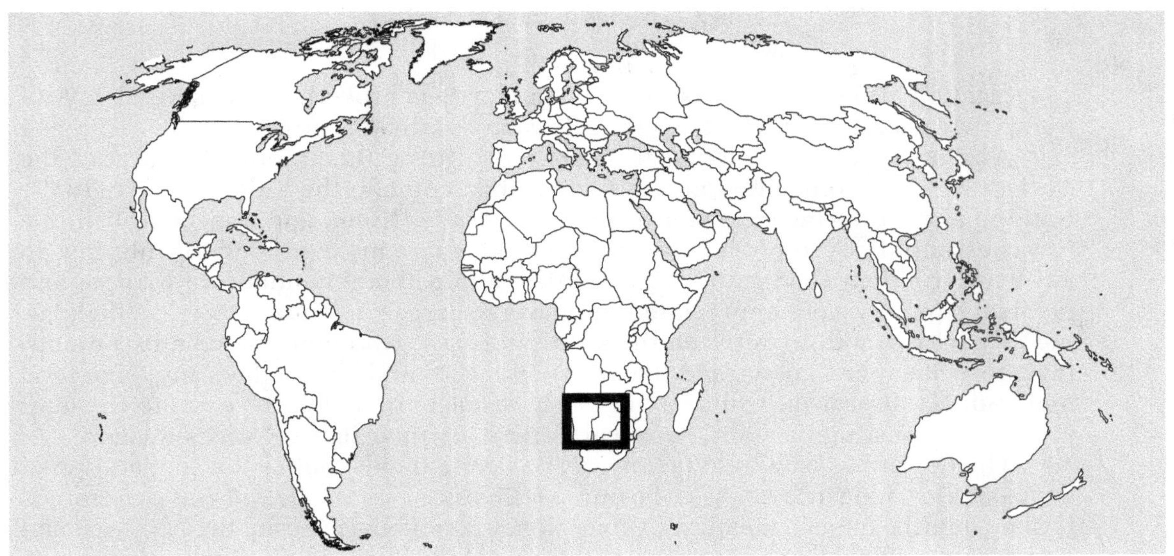

Eating Christmas in the Kalahari

Richard Borshay Lee

*What happens when an anthropologist living among the !Kung of Africa decides to be generous and to share a large animal with everyone at Christmastime? This compelling account of the misunderstanding and confusion that resulted takes the reader deeper into the nature of culture. Richard Lee carefully traces how the !Kung perceived his generosity and taught the anthropologist something about his own culture.**

Listen to the **Chapter Audio** on **myanthrolab.com**

The !Kung Bushmen's knowledge of Christmas is thirdhand. The London Missionary Society brought the holiday to the southern Tswana tribes in the early nineteenth century. Later, native catechists spread the idea far and wide among the Bantu-speaking pastoralists, even in the remotest corners of the Kalahari Desert. The Bushmen's idea of the Christmas story, stripped to its essentials, is "praise the birth of white man's god-chief"; what keeps their interest in the holiday high is the Tswana-Herero custom of slaughtering an ox for his Bushmen neighbors as an annual goodwill gesture. Since the 1930s, part of the Bushmen's annual round of activities has included a December

*From Richard Borshay Lee, "Eating Christmas in the Kalahari," *Natural History*, December 1969, pp. 14–22, 60–64. Reprinted from *Natural History* December 1969; copyright © Natural History Magazine, Inc., 1969.

Eating Christmas in the Kalahari, Richard Borshay Lee, "Eating Christmas in the Kalahari," from Natural History, December 1969; copyright © Natural History Magazine, Inc. 1969.

congregation at the cattle posts for trading, marriage brokering, and several days of trance dance feasting at which the local Tswana headman is host.

As a social anthropologist working with !Kung Bushmen, I found that the Christmas ox custom suited my purposes. I had come to the Kalahari to study the hunting and gathering subsistence economy of the !Kung, and to accomplish this it was essential not to provide them with food, share my own food, or interfere in any way with their food-gathering activities. While liberal handouts of tobacco and medical supplies were appreciated, they were scarcely adequate to erase the glaring disparity in wealth between the anthropologist, who maintained a two-month inventory of canned goods, and the Bushmen, who rarely had a day's supply of food on hand. My approach, while paying off in terms of data, left me open to frequent accusations of stinginess and hardheartedness. By their lights, I was a miser.

The Christmas ox was to be my way of saying thank you for the cooperation of the past year; and since it was to be our last Christmas in the field, I was determined to slaughter the largest, meatiest ox that money could buy, insuring that the feast and trance dance would be a success.

Through December I kept my eyes open at the wells as the cattle were brought down for watering. Several animals were offered, but none had quite the grossness that I had in mind. Then, ten days before the holiday, a Herero friend led an ox of astonishing size and mass up to our camp. It was solid black, stood five feet high at the shoulder, had a five-foot span of horns, and must have weighed 1,200 pounds on the hoof. Food consumption calculations are my specialty, and I quickly figured that bones and viscera aside, there was enough meat—at least four pounds—for every man, woman, and child of the 150 Bushmen in the vicinity of /ai/ai who were expected at the feast.

Having found the right animal at last, I paid the Herero £20 ($56) and asked him to keep the beast with his herd until Christmas day. The next morning word spread among the people that the big solid black one was the ox chosen by /ontah (my Bushman name; it means, roughly, "whitey") for the Christmas feast. That afternoon I received the first delegation. Ben!a, an outspoken sixty-year-old mother of five, came to the point slowly.

"Where were you planning to eat Christmas?"

"Right here at /ai/ai," I replied.

"Alone or with others?"

"I expect to invite all the people to eat Christmas with me."

"Eat what?"

"I have purchased Yehave's black ox, and I am going to slaughter and cook it."

"That's what we were told at the well but refused to believe it until we heard it from yourself."

"Well, it's the black one," I replied expansively, although wondering what she was driving at.

"Oh, no!" Ben!a groaned, turning to her group. "They were right." Turning back to me she asked, "Do you expect us to eat that bag of bones?"

"Bag of bones! It's the biggest ox at /ai/ai."

"Big, yes, but old. And thin. Everybody knows there's no meat on that old ox. What did you expect us to eat off it, the horns?"

Everybody chuckled at Ben!a's one-liner as they walked away, but all I could manage was a weak grin.

That evening it was the turn of the young men. They came to sit at our evening fire. /gaugo, about my age, spoke to me man-to-man.

"/ontah, you have always been square with us," he lied. "What has happened to change your heart? That sack of guts and bones of Yehave's will hardly feed one camp, let alone all the Bushmen around /ai/ai." And he proceeded to enumerate the seven camps in the /ai/ai vicinity, family by family. "Perhaps you have forgotten that we are not few, but many. Or are you too blind to tell the difference between a proper cow and an old wreck? That ox is thin to the point of death."

"Look, you guys," I retorted, "that is a beautiful animal, and I'm sure you will eat it with pleasure at Christmas."

"Of course we will eat it; it's food. But it won't fill us up to the point where we will have enough strength to dance. We will eat and go home to bed with stomachs rumbling."

That night as we turned in, I asked my wife, Nancy, "What did you think of the black ox?"

"It looked enormous to me. Why?"

"Well, about eight different people have told me I got gypped; that the ox is nothing but bones."

"What's the angle?" Nancy asked. "Did they have a better one to sell?"

"No, they just said that it was going to be a grim Christmas because there won't be enough meat to go around. Maybe I'll get an independent judge to look at the beast in the morning."

Bright and early, Halingisi, a Tswana cattle owner, appeared at our camp. But before I could ask him to give me his opinion on Yehave's black ox, he gave me the eye signal that indicated a confidential chat. We left the camp and sat down.

"/ontah, I'm surprised at you; you've lived here for three years and still haven't learned anything about cattle."

"But what else can a person do but choose the biggest, strongest animal one can find?" I retorted.

"Look, just because an animal is big doesn't mean that it has plenty of meat on it. The black one was a beauty when it was younger, but now it is thin to the point of death."

"Well, I've already bought it. What can I do at this stage?"

"Bought it already? I thought you were just considering it. Well, you'll have to kill it and serve it, I suppose. But don't expect much of a dance to follow."

My spirits dropped rapidly. I could believe that Ben!a and /gaugo just might be putting me on about the black ox, but Halingisi seemed to be an impartial critic. I went around that day feeling as though I had bought a lemon of a used car.

In the afternoon it was Tomazo's turn. Tomazo is a fine hunter, a top trance performer . . . and one of my most reliable informants. He approached the subject of the Christmas cow as part of my continuing Bushman education.

"My friend, the way it is with us Bushmen," he began, "is that we love meat. And even more than that, we love fat. When we hunt we always search for the fat ones, the ones dripping with layers of white fat: fat that turns into a clear, thick oil in the cooking pot, fat that slides down your gullet, fills your stomach and gives you a roaring diarrhea," he rhapsodized.

"So, feeling as we do," he continued, "it gives us pain to be served such a scrawny thing as Yehave's black ox. It is big, yes, and no doubt its giant bones are good for soup, but fat is what we really crave, and so we will eat Christmas this year with a heavy heart."

The prospect of a gloomy Christmas now had me worried, so I asked Tomazo what I could do about it.

"Look for a fat one, a young one . . . smaller, but fat. Fat enough to make us //gom (evacuate the bowels), then we will be happy."

My suspicions were aroused when Tomazo said that he happened to know a young, fat, barren cow that the owner was willing to part with. Was Tomazo working on commission, I wondered? But I dispelled this unworthy thought when we approached the Herero owner of the cow in question and found that he had decided not to sell.

The scrawny wreck of a Christmas ox now became the talk of the /ai/ai water hole and was the first news told to the outlying groups as they began to come in from the bush for the feast. What finally convinced me that real trouble might be brewing was the visit from u!au, an old conservative with a reputation for fierceness. His nickname meant spear and referred to an incident thirty years ago in which he had speared a man to death. He had an intense manner; fixing me with his eyes, he said in clipped tones:

"I have only just heard about the black ox today, or else I would have come here earlier. /ontah, do you honestly think you can serve meat like that to people and avoid a fight?" He paused, letting the implications sink in. "I don't mean fight you, /ontah; you are a white man. I mean a fight between Bushmen. There are many fierce ones here, and with such a small quantity of meat to distribute, how can you give everybody a fair share? Someone is sure to accuse another of taking too much or hogging all the choice pieces. Then you will see what happens when some go hungry while others eat."

The possibility of at least a serious argument struck me as all too real. I had witnessed the tension that surrounds the distribution of meat from a kudu or gemsbok kill, and had documented many arguments that sprang up from a real or imagined slight in meat distribution. The owners of a kill may spend up to two hours arranging and rearranging the piles of meat under the gaze of a circle of recipients before handing them out. And I knew that the Christmas feast at /ai/ai would be bringing together groups that had feuded in the past.

Convinced now of the gravity of the situation, I went in earnest to search for a second cow; but all my inquiries failed to turn one up.

The Christmas feast was evidently going to be a disaster, and the incessant complaints about the meagerness of the ox had already taken the fun out of it for me. Moreover, I was getting bored with the wisecracks, and after losing my temper a few times, I resolved to serve the beast anyway. If the meat fell short, the hell with it. In the Bushmen idiom, I announced to all who would listen:

"I am a poor man and blind. If I have chosen one that is too old and too thin, we will eat it anyway and see if there is enough meat there to quiet the rumbling of our stomachs."

On hearing this speech, Ben!a offered me a rare word of comfort. "It's thin," she said philosophically, "but the bones will make a good soup."

At dawn Christmas morning, instinct told me to turn over the butchering and cooking to a friend and take off with Nancy to spend Christmas alone in the bush. But curiosity kept me from retreating. I wanted to see what such a scrawny ox looked like on butchering, and if there *was* going to be a fight, I wanted to catch every word of it. Anthropologists are incurable that way.

The great beast was driven up to our dancing ground, and a shot in the forehead dropped it in its tracks. Then, freshly cut branches were heaped around the fallen carcass to receive the meat. Ten men volunteered to help with the cutting. I asked /gaugo to make the breast bone cut. This cut, which begins the butchering process for most large game, offers easy access for removal of the viscera. But it also allows the hunter to spot-check the amount of fat on an animal. A fat game animal carries a white layer up to an inch thick on the chest, while in a thin one, the knife will quickly cut to bone. All eyes fixed on his hand as /gaugo, dwarfed by the great carcass, knelt to the breast. The first cut opened a pool of solid white in the black skin. The second and third cut widened and deepened the creamy white. Still no bone. It was pure fat; it must have been two inches thick.

"Hey /gau," I burst out, "that ox is loaded with fat. What's this about the ox being too thin to bother eating? Are you out of your mind?"

"Fat?" /gau shot back. "You call that fat? This wreck is thin, sick, dead!" And he broke out laughing. So did everyone else. They rolled on the ground, paralyzed with laughter. Everybody laughed except me; I was thinking.

I ran back to the tent and burst in just as Nancy was getting up. "Hey, the black ox. It's fat as hell! They were kidding about it being too thin to eat. It was a joke or something. A put-on. Everyone is really delighted with it."

"Some joke," my wife replied. "It was so funny that you were ready to pack up and leave /ai/ai."

If it had indeed been a joke, it had been an extraordinarily convincing one, and tinged, I thought, with more than a touch of malice, as many jokes are. Nevertheless, that it was a joke lifted my spirits considerably, and I returned to the butchering site where the shape of the ox was rapidly disappearing under the axes and knives of the butchers. The atmosphere had become festive. Grinning broadly, their arms covered with blood well past the elbow, men packed chunks of meat into the big cast-iron cooking pots, fifty pounds to the load, and muttered and chuckled all the while about the thinness and worthlessness of the animal and /ontah's poor judgment.

We danced and ate that ox two days and two nights; we cooked and distributed fourteen potfuls of meat and no one went home hungry and no fights broke out.

But the "joke" stayed in my mind. I had a growing feeling that something important had happened in my relationship with the Bushmen and that the clue lay in the meaning of the joke. Several days later, when most of the people had dispersed back to the bush camps, I raised the question with Hakekgose, a Tswana man who had grown up among the !Kung, married a !Kung girl, and who probably knew their culture better than any other non-Bushman.

"With us whites," I began, "Christmas is supposed to be the day of friendship and brotherly love. What I can't figure out is why the Bushmen went to such lengths to criticize and belittle the ox I had bought for the feast. The animal was perfectly good and their jokes and wisecracks practically ruined the holiday for me."

"So it really did bother you," said Hakekgose. "Well, that's the way they always talk. When I take my rifle and go hunting with them, if I miss, they laugh at me for the rest of the day. But even if I hit and bring one down, it's no better. To them, the kill is always too small or too old or too thin; and as we sit down on the kill site to cook and eat the liver, they keep grumbling, even with their mouths full of meat. They say things like, 'Oh, this is awful! What a worthless animal! Whatever made me think that this Tswana rascal could hunt!' "

"Is this the way outsiders are treated?" I asked.

"No, it is their custom; they talk that way to each other, too. Go and ask them."

/gaugo had been one of the most enthusiastic in making me feel bad about the merit of the Christmas ox. I sought him out first.

"Why did you tell me the black ox was worthless, when you could see that it was loaded with fat and meat?"

"It is our way," he said, smiling. "We always like to fool people about that. Say there is a Bushman who has been hunting. He must not come home and announce like a braggart, 'I have killed a big one in the bush!' He must first sit down in silence until I or someone else comes up to his fire and asks, 'What did you see today?' He replies quietly, 'Ah, I'm no good for hunting. I saw nothing at all [pause] just a little tiny one.' Then I smile to myself," /gaugo continued, "because I know he has killed something big.

"In the morning we make up a party of four or five people to cut up and carry the meat back to the camp. When we arrive at the kill we examine it and cry out, 'You mean to say you have dragged us all the way out here in order to make us cart home your pile of bones? Oh, if I had known it was this thin I wouldn't have come.' Another one pipes up, 'People, to think I gave up a nice day in the shade for this. At home we may be hungry, but at least we have nice cool water to drink.' If the horns are big, someone says, 'Did you think that somehow you were going to boil down the horns for soup?'

"To all this you must respond in kind. 'I agree,' you say, 'this one is not worth the effort; let's just cook the liver for strength and leave the rest for the hyenas. It is not too late to hunt today and even a duiker or a steenbok would be better than this mess.'

"Then you set to work nevertheless; butcher the animal, carry the meat back to the camp and everyone eats," /gaugo concluded.

Things were beginning to make sense. Next, I went to Tomazo. He corroborated /gaugo's story of the obligatory insults over a kill and added a few details of his own.

"But," I asked, "why insult a man after he has gone to all that trouble to track and kill an animal and when he is going to share the meat with you so that your children will have something to eat?"

"Arrogance," was his cryptic answer.

"Arrogance?"

"Yes, when a young man kills much meat he comes to think of himself as a chief or a big man, and he thinks of the rest of us as his servants or inferiors. We can't accept this. We refuse one who boasts, for someday his pride will make him kill somebody. So we always speak of his meat as worthless. This way we cool his heart and make him gentle."

"But why didn't you tell me this before?" I asked Tomazo with some heat.

"Because you never asked me," said Tomazo, echoing the refrain that has come to haunt every field ethnographer.

The pieces now fell into place. I had known for a long time that in situations of social conflict with Bushmen I held all the cards. I was the only source of tobacco in a thousand square miles, and I was not incapable of cutting an individual off for noncooperation. Though my boycott never lasted longer than a few days, it was an indication of my strength. People resented my presence at the water hole, yet simultaneously dreaded my leaving. In short I was a perfect target for the charge of arrogance and for the Bushman tactic of enforcing humility.

I had been taught an object lesson by the Bushmen; it had come from an unexpected corner and had hurt me in a vulnerable area. For the big black ox was to be the one totally generous, unstinting act of my year at /ai/ai and I was quite unprepared for the reaction I received.

As I read it, their message was this: There are no totally generous acts. All "acts" have an element of calculation. One black ox slaughtered at Christmas does not wipe out a year of careful manipulation of gifts given to serve your own ends. After all, to kill an animal and share the meat with people is really no more than the Bushmen do for each other every day and with far less fanfare.

In the end, I had to admire how the Bushmen had played out the farce—collectively straight-faced to the end. Curiously, the episode reminded me of the *Good Soldier Schweik* and his marvelous encounters with authority. Like Schweik, the Bushmen had retained a thoroughgoing skepticism of good intentions. Was it this independence of spirit, I wondered, that had kept them culturally viable in the face of generations of contact with more powerful societies, both black and white? The thought that the Bushmen were alive and well in the Kalahari was strangely comforting. Perhaps, armed with that independence and with their superb knowledge of their environment, they might yet survive the future.

Study and **Review** on **myanthrolab.com**

Review Questions

1. What was the basis of the misunderstanding experienced by Lee when he gave an ox for the Christmas feast held by the !Kung?
2. Construct a model of cross-cultural misunderstanding, using the information presented by Lee in this article.
3. Why do you think the !Kung ridicule and denigrate people who have been successful hunters or who have provided them with a Christmas ox? Why do Americans expect people to be grateful to receive gifts?

Studying Culture

Studying Culture

PREVIEW

- How did anthropology begin as a discipline? What important figures shaped the development of anthropology?
- What theoretical perspectives do anthropologists bring to their study of cultures?
- What is ethnographic fieldwork? Why is it important in anthropology?
- How do anthropologists use ethnohistories and cross-cultural comparisons in their work?
- Why can the impacts anthropologists have on the people they study be controversial?

Tribal canoes greeting ceremony at Elliot Bay; Seattle Salmon Homecoming Celebration. *Danita Delimont/Alamy*

Listen to the Chapter Audio on myanthrolab.com

Read on myanthrolab.com

Ice had formed ahead of them, and it reached all the way to the sky. The people could not cross it. It was too thick to break. A Raven flew up and struck the ice and cracked it when he came down. Coyote said, "these small people can't get across the ice." Another Raven flew up again and cracked the ice again. Coyote said, "try again, try again." Raven flew up again and broke the ice. The people ran across. (a Northern Paiute narrative of glaciation on the Snake River in Idaho, p. 83)

That in ancient times a herd of these tremendous animals came to the big-bone licks, and began a universal destruction of the bear, deer, elks, buffaloes, and other animals: that the great Man above, looking down and seeing this, was so enraged that he seized his lightning, descended on the earth, seated himself on the neighboring mountain, on a rock of which his seat and the print of his feet are still to be seen, hurled his bolts among them until the whole was slaughtered, except the big bull. (a Delaware narrative of mammoths in Virginia, p. 128)

The time ago, the water of the Pacific flowed through what is now the swamp and prairie between Waatch village and Neah Bay, making an island of Cape Flattery. The water suddenly receded, leaving Neah Bay perfectly dry. It was four days reaching its lowest ebb, and then rose again till it had submerged the Cape That and in fact the whole country, excepting the tops of the mountains at Clyoquot. The water on its rise became very warm, and as it came up to the houses, those who had canoes put their effects into them, and floated off with the current which set very strongly to the north. Some drifted one way, some another; and when the waters assumed their accustomed level, a portion of the tribe found themselves beyond Nootka, where their descendents now reside. (a Quillayute narrative of land transformations in Washington and British Columbia, p. 190)

(Source: Red Earth, White Lies: Native Americans and the Myth of Scientific Fact; Vine Deloria Jr. , 1997, Golden, Colorado: Fulcrum Publishing) Specific sources: Paiute: Julian Steward, " Some Western Shoshoni Myths" Washington DC, Smithsonian Institution, Bureau American Ethnology, Bulletin 136, Anthropological Papers, no. 31, 1943, page 299.

Delaware: as Jefferson, Notes on the State of Virginia, Boston:Thomas & Andrews, J. West, West & Greenleaf et al, 1801, pages 59-61. Quoted in Ludwell H. Johnson III: Man and Elephants in America" Scientific Monthly 75 (October 1952), page 217. Quillayute: James G. Swan, The Indians of Cape Flattery of Washington DC: Smithsonian Contributions to Knowledge, no. 220, 1869, page 57.

These stories can be interpreted on many levels. One kind of reading of narratives told by the Northern Paiute, Delaware, and Quillayute peoples may be made to ancient climatic and ecological events and upheavals in their territories. In this interpretation, the stories give accounts of natural or geological events and explanations for the appearance of animals, glaciations, or the formation of lakes and rivers resulting from floods and other catastrophic events. According to geologist Dr. Eugene Kiver, the "floods may have happened when people were around. Native Americans have myths about floods (Robbins 2004).

Stories that seem to parallel actual occurrences suggest the accuracy of people's memories of their past, even though events may be embellished in the rich, poetic language of tradition. **Narratives** may dramatize real events in symbolic form consistent with cultural practices of storytelling. Thus, they may transmit across generations the memories of people who witnessed events that changed their geographic landscape. We will never know whether these stories encapsulate such memories or whether they imagine an explanation for the landscape that existed when the people developed the narrative. Whatever the particular facts, narratives have the power to create and transmit a people's worldview.

narratives
Stories and myths that dramatize actual memories or events in symbolic form consistent with cultural practices of storytelling.

Without a writing system, indigenous peoples use storytelling to preserve their history. Collecting and interpreting these stories is one of the methods of cultural anthropology. Anthropologists analyze narratives to identify aspects of cultural identity, social values, moral themes, people's practices and attitudes, and artistic principles and motifs.

oral traditions
Cultural narratives that have validity as artifacts of culture and experience.

Traditional narratives may also be dramatic renditions of historical events. The accuracy of chronologies and events may be uncertain, but **oral traditions** like the story of Coyote and Wishpoosh have validity as artifacts of culture and experience. In 1997, for example, the Supreme Court of Canada ruled in a land claims case brought by the Gitksan, an indigenous people of British Columbia, that oral traditions have validity as legal testimony and as records of the past. This chapter explores the theories and methods involved in the anthropological interpretation of culture.

What are some oral traditions from your cultural group (such as your family) that you could analyze from an anthropological perspective?

ANTHROPOLOGY AND THE EXPLANATION OF CULTURAL DIVERSITY

Although the field of anthropology as an academic discipline is only slightly more than a century old, its intellectual roots in Europe go back much farther. Although people everywhere may note cultural differences between themselves and others, anthropology has its roots in the exploration and colonial expansions that originated in Europe in the fifteenth and sixteenth centuries. Explorers, traders, and missionaries, bent on their far-flung journeys of discovery and conquest, often wrote about and commented on the differences they observed in the ways of life of the peoples they encountered.

Europeans wrote many journals, diaries, letters, and memoirs during the first centuries of colonization in North and South America, Africa, Asia, and the Pacific islands. Although many writers were biased and ethnocentric, they nevertheless often left detailed observations of cultures at the time of contact. For example, Jesuit missionaries wrote detailed accounts about working in North America in the seventeenth century. These men were better educated than most of the explorers and adventurers who preceded and followed them. They were familiar with the scholarly literary and philosophical works of their age. Although critical of many of the practices they described, the Jesuits often were astute observers and recorders. They sometimes judged native customs and attitudes to be superior to the French, for example, such as the people's rules for hospitality and generosity and their relatively harmonious, noncompetitive community life. In some ways, these missionaries were like anthropologists, both observers and participants in others' lifeways, although of course they had their own goal of converting native peoples to Christianity.

The sixteenth-century Spanish missionary Bartolome de las Casas' description of the effects of colonial life on Native Americans led to humanitarian reforms.
Father James Driscoll/Father James Driscoll

The goal of anthropology as a discipline is to record and account for the great diversity in human cultures. But today there is diversity in anthropology as well, as anthropologists choose different conceptual frameworks to achieve their goals. This section explores a number of perspectives that have been proposed to account for similarities and differences in human societies. These perspectives differ in their focus and in the kinds of theories that they offer to explain human behavior and cultural diversity. A cultural theory is one that attempts to formulate explanations that help us understand why particular practices originate and how they are developed and maintained in particular populations. From an understanding of cultural diversity, some anthropologists also propose theories that can help explain universal trends and processes.

Some approaches in anthropology that were developed in the nineteenth and early twentieth centuries, such as evolutionism, have been discarded as inadequate or incomplete, either because they were unscientific and based on fragmentary and poorly understood data, or because they were based on social attitudes and prejudices that were then prevalent. Nevertheless, the works of some early anthropologists continue to inform aspects of modern inquiry.

evolutionism
View held by early social philosophers that human differences can be accounted for by different rates of progress, leading to different levels of cultural achievement.

Evolutionism

During the Enlightenment of the eighteenth century, European social philosophers, relying on the writings of earlier observers, took a comparative evolutionary perspective, and understood cultural diversity from the point of view of human "progress." Scholars focused on finding rational, reasoned, and scientific explanations for human differences. They understood that people adapt to their social environments and historical conditions as well as to their physical surroundings, with the goal of progress and the possibility of betterment. Enlightenment philosophers looked for evolutionary trends in the development of human societies. Thus, in **evolutionism,** human differences could be accounted for by different rates of progress, leading to different levels of achievement. Various hypotheses were put forward, demonstrating a progression from stages of "primitive" culture to "civilization." Even though distinct schemes were suggested by different theorists, they had in common an assumption of "unilinear evolution," that is, progression through rigid stages in a set order. Although these theories were ethnocentric, using European culture as a measure of progress, they laid the foundation for nineteenth-century anthropological thinking about sociocultural evolution.

Throughout the nineteenth century, European and American scholars concentrated on developing and refining comparative evolutionary approaches toward understanding the similarities and differences among cultures. The Englishmen Herbert Spencer (1877) and Edward Tylor (1871) and the American Lewis Henry Morgan (1877) proposed models outlining stages of cultural development from the earliest human societies to late nineteenth-century European culture. Both Morgan and Spencer focused on understanding how cultures are integrated and systematized and how the various features of one culture indicate an evolutionary status in comparison with other cultures. For example, Morgan proposed three stages of cultural evolution: savagery, in which people subsist on wild plants and animals; barbarism, in which people start to use agriculture; and civilization, which begins with the invention of writing. Spencer, a social Darwinist, believed that European influence or domination over other peoples was the natural result of evolutionary progress. The social Darwinists applied some aspects of Charles Darwin's theories of biological evolution to social and cultural phenomena, particularly ideas about the survival of better-adapted organisms and the disappearance of maladaptive forms. These theories essentially justified European hegemony and empire throughout the world.

Using eighteenth- and nineteenth-century ideas and data, sources that varied widely in their reliability and accuracy, early anthropologists nevertheless advanced the study of human societies by proposing a more thorough analysis of cultural features and their significance for the development of social forms. For example, Morgan first explained the kinship systems of tribes making up the Iroquois Confederacy and the links between a kinship system and the economic system, family organization, and social structure.

Empiricism

Anthropology began to take modern form as a discipline in the late nineteenth and early twentieth centuries with the work of the German-born American Franz Boas (1896), the Polish-born Briton Bronislaw Malinowski (1922), and several others. In this period, direct fieldwork, rather than speculation based on the data of others, became central to the pursuit of knowledge about human cultures. That is, anthropology came to be seen as a scientific inquiry into facts that can be observed directly.

Boas began his career in Germany as a geographer, but on a trip to the Arctic to investigate northern waters in 1883, he became interested in the indigenous peoples and their cultures. He spent a year living with the Inuit, deepening his appreciation of cultural traits and his conviction that only by living with other people can one truly understand cultural differences. In 1886, Boas traveled to British Columbia to learn about

Margaret Mead's reports about growing up in Samoa and living among the Manus of New Guinea astonished the public. Corbis/Bettmann/Corbis

Bella Coola (Nuxalk) culture, and two years later he immigrated to the United States. While studying the Kwakiutl of the Pacific Northwest and their ceremonial life, he became the major figure and driving force in the development of American anthropology. Boas trained many of the most prominent anthropologists of his and the next generation, including Ruth Benedict and Margaret Mead, sending them into the field to meticulously collect and archive data about many different cultures.

Boas consistently stressed the need for **empiricism,** the practice of formulating theories and analyses after conducting studies based on direct observation and objective description. Emphasis on empirical research stresses the primacy of collecting observable data rather than the construction of theories, although of course theories need to be based on empirical data, and the collection of data leads to the formulation of theories that explain those social facts. Boas also introduced the concept of cultural relativism, and believed that each way of life is a unique adaptation to particular historical conditions, a view that critics referred to as "historical particularism." Boas refuted the earlier theories of cultural evolutionism, criticizing these concepts as being essentially ethnocentric and racist. According to Boas, cultures should be understood and evaluated in their own terms, not in terms of the cultural practices, beliefs, and values of the observer. In his own work and that of his students, Boas stressed the importance of learning the native languages to understand the people's attitudes and beliefs literally in their own terms. Boas's work implicitly questioned Euro-American biases in interpreting other cultures and raised issues that today are concerned with examining the subjectivity of the observer and analyst.

Boas also stressed that similarities and differences should be understood as outcomes of the functions and meanings of cultural traits within a society. He pointed out that the same traits can have different meanings in different cultures. Polygamy, or plural marriage, for example, may occur for different reasons in different societies, depending on the cultural context. Marriage rules allowing men to take more than one wife, for instance, may function to signal a man's comparative wealth, power, and prestige; to relieve women of household burdens by providing additional labor; or to ensure that all women can have husbands in societies where women outnumber men.

Functionalism

If you were a functionalist, how would you argue that even negative practices, such as antisocial behavior, can have positive functions for society as a whole?

Functionalism, or the study of the social functions of cultural traits, was a hallmark of the research of Bronislaw Malinowski, whose work especially influenced British social anthropology. Malinowski believed that the social, economic, and political structures of societies were organized to satisfy human needs and that people's diverse institutions and practices have specific functions that address those needs. According to Malinowski, men and women living together in a community develop an "invisible network of social bonds" made up of shared values, attitudes, and practices that "integrate the group into a whole" (1922). All cultural behaviors and artifacts can be explained by understanding their role in maintaining this whole.

Like Boas, Malinowski was dedicated to fieldwork. Malinowski lived with the Trobriand Islanders of the western Pacific in Melanesia, immersing himself in Trobriand culture and language. Like Boas, he also stressed the importance of anthropologists learning the native language of the people they study, because people express their values and attitudes through their language. Malinowski used functionalism to explain his observations of Trobriand life. Students of Malinowski, such as A. R. Radcliffe-Brown and others, applied functionalist interpretations to field data collected among other Pacific Islanders, Africans, and Australian Aborigines. These interpretations are now sometimes criticized for overemphasizing functional stability rather than acknowledging societal tensions and change as ongoing, continuous processes.

empiricism
The practice of conducting studies through direct observation and objective description.

functionalism
View that cultural traits have social functions that contribute to the smooth operation of the whole society.

Modern Theoretical Perspectives: An Overview

One of the criticisms of earlier theoretical approaches was the tendency to overly generalize about people's behaviors and beliefs and to depict other societies as bounded, homogeneous, and timeless. In contrast, some modern approaches attempt to uncover processes of change and adaptation or to analyze the conflicts and tensions that arise out of societal differences. Although these theories emphasize changes in social practices and beliefs, they differ significantly from eighteenth- and nineteenth-century ideas of unilinear evolution. Instead, concepts of "multilinear" change and adaptation developed which stressed the complexity of historical and cultural processes. One current approach in anthropological theory is to study culture from a materialist perspective, placing technological and economic adaptations at the center of cultural diversity. Another perspective analyzes cultures from a structuralist perspective, emphasizing the role of social structures in fulfilling human needs and integrating social systems. A variation of the structuralist perspective stresses the role of ideas and habits of mind as the sources of diversity. A third orientation, the conflict perspective, places status and power relations at the center of diversity, focusing on how a worldwide system of dominance and subordination, power, and influence operate within and between societies. A fourth perspective is interpretive, with an emphasis on the meanings that people communicate through symbols. Table 1 summarizes some of the modern perspectives in anthropological theory.

materialist perspectives Explanations of cultural differences that emphasize environmental adaptation, technologies, and methods of acquiring or producing food.

cultural ecology Field that studies cultures as dynamic wholes based on the satisfaction of human needs through cultural behaviors.

cultural materialism Explanations of cultural differences as the results of cultural adaptations through economic production.

Materialist Perspectives

Materialist perspectives emphasize environmental adaptation, technologies, and methods of acquiring or producing food in the development of culture. Humans adapt to their environments primarily through culture. Humans address the scarcity of resources by developing methods of extracting, exploiting, storing, and processing whatever foods are available. These behaviors, and the satisfaction of other human needs, form a cultural core from which other aspects of society develop and are integrated. This analytic and explanatory focus in anthropology is called **cultural ecology,** a term introduced by Julian Steward in the 1930s. In societies that depend directly on their environment, ecological factors, such as resources, climate, and topography, have more pervasive effects on cultural development than in societies where people can control and modify their immediate environment.

Another materialist perspective centering on cultural adaptations through economic production is referred to as **cultural materialism,** developed by Marvin Harris (1979). This approach, influenced by the economic views of Karl Marx, gives greatest importance to economic systems and economic relations in the development of culture. Cultural traits are then explained as responses to economic necessities or benefits. Similarly, people need to organize work in order to produce and exchange foods, other goods, and services. From this basic organization, other features of culture

TABLE 1 EXPLAINING CULTURAL DIVERSITY

Materialist Perspectives Marvin Harris	Emphasizes the centrality of environmental adaptation, technology, and methods of acquiring or producing food in the development of culture.
Cultural Ecology	Cultural traits related to the satisfaction of basic human needs form a cultural core that is directly influenced by the physical environment.
Cultural Materialism	All aspects of a society's culture are derived from its economic foundation.
Structuralist Perspectives Claude Lévi-Strauss	Cultural diversity stems from differences in the forms by which people express universal meanings. These forms define and structure their lives and experiences and may serve universal social functions.
Interpretive Perspectives Clifford Geertz	Culture is a unique system of symbols with multiple layers of meaning. Through their behavior, people act out those meanings and communicate them to one another.
Conflict Perspectives	Culture is an expression of power relations within a society and between societies. Distributions of power are linked to distributions of wealth and status and affect gender relations as well as processes such as colonialism.

emic
Subjective, based on insiders' views, as in explanations people have for their own cultural behavior.

etic
Objective, based on outsiders' views, as in explanations of people's behavior by anthropologists or other observers.

structuralism
View that cultural differences can be explained by differences in forms or conceptual categories rather than in meanings.

follow. For example, to ensure adequate supplies of resources, people must regulate the size of their communities, increasing or decreasing population growth depending on resource availability. People also must develop methods of arriving at group decisions and controlling behavior to conform to those decisions. Basic economic behaviors and relationships influence how these traits are developed. In other words, what people do ultimately shapes what they believe, rather than the other way around.

Cultural materialism makes a distinction between *subjective* explanations for cultural behavior that are offered by the people engaged in that behavior—**emic** views—and *objective* explanations for cultural behavior that are given by anthropologists or other observers—**etic** views. Cultural materialists claim that people usually are not aware of the underlying adaptive reasons for their actions. Thus, researchers look for explanations of people's behaviors based on observations and other objective criteria developed from an understanding of broad cultural and historical processes. These explanations are derived, in part, from theories that emerge from the comparative and holistic focus in anthropology. That is, by considering data from many societies, anthropologists can uncover the ways that particular practices are correlated and integrated with environmental constraints, economic systems, and social meanings.

In his popular book *Cows, Pigs, Wars and Witches: The Riddles of Culture* (1974), Harris contrasted emic and etic explanations of why Hindus in India do not eat or even kill cows. According to an emic analysis, Hindus do not kill cows because cows are sacred animals, symbolic of "everything that is alive." This is an explanation that a Hindu believer might give. In an etic analysis, however, the meaning of the sacredness of cows is analyzed in the context of the economic needs of farmers in India. For example, Indian farmers use cattle to pull their plows and they use the dung as fuel for cooking fires and as insulation in their houses. Harris concluded that cattle are considered "sacred" to protect them from slaughter, because they are vital to Indian farming. Harris' work has been influential in its focus on understanding the ecological and materialist meanings and origins of systems of belief and practice. He has shown that such practices are not random but instead are grounded in the necessities of survival and the organization of daily life.

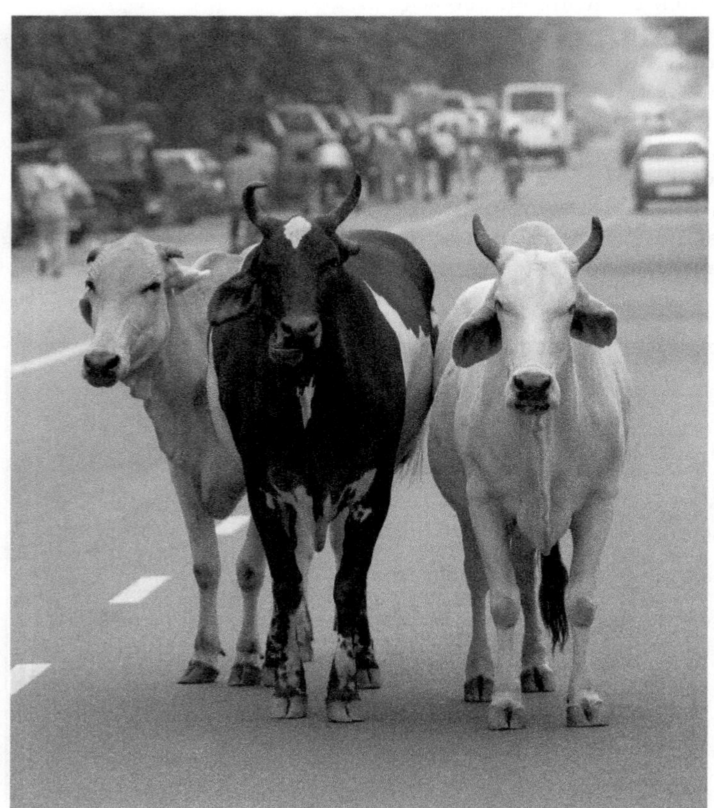

From the perspective of cultural materialism, cattle are too important for agriculture to be slaughtered in India. Alamy Limited/Frank Fredolin/Alamy

Structuralist Perspectives

Taking a different turn in the analysis of culture, some anthropologists emphasize the centrality of forms and structure in the expression of culture, called **structuralism.** For example, the French scholar Claude Lévi-Strauss used theories from structural linguistics (Saussure 1916) to analyze symbolic expressions of culture in terms of their structures or patterns, in addition to their meanings. His goal was to identify the underlying patterns that all the expressions have in common or the underlying codes on which all the expressions are based. Cultures could then be understood in terms of pattern variance.

Lévi-Strauss was interested in explaining why myths from different cultures around the world seem so similar. Treating mythology as a form of language or symbolic communication, he proposed a "principle of opposition" that all myths share, much like novels have a protagonist who engages in some kind of struggle that is somehow resolved. In mythology, heroic struggles involve a contest between opposites, especially between various forms of good and evil, with or without third-party mediation. Myths can be told and retold with elaborations, but the basic structure always stays the same. In this case, understanding cultural differences would involve identifying the particular hero, type of struggle, type of mediation, if any, and type of outcome in each case. One can use Levi-Strauss' approach to uncover a widespread narrative structure and narrative arc recognizable in most myths and folklore. These narrative structures exist as well in popular culture in the form of films, for example, where protagonists are confronted with conflicts or problems that they have to overcome. Finally, these narrative forms can also be found to underlie personal stories that people tell each other about incidents in their lives, demonstrating their ways of dealing with life's challenges.

Lévi-Strauss' work essentially developed a theory of the mind, based on structural analysis, to explain cultural differences as variations in basic themes of universal human thinking. He also applied this method to the study of kinship (1949). He was interested in the fact that kinship structures are limited in the number of basic types and are strongly supported by myths and taboos. He looked for a basic unit of kinship that could explain all the variations. For any society requiring a man to marry outside his own hereditary line, for example, Lévi-Strauss identified a cluster of four roles—brother, sister, father, son. These roles structure the exchanges that maintain the circulation of women in the society and establish cooperative relationships or alliances among kin groups. He proposed that marriage is the means through which people, and men in particular, form alliances that promote social cohesion and stability. Marriages forge alliances through a reciprocal exchange between one group that gives women as wives to another group, receiving gifts in return. This sets up patterned relationships between wife givers and wife receivers that over time establish enduring bonds between the groups. Understanding cultural differences in this case would involve identifying and comparing marriage rules, kin roles, forms of exchanges, and forms of alliances. Although Lévi-Strauss is criticized for his focus on men as the primary social actors in these relationships, the perspective of structuralism remains useful today in its emphasis on patterned relationships among people occupying particular roles in society.

interpretive anthropology View that cultural differences can be understood as complex webs of meaning rather than through forms.

conflict perspectives Understanding cultural differences as a consequence of conflict in the interests and goals of various groups within a society and focusing on issues of power and resistance.

Interpretive Anthropology

In contrast to structural-functional analyses, some anthropologists focus on culture as meanings rather than as forms and functions. American anthropologist Clifford Geertz (1973), for example, focuses on mental and cognitive processes in the development and transmission of culture. This kind of analysis, sometimes called **interpretive anthropology,** stresses the multilayered symbolic meanings of people's actions. From this perspective, cultural behavior is the acting out of those meanings.

Geertz developed his theory while working among the Javanese. According to Geertz, "Man is an animal suspended in webs of significance he himself has spun; I take culture to be those webs, and the analysis of it to be therefore not an experimental science in search of law but an interpretative one in search of meaning" (1973, 4–5). Geertz has called culture an "acted document" that is essentially public and therefore observable and analyzable. Doing ethnography, then, is like trying to read or construct a reading from a manuscript. To understand culture, interpretive anthropologists pay close attention to people's expressions of values, attitudes, meanings, intentions, and the felt importance of their actions (9–10). As the collective characteristics of a group, these meanings help define cultural differences among different groups. In order to uncover cultural meanings, working in the native languages is crucial since interpreters, no matter how adept and knowledgeable in the two languages, cannot translate subtle and symbolic nuances not directly expressed but covertly understood by native speakers.

Anthropologist Eleanor Leacock's (1981) pioneering work on the Montagnais and Naskapi in eastern Canada pointed to the role of colonial government in undermining indigenous culture. Photo Researchers/ Bryan and Cherry Alexander/Photo Researchers, Inc.

Conflict Perspectives and the Analysis of Culture and Power

Conflict perspectives focus on social problems or social issues in societies, especially those that arise as a result of the distribution of power among groups or social categories. Much of this analysis focuses on the relationship between culture and various forms of social, economic, and political power. Its adherents often use a Marxist framework to analyze how capitalist institutions penetrate and transform indigenous societies to suit their own needs.

One important concern in the analysis of power is the issue of gender, which also plays a role in anthropology. Many anthropological writings (by both male and female anthropologists) have a conceptual male bias. This bias often results in the assumption that male dominance exists (and has existed) in all societies. Reconstructions of indigenous social life prior to European contact tell a different story about the roles of men and women, however. Evidence indicates that, in many societies, especially in communities relying on a hunter-gatherer economy, gender relations were often essentially equal, certainly more equal than after European conquest or colonization led to conformity to a European cultural model (Etienne and Leacock 1980; Leacock 1981). This conformity also led to patterns of leadership and decision-making procedures in many of the societies that European powers confronted and overwhelmed. Indigenous societies often were based on **egalitarian ethics**—principles that community members had fundamentally equal rights to available resources and to social respect. Attitudes about communal and family control of land were undermined and altered as notions of private property and individual control of resources became the norm, in keeping with European economic systems. Students of power and colonial control often use conflict perspectives, feminist perspectives, or Marxist frameworks to analyze how indigenous cultures have been transformed.

Have you ever been a newcomer? What preconceptions did you bring with you?

Conflict perspectives are especially helpful in understanding culture change, whether that change is derived from internal processes or from external sources. For example, changes in attitudes and in practices may result from tensions among distinct segments of society based perhaps on class, gender, or ethnic differentiation. These tensions may over time lead to innovations or to fundamental alterations in the ways that societies are ordered and the ways that social roles are understood and enacted. Conflicts resulting from warfare and other sources of aggression between societies may also lead to change as one group may come to dominate another and impose not only their military control but also their cultural norms and practices.

Finally, conflict perspectives can help us understand the kinds of challenges and resistance to power expressed by dominated groups. Such resistance may take overt forms of refusal to acquiesce to power but it may also take covert forms of creative expression through song, artwork, and storytelling as well as through the transmission of secret knowledge.

Interpretive and conflict perspectives, in particular, share an emphasis on including multiple voices and perspectives within a community. From an interpretive framework, meaning is not homogeneous but rather is produced and interpreted by different people depending on their particular experiences and statuses within society. From a conflict framework, a society consists of people with different status- and role-related interests and privileges. And these differences need to be heard and analyzed (see Controversies feature). As Lila Abu-Lughod suggests, "Generalization, the characteristic mode of operation and style of writing of the social sciences can no longer be regarded as neutral description. . . . When one generalizes from experiences and conversations with a number of specific people in a community, one tends to flatten out differences among them and to homogenize them . . . and tends to smooth over contradictions, conflicts of interest, and doubts and arguments, not to mention changing motivations and circumstances" (2008, 58). Anthropologists therefore need to focus on "the particular" to understand the complexity, variability, and inconsistencies of human experience.

Reflexive Anthropology

Reflexive anthropology has been developed and championed by anthropologists in the tradition of postmodernism. The goal of such studies is to understand cultural impacts on the observations and writings of anthropologists, which must be taken into account in understanding other cultures (Clifford and Marcus 1986).

Early anthropologists saw their study populations as "primitive." As a result of colonialism and imperialism, societies were created that often appeared as static, timeless, and "traditional" to later European and American anthropologists, when they were not. Other labels often used but still difficult to define include the terms *non-Western, native,* and *indigenous.*

Today, rather than viewing societies as isolates and ideal types with unique sets of cultural traits, anthropologists investigate how the cultural practices and attitudes of a society relate to processes of globalization, such as modernization and economic development.

egalitarian ethics
Social principles that support equal access to resources and to social prestige within a community

reflexive anthropology
The anthropology of anthropology, which focuses on the labels that anthropologists use, the impacts of anthropologists on the people they study, and professional ethics.

Many anthropologists look for ways to apply their knowledge and theories to address these contemporary problems. In addition, anthropologists recognize that many voices cooperate and compete in the production of meaning, creating **polyphony**—the many sounds and voices of people in all segments or groups in a society. In this context, some anthropologists question the choice of voice in the texts that they produce and their own role in the process of presentation (see the Controversies feature later in this chapter for more discussion of these complex issues).

The discipline of anthropology developed in the nineteenth century; however, some missionaries, explorers, and colonists made detailed accounts of other cultures beginning in the fifteenth and sixteenth centuries. Evolutionism influenced nineteenth-century works by Herbert Spencer, Edward Tylor, and Lewis Henry Morgan. Two important figures in early twentieth-century anthropology are Franz Boas, who called for an anthropology based on cultural relativism and empiricism, and Bronislaw Malinowski, who explained cultural traits from the perspective of functionalism. Anthropologists may also use a materialist perspective (either cultural ecology or cultural materialism), structuralist perspectives and symbolic analyses, or conflict perspectives involving the analysis of culture and power to describe and explain culture. Interpretive anthropology focuses on the interconnectivity, subjectivity, and multiplicity of cultural meanings. And reflexive anthropology seeks to uncover and make visible the perspectives of the anthropologist him/herself in the processes of observation, analysis, and presentation of data about other cultures.

ETHNOGRAPHY AND FIELDWORK

Fieldwork—living with the group under study—remains a hallmark of modern anthropological methods. Writing about fieldwork, Paul Rabinow stated that "Culture is interpretation. The 'facts' of anthropology, the material that the anthropologist has gone to the field to find, are already themselves interpretations" (1977, 155). These interpretations are in effect translations from one cultural system into another. In the past, most anthropologists worked in societies different from their own, but today many work in their own countries and some even in their own communities. In addition, some anthropologists focus on secondary analyses of existing data rather than gathering primary data. Two types of studies based on secondary sources are comparisons using databases and ethnologies based on historical documents.

Cross-Cultural Comparisons

In 1949, anthropologists at Yale University founded the Human Relations Area Files (HRAF) to gather in one database and codify all the known cultural facts and details about the world's peoples. HRAF data consist of facts extracted from ethnographies written by anthropologists doing fieldwork in all parts of the world. The collection is divided into five world areas: Africa, Asia, North America, South America, and Oceania. Hundreds of cultural features and practices are coded and cross-referenced for making **cross-cultural comparisons.** Researchers use the HRAF data to find statistical correlations among certain cultural features or to test hypotheses about what cultural facts or forms are likely to be found in association with other facts or forms. The HRAF database can be accessed through university library systems that subscribe to the service.

For example, a study by Melvin Ember and Carol Ember (1996a) used HRAF data to propose hypotheses about the cultural settings in which couples choose to live near the family of the husband after marriage, in contrast to those in which couples choose to live near the wife's family. Another HRAF-based study by the Embers (1996b) showed a strong correlation among different kinds of violence in societies. Societies that frequently engage in warfare also are more likely to tolerate high levels of violence in other social contexts, such as murder, rape, assault, and domestic abuse.

Although large-scale comparative studies like the Embers's can uncover associations among cultural traits, comparing data that have been collected from numerous ethnographies and articles written by different researchers is difficult. In the first place, the data may not be comparable. In addition, when gleaned from

polyphony
The many voices of people from all the different segments and groups that make up a society; a quality of ethnographic writing today that presents multiple views of a culture.

fieldwork
In anthropology, living and interacting with the people or group under study.

cross-cultural comparisons
Means of understanding cultural differences and similarities through data analysis rather than direct observation.

CULTURE CHANGE

DOCUMENTING CHANGES IN THE LIVES OF AUSTRALIAN ABORIGINES

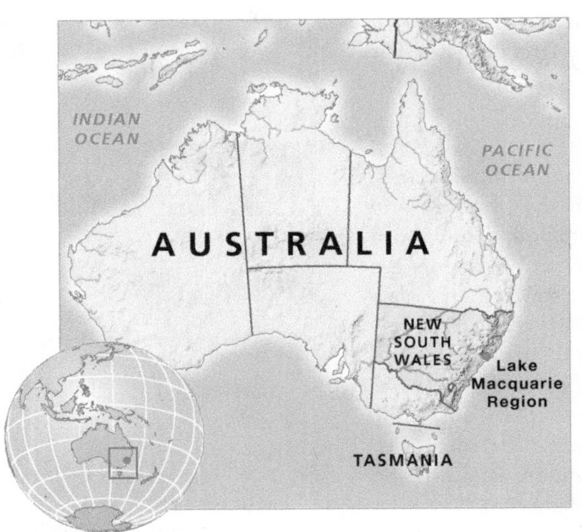

Using historical and ethnographic data, Australian ethnohistorians piece together the processes of transformation in the lives of Aborigines before and after the arrival of Europeans on the continent. They base their studies on documents describing interactions between Aboriginal peoples and Europeans, and on the policies carried out by agents of change, such as explorers, missionaries, traders, settlers, and government officials. Maps, photographs, biographies, and oral traditions are other sources of data ethnohistorians use in understanding change.

Ethnohistorians also document how societies invent and reinvent themselves and their cultures in response to internal and external forces. For example, the Aboriginal Family History Project of the South Australian Museum researches Aboriginal genealogies and community histories. The project uses material collected by museum anthropologists, ethnographers, and historians over the past century, but in particular the records of Norman Tindale and Joseph Birdsell, early twentieth-century anthropologists who collected data on Australian Aborigines. The museum's collection includes thousands of photos taken at Aboriginal sites around Australia.

Among many other Australian ethnohistory databases are hundreds of documents that scholars, writers, and community leaders prepared about the Awaba Aborigines of the Lake Macquarie region, housed at the University of Newcastle, including an 1837 translation of The Gospel of St. Mark in Awabakal. Other documents describe the genocide of Aborigines by Europeans and the forced assimilation of survivors, along with the struggles of present-day Aborigines to gain recognition of their claims to land, improve their economic conditions, and preserve their traditional culture.

Aboriginal Land Rights protest, Sydney, Australia. Alamy Limited/Tim Graham/Alamy

Data uncovered by ethnohistorians and testimony of contemporary Aborigines led Australian Prime Minister Kevin Rudd to issue a formal apology in 2008 for the treatment of Aborigines by Australian authorities. Of special note was the policy of forcibly removing Aboriginal and mixed-race children from their homes and taking them to residential facilities or placing them in foster care. Estimates suggest that more than 50,000 Aboriginal children were removed. Prime Minister Rudd began his statement:

> There is something terribly primal about the firsthand accounts [of victims]. The pain is searing; it screams from the pages. The hurt, the humiliation, the degradation and the sheer brutality of the act of physically separating a mother from her children is a deep assault on our senses and on our most elemental humanity. These stories cry out to be heard; they cry out for an apology. . . . That is what we are doing in this place today. (quoted in *Cultural Survival Quarterly*, 2008, 7)

ethnographies, practices and traits are taken out of their full cultural and historical contexts, which also may make them difficult to compare. Another danger in comparative studies is imputing causality: Although certain traits may appear in association, it may not be clear whether they are causally related at all or whether one trait causes or is an effect of another.

Ethnohistorical Research

A field more concerned with causal relationships in culture change than with comparisons is **ethnohistory,** the reconstruction and interpretation of the history of indigenous peoples from their point of view as well as the points of view of outside observers. Thus, some anthropological work takes place in libraries and archives containing historical records that help researchers learn about past conditions and events relevant to understanding the present lives of the people they are studying. A survey of ethnohistory usually is part of the preparation for conducting fieldwork. Ethnohistorians analyze the processes stemming from historical events and their consequences for changes in indigenous culture. A common focus is the impact of colonialism and conquest on the cultures of colonized peoples.

ethnohistory
Field of study for reconstructing and interpreting the history of indigenous peoples from their point of view as well as the points of view of ethnohistorians.

Imagine that your e-mails or blogs are among the records on which an ethnohistory of Internet culture is based. What kinds of information would your records provide? How could your records be interpreted to explain changes in Internet culture? How could your records help to document the changes we call globalization?

Ethnographic Fieldwork

Much of the work of anthropology consists of collecting and analyzing information about culture—that is, people's activities, beliefs, and attitudes. The reports that result from doing cultural anthropology are called *ethnography* (from the Greek word *ethnos,* meaning "people" or "a division of people"). The methods used in ethnographic work obviously depend on the kind of data required. Because cultural anthropology is concerned with the complex study of living cultures, anthropologists need to obtain many different kinds of information in many different kinds of settings. Anthropologists' initial fieldwork experiences often set the framework in which their research interests develop and continue throughout their careers. Anthropologists traditionally have chosen research problems and sites in foreign countries. This is still a common approach, but today many anthropologists work in their own countries, even in their own communities.

Doing Fieldwork

Fieldwork involves a complex process of observing and participating in another culture. Participant observation is at the core of the fieldwork experience. Anthropologists both observe the activities taking place in the community and participate in them as much as possible and as appropriate. Anthropologists usually live in the community that they are studying, sometimes renting a house or a room in someone else's dwelling. Fieldwork, then, is an ongoing, multifaceted research experience.

Choosing a Problem and Site. Anthropologists begin by choosing a research problem and then the site in which to conduct their study. Most anthropologists do their first research project when they are graduate students. Their interest in a particular subject may develop from an especially exciting course or from an especially stimulating teacher. Some anthropologists have long-standing interests in a particular country or community. Others choose a research site that best suits their theoretical or topical interests. Most graduate students embarking on their first field trip are advised to plan to be on site for about one year. This allows observations during a full annual cycle of economic, social, and ritual activities. Longer field stays are always beneficial but may not be possible due to lack of funding.

Doing Preliminary Research. Before fieldwork trips, researchers gather as much information about their subject of study as they can. They read what other anthropologists have written about the topic, attempting to understand the data and the theoretical approaches that others have used in analyzing the problem. To prepare themselves for entering a foreign country or community, they will want to learn as much as they can about the culture, the history, the conditions, and significant current events of that region, as well as the rules for entering and residing in the country. If possible, anthropologists also study the language of the country so that they can communicate directly with the residents. Before setting out for the site, anthropologists often make contact with local people to make sure that their presence in the community will be acceptable.

Anthropologist Elisha Renne (right) confers with professors Dr. Babatunde Agbaje-Williams and Dr. Aderonke Adesanya in Nigeria. Much anthropological field work today takes place in large-scale societies rather than small indigenous communities. Elisha P. Renne/Elisha P. Renne

Arrival and Culture Shock. In the field, researchers must immediately learn new customs, new faces, new foods, new languages, and ways of communicating. This learning is intense because, unlike tourists, anthropologists are immersing themselves in a new way of life in which they will participate. Often, the unstated rules of decorum and etiquette are most easily, and unknowingly, violated. Anthropologists need to be keenly observant, not only of other people's activities but also of the way other people react. By being sensitive to people's reactions, anthropologists can learn much about attitudes, values, and norms. Their experiences also afford them new insights into their own culture, behavior, and beliefs. Nevertheless, doing fieldwork has emotional ups and downs. At the beginning, anthropologists may feel uncertain, fearful, and lonely as they seek acceptance and cooperation. They may also experience **culture shock**—the feeling of being out of place in unfamiliar surroundings, and the feeling of losing one's cultural bearings.

Have you ever experienced culture shock? What was the situation? How did you respond to it?

Choosing a Place to Live. Once on site, anthropologists obtain a place of residence, arranging to live in or near a household or renting a dwelling. Living in a household has the advantage of proximity to people through family networks and routine participation in household and community events. Of course, the anthropologists need to find someone willing to be a host, sometimes a difficult task. A disadvantage to staying with a family, however, is that members of a household may try to ally themselves with the anthropologists, against the interests of others in the community, or may try to involve the anthropologists on their side in local social and political networks. In many field locations, anthropologists may have high status among the people they study. In poor and marginalized communities, they may be perceived as rich and powerful simply because of their presence and the assumed privilege of their lives, although anthropologists are rarely thought of as such in their own countries or communities. A challenge of fieldwork, then, is to establish good relations without allowing people to use a relationship to gain benefits or advantages over others in the community. Thus, although friendships may develop between an anthropologist and the people in the community, the researcher needs to remain as nonpartisan as possible in village conflicts, disputes, and controversies.

The communities in which anthropologists conduct fieldwork are linked to other communities, the nation, and other nations through local, regional, national, and transnational systems of exchange and the global market economy. A farm family in India, for example, might sell produce and handicrafts in regional markets that link ultimately to international export and import markets. Anthropologists must trace these kinds of connections and understand their impacts on people's daily lives.

Working in an Unfamiliar Language. As fieldwork begins, anthropologists usually hire an interpreter unless they are fluent in the local language. Learning the field language is clearly desirable, and even necessary, if the anthropologists truly want to learn the kinds of meanings people ascribe to their own behavior. Working through translators is very different from speaking directly to people. Many nuances of meaning and attitudes that are conveyed in language are lost in translation, regardless of the interpreter's skill.

Gathering Data. Once they are established, the anthropologists often survey the village or community or other field site. They may draw a map, situating the site within its local environment and the houses, other structures, farm fields, open spaces, or other areas where people congregate and socialize. A social survey, collecting **qualitative data,** may include information about the composition of households and the relationships between members of nearby houses. From these data, anthropologists learn about family ties and neighborhood networks. Anthropologists sometimes hire assistants to help with these tasks. If assistants come from the village, they can provide a personal connection to other people and help broaden the anthropologist's social network.

Gathering data includes interviewing members of the community. Traditional anthropological methodology includes collecting data concerning kinship, that is, how people trace relationships and descent from generation to generation and among members of the same generation. Combining genealogical information with residence histories that record how long people have resided in which houses allows anthropologists to learn about systems of relationships, people's geographic mobility, and intercommunity relations. It is also traditional to gather data about the ways that people obtain their food, earn a living, and provide themselves and others with goods and services. Economic and social networks may link groups and societies through trade, intermarriage, and friendships.

Anthropologists may collect **quantitative data** such as population trends reflected in births, marriages, and mortality statistics, fluctuations in community size, sources of income, and other statistical measures relevant to their specific studies.

In addition to gathering qualitative and quantitative data, some anthropologists use photography and film as methods of recording the lives and voices of community

culture shock
Feeling an anthropologist may have at the start of fieldwork of being out of place in unfamiliar surroundings.

qualitative data
Information obtained through personal interviews, life histories, observation, and interaction with community members.

quantitative data
Statistical information about population, employment and income figures, census reports on births and mortality, and so on, that reflect trends and processes within a community.

members. These visual technologies provide dramatic and authentic reflections by the people themselves. However, their use may raise ethical problems, especially around the issue of anonymity. Someone whose image or voice is recorded can obviously be easily identified. In situations of conflict, the personal safety of participants may be jeopardized.

Researchers also gather data through formal interviews and by attending meetings, informal gatherings, religious activities, and other community events. Anthropologists try to participate as much as possible to the extent that their presence is acceptable to community members. Anthropologists need to be sensitive to villagers' attitudes about an outsider's participation in community life. Outsiders may be welcome in some settings but not in others, particularly in sacred or secret activities or in meetings where controversial issues are discussed. Women anthropologists might find their access to certain men's activities limited, and male anthropologists might likewise find their access to certain women's activities restricted. Anthropologists usually want to interview community political officials, religious functionaries, teachers, and doctors for certain kinds of information. It is important, however, not to become overreliant on local authorities, in order to avoid interpretation of village life from the perspective of the local elite. Despite increasing involvement with villagers, researchers usually remain outsiders, except sometimes for those who are themselves indigenous or native to the group they are studying. Some of the best, most insightful ethnographic accounts are written by native anthropologists.

Interpreting and Reporting Data. During and after fieldwork, anthropologists reflect on their interactions and the data they have collected. New research questions may arise, new opportunities for observation and participation may present themselves, and new understandings of what has happened may be revealed. Field notes are rewritten as ethnographic accounts and papers, which are published and presented at professional meetings. Sharing the results of research is important in a community of scholars and often leads to new research questions to answer. Anthropological reports are framed within the analytic and theoretical perspectives of the researcher. Other anthropologists may undertake reanalyses of data, focusing on additional questions and employing different theoretical frameworks.

When anthropologists return home after living in the field for an extended period of time and becoming comfortable in a different culture, they often go through a period of culture shock, not unlike the culture shock they felt when they first arrived in the field. They may see the behavior of their friends and relatives with new eyes. For a while, they are outside observers of their own culture, once so familiar and taken for granted. Of course, in a short time, they are readily integrated into their own daily lives. The experience of living with other people in another society has profound and lasting meaning. For many, it gives them new insights into their own behavior and their own beliefs.

How could you apply each of the steps described in this section in a fieldwork situation close to home?

Anthropological Research in Urban Societies

When anthropologists conduct research in urban societies, they use many of the same data-collection techniques that they use in rural or isolated communities. Rarely, however, do they study a whole town or city. Instead, they investigate a specific topic within a defined subculture or group. For example, some researchers specialize in **urban anthropology,** a field that focuses on studying the lives of people living in cities or urban neighborhoods. Urban anthropologists may analyze a neighborhood association, a particular occupational group, a school setting, a religious network, a health care delivery system, or a senior citizen center. The people in these groups may or may not reside near one another, but they interact frequently in particular areas of their lives.

In conducting this kind of research, anthropologists use data-gathering techniques similar to those sociologists and other researchers use, including survey research. **Survey research** involves the use of formal questionnaires, administered to a random sample of subjects, to elicit social data such as occupation, income, level of education, marital status, participation in clubs and associations, political and religious affiliations, household size, number of computers in the home, and so on. Questionnaires also elicit information about people's attitudes, values, and practices, which are then tallied and analyzed. Survey data provide information about features and trends in the community under study, including socioeconomic conditions, social participation, social norms, people's attitudes and opinions, and cultural practices. In survey research, data analysis can

urban anthropology
Field that focuses on studying the lives of people living in cities or urban neighborhoods.

survey research
Use of formal questionnaires, administered to a random sample of subjects, eliciting social data that can be analyzed statistically.

In Their Own VOICES

Fieldwork and the Phone

In this excerpt, anthropologist P. L. Sunderland reflects on her discovery of the value of a new research tool—the telephone—as an integral part of her fieldwork conducted among women participating in the mainstream jazz community centered in New York City.

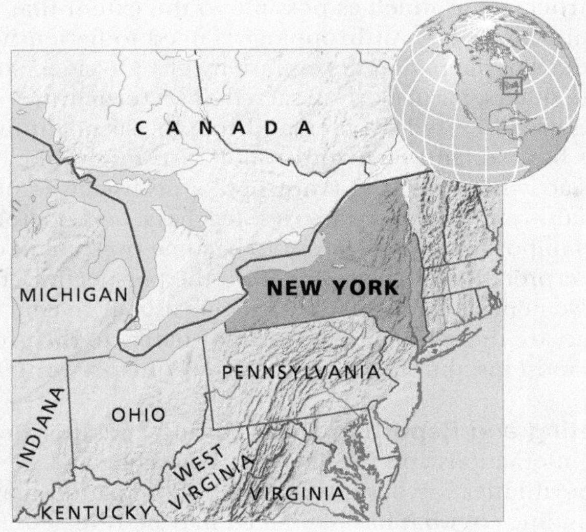

In the United States and in many other parts of the world, day to day interaction with the telephone has changed significantly over the last fifteen to twenty years. On the whole, anthropologists have paid little scholarly attention to the telephone.

I began thinking about this issue in the early 1990s. At the time I was conducting fieldwork in New York City's mainstream jazz community. I had more or less stumbled onto this dissertation topic because of taking up employment during graduate school in Bradley's, at the time not only an important mainstream jazz club, but also the important jazz "hang." Then when I set about to begin the research, I conceived of my fieldwork as having two main components: 1) ethnographic observations and conversations carried out in jazz clubs and at other jazz events; and 2) face-to-face audiotaped interviews with women of the community, carried out in the women's homes. I did both of these things. But I also found myself spending a considerable amount of time on the phone. I soon realized that telephone conversations were not only crucial to the fieldwork, but in many senses constituted the fieldwork. Many of my telephone conversations were participant observation. I was equally interacting and participating with the women in a quotidian form of activity.

I was actually excited. It felt like I had discovered a very new thing—that a way in which urban research is carried out is via the phone. It makes sense. So much of our "other" life, that is our "not-fieldwork" life is carried out via the phone. With the excitement of this realization, there was the simultaneous heightened awareness of anthropologists' lack of mention of the telephone.

As anthropologists we have not generally embraced the telephone as a fieldwork medium, even when we recognize it as "socially key" for ourselves as well as others. Without a doubt, telephone interaction was an extremely important aspect of everyday life for jazz community members. The telephone was also the primary medium that allowed the "everyday" boundaries of the community to extend beyond the geographical limits of the city.

As anthropologists we have recognized the need to dislodge cultural matters from spaces and places, and recognized the validity of arguments that stable, bounded "things" like societies and communities are the product of analytic imagination.

The double-barreled nature of telephone conversations—transmitters of meaning and social relationship glue—are why

emphasize statistical correlations to answer a particular research question, or narrative descriptions to understand the life of the group or community as a whole.

Anthropologists also use participant observation in urban settings. Urban anthropologist Judith Freidenberg (2000) studied elderly Puerto Ricans in New York City's El Barrio, a predominantly Hispanic neighborhood on the Upper East Side of Manhattan. Freidenberg consulted archival and historical records on immigration from Puerto Rico, neighborhood residency, and age and gender distribution of the Puerto Rican community in New York in order to situate her field community within its larger geographic, social, and historical contexts. She gathered statistics on income, occupation, and education to obtain a social and economic profile of the community. Then, before entering the field, she made a survey of neighborhood associations, church groups, after-school programs, and clinics and hospitals to understand the extent of Puerto Rican involvement in community services and networks.

After obtaining enough background information, Freidenberg attended community functions and visited senior centers and health care clinics so that she could get to know the people who used these services and they could get to know her. She then talked with

Alamy Limited/mambo/Alamy

I say that in some ways my telephone conversations were the quintessential aspects of my fieldwork experience.

But as much as I was excited about these interactions as fieldwork interactions, I sometimes did not feel as good or comfortable about these interactions as fieldwork as I did when I was in jazz clubs or at other jazz events. It often did not feel quite right.

Participant observation can be a murky, personally messy business. A major source of the personal messiness of participant observation can come from the attempt to do what others do in a setting—and as a consequence, establish relations based on that activity—but with a different, outside-of-that-sphere goal in mind.

Fieldnotes are considered a necessity for us after face-to-face encounters and also would probably be quickly understood by others. For friendly conversations on the telephone there was no such model—for any of us—and I believe this was also part of the discomfort.

An underlying sense that telephone interactions are not the "real" stuff of community or social life also undoubtedly influences our anthropological hesitation to utilize the telephone in fieldwork. As we fully recognize the telephone as an important medium of contemporary social life and as we incorporate the telephone into our ethnographic toolkit, we open the door for another kind of fieldwork.

Anthropologists' commitment to long-term intensive involvement with people continues to distinguish our scholarship. This merit should not be lost. [But] we must be sure that we do not wear methodological blinders. Anthropological methodology was developed in social situations where the telephone was virtually nonexistent. When we find ourselves using the telephone in our fieldwork, it is important that we do not have to hide from that use. We know that telephones are in homes, offices, pockets, purses, and public places. We also know we participate in telephone interactions with other scholars, friends, family, and so on. It is also time that we included them, and admitted to including them, as integral parts of our fieldwork.

From P. L. Sunderland. 1999. "Fieldwork and the Phone." *Anthropological Quarterly* 72(3): 105–17.

CRITICAL THINKING QUESTIONS

Think about how you would go about writing an ethnography of your own use of telephones. What questions might you investigate? Here are some possibilities: For what purposes do you use telephones? Do you always answer the phone when it rings? What do you think you accomplish through phone use? Could you accomplish these goals by some other means? What's the difference?

individuals whom she thought would be interested in working with her and began conducting in-depth interviews with them. She also accompanied her consultants in their daily activities, such as shopping, attending church, going to the doctor, and visiting with friends.

Over time, Freidenberg gained firsthand knowledge about the people's activities, attitudes, and opinions on a wide range of subjects. By collecting extended **life histories,** she got a fairly complete picture of people's experiences throughout their lives. She was able to understand their perspective on what it means to grow older as immigrants in a large city and to need health care and social services. As years passed, Freidenberg became part of their lives and they part of hers. She used the knowledge she had gained to make policy recommendations about the delivery of medical and social services to the elderly in New York City.

life histories
A research methodology focusing on collecting narratives of the life experiences of research participants, including their places of residence, work, family composition, social interactions, and roles within their communities.

Just as Freidenberg studied elderly Puerto Ricans in New York City, Scott Youngstedt (2004) focused his research on how Hausa migrants to Niamey, the capital of Niger in western Africa, build social networks in their new settings to create or re-create a sense of community and familiarity as they adjust to living far from "home." When new arrivals come to the city, they immediately attempt to locate other people from their hometowns, re-creating the kinds of social support familiar to them from traditional ethics of reciprocity and mutual aid.

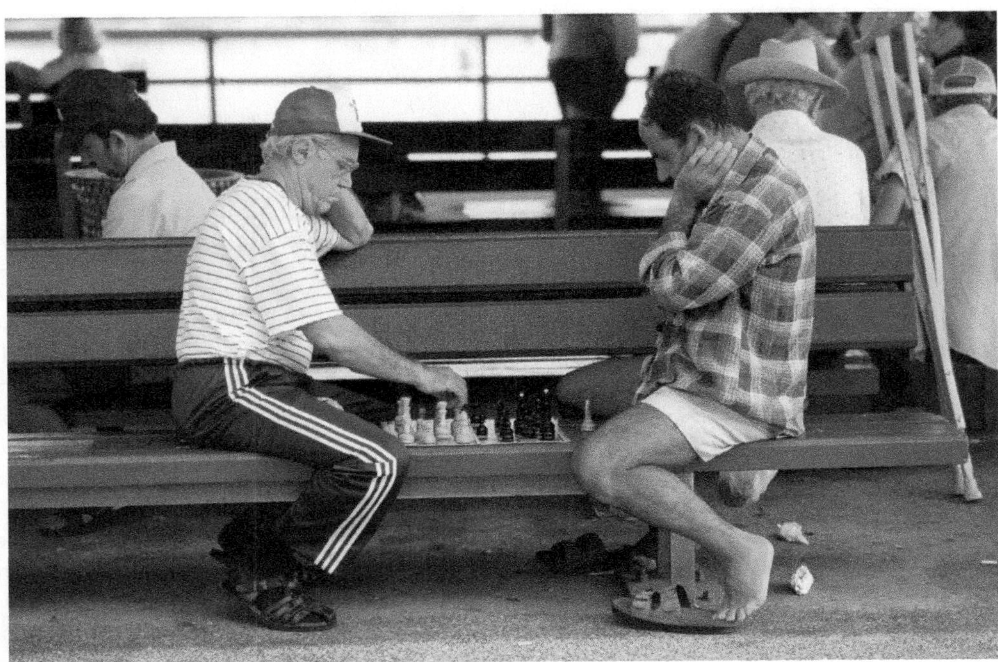

As an urban anthropologist, how might you go about studying this Puerto Rican community in New York City? What aspects of the culture of this community would you want to try to understand through your study? Corbis/Mark Peterson/Corbis

In 1960, at the time of Niger's independence, the city had a population of 30,000, approximately 3,600 (or 12 percent) of whom were Hausa. By 2003, slightly more than half of the city's 800,000 residents were Hausa (Youngstedt 2004, 96). Most Hausa migrants to Niamey hope to return to their home villages once they achieve comparative economic success. However, few are able to do so. Few jobs provide steady employment or sufficient salaries to enable workers to save money. Instead, life becomes a struggle to pay for the basic necessities of food and housing. That Hausa and members of other groups continue to be drawn to Niamey indicates the degree of poverty in rural communities. Indeed, a report by the United Nations Human Development Programme in 2002 ranked Niger 173rd out of 174 nations studied (Youngstedt 2004, 94).

Hausa men meet daily in coffee shops and public squares where they exchange information about jobs or housing, get news from their hometowns, and debate issues. Youngstedt's interactions with Hausa consultants in these "conversation groups" revealed that the men developed and transmitted their understandings of how the position of their nation in the global economy contributes to creating their own conditions of poverty and disadvantage. Urban studies unveil the complex layers of activities and meanings that connect individuals to one another and to the global contexts in which their lives are situated.

Another topic of research in cities is analysis of occupational groups in their urban and national environments. Florence Babb's research on market women in the city of Huarez in northwestern Peru centered on both the activities of individual traders and the government policies aimed at restricting their work (Babb 1989). Babb's study uncovered the precarious but essential role that tradeswomen render to settled urban populations. For the women, trading provided one of the few income-generating occupations available for people with few or no formal work skills. Marketing is one of the two most common occupations for women in Peru, second only to domestic service. Women are a large majority of the traders throughout the country (Babb 1989, 3). Trading enables women to keep the flexible hours that allow them to fulfill other family responsibilities. Despite the hard work and long hours, most traders make little money. They are increasingly overshadowed by more formal commercial establishments. In addition, men have many more job options because of better education and training.

Peruvian government policies contribute to marginalizing traders, most of whom are members of indigenous communities, in part because their activities are difficult to regulate and their income is difficult to tax. They are also seen as symptoms of economic backwardness. But studies of tradespeople in urban centers, not only in Peru but also throughout Latin America and Africa, demonstrate that they provide a wide range of products including raw and cooked foods, meat, and clothing.

In addition to focusing on particular groups, occupations, and neighborhoods, urban anthropologists may analyze the cultural and structural linkages among diverse populations within a city. They may also focus on structural linkages between communities, larger urban contexts, and national social and political entities. This focus guided the research of Jagna Sharff (1998), who led a team of three urban anthropologists in a long-term (fifteen-year) research project in a poor, predominantly Hispanic neighborhood on the Lower East Side of New York City.

CASE STUDY

Life in Riverfront: A Midwestern Town Seen through Japanese Eyes

In their book, *Life in Riverfront: A Middle-Western Town Seen Through Japanese Eyes* (2001), two Japanese anthropologists, Mariko Fujita Sano and Toshiyuki Sano, write about the process of doing ethnography of a foreign culture in a complex, heterogeneous society made up of people of different social classes and ethnic and religious groups. They tell about their expectations before embarking on fieldwork and about their gradual immersion as both observers and participants in community life. The town, located in central Wisconsin, has about 22,000 residents, nearly all of European American ancestry. Both anthropologists were born and raised in Japan and received PhDs in anthropology from Stanford University in California. They had absorbed stereotypes about "Middle America" that they feared might affect their observations, and were concerned that they might not be readily accepted or trusted in Riverfront, which had few Asian residents: As "foreigners . . . everything that we do would stand out."

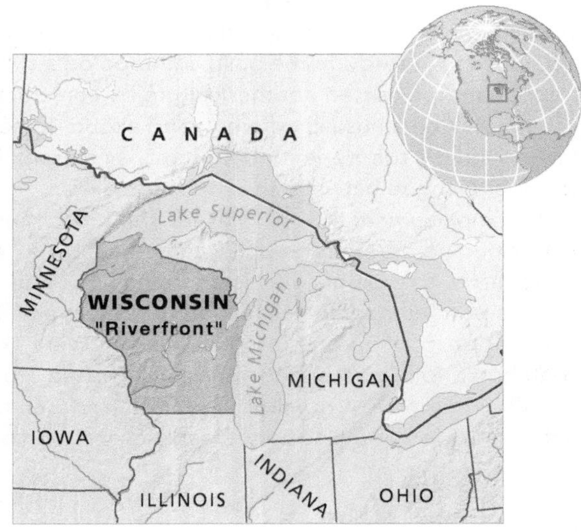

The couple also worried about finding a place to live, especially after the owner of the first apartment they looked at asked, "Which church do you go to?" They were afraid that people might be hostile to them because Japan was an enemy of the United States in World War II. Mariko Sano was concerned that "conservative Middle Americans" would think of her as a housewife accompanying her husband, rather than as a well-educated professional. Another preconception that the Sanos brought to Riverfront was that the town would be ethnically uniform. "Although we had known that American society is ethnically diverse, we tended to associate ethnicity with racial minorities such as African Americans, Hispanics, and Asians and tended to see European-American people as a uniform ethnicity" (2001, 1). Yet Europeans proved equally diverse.

The Sanos imagined Riverfront as a rural community in the midst of farms and open country. They thought that life would be simpler than in a large city, although they hadn't really thought about what "simpler" might mean. They found, of course, that "Middle America" is much more complex than they had anticipated based on their preconceived notions and stereotypes. They also found that Riverfront is embedded not only in a geographic context but also in an economic and political context of competing interests and identities.

The Sanos combined several research methodologies. They delved into archival material to understand the town's development since its incorporation in 1856. They traced the geographic spread and economic growth of the town and its relationship to a campus in the University of Wisconsin system. They also collected life histories from older residents and used them to "sketch a picture" of life in Riverfront as early as the 1920s and 1930s. They were careful to obtain life histories representative of the various ethnic groups there to ascertain similarities and differences in the immigrant experience. In addition, the Sanos analyzed quantitative statistical data from official census lists dating back to the mid-nineteenth century, detailing population, ethnic and national origin, and residential mobility within the town. The Sanos also volunteered at a senior citizen center, helping to serve meals for elderly townspeople. This activity enabled the Sanos to

CONTROVERSIES

How Do Anthropologists Present Knowledge About the People They Study?

Since the 1960s, anthropologists have questioned their roles as agents of change, as they intentionally or unwittingly facilitate worldwide economic and political processes (Gough 1968). Some anthropologists also side with the people they study against oppressive policies that destroy the people's land and resources or pressure them to abandon their way of life.

Anthropologists interested in the impacts of the researcher's ideologies on other peoples look at the ways groups represent themselves and others, and structure people's ideas about these groups. As people involved in the processes of "writing culture," anthropologists influence the representation of the peoples they study. In the past, anthropologists often wrote about and presented another culture by constructing the "other" as alien, unusual, different, and exotic. To counteract this tendency, some anthropologists today present their findings as a dialogue between themselves and members of the society among whom they have lived. The production of any text, including an ethnography, can be seen as a "dialogic" process with multiple voices and meanings (Bakhtin 1981). In the past, ethnographies tended to present a unified voice in their description of a people's lifeways. Very likely, they contributed to cultural stereotypes and depicted greater conformity, uniformity of opinion, and idealized behavior than actually existed in the society. Deeply contested issues were often glossed over. Because ethnographies focused on a view of culture from the perspective of people with greater prestige and privilege, the voices of marginalized members of communities were muted or unheard.

In addition, because most anthropologists were male in the past, and because they worked primarily with male consultants, ethnographies tended to be told from a male perspective. Women's concerns, lives, and voices were relatively unknown and unheard. Examples of gender bias in ethnological interpretation are common. Writing about the Nuer of southern Sudan, for example, the British social anthropologist E. E. Evans-Pritchard concluded that Nuer family life was "remarkably harmonious on the surface" (1955, 133). Yet his research, based entirely on the testimony of men, disclosed culturally sanctioned wife abuse and the wishes of both husbands and wives (reported by the husbands) for their spouse's death! Not a harmonious picture, even on the surface. More recently, the writings of Napoleon Chagnon (1997) among the Yanomami of Brazil and Venezuela downplay the significance of the violence husbands inflict on women. And many anthropologists overemphasize the male role of hunting in comparison to the female role of gathering.

The male bias in anthropology extends to theories about human evolution and cultural origins. For example,

meet people, establish friendly relations, and contribute to the community. It also gave them opportunities for informal conversations and interviews.

After a year in Riverfront, life changed for the Sanos and their relations with people when Mariko gave birth to their first child. As they point out, "Anthropologists in the field often reach a turning point at which the nature of the relationship with their interviewees changes dramatically. For us, the turning point was the birth of our son." Even before the baby was born, people began to give advice about how to take care of the child, in effect beginning the process of integrating the child into the culture of Riverfront. From being outsiders and strangers, the Sanos became friends and community members, especially to regulars at the senior citizens center. People commented that the child, because of its birth in Riverfront, would be an American.

The Sanos left Riverfront after nearly two years of fieldwork. They returned some twelve years later to see many economic changes, as old industries disappeared and new shopping malls were constructed. Immigrants continued to arrive in town, some from Europe and others from urban and rural American communities. The Sanos realized that these immigrants were much like themselves, arriving in a new place and adapting to its culture. As they conclude, "We have carried on cultural dialogues between 'them' and 'us' and among 'ourselves.'" And they note that these are the same "cultural-dialogical experiences" that all newcomers have, whatever their origins and whatever their purposes. Read the Document on myanthrolab.com since the earliest known tools were found in association with animal bones (dating from about 2 million years ago), and since hunting is assumed to have been primarily a male role, researchers have proposed theories of human development that privilege male inventiveness and initiative while portraying females as passive onlookers to cultural evolution. These conclusions are controversial for many reasons, not the least because there may have been earlier tools made of fiber for use in containers for carrying gathered plant resources, presumably the work of females (Ehrenberg 1989). The point is that although we know quite a bit about physical evolution, we know little about the lives of our earliest ancestors. And as Linda Fedigan (1986) suggests, models of human origins are "symbolic statements about and prescriptions for human nature." They tell us more about the people making the theories than they do about early human populations.

Because of these problems with the ethnographer's voice, some anthropologists are producing "polyphonous" ethnographies with a multitude of voices. Rather than relying on a single, dominant perspective, they give multiple interpretations of activities and opinions from the points of view of people with different roles in the community. The voices of men and women, of the elites and the marginal contribute to a diversity of representations. By focusing on dialogue and polyphony, anthropologists locate culture not only in behavior but also in conversation about behavior, ideas, attitudes, and emotions. Ethnographers also focus on their own issues of power, their relations with communities in their own societies, and their relations with people in the communities they study. And they need to pay more attention to looking past their own subjectivity to more fully represent others.

Controversies within the discipline about the role of the anthropologist and the focus of ethnography do not weaken the field but, rather, invigorate it, bringing out issues for thought and dialogue. Anthropology plays a vital role in today's world. It has the tools with which to understand and analyze complex issues of power that structure and confront our world. The theories and methods that anthropologists use provide the knowledge and techniques for understanding people's behavior and how they organize, transmit, evaluate, and express their experiences. Anthropologists can contribute to debates about public policy in national and international arenas. They can help inform people about the value of all cultures.

CRITICAL THINKING QUESTIONS

How do you think your roles and status as a member of your society might affect your observations of other people? How might they color what you say to an anthropologist interviewing you about your people's way of life?

If you were writing an ethnography of your community, whose voices might you want to represent or include? Why?

The Sharff team collected economic data on income and employment, information on household composition and residence, and social indicators such as health, education, and friendship networks. They opened an office in the neighborhood as headquarters and space for their team to meet together and with community residents. The researchers interacted with people daily, but they framed their research and interpretation of data in terms of a larger picture: the city's economy and national policies affecting poor people. The researchers were untangling the web of economic and political relationships that impacted the daily lives of low-income Hispanics. That web included deindustrialization, leading to loss of employment, and interrelated problems stemming from lack of educational opportunity, cuts in social service spending, neighborhood deterioration, and increased crime and drug use. According to Sharff and her colleagues, the violence in the community resulted from the "violence of poverty" inflicted on poor people by national and local forces beyond their control.

As you can imagine, doing fieldwork in one's own society poses special problems of objectivity. Many anthropologists believe that being completely objective when studying any culture is impossible because all observers bring with them their own learned values, attitudes, and expectations. At the same time, anthropologists need to "know" something about the subjects of study. The challenge, then, is to "learn" about them in a different way, taking account of what the researchers think they already know but looking afresh from an anthropological perspective.

Watch the **Video:** *Corporate Ethnography* on **myanthrolab.com**

REVIEW

Boas, Malinowski, and other early twentieth-century anthropologists emphasized fieldwork. Ethnohistory and cross-cultural comparisons using databases such as the Human Relations Area Files are examples of anthropological approaches based on records and data rather than on direct observations. When anthropologists do fieldwork, they often write descriptive accounts called ethnographies. Conducting fieldwork involves many steps before even entering the field, at which time most first-time anthropologists experience culture shock. Fieldwork can focus on entire small-scale societies or on subcultures or subgroups within a larger society. Anthropologists also study groups, communities, and institutions within their own societies. Using methods such as interviews and survey research as well as participant observation, researchers in urban anthropology focus on segments of larger societies and their connections with other societies and the world.

THE ANTHROPOLOGY OF ANTHROPOLOGY

The study of anthropology by anthropologists has been a growing interest for many in the past several decades. Anthropologists are concerned both about the role of the discipline of anthropology in relation to indigenous societies and about the unspoken and largely invisible assumptions that anthropologists may use in developing theories, formulating analyses, and presenting data about other peoples.

Ethical Issues in Anthropology

Other issues concerning anthropology relate to the ethics of conducting research involving human subjects. Cultural anthropologists make their living and build their careers by studying other people. They live among them, learn from them, and write about them. As a result, the most important ethical issues they face involve their relationships with and obligations to those people.

The American Anthropological Association, the professional association to which most anthropologists belong, formulated a Code of Ethics, setting out a number of principles that it recommends to its members (American Anthropological Association 1998). The code mandates intellectual honesty, forbidding any falsification or intentional biasing of data. Stage-directing ethnographic film footage would be regarded as unethical, for example. The code also advises that an anthropologists' ethical obligations to the people they study are more important than the pursuit of knowledge or the completion of research projects. Ethical obligations include avoiding harm to or exploitation of the people, and fully disclosing the goals and uses of the research. Anthropologists also must consider the social and political implications of the material that they produce. Finally, the code notes that, although some anthropologists use their research to advocate for the people they study, this is not an ethical responsibility but rather an individual choice. Anthropologists are also guided by federal legal requirements safeguarding the rights of human subjects in any type of research project. These rights include **informed consent,** that is, full disclosure of research goals, research methods, types of analyses, and reporting procedures.

Anthropologists do not agree on their proper roles in relation to the people they study. For some anthropologists, research is an end in itself. People in the community extend their hospitality voluntarily. And although anthropologists should certainly avoid doing anything that they feel may be harmful to the community (in the short or long term), some believe that they have no continuing obligation to the people. Other anthropologists believe that they have ongoing responsibilities to the community, and they lend their help. Anthropologists may be able to collect and analyze documents or testify in court proceedings regarding native territories and indigenous land claims cases. Others can use their training and knowledge to represent native interests in dealings with local and national governments. At the least, anthropologists can present information about the needs of indigenous communities to the public in their writings and in classes. As experts, they can talk to the media, countering negative stereotypes about poor and marginalized peoples. Applied anthropologists focus on many of these goals.

informed consent
The full disclosure to research participants of the research goals, methods, types of analyses, and reporting procedures.

ANTHROPOLOGY APPLIED

Human Terrain System

In 2007, the United States Department of Defense inaugurated a program termed Human Terrain System (HTS) with the goal of providing cultural sensitivity training to military officers and soldiers stationed in Iraq and Afghanistan. The training would be the responsibility of cultural anthropologists and other social scientists. The term "human terrain" refers to the social, cultural, economic, and political features of the people in communities where military units operate. Cultural researchers are "embedded" in military units in the target countries. They are organized into "Human Terrain Teams" led by a military officer and staffed by four additional members: one cultural analyst, a regional studies analyst, and two staffers with a military intelligence background. Anthropologists (possibly working as both cultural analysts and regional studies analysts) provide background cultural data concerning such matters as local tribal organizations, leadership patterns, family and clan structures, and norms for conflict resolution. They also teach military personnel the local practices of interpersonal interaction (e.g., how to greet people, how to engage in conversation, how to ask questions, etc.). Beginning as an experimental project, the Human Terrain System was awarded a fund of $40 million by the Department of Defense to expand services to twenty-six U.S. combat brigades stationed in Iraq and Afghanistan.

Dr. Montgomery McFate helped design the program beginning in 2003 and has since become its senior social science adviser (2004). She is also one of the co-authors of a military manual on counterinsurgency. McFate is an advocate of anthropologists working with the military in order to help achieve goals of community involvement and support for enhancing the role of local leaders, for developing rapport for military personnel and objectives, strengthening security, and building resistance to Taliban insurgents in Afghanistan.

Military officials claim that the program has enabled them to reduce combat operations and instead focus on improving security by building relationships with people and understanding and addressing their concerns. However, the Human Terrain System project is not without its strong detractors among anthropologists. Indeed, shortly after the project's inauguration in 2007, the American Anthropological Association published a statement opposing HTS on the grounds that it could potentially lead to a violation of professional ethics and endanger research subjects. Two years later, the Association released a report again critical of HTS, stating that "When ethnographic investigation is determined by military missions, where data collection occurs in the context of war, integrated into the goals of counterinsurgency in a potentially coercive environment . . . it can no longer be considered a legitimate professional exercise of anthropology." Furthermore, anthropologists embedded with combat troops may have their data unwittingly used to make decisions concerning military targets and attacks.

Defense Imagery.mil/DoD photo by Spc. Tobey White, U.S. Army

Anthropologist David Price points out that HTS is only the latest in a series of interconnections between anthropology, other social sciences, and military and intelligence agencies. In his opinion, anthropological research and findings have been misused in order to promote the government's political and social agendas both at home and abroad. In *Weaponizing Anthropology* (2011), Price examines what he calls the increasing "militarization of anthropology and education" since the attacks on the World Trade Center on September 11, 2001.

Still, both supporters and opponents of HTS acknowledge the difficulty in assessing the program's effectiveness. To date, research is lacking concerning the success or failure of meeting the goals of enhancing cultural sensitivity among military personnel or of winning the "hearts and minds" of Iraqi or Afghan citizens. However, one documented outcome has been the deaths of at least three anthropologists serving as members of HTS teams in Iraq and Afghanistan.

CRITICAL THINKING QUESTIONS

Do you think that anthropologists can remain objective and neutral if they are "embedded" in military combat units? Do you think that local residents are likely to perceive them as such?

REVIEW

Reflexive anthropology focuses on anthropology itself, the language it uses to describe people, and its impacts on both knowledge and people. Today, many ethnographies are written to reflect polyphony—the many voices of people from all the different segments and groups that make up a society. Concern about the impacts of anthropologists on study populations has led to a professional Code of Ethics for the conduct of anthropology.

Study and **Review** on **myanthrolab.com**

CHAPTER SUMMARY

Anthropology and the Explanation of Cultural Diversity

- Although anthropology as an academic discipline is only slightly more than a century old, it has its origins in the colonial expansion of Europe that began in the fifteenth and sixteenth centuries when explorers, traders, and missionaries visited and commented on the peoples and cultures they encountered. During the eighteenth century, European social philosophers consulted the journals and writings of earlier observers. Their evolutionism—hypotheses about the progress of humankind from one cultural stage to the next—established a basis for anthropological theories.
- The anthropology that emerged in the late nineteenth and early twentieth centuries in the United States and Europe focused on classifying and comparing peoples and cultures throughout the world, attempting to determine their evolutionary relationships to one another. Two important figures were Franz Boas, who championed attention to historical details, empiricism, and cultural relativism, and Bronislaw Malinowski, who contributed the perspective of functionalism. Their work, emphasizing fieldwork and direct interactions with and observations of other cultures, forms the core of anthropology.
- Anthropologists have developed a number of conceptual frameworks to explain human cultures. Materialist perspectives emphasize the centrality of environmental adaptation, technology, and methods of acquiring or producing food. Cultural ecology focuses on how the physical environment directly influences the satisfaction of basic human needs and how people's adaptive behaviors interact with other aspects of culture. Cultural materialists often distinguish between emic explanations of behavior, based on the reasons people themselves offer for what they do, and etic explanations, based on the analysts' observations of people's behavior and other objective criteria.
- Structuralist approaches look at the role of concepts in structuring experiences and relationships. Interpretive anthropologists focus on relationships among meanings in the development and transmission of culture. Conflict perspectives focus on social and cultural inequalities and power relations.
- Some anthropologists emphasize forms of social, economic, and political power in shaping culture. Some of their attention is directed toward anthropology itself, uncovering unstated biases in the field and in the analysis of culture. Today, anthropologists are rethinking notions about "traditional" society and focusing more on the complex ways in which traditional societies reshaped themselves, and were reshaped by the impacts of European expansion and colonial control. Worldwide processes of modernization and globalization also raise issues about how people are enmeshed in economic institutions and political forces beyond their control.

Ethnography and Fieldwork

- The central tool of anthropological research is fieldwork, especially participant observation. Anthropologists live among the people they are studying for an extended time to gain an understanding of their culture from the people's point of view. As participant observers, anthropologists observe and record the communities' activities and participate in them as much as possible and appropriate. Earlier anthropologists focused on small, seemingly isolated indigenous societies. Today, however, many anthropologists work in larger societies, including their own, focusing on specific subcultures or communities.
- In addition to fieldwork, some anthropologists use ethnohistory, researching in libraries and archives to learn about past conditions and events relevant to understanding the lives of the people they are studying. Anthropologists also employ the comparative method in understanding cross-cultural similarities and differences in human cultures.

The Anthropology of Anthropology

- Cultural anthropologists are concerned with ethical issues involving their relationships with the people they study. Some anthropologists become advocates for the communities they have studied, whereas others seek to disseminate information that counters negative stereotypes about poor and marginalized peoples.

REVIEW QUESTIONS

1. How did anthropology become an academic discipline? What were the principal goals of early anthropologists?
2. How did Boas and Malinowski influence the development of anthropology?
3. What main theoretical perspectives do anthropologists use to describe and explain cultural differences and changes?
4. What are the differences between an emic and an etic perspective?
5. How might a cultural event be analyzed differently by a conflict theorist and an interpretivist?
6. How do anthropologists prepare for fieldwork? What are the key benchmarks in conducting fieldwork?
7. What are some pitfalls of living and participating in family and community life while doing fieldwork?
8. What is the anthropology of anthropology? What are some issues about the roles of anthropologists and the writing of ethnographies?

MyAnthroLab Connections

Watch. Listen. View. Explore. Read. MyAnthroLab is designed just for you. Dynamic visual activities, videos, and readings found in the multimedia library will enhance your learning experience.

Resources from this chapter:

Watch on **myanthrolab.com**

- *Corporate Ethnography*

Explore on **myanthrolab.com** In MySearchLab, enter the Anthropology database to find relevant and recent scholarly and popular press publications. For this chapter, enter the following keywords: urban anthropology, ethnohistory, cross-cultural

Read on **myanthrolab.com**

- *Glebo: Civilizing the Anthropologist* by Mary H. Moran
- *Morocco: Adolescents in a Small Town by Susan Schaefer David*

Fieldwork on Prostitution in the Era of AIDS

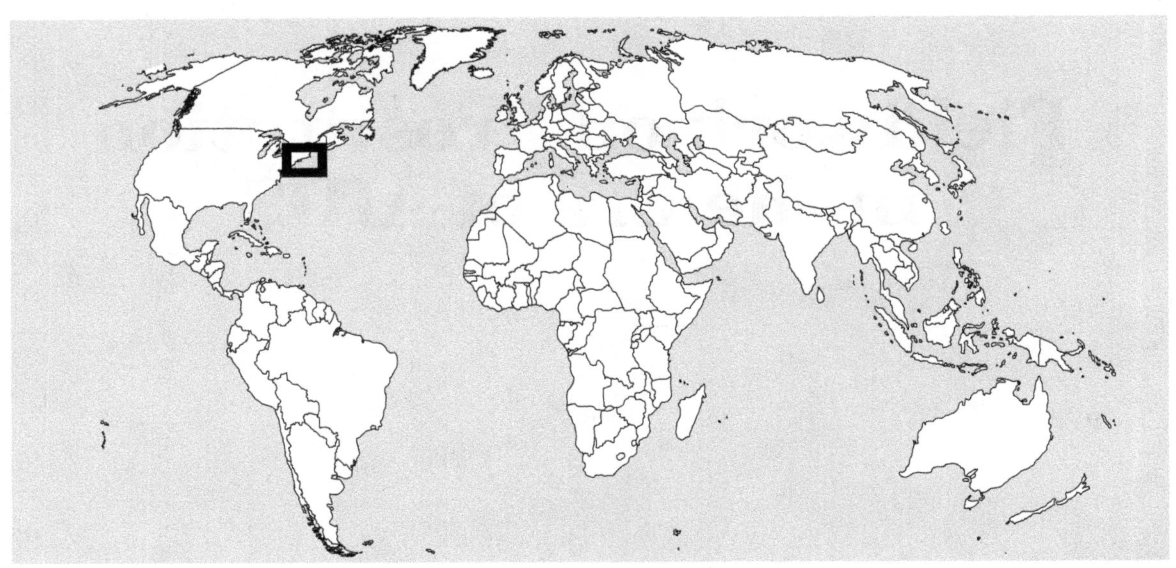

Fieldwork on Prostitution in the Era of AIDS

Claire E. Sterk

Many Americans associate social research with questionnaires, structured interviews, word association tests, and psychological experiments. They expect investigators to control the research setting and ask for specific information, such as age, income, place of residence, and opinions about work or national events. But ethnographic fieldwork is different. Cultural anthropologists may administer formal research instruments such as questionnaires, but largely their goal is to discover culture, to view the actions and knowledge of a group through the eyes of its members. In this sense, ethnographers are more like students; cultural informants are more like teachers. To implement ethnographic research, anthropologists must often become part of the worlds they seek to understand. They arrive as strangers, seek entrance into a group, meet and develop relationships of trust with informants, and wrestle with the ethical dilemmas that naturally occur when someone wants to delve into the lives of others.

These are the challenges discussed in this selection by Claire Sterk. Working inside the United States, as many anthropologists do these days, she engaged in a long-term study of prostitutes in New York City and Atlanta. Her research required her to discover the places where her informants worked and hung out, introduce herself, develop rapport, and conduct open-ended interviews that permitted informants to teach her about their lives. During this process, she learned not to depend too much on contacts (gatekeepers) she met initially, that it was helpful to know something about respondents but to avoid an "expert" role, to

Fieldwork on Prostitution in the Era of AIDS, from Tricking and Tripping by Claire E. Sterk (Putnam Valley, NY: Social Change Press, 2000), pp. 14–20. Reprinted by permission.

*refrain from expressing her own opinions about the culture and lives of her subjects, and to manage a variety of ethical questions. She ends by listing six themes that emerged from her ethnographic study.**

Prostitution is a way of life. IT IS THE LIFE.
We make money for pimps who promise us
love and more,
but if we don't produce, they shove us out the door.
We turn tricks who have sex-for-pay.
They don't care how many times we serve
every day.
The Life is rough. The Life is tough.
We are put down, beaten up, and left for dead.
It hurts body and soul and messes with
a person's head.
Many of us get high. Don't you understand it is
a way of getting by?
The Life is rough. The Life is tough.
We are easy to blame because we are lame.

—Piper, 1987[1]

Listen to the **Chapter Audio** on **myanthrolab.com**

One night in March of 1987 business was slow. I was hanging out on a stroll with a group of street prostitutes. After a few hours in a nearby diner/coffee shop, we were kicked out. The waitress felt bad, but she needed our table for some new customers. Four of us decided to sit in my car until the rain stopped. While three of us chatted about life, Piper wrote this poem. As soon as she read it to us, the conversation shifted to more serious topics—pimps, customers, cops, the many hassles of being a prostitute, to name a few. We decided that if I ever finished a book about prostitution, the book would start with her poem.

✱ This book is about the women who work in the lower echelons of the prostitution world. They worked in the streets and other public settings as well as crack houses. Some of these women viewed themselves primarily as prostitutes, and a number of them used drugs to cope with the pressures of the life. Others identified themselves more as drug users, and their main reason for having sex for money or other goods was to support their own drug use and often the habit of their male partner. A small group of women interviewed for this book had left prostitution, and

*From *Tricking and Tripping* by Claire E. Sterk (Putnam Valley, NY: Social Change Press, 2000), pp. 14–20. Reprinted by permission.

[1]The names of the women who were interviewed for this study, as well as those of their pimps and customers, have been replaced by pseudonyms to protect their privacy.

most of them were still struggling to integrate their past experiences as prostitutes in their current lives.

The stories told by the women who participated in this project revealed how pimps, customers, and others such as police officers and social and health service providers treated them as "fallen" women. However, their accounts also showed their strengths and the many strategies they developed to challenge these others. Circumstances, including their drug use, often forced them to sell sex, but they all resisted the notion that they might be selling themselves. Because they engaged in an illegal profession, these women had little status: their working conditions were poor, and their work was physically and mentally exhausting. Nevertheless, many women described the ways in which they gained a sense of control over their lives. For instance, they learned how to manipulate pimps, how to control the types of services and length of time bought by their customers, and how to select customers. While none of these schemes explicitly enhanced their working conditions, they did make the women feel stronger and better about themselves.

In this [article], I present prostitution from the point of view of the women themselves. To understand their current lives, it was necessary to learn how they got started in the life, the various processes involved in their continued prostitution careers, the link between prostitution and drug use, the women's interactions with their pimps and customers, and the impact of the AIDS epidemic and increasing violence on their experiences. I also examined the implications for women. Although my goal was to present the women's thoughts, feelings, and actions in their own words, the final text is a sociological monograph compiled by me as the researcher. . . .

The Sample

. . . The research was conducted during the last ten years in the New York City and Atlanta metropolitan areas. One main data source was participant observation on streets, in hotels and other settings known for prostitution activity, and in drug-use settings, especially those that allowed sex-for-drug exchanges. Another data source was in-depth, life-history interviews with 180 women ranging in age from 18 to 59 years, with an average age of 34. One in two women was African-American and one in three white; the remaining women were Latina. Three in four had completed high school, and among them almost two-thirds had one or more years of additional educational training. Thirty women had graduated from college.

Forty women worked as street prostitutes and did not use drugs. On average, they had been prostitutes for 11 years. Forty women began using drugs an average of three years after they began working as prostitutes, and the average time they had worked as prostitutes was nine years. Forty women used drugs an average of five years before they became prostitutes, and on the average they had worked as prostitutes for eight years. Another forty women began smoking crack and exchanging sex for crack almost simultaneously, with an average of four years in the life. Twenty women who were interviewed were ex-prostitutes.

Comments on Methodology

When I tell people about my research, the most frequent question I am asked is how I gained access to the women rather than what I learned from the research. For many, prostitution is an unusual topic of conversation, and many people have expressed surprise that I, as a woman, conducted the research. During my research some customers indeed thought I was a working woman, a fact that almost always amuses those who hear about my work. However, few people want to hear stories about the women's struggles and sadness. Sometimes they ask questions about the reasons why women become prostitutes. Most of the time, they are surprised when I tell them that the prostitutes as well as their customers represent all layers of society. Before presenting the findings, it seems important to discuss the research process, including gaining access to the women, developing relationships, interviewing, and then leaving the field.

Locating Prostitutes and Gaining Entree

One of the first challenges I faced was to identify locations where street prostitution took place. Many of these women worked on strolls, streets where prostitution activity is concentrated, or in hotels known for prostitution activity. Others, such as the crack prostitutes, worked in less public settings such as a crack house that might be someone's apartment.

I often learned of well-known public places from professional experts, such as law enforcement officials and health care providers at emergency rooms and sexually transmitted disease clinics. I gained other insights from lay experts, including taxi drivers, bartenders, and community representatives such as members of neighborhood associations. The contacts universally mentioned some strolls as the places where many women worked, where the local police focused attention, or where residents had organized protests against prostitution in their neighborhoods.

As I began visiting various locales, I continued to learn about new settings. In one sense, I was developing ethnographic maps of street prostitution. After several visits to a specific area, I also was able to expand these maps by adding information about the general atmosphere on the stroll, general characteristics of the various people present, the ways in which the women and customers connected, and the overall flow of action. In addition, my visits allowed the regular actors to notice me.

I soon learned that being an unknown woman in an area known for prostitution may cause many people to notice you, even stare at you, but it fails to yield many verbal interactions. Most of the time when I tried to make eye contact with one of the women, she quickly averted her eyes. Pimps, on the other hand, would stare at me straight on and I ended up being the one to look away. Customers would stop, blow their horn, or wave me over, frequently yelling obscenities when I ignored them. I realized that gaining entree into the prostitution world was not going to be as easy as I imagined it. Although I lacked such training in any of my qualitative methods classes, I decided to move slowly and not force any interaction. The most I said during the initial weeks in a new area was limited to "How are you" or "Hi." This strategy paid off during my first visits to one of the strolls in Brooklyn, New York. After several appearances, one of the women walked up to me and sarcastically asked if I was looking for something. She caught me off guard, and all the answers I had practiced did not seem to make sense. I mumbled something about just wanting to walk around. She did not like my answer, but she did like my accent. We ended up talking about the latter and she was especially excited when I told her I came from Amsterdam. One of her friends had gone to Europe with her boyfriend, who was in the military. She understood from her that prostitution and drugs were legal in the Netherlands. While explaining to her that some of her friend's impressions were incorrect, I was able to show off some of my knowledge about prostitution. I mentioned that I was interested in prostitution and wanted to write a book about it.

Despite the fascination with my background and intentions, the prostitute immediately put me through a Streetwalker 101 test, and apparently I passed. She told me to make sure to come back. By the time I left, I not only had my first conversation but also my first connection to the scene. Variations of this entry process occurred on the other strolls. The main lesson I learned in these early efforts was the importance of having some knowledge of the lives of the people I wanted to study, while at the same time refraining from presenting myself as an expert.

Qualitative researchers often refer to their initial connections as gatekeepers and key respondents. Throughout my fieldwork I learned that some key respondents are important in providing initial access, but they become less central as the research evolves. For example, one of the women who introduced me to her lover, who was also her pimp, was arrested and disappeared for months. Another entered drug treatment soon after she facilitated my access. Other key respondents provided access to only a segment of the players on a scene. For example, if a woman worked for a pimp, [she] was unlikely . . . to introduce me to women working for another pimp. On one stroll my initial contact was with a pimp whom nobody liked. By associating with him, I almost lost the opportunity to meet other pimps. Some key respondents were less connected than promised—for example, some of the women who worked the street to support their drug habit. Often their connections were more frequently with drug users and less so with prostitutes.

Key respondents tend to be individuals central to the local scene, such as, in this case, pimps and the more senior prostitutes. Their function as gatekeepers often is to protect the scene and to screen outsiders. Many times I had to prove that I was not an undercover police officer or a woman with ambitions to become a streetwalker. While I thought I had gained entree, I quickly learned that many insiders subsequently wondered about my motives and approached me with suspicion and distrust.

Another lesson involved the need to proceed cautiously with self-nominated key respondents. For example, one of the women presented herself as knowing everyone on the stroll. While she did know everyone, she was not a central figure. On the contrary, the other prostitutes viewed her as a failed streetwalker whose drug use caused her to act unprofessionally. By associating with me, she hoped to regain some of her status. For me, however, it meant limited access to the other women because I affiliated myself with a woman who was marginal to the scene. On another occasion, my main key respondent was a man who claimed to own three crack houses in the neighborhood. However, he had a negative reputation, and people accused him of cheating on others. My initial alliance with him delayed, and almost blocked, my access to others in the neighborhood. He intentionally tried to keep me from others on the scene, not because he would gain something from that transaction but because it made him feel powerful. When I told him I was going to hang out with some of the other people, he threatened me until one of the other dealers stepped in and told him to stay away. The two of them argued back and forth, and finally I was free to go. Fortunately, the dealer who had spoken up for me was much more central and positively associated with the local scene. Finally, I am unsure if I would have had success in gaining entrance to the scene had I not been a woman.

Developing Relationships and Trust

The processes involved in developing relationships in research situations amplify those involved in developing relationships in general. Both parties need to get to know each other, become aware and accepting of each other's roles, and engage in a reciprocal relationship. Being supportive and providing practical assistance were the most visible and direct ways for me as the researcher to develop a relationship. Throughout the years, I have given countless rides, provided child care on numerous occasions, bought groceries, and listened for hours to stories that were unrelated to my initial research questions. Gradually, my role allowed me to become part of these women's lives and to build rapport with many of them.

Over time, many women also realized that I was uninterested in being a prostitute and that I genuinely was interested in learning as much as possible about their lives. Many felt flattered that someone wanted to learn from them and that they had knowledge to offer. Allowing women to tell their stories and engaging in a dialogue with them probably were the single most important techniques that allowed me to develop relationships with them. Had I only wanted to focus on the questions I had in mind, developing such relationships might have been more difficult.

At times, I was able to get to know a woman only after her pimp endorsed our contact. One of my scariest experiences occurred before I knew to work through the pimps, and one such man had some of his friends follow me on my way home one night. I will never know what plans they had in mind for me because I fortunately was able to escape with only a few bruises. Over a year later, the woman acknowledged that her pimp had gotten upset and told her he was going to teach me a lesson.

On other occasions, I first needed to be screened by owners and managers of crack houses before the research could continue. Interestingly, screenings always were done by a man even if the person who vouched for me was a man himself. While the women also were cautious, the ways in which they checked me out tended to be much more subtle. For example, one of them would tell me a story, indicating that it was a secret about another person on the stroll. Although I failed to realize this at the time, my field notes revealed that frequently after such a conversation, others would ask me questions about related topics. One woman later acknowledged that putting out such stories was a test to see if I would keep information confidential.

Learning more about the women and gaining a better understanding of their lives also raised many ethical questions. No textbook told me how to handle situations in which a pimp abused a woman, a customer forced a woman to engage in unwanted sex acts, a customer requested unprotected sex from a woman who knew she was HIV infected, or a boyfriend had unrealistic expectations regarding a woman's earnings to support his drug habit. I failed to know the proper response when asked to engage in illegal activities such as holding drugs or money a woman had stolen from a customer. In general, my response was to explain that I was there as a researcher. During those occasions when pressures became too severe, I decided to leave a scene. For example, I never returned to certain crack houses because pimps there continued to ask me to consider working for them.

Over time, I was fortunate to develop relationships with people who "watched my back." One pimp in particular intervened if he perceived other pimps, customers, or passersby harassing me. He also was the one who gave me my street name: Whitie (indicating my racial background) or Ms. Whitie for those who disrespected me. While this was my first street name, I subsequently had others. Being given a street name was a symbolic gesture of acceptance. Gradually, I developed an identity that allowed me to be both an insider and an outsider. While hanging out on the strolls and other gathering places, including crack houses, I had to deal with some of the same uncomfortable conditions as the prostitutes, such as cold or warm weather, lack of access to a rest room, refusals from owners for me to patronize a restaurant, and of course, harassment by customers and the police.

I participated in many informal conversations. Unless pushed to do so, I seldom divulged my opinions. I was more open with my feelings about situations and showed empathy. I learned quickly that providing an opinion can backfire. I agreed that one of the women was struggling a lot and stated that I felt sorry for her. While I meant to indicate my genuine concern for her, she heard that I felt sorry for her because she was a failure. When she finally, after several weeks, talked with me again, I was able to explain to her that I was not judging her, but rather felt concerned for her. She remained cynical and many times asked me for favors to make up for my mistake. It took me months before I felt comfortable telling her that I felt I had done enough and that it was time to let go. However, if she was not ready, she needed to know that I would no longer go along. This was one of many occasions when I learned that although I wanted to facilitate my work as a researcher, that I wanted people to like and trust me, I also needed to set boundaries.

Rainy and slow nights often provided good opportunities for me to participate in conversations with groups of women. Popular topics included how to work safely, what to do about condom use, how to make more money. I often served as a health educator and a supplier of condoms, gels, vaginal douches, and other feminine products. Many women were very worried about the AIDS epidemic. However, they also were worried about how to use a condom when a customer refused to do so. They worried particularly about condom use when they needed money badly and, consequently, did not want to propose that the customer use one for fear of rejection. While some women became experts at "making" their customers use a condom—for example, by hiding it in their mouth prior to beginning oral sex—others would carry condoms to please me but never pull one out. If a woman was HIV positive and I knew she failed to use a condom, I faced the ethical dilemma of challenging her or staying out of it.

Developing trusting relationships with crack prostitutes was more difficult. Crack houses were not the right environment for informal conversations. Typically, the atmosphere was tense and everyone was suspicious of each other. The best times to talk with these women were when we bought groceries together, when I helped them clean their homes, or when we shared a meal. Often the women were very different when they were not high than they were when they were high or craving crack. In my conversations with them, I learned that while I might have observed their actions the night before, they themselves might not remember them. Once I realized this, I would be very careful to omit any detail unless I knew that the woman herself did remember the event.

In-Depth Interviews

All interviews were conducted in a private setting, including women's residences, my car or my office, a restaurant of the women's choice, or any other setting the women selected. I did not begin conducting official interviews until I developed relationships with the women. Acquiring written informed consent prior to the interview was problematic. It made me feel awkward. Here I was asking the women to sign a form after they had begun to trust me. However, often I felt more upset about this technicality than the women themselves. As soon as they realized that the form was something the university required, they seemed to understand. Often they laughed about the official statements, and some asked if I was sure the form was to protect them and not the school. None of the women refused to sign the consent form, although some refused to sign it right away and asked to be interviewed later.

In some instances the consent procedures caused the women to expect a formal interview. Some of them were disappointed when they saw I only had a few structured questions about demographic characteristics, followed by a long list of open-ended questions. When this disappointment occurred, I reminded the women that I wanted to learn from them and that the best way to do so was by engaging in a dialogue rather than interrogating them. Only by letting the women identify their salient issues and the topics they wanted to address was I able to gain an insider's perspective. By being a careful listener and probing for additional information and explanation, I as the interviewer, together with the women, was able to uncover the complexities of their lives. In addition, the nature of the interview allowed me to ask questions about contradictions in a woman's story. For example, sometimes a woman would say that she always used a condom. However, later on in the conversation she would indicate that if she needed drugs she would never use one. By asking her to elaborate on this, I was able to begin developing insights into condom use by type of partner, type of sex acts, and social context.

The interviewer becomes much more a part of the interview when the conversations are in-depth than when a structured questionnaire is used. Because I was so integral to the process, the way the women viewed me may have biased their answers. On the one hand, this bias might be reduced because of the extent to which both parties already knew each other; on the other, a woman might fail to give her true opinion and reveal her actions if she knew that these went against the interviewer's opinion. I suspected that some women played down the ways in which their pimps manipulated them once they knew that I was not too fond of these men. However, some might have taken more time to explain the relationship with their pimp in order to "correct" my image.

My background, so different from that of these women, most likely affected the nature of the interviews. I occupied a higher socioeconomic status. I had a place to live and a job. In contrast to the nonwhite women, I came from a different racial background. While I don't know to what extent these differences played a role, I acknowledge that they must have had some effect on this research.

Leaving the Field

Leaving the field was not something that occurred after completion of the fieldwork, but an event that took place daily. Although I sometimes stayed on the strolls all night or hung out for several days, I always had a home to return to. I had a house with electricity, a warm shower, a comfortable bed, and a kitchen. My house sat on a street where I had no fear of being shot on my way there and where I did not find condoms or syringes on my doorstep.

During several stages of the study, I had access to a car, which I used to give the women rides or to run errands together. However, I will never forget the cold night when everyone on the street was freezing, and I left to go home. I turned up the heat in my car, and tears streamed down my cheeks. I appreciated the heat, but I felt more guilty about that luxury than ever before. I truly felt like an outsider, or maybe even more appropriate, a betrayer.

Throughout the years of fieldwork, there were a number of times when I left the scene temporarily. For example, when so many people were dying from AIDS, I was unable to ignore the devastating impact of this disease. I needed an emotional break.

Physically removing myself from the scene was common when I experienced difficulty remaining objective. Once I became too involved in a woman's life and almost adopted her and her family. Another time I felt a true hatred for a crack house owner and was unable to adhere to the rules of courteous interactions. Still another time, I got angry with a woman whose steady partner was HIV positive when she failed to ask him to use a condom when they had sex.

I also took temporary breaks from a particular scene by shifting settings and neighborhoods. For example, I would invest most of my time in women from a particular crack house for several weeks. Then I would shift to spending more time on one of the strolls, while making shorter and less frequent visits to the crack house. By shifting scenes, I was able to tell people why I was leaving and to remind all of us of my researcher role.

While I focused on leaving the field, I became interested in women who had left the life. It seemed important to have an understanding of their past and current circumstances. I knew some of them from the days when they were working, but identifying others was a challenge. There was no gathering place for ex-prostitutes. Informal networking, advertisements in local newspapers, and local clinics and community settings allowed me to reach twenty of these women. Conducting interviews with them later in the data collection process prepared me to ask specific questions. I realized that I had learned enough about the life to know what to ask. Interviewing ex-prostitutes also prepared me for moving from the fieldwork to writing.

It is hard to determine exactly when I left the field. It seems like a process that never ends. Although I was more physically removed from the scene, I continued to be involved while analyzing the data and writing this book. I also created opportunities to go back, for example, by asking women to give me feedback on parts of the manuscript or at times when I experienced writer's block and my car seemed to automatically steer itself to one of the strolls. I also have developed other research projects in some of the same communities. For example, both a project on intergenerational drug use and a gender-specific intervention project to help women remain HIV negative have brought me back to the same population. Some of the women have become key respondents in these new projects, while others now are members of a research team. For example, Beth, one of the women who has left prostitution, works as an outreach worker on another project.

Six Themes in the Ethnography of Prostitution

The main intention of my work is to provide the reader with a perspective on street prostitution from the point of view of the women themselves. There are six fundamental aspects of the women's lives as prostitutes that must be considered. The first concerns the women's own explanations for their involvement in prostitution and their descriptions of the various circumstances that led them to become prostitutes. Their stories include justifications such as traumatic past experiences, especially sexual abuse, the lack of love they experienced as children, pressures by friends and pimps, the need for drugs, and most prominently, the economic forces that pushed them into the life. A number of women describe these justifications as excuses, as reflective explanations they have developed after becoming a prostitute.

The women describe the nature of their initial experiences, which often involved alienation from those outside the life. They also show the differences in the processes between women who work as prostitutes and use drugs and women who do not use drugs.

Although all these women work either on the street or in drug-use settings, their lives do differ. My second theme is a typology that captures these differences, looking at the women's prostitution versus drug-use identities. The typology distinguishes among (a) streetwalkers, women who work strolls and who do not use drugs; (b) hooked prostitutes, women who identify themselves mainly as prostitutes but who upon their entrance into the life also began using drugs; (c) prostituting addicts, women who view themselves mainly as drug users and who became prostitutes to support their drug habit; and (d) crack prostitutes, women who trade sex for crack.

This typology explains the differences in the women's strategies for soliciting customers, their screening of customers, pricing of sex acts, and bargaining for services. For example, the streetwalkers have the most bargaining power, while such power appears to be lacking among the crack prostitutes.

Few prostitutes work in a vacuum. The third theme is the role of pimps, a label that most women dislike and for which they prefer to substitute "old man" or "boyfriend." Among the pimps, one finds entrepreneur lovers, men who mainly employ streetwalkers and hooked prostitutes and sometimes prostituting addicts. Entrepreneur lovers engage in the life for business reasons. They treat the women as their employees or their property and view them primarily as an economic commodity. The more successful a woman is in earning them money, the more difficult it is for that woman to leave her entrepreneur pimp.

Most prostituting addicts and some hooked prostitutes work for a lover pimp, a man who is their steady partner but who also lives off their earnings. Typically, such pimps employ only one woman. The dynamics in the relationship between a prostitute and her lover pimp become more complex when both partners use drugs. Drugs often become the glue of the relationship.

For many crack prostitutes, their crack addiction serves as a pimp. Few plan to exchange sex for crack when they first begin using; often several weeks or months pass before a woman who barters sex for crack realizes that she is a prostitute.

Historically, society has blamed prostitutes for introducing sexually transmitted diseases into the general population. Similarly, it makes them scapegoats for the spread of HIV/AIDS. Yet their pimps and customers are not held accountable. The fourth theme in the anthropological study of prostitution is the impact of the AIDS epidemic on the women's lives. Although most are knowledgeable about HIV risk behaviors and the ways to reduce their risk, many misconceptions exist. The women describe the complexities of condom use, especially with steady partners but also with paying customers. Many women have mixed feelings about HIV testing, wondering how to cope with a positive test result while no cure is available. A few of the women already knew their HIV-infected status, and the discussion touches on their dilemmas as well.

The fifth theme is the violence and abuse that make common appearances in the women's lives. An ethnography of prostitution must allow the women to describe violence in their neighborhoods as well as violence in prostitution and drug-use settings. The most common violence they encounter is from customers.

These men often assume that because they pay for sex they buy a woman. Apparently, casual customers pose more of a danger than those who are regulars. The types of abuse the women encounter are emotional, physical, and sexual. In addition to customers, pimps and boyfriends abuse the women. Finally, the women discuss harassment by law enforcement officers.

When I talked with the women, it often seemed that there were no opportunities to escape from the life. Yet the sixth and final theme must be the escape from prostitution. Women who have left prostitution can describe the process of their exit from prostitution. As ex-prostitutes they struggle with the stigma of their past, the challenges of developing a new identity, and the impact of their past on current intimate relationships. Those who were also drug users often view themselves as ex-prostitutes and recovering addicts, a perspective that seems to create a role conflict. Overall, most ex-prostitutes find that their past follows them like a bad hangover.

Study and **Review** on **myanthrolab.com**

Review Questions

1. Based on reading this selection, how is ethnographic research different from other social science approaches to research?
2. What can ethnographic research reveal that other forms of research cannot? What can the use of questionnaires and observational experiments reveal about people that ethnographic research might miss?
3. What were some of the techniques used by Sterk to enter the field, conduct her research, and leave the field? What problems did she face?
4. What advice does Sterk have for aspiring ethnographers?
5. What are some of the ethical issues faced by anthropologists when they conduct ethnographic research?

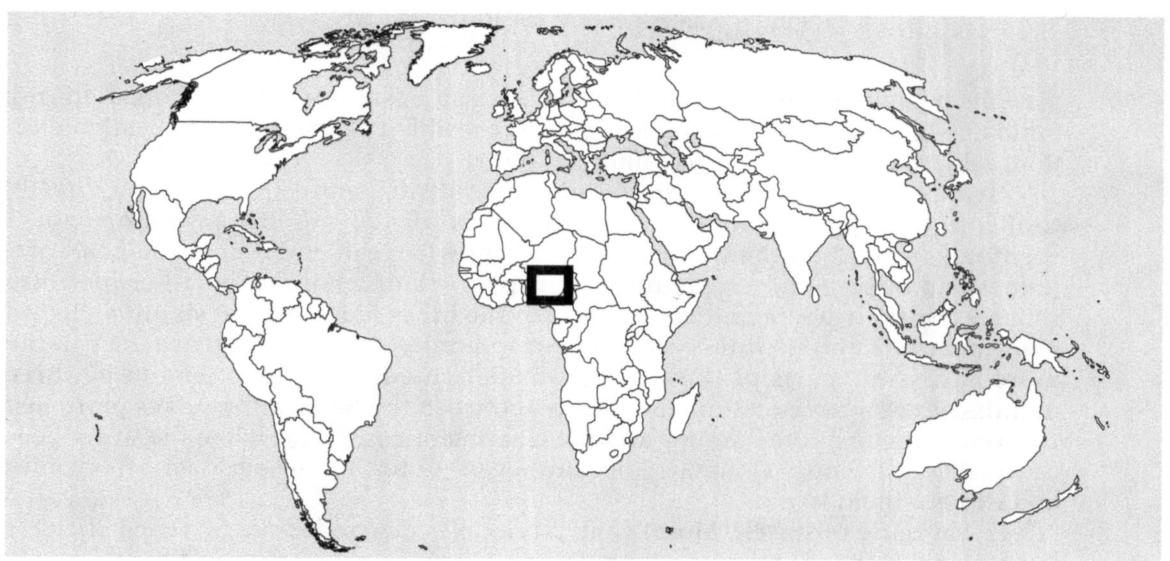

Shakespeare in the Bush

Laura Bohannan

*All of us use the cultural knowledge we acquire as members of our own society to organize our perception and behavior. Most of us are also naive realists: we tend to believe our culture mirrors a reality shared by everyone. But cultures are different, and other people rarely behave or interpret experience according to our cultural plan. In this article, Laura Bohannan describes her attempt to tell the classic story of Hamlet to Tiv elders in West Africa. At each turn in the story, the Tiv interpret the events and motives in Hamlet using their own cultural knowledge. The result is a very different version of the classic play and an excellent example of cross-cultural miscommunication.**

Just before I left Oxford for the Tiv in West Africa, conversation turned to the season at Stratford. "You Americans," said a friend, "often have difficulty with Shakespeare. He was, after all, a very English poet, and one can easily misinterpret the universal by misunderstanding the particular."

I protested that human nature is pretty much the same the whole world over; at least the general plot and motivation of the greater tragedies would always be clear—everywhere—although some details of custom might have to be explained and difficulties of translation might produce other slight changes. To end an argument we could not conclude, my friend

*From Laura Bohannan, "Shakespeare in the Bush." Used by permission.

Shakespeare in the Bush, from Laura Bohannan, "Shakespeare in the Bush." Used by permission.

From Chapter 5 of *Conformity and Conflict: Readings in Cultural Anthropology.* Fourteenth Edition. James Spradley, David W. McCurdy.

gave me a copy of *Hamlet* to study in the African bush: it would, he hoped, lift my mind above its primitive surroundings, and possibly I might, by prolonged meditation, achieve the grace of correct interpretation.

It was my second field trip to that African tribe, and I thought myself ready to live in one of its remote sections—an area difficult to cross even on foot. I eventually settled on the hillock of a very knowledgeable old man, the head of a homestead of some hundred and forty people, all of whom were either his close relatives or their wives and children. Like the other elders of the vicinity, the old man spent most of his time performing ceremonies seldom seen these days in the more accessible parts of the tribe. I was delighted. Soon there would be three months of enforced isolation and leisure, between the harvest that takes place just before the rising of the swamps and the clearing of new farms when the water goes down. Then, I thought, they would have even more time to perform ceremonies and explain them to me.

I was quite mistaken. Most of the ceremonies demanded the presence of elders from several homesteads. As the swamps rose, the old men found it too difficult to walk from one homestead to the next, and the ceremonies gradually ceased. As the swamps rose even higher, all activities but one came to an end. The women brewed beer from maize and millet. Men, women, and children sat on their hillocks and drank it.

People began to drink at dawn. By midmorning the whole homestead was singing, dancing, and drumming. When it rained, people had to sit inside their huts: there they drank and sang or they drank and told stories. In any case, by noon or before, I either had to join the party or retire to my own hut and my books. "One does not discuss serious matters when there is beer. Come, drink with us." Since I lacked their capacity for the thick native beer, I spent more and more time with *Hamlet*. Before the end of the second month, grace descended on me. I was quite sure that *Hamlet* had only one possible interpretation, and that one universally obvious.

Early every morning, in the hope of having some serious talk before the beer party, I used to call on the old man at his reception hut—a circle of posts supporting a thatched roof above a low mud wall to keep out wind and rain. One day I crawled through the low doorway and found most of the men of the homestead sitting huddled in their ragged cloths on stools, low plank beds, and reclining chairs, warming themselves against the chill of the rain around a smoky fire. In the center were three pots of beer. The party had started.

The old man greeted me cordially. "Sit down and drink." I accepted a large calabash full of beer, poured some into a small drinking gourd, and tossed it down. Then I poured some more into the same gourd for the man second in seniority to my host before I handed my calabash over to a young man for further distribution. Important people shouldn't ladle beer themselves.

"It is better like this," the old man said, looking at me approvingly and plucking at the thatch that had caught in my hair. "You should sit and drink with us more often. Your servants tell me that when you are not with us, you sit inside your hut looking at a paper."

The old man was acquainted with four kinds of "papers": tax receipts, bride price receipts, court fee receipts, and letters. The messenger who brought him letters from the chief used them mainly as a badge of office, for he always knew what was in them and told the old man. Personal letters for the few who had relatives in the government or mission stations were kept until someone went to a large market where there was a letter writer and reader. Since my arrival, letters were brought to me to be read. A few men also brought me bride price receipts, privately, with requests to change the figures to a higher sum. I found moral arguments were of no avail, since in-laws are fair game, and the technical hazards of forgery difficult to explain to an illiterate people. I did not wish them to think me silly enough to look at any such papers for days on end, and I hastily explained that my "paper" was one of the "things of long ago" of my country.

"Ah," said the old men. "Tell us."

I protested that I was not a storyteller. Storytelling is a skilled art among them; their standards are high, and the audiences critical—and vocal in their criticism. I protested in vain. This morning they wanted to hear a story while they drank. They threatened to tell me no more stories until I told them one of mine. Finally, the old man promised that no one would criticize my style "for we know you are struggling with our language." "But," put in one of the elders, "you must explain what we do not understand, as we do when we tell you our stories." Realizing that here was my chance to prove *Hamlet* universally intelligible, I agreed.

The old man handed me some more beer to help me on with my storytelling. Men filled their long wooden pipes and knocked coals from the fire to place in the pipe bowls; then, puffing contentedly, they sat back to listen. I began in the proper style, "Not yesterday, not yesterday, but long ago, a thing occurred. One night three men were keeping watch outside the homestead of the great chief, when suddenly they saw the former chief approach them."

"Why was he no longer their chief?"

"He was dead," I explained. "That is why they were troubled and afraid when they saw him."

"Impossible," began one of the elders, handing his pipe on to his neighbor, who interrupted, "Of course it wasn't the dead chief. It was an omen sent by a witch. Go on."

Slightly shaken, I continued. "One of these three was a man who knew things"—the closest translation for scholar, but unfortunately it also meant witch. The second elder looked triumphantly at the first. "So he spoke to the dead chief, saying, 'Tell us what we must do so you may rest in your grave,' but the dead chief did not answer. He vanished, and they could see him no more. Then the man who knew things—his name was Horatio—said this event was the affair of the dead chief's son, Hamlet."

There was a general shaking of heads around the circle. "Had the dead chief no living brothers? Or was this son the chief?" "No," I replied. "That is, he had one living brother who became the chief when the elder brother died."

The old men muttered: such omens were matters for chiefs and elders, not for youngsters; no good could come of being behind a chief's back; clearly Horatio was not a man who knew things.

"Yes, he was," I insisted, shooing a chicken away from my beer. "In our country the son is next to the father. The dead chief's younger brother had become the great chief. He had also married his elder brother's widow only about a month after the funeral."

"He did well," the old man beamed and announced to the others, "I told you that if we knew more about Europeans, we would find they really were very like us. In our country also," he added to me, "the younger brother marries the elder brother's widow and becomes the father of his children. Now, if your uncle, who married your widowed mother, is your father's full brother, then he will be a real father to you. Did Hamlet's father and uncle have one mother?"

His question barely penetrated my mind; I was too upset and thrown too far off balance by having one of the most important elements of *Hamlet* knocked straight out of the picture. Rather uncertainly I said that I thought they had the same mother, but I wasn't sure—the story didn't say. The old man told me severely that these genealogical details made all the difference and that when I got home I must ask the elders about it. He shouted out the door to one of his younger wives to bring his goatskin bag.

Determined to save what I could of the mother motif, I took a deep breath and began again. "The son Hamlet was very sad because his mother had married again so quickly. There was no need for her to do so, and it is our custom for a widow not to go to her next husband until she has mourned for two years."

"Two years is too long," objected the wife, who had appeared with the old man's battered goatskin bag. "Who will hoe your farms for you while you have no husband?"

"Hamlet," I retorted without thinking, "was old enough to hoe his mother's farms himself. There was no need for her to remarry." No one looked convinced. I gave up. "His mother and the great chief told Hamlet not to be sad, for the great chief himself would be a father to Hamlet. Furthermore, Hamlet would be the next chief: therefore he must stay to learn the things of a chief. Hamlet agreed to remain, and all the rest went off to drink beer."

While I paused, perplexed at how to render Hamlet's disgusted soliloquy to an audience convinced that Claudius and Gertrude had behaved in the best possible manner, one of the younger men asked me who had married the other wives of the dead chief.

"He had no other wives," I told him.

"But a chief must have many wives! How else can he brew beer and prepare food for all his guests?"

I said firmly that in our country even chiefs had only one wife, that they had servants to do their work, and that they paid them from tax money.

It was better, they returned, for a chief to have many wives and sons who would help him hoe his farms and feed his people; then everyone loved the chief who gave much and took nothing—taxes were a bad thing.

I agreed with the last comment, but for the rest fell back on their favorite way of fobbing off my questions: "That is the way it is done, so that is how we do it."

I decided to skip the soliloquy. Even if Claudius was here thought quite right to marry his brother's widow, there remained the poison motif, and I knew they would disapprove of fratricide. More hopefully I resumed, "That night Hamlet kept watch with the three who had seen his dead father. The dead chief again appeared, and although the others were afraid, Hamlet followed his dead father off to one side. When they were alone, Hamlet's dead father spoke."

"Omens can't talk!" The old man was emphatic.

"Hamlet's dead father wasn't an omen. Seeing him might have been an omen, but he was not." My audience looked as confused as I sounded. "It *was* Hamlet's dead father. It was a thing we call a 'ghost.' " I had to use the English word, for unlike many of the neighboring tribes, these people didn't believe in the survival after death of any individuating part of the personality.

"What is a 'ghost'? An omen?"

"No, a 'ghost' is someone who is dead but who walks around and can talk, and people can hear him and see him but not touch him."

They objected. "One can touch zombis."

"No, no! It was not a dead body the witches had animated to sacrifice and eat. No one else made Hamlet's dead father walk. He did it himself."

"Dead men can't walk," protested my audience as one man.

I was quite willing to compromise. "A 'ghost' is a dead man's shadow."

But again they objected. "Dead men cast no shadows."

"They do in my country," I snapped.

The old man quelled the babble of disbelief that rose immediately and told me with that insincere, but courteous, agreement one extends to the fancies of the young, ignorant, and superstitious, "No doubt in your country the dead can also walk without being zombis." From the depths of his bag he produced a withered fragment of kola nut, bit off one end to show it wasn't poisoned, and handed me the rest as a peace offering.

"Anyhow," I resumed, "Hamlet's dead father said that his own brother, the one who became chief, had poisoned him. He wanted Hamlet to avenge him. Hamlet believed this in his heart, for he did not like his father's brother." I took another swallow of beer. "In the country of the great chief, living in the same homestead, for it was a very large one, was an important elder who was often with the chief to advise and help him. His name was Polonius. Hamlet was courting his daughter, but her father and her brother . . . [I cast hastily about for some tribal analogy] warned her not to let Hamlet visit her when she was alone on her farm, for he would be a great chief and so could not marry her."

"Why not?" asked the wife, who had settled down on the edge of the old man's chair. He frowned at her for asking stupid questions and growled, "They lived in the same homestead."

"That was not the reason," I informed them. "Polonius was a stranger who lived in the homestead because he helped the chief, not because he was a relative."

"Then why couldn't Hamlet marry her?"

"He could have," I explained, "but Polonius didn't think he would. After all, Hamlet was a man of great importance who ought to marry a chief's daughter, for in his country a man could have only one wife. Polonius was afraid that if Hamlet made love to his daughter, then no one else would give a high price for her."

"That might be true," remarked one of the shrewder elders, "but a chief's son would give his mistress's father enough presents and patronage to more than make up the difference. Polonius sounds like a fool to me."

"Many people think he was," I agreed. "Meanwhile Polonius sent his son Laertes off to Paris to learn the things of that country, for it was the homestead of a very great chief indeed. Because he was afraid that Laertes might waste a lot of money on beer and women and gambling, or get into trouble by fighting, he sent one of his servants to Paris secretly, to spy out what Laertes was doing. One day Hamlet came upon Polonius's daughter Ophelia. He behaved so oddly he frightened her. Indeed"—I was fumbling for words to express the dubious quality of Hamlet's madness— "the chief and many others had also noticed that when Hamlet talked one could understand the words but not what they meant. Many people thought that he had become mad." My audience suddenly became much more attentive. "The great chief wanted to know what was wrong with Hamlet, so he sent for two of Hamlet's age mates [school friends would have taken long explanation] to talk to Hamlet and find out what troubled his heart. Hamlet, seeing that they had been bribed by the chief to betray him, told them nothing. Polonius, however, insisted that Hamlet was mad because he had been forbidden to see Ophelia, whom he loved."

"Why," inquired a bewildered voice, "should anyone bewitch Hamlet on that account?"

"Bewitch him?"

"Yes, only witchcraft can make anyone mad, unless, of course, one sees the beings that lurk in the forest."

I stopped being a storyteller, took out my notebook and demanded to be told more about these two causes of madness. Even while they spoke and I jotted notes, I tried to calculate the effect of this new factor on the plot. Hamlet had not been exposed to the beings that lurk in the forest. Only his relatives in the male line could bewitch him. Barring relatives not mentioned by Shakespeare, it had to be Claudius who was attempting to harm him. And, of course, it was.

For the moment I staved off questions by saying that the great chief also refused to believe that Hamlet was mad for the love of Ophelia and nothing else. "He was sure that something much more important was troubling Hamlet's heart."

"Now Hamlet's age mates," I continued, "had brought with them a famous storyteller. Hamlet decided to have this man tell the chief and all his homestead a story about the man who had poisoned his brother because he desired his brother's wife and wished to be chief himself. Hamlet was sure the great chief could not hear the story without making a sign if he was indeed guilty, and then he would discover whether his dead father had told him the truth."

The old man interrupted, with deep cunning. "Why should a father lie to his son?" he asked.

I hedged: "Hamlet wasn't sure that it really was his dead father." It was impossible to say anything, in that language, about devil-inspired visions.

"You mean," he said, "it actually was an omen, and he knew witches sometimes send false ones. Hamlet was a fool not to go to one skilled in reading omens and divining the truth in the first place. A man-who-sees-the-truth could have told him how his father died, if he really had been poisoned, and if there was witchcraft in it; then Hamlet could have called the elders to settle the matter."

The shrewd elder ventured to disagree. "Because his father's brother was a great chief, one-who-sees-the-truth might therefore have been afraid to tell it. I think it was for that reason that a friend of Hamlet's father—a witch and an elder—sent an omen so his friend's son would know. Was the omen true?"

"Yes," I said, abandoning ghosts and the devil; a witch-sent omen it would have to be. "It was true, for when the storyteller was telling his tale before all the homestead, the great chief rose in fear. Afraid that Hamlet knew his secret, he planned to have him killed."

The stage set of the next bit presented some difficulties of translation. I began cautiously. "The great chief told Hamlet's mother to find out from her son what he knew. But because a woman's children are always first in her heart, he had the important elder Polonius hide behind a cloth that hung against the wall of Hamlet's mother's sleeping hut. Hamlet started to scold his mother for what she had done."

There was a shocked murmur from everyone. A man should never scold his mother.

"She called out in fear, and Polonius moved behind the cloth. Shouting 'A rat!' Hamlet took his machete and slashed through the cloth." I paused for a dramatic effect. "He had killed Polonius!"

The old men looked at each other in supreme disgust. "That Polonius truly was a fool and a man who knew nothing! What child would not know enough to shout, 'It's me!'" With a pang, I remembered that these people are ardent hunters, always armed with bow, arrow, and machete; at the first rustle in the grass an arrow is aimed and ready, and the hunter shouts "Game!" If no human voice answers immediately, the arrow speeds on its way. Like a good hunter Hamlet had shouted, "A rat!"

I rushed in to save Polonius's reputation. "Polonius did speak. Hamlet heard him. But he thought it was the chief and wished to kill him to avenge his father. He had meant to kill him earlier that evening. . . ." I broke down, unable to describe to these pagans, who had no belief in individual afterlife, the difference between dying at one's prayers and dying "unhousell'd, disappointed, unaneled."

This time I had shocked my audience seriously. "For a man to raise his hands against his father's brother and the one who has become his father—that is a terrible thing. The elders ought to let such a man be bewitched."

I nibbled at my kola nut in some perplexity, then pointed out that after all the man had killed Hamlet's father.

"No," pronounced the old man, speaking less to me than to the young men sitting behind the elders. "If your father's brother has killed your father, you must appeal to your father's age mates; *they* may avenge him. No man may use violence against his senior relatives." Another thought struck him. "But if his father's brother had indeed been wicked enough to bewitch Hamlet and make him mad, that would be a good story indeed, for it would be his fault that Hamlet, being mad, no longer had any sense and thus was ready to kill his father's brother."

There was a murmur of applause. *Hamlet* was again a good story to them, but it no longer seemed quite the same story to me. As I thought over the coming complications of plot and motive, I lost courage and decided to skim over dangerous ground quickly.

"The great chief," I went on, "was not sorry that Hamlet had killed Polonius. It gave him a reason to send Hamlet away, with his two treacherous age mates, with letters to a chief of a far country, saying that Hamlet should be killed. But Hamlet changed the writing on their papers, so that the chief killed his age mates instead." I encountered a reproachful glare from one of the men whom I had told undetectable forgery was not merely immoral but beyond human skill. I looked the other way.

"Before Hamlet could return, Laertes came back for his father's funeral. The great chief told him Hamlet had killed Polonius. Laertes swore to kill Hamlet because of this; and because his sister Ophelia, hearing her father had been killed by the man she loved, went mad and drowned in the river."

"Have you already forgotten what we told you?" The old man was reproachful. "One cannot take vengeance on a madman; Hamlet killed Polonius in his madness. As for the girl, she not only went mad, she was drowned. Only witches can make people drown. Water itself can't hurt anything. It is merely something one drinks and bathes in."

I began to get cross. "If you don't like the story, I'll stop."

The old man made soothing noises and himself poured me some more beer. "You tell the story well, and we are listening. But it is clear that the elders of your country have never told you what the story really means. No, don't interrupt! We believe you when you say your marriage customs are different, or your clothes and weapons. But people are the same everywhere; therefore, there are always witches and it is we, the elders, who know how witches work. We told you it was the great chief who wished to kill Hamlet, and now your own words have proved us right. Who were Ophelia's male relatives?"

"There were only her father and her brother." Hamlet was clearly out of my hands.

"There must have been many more; this also you must ask of your elders when you get back to your country. From what you tell us, since Polonius was dead, it must have been Laertes who killed Ophelia, although I do not see the reason for it."

We had emptied one pot of beer, and the old men argued the point with slightly tipsy interest. Finally one of them demanded of me, "What did the servant of Polonius say on his return?"

With difficulty I recollected Reynaldo and his mission. "I don't think he did return before Polonius was killed."

"Listen," said the elder, "and I will tell you how it was and how your story will go, then you may tell me if I am right. Polonius knew his son would get into trouble, and so he did. He had many fines to pay for fighting, and debts from gambling. But he had only two ways of getting money quickly. One was to marry off his sister at once, but it is difficult to find a man who will marry a woman desired by the son of a chief. For if the chief's heir commits adultery with your wife, what can you do? Only a fool calls a case against a man who will someday be his judge. Therefore Laertes had to take the second way: he killed his sister by witchcraft, drowning her so he could secretly sell her body to the witches."

I raised an objection. "They found her body and buried it. Indeed Laertes jumped into the grave to see his sister once more—so, you see, the body was truly there. Hamlet, who had just come back, jumped in after him."

"What did I tell you?" The elder appealed to the others. "Laertes was up to no good with his sister's body. Hamlet prevented him, because the chief's heir, like a chief, does not wish any other man to grow rich and powerful. Laertes would be angry, because he would have killed his sister without benefit to himself. In our country he would try to kill Hamlet for that reason. Is this not what happened?"

"More or less," I admitted. "When the great chief found Hamlet was still alive, he encouraged Laertes to try to kill Hamlet and arranged a fight with machetes between them. In the fight both the young men were wounded to death. Hamlet's mother drank the poisoned beer that the chief meant for Hamlet in case he won the fight. When he saw his mother die of poison, Hamlet, dying, managed to kill his father's brother with his machete."

"You see, I was right!" exclaimed the elder.

"That was a very good story," added the old man, "and you told it with very few mistakes. There was just one more error, at the very end. The poison Hamlet's mother drank was obviously meant for the survivor of the fight, whichever it was. If Laertes had won, the great chief would have poisoned him, for no one would know that he arranged Hamlet's death. Then, too, he need not fear Laertes's witchcraft; it takes a strong heart to kill one's only sister by witchcraft.

"Sometime," concluded the old man, gathering his ragged toga about him, "you must tell us some more stories of your country. We, who are elders, will instruct you in their true meaning, so that when you return to your own land your elders will see that you have not been sitting in the bush, but among those who know things and who have taught you wisdom."

Study and **Review** on **myanthrolab.com**

Review Questions

1. In what ways does Bohannan's attempt to tell the story of Hamlet to the Tiv illustrate the concept of naive realism?
2. Using Bohannan's experience of telling the story of *Hamlet* to the Tiv and the response of the Tiv elders to her words, illustrate cross-cultural misunderstanding.
3. What are the most important parts of *Hamlet* that the Tiv found it necessary to reinterpret?

Colonialism and Cultural Transformations

Colonialism and Cultural Transformations

PREVIEW

- What is colonialism, and what types of colonies were established?
- What are the patterns of relationships between colonists and their countries of origin and between colonists and indigenous peoples?
- How did the European slave trade differ from traditional forms of African slavery?
- How did the European slave trade change African societies and cultures?
- How does the history of the North American fur trade illustrate culture change?
- How did the buffalo trade and the horse change the Lakota way of life?
- How were patterns of colonization and change different in North and South America?
- How did plantations, missions, mines, and epidemics change indigenous South American societies?
- Who were the agents of change, and what were their goals?
- How did native peoples react to colonialism?
- How did native peoples lose their lands, and how did Europeans justify their land seizures?
- How did colonialism and the post-colonial era help set the stage for present-day globalization?

"Sunday school, Indians and white[s]." Indian Territory [Oklahoma], ca. 1900. *The National Archives*

Colonialism and Cultural Transformations

The commerce which may be carried on with the people inhabiting the line you will pursue, renders a knowledge of those people important. You will therefore endeavour to make yourself acquainted, as far as a diligent pursuit of your journey shall admit, with the names of the nations and their numbers;

Listen to the Chapter Audio on myanthrolab.com

Read on myanthrolab.com

The extent and limits of their possessions;
Their relations with other tribes or nations;
Their language, traditions, monuments;
Their ordinary occupations in agriculture, fishing, hunting, war, arts, and the implements for these;
Their food, clothing, and domestic accommodations;
The diseases prevalent among them, and the remedies they use;
Moral and physical circumstances which distinguish them from the tribes we know;
Peculiarities in their laws, customs, and dispositions;
And articles of commerce they may need or furnish, and to what extent.

And, considering the interest which every nation has in extending and strengthening the authority of reason and justice among the people around them, it will be useful to acquire what knowledge you can of the state of morality, religion, and information among them; as it may better enable those who may endeavour to civilize and instruct them, to adapt their measures to the existing notions and practices of those on whom they are to operate....

In all your intercourse with the natives, treat them in the most friendly and conciliatory manner which their own conduct will admit; allay all jealousies as to the object of your journey; satisfy them of its innocence; make them acquainted with the position, extent, character, peaceable and commercial dispositions of the United States; of our wish to be neighbourly, friendly, and useful to them, and of our dispositions to a commercial intercourse with them; confer with them on the points most convenient as mutual emporiums, and the articles of most desirable interchange for them and us. If a few of their influential chiefs, within practicable distance, wish to visit us, arrange such a visit with them, and furnish them with authority to call on our officers on their entering the United States, to have them conveyed to this place at the public expense. If any of them should wish to have some of their young people brought up with us, and taught such arts as may be useful to them, we will receive, instruct, and take care of them. Such a mission, whether of influential chiefs, or of young people, would give some security to your own party.

From Thomas Jefferson letter to Meriwether Lewis, 1803, http://www.mt.net/~rojomo/landc.htm.

Thomas Jefferson's 1803 letter to Meriwether Lewis at the start of what came to be called the Lewis and Clark expedition reveals the thinking behind a common pattern of state expansion. The newly independent United States was expanding the territory it perceived itself as owning in North America. That thinking also helped Europeans and Americans rationalize colonialism and aggression against native populations on a global scale.

State societies are driven to expand their borders or spheres of influence, thus requiring a continuous influx of wealth, either as goods or laborers to produce more goods. The steady and growing supply of wealth enriches the elites and allows them to increase their control within their own territories and to exert influence outside. Conquest and colonialism are the results.

The early state societies in the Middle East, North Africa, China, Peru, and Mexico gained their wealth by conquering neighboring territories and incorporating the defeated peoples into their empires. Of these, the most long-lasting societies have been the Chinese state and Arabs in the Middle East and North Africa. The extent to which conquerors forced defeated groups to alter their indigenous cultures varied in different parts of the world and at different times. This chapter focuses on processes of state expansion that originated in Europe in the fifteenth and sixteenth centuries.

colonies
Settlements of foreign nationals with controlling interests in indigenous territories.

imperialism
Empire building through state expansion in both commerce and territory.

EUROPEAN COLONIALISM

European states did what earlier states elsewhere in the world had done before them, but the Europeans were in many ways the most successful. Other states, such as China and the Incas in Peru and Ecuador, enlarged their borders through expansion into adjacent lands, continuously increasing conquered territory as their borders were extended bit by bit. People who lived at great distances from the center of the state saw the space between them and the state shrink until they were the next group to be engulfed. European expansion eventually reached worldwide not only by expanding the borders of their countries but also by increasing their control over societies hundreds or thousands of miles from their shores. Similarly, Arab influence has extensive reach in large regions of the world, especially through the spread of Islam.

Technological advances unique to Europe enabled colonial expansion and control. The ability to travel long distances was made possible by improvements in sailing vessels, navigation, and mapmaking, enabling European explorers, traders, soldiers, and missionaries to venture to all parts of the world. Technological improvements in armaments also allowed Europeans to threaten or conquer people who resisted them.

Although colonialism as a consequence of economic and political expansion was a characteristic of developing state societies in many parts of the world, this chapter focuses specifically on European colonialism because Europeans were able to establish, at one time or another, the most far-flung and extensive system of colonies throughout the world. In addition, the legacies of European colonialism(s) have affected and are affecting many countries in the contemporary world. However, we should be mindful of the fact that colonial and neocolonial policies emanate from other parts of the world today, as in the past.

Colonialism Defined

European powers, specifically Great Britain, France, Spain, Portugal, and Holland, endeavored to solidify their control and influence in far-flung regions through the establishment of **colonies**—settlements of foreign nationals with controlling interests in indigenous territories. Colonies were intimately tied to the host country, but colonists remained politically and economically subordinate to their home countries. Residents of the colonies did not have equal legal or social standing with the residents of the home country. Their purpose was to produce wealth that could be extracted from the territories they occupied to enrich the home country as the colonial power. A complex system of trade tied the colonies to the home country. The home country's policies governed the ways that colonial subjects had to behave.

As Jurgen Osterhammel defines it: "A colony is a new political organization created by invasion (conquest and/or settlement colonization) but built on pre-colonial conditions. Its alien rulers are in sustained dependence on a geographically remote (mother country) or imperial center, which claims exclusive rights (possession) of the colony" (1997, 10). Osterhammel defines **colonialism**, then, as the following:

> [a] relationship of domination between an indigenous (or forcibly imported) majority and a minority of foreign invaders. The fundamental decisions affecting the lives of a colonized people are made and implemented by the colonial rulers in pursuit of interests that are often defined in a distant metropolis. Rejecting cultural compromises with the colonized population, colonizers are convinced of their own superiority and of their ordained mandate to rule. (1997, 16–17)

This wall painting of the Chinese attacking the Tibetans during the T'ang Dynasty (A.D. 618–907) shows that empire building is not a recent European phenomenon. China's territory and influence on other Asian peoples reflect thousands of years of state expansion and colonization. Bridgeman Art Library/Mogao Caves, Dunhuang, Gansu Province, NW China/The Bridgeman Art Library

Colonialism is often linked with **imperialism**, or empire building—an extension of nation building using other people's lands and resources. Osterhammel defines imperialism as the following:

> a concept that comprises all forces and activities contributing to the construction and the maintenance of trans-colonial empires. Imperialism presupposes the will and the ability of an imperial center

> to define as imperial its own national interests and enforce them worldwide in the anarchy of the international system. Imperialism thus implies not only colonial politics, but international politics for which colonies are not just ends in themselves, but also pawns in global power games. (1997, 21)

There were both similarities and differences in the tactics and policies of the various European states as they imposed their will and controlled the peoples of distant lands.

A World System

European expansionism did not just extend political and economic control but created a new order that came to dominate and entangle most regions of the world in global networks of resource extraction, new forms of labor in the production of goods, and ever widening cycles of wealth. To use the phrase introduced by Immanuel Wallerstein (1974), a "modern world system" was generated, with roots in European economies of the late feudal period that were radically transformed beginning in the late fifteenth and early sixteenth centuries into capitalist forms of production and consumption. Colonialism was both a response to the new economic order and a means of furthering its development by finding abundant resources far from home and creating markets for the goods produced.

In world systems theory, a basic distinction is drawn between countries and regions described as constituting the "core" and the "periphery." Core countries are those that control production and the flow of goods by exploiting the raw materials of peripheral regions and turning those resources into manufactured goods that are then sold domestically or internationally, often back to the same people whose raw materials were first expropriated. Core countries also determine the costs of production (labor, equipment) and rates of exchange in ways that benefit them by increasing their profits. The distinction between core and periphery is a distinction in the structural arrangement of the world system and although the structure remains constant, the regions of the world that can be characterized as core or periphery may vary through history and the relations between countries may vary as well.

The terminology now often used to differentiate the economic standing of regions or countries—"developed" or "underdeveloped" (or "developing")—essentially refers to the same constructs as "core" and "periphery." The relationships between developed and underdeveloped regions are basically ones of unequal participation in the world economy such that increasing profits flow to the developed world from the resources and labor of underdeveloped countries. Indeed, this process has been called the "development of underdevelopment" to emphasize the fact that underdeveloped regions did not just happen, but were created (Franck 1964). Finally, this distinction can be seen as the modern reflection of colonial processes that began centuries ago as the colonies (or periphery) were subject to the control of the core countries.

Types of Colonies

There are three main types of colonies, depending on the purpose of contact or conquest: exploitation colonies, maritime enclaves, and settlement colonies. **Exploitation colonies** usually result from military conquests in which the colonial power seeks to exploit the economic resources of the region. The power usually sends a relatively small number of its citizens to invade as soldiers. Then it continues to control the colony through government functionaries and traders. In exploitation colonies, the home country exerts complete dominance over the political functioning of the colony and over its soldiers, bureaucrats, and traders.

Maritime enclaves develop from sea trade and coastal exploration. Their purpose is to control trade at the ports of foreign lands and to have an indirect control over internal trade in foreign territories. The colonized country remains formally independent, but the colonizing power has some degree of influence over the political and commercial policies of the supposedly independent state through its maritime enclaves.

Settlement colonies result from military invasions that support permanent settlement by the invader's citizens. By encouraging settlement, the home country aims to acquire abundant cheap land and labor. In establishing a permanent presence, foreign settlers appropriate land from indigenous inhabitants.

exploitation colonies
Colonies established by military conquest for the purpose of exploiting the economic and natural resources of a region.

maritime enclaves
Colonies established as a result of sea trade and coastal exploration for the purpose of controlling trade at foreign ports.

settlement colonies
Permanent colonies established through exploration or conquest for the purpose of occupying land and controlling labor.

In the 1990s, 250,000 Tatars who had been deported in 1944 by the former USSR returned to their Crimean homeland and gathered here to honor those who died. Corbis/GLEB GARANICH/Reuters/Corbis

In settlement colonies, colonists have some degree of self-rule, although the home country wields ultimate control. The rights of the indigenous population may be disregarded, and their land taken. Where they resist, they may be killed and, sometimes, whole groups may be exterminated. Different strategies develop for controlling the labor supply and acquiring land in the colony. In colonial New England and the later United States, after an initial period of coexistence, indigenous peoples were seen as economically unnecessary and were displaced or killed if they refused to move. And because of both the continual influx of settlers from Europe and indigenous deaths from war and disease, the European colonists and their descendants came to outnumber the native population.

In contrast, colonial settlers in Africa remained economically dependent on the indigenous population. Because their labor was needed on plantations and in mines, colonists could not afford to entirely displace or annihilate them. And Europeans were always a minority in African colonies. In the Caribbean and parts of North and South America, slaves were imported from Africa as the indigenous populations began to die off in the seventeenth and eighteenth centuries. Slaves performed the vital economic functions of producing crops and manufactures in colonial cities and plantations.

In Africa and elsewhere, Europeans sought to instill their values both directly and indirectly through **missionism**—settlement for the purpose of religious conversion—and education, as well as through social, economic, and political control. For example, a 1919 French reader proclaimed: "It is an advantage for a native to work for a white man, because the whites are better educated, more advanced in civilization than the natives, and because, thanks to them, the natives will make more rapid progress . . . and become one day really useful men. . . . You who are intelligent and industrious, my children, always help the Whites in their tasks. This is a duty" (Buell 1928, 63). In East African colonies under Italian control, African children read textbooks that contained such sayings as "I am happy to be subject to the Italian government and I love Italy with the affection of a son" or "Help me, oh God, to become a good Italian!" (DeMarco 1943, 36, 40).

Christian missionaries competed with one another for influence and converts to their particular sect. Missionaries of Islam and Buddhism vied for converts as well. Islam and its cultural influences have spread, especially to North and Central Africa and Asia, from its Middle Eastern origins. More recently, it has spread to Europe and North America. Buddhist missionaries have been primarily successful in Asia. These religions have also aided processes of state consolidation and cultural transformation.

missionism
Settlement for the purpose of religious conversion.

resettlement policies
Efforts of colonial authorities to relocate indigenous people to permanent settlements, usually on less desirable land, to control and influence them.

Colonial governments often attempted to settle nomadic people in more permanent communities—a common policy in North America in the nineteenth century. Even today, in Africa and the Middle East, where nomadic pastoralists use vast tracts of land for grazing their animals, the governments of Iran, Morocco, the Sudan, and Kenya, for example, institute policies restricting people's access to territory, thus compelling them to abandon their traditional economies and settle in towns and villages. **Resettlement policies** continue today in other parts of the world as well in order to control and influence indigenous peoples.

Imperialism, or empire building, in state societies is achieved through conquest and absorption of neighboring peoples and the establishment of colonies in distant lands. Colonialism involves the domination and exploitation of indigenous peoples. Colonies were also established as military enclaves and settlements. Settlement colonies involved forcing native peoples to relocate. Motivations for colonization included enriching the home country, gaining religious converts, and extending power and influence.

THE EUROPEAN SLAVE TRADE

The slave trade was instrumental in developing a globalized system of economic and political networks from which Europeans directed and profited. The slave trade both benefited from and accelerated the growth of manufacturing in Europe, which led to the Industrial Revolution and the worldwide dominance of European commerce for centuries to come.

The scope in numbers alone of the European **slave trade** is staggering. Between 1451 and 1600, about 275,000 Africans were forcibly sent to Europe and the Americas. During the seventeenth century, about 1,341,000 Africans were enslaved, sent mainly to sugarcane plantations in the Caribbean (Wolf 1982, 195–96). In the eighteenth century, more than 6 million people were taken from Africa, two-thirds to the Caribbean and most of the rest to other European colonies in the Americas. Even though Great Britain banned the slave trade in 1807, an additional 2 million Africans were sold into slavery in the nineteenth century. These figures combine to a total of about 10 million people who were stolen from their communities in Africa and sent to labor for the rest of their lives on plantations many thousands of miles away. The wealth produced by slaves in the Americas contributed to the accumulation of capital and resources in Europe, directly and indirectly leading to the Industrial Revolution in the late eighteenth and early nineteenth centuries (Williams 1944).

The Portuguese initiated the European international slave trade along the western coast of Africa. At first, they were interested in obtaining gold and spices, but then they shifted to a focus on extracting people to work on the plantations that they were developing in South America, principally in Brazil. Competition soon began as Dutch slave traders were supplying their sugar plantations in the Caribbean. By the late seventeenth century, the British and the French were deeply involved in the slave trade as well. The purchase of slaves was made possible by a rise in production of goods in Europe.

Slavery in Africa

Slavery was practiced in Africa and the Middle East long before European powers arose. Slavery was seen as a source of labor, a means of absorbing conquered peoples, and a solution for people who became destitute for any reason. The growth in the international slave trade depended on preexisting indigenous systems of slavery in West Africa that contributed to the capture and transshipment of other Africans. However, it is unknown whether the African people involved in facilitating the European slave trade knew anything about the conditions to which African slaves were destined.`

Many societies in West Africa had extensive networks of long-distance trade that could be used to funnel people forced into slavery or coerced labor. War captives were often taken from enemy communities and forced to work for their captors. Some West African societies also had systems of indenture in which people pawned themselves if they became indebted to another person and were unable to repay a loan. Selling children

slave trade
Buying and selling of people into servitude.

This slave family living in Savannah in the 1860s contributed to their master's wealth but did not share his standard of living. In contrast, slaves in Africa lived with their masters and had similar comforts.
Corbis/Bettmann/Corbis

CULTURE CHANGE

IMPACTS OF THE EUROPEAN SLAVE TRADE ON AFRICAN STATES

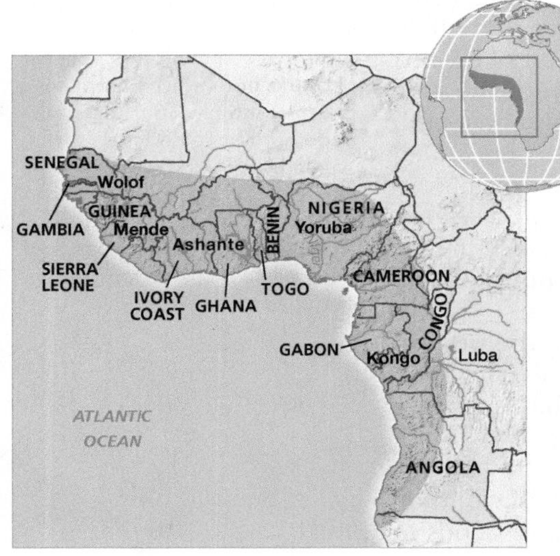

The effects of the European slave trade were borne primarily by its direct victims who were captured and sold into servitude for the rest of their lives, but it also deprived people who survived in their home communities of family members to aid in their subsistence and welfare. The slave trade tore apart households and disturbed networks of people who shared rights and responsibilities toward one another.

However, some Africans benefited economically and politically from the slave trade. For example, the elites in West African chiefdoms and kingdoms, which existed before European contact, amassed wealth and power by participating in the European slave trade and acting as intermediaries and distributors of European goods, which they gained from selling slaves, to other members of their communities.

Elite accumulation of wealth and power contributed to the formation of state societies in West Africa whose rulers gained even more control, particularly in Nigeria and in the Congo. The Ashantis in the Gold Coast (modern Ghana) and Nigeria extended their power both locally and regionally. Ashanti slave traders gained from Europeans in exchange for slaves. The Yorubas subjugated small states and demanded slaves as tribute from conquered tribes. Through successful campaigns, they extended their trading networks into Central Africa (Wolf 1982). In contrast, the precolonial kingdom of the Kongo dissolved because competing elites vied for control of the slave trade.

The political consequences of the European slave trade for African societies, therefore, depended on the access to slaves and the role of local elites. Some states were founded; others consolidated their power; still others broke apart during the centuries of upheaval that slave trade caused. In addition, as the trade intensified, West Africans moved from their coastal villages inland to escape slave-raiding expeditions. Raiders targeted small autonomous societies that lacked strong centralized governments or armed militaries. As people moved eastward, however, they sometimes came into contact with newly emerging states that took part in slave trading in their regions. Thus, the trade that began in West Africa radiated throughout the continent. And in East Africa, Arab traders took slaves to supply demands for labor in the Middle East and Asia.

The slave trade strengthened principles of patrilineal descent. In precolonial times, some Western and Central African societies reckoned descent patrilineally, whereas others were based on matrilineal kinship. However, men gained greater power and authority through involvement in the slave trade and by using the sons of their slave women as warriors against other groups (Wolf 1982). This shift may have strengthened patrilineal kinship in previously matrilineal societies.

Although the slave trade ended in the middle of the nineteenth century, the legacies of both the slave trade and European colonization can be seen today in many African countries. So-called "ethnic" or "tribal" conflicts, political instability, and the cruelties of civil wars continue to wreak havoc in the Congo, Sierra Leone, Chad, Uganda, and elsewhere.

From a cross-cultural perspective, how would you define the social functions of slavery? How would you account for the continuation of an international slave trade in Africa and the Middle East today?

into slavery or service to prevent their starvation was also an option. In addition, a period of indentured labor was often used as a punishment for wrongdoing in traditional systems of justice. However, people thus enslaved did not usually receive harsh treatment. They resided with the families who controlled them and therefore their living conditions were similar to that of others in the community.

Slavery in the Americas

Europeans and colonists saw African slaves as racially inferior and not deserving of rights and dignity. The voyage from Africa to the Americas, called the "Middle Passage," began the slaves' experience of degradation and isolation. Once in the Americas, slaves were completely cut off from their kin and home communities. Families were often broken apart and each person "sold" to different owners, adding to their sense of helplessness and loss. A person's duration of enslavement was indefinite, with no hope of release and return. Slaves were not seen as economic partners, though they certainly were economic assets. They could be, and were, bought and sold as commodities with no regard to their well-being, family ties, or their personal autonomy and feelings. They could be subjected to whatever treatment or maltreatment their owners decided to heap upon them.

fur trade
Exchange of animal pelts or hides between Native Americans and colonists in exchange for European trade goods.

The European Industrial Revolution was built on the African slave trade and on colonial materials and markets. The internationalization of the slave trade had profound human costs; in Africa, it led to the consolidation of kingdoms, greater competition and conflict between groups (as well as greater cooperation), and changes in families and kinship. The European slave trade contributed to the globalization that we see today.

TRADE AND SETTLEMENT IN NORTH AMERICA

The colonial enterprise in North America took the form of both trading and settler colonies. Europeans first came to North America in the late fifteenth century when Portuguese, Spanish, and French fishermen caught fish in the ocean off the coasts of Newfoundland and Québec. The first European to make an official landfall on the northeastern coast of North America, however, was John Cabot, who arrived in 1497 and promptly declared Newfoundland a possession of England. By 1550, approximately fifty fishing boats from each of the European countries (England, France, Portugal, Spain) were making annual visits to the Atlantic waters. By the end of the sixteenth century, the numbers had tripled (Sauer 1971).

Intermittent commercial relations in the northeast soon expanded to become the focus of European activities there. Native peoples gradually became enmeshed in trading networks that had far-reaching effects on their cultures and histories. At the same time that French, British, and Dutch traders were establishing commercial ties with indigenous nations in the northeast, Spanish adventurers were invading and plundering Mexico in the south and northward into what later became the southern United States. Although the early history of regional contact in the Western Hemisphere reveals different colonial motives, the eventual impact of European contact followed similar patterns throughout the continent. Trade, conquest, and colonization spread everywhere, and all native peoples were engulfed and their cultures transformed within a few centuries.

The Fur Trade

The involvement of Native Americans in the **fur trade**, at first peripheral to their economies, transformed their societies materially as durable metal goods became mainstays of material culture. Dependence on trade also had unforeseen negative effects. Native trappers could not control the market for furs, which made them vulnerable to changes in demand. When demand was high, people abandoned some traditional practices in an effort to keep pace. They overtrapped nearby territories, leading to a rapid depletion of beaver, otter, and other animals. People had to travel greater distances from their communities to find the desired resource, often entering territories of others who were similarly engaged in trapping and trading. Competition sometimes led to open conflict. When the demands of the fur market declined, people were left without the ability to acquire desired goods. In addition, some desired European products, such as guns and liquor, had negative effects on indigenous communities.

At first, native peoples were often eager to trade furs, such as these beaver pelts, for metal European tools and utensils. (North Wind Picture Archives)
North Wind Pictures/North Wind/North Wind Picture Archives

Involvement in the fur trade also led to other changes. As early as the seventeenth century in some eastern nations, trapping and trading became men's central economic activities. Among farming people

depopulation
Reduction in population size as a result of war, conquest, colonization, or disease.

where farmwork was the responsibility of women, food supplies were maintained; however, among foragers who depended more heavily on the meat and fish brought in by hunters, traditional food resources were not exploited as fully as previously. Many people then traded with Europeans for food as well as for manufactured goods. This process eventually led to increased dependence on traders, further deepening the need to spend even more time trapping animals.

Women were also involved in the fur trade because their labor was necessary to prepare the pelts for market. As the economic roles of both men and women focused more on tasks related to the fur trade, people grew more dependent on trade to supply their needs and wants. Economic systems shifted from subsistence to a focus on trapping and trading. Thus, the shift in gender roles and a new emphasis on acquiring personal wealth and private property also developed.

Through indigenous peoples' contact with Europeans, the concept of personal private property developed, which contrasted fundamentally with most traditional beliefs about ownership of resources either communally or by kinship groups as collective entities. As people lost access to their own territory, competition grew to own or control lands and resources that remained, often leading to warfare. In addition, formerly nomadic communities gradually established temporary and then permanent settlements near trading posts. This change was most marked in Canada and the Arctic. Small groups began to camp near riverbanks and coastal trading posts for access to European goods. Other demographic changes included great losses in population.

Westward Expansion and Depopulation

As trade and European settlement moved steadily westward in the eighteenth and nineteenth centuries, intense wars of survival pitted native groups against one another. Conflicts were often prompted and made worse by Europeans, who forged commercial and military alliances with native peoples in opposition to other European countries and their respective indigenous allies. In this new form of warfare, thousands of people were killed, and thousands more were routed from their homes or forced to flee to safety.

The Europeans' desires for settlement intensified competition over land. The British were most successful in establishing growing communities in North America, while French settlements remained comparatively small and isolated along the rivers and ports of their primary areas of dominance in what are now Québec and New Orleans. The Spanish foothold in North America was concentrated in Mexico and in what is now the southern United States and California. Beginning in the early seventeenth century, English colonists established villages from the Atlantic coast moving steadily westward. In doing so, they expropriated indigenous lands and dispersed, annihilated, or assimilated the original inhabitants.

European expropriation was aided by the spread of diseases of European origin that had never been seen in North America, especially smallpox, measles, and influenza. Native peoples had no natural resistance or immunity to these diseases. In the early 1600s, the Powhatan chief, Wahunsonacock, told John Smith in Virginia: "I have seen two generations of my people die. Not a man of the two generations is alive now but myself" (Hariot 1972). In Massachusetts, Massasoit, a Wampanoag chief, concluded, "Englishmen, take that land, for none is left to occupy it" (Brasser 1978, 66). As settlers moved westward, carrying their diseases with them, they caused untold numbers of deaths when they settled in the plains in the early and mid-nineteenth century. As Little Wolf of the Cheyenne noted, "Many have died of diseases we have no name for" (Thornton 1987, 134).

Depopulation was a global phenomenon, not limited to European colonies in the Americas. European colonies in Indonesia and the Pacific islands and in Australia also led to depopulation among indigenous peoples.

Estimates for the indigenous population of North America vary widely. Today, accepted figures range from more than 2 million (Ubelaker 1976) to more than 7 million (Thornton 1987). Whatever the number, rates of decline from the sixteenth through the nineteenth centuries were undoubtedly enormous. By the end of the nineteenth century, only about 250,000 Native Americans survived in the United States. This steep **depopulation** had significant social, economic, and political consequences, in addition to the human tragedy. Whole families—sometimes entire lineages or clans—were wiped out in just a few years. Not only did the most vulnerable, such as young children and elders, die in great numbers, but men and women in their prime also succumbed. Their deaths left survivors without the farmers, gatherers, hunters, artisans, and leaders they needed to sustain themselves and their ways of life.

European trade and settlement in North America began with the fur trade and led to the depopulation of Native Americans through displacement, warfare, and disease. Participation in European trading networks transformed native peoples' subsistence activities, settlement patterns, land use, gender relations, political organization, and economic systems.

SPANISH COLONIZATION IN THE AMERICAS

The Spanish began their invasions and conquests in Mexico and Central and South America in the early sixteenth century. Their goal was originally to find gold and other precious metals. It later shifted to acquiring territory to establish large plantations for growing domestic and imported crops. Spain lost Brazil to Portugal, but the Spanish took land and resources elsewhere on the continent. At first, both groups confiscated indigenous people's land and forced them to work on plantations. Other native people were forced to work in mines, extracting silver and other precious minerals.

An early catastrophic effect of European invasion was loss of life through disease. Reliable figures are not available for the pre-Columbian populations of South America, but estimates for Mexico suggest a native population of approximately 30 million at the time of the Spanish invasions in 1519. The indigenous population of Mexico fell to 3 million by 1568, a loss of 90 percent in barely fifty years (Cowley and Talbot 2001, 281).

In the Andes as well, Spanish invasions took a toll as a result of direct military conflict and the spread of European diseases. Examination of Inca skeletal samples from Ecuador indicates that, just prior to contact, the health of native populations was beginning to deteriorate (Ubelaker 1994). These health deficits resulted from sedentary lifestyles and higher population densities associated with farming as the Inca Empire expanded. Recall from chapter entitled, "Economic Systems" the benefits and risks of agriculture as a mode of subsistence. These conditions accelerated in the period following the Spanish invasions. Life expectancy dropped further, especially for people under the age of 15, and maximum longevity in years also declined. These health effects were directly caused by trauma and exposure to infectious diseases. As mentioned earlier, one consequence of this die-off of Native Americans was the importation of African slaves to Spanish and Portuguese colonial plantations.

CASE STUDY

Lakota Trade and the Consequences of Change in Economic Production

The Lakotas were a loose alliance of nations whose original homeland was in central Minnesota. Their economy combined farming and foraging. Women did the planting and gathered wild foods, and men were hunters. Lakotas also exchanged meat and hides for crops from settled farming peoples.

Although Lakotas were well adapted to their prairie environment, the arrival of European settlers and traders made their stay in that region difficult. Eastern Indians fled toward the west and entered territories inhabited by other nations, leading to competition for land and resources. In the early eighteenth century, Lakotas crossed west into the Great Plains, where they became nomadic foragers, extending into the Dakotas, Nebraska, and Wyoming.

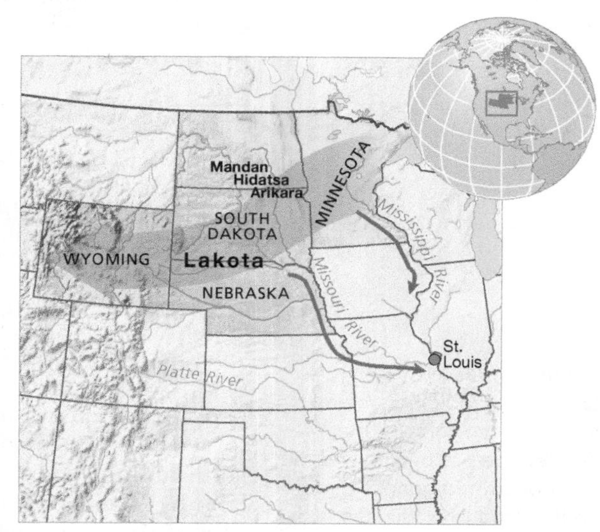

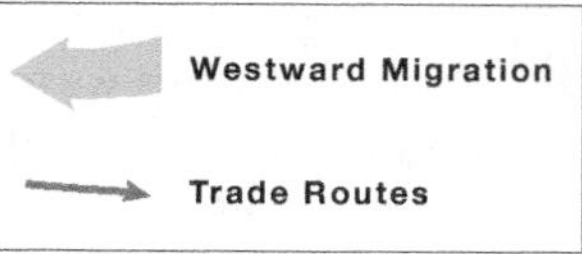

The most important innovation in eighteenth-century native culture was horses, originally obtained through trading networks from Spanish sources in the Southwest. Plains Indians immediately realized these animals' potential for travel and transport. Horsemen continued their roles as traders and hunters, especially for buffalo, which became important in European and American trade.

European trade increased the people's fortunes. Trade between Lakotas and the French began in the late seventeenth century when the people still inhabited lands in Minnesota. After the people migrated into the plains, they obtained European goods through intermediary nations such as the Mandans, Hidatsas, and Arikaras living along the Missouri River. Then, in the early 1800s, Americans from St. Louis traded with Lakotas for animal hides and meat. Lakota soon became middlemen between American traders and other native peoples living in the plains, thereby asserting economic dominance in the region.

As trade deepened, both men and women spent more time procuring and preparing animal products for market. Hunters killed many more animals than their subsistence required. Women spent more time processing buffalo meat into dried pemmican and tanning hides for trade (Klein 1980).

Economic changes promoted shifts in cultural values and social relations. In contrast to traditional ethics of equality and generosity, greater differences in wealth and rank emerged. The number of horses people owned became a symbol of their fortunes, as the accumulation of property became a desired goal. People increased the number of their horses by buying them, or, more commonly, by raiding other peoples. Wealthy families enhanced their social prestige by being generous to others. However, unlike past practices, when successful people gave away all or most of their surplus abundance, now wealthy families kept more of their personal goods, thereby leading to differences in standards of living.

A complex relationship developed between gender and wealth. To accumulate property and increase status, a man needed women's services to transform raw products into marketable items. However, one woman working alone could not keep pace with the supply of animals that a man could hunt. Three to ten days of work were probably required to tan one buffalo hide, yielding a seasonal rate of twenty to thirty hides (Klein 1983, 155). Thus, men sought to have more than one wife. Age at marriage rose for men, therefore, as only experienced hunters and warriors could acquire enough horses to give as obligatory gifts to a woman's parents upon proposal of marriage. Marriage age for women declined, as fathers agreed to daughters' unions in exchange for the horses they would receive. The widening gap in age between spouses strengthened husbands' control because seniority conferred prestige in Lakota society.

Interaction with American traders destabilized power relations among the Lakotas. Traders and government officials established ties with individuals who they thought could control hunters and warriors, shifting the economic balance in favor of hunting and trapping for the market. Although the "chiefs" that Americans contacted did not traditionally dominate their communities, "the more the agents treated them as powerful, the more powerful they became" (Schusky 1994, 263–64). As native leaders became the conduit for wealth to their nation, they used the situation to their material and social advantage.

Thus, trade had complex, interconnected consequences for the Lakotas and other indigenous nations of North America (and elsewhere). Changes in subsistence strategies, settlement patterns, gender relations, and the social order were mutually reinforcing in transforming indigenous ways of life. Read the **Document** on **myanthrolab.com**

Indigenous depopulation as a direct or indirect consequence of colonialism has been estimated for a number of countries worldwide, such as those shown in Table 1.

Spanish Landholding in the Colonies

encomiendas
Spanish landholding system in the American colonies that granted the use of land and the labor of any indigenous people on that land to soldiers, priests, and settlers.

haciendas
Estates made up of lands directly owned by Spanish settlers.

The Spanish crown gave land grants, called **encomiendas,** to soldiers, priests, and settlers. Encomiendas gave the holder rights to use the land and the labor of the native people residing on that land. The native people were essentially conscripted laborers, forced to work for others on the very land that they once held themselves. Another landholding system was the estates, or **haciendas,** resulting from direct ownership of land by Spanish settlers. Native people on haciendas worked as sharecroppers, owing part of their produce to the owners. A third type of landholding was the mission village, populated by Spanish priests and their forced converts. People in surrounding communities were compelled to relocate to the missions and to provide labor on mission farms. New Spanish settlers promptly confiscated land vacated by the indigenous population.

TABLE 1 ESTIMATED DEPOPULATION IN THE AMERICAS AND THE PACIFIC

	Precontact Population	Population Low Point	Depopulation
United States and Canada	7,000,000	390,000	6,610,000*
South America	8,500,000	450,000	8,050,000
Oceania/Polynesia	1,100,000	180,000	920,000
Micronesia	200,000	83,000	117,000
Melanesia/Fiji	300,000	85,000	215,000
New Caledonia	100,000	27,000	73,000
Australia	300,000	60,500	239,500

*According to the 2010 U.S. Census, Native American and Alaskan Native populations have rebounded to nearly 2.9 million people, about a third of the original estimated population. Native Hawaiians, Samoans, Tongans, Tahitians, and other Pacific Islanders numbered 540,000 in 2010. U.S. Bureau of the Census 2011.

Source: John Bodley, *Victims of Progress*, 5th ed., p. 50. © 2008. Altamira Press. Reprinted by permissionof Rowman & Littlefield.

mita
Traditional Incan system of conscripted labor for public works, adapted by the Spanish for use in obtaining indigenous workers for their mines.

Mining Quotas

Mining interests were spurred by the discovery of silver in Bolivia in 1545. At first, the Spanish obtained indigenous workers for their mines using the model of community service already present in the Inca Empire. In this system, called **mita,** each community was obligated to provide a specified number of workers for state projects. Under Incan control, men worked on public construction projects such as roads and irrigation works, and both men and women worked on farms owned by the Incan elite and priesthood. The Spanish used the same system of labor but for Spanish profit rather than public works. The system became increasingly brutal as people died from disease and the rigors of the work. Burdens on each worker increased as the population shrank and service quotas for each community remained constant. The Spanish also obtained workers for their mines by dispossessing people from their land, turning them into "free" laborers. Unable to earn a living from their land, free laborers found it necessary to take whatever work they could find, essentially consigning themselves to the mines. Later, African slaves were used in the mining industry, especially in the processing of silver with mercury (Wolf 1982).

Intermarriage

In both South America and Mexico, Spaniards replaced the indigenous social elites but also used some elites to control local populations. Local elites were permitted to continue receiving tribute in produce and labor from members of the common classes. They functioned as supervisors of local populations, helping to keep rebellion in check in their own interests as well as those of Spanish colonists.

Marriage customs reinforced this social system. In Mexico, for example, the Spanish government encouraged intermarriage between Spanish men and native women, often through capture and rape. Because, in the early periods of colonization, most of the Spanish immigrants into Mexico were men, they needed the services, sexual and domestic, of indigenous women. In addition, Spanish authorities believed that intermarriage would create a mixed-race class of people that would stabilize social tensions created by invasion and conquest.

The Mission System

In the southwestern United States and California, the building of missions and military forts more directly destroyed indigenous culture. By the end of the eighteenth century, colonists had enslaved tens of thousands of native people, who were rounded up, removed from their homes, compelled to convert to Roman Catholicism, and forced into labor. Mission Indians typically lived in virtual slavery. Infractions or resistance were often punished by beatings, solitary confinement, mutilation, branding, or execution (Castillo 1978; Jackson and Castillo 1995). The brutal treatment, as well as malnutrition, led to a precipitous decline in the native population. As elsewhere in North America, disease was the most significant cause of death, accounting for about one-half of deaths (Cook 1976; 1978).

REVIEW

Spanish colonization of Mexico, Central America, the Caribbean, and South America was based on plantation farming and mining using forced native labor and the mita system. Encomiendas, haciendas, and the mission system removed land and resources from indigenous access or control. Intermarriage created a unique system of social stratification with Native Americans at the bottom of the hierarchy.

AGENTS OF DIRECTED CULTURE CHANGE

Colonial authorities attempted to subdue indigenous populations through military actions and the establishment of law and order in the colonies. They also applied social, economic, and political pressures on indigenous peoples to persuade them to change their cultural practices to be more consistent with European values and behaviors. Indoctrination was achieved through the work of missionaries, teachers, and enforcers of the rule of law.

Missionaries

Missionaries were a powerful force for cultural transformation in indigenous communities. From the sixteenth century, missionaries preceded, accompanied, and followed military and exploratory campaigns into the Americas. At first, they generally saw their role as compatible with their country's goals, which included converting, civilizing, and, they thought, helping pagan inhabitants, while at the same time exploiting any resources that might benefit their home country and the church. In later periods, though, missionaries sometimes came into conflict with civilian authorities, whose actions and policies toward native people became increasingly brutal at a time when European moral standards had begun to change.

Different groups of missionaries had different approaches to conversion. Many thought that indigenous people were subhuman and should be controlled as one would control animals. As soon as they entered a region and gained control, they forced the people to build churches, destroyed traditional ceremonial structures and paraphernalia, and beat and tortured native religious leaders into submission.

Others assumed that indigenous people were fully human and capable of intelligent thought and reasoning (Vecsey 1997). Jesuits, for example, believed that pagan religious and intellectual errors resulted from the powers that the devil had over them or from the control exerted by native people who masqueraded as shamans and religious practitioners. Many missionaries saw their role as enlightening misguided but sincere people. They also made use of economic and political arguments to gain converts. Trading posts gave favorable terms and provided guns to Christian Indians but not to pagans (Bonvillain 1986).

A Spanish hacienda in Tarahuasi, Peru. Alamy Limited/Travelscape Images/Alamy

Later, British missionaries came to convert indigenous people to Protestantism. They emphasized the spiritual rewards of Christianity along with advantages of protection supposedly bestowed upon converts by the British crown. Christian Indians were favored through trade and military alliances. Missionaries taught people, directly or indirectly, to be ashamed of their culture, their heritage, and themselves. They transferred the Christian notion of sin to people who had no concept of innate sinfulness. In the words of a modern Coast Salish Catholic from the state of

Washington, "The priests said, 'You are sinful, vile,' and the Indians wondered, 'What have I done?'" (Hilbert 1987, quoted in Vecsey 1997, 351).

The missionaries advocated changes in native settlement patterns and systems of leadership and social control (Bonvillain 1986). They encouraged people who were previously nomadic to settle permanently, preferably near European ports and trading posts, where they were more easily contacted and controlled. The priests tried to convince their converts to obey laws, their superiors, and colonial government personnel. Many tried to supplant indigenous child-rearing practices that they saw as lenient with more authoritarian measures, including corporal punishment as a means of controlling a child's will and compelling obedience. Missionaries also condemned native ethics concerning sexuality, which generally regarded premarital sexual relations as normal and natural. They also criticized marital flexibility and the relative ease of divorce found in most indigenous societies. Last, they attempted to transform the basically egalitarian gender relations that they observed in most native societies into the system of patriarchal dominance and authority that was typical of Europe.

Schoolteachers

In all countries under colonial control, authorities used education as a means of reorienting indigenous cultures. Forced attendance at boarding schools, for example, separated children from their parents and communities, with the result that children lost touch with traditional ways of interacting, sacred knowledge and rituals, and even their native languages. Values inculcated in schools encouraged children to identify with their teachers while at the same time making them ashamed of their parents and their heritage. They were taught that their people's customs were backward, immoral, and irrational. They were made to believe that civilization, as reflected in European customs, was desirable, if not fully attainable. These lessons were taught subtly in the context of general education, religious instruction, and industrious work. The values of hard work and obedience to authority (whether it be teacher, administrator, or king) were transmitted as necessary attributes of a civilized and educated person. For example, an order issued in 1887 by John Atkins, Commissioner of the U.S. Bureau of Indian Affairs dealing with education and language policies, stated, "The instruction of the Indians in the vernacular is not only of no use to them, but is detrimental to the cause of their education and civilization, and no school will be permitted on the reservation in which the English language is not exclusively taught" (Commissioner of Indian Affairs 1887, xxii).

Throughout the world, European colonizers banned ceremonial practices they saw as contrary to Christian beliefs and ethics. Also, missionaries, teachers, and government officials distributed clothing to native peoples in the Americas, Africa, and the Pacific. They especially insisted that women wear blouses or dresses to cover their breasts and that men wear shorts or pants instead of traditional clothing styles that revealed all or part of their genitals. Today, the same type of native clothing may be found on an Amazonian Indian and a Belgian tourist in New York City or Tokyo.

Missionaries, teachers, and government officials also condemned indigenous religious ceremonies and practitioners. Some practices, especially shamanism, were seen as backward, ignorant, and dangerous. In North America, the U.S. government outlawed the Sun Dance ceremony of the Plains Indians, and the Canadian government outlawed the potlatch ceremonial complex of the Pacific Northwest peoples.

Government Officials

Colonial administrators imposed Eurocentric patterns of law and social control in indigenous and tribal societies, which they saw as essentially disorderly. European jurisprudence, based solely on the facts in a criminal case or civil dispute, was antithetical to native justice, which was based on social context. This social context included common knowledge about the parties in a dispute and the reciprocal obligations that people have toward one another in relatively small, face-to-face communities. To indigenous peoples, the goal of adjudication was conflict resolution—a negotiated settlement that repairs social relations. To colonial administrators, the goal of adjudication was the determination of guilt or fault and its assignment to one of the parties in a dispute.

By imposing European concepts and systems of law, colonial authorities disturbed traditional systems of social relationships and ethical values, creating far-reaching changes in behavior and attitudes. Law has been described as "the cutting edge of colonialism" (Chanock 1985, 4) because of its effect on the fabric of indigenous society. Furthermore, by establishing courts and judicial systems based on European principles, the problems of indigenous people were reinterpreted in a language of law that distorted the indigenous experience. Concepts such as "equality under the law" and "innocent until proven guilty," for instance, were not traditional in native justice.

customary law
Selected aspects of native justice and jurisprudence codified into law by colonial authorities, mainly to secure greater control over indigenous populations.

cash economies
Systems of exchange based on the use of currency in modern markets.

In some regions, colonial authorities recognized "native courts" that enforced "customary law" (Merry 1991, 893). However, **customary law** was often an inaccurate creation of colonial regimes. For example, in Zambia and Malawi, colonial authorities transformed indigenous systems of adjudication that were flexible and adaptable to different contexts and different social needs into a system of customary law that was based on a rigid written code (Chanock 1985). Enshrining a particular set of indigenous practices in a written code privileges some practices over others and creates an artificial "tradition" that then becomes identified as part of indigenous culture. Colonial authorities manipulated this process to reflect their interests in the region. When countries in Africa and elsewhere gained their independence, they sometimes used these codes of customary law to establish judicial procedures. These borrowed procedures then became central ingredients in developing statehood, a national culture, and nationalistic pride.

A Cash Economy

Colonial law and administrative control benefited elites and their wealth in both the colonies and the home country. Imposed taxes obtained income for the state and compelled changes in indigenous economic systems. In Africa, both British and French administrations used taxation as a means of collecting revenue and as a method of encouraging economic changes in indigenous communities. Households were required to pay taxes in cash, but people's access to money was limited, because their economies were based on subsistence farming or cattle herding. Access to manufactured goods, foods, and luxury items also required cash. As a result, some members of the family, usually men, had to obtain work outside of their local communities for which they would be paid in cash. In some areas, women sold milk and home-brewed beer for cash.

In Africa, most of the work available was on plantations producing crops for export or in mines extracting valuable mineral resources. Migration from rural areas to plantations, mines, and towns disturbed the social cohesiveness of local communities; families were splintered by the need for employment to buy the goods that had come to symbolize the good life. Women who remained in the local communities were burdened by additional responsibilities in their households and in the subsistence farming that supported their families. Colonial **cash economies** and systems of taxation thus continued the household and community fracturing that had occurred during the slave trade era.

REVIEW

Agents of directed culture change included missionaries, schoolteachers, and government officials. They discouraged or outlawed traditional ways of life, changing how people ate, dressed, and raised their children. They also imposed European values. Finally, they introduced a cash economy, which led to labor migration and changes in family relations and replaced traditional systems of reciprocity and redistribution.

JUSTIFICATIONS FOR COLONIAL RULE

Throughout the eighteenth and nineteenth centuries, European control increased in many parts of the world. The colonial presence of the Portuguese, Spanish, and Dutch was gradually replaced by that of Great Britain, France, Germany, Italy, Belgium, and the United States. As they set up colonial regimes in Africa, Asia, and the Pacific, they developed new justifications for their rule to replace the earlier rationale that Europeans could take lands they conquered simply by self-declared "right of discovery."

The British used the model of European landholding patterns and practices to claim that, in order to "own" land, one had to transform it through labor. This agrarian model did not always fit indigenous economies in other parts of the world. Thus, British authorities recognized that indigenous people "used" land but questioned whether they "owned" it. Lack of proof of ownership thus became a rationale for ignoring indigenous claims to land and resources.

The same principle of landownership through farming was used in the United States to justify settler expansion in the plains and the West in the nineteenth century. Many indigenous peoples were nomadic foragers without fixed or permanent settlement sites. American authorities viewed hunting territories as open and unsettled because they did not find permanent villages and plowed fields. In Australia as well, the British and, later, Australian governments ignored the rights of Aborigines to their accustomed territories. They claimed that the land was "unoccupied wasteland" and therefore could be appropriated by the Australian state (Bodley 1999, 88).

white man's burden
Paternalistic, racist, colonial attitude that treated colonized peoples as inferiors in need of protection and instruction on how to live.

pacification
Colonial goal of forcing indigenous people to be peaceful and nonresistant so that settlers could safely inhabit their lands.

White Man's Burden

European colonizers also justified their control of indigenous peoples by claiming cultural and moral superiority. Administering to these people responsibly was the **"white man's burden."** Various versions of the white man's burden were used to justify the eradication of indigenous practices and their replacement with behaviors, values, and attitudes more consistent with those of Europeans. Missionaries working in North and South America in the sixteenth and seventeenth centuries embodied the idea that they were saving the natives and doing God's work by converting them.

In Africa, Asia, and the Pacific, educators and government officials spoke the same Eurocentric and essentially racist attitudes in a language of science and reason. For example, Herman Merivale, a British professor of political economy, wrote in 1861 that the natives deserved protection from the excesses of colonial settlers and also deserved to be civilized by the guidance and superiority of the white men. As Merivale advocated, "Colonial authorities should act upon the assumption that they have the right, in virtue of the relative position of civilized and Christian men to savages, to enforce abstinence from immoral and degrading practices" such as cannibalism, infanticide, and wife abuse (1988, 101). Furthermore, "[T]here should be no hesitation in acting on the broad principle that the natives must, for their own protection, be placed in a situation of acknowledged inferiority, and consequently of tutelage" (p. 103).

View the **Map:** *World Colonial Empires, 1900* on **myanthrolab.com**

In 1841, the British House of Commons Select Committee on South Australia issued an official report (*British Parliamentary Papers,* 1841, vol. IV, no. 394) generally deploring the harsh treatment of Aborigines by colonial authorities. It observed that government policy "has thrown impediments in the way of successful colonization; it has engendered wars, and it has vanished from our confines, or exterminated, the native, who might have been profitable workmen, good customers, and good neighbors" (quoted in Bodley 1988, 68). British colonial authorities in the twentieth century elaborated on the white man's burden. In the words of Sir Hubert Murray, lieutenant governor of Papua New Guinea, in the 1930s, colonial governments have a duty "towards subject races"—the duty of "association and collaboration." As he stated, "We are not trying to make the brown man white; we are trying to make him a better brown man than he was before" (Murray 1933, in Bodley 1988, 43).

In your opinion, should Europeans have refrained from interfering in native practices of cannibalism, infanticide, and domestic abuse? Why or why not?

A Sacred Trust

The British colonial attitude of "sacred trust" toward indigenous peoples justified their efforts to "civilize" them. Murray advocated a policy of "peaceful pacification" of indigenous peoples through "indirect rule." As he said, a "scientific method of **pacification**" rests on "knowledge of the people whom you propose to pacify, and some idea of what you are going to do with them when they are pacified" (1988/1933, 43).

Murray emphasized that "native races are no longer deliberately exterminated" and that colonial governments should refrain from punitive attacks on native villages as a punishment for rebellious acts. Such a policy, he said, was both morally untenable and impractical because it led to hostility on the part of indigenous peoples and therefore thwarted colonial efforts at "peaceful pacification." Instead, Murray advocated the establishment of a local police force made up of members of the indigenous community. This would foster loyalty to the government and help administer indigenous regions. The police would develop "pride in their uniform." This tactic proved to be divisive in indigenous communities, however, as native police upheld colonial authority and sometimes abused their powers.

Listen to the **Audio:** *How We Got Here: The Birtish Legacy in Iraq* on **myanthrolab.com**

reservations
Land guaranteed by treaty for native residents' ownership and control.

Murray also advocated winning over local leaders who would then convince members of their communities to support or at least not oppose colonial authority. This strategy, too, caused divisions within indigenous communities, pitting one faction against another. Colonial administrators were advised

- To establish posts in interior districts in order to deepen their control and create multiple centers of influence;
- To demonstrate benevolence and create goodwill, for example, by returning prisoners to their communities as "ambassadors of peace";
- To bring gradual rather than abrupt change to the lives of indigenous people;
- And to permit the preservation of indigenous customs so long as they did not contribute to disorder and resistance (1988, 49).

The Reservation System

In the nineteenth century in the United States and Canada, the federal governments obtained land from native peoples through ostensibly legal means, replacing the outright confiscation of territory and annihilation of indigenous peoples. The U.S. government was consistent in its goal of removing native peoples to lands outside areas of American settlement. The philosophy of Manifest Destiny was at the heart of these efforts, as Americans believed that the land was rightfully theirs. They acquired land through the procedural legality of signing treaties with native leaders and establishing reservations (or reserves, as they are called in Canada) for native peoples.

Reservations consisted of land guaranteed by treaty for native residents' ownership and control. Treaty language promised that the government would protect reservations from confiscation or settlement by nonnative people. In exchange, people agreed to cede their territory for protection and the perpetual right to live on their remaining land. Through these treaties, the United States acquired millions of acres of native land and created hundreds of reservations.

However, settlers nevertheless frequently intruded on these protected lands. Once this happened, government officials, claiming they were powerless to stop the settlers, urged the indigenous people to abandon their lands and move farther west, out of the way. Some native groups moved three or four times before finally ending up in "Indian Territory," now Oklahoma.

When people resisted giving up their homelands, however, Americans resorted to intimidation and threat of military force, and no justifications were offered. For example, speaking in 1831 to a delegation of Sauk leaders who balked at moving from their Illinois villages, General Edmund Gaines told them: "I came here neither to beg nor hire you to leave your village. My business is to remove you, peaceably if I can, but forcibly if I must" (Jackson 1964, 111–12). In 1851, Luke Lea, the federal Commissioner of Indian

These native children photographed before (left) and after (right) they entered the Hampton Institute in Hampton, Virginia to learn new values, languages, and beliefs. (left) Library of Congress/Johnston, Frances Benjamin/Library of Congress Prints and Photographs Division [LC-USZ62-78702]; (right) Library of Congress/Johnston, Frances Benjamin/Library of Congress Prints and Photographs Division [LC-USZ62-78701]

Affairs, told Santee delegates in South Dakota, "Suppose your Great Father wanted your land and did not want a treaty for your good, he would come with 100,000 men and drive you off to the Rocky Mountains" (Meyer 1993, 78).

CASE STUDY

Indigenous Colonized Societies of Australia and Tasmania

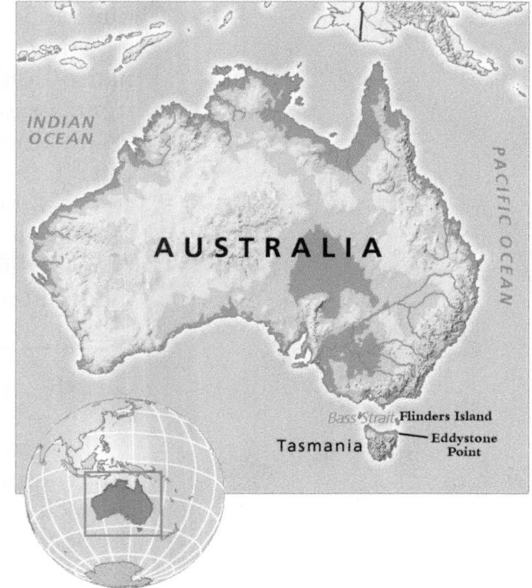

In Australia, Aboriginal ownership of land had been denied from the outset of British colonization. Because Aborigines were nomadic foragers, their entitlement to the territories they inhabited and where they gathered and hunted resources was invisible to British farmers, sheep ranchers, and government officials. The people traditionally lived in small, scattered, seasonal encampments. Their presence was barely acknowledged by colonial administrators, who saw them as nuisances to be pushed away from the newly founded and growing towns and cities of colonial Australia. White officials took young Aboriginal children from their families. The children were placed in institutions or in white foster homes as servants and denied contact with their families. Ironically, this practice was seen as a humane way to assimilate natives into colonial society and culture. According to Australian government reports, 10 percent to 33 percent of Aboriginal children were part of this "Stolen Generation." This policy was not officially rescinded until 1969.

Today, Aboriginal Australians constitute a small but growing percentage of the country's population, accounting for about 2 percent of a total population of approximately 20 million. They are a relatively youthful population; 70 percent of Aboriginal Australians are aged 25 or younger. However, according to all sets of economic and social data, they live in comparative disadvantage. Indeed, Aboriginal life expectancy averages seventeen years less than for non-Aboriginal Australians, while their unemployment rate is three times that of non-Aboriginals (Johnston 2008). The Aboriginal infant mortality rate is three times that of other Australians, the average Aboriginal household income is 62 percent of the national average, the school dropout rate for Aboriginal youth is twice that of other Australians, and Aboriginal Australians suffer higher rates of chronic diseases and disabilities (*Cultural Survival* 2010).

In response to pressure from Aboriginal communities and their supporters, Prime Minister Kevin Rudd apologized to Aboriginal peoples in February 2008 (BBC News 2008). He also acknowledged the gap between contemporary Aboriginal and non-Aboriginal Australians in their "life expectancy, educational achievement, and economic opportunity." Although many Aboriginal leaders welcomed Rudd's apology and its recognition of past injustices, they also point out that the government is not willing to compensate members of the Stolen Generation or their communities.

Aboriginal people are now using the Australian court system in order to file land claims cases seeking recognition of their title to ancestral territory. Beginning with a High Court ruling in a case decided in 1988, referred to as the *Mabo* ruling after the lead Aboriginal litigant Eddie Mabo, Australian courts have found that Aboriginal traditional occupancy and use of land justifies the people's claims. Most of the claims have been for territory in rural areas where Aboriginal communities are situated. But in 2006, a federal judge ruled that the Noongar people had title to an area of 2,300 square miles that included the city of Perth, with a population of 1.7 million (Cherrington 2006). According to the ruling, the Noongar people maintained their cultural identity and traditions even though they had been displaced from their lands when white settlement began in 1892. Although they have been granted native title to the area, the Noongar will not take possession because, according to Australian law, "freehold title" (i.e., private ownership of houses and buildings) supersedes native title. Still, the ruling is an important recognition of Aboriginal claims.

In Tasmania, an island off the southeastern coast of Australia, nineteenth-century British colonial policies led to the near extinction of the Tasmanian people. When Tasmanians resisted attempts to confiscate their settlement and hunting areas, Australian settlers killed or captured whole villages and communities. The native people retaliated against Anglo ranchers and farmers.

In 1828, Governor Sir Arthur Lawley warned settlers to cease attacking Tasmanians, but he also ordered Tasmanians to keep clear of Anglo settlements unless they had received official passports allowing them entry. When he was ignored, Lawley ordered his soldiers to round up the natives and remove them for their own safety. Rewards were offered for natives taken alive, but many more were killed than captured. In the end, the few hundred native Tasmanians who survived were taken to Flinders Island, off the coast of Tasmania. By 1854, it was reported that only sixteen Tasmanians were left, and only one was left by 1870. She died in 1876 (Howells 2001, 263).

However, some of the people's descendants had eluded the settlers and soldiers. Today native Tasmanians, preferring their own name, Palawa, are demanding recognition of their rights to some of their land and sacred sites. In particular, they are reclaiming Eddystone Point, a traditional trading base and ceremonial center. When the Australian government offered the site for public bidding, the Palawa held demonstrations. The government then stopped the bidding process. Meanwhile, Aboriginal peoples from Tasmania and Australia use the site as a place to express their solidarity and perform sacred rituals (*Cultural Survival Quarterly* 2002, 13). In 2006, the Tasmanian government formally apologized for the treatment of the Tasmanians. **Read** the **Document** on **myanthrolab.com**

Another land-grabbing strategy, popular through the 1870s, was collusion between government and traders to force native representatives to sign land-cession agreements in exchange for the forgiveness of debts that their community members incurred. Traders gave credit to indigenous families that amounted to more than they could ever repay. Officials then demanded land in exchange for the debts owed. Bribing and intoxicating indigenous delegates to treaty negotiations was another strategy in which leaders signed away their people's land without even knowing what they were doing.

Once native people were settled on reservations and reserves, the U.S. and Canadian federal governments implemented policies aimed at "civilizing" them. "Civilized" native people were sedentary farmers who lived in nuclear family households, wore Anglo clothing, spoke English, and attended church. Missionaries often took control of local education and merged religious doctrines with secular training in farming, manual skills, and domestic duties. Participation in traditional religious ceremonies was forbidden.

REVIEW

European justifications for their treatment of indigenous peoples in colonized lands were based on Eurocentric and racist ideas. These ideas, such as the right of discovery, the white man's burden, and the sacred trust, made Europeans the stewards of people they viewed as racially "inferior," culturally "primitive," or simply "wild." "Pacification" was followed by the establishment of the reservation system designed to "civilize" the natives.

REACTIONS OF INDIGENOUS PEOPLES TO EUROPEAN COLONIZERS

Watch the **Video:** *Defining Indigenous Peoples* on **myanthrolab.com**

When indigenous peoples first encountered Europeans sailing in the waters off their shores or arriving in their territories, they reacted in different ways. Coastal peoples were amazed at the sight of strange-looking, pale, absurdly dressed men atop huge moving sailing vessels that looked to them like "floating houses" or "hovering clouds" (Bitterli 1989, 21). The open and friendly manner of many indigenous peoples struck European explorers as simple and straightforward. The following is from the journals of Christopher Columbus, writing in October 1492 about his first contact with indigenous people in Hispaniola (now divided between Haiti and the Dominican Republic):

> I, in order that they might feel great amity towards us, because I knew they were a people to be delivered and converted to our holy faith rather by love than by force, gave to some among them some red caps and glass beads, which they hung round their neck, and many other things of little value. At this they were greatly pleased and became so entirely our friends that it was a wonder to see. Afterwards they came swimming to the ship's boats, where we were, and brought us parrots and cotton thread in balls, and spears and many other things. (Vigneras 1960, 23)

Columbus also remarked that the residents of the territory would make good servants.

Slightly more than a century later, Samuel de Champlain described his meeting with Algonquian Indians in Maine in 1604, which began with speeches of friendship. Champlain referred to the desire of the French to visit the country and trade with the inhabitants:

> They signified their great satisfaction, saying that no greater good would come to them than to have our friendship,. . . and we should dwell in their land, in order that they might in future more than ever before engage in hunting beavers, and give us a part of them in return for our providing them with things which they wanted. After he finished his discourse, we presented them with hatchets, caps, knives, and other little knick knacks. (Champlain 1907, 50)

Trade Goods and Gods

Indigenous peoples were usually willing, and often eager, to acquire goods of European manufacture. These were utilitarian objects, especially made of metal, or decorative objects, which Europeans thought of as relatively worthless baubles and trinkets. The eagerness with which natives sought foreign goods confirmed the Europeans' sense of superiority and their view of indigenous peoples as somewhat childish.

Some indigenous peoples had to make compromises between their desire for trade goods and their wariness of the strangers. In some cases, they managed this compromise through indirect or distant exchanges, as in the following example, reported by a French trader exploring the West African coast of Guinea:

> These barbarous people would not venture close to us in order to exchange their fish and water for our tobacco and ship's biscuit. They behaved rather as we behave towards victims of the plague; our people were obliged to take the goods they wanted to exchange for fish some distance from the ship and then turn back. After the natives had observed this, they approached to what had been brought to them, put their fish in the same place, and returned to their huts. (Jannequin 1643, 43–44)

Native North Americans typically saw Europeans as childish, stupid, and cruel. They were shocked at what they perceived as coldness toward human suffering and unwillingness to be generous to people in need. They saw foreigners as stupid for always getting lost in the woods and failing to notice features of the landscape. They were also dismayed by the Europeans' tendency to complain about discomfort, hunger, and pain (Thwaites 1906).

In other parts of the world, some native peoples endowed Europeans with extraordinary powers. They were awed by technological wonders that Europeans possessed. Such reactions may have exaggerated Europeans' feelings of cultural superiority and self-importance. For the Aztecs and Incans, the timing of contact happened to coincide with prophecies of the return of divine beings or strange creatures with supernatural powers. One of these prophecies concerned the Incan creator god Viracocha, who was a bearded white man, just like the Spaniards. When Cortés arrived in Mexico in 1519 and Pizarro came to Peru in 1526, they, with their horses, were greeted and welcomed as returning gods. However, it is possible that some accounts of these encounters were embellished (or even fabricated) by Europeans as justifications for their presence in Native communities.

People soon realized their mistake, however. The following are the words of an Incan chronicler, recorded by a Spanish monk in Peru soon after the conquest of the Inca Empire:

> I thought they were kindly beings sent (as they claimed) by Tecsi Viracocha, that is to say, by God; but it seems to me that all has turned out the very opposite from what I believed; so let me tell you, brothers, from proof they have given me since their arrival in our country, they are the sons not of Viracocha, but of the devil. (Wachtel 1977, 22; note here that it is the Spaniards who claimed to be sent by God)

These words reveal not only the Incan attitude but also the Spaniards' manipulation of native beliefs. The Spanish claimed to be kindly beings sent by God, giving greater importance to indigenous prophecies as a cause of the conquest than was the case. Native peoples may later have reinterpreted their histories to fit their circumstances, using concepts from Christianity to explain events.

Guns and Other Technological Wonders

How is the theme of technologically superior strangers with unknown intentions played out in American popular culture today?

Europeans used their technology to instill awe, confusion, and sometimes fear. For example, Jesuit missionaries working among the Hurons in Ontario in the 1630s used clocks to inspire awe. The Hurons were surprised by the "voice" that the clock made when it struck on the hour. They interpreted this "voice" as the sound of the spirit of the clock and were amazed that the missionaries could order the clock to use its voice at will. The Hurons did not know that the Jesuits could predict when the clock would strike because they could tell the time. The Hurons interpreted European behavior in their own terms, as all peoples do. As animists, believing that objects may be imbued with spirit power and may have voices and wills, the Hurons interpreted the new objects in terms of their prior beliefs.

Guns had more damaging effects. They created fear when fired into the air as a display or directly at animals or people, causing injury and death. The arbitrary, random, and unforeseen manner in which the Europeans used their weapons also instilled fear. In 1606, in the waters off the coast of New Guinea, for example, Luis Baez de Torres had his soldiers shoot at people in their canoes as they were rowing toward him in a friendly greeting. According to de Torres, "On reaching them, we saluted them with our arquebuses and killed some, and when any fell dead they gave them blows with their clubs to make them get up, thinking that they were not dead" (Hilder 1980, 28).

Since the 1940s, as dozens of countries have won their independence, much of the world has become free of direct colonial rule. Independence movements spread through forces of globalization are still at work in the world today.

Native Resistance and Retaliation

Indigenous peoples tended to treat Europeans with generosity and friendliness, until they learned from experience that the strangers were not to be trusted and that they desired their land, resources, and labor. From most reports, attacks on Europeans seem

The Aztecs are reported to have recoiled in horror at the display of Spanish artillery: "[I]t was as if one had lost one's breath; it was as if for the time being there was stupefaction, as if one were affected by mushrooms. Fear prevailed. It was as if everyone had swallowed his heart. Even before it had grown dark, there was terror, there was astonishment, there was apprehension, there was a stunning of the people" (Sahagun 1975, 47). Art Resource, Inc./bpk, Berlin/Kunstbibliothek, Staatliche Museen/Art Resource, NY

In Their Own VOICES

Nelson Mandela on the Struggle Against Apartheid in South Africa

In this excerpt, Nelson Mandela discusses the beginnings of the antiapartheid struggle. This was part of the struggle against colonial rule in Africa in the 1950s and 1960s. In South Africa, it took decades to achieve victory but, finally, in 1994, with all South Africans able to vote, a new government led by the African National Congress (ANC) was elected. Nelson Mandela was its first president.

Since 1912 and year after year thereafter, in their homes and local areas, in provincial and national gatherings, on trains and buses, in the factories and on the farms, in cities, villages, shanty-towns, schools and prisons, the African people have discussed the shameful misdeeds of those who rule the country.

Year after year they have raised their voices in condemnation of the grinding poverty of the people, the low wages, the acute shortage of land, the inhuman exploitation, and the whole policy of white domination. But instead of more freedom, repression began to grow in volume and intensity and it seemed that all their sacrifices would end in smoke and dust.

Today the whole country knows that their labours were not in vain, for a new spirit and new ideas have gripped our people. Today the people speak the language of action: there is a mighty awakening among the men and women of our country and the year 1952 stands out as the year of this upsurge of national consciousness. In June 1952, the African National Congress and the South African Indian Congress, bearing in mind their responsibility as the representatives of the downtrodden and oppressed people of South Africa, took the plunge and launched the Campaign for the Defiance of the Unjust Laws. . . . It spread throughout the country like wildfire. Factory and office workers, doctors, lawyers, teachers, students, and the clergy; Africans, Coloureds, Indians, and Europeans, old and young, all rallied to the national call. . . . The Campaign called for immediate and heavy sacrifices. Workers lost their jobs, chiefs and teachers were expelled from the service, doctors, lawyers, and businessmen gave up their practices and businesses and elected to go to jail. Defiance was a step of great political significance. It released strong social forces which affected thousands of our countrymen.

It was an effective way of getting the masses to function politically; a powerful method of voicing our indignation against the reactionary policies of the government. It was one of the best ways of exerting pressure on the government and extremely dangerous to the stability and security of the State. It inspired and aroused our people from a conquered and servile community of "yes-men" to a militant and uncompromising band of comrades-in-arms. . . .

The entire continent is seething with discontent, and already there are powerful revolutionary eruptions in the Gold Coast, Nigeria, Tunisia, Kenya, the Rhodesia, and South Africa. The oppressed people and the oppressors are at loggerheads. The day of reckoning between the forces of freedom and those of reaction is not very far off. I have not the slightest doubt that when that day comes truth and justice will prevail.

From Nelson Mandela, "No Easy Walk to Freedom," excerpt from speech given in 1953. Reprinted by permission of the Nelson Mandela Foundation.

CRITICAL THINKING QUESTIONS

How does Nelson Mandela suggest that oppressed peoples can achieve political and social justice? Why did the ANC succeed in defeating apartheid?

to have been well motivated, as friendliness turned to retaliation, against either a particular offending group or the next party of European intruders. In Spanish colonies in the Americas, for example, residents of marginal regions in central Mexico resisted foreign control. This resistance was most marked in the north among the Yaqui and Apache in Sonora, the northernmost Mexican state. Not until the middle and late nineteenth century were these two groups "pacified" with the help of the U.S. military.

Farther north, the Pueblo peoples (Hopi, Zuni, Cochiti, Tewa, and others), living along the Rio Grande in what is now New Mexico, staged a revolt in 1680. After more than a century of rule by Spanish colonizers and priests, the various communities united to oust the foreigners, killing 21 priests and about 400 settlers out of a population of 2,500 (Dozier 1970, 59). Then, twelve years later, the Spanish sent another invading force and reestablished control in 1692. Eventually, this region became part of the United States after the Mexican-American War ended in 1846 with the signing of the Treaty of Guadalupe Hidalgo.

In the south of Mexico, Spanish authorities also had a difficult time establishing permanent control, especially in Chiapas. There, members of indigenous Tzotzil and Tzeltal communities put up active resistance through military defense as well as passive resistance through retreat to remote mountain areas. Even in later centuries, their resistance simmered, most recently manifested in the Zapatista movement of the 1990s.

Indigenous reactions to European colonizers were diverse, but a common pattern was awe, friendship, interest in trade goods, treaties, acts of resistance or aggression, and ultimate defeat in armed conflict. Some resistance movements have persisted to the present day.

GLOBALIZATION IN THE POSTCOLONIAL ERA

In 1947, India became one of the first large colonized countries to free itself of European control from Great Britain. The independence movement accelerated in the 1950s and 1960s, when many African countries became independent of Great Britain, France, and Belgium. Similar processes occurred in Asia and in the Pacific in the following decades. Indigenous peoples nevertheless seldom obtained equal social, economic, or political rights in their new nations. They often remained marginalized groups under pressure from newly formed central governments to conform to national practices and values. Central authorities justified this pressure in the name of **nationalism,** focusing on the importance of building a common culture to strengthen national unity. In the process of nation building, cultural diversity was often a casualty, as indigenous ways were targeted as backward and obstacles to growth.

Land grabbing did not end with independence. National governments in Peru, Bolivia, Colombia, Venezuela, Brazil, and Chile, for example, changed land policies that had favored Indians' rights and permitted outside interests to exploit native lands and resources. In the United States today, successes in Native American land claims are balanced against the appropriation of resources on those lands, such as oil, uranium, and platinum.

Which nations can be characterized as xenophobic today? Why?

Similar patterns developed in Africa and the Middle East, sometimes contributing tragically to internal competition and intertribal genocide. In **xenophobic** reactions, the governments of newly independent states sought to selectively expel or decimate tribes, ethnic minorities, foreign laborers, merchant elites, or former colonial overlords. Issues over land and resources aggravated these conflicts.

nationalism
Movement in independent states to build national identity, pride, and unity.

xenophobic
Having to do with fear, hatred, and envy of strangers, outsiders, or foreign-born minorities within the society.

postcolonial era
Period (roughly since 1965) following the independence of the last former European colonies as new nations under indigenous leadership and control.

Table 2 summarizes data on indigenous populations in selected countries and the land under their control during the height of the colonial period, prior to 1960.

Colonialism began a process of global transformation in all areas of society and culture, affecting economic systems, social life, political organization, and more. In the **postcolonial era,** processes have continued to integrate national societies throughout the world. Migration of peoples from rural to urban areas within their own countries and migration to foreign lands have contributed to the creation of a very different world than existed in 1500. As people have traveled from one place to another, they have brought with them their cultural practices and beliefs, their languages, and their expectations for a new way of life. They have also brought with them some of the plants and animals native to their home regions. This process, begun on a worldwide scale many centuries ago, has had a global impact on environments and economic systems, as well as on an emerging global culture.

When Christopher Columbus made his second voyage to Hispaniola in 1493, he brought seeds and cuttings for planting wheat, chickpeas, melons, onions, radishes, greens, grapevines, sugarcane, and fruit stones (Crosby 1972, 67). Not all of these plants were successfully grown in that region, but many did prosper. Sugar, in particular, came to dominate the economies of Central and South America, and wheat is grown all over North and South America. According to Crosby, who dubbed this process "the Columbian exchange," many of the European plants and animals that were transplanted to the Americas were brought deliberately, but many seeds also came inadvertently, "in the folds of textiles, in clods of mud, in dung, and in a thousand other ways" (p. 73). Many weeds and grasses that are now common in North America are European in origin, including bluegrass, daisies, and dandelions.

In what other ways can present-day globalization be attributed to European colonialism? In what sense, according to some, is colonialism still going on today?

TABLE 2 AMOUNT OF LAND RESERVED FOR INDIGENOUS POPULATIONS IN DIFFERENT COUNTRIES

	Native Population as Percentage of Total Population	Native Lands as Percentage of Total Area
Bechuanaland	99+	38
Swaziland	98	48
New Guinea	98	97
Zimbabwe	95	33
Botswana/Namibia	87	25
Canada	3	0.2
Chile	2	0.6
United States	0.3	1

Note: These figures are pre-1960. As countries gained independence, native lands as a percentage of total land area rose, by definition, to nearly 100 percent (depending on the amount of foreign-owned land). Most African countries achieved independence with majority rule by 1970. For example, Bechuanaland, a British protectorate, became the independent Republic of Botswana in 1966. Papua New Guinea achieved independence in 1975, but the western part of the island, Irian Jaya, was annexed by Indonesia in 1968. In Canada, the United States, and South America, both native population as a percentage of total population and native lands as a percentage of total land area generally rose, the latter through recent successful land claims.

Source: John Bodley, *Victims of Progress*, 5th ed., p. 107. © 2008. Altamira Press. Reprinted by permission of Rowman & Littlefield.

Indigenous peoples in the Americas gradually adopted European livestock. Sheep and goats were incorporated into the economies of southwestern peoples, who utilized the animals' wool, milk, and meat. Cattle, chickens, and pigs were also kept as sources of food. And horses, originally brought by the Spanish, revolutionized the economies of many native peoples in North America, especially the inhabitants of the Great Plains, who utilized horses as pack animals to carry heavy loads and as mounts to make travel easier, make hunting more efficient and productive, and make warfare more deadly.

In turn, Native American plants have been carried to the other continents as well. Among the most important food crops are maize, beans, peanuts, potatoes, sweet potatoes, manioc (cassava), squashes, pumpkin, papaya, avocado, pineapple, tomato, chili pepper, and cacao (the source of cocoa) (Crosby 1972, 170). Many of these crops, particularly potatoes, maize, manioc, beans, and peanuts, have contributed to population growth in Europe and Africa, as well as in the Americas. Today, some native foods of the Americas are major export crops of other countries. For example, India is one of the world's largest producers of peanuts, and China produces more sweet potatoes than any other country. Peanuts and cocoa are important export crops for countries in West Africa, whereas maize and manioc are critical for domestic consumption there. Finally, national cuisines make us realize the impact that worldwide exploration and exchange have made. For instance, the pasta and tomato sauces so common in Italian recipes are the gifts of China and Mexico. And Mexico has given the gift of chocolate to the entire world!

REVIEW

Since the 1940s, as people gained independence from colonial rulers, nationalism and globalization continued the legacies of colonialism. Newly independent nations evicted foreigners and competed internally for power. Ethnic or tribal minorities were often persecuted, marginalized, or pressured to sacrifice their ways of life. The global economy has transformed production and resource use in the new nations.

ANTHROPOLOGY APPLIED

Establishing the Xingu National Park

In the Amazon, national governments have vacillated between recognizing and guaranteeing indigenous peoples' rights to land and uprooting them to make way for settlement and economic development. In Brazil, constitutions written between 1891 and 1946 respected native peoples' rights to their lands, and some Brazilian states set aside lands under the guardianship of the Indian Protection Service. By 1961, however, settlers and land speculators had reduced the largest of these reserves from 33,000 to 8,500 square miles. At that time, the reserve, later expanded to 11,500 square miles, became the Xingu National Park (Bodley 1999, 83). The Brazilian National Indian Foundation (FUNAI) supposedly protects this park and other native reserves, but Brazilian governments have permitted mining on native lands (Gray 1990).

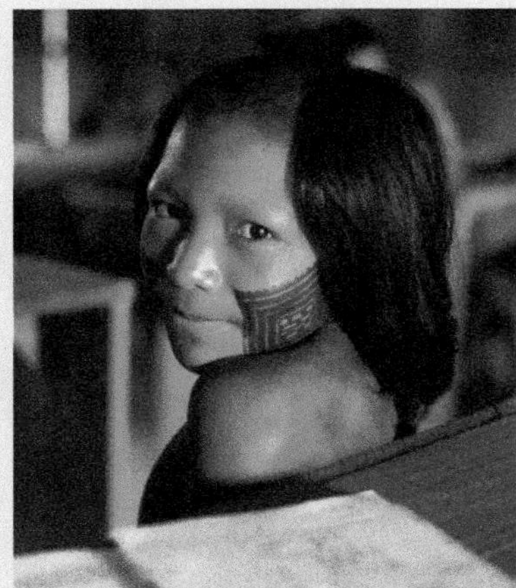
Specialist Stock/GERARD & MARGI MOSS/Still Pictures/Specialist Stock

Alamy Limited/Sue Cunningham/Worldwide Picture Library/Alamy

Anthropologists helped establish the Xingu National Park and work today to protect the people who live there. Ethnographies of the Amazonian people date back to the 1880s and 1930s. In the early 1960s, anthropologists Robert Carneiro and Gertrude Dole supported the efforts of the Brazilian champion of Indians, Claudio Villas-Boas, and his brothers to save the indigenous peoples of the Xingu River valley by creating a preserve. In 1965, only an estimated 542 people remained, but today more than 6,000 people in thirty villages representing seventeen nations live in the Xingu National Park.

CRITICAL THINKING QUESTION

Why do governments decide to protect indigenous peoples or exploit protected lands?

Study and Review on myanthrolab.com

CHAPTER SUMMARY

European Colonialism

- Conquest and colonialism have occurred in many parts of the world as state societies expanded their borders or spheres of influence. In the process, conquerors and colonizers changed the cultures of indigenous peoples. Europeans established colonies, that is, settlements of foreign nationals with controlling interests in indigenous territories, on every continent. These colonies were tied to the home country both politically and economically. The home country governed how colonial subjects behaved and extracted resources.
- There were three major types of colonies: exploitation colonies (resulting from military conquests in which the colonial power exploits economic resources), maritime enclaves (resulting from sea trade and coastal exploration to control trade at foreign ports and territories), and settlement colonies (resulting from military invasion supporting permanent colonial settlement).

The Slave Trade

- The slave trade took West Africans to work on plantations in the Caribbean, South America, and the United States. About 10 million people were taken from Africa by the time the slave trade ended in the nineteenth century.
- The wealth the slaves in the Americas produced enriched their owners and contributed to the accumulation of capital and resources that led to the Industrial Revolution.
- Many African societies had systems of slavery or coerced labor.
- Conditions of slavery in the Americas were likely worse than those in traditional African societies. European colonists typically saw African slaves as racially inferior. They were the property of the masters, who could treat them any way they decided.
- The slave trade changed West African societies. Some African elites were able to centralize their wealth and power, but other African societies fell apart because rival factions competed for war captives who could be sold as slaves.

Trade and Settlement in North America

- In North America, settler colonies relegated indigenous peoples to small portions of their ancestral homelands or to unknown lands.
- European and American settlers benefited from the spread of epidemic diseases such as measles and smallpox. The destruction of resources and military intervention persuaded native leaders to cede most of their land to the U.S. government.
- European powers focused their economic interests in North America on the fur trade. Most native communities participated in the fur trade to procure European manufactured goods.
- Native people could not control the market for furs, which made them vulnerable to changes in demand. They overtrapped their territories and then competed with other indigenous groups. As settlers pushed west, indigenous peoples fled, increasing competition and warfare.

Spanish Colonies in the Americas

- Spanish colonization in the Americas was focused on exploiting resources, especially precious metals, and on establishing plantations that would produce marketable crops, principally sugarcane, in the Caribbean and South America.
- At first, indigenous inhabitants of the regions were compelled to work in mines and on plantations, but African slaves replaced them due to depopulation in some regions. Landholding patterns included encomiendas, haciendas, and mission villages.
- The Spanish intermarried with indigenous peoples, creating a social class of mixed ancestry. This group functioned as intermediaries and as an elite class.

Agents of Directed Culture Change

- Throughout the world, colonial authorities have pressed indigenous peoples to change their cultural practices to be more consistent with European values and behaviors. Missionaries aided in this process by attempting to convert indigenous peoples to Christianity. Schoolteachers inculcated European values and norms. Native children in boarding schools lost touch with their traditional ways, religious beliefs, and languages.
- Colonial administrators imposed Eurocentric patterns of law and social control, disturbing traditional social relationships and ethical values. The introduction of cash economies based on market principles changed economic relationships.

Justifications for Colonial Rule

- Europeans believed that they could take land they conquered simply by their self-declared "right of discovery." Lack of proof of ownership was also a rationale for ignoring indigenous claims to land and resources. Nationalism and imperialism helped to justify colonialism.
- European colonizers claimed a "white man's burden" of cultural, moral, and racial superiority. Europeans believed that they had a "sacred trust" to pacify and civilize the natives.

Indigenous Reactions to European Colonizers

- Some indigenous peoples were awed by European technology and manufactures or believed that Europeans were gods.
- Indigenous communities differed in their attitudes toward Europeans. Many were eager trading partners. Once people realized Europeans wanted to control their lands and lives, however, disagreements often arose.

Globalization in the Postcolonial Era

- Since the 1940s, much of the world has been freed from direct colonial control. Competition for power and authority among tribes or elites has led to violence. Indigenous peoples often remain marginalized in the newly established nations. Nationalism is hard to achieve in culturally diverse societies.
- Indigenous foragers and nomadic pastoralists have been encouraged or compelled to settle permanently in one area and farm or work for wages. Efforts to spread a national language have lessened cultural diversity.

REVIEW QUESTIONS

1. What were European motivations for colonialism and patterns of colonization?
2. How did the European slave trade spread colonialism and undermine African states?
3. How did indigenous peoples of North America become involved in European trading networks? How did that affect their modes of subsistence?
4. How did systems of Spanish landholding and mining affect native peoples?
5. Why was intermarriage between Spaniards and indigenous people encouraged? What role did their descendants have in colonial society?
6. What were the three principal agents of directed culture change, and what impacts did they have on indigenous peoples?
7. How did Europeans justify colonial rule? What are some legacies of colonialism in postcolonial nations today?
8. How did indigenous peoples react to European colonizers?

MyAnthroLab Connections

Watch. Listen. View. Explore. Read. MyAnthroLab is designed just for you. Dynamic visual activities, videos, and readings found in the multimedia library will enhance your learning experience.

Resources from this chapter:

Watch on **myanthrolab.com**
- *Defining Indigenous Peoples*

Listen on **myanthrolab.com**
- *How We Got Here: The British Legacy in Iraq*

View on **myanthrolab.com**
- *World Colonial Empires, 1900*

Explore on **myanthrolab.com** In MySearchLab, enter the Anthropology database to find relevant and recent scholarly and popular press publications. For this chapter, enter the following keywords: imperialism, nationalism, xenophobic, postcolonial era

Read the **Document**
- *Yuqui: Fighting the Odds for Cultural Survival* by Allyn MacLean Stearman
- *Kiowa: An Emergent People* by Nancy P. Hickerson

Do Muslim Women Really Need Saving?

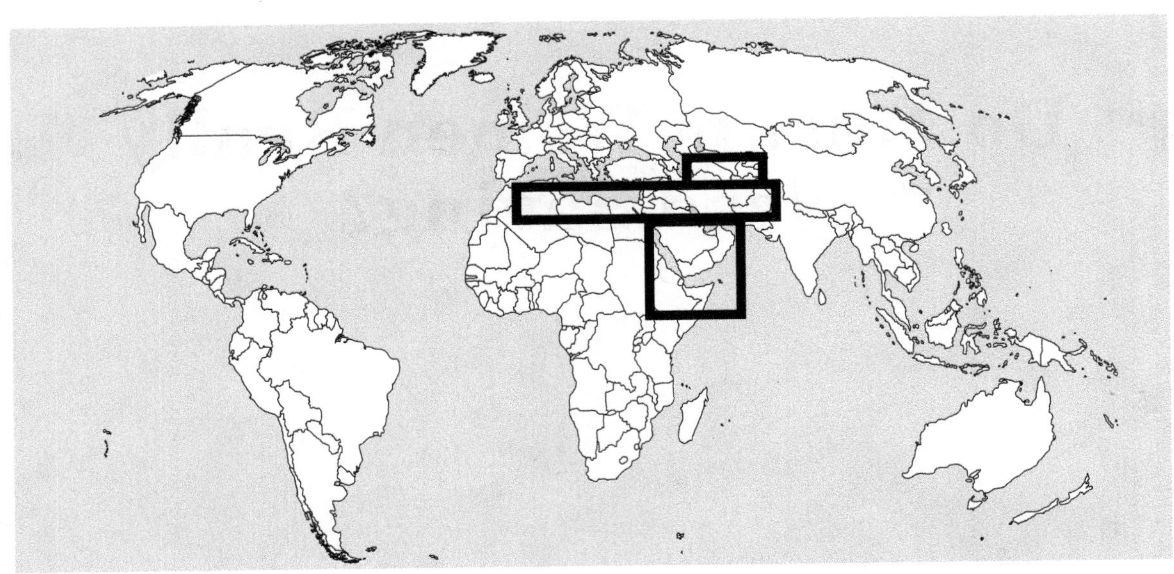

Do Muslim Women Really Need Saving?

Lila Abu-Lughod

Should our government use the "liberation of women" to justify going to war (as Laura Bush suggested in a 2002 speech supporting the war in Afghanistan)? Not in the case of Afghanistan and other Muslim countries argues Lila Abu-Lughod in this article, if by liberation one means freeing women from a culture based on the importance of family and religion. In Afghanistan, as in many Muslim societies, there is a clear separation between the women's world, which is most often focused on the family and household, and the more public role assumed by men. Nothing marks this separation more clearly than women's public dress, which consists of the burqa, an article of clothing that covers women completely from head to toe, or scarves that cover the head but not the face. For Westerners and especially some Western feminists, the burqa has been a symbol of male exploitation and control of women; for most Muslim women, however, these garments signify modesty and the separation of private family-oriented lives from the public realm. Indeed, as Abu-Lughod puts it, the burqa serves as a kind of "mobile home" for women in public spaces, and the Western perspective seems ethnocentric as a result. The meaning of the burqa was complicated in Afghanistan by its extension under Taliban rule to all women living in multi-ethnic Afghanistan, despite its original use only by Pashtuns. For the Taliban, the burqa was a sign of religious piety, not only one that signified public modesty. Although some Afghan women may have adopted its religious meaning, its not surprising that many women, motivated by its usual significance, continued to wear the garment despite liberation by NATO troops. Abu-Lughod concludes that instead of saving

*Afghan women from their own cultural customs and values, Western feminists should concentrate their efforts on helping to bring "justice" to women's lives by preventing war and increasing education and freedom from want. What are the ethics of the current "War on Terrorism," a war that justifies itself by purporting to liberate, or save, Afghan women? Does anthropology have anything to offer in our search for a viable position to take regarding this rationale for war?**

Listen to the **Chapter Audio** on **myanthrolab.com**

I want to point out the minefields—a metaphor that is sadly too apt for a country like Afghanistan, with the world's highest number of mines per capita—of this obsession with the plight of Muslim women. I hope to show some way through them using insights from anthropology, the discipline whose charge has been to understand and manage cultural difference.

The question is why knowing about the "culture" of the region, and particularly its religious beliefs and treatment of women, was more urgent than exploring the history of the development of repressive regimes in the region and the U.S. role in this history. Such cultural framing, it seemed to me, prevented the serious exploration of the roots and nature of human suffering in this part of the world. Instead of political and historical explanations, experts were being asked to give religio-cultural ones. Instead of questions that might lead to the exploration of global interconnections, we were offered ones that worked to artificially divide the world into separate spheres—recreating an imaginative geography of West versus East, us versus Muslims, cultures in which First Ladies give speeches versus others where women shuffle around silently in burqas.

Most pressing for me was why the Muslim woman in general, and the Afghan woman in particular, were so crucial to this cultural mode of explanation, which ignored the complex entanglements in which we are all implicated, in sometimes surprising alignments. Why were these female symbols being mobilized in this "War against Terrorism" in a way they were not in other conflicts? Laura Bush's radio address on November 17 reveals the political work such mobilization accomplishes. On the one hand, her address collapsed important distinctions that should have been maintained. There was a constant slippage between the Taliban and the terrorists, so that they became almost one word—a kind of hyphenated monster identity: the Taliban-and-the-terrorists. Then there was the blurring of the very separate causes in Afghanistan of women's continuing malnutrition, poverty, and ill health, and their more recent exclusion under the Taliban from employment, schooling, and the joys of wearing nail polish. On the other hand, her speech reinforced chasmic divides, primarily between the "civilized people throughout the world" whose hearts break for the women and children of Afghanistan and the Taliban-and-the-terrorists, the cultural monsters who want to, as she put it, "impose their world on the rest of us."

Most revealingly, the speech enlisted women to justify American bombing and intervention in Afghanistan and to make a case for the "War on Terrorism" of which it was allegedly a part. As Laura Bush said, "Because of our recent military gains in much of Afghanistan, women are no longer imprisoned in their homes. They can

*From "Do Muslim Women Really Need Saving? Anthropological Reflections on Cultural Relativism and Its Others," *The American Anthropologist* 104 (2002), no. 3. Reprinted by permission of Wiley-Blackwell Publishing.

listen to music and teach their daughters without fear of punishment. . . . The fight against terrorism is also a fight for the rights and dignity of women."[1]

These words have haunting resonances for anyone who has studied colonial history. Many who have worked on British colonialism in South Asia have noted the use of the woman question in colonial policies where intervention into sati (the practice of widows immolating themselves on their husbands' funeral pyres), child marriage, and other practices was used to justify rule. As Gayatri Chakravorty Spivak has cynically put it: white men saving brown women from brown men. The historical record is full of similar cases, including in the Middle East. In *Turn of the Century Egypt*, what Leila Ahmed has called "colonial feminism" was hard at work. This was a selective concern about the plight of Egyptian women that focused on the veil as a sign of oppression but gave no support to women's education and was professed loudly by the same Englishman, Lord Cromer, who opposed women's suffrage back home.

Sociologist Marnia Lazreg has offered some vivid examples of how French colonialism enlisted women to its cause in Algeria. She describes skits at awards ceremonies at the Muslim Girls' School in Algiers in 1851 and 1852. In the first skit, written by "a French lady from Algiers," two Algerian Arab girls reminisced about their trip to France with words including the following:

> *Oh! Protective France: Oh! Hospitable France! . . .*
> *Noble land, where I felt free*
> *Under Christian skies to pray to our God: . . . .*
> *God bless you for the happiness you bring us!*
> *And you, adoptive mother, who taught us*
> *That we have a share of this world,*
> *We will cherish you forever!*[2]

These girls are made to invoke the gift of a share of this world, a world where freedom reigns under Christian skies. This is not the world the Taliban-and-the-terrorists would "like to impose on the rest of us."

Just as I argued above that we need to be suspicious when neat cultural icons are plastered over messier historical and political narratives, so we need to be wary when Lord Cromer in British-ruled Egypt, French ladies in Algeria, and Laura Bush, all with military troops behind them, claim to be saving or liberating Muslim women.

Politics of the Veil

I want now to look more closely at those Afghan women Laura Bush claimed were "rejoicing" at their liberation by the Americans. This necessitates a discussion of the veil, or the burqa, because it is so central to contemporary concerns about Muslim women. This will set the stage for a discussion of how anthropologists, feminist anthropologists in particular, contend with the problem of difference in a global world.

[1]U.S. Government. 2002. Electronic document, http://www.whitehouse.gov/news/releases/2001/11/20011117. Accessed January 10.

[2]Lazreg, Marnia. 1994. *The Eloquence of Silence: Algerian Women in Question*. New York: Routledge.

In the conclusion, I will return to the rhetoric of saving Muslim women and offer an alternative.

It is common popular knowledge that the ultimate sign of the oppression of Afghan women under the Taliban-and-the-terrorists is that they were forced to wear the burqa. Liberals sometimes confess their surprise that even though Afghanistan has been liberated from the Taliban, women do not seem to be throwing off their burqas. Someone who has worked in Muslim regions must ask why this is so surprising. Did we expect that once "free" from the Taliban they would go "back" to belly shirts and blue jeans, or dust off their Chanel suits? We need to be more sensible about the clothing of "women of cover," and so there is perhaps a need to make some basic points about veiling.

First, it should be recalled that the Taliban did not invent the burqa. It was the local form of covering that Pashtun women in one region wore when they went out. The Pashtun are one of several ethnic groups in Afghanistan and the burqa was one of many forms of covering in the subcontinent and Southwest Asia that has developed as a convention for symbolizing women's modesty or respectability. The burqa, like some other forms of "cover" has, in many settings, marked the symbolic separation of men's and women's spheres, as part of the general association of women with family and home, not with public space where strangers mingled.

Twenty years ago the anthropologist Hanna Papanek, who worked in Pakistan, described the burqa as "portable seclusion." She noted that many saw it as a liberating invention because it enabled women to move out of segregated living spaces while still observing the basic moral requirements of separating and protecting women from unrelated men. Ever since I came across her phrase "portable seclusion," I have thought of these enveloping robes as "mobile homes." Everywhere, such veiling signifies belonging to a particular community and participating in a moral way of life in which families are paramount in the organization of communities and the home is associated with the sanctity of women.

The obvious question that follows is this: If this were the case, why would women suddenly become immodest? Why would they suddenly throw off the markers of their respectability, markers, whether burqas or other forms of cover, which were supposed to assure their protection in the public sphere from the harassment of strange men by symbolically signaling to all that they were still in the inviolable space of their homes, even though moving in the public realm? Especially when these are forms of dress that had become so conventional that most women gave little thought to their meaning.

To draw some analogies, none of them perfect, why are we surprised that Afghan women do not throw off their burqas when we know perfectly well that it would not be appropriate to wear shorts to the opera? At the time these discussions of Afghan women's burqas were raging, a friend of mine was chided by her husband for suggesting she wanted to wear a pantsuit to a fancy wedding: "You know you don't wear pants to a WASP wedding," he reminded her. New Yorkers know that the beautifully coiffed Hasidic women . . . are wearing wigs. This is because religious belief and community standards of propriety require the covering of the hair. They also alter boutique fashions to include high necks and long sleeves. As anthropologists know perfectly well, people wear the appropriate form of dress for their social communities and are guided by socially shared standards, religious beliefs, and moral ideals, unless they deliberately transgress to make a point or are unable to afford proper cover. If we think that U.S. women live in a world of choice regarding clothing, all we need to do is remind ourselves of the expression, "the tyranny of fashion."

What had happened in Afghanistan under the Taliban is that one regional style of covering or veiling, associated with a certain respectable but not elite class, was imposed on everyone as "religiously" appropriate, even though previously there had been many different styles, popular or traditional with different groups and classes—different ways to mark women's propriety, or, in more recent times, religious piety. Although I am not an expert on Afghanistan, I imagine that the majority of women left in Afghanistan by the time the Taliban took control were the rural or less educated, from nonelite families, since they were the only ones who could not emigrate to escape the hardship and violence that has marked Afghanistan's recent history. If liberated from the enforced wearing of burqas, most of these women would choose some other form of modest headcovering, like all those living nearby who were not under the Taliban—their rural Hindu counterparts in the North of India (who cover their heads and veil their faces from affines) or their Muslim sisters in Pakistan.

Even The *New York Times* carried an article about Afghan women refugees in Pakistan that attempted to educate readers about this local variety. The article describes and pictures everything from the now-iconic burqa with the embroidered eyeholes, which a Pashtun woman explains is the proper dress for her community, to large scarves they call chadors, to the new Islamic modest dress that wearers refer to as *hijab*. Those in the new Islamic dress are characteristically students heading for professional careers, especially in medicine, just like their counterparts from Egypt to Malaysia. One wearing the large scarf was a school principal; the other was a poor street vendor. The telling quote from the young street vendor is, "If I did [wear the burqa] the refugees would tease me because the burqa is for 'good women' who stay inside the home."[3] Here you can see the local status associated with the burqa—it is for good respectable women from strong families who are not forced to make a living selling on the street.

The British newspaper *The Guardian* published an interview in January 2002 with Dr. Suheila Siddiqi, a respected surgeon in Afghanistan who holds the rank of lieutenant general in the Afghan medical corps.[4] A woman in her sixties, she comes from an elite family and, like her sisters, was educated. Unlike most women of her class, she chose not to go into exile. She is presented in the article as "the woman who stood up to the Taliban" because she refused to wear the burqa. She had made it a condition of returning to her post as head of a major hospital when the Taliban came begging in 1996, just eight months after firing her along with other women. Siddiqi is described as thin, glamorous, and confident. But further into the article it is noted that her graying bouffant hair is covered in a gauzy veil. This is a reminder that though she refused the burqa, she had no question about wearing the chador or scarf.

Finally, I need to make a crucial point about veiling. Not only are there many forms of covering, which themselves have different meanings in the communities in which they are used, but also veiling itself must not be confused with, or made to stand for, lack of agency. As I have argued in my ethnography of a Bedouin community in Egypt in the late 1970s and 1980s, pulling the black head cloth over the face in front of older respected men is considered a voluntary act by women who are deeply committed to being moral and have a sense of honor tied to family. One of the ways they show their standing is by covering their faces in certain contexts. They decide for whom they feel it is appropriate to veil.

[3]Fremson, Ruth. 2001. Allure Must Be Covered. Individuality Peeks Through. *New York Times*, November 4:14.

[4]Goldenberg, Suzanne. 2002. The Woman Who Stood Up to the Taliban. *The Guardian*, January 24. Electronic document, http://222.guardian.co.uk/afghanistan/story/0,1284,63840.

To take a very different case, the modern Islamic modest dress that many educated women across the Muslim world have taken on since the mid-1970s now both publicly marks piety and can be read as a sign of educated urban sophistication, a sort of modernity. As Saba Mahmoodhas so brilliantly shown in her ethnography of women in the mosque movement in Egypt, this new form of dress is also perceived by many of the women who adopt it as part of a bodily means to cultivate virtue, the outcome of their professed desire to be close to God.[5]

Two points emerge from this fairly basic discussion of the meanings of veiling in the contemporary Muslim world. First, we need to work against the reductive interpretation of veiling as the quintessential sign of women's unfreedom, even if we object to state imposition of this form, as in Iran or with the Taliban. (It must be recalled that the modernizing states of Turkey and Iran had earlier in the century banned veiling and required men, except religious clerics, to adopt Western dress.) What does freedom mean if we accept the fundamental premise that humans are social beings, always raised in certain social and historical contexts and belonging to particular communities that shape their desires and understandings of the world? Is it not a gross violation of women's own understandings of what they are doing to simply denounce the burqa as a medieval imposition? Second, we must take care not to reduce the diverse situations and attitudes of millions of Muslim women to a single item of clothing. Perhaps it is time to give up the Western obsession with the veil and focus on some serious issues with which feminists and others should indeed be concerned.

Ultimately, the significant political-ethical problem the burqa raises is how to deal with cultural "others." How are we to deal with difference without accepting the passivity implied by the cultural relativism for which anthropologists are justly famous—a relativism that says it's their culture and it's not my business to judge or interfere, only to try to understand. Cultural relativism is certainly an improvement on ethnocentrism and the racism, cultural imperialism, and imperiousness that underlie it; the problem is that it is too late not to interfere. The forms of lives we find around the world are already products of long histories of interactions.

We need to look closely at what we are supporting (and what we are not) and to think carefully about why. . . . I do not know how many feminists who felt good about saving Afghan women from the Taliban are also asking for a global redistribution of wealth or contemplating sacrificing their own consumption radically so that African or Afghan women could have some chance of having what I do believe should be a universal human right—the right to freedom from the structural violence of global inequality and from the ravages of war, the everyday rights of having enough to eat, having homes for their families in which to live and thrive, having ways to make decent livings so their children can grow, and having the strength and security to work out, within their communities and with whatever alliances they want, how to live a good life, which might very well include changing the ways those communities are organized.

. . . For that, we need to confront two more big issues. First is the acceptance of the possibility of difference. Can we only free Afghan women to be like us or might we have to recognize that even after "liberation" from the Taliban, they might want different things than we would want for them? What do we do about that? Second,

[5]Mahmood, Saba. 2001. Feminist Theory, Embodiment, and the Docile Agent: Some Reflections on the Egyptian Islamic Revival. *Cultural Anthropology* 16(2): 202–235.

we need to be vigilant about the rhetoric of saving people because of what it implies about our attitudes.

Again, when I talk about accepting difference, I am not implying that we should resign ourselves to being cultural relativists who respect whatever goes on elsewhere as "just their culture." I have already discussed the dangers of "cultural" explanations; "their" cultures are just as much part of history and an interconnected world as ours are. What I am advocating is the hard work involved in recognizing and respecting differences—precisely as products of different histories, as expressions of different circumstances, and as manifestations of differently structured desires. We may want justice for women, but can we accept that there might be different ideas about justice and that different women might want, or choose, different futures from what we envision as best? We must consider that they might be called to personhood, so to speak, in a different language.

Reports from the Bonn peace conference held in late November to discuss the rebuilding of Afghanistan revealed significant differences among the few Afghan women feminists and activists present. RAWA's position was to reject any conciliatory approach to Islamic governance. According to one report I read, most women activists, especially those based in Afghanistan who are aware of the realities on the ground, agreed that Islam had to be the starting point for reform. Fatima Gailani, a U.S.-based advisor to one of the delegations, is quoted as saying, "If I go to Afghanistan today and ask women for votes on the promise to bring them secularism, they are going to tell me to go to hell."

One of the things we have to be most careful about in thinking about Third World feminisms, and feminism in different parts of the Muslim world, is how not to fall into polarizations that place feminism on the side of the West. I have written about the dilemmas faced by Arab feminists when Western feminists initiate campaigns that make them vulnerable to local denunciations by conservatives of various sorts, whether Islamist or nationalist, of being traitors. As some like Afsaneh Najmabadi are now arguing, not only is it wrong to see history simplistically in terms of a putative opposition between Islam and the West (as is happening in the United States now and has happened in parallel in the Muslim world), but it is also strategically dangerous to accept this cultural opposition between Islam and the West, between fundamentalism and feminism, because those many people within Muslim countries who are trying to find alternatives to present injustices, those who might want to refuse the divide and take from different histories and cultures, who do not accept that being feminist means being Western, will be under pressure to choose, just as we are: Are you with us or against us?

My point is to remind us to be aware of differences, respectful of other paths toward social change that might give women better lives. Can there be a liberation that is Islamic? And, beyond this, is liberation even a goal for which all women or people strive? Are emancipation, equality, and rights part of a universal language we must use?

Might other desires be more meaningful for different groups of people? Living in close families? Living in a godly way? Living without war? I have done fieldwork in Egypt over more than 20 years and I cannot think of a single woman I know, from the poorest rural to the most educated cosmopolitan, who has ever expressed envy of U.S. women, women they tend to perceive as bereft of community, vulnerable to sexual violence and social anomie, driven by individual success rather than morality, or strangely disrespectful of God.

Beyond the Rhetoric of Salvation

Let us return, finally, to my title, "Do Muslim Women Need Saving?" The discussion of culture, veiling, and how one can navigate the shoals of cultural difference should put Laura Bush's self-congratulation about the rejoicing of Afghan women liberated by American troops in a different light. It is deeply problematic to construct the Afghan woman as someone in need of saving. When you save someone, you imply that you are saving her from something. You are also saving her to something. What violences are entailed in this transformation, and what presumptions are being made about the superiority of that to which you are saving her? Projects of saving other women depend on and reinforce a sense of superiority by Westerners, a form of arrogance that deserves to be challenged. All one needs to do to appreciate the patronizing quality of the rhetoric of saving women is to imagine using it today in the United States about disadvantaged groups such as African American women or working-class women. We now understand them as suffering from structural violence. We have become politicized about race and class, but not culture.

Could we not leave veils and vocations of saving others behind and instead train our sights on ways to make the world a more just place? The reason respect for difference should not be confused with cultural relativism is that it does not preclude asking how we, living in this privileged and powerful part of the world, might examine our own responsibilities for the situations in which others in distant places have found themselves. We do not stand outside the world, looking out over this sea of poor benighted people, living under the shadow—or veil—of oppressive cultures; we are part of that world. Islamic movements themselves have arisen in a world shaped by the intense engagements of Western powers in Middle Eastern lives.

A more productive approach, it seems to me, is to ask how we might contribute to making the world a more just place. A world not organized around strategic military and economic demands; a place where certain kinds of forces and values that we may still consider important could have an appeal and where there is the peace necessary for discussions, debates, and transformations to occur within communities. We need to ask ourselves what kinds of world conditions we could contribute to making such that popular desires will not be overdetermined by an overwhelming sense of helplessness in the face of forms of global injustice. Where we seek to be active in the affairs of distant places, can we do so in the spirit of support for those within those communities whose goals are to make women's (and men's) lives better? Can we use a more egalitarian language of alliances, coalitions, and solidarity, instead of salvation?

Even RAWA, the now celebrated Revolutionary Association of the Women of Afghanistan, which was so instrumental in bringing to U.S. women's attention the excesses of the Taliban, has opposed the U.S. bombing from the beginning. They do not see in it Afghan women's salvation but increased hardship and loss. They have long called for disarmament and for peacekeeping forces. Spokespersons point out the dangers of confusing governments with people, the Taliban with innocent Afghans who will be most harmed. They consistently remind audiences to take a close look at the ways policies are being organized around oil interests, the arms industry, and the international drug trade. They are not obsessed with the veil, even though they are the most radical feminists working for a secular democratic Afghanistan. Unfortunately, only their messages about the excesses of the Taliban have been heard, even though their criticisms of those in power in Afghanistan have included previous regimes. A first step in hearing their wider message is to break with the language of alien cultures, whether to understand or eliminate them. Missionary work and colonial feminism belong in the past. Our task is to critically explore what we might do to help create a world in which those poor Afghan women, for whom "the hearts of those in the civilized world break," can have safety and decent lives.

Study and **Review** on **myanthrolab.com**

Review Questions

1. What is meant by colonial feminism? Can you think of other examples of changes to local custom promoted by colonial administrations?
2. How did Laura Bush and other U.S. officials use the lives of Afghan women to justify the invasion and bombing of Afghanistan?
3. What is the American perception of the burqa and how does that differ from the way women who wear the garment perceive its meaning? How has the American perception of the burqa influenced policy toward military intervention?
4. What meaning has the Taliban given the burqa and how is that related to the meaning given the garment by Americans?
5. What do the concepts of ethnocentrism and cultural relativism mean? How do they relate to Abu-Lughod's argument?
6. Can Americans find ways of helping Afghan women without "saving them"? What might some of these ways be?

Gender

PREVIEW

- What is the difference between sex and gender?
- How do gender roles and gender relations vary across cultures?
- How does subsistence strategy relate to gender roles and relationships?
- How do gender constraints relate to a culture's ideological system?
- How does male dominance or gender equality affect a society?
- What global factors affect women's participation in the work force?
- How have ideologies affected gender constructs in the industrial and postindustrial eras?

A Benin Bronze Plaque, one of many which decorated the palace of the Obas of Benin, Nigeria. This bronze represents a leopard. This selection is now located in the: Ethnologisches Museum, Staatliche Museen, Berlin, Germany. *Werner Forman/Art Resource, NY*

((•–[Listen to the Chapter Audio on myanthrolab.com

[Read on myanthrolab.com

A man and a woman were once making a hard journey through the bush. The woman had her baby strapped upon her back.... They had nothing to eat with them, and as they traveled on they became very hungry.

Suddenly,...they came upon a herd of bush cows grazing quietly.

The man said to the woman, "You have the power of transforming yourself into whatever you like; change now to a leopard and capture one of the bush cows, that I may have something to eat and not perish." The woman...said, "Do you really mean what you ask, or are you joking?" "I mean it," said the man, for he was very hungry.

The woman untied the baby from her back, and put it upon the ground. Hair began growing upon her neck and body. She dropped her loincloth; a change came over her face. Her hands and feet turned into claws. And, in a few moments, a wild leopard was standing before the man, staring at him with fiery eyes. The poor man was frightened nearly to death and clambered up a tree....When he was nearly to the top, he saw that the poor little baby was almost within the leopard's jaws, but he was so afraid, that he couldn't make himself come down to rescue it.

When the leopard saw that she already had the man...full of terror, she ran away to the flock of cattle to do for him as he had asked her to. Capturing a large young heifer, she dragged it back to the foot of the tree. The man, who was still as far up in its top as he could go,...begged the leopard to transform herself back into a woman.

Slowly, the hair receded, and the claws disappeared, until finally, the woman stood before the man once more. But...he would not come down until he saw her take up her clothes and tie her baby to her back. Then she said to him, "Never ask a woman to do a man's work again."

This narrative of the leopard woman from Liberia shows attitudes about the proper work of women and men and the dangers of violating social norms about gender. This chapter explores the cross-cultural study of gender and gender relations, about which every human society has something to say. People's norms for gender behavior vary widely, yet common patterns exist. These patterns of thought and behavior relate in part to the way people make their living and the ideologies that support those ways.

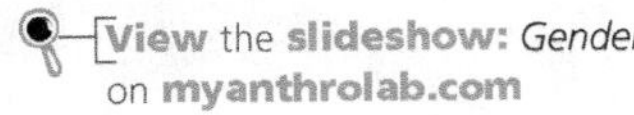
View the slideshow: *Gender* on myanthrolab.com

SEX AND GENDER

As anthropologists use the word, **gender** refers to the roles that people perform in their households and communities and the values and attitudes that people have regarding men and women. Thus, gender is a cultural category. Gender is not the same as **sex,** which is a biological category. That is, females and males are born, but women and men are products of their culture's definitions of how females and males should act.

The term *gender identity* refers to how people internalize and enact those attitudes and expectations that are associated with their gender category. Gender identity is conveyed, for example, by how people dress, walk, and speak. And it is shown by the activities that people engage in and the attitudes they have about themselves and others. The term **gender construct (gender model)** refers to the set of cultural assumptions about gender roles and values and the relations between the genders that people learn as members of their societies. Unlike sex, gender is in every way "culturally constructed." Indeed, gender constructs are deeply ingrained beginning in earliest socialization experiences and become naturalized so that they are taken to be part of a person's "nature" and not usually recognized as culturally derived.

People in every culture maintain and transmit ideas about the roles that are appropriate for women and men to fill, the rights they have in relation to one another, and the values associated with their activities. These gender constructs vary widely across cultures.

gender
The roles that people perform in their households and communities and the values and attitudes that people have regarding men and women.

sex
Biological differences between males and females.

gender construct (gender model)
The set of cultural assumptions about gender roles and values and the relations between the genders that people learn as members of their societies.

In many societies, however, the contrasting activities of men and women are constrained to some degree by the reproductive role that is exclusive to women. For example, engaging in exceptionally arduous physical activities during pregnancy and nursing is dangerous for women and their offspring and might jeopardize the survival of the group.

Evolutionary Perspectives

Anthropologists have sometimes looked to the evolutionary and archaeological records to explore the origins of gendered roles and behaviors. What can we learn about our earliest hominid ancestors? What data can we use to develop models of hominid and human behavior?

Based on DNA evidence, biological anthropologists suggest that the ancestors of humans and nonhuman primates such as chimpanzees and gorillas diverged some 5 or 6 million years ago (Zihlman 1981, 85–86). Complex adaptations deriving from climatic changes in southern and eastern Africa led to species differentiation and the exploitation of distinct ecological zones. Fossil evidence indicates that the hominid ancestors of modern humans (the australopithecines) were established by about 3.5 million years ago. These creatures were small by modern standards but were markedly different from other primates, principally because they could walk upright. Among the critical adaptations they had undergone were changes in the knees, allowing them to lock to support extended legs, the development of arches in the feet to support body weight and shift balance from heel to toe in walking, and repositioning the spine and pelvis to support upright posture.

Gender identity is signaled in many ways, including one's attire and presentation of self. This street scene in Dubai, United Arab Emirates, contrasts the burkhas of Muslim women with an advertisement featuring Britney Spears. Corbis/Steve Raymer/Encyclopedia/Corbis

The skeletal features distinguishing hominid males and females had also evolved. Nonhuman primate species have different degrees of sexual dimorphism. Some species have relatively slight differences in height, weight, and structural features between males and females, whereas these differences are marked in others. A general decline in sexual dimorphism in human evolution was due to the dual factors of decreases in male body size and increases in female stature (Hager 1991, 48). The significant contrasts in the size and shape of the female and male pelvis, a critical factor in human evolution, first appeared about 2 million years ago. This adaptation was interrelated with the enlargement of the brain. As cognitive complexity increased, presumably to process information and solve problems, the brain itself became bigger. This growth eventually posed dangers to pregnant females because their infants' heads would be too large to pass through the pelvic opening without endangering the mother's life. Adaptive changes in the size and positioning of the female pelvis responded to these dangers, allowing for safe births. However, human babies also had to adapt, so that their muscular coordination at birth now is relatively undeveloped compared to that of other mammals and even other primates. They are therefore dependent on adult caregivers for a long time. This dependency had critical consequences for the development of social bonds, especially between mother and child but also with other family and community members.

Although scientists have learned much about the physical structure of early hominids, they know little about how they lived. The first direct evidence of cultural patterns comes from about 2 million years ago with the manufacture and use of stone tools. Although there is controversy about how these earliest tools were used, they are often found along with animal bones (McBrearty and Moniz 1991, 72). Some bones have cut marks made by stone tools, and stone hammers may have been used to smash bones to extract the marrow.

The association of tools and animal bones has led some researchers to emphasize the significance of meat eating and therefore of hunting in the development of human culture. However, it is not clear that early hominids obtained their meat by hunting. Nonhuman primates obtain meat by scavenging as often as by hunting, and presumably so did some early hominid groups; however, the archaeological record supplies no clear evidence that distinguishes hunting from scavenging.

Still, despite a lack of supporting data, anthropologists have theorized that the dietary emphasis on hunting privileged males as the major agents of human cultural advances. Because males are assumed to have been the primary hunters in early hominid groups, they are also assumed to have invented tools and weapons, artifacts considered the hallmarks of humanity, differentiating us from other primates. From these assumptions, early hominid males are represented as using their intelligence and skills to provide food for themselves and others. In contrast, females are represented as passive recipients of meat provided by males and as leading relatively sedentary lives at home bases where they cared for their offspring and for sick or elderly members of the group. In this model, males shaped human culture, supplying women and children with necessary resources (Zihlman 1981, 75).

This "man-the-hunter" model is a modern manifestation of assumptions that first became popular through the works of Charles Darwin in the mid- and late nineteenth century and reflect the cultural practices and attitudes prevalent in Europe at that time. When twentieth-century anthropologists revisited questions of human cultural origins, they again privileged "man the hunter" as the key to human development that differentiates us from other primates. However, it is crucial not to impose contemporary attitudes and constructs on hominid ancestors living hundreds of thousands, if not millions, of years ago. The model of "man the hunter" as the primary actor in human origins and agent of cultural innovation and progress is a projection backward into history and prehistory of contemporary constructs of gender.

Despite their seeming logic, models of "man the hunter" are based on questionable or even faulty assumptions. First, hominid species evolved about 2 million years before evidence of stone tool use. Although it has been suggested that bipedalism (walking on two feet) was an adaptation to the need to see prey animals over tall savanna grasses and to throw simple weapons at them, structural changes allowing bipedalism evolved millennia before stone tools were being made. According to Margaret Ehrenberg (1989, 42), bipedalism more likely developed because early hominid mothers had to carry their infants because the infants were unable to cling to their mothers as earlier primate young had. Infants could not cling because the hominid loss of body hair left the baby nothing to cling to and because changes in the feet did not permit gripping.

In addition, stone tools were not necessarily the first kind of tools that hominids invented. Other types of tools made from plant fibers might have been used at earlier stages of development, but because they disintegrated and have not become part of the fossil or archaeological record, they have therefore not influenced theories about human cultural origins. Indeed, some researchers suggest that the earliest tools were artifacts used to dig for plants because gathering preceded hunting as a strategy for resource exploitation (Ehrenberg 1989, 46). Furthermore, early inventions might have focused on containers and devices to carry infants, young children, and gathered foods. Females probably invented these devices and taught others how to make them because females are the primary caregivers of children in all species of primates.

Moreover, no clear evidence supports assumptions about the importance of meat eating in the diet of early hominids. Early hominid teeth were adapted for an omnivorous diet, and we have no way of knowing the percentages of plants, seeds, and meat they ate (Fedigan 1986, 52). Unlike the connection between meat eating and stone tools, evidence of plants or seeds in the diet would not be preserved because of the impermanence of these foods and of wooden or fiber tools used to process or transport them. Hominid front teeth were smaller and their back teeth larger and flatter than those of nonhuman primates, indicating an adaptation to chewing fibrous foods. And although the canine teeth of nonhuman male primates are typically much larger than those of females, male and female hominids had similar-sized canines, perhaps indicating decreased emphasis on male dominance and aggression.

Furthermore, although there is evidence of the association between stone tools and animal bones, we do not know all of the uses to which early hominids put these tools. The earliest tools have been called "scrapers" or "choppers," but their actual function is unclear. The wear patterns on some of them indicate that they were used for a number of different functions, such as processing meat, plants, and hides, but many may have been used for other purposes (McBrearty and Moniz 1991, 76; Ehrenberg 1989, 46).

The "man-the-hunter" construct emphasizes male dominance behavior. Hominid males and their human descendents are seen as protectors of dependent females and children. However, this too is impossible to verify. Although male dominance is a feature of many, but not all, nonhuman primate groups, its role in human evolution is unknown. Some researchers, especially those in sociobiology, emphasize the importance of dominant males in selecting mates and therefore in transmitting their genes to future generations. Other theorists question the centrality of dominance in mate selection. Zihlman (1981), for example, notes that in most species, the sex investing the greatest amount of energy and time in offspring chooses mates and therefore has the greatest influence on gene flow (1981, 88). Given this observation, what kind of mate would a female favor if she were looking forward to years of caring for dependent children? Zihlman has suggested that such females would select mates who are "sociable" and "willing to share food and protect them and their offspring" (1981, 91). Smuts (2001) cites comparative evidence from nonhuman primate studies indicating that females mate with males who are cooperative and nonaggressive. Data from observations of chimpanzees also find that females do not mate with aggressive males (Ehrenberg 1989, 49). Such evidence leads Ehrenberg to conclude that hominid females probably preferred sociable and friendly males. Furthermore, Lancaster and Whitten (1993) agree that sharing is both a behavior and an attitude that distinguishes human beings from all other primates. Through sharing and cooperation, people forge bonds of mutual interdependence. These ethics are the foundations of human families and community life.

During periods of early human evolution, female roles combined reproduction, food procuring, and social responsibilities. Males also gathered plant foods, at first primarily for themselves, following the primate pattern. Gradually, traits of sharing and cooperation were favored as females selected mates and established pair bonds. As a result, males' emotional investments in their children increased (Zihlman 1981, 93). Indeed, rather than hunting providing the template for human society, hunting patterns may have been built on behaviors developed in gathering and sharing plant resources.

Although we do not know how social roles developed in the evolutionary or prehistoric past, researchers have suggested theories that account for the development of the role of fathers in social interaction with their children. Male involvement with children may have developed from men's hunting and sharing the meat with women and children (Lancaster 1983; Mackey 1985). Other theories emphasize the evolutionary trends toward greater dependency of infants and young children due to larger brain size and the consequent need for birth earlier in the developmental process (Smuts 1985; Hewlett 1991). Hewlett suggests that the critical factor in the evolution of the role of fathers was the kind of male–female relationship that developed early in human evolution. As social bonds among our earliest hominid ancestors (the australopithecines) were strengthened between a male and female pair, associated with ongoing and consistent sexual relations, males formed bonds with offspring, essentially the offspring of the female with whom they mated. Males provided meat and offered protection primarily to their female mate, but their offspring benefited indirectly from the male's investment in the female (Hewlett 1991, 160). Later, transmission of cultural knowledge based on experience became another feature of fathers' involvement with their children.

All of these various theories need to be considered in formulating ideas about the prehistoric past. And in this, caution needs to be used so that we don't project our own ideas onto the lives of people who can't speak for themselves.

The Cultural Construction of Gender Identity

Gender as a social or cultural construct is a primary aspect of one's personal and social identity. It develops in earliest socialization through the ways that a baby is handled, treated, and spoken to. **Cultural constructs** are models of behavior and attitudes that a particular culture transmits to its members. These constructs are shared beliefs and values that become taken for granted as guiding principles. Childhood learning teaches appropriate behavior and molds personality to conform to cultural norms. Girls and boys learn skills and attitudes that make them functioning members of their community. In addition, most (but not all) cultures use two sets of personal names, one appropriate for

cultural constructs
Models of behavior and attitudes that a particular culture transmits to its members.

transvestism
Dressing in the clothes usually worn by members of the opposite gender.

females and one appropriate for males.

Ideological messages about women's and men's places in their families and communities and about their social value may be conveyed through religious beliefs and practices, language, and daily interactions between men and women in their families, communities, and wider social arenas. Rights to make decisions, to speak, and to participate in particular activities reflect cultural valuations and privileges allocated to people. Consider the differences in how English-speaking women and men use language not only to communicate their ideas and feelings but also to transmit their gender identity. For example, studies of conversational practice suggest that women tend to be more polite, deferential, and attentive to others, whereas men tend to be more assertive and interruptive when speaking with others.

One universal expression of gender identity is the signaling of gender differences by bodily adornments and comportment. For example, men and women generally wear different kinds of clothing or jewelry. They may fashion their hair in different styles or use body decorations such as tattoos or makeup. In North American and European countries, pants have only been considered appropriate attire for women since the middle of the twentieth century. Even so, styles, colors, and designs used for women's clothing may differ from those commonly used for men. Moreover, although wearing garments styled like men's pants and shirts may be acceptable for women, wearing dresses and skirts is not at all acceptable for men in most American settings. It was not until 1995 that **transvestism,** or cross-dressing to look and act like someone of the opposite gender, was removed from the official list of mental illnesses.

Other kinds of gender-differentiating behavior are subtler and less conscious but just as powerful. Social presentation includes dynamics of walking, sitting, and general body posture. Speech styles employed by women or men are also often distinct. Nonverbal communication, such as gestures, smiling, eye contact, and touch, may be differentially employed.

Gender and Sexuality

Although we commonly think of sexual feelings and practices as part of our nature, they are also shaped by culture. Our culture teaches us what kinds of sexual feelings and practices are "normal" or "natural" and what kinds are "deviant." We learn who are appropriate sexual partners, when and where sexual relations are appropriate, and the proper ways to engage in sex. With few exceptions, these expectations are culturally constructed.

In this ancient symbol of yin (femaleness) and yang (maleness), the light area represents the greater sunlight of the summer solstice, which is associated with maleness; the dark area represents the greater moonlight of the winter solstice, associated with femaleness. The Image Works/Charles Walker/Topfoto/The Image Works

All societies institute some form of the incest taboo that bans sex between members of the nuclear family and certain other relatives. Many societies also set an appropriate age to begin sexual relations. In the United States, for example, it is illegal for an adult to have sex with someone younger than 16, a crime called statutory rape. This obviously does not mean that no one under the age of 16 has sex, but it does formalize cultural attitudes and criminalize specific behaviors. American society also has gender-based attitudes about the relative ages of men and women engaging in consensual sex. In many "normal" couples, a man may be fifteen or twenty years older than the woman, but it is rare to hear of a couple in which a woman is significantly older than the man. One reason may have to do with reproductive potential. That is, an old man can still have children with a young woman, but a young man cannot have children with a much older woman. Nevertheless, negative attitudes about younger men who choose much older women reveal cultural values about both sex and gender.

Another cultural element in attitudes about sexuality is the accepted relationship between sex and marriage. In American society, public discourse regards sex between unmarried people as inappropriate or less appropriate than sex between a husband and wife. Actual practice contradicts public morality, but the fact that political and religious leaders are reluctant to condone sex outside of marriage indicates the strength of underlying cultural constructs.

In contrast, it is considered normal and natural that unmarried people engage in sex in many other societies. In some societies, proving one's ability to conceive is a prerequisite for marriage. And although no society encourages extramarital sexual activities, the punishment for adulterers varies widely and is not severe everywhere. In addition, patriarchal societies often have double standards about these issues. Men are permitted and even encouraged to have premarital sexual experiences, whereas women are taught to remain chaste before marriage. In some patrilineal societies, a woman's virginity is a prerequisite for marriage, and adultery may be more severely punished if committed by a woman than by a man. In some Islamic countries, adultery is a capital offense for both partners. In others, only the woman is singled out for punishment. In 2003, for example, a divorced Nigerian woman, Amina Lawal, was condemned to death by stoning by an Islamic court for bearing a child out of wedlock; the man, who denied he was the father, received no punishment. However, an appeals court acquitted and released Lawal later that year, in large part because of international pressure.

Gender and Homosexuality

Attitudes about homosexuality are a further reflection of cultural learning. Judeo-Christian-Islamic teachings consider homosexuality a violation of natural law. Many nations dominated politically by religious thinking have laws that criminalize homosexual conduct and institute policies that discriminate against homosexuals. As recently as 1986 in the United States, the U.S. Supreme Court, in *Bowers v. Hardwick,* upheld the right of the state of Georgia to make private sexual relations between consulting adult homosexuals a crime punishable by imprisonment. This ruling was superseded, however, in 2003. Attitudes about homosexuality are continuously debated in many countries, most recently over gay marriage and gay people in the ministry. In 2003, the Episcopal Church installed an openly gay priest, Gene Robinson, as bishop of New Hampshire, setting off a controversy that led to Anglican dioceses in Africa and Latin America threatening to break from the central Church in Britain.

Listen to the **Audio:** *The Connection between Gender Roles and Sex* on **myanthrolab.com**

Antihomosexual attitudes are far from universal. In India, for example, Hindu belief regards homosexuality as one of the possible expressions of human desire. Mythic stories portray both heterosexual and homosexual experience as natural and joyful. In addition, the pantheon of Hindu deities includes some who are sexually ambiguous, combining aspects of maleness and femaleness, or who transform themselves from one gender into the other. Finally, some Indian male homosexuals and transvestites adopt the role of *hijras,* people thought of as "neither man nor woman" (Nanda 1990). Although *hijras* are sometimes feared and ridiculed, they are also considered sacred, combining and mediating between female and male aspects believed to exist in all humans.

Why do you think that third gender roles such as the *hijras* exist?

As another example, the Etoro and several other horticultural societies in New Guinea insist on male homosexual activity to ensure a man's physical growth and enhance his physical and spiritual strength. According to Etoro beliefs, people have a kind of spirit essence called *hame* that is needed to develop and maintain one's energy and vitality. At birth, only a small amount of *hame* is placed in a child, not enough to protect it for a long, healthy life. So, as people mature, they must try to augment their store of *hame* or life force. They must also protect it from potential sources of depletion, and one of the major causes of depletion is heterosexual intercourse. Men protect themselves from depleting their *hame* by avoiding sexual intercourse with women during periods associated with farming and trading cycles, estimated by anthropologist Raymond Kelly (1976) to amount to between 205 and 260 days per year. Protection against depletion is not enough, however, because the Etoro also believe that boys lack semen, which contains *hame.* Youths can acquire *hame* only by receiving semen from adult men. Boys orally consume a man's semen after manipulating his penis to the point of ejaculation.

In contrast to men, women are thought (at least by men) to have a limited amount of *hame,* thus explaining their relative weakness compared to men. Kelly did not collect women's beliefs about *hame,* however, because "a male anthropologist cannot develop an informant relationship with a female" (p. 47). Although Etoro men claimed that "only the women know what the women do," they believe that women engage in some form of homosexual activity through which adult women may transmit menstrual blood to young girls to initiate their reproductive capacity.

CASE STUDY

Two-Spirits: A Third Gender

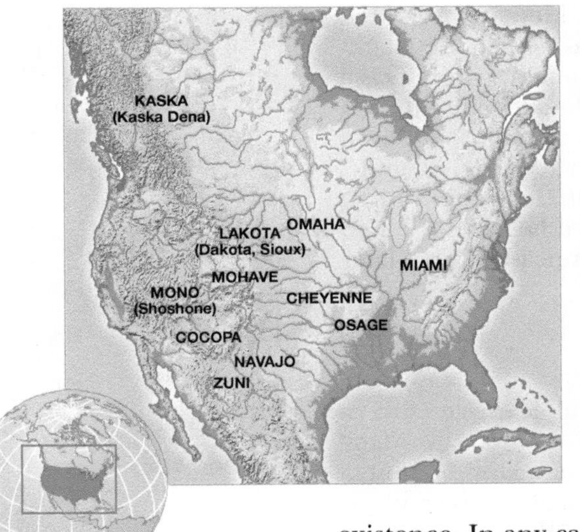

Although the division of humans into two gender categories is the most common cultural pattern, other possibilities exist. For example, many native cultures in North America recognized a third gender category. The concept of a third gender was based on separating the social being (the gender category) from the biological body (the facts of sex). The third gender was a social concept that included biological males and females who assumed social roles other than (or sometimes in addition to) the roles usually associated with their sex. This third gender was a distinct gender category, different from woman and man. Western observers formerly misused the term **berdaches** to refer to third-gender individuals in a derogatory way.

According to documentary evidence reviewed by Charles Callender and Lee Kochems (1983), 113 native North American societies provided a third gender status as a possibility for their members. Lack of mention of third genders, now often called **Two-Spirits,** in other cultures does not necessarily mean that they were absent. Rather, Euro-American observers may not have noted their existence. In any case, third genders were well established in most of North America. Callender and Kochems find no correlation between types of social or economic systems and the ability of individuals to choose a third gender, except that Two-Spirits were least likely in societies that relied heavily on hunting.

People became Two-Spirits as a result of personal inclination, spiritual calling, or parental selection. A young girl or boy might take an interest in the occupations and demeanors usually displayed by people of the opposite gender. Parents thereafter trained the child in the subsistence skills appropriate to the child's chosen role. Among some groups, parents who had no sons might choose a daughter to learn hunting skills as a son would.

A more common mode of recruitment was to receive a spiritual calling through a vision or dream. Dreaming to assume the third gender gave both spiritual and social validation to a male's or female's gender transformation. Two-Spirits who came to their status through a spiritual calling were often thought to have extraordinary powers to heal and to foretell the future.

A Two-Spirits' social role was formally validated with rituals that publicly marked their special status. Among the Kaska of Yukon Territory, the parents of a female Two-Spirit tied a bear's dried ovaries to her belt to protect her from becoming pregnant when she reached the age of 5. At puberty, female Two-Spirits of the Cocopa had their noses pierced like men rather than tattoos on their chins like women. Among the Mohave, a male Two-Spirit participated in a public ceremony in which he was led into a circle surrounded by an audience and a singer when he was about 10 years old. When the singer sang initiation songs, the Two-Spirit danced as women did and was proclaimed an *aylha* (Two-Spirit) after the fourth dance. The Two-Spirit was then ritually bathed, given a woman's skirt, and announced a new woman's name.

Two-Spirits typically performed economic duties usually appropriate to the opposite sex, sometimes in addition to those associated with their biological sex. Female Two-Spirits were hunters and trappers. Male Two-Spirits worked as farmers (where economies included horticulture) and were trained in domestic skills, such as sewing, embroidery, and cooking.

Although male Two-Spirits generally did not participate in warfare, they joined war parties in some societies, either as fighters or carriers of supplies. Among the Cheyenne, they accompanied war expeditions, serving as healers of the wounded and guardians of scalps obtained in battle. They also had charge of the Scalp Dances that followed raids. Some female Two-Spirits became famous for their military skills.

Two-Spirits were often more prosperous than other members of their community. Their ability to perform both women's and men's work gave them economic advantages. In some societies, Two-Spirits had unique sources of income because they performed ritual functions specifically assigned to them. For example, Lakota Two-Spirits received horses in return for bestowing secret, spiritually powerful names on children. In several

berdaches
Male Two-Spirits in some Native American societies who adopted some of the economic and social roles of women.

Two-Spirits
In Native American societies, males who adopted some of the social and economic roles of women, and females who adopted some of the social and economic roles of men.

California groups, Two-Spirits were responsible for burial and mourning rituals. In societies such as the Diné, Cheyenne, and Omaha, they were often paid for resolving conflicts between spouses or arranging liaisons and marriages (Williams 1986, 70–71).

One of the consistent features of third-gender tradition was that members wore clothing and hairstyles associated with their chosen social role rather than with their biological sex. This demonstrates that gender distinctions are given both symbolic and practical value. In a literal as well as figurative sense, people wear the markings of the gender with which they are associated. Some Two-Spirits changed their clothing to reflect the gender identity of the work. For instance, Western Mono Two-Spirits wore men's clothing when hunting and women's dress when gathering, and male Osage and Miami Two-Spirits wore men's clothing when they joined war expeditions but dressed like women when they returned home. Deceased male Zuni Two-Spirits were buried in women's dress and men's trousers (Williams 1986, 454).

This drawing from the 1800s shows Sac and Fox warriors competing to attract the attention of a male Two-Spirit. (Smithsonian American Art Museum, Washington, DC/Art Resource, NY) Art Resource, Inc./Smithsonian American Art Museum, Washington, DC/Art Resource, NY

The social and sexual lives of Two-Spirits were consistent with their gender roles. Sexual activity and marriage usually involved relationships with members of the opposite social gender. That is, female Two-Spirits had sexual relations with and might marry women, and male Two-Spirits had sexual relations with and might marry men. Two-Spirits were often highly desired mates because of their prosperity, productive skills, and spiritual knowledge. According to recorded accounts, they had little difficulty marrying and establishing successful households. The wives of female Two-Spirits sometimes had children fathered by men but claimed by the Two-Spirit husband in an expression of social fatherhood. In some societies, Two-Spirits might marry either men or women. Significantly, Two-Spirits never married other Two-Spirits because two people with the same social gender could not marry.

Native Americans did not view sexual relations between Two-Spirits and their mates as either homosexual or heterosexual because Two-Spirits were not men or women. They were a distinct third gender. Symbolic transformation made gender, not biological sex, the important factor. Two-Spirits' sexual activity, like all their behavior, was seen as private and specific to them as members of a distinct third gender. Native American worldview extended this privacy to all sexual activity, including homosexuality and heterosexuality.

Gender equality is a prerequisite for the respect and high status conferred on Two-Spirits because it meant that neither males nor females gave up or acquired social prestige by abandoning roles usually associated with their sex and instead assuming other roles. Euro-American observers did not understand this underlying gender equality, however. They could not understand why males chose not to identify as men, interpreting this choice as a voluntary decline in status. In contrast to Euro-American values, males in most Native American societies did not give up dominance by abandoning men's roles because men's roles did not include rights to dominate. Most examples of men's dominance over women occurred in native societies that contact with European and American traders, officials, and missionaries had already transformed.

By the late nineteenth and early twentieth centuries, the number of Two-Spirits declined due to voluntary or forced adoption of Euro-American attitudes and practices. These insisted on only a two-category system of gender, denigrated males who dressed like women or assumed women's roles, and proclaimed homosexuality to be a violation of natural and divine laws. Agents of the U.S. and Canadian governments who supervised native reservations tried to force male Two-Spirits to wear men's clothing and short hair. The following are the words of a Lakota religious leader speaking of events that occurred in the 1920s:

> When the people began to be influenced by the missions and the boarding schools, a lot of them forgot the traditional ways and the traditional medicine. Then they began to look down on the *winkte,* Two-Spirits, and lose respect. Some changed their ways and put on men's clothing. But others, rather than change, went out and hanged themselves. (quoted in Williams 1986, 182)

Female Two-Spirits were also forced to abandon their social and sacred roles. Despite decades of concerted social and ideological pressures, however, Two-Spirits continue to exist in some Native American societies. Indeed, with the growing cultural acceptance in North America about nontraditional lifestyles and about flexibility in gender roles, Native American Two-Spirits are more and more willing to assert their identities publicly and to seek support from one another and from their relatives and community members. There are now regional and national get-togethers so that people can share their experiences and seek solidarity.

REVIEW

Gender, cultural constructs that refer to the roles people perform in their households and communities, differs from sex, which is a biological category. Gender identity is expressed in clothing, makeup, personal names, speech, nonverbal communication, economic roles, and how people are enculturated into appropriate behaviors for men and women. Attitudes and practices concerning homosexual and heterosexual sexual behavior are also culturally constructed. Gender constructs also include third gender roles, such as Two-Spirits and berdaches, people who are biologically male or female but take on the cultural and economic roles of the opposite gender.

GENDER ROLES AND RELATIONS

In all societies, certain behaviors and activities are deemed appropriate for women and others for men, with some overlap for both genders. Constellations of behaviors that are culturally associated with each gender are referred to as **gender roles.** Gender roles include the kind of work typically assigned to men and women, the familial roles that people play, the positions of leadership at home or in the community, and the ritual practices in which they engage. In some societies, women's and men's roles may be quite distinct with little overlap, whereas gender roles may be flexible in other societies.

Read the **Document** *Yap: Changing Roles of Men and Women* on **myanthrolab.com**

Men and women carry out their gender roles in relation to one another, interacting in their households and their communities in nearly every aspect of life. Even in activities in which women and men are separated from each other, same-gender groups usually act in a way that is mindful of the other group. Coming-of-age rituals for girls and boys, for example, may be organized around gender differences.

Gender relations consist of interactions between men and women, which may reflect differences in the relative status, prestige, and power of women and men. In some societies, gender equality generally prevails. Women and men are thought of as equal, having the same rights to respect, autonomy, and independence. Although men and women may have different roles in their households and communities, their work and activities are equally valued and socially rewarded. In other societies, the genders are not considered equal, and some degree of male dominance prevails. Men are thought of as superior to women, as more capable, intelligent, or spiritually endowed. Men occupy more prestigious roles in their societies as leaders and decision makers. In their homes, men may have control over the activities of their wives. Extreme forms of male dominance may be reflected in physical abuse and rape. These behaviors tend to be more acceptable in strongly patriarchal societies, where men hold positions of authority and power to the exclusion of women. There are no known examples of matriarchal societies in which women have exclusive power.

gender roles
Constellations of rights, duties, attitudes, and behaviors that are culturally associated with each gender.

gender relations
Norms of interaction between men and women, which may reflect differences in the relative status, prestige, and power of women and men.

Division of Labor by Gender

Some form of division of labor by gender influences the range of daily work that an individual carries out in all societies. Men's and women's work is often complementary, both contributing to the maintenance of their households by providing food, shelter, clothing, and necessary equipment. There is a great deal of cross-cultural variation in the allocation of work according to gender, but certain patterns tend to be found in most societies. Table 1 summarizes some of these frequent associations between tasks and gender.

TABLE 1 TASKS AND GENDER	
Tasks Usually Performed by Women	**Tasks Usually Performed by Men**
Gathering plants, seeds, fruits, nuts	Hunting animals
Caring for children	Fishing as a primary responsibility
Caring for the sick and elderly	Herding large animals
Keeping up dwellings	Clearing fields for planting
Making clothing	Conducting warfare
	Conducting long-distance trade
Variable Gender Assignment or Cooperative Tasks	
Hunting small animals	Making crafts: pottery, basketry, tools
Fishing as a secondary resource	Building houses
Herding small animals	Conducting local trade
Planting/harvesting crops	

Inferences about division of labor by gender can be made from data concerning nonhuman primate behavior and traditional foraging societies whose cultural patterns are well documented. Such data led Lila Leibowitz to postulate that a division of labor was not necessary when human ancestors engaged in "unspecified and undifferentiated" production (1983, 123). Our early hominid ancestors, like modern nonhuman primates (chimpanzees and gorillas, for example), spent their days in the same pursuits. They moved from one resource site to another, gathered and ate fruits and plants, and socialized together. Male and female tasks were not differentiated except for childbearing, nursing, and caring for the young, all obviously female responsibilities. However, at some point in our ancestral past, a division of labor developed when people began to engage in more specialized economic techniques, requiring more complex skills and learning. A division of labor was efficient because it allowed different people to learn different sets of skills, enabling them to specialize, refine, and deepen their knowledge and proficiency.

A division of labor based on gender contributed to coordinating a group's activities, due to the fact that women were restricted in their mobility because of their reproductive roles. That is, unlike other mammals whose young are able to walk and feed themselves fairly soon after birth, human infants remain dependent on adults for a protracted period of many years. As a consequence, caregivers are limited in their own activities. Pregnancy, childbearing, and nursing limit women's ability to travel during significant periods of their lives. Travel becomes more burdensome and also more dangerous to a mother's and child's survival. In almost all cultures, women are allotted the care of infants and young children. Presumably as an extension of these duties, women generally perform other caretaker activities, such as preparing family meals and caring for the sick, disabled, or aged individuals within the household.

The division of labor based on gender is also an efficient allocation of human resources and energy in cultures where different kinds of labor require different outputs of energy and strength. Furthermore, it is efficient to teach people skills they are going to use during most of their lives. Skills needed to recognize and utilize edible plants, roots, herbs, and fruits or to track, locate, and kill animals require many years of careful instruction and practice. Therefore, specialization by gender and other factors such as age is efficient and provides for the survival of all.

Women in foraging societies gather wild plants, fruits, and nuts and may also hunt small animals. In contrast, hunting and trading, which may require one to be absent from the home settlement for days, are typically the work of men. Anthropologists extrapolate from these data to make assumptions about the lives of prehistoric peoples.

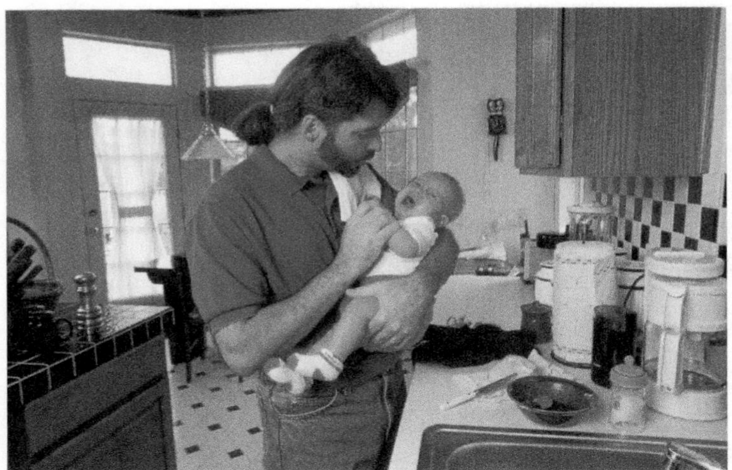

What socioeconomic and sociocultural changes in the United States permitted the changes in gender roles that this photograph represents?
The Image Works/Bob Daemmrich/The Image Works

In addition to considerations of energy and mobility, foraging societies may assign home-based activities to women and external hunting and traveling to men because of the need to protect women against possibilities of accidents and deaths that might occur away from local settlements (Friedl 1975, 135). Because the survival and continuity of a community depend on the successful reproductive life of women, protecting them from unnecessary danger is adaptive. At the same time, cooperative labor may include both men and women within a community. For example, communal hunting and farming might involve adults and youths of both genders.

In addition, gender roles change as economic and material factors change (for example, when foragers become agriculturalists). Cultural forms arise in specific conditions and are changeable when those conditions no longer obtain. Although gender roles may have arisen because women and men have different reproductive functions and different energy and mobility requirements, the adaptive basis of earlier division of labor by gender is lost when productive work is historically transformed and can be performed equally well by women or men. However, more than economic and material factors are involved. For example, in modern industrial societies, most jobs can be accomplished equally well by women or men, but many jobs are held predominantly by one gender or the other. Men or women equally could be brain surgeons or typists, but most brain surgeons are men and most typists are women. Therefore, we need to explain gender roles in noneconomic terms as well.

One explanation is the social organization of households. All societies structure households on the basis of families, regardless of family composition and household organization. Economic cooperation helps sustain family units because members perform different kinds of work that complement each other's tasks, becoming interdependent in providing basic necessities. Households are established and maintain stability on this basis, so the gender division of labor remains a convenient method of organizing household production even when it is no longer an economic necessity.

Another explanation is that attitudes about work and its association with gender are part of the background ideologies that members of a society take for granted. These beliefs and attitudes are naturalized and thought of as human nature rather than understood as endowments of one's culture. Ideological processes, then, contribute to the maintenance of a gender division of labor, regardless of economic or other considerations.

One aspect of these ideologies is the evaluation of some work roles as inherently more attractive or fitting for men and others as inherently more appropriate and appealing to women. For example, women are thought to make good nurses because they have an innate desire to be nurturing. They also make good elementary school teachers because they like to work with children, an extension of their motherly roles. Men, in contrast, are thought to make good leaders and heads of corporations because they are innately assertive and like to be in control. Nurturance and dominance, however, are learned behaviors. Nevertheless, positive judgments become associated with the proper performance of one's gender roles, whereas people who resist assuming their culturally prescribed gender identities are viewed negatively.

Gender and Status

Gender roles are complicated by the fact that work and other tasks assigned to men and women may not be considered equivalent or equally valuable. In theory, gender relations may be characterized on a continuum from approximate equality to the complete domination of members of one gender by members of the other. In practice, whenever there is gender domination, as in strongly patriarchal societies, it is always the domination of women by men.

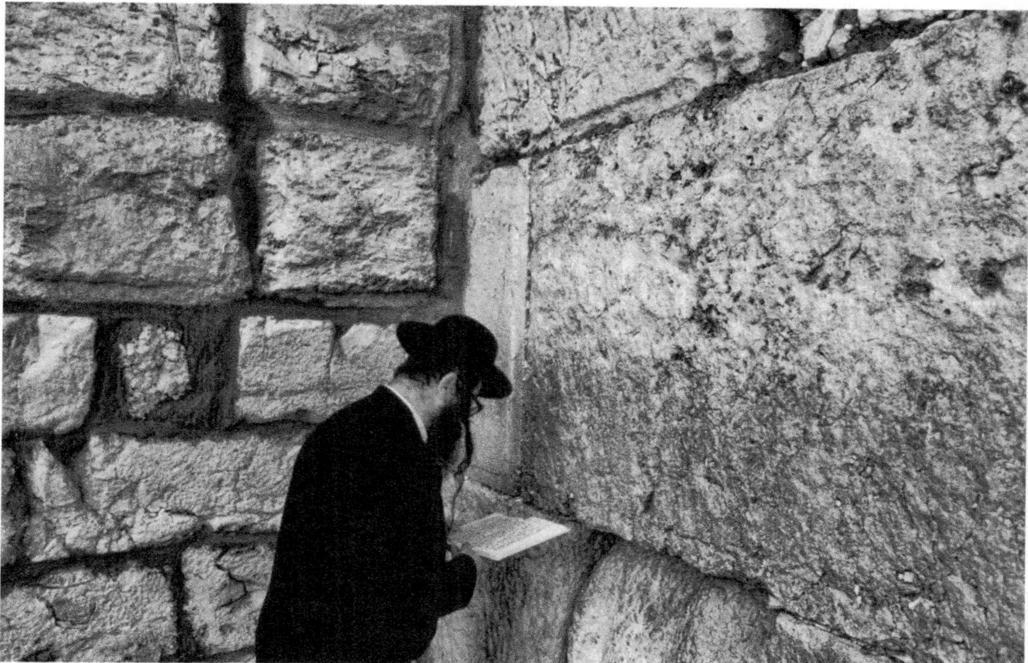

This Orthodox Jewish man is praying at the Wailing Wall in Jerusalem. Women are not permitted to pray at the same section of the wall as men. Alamy Limited/Bill Bachmann/Alamy

Gender equality refers to a constellation of behaviors, attitudes, and rights that support the autonomy of both women and men. In a gender-equal society, women and men may have different economic, social, and political roles but the rewards given to them are roughly similar. For example, in Mohawk communities, women did most of the farmwork and household tasks while men hunted, fished, and traded. Although their activities were distinct, their work and contributions to their households were equally valued. Both men and women could hold positions of prestige and influence in their communities. Gender equality is more likely to exist in foraging and horticultural societies, where all individuals make important contributions to subsistence and where hierarchical leadership is absent or minimal.

In contrast, **gender inequality** refers to denial of autonomy and equal rights to one group of people based on their gender. Gender inequality tends to be most marked in societies with strong economic specialization, where social and political stratification affects the allocation of rights and privileges among social categories, including class and gender. In patriarchal societies, such as in India, Pakistan, and many Middle Eastern countries, women generally do not occupy positions of authority and are restricted in many of their daily activities. In these and other male-dominated societies, men contribute most of the productive labor that supports their families. They make most of the important decisions that affect their families, and they serve their communities as political or religious leaders.

How does a religion with which you are familiar define the status and roles of women and men?

Cultural values and social rewards mold people's attitudes about themselves and their relations to others. In societies where **male dominance** is pervasive, men learn to disvalue women and to assume rights to control women's activity. Women in these cultures learn to disvalue themselves and accept male domination. These gender models are often conveyed nonconsciously and go unquestioned. They are automatically accepted and followed and thus are strengthened in the society.

In all societies, ideological constructs support and perpetuate existing ways of living. For example, religion often provides explanations and justifications for existing social relations. Religious beliefs sanction the status and roles of women and men, explaining divine origins for personal freedoms or restrictions, for differences in the prestige or power of men and women, and for the rights and obligations that they have. Myths of creation may give greater or lesser prominence to male or female deities, justifying the social value of human women and men (Sanday 1981). For example, religious practice affects gender by allowing or restricting the ability of men and women to perform rituals. Barring women from sacred roles limits their status and prestige.

gender equality
A constellation of behaviors, attitudes, and rights that support the autonomy of both women and men.

gender inequality
The denial of autonomy and equal rights to one group of people based on their gender.

male dominance
A constellation of behaviors and attitudes that grant men access to roles of prestige and reward and deny the same to women.

CONTROVERSIES

Is Male Dominance Universal?

Anthropologists long maintained that, in all societies, the status of women was at least to some extent subordinate to that of men (Friedl 1975, 7; Rosaldo 1974, 17). In other words, although women's status varied from society to society, in no society were they fully equal to men. But are there (or were there) genuinely equal or superior to egalitarian societies? From the data, it seems that the answer is *yes*. But this is a complex issue, for several reasons. One is that there has been a long history of Western male bias in reporting behavior and beliefs in non-Western cultures (Leacock 1981, 17; Rohrlich-Leavitt, Sykes, and Weatherford 1975, 110–11). Explorers, missionaries, soldiers, and travelers in European colonization of the Americas, Africa, Asia, and the Pacific were almost exclusively men, who interpreted the cultures of native peoples through their own ethnocentric worldviews.

Later observers, including anthropologists, economists, and historians, were also predominantly men. Notwithstanding their supposed objectivity, they brought with them, as all people do, biases and frames of reference dominant in their own cultures. They usually asked for the opinions of men, partly because interacting with women was difficult for a foreign man, but also partly because male investigators considered men's opinions to be more significant than those of women. As Joseph Lafitau, a French observer of Native American cultures, commented in 1974, "authors who have written on the customs of the Native Americans concerning the rights and status of women have formed their conceptions, in this as in everything else, on European ideas and practices" (1974, 344).

Colonial contact also often swiftly and dramatically altered traditional gender relations by transforming indigenous cultures (Leacock 1981; Etienne and Leacock 1980; Gailey 1987; Wolf 1982). Emphases on external trade rather than household production and consumption undermined women's contributions and enhanced male control over resources. As a result, the allocation of productive roles changed.

Rapid realignments of indigenous political formations to meet colonizers' demands often accompanied changes in production. Among the Iroquois, for example, British, French, and American officials dealt only with male chiefs, ignoring the authority and opinions of women. However, among the Iroquois, female heads of matrilineal clans chose men of their group as leaders and appointed spokespersons to voice their opinions in council meetings.

Also, in Africa, the European colonizers bypassed female chiefs and warriors in favor of male leaders. Among the Igbo of Nigeria, for example, villages traditionally had a male leader for men and a female leader for women, but British officials undermined the power of the female leaders. Changes in political organization following European colonization usually enhanced the public prestige of men and increased their control over their localities and families.

CRITICAL THINKING QUESTIONS

How could changes in gender relations caused by colonialism be interpreted as proof of the theory of universal male dominance? Why would that interpretation be wrong?

Even in societies that restrict women's public participation, however, women nevertheless have some power and informally control much of what happens in their households. Women's lives are sometimes described as focused on the "domestic sphere" and men's lives as taking place in the "public sphere." This distinction may be fitting for some societies, especially agrarian or industrial states where labor tasks are highly specialized and gender roles are rigidly defined. But the distinction loses its value when applied to foraging or horticultural societies (Lamphere 2001). In these societies, there is little differentiation between a public and private domain. Most activities take place communally, often out in the open or indoors in dwellings inhabited by multiple family groups. Much work requires the cooperative efforts of men and women. Although these societies certainly have gender distinctions as well, a demarcation of domains is generally less rigid.

Women are sometimes able to exert influence, even in the most rigidly segregated communities, through direct personal religious experiences. In Ethiopia, for example, women may be possessed by spirits known as *zars*, whose presence is manifested through ecstasy and out-of-body experiences. Women who are possessed by spirits must attend a communal ceremony in the company of other afflicted individuals. At these rituals, held regularly about once every month, healers cure the women in an atmosphere of festivity and abandon (Boddy 2001). In addition to the ritual functions of *zar* beliefs, afflicted women have the opportunity to socialize together away from the control and supervision of their fathers or husbands. *Zar* spirits may possess any individual, but their most frequent targets are married women. It has been hypothesized that, in the context of a male-dominated society, *zar* beliefs and practices provide married women with an outlet for frustrations, a release from restrictions imposed upon them, and an escape from household responsibilities (Lewis 1989).

In societies with gender equality, men and women are equally able to occupy positions of prestige and authority in their communities. Both contribute to making decisions that affect themselves and their families, and their rights to act independently and autonomously are equally respected. Gender equality does not necessarily mean that women and men do the same kinds of work or have the same social roles and responsibilities but that their contributions are equally valued. In addition, attitudes about males and females reflect positive evaluations. In family and personal life, women and men have the same opportunities and rights. Attitudes toward male and female sexuality are comparable. If premarital sex is permitted for men, it is permitted for women as well. If men can initiate divorce, women may also end their unhappy marriages.

Beginning in the fifteenth century, European explorers and colonizers directly and indirectly altered the gender roles, status, and relations of people in the societies with which they came into contact. Europeans imposed their own cultural beliefs and attitudes on those peoples, devaluing women and regarding men as dominant.

Although the status of men is generally secure in most societies, the status of women varies greatly across cultures. Anthropologists attempt to explain this variability by drawing attention to economic, structural, and ideological factors. A basic feature of society and influence on gender status is the productive contribution that women and men make to their household and community economies. Ownership or control over resources interrelates with participation in economic production. As well, risk taking in hunting and warfare further influences the relative status of men and women.

Would you say that gender equality exists in the United States? How would you defend your answer?

In general, women's status is higher in societies where their labor contributes the major share of food that their families consume. For example, among foragers such as the Ju/'hoansi of Namibia and Botswana, the plants, roots, and nuts that women gather make up about 70 percent of the people's yearly caloric intake (Lee 2003). Significantly, women's social rights are also respected and their independence is secure. In contrast, in foraging societies such as the Inuit of the Alaskan and Canadian Arctic, where the percentage of food obtained by women's direct labor is relatively low, women's status is correspondingly lower.

In farming societies, a generally consistent relationship can be seen between the amount of farmwork that women do and their social and political rights. For example, among the northeastern Iroquois, women's labor (planting and harvesting crops) supplied most of the food that people ate, supplemented by meat and fish that the men brought in. In addition to their direct labor, women controlled the allocation of land through the matrilineages that they headed. They also controlled the distribution of food to families within their kinship groups. All these responsibilities in production and distribution gave women a secure basis for their high social status. In contrast, among the farming and hunting peoples of the Amazon region in South America, women's relatively low status can be understood partly as consistent with their minor roles in obtaining food, as men do most of the planting, hunting, and fishing.

Historical evidence shows that when relations of production are transformed in a way that limits women's participation, then women's social and political rights become restricted and their social value declines. Recall that patterns of postmarital residence also play a role in women's security and independence. Matrilocal societies provide women with continued emotional support from their kin, whereas patrilocal residence patterns remove women from their kin groups and the support they can provide when conflicts arise. In addition, social and political complexity and the patterns of community leadership also affect gender status.

The degree and type of warfare in a region also influence gender constructs. Success in warfare usually confers social prestige on men. However, men's ability to translate their military achievements into control over women in their communities is in part related to the frequency of warfare and to characteristics of warfare. Where warfare is frequent and directed against distant enemies, warriors are absent from home for long periods of time and are less able to dominate the households they leave behind. Women in these societies have higher status. Warfare directed against nearby settlements, however, creates conditions in which warriors can extend their military dominance to other aspects of social life, including gender dominance. Furthermore, frequent internal warfare endangers noncombatants, affirming men's roles as defenders and protectors.

REVIEW

In some societies, gender roles are more segregated than in others. Gender roles strongly affect gender relations. Societies exhibit either gender equality or gender inequality, which usually means male dominance. All societies have some division of labor by gender, which allows people to specialize in a few skill areas rather than having to master all the survival skills of their culture. All societies also have cooperative labor. Gender division of labor reflects biological, economic, and cultural realities. Women's status in a society is based in part on the importance of their roles in the production of goods or provision of food; on their importance as householders, depending on the type and frequency of warfare; and on their access to kin support based on postmarital residence patterns.

GENDER AND SUBSISTENCE

As mentioned, modes of subsistence relate to gender roles, gender status, and gender relations. Foraging societies tend to have gender equality and egalitarian gender relations, except where men's economic or political roles are critical to the survival of the group, a situation that favors male dominance. Horticultural, pastoral, and agricultural societies tend to have greater gender inequality, depending on the control of subsistence resources and other factors, with the likelihood of some degree of male dominance. This pattern, however, varies considerably. Industrial societies, with economies built on agricultural bases, tend to retain ideological male dominance while gradually enlarging economic opportunities for women and extending legal and institutional equalities to both genders.

Foragers and Gender

In many foraging bands, women's and men's interdependent contributions to their households were (and in some cases still are) reflected in equality of social relations and social status. However, among others, male dominance is apparent. We can compare two foraging societies, the Ju/'hoansi of southern Africa and the Inuit of the North American Arctic, to understand similarities and differences. Both these small, nomadic societies were traditionally organized around bilaterally related kin groups. Economic roles were defined according to gender, but flexibility and overlap were also found. The productive

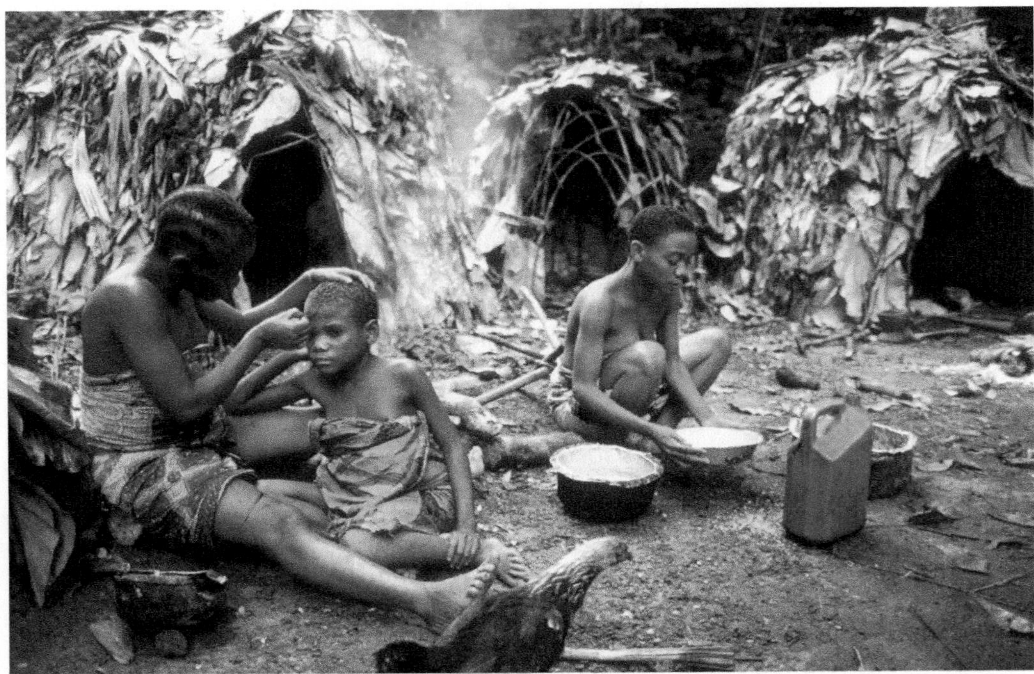

These Mbuti Pygmy women live in a foraging society in the Ituri rain forest in Congo in Central Africa. In Mbuti society women are valued artists and have greater gender equality than women have in groups that live in more hostile environments. Corbis/Wendy Stone/Corbis

CULTURE CHANGE

TRANSFORMATION OF GENDER STATUS IN A FORAGING SOCIETY

The role of subsistence in gender constructs can be seen clearly in well-documented cases of culture change. Economic and political changes among the Inuit, for example, have significantly affected gender roles, relationships between women and men, and cultural evaluation of the genders. Trade with Europeans, Canadians, and Americans encouraged Inuit men to spend more time and energy trapping animals for furs instead of subsistence hunting. Men who engaged in trade could accumulate valued manufactured goods, especially items related to men's work, such as fishing nets, metal fishhooks, guns, ammunition, steel traps, modern boats, and outboard motors (Graburn 1969, 129–30). As Arctic economies focused on trapping, families congregated near trading posts, becoming more dependent on the goods and foods they received in exchange for furs. In the twentieth century, Canadian and U.S. authorities accelerated this relocation by establishing administrative offices, schools, and nursing stations in settled villages.

Inuit attitudes toward ownership changed. Formerly, anyone in the area shared land and resources. Later, trapping lines and the animals they snared were considered individual property. Because inspecting trapping lines and retrieving animals were done individually rather than collectively, cooperation in most economic activities became unnecessary. Emphases on individual property and accumulation of wealth enhanced the status of young men who were successful trappers.

After World War II, the pace of change throughout the Artic accelerated. Towns grew through consolidation of neighboring communities, influx of people from distant camps, and natural population increases. Exploration for oil, particularly in Alaska, by transnational corporations created numerous jobs, and thousands of nonnatives immigrated to the region (Chance 1990).

Today wage work is available to some Inuit women and men, often in gender-linked occupations. Men typically are employed in construction, mining, building maintenance, and work at Canadian and U.S. military bases. Women work in service jobs and as nurse's aides, teachers, and school aides. Since the 1980s, however, women have joined men in technical, managerial, and professional fields (Bodenhorn 1993, 184). Both men and women also gain income from skilled craftwork, including sculpture, painting, and basketry. Wage-earning work has increased the economic independence of contemporary Inuit women, leading to gender equality.

---

labor of both women and men was essential for survival and was socially recognized and rewarded. Formal political structures and formalized leadership were absent. Settlements were politically and economically autonomous.

In Ju/'hoansi and Inuit societies, marriages are usually monogamous, although polygyny and polyandry occur infrequently. Initial postmarital residence is matrilocal, providing a young wife with support from her kin until children are born and her marriage becomes stable. Divorce, though, is common, particularly in the early years of marriage, and can be initiated by either spouse. Fathers in both cultures take an active role in child care and are affectionate and playful with their children. In general, attitudes toward premarital sexual activity are permissive for both girls and boys. And although adultery is not condoned, its only punishment is gossip and criticism. Despite these similarities, important differences in the two cultures help us understand the conditions under which egalitarian gender relations are maintained and, conversely, some of the conditions that promote male dominance.

In contrast to Ju/'hoansi society, where annual caloric intake consisted mainly of plant products, the Inuit diet was almost exclusively based on meat and fish. Because men supplied these resources primarily, their labor was seen as more directly producing conditions for survival. Women's contributions, although substantial and essential, were seen as supplemental. An emphasis on male labor among the Inuit led to preferences for patrilocal residence following an initial period with the wife's kin. Camp affiliation was commonly based on kinship bonds among men. Collective male labor was essential for many economic pursuits, especially among coastal peoples engaged in hunting sea animals.

The Inuit situation contrasted with that of Ju/'hoansi economies. Ju/'hoansi hunters were respected and socially rewarded, but Ju/'hoansi women were also recognized for contributing to and controlling the major food supply. The Inuit division of labor that required men to leave their camps for individual or collective hunting resulted in the physical separation of men and women. Primary social interactions were with members of one's own gender. In contrast, physical and social separation of women and men was not common among the Ju/'hoansi. Conversational and interactional groupings formed casually without regard to gender.

The conditions under which men pursued their economic roles added to their prestige because of the risks involved. The Arctic environment presents severe constraints, and a man's efforts, however skilled and fearless the hunter, were likely to fail. Daily risks to survival, compounded by the likelihood of failure, encouraged hunters to attempt to establish some control over their situation. Their religious beliefs revolved around ritualized precautions, taboos, and prayers to forestall disaster. The greater risks they took were rewarded with greater social prestige. Arctic survival depended on men's ability to control resources in dangerous situations involving violent acts against large, aggressive animals (Sanday 1981). This control extended to dominance over women. In a society where interpersonal aggression was condemned and where cooperative, friendly, and hospitable behavior was preferred, men were permitted to act violently toward women. Wife beating and rape were not uncommon (Briggs 1982).

Gender in Pastoral Societies

Anthropological studies of pastoralist societies, especially in Africa, have emphasized their patriarchal social and political organization. Men control access to land and herds. They own the animals, particularly cattle, that form the basis of subsistence and of ideology. That is, the people think of themselves as pastoralists centering on male pursuits, male interests, and male norms. For example, to be a Maasai (cattle herders of Kenya and Tanzania) is to be a pastoralist. Maasai men, therefore, fit this ideal, but Maasai women are marginalized because they are not herders. If women do partake in the self-conception of Maasai, it is as wives of men and mothers of sons, who they socialize into the male-centered ideal.

Although persuasive, this portrayal of pastoral societies is problematic. One problem concerns male bias in the analysis—most of the anthropologists who first described East African pastoral societies were men. A second problem concerns the historical transformations of pastoral societies resulting from European colonial influences. These transformations have become the focus of critical study to uncover earlier cultural practices and norms and to understand the processes that have shaped contemporary pastoral societies.

For example, in the late 1800s, when German colonial authorities first entered Maasai territory in what was then called Tanganyika, Maasai familial and community roles were distinguished by gender, but both men and women had autonomy in their own spheres. Women and men could achieve respect by their oratorical skills, generosity, and other personality traits (Hodgson 1999, 45). Subsistence responsibilities were allocated by gender. Women took care of calves, sheep, and goats, milked the cows, distributed milk within their households, and traded surplus milk. Young boys herded the goats and sheep. Adult men and older boys herded the cattle and decided where and when to graze the animals. Although their roles were separate, husbands and wives cooperated in deciding whether to slaughter, trade, or give away the animals. Women as well as men could give cattle and other animals to other people. After marriage, a husband gave some cattle to his wife as "house-property" under her control (Hodgson 1999, 47). Finally, women traded animals (mostly goats and sheep), milk, and hides to neighboring farming peoples to obtain grain and other crops.

Men held the major public political roles, as heads of lineages, ceremonial leaders, and members of village councils. Women could contribute to group decisions either indirectly through their husbands and sons or directly by speaking at meetings. Both men and women participated in negotiations for the marriages of their sons and daughters, and both could benefit from the cattle received as bridewealth when their daughters married.

German authorities sought to "pacify" indigenous groups to make the territory safe for European settlement. When the British replaced the Germans in 1920, after World War I, government intervention increased, affecting Maasai economic activities, leadership, and religious practices, and consequently also traditional gender roles.

Colonial authorities sought out Maasai elders who they thought could help them control the military impulses of younger men. The elders took this opportunity to increase their power.

British agents also contributed to the marginalization of Maasai women by restricting and regulating trade in ways that favored men. Men were enticed or coerced into the growing cash economy. They were considered "heads of households" and forced to pay taxes. To pay these taxes, however, men had to obtain cash by selling cattle, which increasingly became commodities to be bought and sold in the marketplace, or by working for wages. Because the British considered men the owners of cattle, the rights of women to share in the control of animals were diminished. To raise taxes, the British also began to regulate the casual, small-scale trade carried on by women. Once trade came under government supervision, men were privileged because of their greater familiarity with cash transactions. Finally, British authorities initiated programs aimed at economic "development." Men were taught new techniques of animal care and health to improve their stock.

As a consequence of these colonial policies, Maasai men gained economic and political centrality, excluding women from shared control over resources and from family and community decision making. Therefore, contemporary gender norms and attitudes that privilege Maasai men in most domains of life are an outgrowth of cultural transformations first initiated by colonial processes and then used by men to benefit themselves as a group.

Studies of other African pastoralist societies document complexities of gender roles and relations, not neatly subsumed under assumptions of patriarchy. Among the Turkana of Kenya, a mixture of patrilateral and matrilateral patterns prevails (Broch-Due 2000). Although kin-group membership follows patrilineal descent and postmarital residence is typically patrilocal, houses and their contents are the property of women. In polygynous households, each wife has her own dwelling. Her children reside with her, viewing her as the central node in their familial relationships. Mothers' houses are also the sites of ceremonial activities for births, marriages, and deaths. Women can also inherit property.

Residence compounds pass through different cycles, some of which are patrifocal and some matrifocal. The male focus centers on the senior male, his wife or wives, and his control of the cattle herd. The female focus centers on the senior female, usually an elder grandmother, her daughters-in-law, and their children. Because husbands are usually much older than their wives, women usually outlive their husbands and become the center of a growing household. When the grandmother dies, the household eventually splinters into new core groups, each composed of one of the elder woman's sons and his wife or wives. Then, when the senior man dies, the focus shifts to his wife. This view of the changing household unveils the complementarity of gender in cyclical patterns.

Attitudes about kinship also reflect Turkana ideologies of gender. For them, kinship is not based on relations forged by sex but rather on those forged by eating together (Broch-Due 2000, 171). In this realm, too, women are central because they milk the cows and allocate the milk. Women therefore control the physical flow of milk, whereas men control the social flow of cattle, given and received in bridewealth.

Turkana social and political prestige revolves more around issues of seniority than of gender. The numbers of cattle necessary for bridewealth have increased as people have moved into a cash economy. But bridewealth still must be given in cattle, so that access to herds has become increasingly competitive. Younger men who cannot secure enough cattle may never be able to contract suitable unions. Elder men have therefore monopolized both their access to cattle and their ability to marry. The age difference between husbands and wives has consequently widened, leading to more rapid cyclical changes from patrifocal to matrifocal households.

The conversion of many communities to Islam has also affected women's roles in Africa. For example, among the Boorana of northern Kenya, men viewed their conversion to Islam as a link to other Africans living under colonialism. The height of the conversions took place in the 1930s when British control over the region intensified (Aguilar 2000, 253). Women were less drawn to Islam because many of its practices and values undermined their autonomy. Previously monogamous, Boorana men began to follow the Islamic pattern of polygynous marriages, which Boorana women opposed. In addition, Muslim husbands could divorce their wives if the woman failed to bear a child, without questioning whether infertility was in fact due to the wife or the husband. Social stigma also made remarrying or finding households that would accept them difficult for divorced women, so the number of single-person households grew.

Today, Boorana women have begun to regain their centrality in their households, as owners of the dwelling and its contents and as keepers of Boorana identity and customs. Many younger men are abandoning Islam for indigenous traditions. Women are contributing to this change through their traditional ritual practices and their ability to communicate with the spirit world.

Gender in Horticultural Societies

In horticultural societies, control over the distribution of produce and goods influences gender status. In societies that are generally egalitarian, women exert their rights to make decisions concerning economic activities. In Iroquoian economies, for example, women performed most of the farmwork, including planting and tending crops and harvesting. In addition, women gathered a wide assortment of fruits, nuts, and roots and were responsible for domestic tasks and child care. Men's subsistence roles included hunting and fishing to supplement the basic plant diet. Trading with other native peoples for animal skins and utilitarian and luxury articles was also the work of men (Thwaites 1906, 15–155). Both women's and men's work was highly valued, socially recognized, and rewarded.

Women were not only responsible for food production but also controlled distribution of both the food and the resources that their husbands and sons contributed. This control over resources was a crucial factor in Iroquoian women's high status in their households and communities (Brown 1975, 236; Bonvillain 1980, 50). In addition to allotting food for daily consumption, women collected and distributed supplies for public feasts and ceremonial occasions (Lafitau 1974, 318). Their economic roles in household production and as resource distributors were thus extended into public domains.

Household organization centered around matrilineal clans that formed the basis of Iroquoian kinship. Matrilocality was the preferred residence pattern, so a house typically consisted of an elder woman, her husband, their daughters and daughters' families, and the couple's unmarried sons.

Iroquoian behaviors and attitudes related to sexuality and marriage reflected the independence and autonomy of women and men. People freely chose to engage in sexual relationships and to form marriages. Marriages were monogamous. Violence against women in the form of wife beating or rape was unheard of (Bonvillain 1980).

Iroquoian women's prestige was strengthened through many features of their roles within clans. Senior women of matrilineages composing each clan had responsibility for overseeing domestic tasks performed in their households and for allocating farmland to their kinswomen (Lafitau 1974, 69). Clan mothers chose lineage and clan chiefs from among prominent men in their kin groups. Thus, both men and women made important, socially valued contributions to their society and had ultimate control over their own behavior.

In contrast, among the Igbo of Nigeria, both men and women contribute to subsistence through their farm labor, but men control land and resources. Patrilineal kinship groups communally hold land. The elders of the patrilineage allocate land to each male member as needed (Njoku 1990). Preferred postmarital residence is patrilocal, consolidating bonds between fathers and sons and between brothers. Men occupy most major decision-making and influential roles in political life. However, women dominate village and regional trade. Therefore, although Igbo culture contains overtly expressed attitudes of male superiority, Igbo tradeswomen control market exchanges and benefit both economically and socially from their expertise in this sphere of life. Women trade their own farm products and crafts as well as those goods made by their husbands. Women's control over local trade is key to their ability to establish a high degree of autonomy in a culture that otherwise is dominated by men.

Igbo subsistence is based on horticulture. Tasks are strongly demarcated according to gender. Men plant yams, considered to be the staple crop. Men also plant cassava, another root crop. Rice, a product introduced in the early twentieth century, is the only crop both men and women grow. Women plant and harvest all other crops, including maize, melons, okra, and varieties of beans (Njoku 1990, 53). These plants are interspersed among the yams and cassavas. Women also weed their husbands' yam gardens. Even when work has a collective focus, tasks are performed according to gender. For example, men harvest yams, but women and children carry the yams to the household yam barn (Ottenberg 1965, 7; Ottenberg and Ottenberg 1962, 119). A man's social prestige depends in part on the output of his yam gardens. Men whose gardens produce a great excess of yams beyond his family subsistence needs has the right to take the title of Eze-ji ("yam king") (Njoku 1990, 54). His children then can take yam-related names, indicating the respect shown to their father.

Other subsistence and household activities are likewise allocated according to gender. Men obtain fish from nearby rivers; women fish in ponds and streams. Men make bamboo frames for houses, women collect and carry mud for house walls; men put mud on the frames, women smooth it when dry. Gender differentiation is extended to craft production as well: Women are potters and men make mats (Ottenberg 1965, 9–10).

Most Igbo women engage in trade, as do the women of a majority of cultures throughout West Africa. Men also trade, but their participation was traditionally less extensive than that of women. Women's marketing expertise encompasses men's products as well because women usually sell agricultural products grown by their husbands in addition to those in their own domain. Most Igbo women are not full-time traders but engage in marketing as an extension of their roles in agricultural production. However, some women do engage in more complex trading activities, functioning as intermediaries and buying from local producers and reselling produce in regional markets. Others buy in large quantities from markets and then resell to villagers who do not go to market (Ukwu 1969, 177). Through these various efforts, women function as catalysts for wide redistributive networks.

Tradeswomen's husbands avoid interfering with their activities or making too many demands on their labor. Successful women have the income and prestige to manage on their own and, therefore, are able to leave an abusive or domineering husband. If divorced or widowed, successful tradeswomen do not feel compelled to remarry because they know that they can support themselves and their children.

In contrast to the Iroquois and Igbo, among the Yanomamo of Amazonia, women are excluded from direct productive work. This exclusion is then used as justification for their social subordination. Yanomamo culture sanctions men's dominance over women in every feature of ideology and practice (Chagnon 1973; 1997). Settlement patterns, social systems, subsistence activities, and village leadership are all dominated by men. These conditions of Yanomamo society have been strongly influenced by economic changes as a result of culture contact (Kellman 1982).

Residence patterns are patrilocal, based on affiliation among patrilineal kin. Marriages are usually arranged by men, a father giving his daughter to be wed to a man with whom he wishes to forge an alliance. Young girls, often as young as 8 or 9 years old, are married to men in their 20s or 30s. Polygyny is common and desired by all men but not economically possible for everyone. A man may contract multiple marriages through establishing alliances with several men who have daughters. Men also obtain wives by capture when raiding other villages.

Prestige in Yanomamo culture is principally based on success in two roles held exclusively by men: warrior and shaman, a type of ritual practitioner who makes contact with the spirit world and performs ceremonies to heal the sick and protect warriors. Successful warriors also function as influential village leaders. Warfare is common and is characterized by

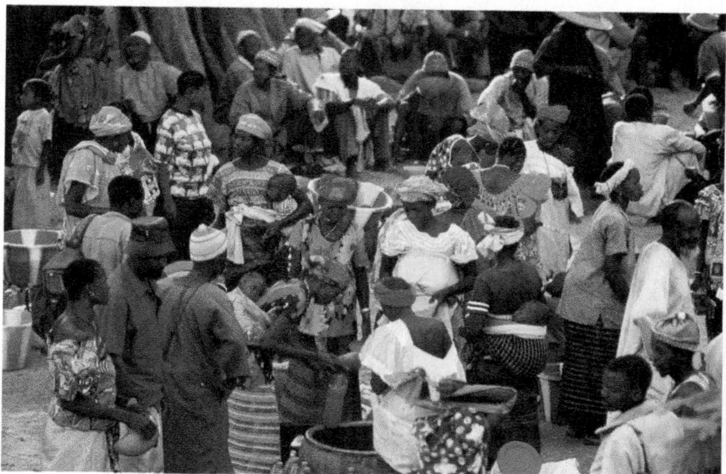

Many West African women are prominent traders, supplying their families and communities with produce and crafts, as shown in this market in Nombori, Mali. Corbis/David Sutherland/Corbis

raids against nearby villages with the aim of killing as many inhabitants as possible. Young women, however, are often captured and brought back to become wives.

Although men are more likely than women to die as the result of raiding, there is still a relative lack of women in most communities because of the practice of female infanticide, a dramatic reflection of the unworthiness of females. This artificially created scarcity of women is a motivation for warfare, giving men the opportunity to capture a wife from a neighboring village (Harris 1974). Warfare creates a dangerous situation for noncombatants, enhancing men's status in their role as defenders. Thus, men's success is rewarded by both high social prestige and the subordination of women. Women's subordination is demonstrated by frequent violence in the form of beatings and rapes.

Finally, in an area of scarce resources, practices may develop in order to disperse populations (Siskind 1973). The scarcity of women, created by female infanticide and polygyny, helps limit population growth and also generates conditions of warfare conducive to forcing people to relocate away from centers of conflict.

Gender in Agricultural States

Agrarian states are complex societies with centralized political systems that maintain some degree of control over local areas within the state. They have economies based on intensive farming and produce surpluses that are used to support a ruling elite. These communities have marked segmentation of the population into classes that occupy different positions in society, and have different kinds of occupations and different standards of living. Many such societies are (or were) characterized by male dominance in gender relations. As in other types of societies, however, the degree of male dominance varies widely, depending on economic, political, and historical factors, as well as on patterns of kinship, marriage, and family.

Culture change through government mandate is a force in the process of globalization. As in the case of China, central governments that have unified or expanded their countries through revolution or territorial conquest often have the power to compel obedience to laws that affect gender and other relationships.

Industrialism, Postindustrialism, and Gender

In Europe and the United States of the late eighteenth century, innovations in productive modes began a process that transformed agricultural societies into industrial nations. Industrialization began in the manufacture of textiles, using mainly women's labor for the first several decades and then marginalizing women as manufacturing became fully established as the dominant productive mode. During the early nineteenth century, the independent self-sufficiency of farming families was gradually eroded by the need to purchase commodities. At the same time, transformations of production in manufacturing resulted in owners hiring workers for the burgeoning industrial sector. These two processes coalesced in the growth of industrial production.

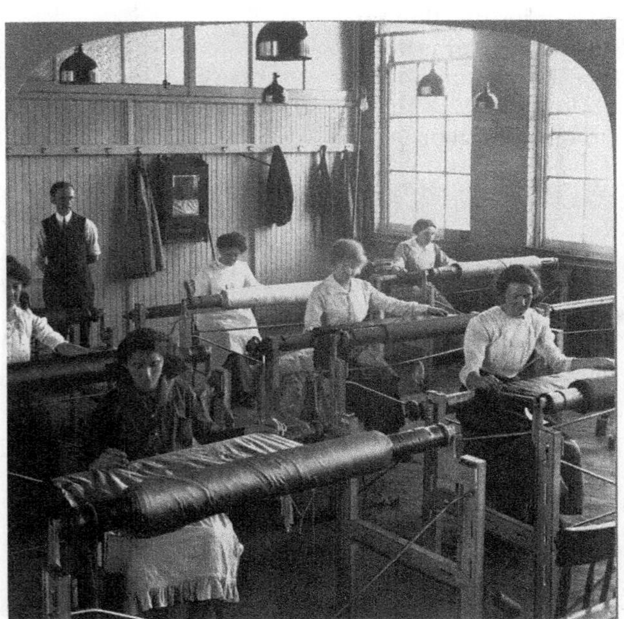

Mill life reproduced the patriarchal relations that existed in households. Men controlled the organization of production, whereas young, unmarried women labored as subordinate workers. Corbis/Corbis

Textile manufacture, centered in Massachusetts, was one of the first industries to develop in the United States, as it had been in Great Britain as well. Manufacturing began in the early 1800s and became well established by the 1820s. Young women, the daughters of farmers, constituted the bulk of mill operators. Unmarried daughters were available for outside employment because their direct productive contribution to their families was not as critical as that of sons. In the farming economy, daughters generally helped in farmwork and housework, but sons were central to agricultural production because they, along with their fathers, contributed the major share of labor on the farms.

American women's participation in mill work began to decline by the 1840s, when working conditions in the mills deteriorated due to competition from abroad and the desire of mill owners to cut costs. Women at mills in Lowell, Massachusetts, went on strike in the 1830s, but their efforts to protect their jobs and improve working conditions failed because the owners were able to find immigrant, especially Irish, women and men willing to work for lower wages. Except in textiles, native-born men also made up a large percentage of the work force in the growing industries of the northeastern and central states (Goldfield et al. 2004). However, they, too, faced competition from immigrant workers willing to work for lower pay.

Women were marginalized in the industrial sector through intersecting links between gender segregation in employment and unequal pay. Some occupations were considered appropriate for women and others for men. For example, industrial jobs requiring operation of large, heavy machinery were open to men, whereas women were employed in industries that relied on handwork and small machinery that produced such items as soap, hats, and cigars (Hartmann 1979). Even where both men and women worked in the same industry, they were differentiated according to specialization. In the manufacture of boots and shoes, for instance, men were employed as cutters and finishers, and women were stitchers and sewers (Matthaei 1982, 189).

In addition, women generally received lower wages than did men, even when both performed the same jobs. This differential in pay, or **gender gap,** as it is now called, was—and is—often masked by the segregation of work and workplaces. Men's social dominance can then be justified by the fact that they earn more money than do women. Paying women lower wages was justified by an ideology that women were only interested in working until they married and would leave the labor force to become wives and mothers.

In the early and mid-nineteenth century, a cultural construct currently referred to as the **cult of domesticity** became popular and justified separation of the genders, relegating women to the domestic sphere. Its popularity grew throughout the nineteenth century and remains in one form or another as a gender construct in American society. According to this cultural ideal, separate roles and domains are appropriate for women and men. Men provide material support for their families; women are suited to perform domestic tasks. Married women who joined the labor force as an economic necessity were told that they were neglecting their proper duties to nurture their husbands and children by working outside the home. Husbands of working women were similarly made to feel derelict in their duty. Because the ideal man was one who supported his wife and children, a man whose wife worked was less than a real man.

gender gap
The difference in wages and income earned by men and women for comparable work.

cult of domesticity
A constellation of beliefs popular in the late nineteenth and early twentieth centuries that promoted the notion that women were, by nature and biology, suited to the domestic tasks of nurturing and caring for their husbands and children.

CASE STUDY

Male Dominance in Traditional Chinese Culture

Patriarchal gender relations were developed through millennia of Chinese history. To underpin political and military power, China's ruling classes adopted philosophies that supported state control. The thoughts of Confucius (551–479 B.C.) and his disciples were especially influential. A cornerstone of Confucianism is the notion of "filial piety," which ordains obedience to one's social superiors. Thus, all Chinese owed obedience to the emperor, sons to their fathers, and women to their husbands.

Male dominance was manifested in numerous social, economic, political, and religious spheres. Households consisted of members of patrilineages, headed by the eldest male. His wife, unmarried children, and married sons and their wives and children were all under his authority. The rule of a head of household was potentially harsh, involving culturally sanctioned beatings of wives and children. Because postmarital residence was patrilocal, wives could rarely depend on their relatives for support in conflicts with their in-laws (Wolf 1974, 158). A wife was subordinate within her husband's household, especially when young and not yet the mother of sons to carry on her husband's lineage.

Mothers-in-law often acted as "surrogates for male authority" (Diamond 1975, 376). Although subordinate to their own husbands, they asserted authority over their sons' wives, who had few, if any, allies in their husbands' households. In keeping with notions of filial piety, a man's allegiance was first and foremost to his parents. His wife could not

With four sons, this traditional Chinese family has a strong future. Families depended on sons for labor and crucial religious functions.
Corbis/Hulton-Deutsch Collection/Corbis

depend on him for social support. Women began to receive deferential treatment after they reached middle or old age and had adult sons. Sons were a woman's main allies, and mothers could attempt to control their sons through strong emotional bonds (Wolf 1974, 168). Sons gravitated toward their mothers' emotional warmth in contrast to the authoritarian relationship they had with their fathers.

A marked preference for sons reflected patriarchal attitudes. Sons were necessary for the social, material, and spiritual well-being of their parents. Through sons, patrilineages maintained their continuity. The division of labor was gender assigned and contributed to the preference for sons over daughters. China was an agricultural country, and although peasant women did work in the fields at harvest time, men were primarily responsible for agricultural production. Women's work was usually confined to domestic tasks.

Women living in prosperous households seldom left the home. The Chinese word for wife, *neiran,* literally means "inside person" (Croll 1982, 224). By keeping his wife in the home, a man demonstrated his wealth and that he did not need her to work in the fields. Thus, women's economic dependence on men reinforced their social subordination (Wong 1974, 234).

Fathers arranged marriages without consulting the bride or groom. Girls generally were married in their late teens but were often betrothed as children. These betrothals solidified alliances between men. Girls' chastity before marriage was essential to maintain the honor of the girl and that of their families, but men had no premarital restrictions and frequented brothels to gain sexual experience (Wong 1974, 236–37). This double standard was another instance of male privilege.

Customs regarding divorce further discriminated against women. Only husbands could initiate divorce, often because of a wife's disobedience or failure to produce a son (Wong 1974, 234). Divorce shamed a woman but carried no stigma for a husband.

Ideally, widows were not supposed to remarry, but poor men who were unable to find suitable wives sometimes sought them (Wong 1974, 236). Widows often agreed to such unions to escape the social stigma and economic hardships of widowhood.

The practice of foot binding symbolized restrictions on girls and women in traditional Chinese society. The feet of young girls at age 4 or 5 were tightly bound with cloth, so that their toes curled under their feet. As the girls grew to adulthood, their feet became deformed, and normal walking was impossible. Adult women took tiny, faltering steps on feet as small as three inches long (Wong 1974, 232). Only among the very poor, where women's agricultural labor was necessary for family survival, did daughters escape this practice.

In the early twentieth century, some customs began to change because of the influence of Chinese intellectuals and administrators, as well as British and French imperial agents (who had defeated the Chinese in a series of nineteenth-century wars). Although men certainly dominated British and French societies, their influence improved women's status in China. For instance, foot binding was outlawed in 1902, although the ban was widely ignored until the 1950s, when the new Communist government eliminated it.

After coming to power in 1949, the Chinese Communists attempted to transform social and familial relationships between women and men. The Marriage Law of 1950 declared that the "New-Democratic marriage system is based on the free choice of partners, on monogamy, on equal rights for both sexes, and on the protection of the lawful interests of women and children" (quoted in Wong 1974, 242). Additional laws banned child-marriage and dowry.

However, patriarchal attitudes continue in a preference for sons, even in the face of government reforms and programs for population control. To limit population growth, the Chinese government began a "One-Child Certificate Program" in 1979. A couple who pledge to have only one child receive cash bonuses, preferential housing, job assignments, and educational opportunities for their child. According to a 1986 study conducted by Fred Arnold and Liu Zhaoxiang (1986), 37 percent of Chinese couples with one child enrolled in the program, but a disparity exists between those with one son and those with one daughter. Sixty percent of holders of one-child certificates have sons; only 40 percent have daughters (Arnold and Liu 1986, 227–28). The Population and Family Planning Law allows a couple to have a second child if both mother and father were themselves the only child in their natal families (Hu 2002). Rural couples may also have a second child if the first child is a girl. This provision recognizes the importance of sons' labor to farm families and is aimed at protecting the life of a first-born girl because without it, parents might be tempted to eliminate their daughter. Some families, however, use prenatal ultrasound to learn the sex of an unborn fetus and abort a female child. Moreover, wealthier families sometimes prefer to pay the large fines imposed on couples who violate the law, leading to disparities in family size between rich and poor. The government is therefore considering imposing higher fines on wealthier families. However, after a devastating earthquake hit China in 2008, couples whose only child was either killed or seriously injured were allowed to have another child (Jacobs 2008).

The one-child program has reduced population growth, a matter of critical importance in China. In 1985, the natural growth rate was 15.73, but it had fallen to 5.89 by 2005 (China Statistical Yearbook 2005) and in 2009, the population growth rate was a low 0.5%, less than half the world average (World Bank, World Development Indicators 2010). However, the gender disparity is troubling and has consequences for future opportunities of men and women. According to the census of 2010, the Chinese sex ratio at birth was 118 males/100 females (Wines and LaFraniere 2011, A9). For children under 15 years of age, it was 117 males/100 females, and for adults 15 to 64 years, it was 106 males/100 females (CIA World FactBook 2010). These figures indicate that males are favored at birth, reflecting the frequent use of abortion to eliminate female fetuses. Favoritism toward males in early childhood presumably leads families to pay less attention to the nutrition and health care needs of girls. The sex ratio evens out as people age due to the usual greater longevity of women. Read the Document on myanthrolab.com

---

Labor leaders also used these attitudes to restrict women's involvement in wage work as competition between employed women and men intensified at the beginning of the twentieth century. Although ostensibly dedicated to bettering conditions for all workers, most unions in the nineteenth and early twentieth centuries discriminated against women, barring them from membership or relegating them and their interests to auxiliary status (Berch 1982). When men were faced with competition from women, who often were willing to work for lower wages, unions had two possible responses: They could advocate equality of pay for all workers, to remove the financial incentive for employers to hire women rather than men; or they could advocate restrictions on women's employment as a strategy for maintaining men's advantages. They chose the latter course.

In another response to competition from women workers, labor leaders and public figures advocated enactment of "protective legislation" to protect women from harmful conditions on the job. Hours for women were decreased, night work in some occupations was forbidden, and exposure to dangerous chemicals, materials, or machinery was banned. But the same protections were not extended to men. Although the rules protected women from dangers on the job, they carried hidden costs, rendering women less attractive as employees and, therefore, hurting their chances of being hired.

Despite strong pressures to keep women in the home, some women sought to obtain higher education and to participate in the work force, spurring social changes in gender roles and expectations. Their political activism also increased. As early as the mid-nineteenth century, women sought political rights equal to men. Organizing at the Seneca Falls (New York) Convention in 1848, Elizabeth Cady Stanton and Lucretia Mott (later joined by Susan B. Anthony) issued a Declaration of Sentiments and Resolutions modeled on the U.S. Declaration of Independence, calling for equal rights for women (Sapiro 1986). The women's suffrage movement culminated in 1920 with the ratification of the Nineteenth Amendment to the U.S. Constitution, which gave women the right to vote.

CULTURE CHANGE

TRANSFORMATION OF AMERICAN WORK IN THE TWENTIETH AND TWENTY-FIRST CENTURIES

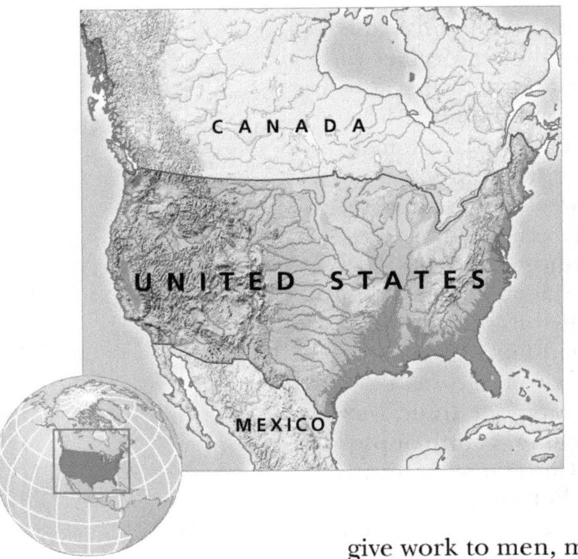

Many factors came together to change the economic and social roles of men and women in the twentieth century. New demands for workers, rising standards of living, and growing awareness of inequalities all led to increased participation of women in paid employment. During World War I (1914–1918), women replaced men who had joined the military, obtaining jobs that had previously been barred to them and including managerial positions and jobs in heavy industry. Patterns of employment among women also changed. As white women were increasingly hired as office workers, teachers, saleswomen, and telephone operators, black women moved into domestic and service occupations (Amott and Matthaei 1991).

After the war, many women remained in the work force to help support their families as inflation rose, real wages fell, and the demand for consumer goods increased. Many mothers also worked to support children through college.

The years of the Great Depression, beginning in 1929 and lasting through the 1930s, witnessed another cycle of shifts in employment. Millions of men lost jobs in industry and construction. To give work to men, many people, including wives of unemployed men, attacked married working women, and states passed laws barring their employment.

The Depression was followed by World War II (1939–1945). Millions of men entered the military, leaving millions of jobs unfilled. Women again heeded the patriotic call to join the work force. Job opportunities for all women improved. Black women worked in industries that had previously been closed to them (Bose 1987, 279). The numbers of married working women increased, and women with young children entered public labor. After the war, men again pushed women out of work or at least out of the positions they had occupied during the war. Many women, though, remained in the work force, motivated by necessity and personal interest.

Workers from different social categories have fed each increase in women's employment. At first, most women workers were young and unmarried. Then immigrant women, single and married, entered the work force. Married, native-born women entered and stayed in paid employment in large numbers in the 1940s. Subsequently, most married working women were older women whose children had grown up. Since the 1960s, however, working mothers with young children have taken jobs in addition to their domestic responsibilities (Fox and Hesse-Biber 1984, 27–28).

Today, costs of living make it necessary for married women and for mothers to earn money. Thus, the two-worker family has become commonplace. In addition, many mothers are single, either because of divorce or of never having married. Many women also choose to pursue a career or to escape the social isolation of their homes.

By 2008, about 70.6 percent of women aged 20 to 64 were in the labor force, as were 83.2 percent of men (U.S. Bureau of the Census, American Community Survey 2008), with the highest levels of employment for men and women between the ages of 25 and 55.

Most women with children of all ages were in the labor force in 2009 (U.S. Department of Labor). That is, 71.6 percent of mothers with children under the age of 18 were working. This is a large increase since 1975, when only 47 percent of mothers with children under 18 were working. The increase comes primarily from mothers with young children. However, those with younger children tended to work fewer hours than those with older children. Table 2 gives the data for labor force participation rates and employment rates for mothers of children under age 18 (U.S. Department of Labor 2008). Data from 2009 indicate that unmarried mothers had higher rates of employment (75.8 percent) than married mothers (69.8 percent) (U.S. Department of Labor 2010).

Labor force participation rates for married women with children under the age of 18 grew steadily in the second half of the twentieth century but leveled off in the 1990s. Since 1997, labor force participation and employment rates for mothers have slightly declined for all categories of women. Although the educational levels of these mothers

TABLE 2 LABOR FORCE PARTICIPATION FOR MOTHERS WITH YOUNG CHILDREN, 2009

Mothers with Children 6–17	Mothers with Children 3–6	Mothers with Children Under 3
78.2%	63.6%	61.1%

Source: U.S. Department of Labor, Current Population Survey 2009, Table 5.

had no effect on the rate of decrease, their husbands' earnings did. Women whose husbands' earnings were in the top 20 percent and in the bottom 20 percent were more likely to stay at home than women whose husbands' incomes were in the middle range (Cohany and Sok 2007, 15). Racial and ethnic differences also affected whether married mothers with young children are likely to be in paid employment. African American mothers were the most likely to work outside the home, at a rate of 65 percent. Most white (58 percent) and Asian mothers (51 percent) were also in the labor force. In contrast, only about one-third (34 percent) of Hispanic mothers sought employment (Cohany and Sok 2007, 12). Finally, married mothers born in the United States were more likely than immigrant mothers to be in the labor force (59 percent compared to 35 percent). In 2008, in 57.3 percent of married-couple households, earnings were contributed from the work of both wife and husband, while 17.8 percent of such households were supported by the earnings of only the husband and 5.8 percent were supported by wives only (U.S. Department of Labor, Current Population Survey 2011, Table 23). Overall married couple households, women's earnings contributed 36.0 percent of total family income (US Department of Labor, Current Population Survey 2011, Table 24).

Women and men are not equally represented in most occupations. The rates of employment by gender in selected occupations are given in Table 3. Women continue to face

TABLE 3 WOMEN AS A PERCENTAGE OF WORKERS IN SELECTED OCCUPATIONS, 2009

Occupation	Women as % of Total (2009)
Total	47.3%
Management, professional, and related occupations	51.4%
Management, business, and financial operations occupations	42.7%
Professional and related occupations	57.5%
Service occupations	57.2%
Sales and office occupations	63.0%
Sales and related occupations	49.6%
Office and administrative support occupations	74.5%
Natural resources, construction, and maintenance occupations	4.4%
Farming, fishing, and forestry occupations	20.5%
Construction and extraction occupations	2.6%
Installation, maintenance, and repair occupations	4.2%
Production, transportation, and material moving occupations	21.4%
Production occupations	28.1%
Transportation and material moving occupations	15.3%

Source: U.S. Department of Labor, U.S. Bureau of Labor Statistics, Current Population Survey 2011, Table 11.

occupational segregation in the types of jobs for which they are hired. These differences reflect continuing tendencies to stereotype certain types of work as appropriate for one gender or the other. Although rates of women employed in managerial and professional occupations have grown in the last several decades, they tend to cluster in lower-paying occupational fields such as education and health care (68 percent) rather than in higher-paying computer and engineering fields (9 percent) (U.S. Bureau of Labor Statistics 2009).

Why is housework devalued? What role does household labor play in statistics about the productivity of the American economy?

Although the number of women in paid employment has grown, discrimination in wages and lack of access to some jobs still hinder their equality as workers, even though the wage gap has narrowed in most occupations. Today, the total U.S. median annual earnings of full-time, year-round workers for women stand at 77.0 percent of men's annual earnings. Using a different measure, the median weekly earnings rate for women is 80.2 percent of men's weekly earnings (Institute for Women's Policy Research 2010). As Table 4 shows, women are paid, on average, less than men in all occupations and for all age cohorts. When salaries are compared for women and men with comparable education and years of experience, the gender gap remains. By age, the youngest group of working women (aged 16 to 24) experienced the smallest gender gap in pay, earning 93 percent of young men's wages (U.S. Bureau of Labor Statistics 2009). As workers age, the discrepancy in earnings increases.

Although the gender gap in pay exists for all races, African American and Hispanic women's wages are closer to those of men of their own group than is true for whites. In 2009, African American women earned 93.7 percent of African American men's wages, and Hispanic women's wages were 89.5 percent of Hispanic men's earnings. In addition, Asian women's earnings were 81.8 percent of Asian men's salaries, while white women had the lowest rate, at 79.2 percent of white men's earnings (U.S. Department of Labor,

TABLE 4 OCCUPATION AND WOMEN'S MEDIAN WEEKLY EARNINGS AS A PERCENTAGE OF MEN'S WEEKLY EARNINGS

Occupation	
Management	72.4
Business and financial	76.3
Computer and mathematical operations	88.1
Architecture and engineering	80.5
Life, physical, and social science	79.0
Community and social services	82.6
Legal occupations	56.6
Education and library occupations	78.3
Arts, entertainment, sports, and media	80.7
Health care practitioner and technical occupations	78.0
Health care support occupations	85.3
Protective service occupations	75.1
Food preparation and serving occupations	90.9
Sales and related occupations	66.2
Office and support occupations	91.6
Farming, fishing, forestry	86.9
Construction and extraction	93.6
Transportation and moving	76.4

Source: U.S. Department of Labor, Current Population Survey 2011, Table 18.

TABLE 5 WOMEN'S EARNINGS BY RACE/ETHNICITY AS PERCENTAGE OF WHITE MEN'S EARNINGS

Race/Ethnicity	Male	Female	Women's Earnings as % of White Men's Earnings
All races	47,127	36,278	77.0%
White alone, not Hispanic	51,405	38,533	75.0%
Black or African American	37,496	31,824	61.9%
Asian	51,760	42,331	82.3%
Hispanic or Latino	31,393	27,181	52.9%

Source: Institute for Women's Policy Research, Current Population Survey Labor Force Statistics 2009.

Current Population Survey 2011, Table 16). However, these data reflect the relatively lower wages of nonwhite men rather than higher wages for nonwhite women. Table 5 presents comparisons of the earnings of different groups of women compared to those of white men. As shown, Asian women's earnings are closest to those of white men (82.3 percent), while those of Hispanic women are furthest (52.9 percent).

social reproduction The care and sustenance of people who will be able to contribute productively to society.

Women who remain at home and fulfill the traditional ideal of domestic roles are involved in the important work of social reproduction. **Social reproduction** entails the care and sustenance of people who will be able to contribute productively to society. Necessary tasks include obtaining and preparing food, maintaining the physical premises of the home, purchasing clothing and other material goods, tending family members when they are ill, and planning and supervising the education of children. However, the worth of labor contributed by stay-at-home wives and mothers is socially devalued, reflected, for example, in the phrase "just a housewife," which women themselves often use as a self-definition. However, the work of social reproduction that such women perform is vital to society and to the economic system. Although nonemployed wives are perceived as dependent on their husbands, husbands also depend on their wives. Just as men contribute their wages to support their families, women contribute their unpaid labor to family survival.

Relationships between subsistence and gender relations depend on the allocation of power, control of resources, and other factors. Some forager and horticultural societies had gender equality, whereas others had male dominance. Agrarian societies were generally male dominated. Industrialism changed gender relations. Segregation and a gender gap (unequal pay) developed in factory work. More women have entered the American work force in the twentieth century. Unemployed women who stay at home came to be seen as nonproductive, an attitude contributing to the subordination of women.

GLOBALIZATION AND GENDER

Agricultural and industrial development programs sponsored by national governments or international agencies aim to strengthen economies, raise living standards, and improve health in impoverished rural communities. Development theory emphasizes the importance of modernization in technology, agricultural production for trade, and industrialization dependent on a mobile labor force. When measured by gross national product (GNP), median family or household income, and longer life expectancy, advances can be demonstrated, but researchers still question the impact of economic development on different sectors of the population.

When the differential effects of development on men and women were first systematically explored, evidence suggested that modernization contributed to a decline in

European colonization had a significant impact on gender roles and attitudes. European traders preferred to deal with men and thus ignored or subverted the economic contributions of women. Missionaries affected gender relations directly and indirectly by redefining marriage and family in terms of European principles. Colonizers also tended to legitimate men's political authority and diminish women's public political roles.

women's status, especially in Africa and Asia (Boserup 1970). In Africa, landownership has passed from the collective control of kinship groups to individual control, increasingly concentrated in the hands of men. As land utilization has changed from an emphasis on subsistence to production for trade in national and global markets, women have seen their role in subsistence farming diminished. As their centrality in family production shrinks, their status has also declined. In Asia, mechanization and technological advances in farming have tended to favor male farmworkers.

An additional element in weighing the changes in women's status is their role in social reproduction and the gender division of labor in the household. The domestic labor that women do helps support family members and makes their participation in agriculture or industry possible. Policy planners and analysts of economic development often ignore this element (Beneria and Sen 1986). Furthermore, in societies where attitudes about gender limit women's ability to participate in work outside the home, their social status declines as societal value is placed on wage-earning activities.

Women's actual contributions to the world economy are often distorted and rendered invisible because of the inadequacy of research and statistics on labor force participation in the public sphere and because women's economic contributions in the home are ignored. Productive work or "active labor" is generally interpreted as participation in income-earning activities. Because much of women's work is in subsistence agriculture, home craft production, or the "informal" labor sector in urban environments (peddling, domestic service), their economic contributions are often seriously underestimated. In addition, census classifications of workers according to their "main" occupation tend to ignore women's economic contributions because they are classified as home workers without detailing their specific contributions to subsistence and also to extra household income such as making foods or crafts for sale. Finally, development programs often focus on the generation of work itself rather than on the reasons that women are not qualified, rooted in their lack of training and education because of discriminatory attitudes.

Women's Roles in Urban and Rural Economic Development

In some countries, industrial development favors women's employment in certain sectors. For example, in Malaysia, Singapore, and Taiwan, national and multinational corporations have established factories, especially in electronics and garment assembly, which employ mainly young women. According to some estimates, about 80 percent of workers in light manufacturing plants worldwide are women between the ages of 13 and 25 (Moore 1988, 100). In Singapore, labor force participation rates for women have increased dramatically since the government embarked on rapid industrialization, providing tax incentives to foreign investment and curtailing labor union organizing (Wong 1986, 208). By 1995, women's economic activity rate had risen to 51 percent (United Nations, Division for the Advancement of Women 2000). Factories in Malaysia have also increased the wage-earning opportunities of young women (Ong 1983). There, and in other Asian and Latin American countries, rural women leave their homes to improve their skills and chances of economic advancement. Their needs are especially acute in the context of increasing poverty in the countryside and the resulting dislocation. In the decade of the 1970s alone, shortly after the government began its industrialization program, the number of Malay women factory workers increased dramatically, from about 1,000 to more than 60,000 (Ong 1983, 429).

Young women benefit from their job opportunities by earning an income that gives them some economic independence and greater status in their families. They also escape the intense control traditionally exerted over them in their households, and they meet friends and socialize in the industrial centers. The wages they earn are higher than those available in other jobs. However, the companies take advantage of the workers' poverty, lack of skills, and lack of alternative opportunities, paying them relatively low wages and offering few benefits.

Today, economic development increasingly affects small, relatively isolated communities. For example, the Pacific islands of Melanesia and Polynesia have become incorporated into national and global export networks. The production of copra (dried coconut) as a cash crop on the Melanesian island of Vanuatu (formally called New Hebrides) has gradually involved villagers in globalization while also maintaining a diversified subsistence and cash economy (Rodman 1993). The people of Vanuatu first became involved in coconut production in the 1930s, but by the early 1980s, world prices for copra had

In Their Own VOICES

Tsetsele Fantan on Women and AIDS in Botswana

In this address from a 2003 conference on Botswana's Strategy to Combat HIV/AIDS, Tsetsele Fantan, from the African Comprehensive HIV/AIDS Partnership, discusses the cultural constraints affecting HIV/AIDS prevention and treatment programs in Botswana. She mentions attitudes about sex, marriage, and women's roles that hamper the effectiveness of these programs. And she emphasizes the need to involve men and women to achieve change. Africa is the continent hardest hit by HIV/AIDS. In Botswana, 67 percent of HIV-infected people ages 16 to 49 are women. Women are also the principal caretakers for AIDS sufferers in their households. And because eight out of ten farmers are women, their illness and death from AIDS affect their entire communities.

Globally, women are exposed to HIV transmission because of four main vulnerabilities: the social/cultural context, economic subordination, sexual subordination, and the female biological makeup. As far as the social/cultural context in Botswana is concerned, boys and girls are socialized differently, predominantly along traditional norms that emphasize female subordination throughout the life cycle. This is also emphasized when young women get married. We remind them that they need to honor and obey. This becomes extremely difficult when women are abused in marriage because as they go to uncles and aunts for counsel, they are reminded of their marriage vows. This gender power differential is compounded by age differences.

As far as economic subordination is concerned, poverty does force some women to adopt economic strategies, survival strategies, such as transactional sex. As far as sexual subordination is concerned, women are expected to have one lifetime partner, while male deviation is condoned, generally expected, or even encouraged. Women are also vulnerable to coerced sex, including rape and other sexual abuse, both inside and outside of the family, including marital rape. Young women and girls are increasingly targeted by older men seeking safe and/or subservient sexual partners, or just sexual adventure.

In addition to all the education that is being given about HIV and AIDS, I would like to mention three areas where I believe work needs to be done. The first is a need to redefine traditional gender images. There is an urgent need to redefine images of masculinity and femininity through culturally relevant public education, and this is an area where the media can play a very important role. We need to emphasize the role of men, not only as breadwinners, but as ensuring the protection of the health of themselves and their families. We need to clearly articulate the imperative for men to change attitudes and behaviors in a nonthreatening way. We need transformational programs that acknowledge that men are partners in the fight against HIV and AIDS. Secondly, we need to engage men in the empowerment of women. We need to recognize and come to terms with the realities of women in Botswana, and the realities of our social circumstances in Botswana, and recognize that women's empowerment cannot be realized without full involvement and engagement of the men. We therefore need to develop initiatives, innovative community-based programs that empower grassroots men to work with women. We need to develop programs that assist men and women to effectively negotiate for space, recognition, and acknowledgment of each other. To develop targeted programs for men that utilize informal, traditional structures, led by traditional and opinion leaders in the districts.

We need to develop gender and culturally sensitive programs and support services that address the vulnerability of women to HIV and AIDS. We need to develop women's entrepreneurial skills, as well as giving them or facilitating their access to credit, because acquiring skills without the capital to start a business which has a market will not change much.

Attitudes and practices that are deeply rooted in culture are unlikely to change in the short term. Programs to address this will require long-term commitment from development partners. Local traditional leaders must be empowered to advocate for and effect these changes at the community level. This should be done through proper dialogue. We need to identify and liberate the positive aspects of culture for gender-sensitive prevention initiatives. Lastly, we need to make sure that the valuable elements in our culture must be preserved and passed on to the next generation.

Watch the **Video:** ***A Generation of Hope*** on **myanthrolab.com**

CRITICAL THINKING QUESTIONS

What aspects of traditional culture encourage the spread of HIV/AIDS among women in Botswana? What features of traditional culture can best prevent this spread?

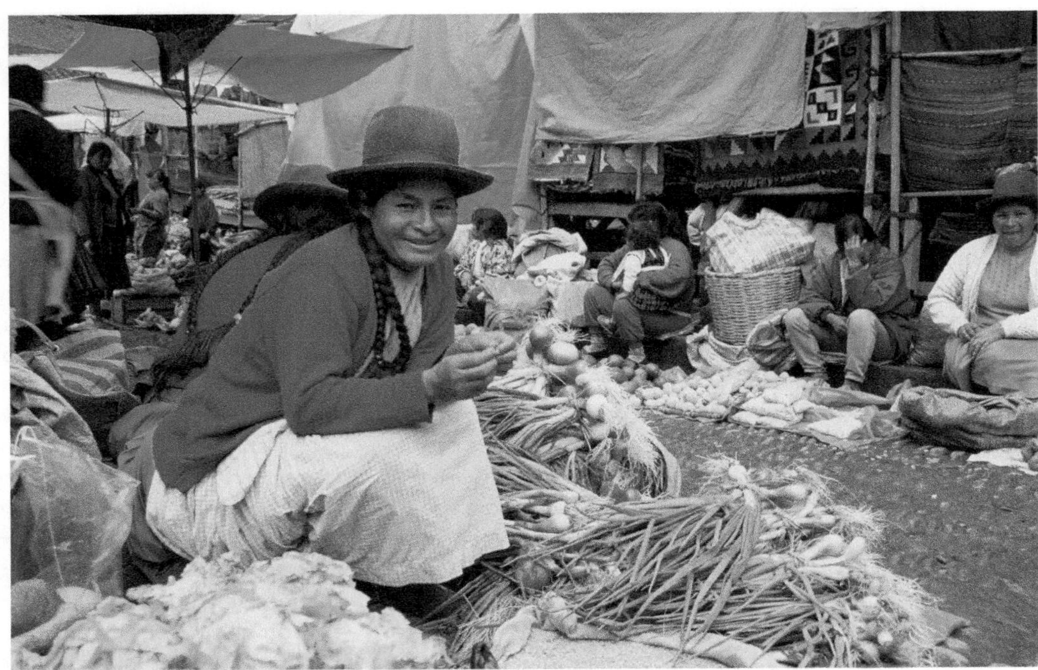

Women in street markets throughout the Andes, as shown here in Pisac, Peru, sell many kinds of produce, prepared foods, and crafts. Superstock/Angelo Cavalli/SuperStock

declined, and the local market collapsed. At that time, the Vanuatu government sponsored a fisheries development program to diversify sources of income and employment.

The shift from copra to fishing has had an impact on gender relations and contributions to household economies. Although most land under copra production was owned or controlled by men, men and women worked cooperatively in the fields. The fisheries industries, however, tend to recruit men because deep-water fishing is an occupation reserved to men. Still, women continue some traditional roles by marketing the fish locally. In addition, although people have become involved in the global economy, they have also continued subsistence farming, fishing, and craft production. Melanesian women have thus been able to maintain much of their traditional status and equality.

In Polynesia, Tahitian women have also been able to retain or even enhance their status in the context of economic change because cultural values supporting gender equality have remained intact. Local governments initiated agricultural development projects oriented toward growing potatoes and green vegetables. These programs are largely successful, involving both men and women by granting financial support and technological training to all. By the early 1990s, approximately 43 percent of potato farmers were women (Lockwood 1997, 511–12). Women's involvement in farming represented a break with the traditional division of labor that had limited women to performing domestic tasks. But they were able to use their customary access to communal land and their new access to government programs to produce crops for export. In addition, women's crafts, such as woven mats, hats, and quilts, have become major income-generating occupations, allowing women's economic contributions to be seen as central to the welfare of their families. Women's rights are protected by the traditional view that people control the products of their labor and the income received.

Women in Changing Socialist States

Most socialist nations have or had made great strides in a relatively short time in increasing women's participation rates in paid employment. Full employment is an underlying principle both for national economic growth and social equality of all citizens. Universal education has helped women acquire the necessary skills and training for industrial and professional occupations. However, serious discrepancies remain between the wages received by men and women for comparable work. For example, women agricultural workers in four socialist societies (the former Soviet Union, China, Cuba, and Tanzania) are concentrated in less-skilled, nonspecialist, low-paying, and low-prestige jobs (Croll 1986). Women's contributions to the total economy are minimized by official definitions of "economically active" that omit family subsistence production, a sector in which women are concentrated (Kruks and Wisner 1989). Furthermore, women often perform the major share of household responsibilities, leading to the "double day" typical of women in many industrial societies.

Although women work in all sectors of the industrial and professional economy, occupations in which women are concentrated tend to have low prestige. Although most socialist governments officially advocate policies aimed at combating discrimination against women, in varying degrees they all fail to recognize the critical link between public production and social or household reproduction. Women's roles in their households make entering the public work force as equals more difficult for them.

The fragility of the advances made by women in socialist countries in terms of economic participation, legal protections, and social equality is demonstrated by changes that have taken place in the former Soviet Union and Eastern Europe since the collapse of the socialist systems in the early 1990s. In the former Soviet Union, for instance, a market system has, among other things, resulted in drastic reductions in employment. Although all sectors of the economy have experienced declines, women have suffered disproportionately. For example, in 1993, approximately 70 percent of people officially listed as unemployed were women (Waters and Posadskaya 1995, 353). In addition, men are nearly twice as likely as women to hold positions of authority in both public and private organizations and enterprises, except in the fields of health care and education, professions long dominated by women (Russian Federation State Statistics Service 2006). Even in fields with numerical majorities of women, men are often found in positions of authority. Because of fears of population decline and falling birth rates (so low that Russia now experiences a negative population growth rate), pressure on women to become full-time mothers and housewives has increased considerably. The resurgence in defining women as childbearers and homemakers indicates that changes in social attitudes necessary to protect advances in women's status have not been realized.

A further indicator of the fragility of women's status in the former Soviet Union is the fact that women's political representation on the national level has plummeted. In the 1980s, women constituted approximately 33 percent of the deputies in the Supreme Soviet (the highest government body in the USSR) and approximately 50 percent or more in lower-level government organizations. After the elections of 1991, however, women accounted for only 5.6 percent of national deputies and were even less represented in regional and local governing bodies (Waters and Posadskaya 1995, 352–53). Similar dramatic declines in women's political representation and increases in unemployment rates have occurred throughout Eastern Europe.

Gender and Political Representation

Although the political leaders of countries worldwide are overwhelmingly men, women's representation in national and local politics has increased dramatically in the last several decades. A study entitled "Women in Parliament in 2008" (Inter-Parliamentary Union) demonstrated several important trends. First, women were elected to 20.6 percent of all parliamentary seats up for renewal worldwide. Second, 15 percent of parliaments reached the United Nations' stated minimum goal of 30 percent women members. Ten years ago, all of the parliaments that had reached that goal were located in Europe, but currently some governing chambers in Africa, Asia, and Latin America have also achieved this minimum target. Third, several countries have instituted special measures to ensure women's participation in the electoral process and women's representation in governing bodies, especially including minimum percentages of seats apportioned to women. And women are elected at higher rates in political systems with proportional representation as compared to majority electoral systems.

Of all countries in the world, only Rwanda had a majority of parliamentary seats (56 percent) occupied by women. Countries with 40 percent or more women parliamentarians include Sweden (45.0 percent), South Africa (44.5 percent), Cuba (43.2 percent), Iceland (42.9 percent), The Netherlands (40.7 percent), and Finland (40.0 percent). At the other end of the international spectrum, in 2008, there were 42 countries having between 1 percent and 10 percent women's representation and an additional ten countries with no women parliamentarians. Among the latter group were countries in the Middle East and the Pacific islands.

Norway and Sweden have the highest percentage of women in elected parliaments (about 40%). Pictured here are leaders of three of Norway's major parties: Kristen Halvorsen, leader of the Socialist Party, Jens Stoltenberg of the Labour Party, and Aslaug Haga of the Centre Party. AP Photos/Tor Richardsen/Scanpix/AP Images

Impacts of Ideology on Gender Constructs

Ideological influences can be seen clearly in the history of American women's participation in the labor force. Since the nineteenth century, each increase in women's participation has evoked an ideological attack by supporters of patriarchal values. At first these attacks focused on beliefs about the divine and innate origins of the gender division of labor. Following World War II, ideological bias socialized men and women to want to do different kinds of work. Interest in popular psychology spread the ideas that men were inherently aggressive and driven to competition and domination, whereas women were passive, docile, and wanted to be dominated. It was widely believed that attempts to behave in ways that contradicted one's innate gender roles were not merely futile but also produced warped, destructive personalities.

Mothers' responsibility for their children's mental health became paramount. A mother's job, then, consisted of selfless devotion to the interests of her children. Mothers who, by poverty or through divorce or widowhood, were compelled to work outside the home received some sympathetic understanding, but middle- and upper-class women who sought professional careers were thought to be selfish and destructive.

Attitudes change to reflect realities, and a reality today is that a majority of households is composed of people in quite different circumstances than the earlier cultural ideal. Couples who both work, unemployed husbands, separated or divorced people, widows or widowers, single parents, and unmarried people living alone constitute a larger percentage of households. Table 6 presents data on various types of family composition, indicating a trend toward both fewer married-couple families and fewer households with nonemployed wives (Ries and Stone 1992, 253).

Government statistics thus indicate that, in 2000, 77 percent of American households consisted of a married couple. Of these, more than half of the wives were in the paid labor force. Therefore, less than one-third of all American households consisted of a husband and nonemployed wife. According to figures released by the U.S. Department of Labor for 2001, 59 percent of married-couple families were supported by the incomes of both husband and wife. This figure shows an increase from 1967, when only 44 percent of married-couple households had incomes from both spouses (U.S. Department of Labor 2001).

TABLE 6 TYPES OF FAMILY COMPOSITION, 1970–2006

Type	1970	1980	1989	2000	2006
Married-couple families	86.7	81.7	79.2	77.0	75.2
Wife in paid labor force	—	41.0	45.7	51.0	—
Wife not in paid labor force	—	40.0	33.5	22.0	—
Male householders, no spouse present	2.4	3.2	4.4	5.0	6.6
Female householders, no spouse present	10.9	15.1	16.5	17.0	18.2

Sources: From U.S. Bureau of the Census, cited in Ries and Stone (1992, 253); U.S. Bureau of the Census (2000; 2006).

As women's roles have been transformed, men's roles have also changed. Husbands are no longer the sole supporters of their families, relieving them of an intense economic and psychological burden. They no longer need to feel that their wives and children are completely dependent on their incomes but can look to their wives for support as well. Some men have taken on the role of "house-husband" or "stay-at-home dad," adopting many of the caretaking responsibilities formerly identified with mothers. This new alignment of roles within the household frees both men and women and enables them to do what suits them best as individuals. Another change has been around issues of child custody in cases of divorce. Courts are no longer automatically granting custody to mothers but instead are weighing multiple factors in their decisions, sometimes assigning custody to fathers.

Although gender roles and relations in any given culture can be analyzed at specific historical periods, it is crucial to understand the forces of change that transform people's behavior and their concepts about themselves and others. The possibility of change always exists, and this is what makes culture a dynamic rather than a static system. Gender relations can become more or less equal or hierarchical, depending on the specific context and operative forces experienced by members of each social category.

The relations between ideology and behavior are extremely complex. Although ideological systems develop in response to structural conditions, changes in these structural conditions usually occur much more rapidly than do changes in the ideological constructs that validate them. People's beliefs may persist despite changes in the contexts that produced them. Therefore, people sometimes have difficulty accepting a new social order and new social concepts.

Additional difficulties in changing ideologies derive from the fact that ideological constructs are often embedded in powerful systems of religious teachings and in attitudes expressed through daily interactions. Individuals usually experience their own behavior as "normal" and "natural" rather than as motivated and mediated by cultural constraints. They are, therefore, largely unaware of the underlying rationales influencing their actions and responses.

Analyses of gender roles and constructs in societies throughout the world demonstrate the diversity of possibilities of human life. People are not forever bound by traditional beliefs and practices. They can accept changes in their actions and they can adopt new ideological concepts relevant to their own experience. Just as we can uncover and understand the transformative dynamics that have occurred in the past, we can also witness and appreciate changes occurring in the present and into the future.

REVIEW

Cultural ideologies are used both to maintain and change gender constructs. Ideological attacks on working women in the United States were designed to discourage participation, just as later ideological inducements encouraged participation during wartime. Contact with Europeans influenced many indigenous groups to adopt more patriarchal or male-dominant ideologies and behaviors. In other instances, European contact improved the status of women. Ideological frameworks create, maintain, and change gender roles and constructs that a society considers acceptable. Behavior usually changes before ideology does.

ANTHROPOLOGY APPLIED

Advocacy for Women

Anthropologists work in organizations that champion women's rights, economic independence, and quality of life. For example, anthropologists conduct and report research on the impacts of economic development on women as well as on their households and communities. Women have been found to play an important role in the economies of developing countries as both producers and consumers, even in strongly patriarchal societies that tend to ignore women's contributions outside the home.

AP Photos/David Longstreath/AP Images

Newscom/MYANMAR NEWS AGENCY/EPA/Newscom

Corbis/Justin Guariglia/Corbis

International organizations involved in advocacy for women include, for example, the Women's Environment and Development Organization (WEDO), the International Center for Research on Women, and the Women's Rights Project of EarthRights International. Through the efforts of organizations such as EarthRights International, rural Burmese women were able to address the United Nations about human rights abuses against women in their country. They reported on their dislocation, forced labor, abandonment, and abuse related to the construction of the Burma–Bangladesh–India natural gas pipeline. The International Fund for Agricultural Development (IFAD), another example, is concerned with ending poverty for rural people. IFAD attempts to strengthen the roles of women in their communities by ensuring that they serve as advisers in projects and as intermediaries between women's organizations and the government. IFAD also attempts to involve both women and men in the outcomes of development projects, thus avoiding the tendency for these initiatives to favor men's interests.

IFAD contends that gender inequality helps perpetuate poverty. To break the cycle of poverty, IFAD attempts to increase women's access to resources (including food, water, and education) and enable them to attain political positions. IFAD also seeks to involve men in the new roles of women because women need the support of men to become empowered to change their roles and status. The idea is that, with equal access to resources, women and men in poverty can help each other and their society.

CRITICAL THINKING QUESTIONS

How does gender inequality perpetuate poverty? As a cultural anthropologist, how might you determine if goals like those of IFAD are viable?

Study and Review on myanthrolab.com

CHAPTER SUMMARY

Sex and Gender

- Gender is a cultural construct that assigns an identity and appropriate roles to people based partly on sexual differences and partly on cultural beliefs about sex and behavior. Gender models make use of sexual differences between males and females, but cultures vary in the roles that women and men perform, the rights they have in relation to each other, and the values associated with their activities. People learn their gender identity from their earliest socialization in infancy through their childhood, learning appropriate behavior and molding personality to conform to cultural norms. Females and males are born, but women and men are products of their culture.
- Most cultures organize their concepts of gender into a dual division of man and woman. However, some cultures allow males and females to identify as a third gender with different roles and behaviors.
- Our culture shapes our sexual feelings and practices and teaches us what is "normal" and what is "deviant." We learn who are appropriate sexual partners, and when, where, and how it is appropriate to have sexual relations. Attitudes about the relationship between sex and marriage and about homosexuality also reflect cultural learning. Some societies view homosexuality as unnatural, sinful, or criminal; others regard it as an expression of human desire.

Gender Roles and Gender Relations

- In all societies, gender influences work. Women's work always includes caring for young children and performing household tasks. Men's work always includes hunting and warfare. Men, women, or both may perform other economic activities, such as farming. Like other elements of culture, gender roles change as economic and material factors change.
- Gender equality is likely in foraging societies where all individuals contribute to subsistence and where hierarchical leadership and control are minimal. In other societies, male dominance may be reflected in men's control over access to resources, economic production and distribution, decision making and leadership, and ritual activity. The most intense male dominance tends to occur in agricultural states. However, in male-dominated societies, women may have independence and power in some spheres of life.
- Some anthropologists suggest that some form of male dominance exists in all societies. Others point to societies in which women and men have or had equal rights and privileges. Rapid culture change brought about by European colonization enhanced men's status and power.

Gender and Subsistence

- Egalitarian relationships develop among foragers and in industrial and postindustrial societies. In the United States, women were central to the industrializing economy. Many women entered the work force outside the home during World Wars I and II. Although there is a "gender gap" in pay between men and women, more than half of women with children of all ages were in the work force by 1996.

Globalization and Gender

- Globalization has affected men and women differently. Women often lose their central roles as subsistence farmers when land is taken out of household production and dedicated to growing crops for national and global trade. Multinational corporations build light manufacturing plants that employ young, unmarried women at low pay.
- Most socialist and former socialist societies have promoted women's participation in production and equal rights. However, working women remain burdened by a "double day," combining paid employment with household responsibilities. Women's unemployment has been disproportionately high in Eastern Europe and the former Soviet Union as socialist economies have changed to a free market. In most countries, women constitute only a small fraction of elected officials or appointed administrators with decision-making powers.

Impacts of Ideology on Gender Constructs

- Despite the significant contributions of women to U.S. economic development and to their families, ideological pressures continue to undermine gender equality. Some people promote the nineteenth-century "cult of domesticity," claiming that men and women are suited for different roles because of their biological needs, psychological orientations, and social wants. Men are supposedly inherently aggressive and assertive, whereas women are innately nurturing and passive. However, many other people support the goal of gender equality.

REVIEW QUESTIONS

1. What are cultural constructs? How are they used to define gender in societies?
2. What are some economic roles typically undertaken by women, and how are those roles different from those of men?
3. What is a third gender identity? How do third gender concepts relate to sexuality and homosexuality?
4. How do production, postmarital residence, and warfare patterns affect the status of women?
5. How are gender roles and relations related to subsistence strategies?
6. How did gender relations among the Ju/'hoansi, Inuit, Iroquois, and Chinese change as a result of both external contact and internal change?
7. How do ideologies affect changes in gender constructs?

MyAnthroLab Connections

Watch. Listen. View. Explore. Read. MyAnthroLab is designed just for you. Dynamic visual activities, videos, and readings found in the multimedia library will enhance your learning experience.

Resources from this chapter:

Watch on **myanthrolab.com**

- *A Generation of Hope*

Listen on **myanthrolab.com**

- *The Connection between Gender Roles and Sex*

View on **myanthrolab.com**

- *Gender*

Explore on **myanthrolab.com** In MySearchLab, enter the Anthropology database to find relevant and recent scholarly and popular press publications. For this chapter, enter the following keywords: gender, gender roles, male dominance, globalization and gender

Read on **myanthrolab.com**

- *Times Are Changing*
- *Women's Movements and Feminism in a Transnational World* by Florence E. Babb
- *Yap: Changing Roles of Men and Women* by Sherwood G. Lingenfelter

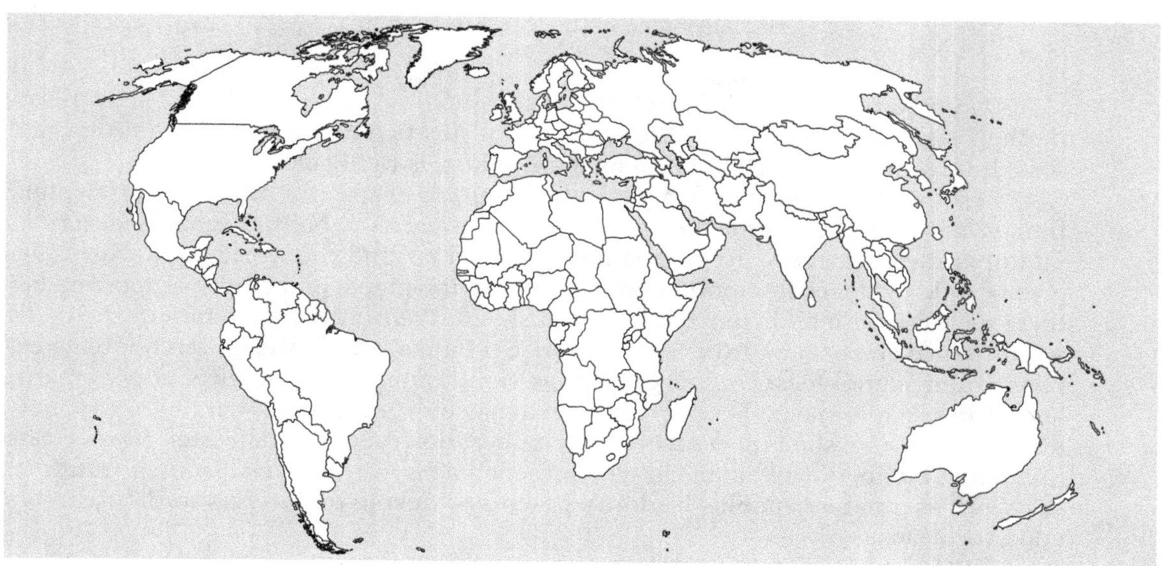

Global Women in the New Economy

Barbara Ehrenreich and Arlie Russell Hochschild

*Movement is a key feature of today's world economy. Manufacturing jobs move from wealthier nations to poorer ones. An enormous variety of goods and raw materials travels by sea and rail to every part of the world. And more and more, so do people. Most come from poor nations to find work in rich ones. At first most were men; today many are women. In this selection, Barbara Ehrenreich and Arlie Russell Hochschild describe the history of female immigration, the reasons women migrate, the kinds of jobs they take in wealthier nations, the stresses their absence has on their own families, their lives in the families of others when they serve as nannies, and consequences for relative wealth among the world's nations. The authors conclude that women, both rich and poor, seek to better their condition and that migration increases interdependence among nations.**

Listen to the **Chapter Audio** on **myanthrolab.com**

"Whose baby are you?" Josephine Perera, a nanny from Sri Lanka, asks Isadora, her pudgy two-year-old charge in Athens, Greece.

Thoughtful for a moment, the child glances toward the closed door of the next room, in which her mother is working, as if to say, "That's my mother in there."

*Introduction and excerpt from Notes from *Global Woman: Nannies, Maids, and Sex Workers in the New Economy* by Barbara Ehrenreich and Arlie Hochschild. Reprinted by permission of Henry Holt and Company, LLC.

"No, you're *my* baby," Josephine teases, tickling Isadora lightly. Then, to settle the issue, Isadora answers, "Together!" She has two mommies—her mother and Josephine. And surely a child loved by many adults is richly blessed.

In some ways, Josephine's story—which unfolds in an extraordinary documentary film, *When Mother Comes Home for Christmas,* directed by Nilita Vachani—describes an unparalleled success. Josephine has ventured around the world, achieving a degree of independence her mother could not have imagined, and amply supporting her three children with no help from her ex-husband, their father. Each month she mails a remittance check from Athens to Hatton, Sri Lanka, to pay the children's living expenses and school fees. On her Christmas visit home, she bears gifts of pots, pans, and dishes. While she makes payments on a new bus that Suresh, her oldest son, now drives for a living, she is also saving for a modest dowry for her daughter, Norma. She dreams of buying a new house in which the whole family can live. In the meantime, her work as a nanny enables Isadora's parents to devote themselves to their careers and avocations.

But Josephine's story is also one of wrenching global inequality. While Isadora enjoys the attention of three adults, Josephine's three children in Sri Lanka have been far less lucky. According to Vachani, Josephine's youngest child, Suminda, was two—Isadora's age—when his mother first left home to work in Saudi Arabia. Her middle child, Norma, was nine; her oldest son, Suresh, thirteen. From Saudi Arabia, Josephine found her way first to Kuwait, then to Greece. Except for one two-month trip home, she has lived apart from her children for ten years. She writes them weekly letters, seeking news of relatives, asking about school, and complaining that Norma doesn't write back.

Although Josephine left the children under her sister's supervision, the two youngest have shown signs of real distress. Norma has attempted suicide three times. Suminda, who was twelve when the film was made, boards in a grim, Dickensian orphanage that forbids talk during meals and showers. He visits his aunt on holidays. Although the oldest, Suresh, seems to be on good terms with his mother, Norma is tearful and sullen, and Suminda does poorly in school, picks quarrels, and otherwise seems withdrawn from the world. Still, at the end of the film, we see Josephine once again leave her three children in Sri Lanka to return to Isadora in Athens. For Josephine can either live with her children in desperate poverty or make money by living apart from them. Unlike her affluent First World employers, she cannot both live with her family and support it.

Thanks to the process we loosely call "globalization," women are on the move as never before in history. In images familiar to the West from television commercials for credit cards, cell phones, and airlines, female executives jet about the world, phoning home from luxury hotels and reuniting with eager children in airports. But we hear much less about a far more prodigious flow of female labor and energy: the increasing migration of millions of women from poor countries to rich ones, where they serve as nannies, maids, and sometimes sex workers. In the absence of help from male partners, many women have succeeded in tough "male world" careers only by turning over the care of their children, elderly parents, and homes to women from the Third World. This is the female underside of globalization, whereby millions of Josephines from poor countries in the south migrate to do the "women's work" of the north—work that affluent women are no longer able or willing to do. These migrant workers often leave their own children in the care of grandmothers, sisters, and sisters-in-law. Sometimes a young daughter is drawn out of school to care for her younger siblings.

This pattern of female migration reflects what could be called a worldwide gender revolution. In both rich and poor countries, fewer families can rely solely on a male breadwinner. In the United States, the earning power of most men has declined since 1970, and many women have gone out to "make up the difference." By one recent estimate, women were the sole, primary, or coequal earners in more than half of American families. So the question arises: Who will take care of the children, the sick, the elderly? Who will make dinner and clean house?

While the European or American woman commutes to work an average twenty-eight minutes a day, many nannies from the Philippines, Sri Lanka, and India cross the globe to get to their jobs. Some female migrants from the Third World do find something like "liberation," or at least the chance to become independent breadwinners and to improve their children's material lives. Other, less fortunate migrant women end up in the control of criminal employers— their passports stolen, their mobility blocked, forced to work without pay in brothels or to provide sex along with cleaning and child-care services in affluent homes. But even in more typical cases, where benign employers pay wages on time, Third World migrant women achieve their success only by assuming the cast-off domestic roles of middle- and high-income women in the First World—roles that have been previously rejected, of course, by men. And their "commute" entails a cost we have yet to fully comprehend.

The migration of women from the Third World to do "women's work" in affluent countries has so far received little media attention—for reasons that are easy enough to guess. First, many, though by no means all, of the new female migrant workers are women of color, and therefore subject to the racial "discounting" routinely experienced by, say, Algerians in France, Mexicans in the United States, and Asians in the United Kingdom. Add to racism the private "indoor" nature of so much of the new migrants' work. Unlike factory workers, who congregate in large numbers, or taxi drivers, who are visible on the street, nannies and maids are often hidden away, one or two at a time, behind closed doors in private homes. Because of the illegal nature of their work, most sex workers are even further concealed from public view.

At least in the case of nannies and maids, another factor contributes to the invisibility of migrant women and their work—one that, for their affluent employers, touches closer to home. The Western culture of individualism, which finds extreme expression in the United States, militates against acknowledging help or human interdependency of nearly any kind. Thus, in the time-pressed upper middle class, servants are no longer displayed as status symbols, decked out in white caps and aprons, but often remain in the background, or disappear when company comes. Furthermore, affluent careerwomen increasingly earn their status not through leisure, as they might have a century ago, but by apparently "doing it all"—producing a full-time career, thriving children, a contented spouse, and a well-managed home. In order to preserve this illusion, domestic workers and nannies make the house hotel-room perfect, feed and bathe the children, cook and clean up—and then magically fade from sight.

The lifestyles of the First World are made possible by a global transfer of the services associated with a wife's traditional role—child care, home-making, and sex—from poor countries to rich ones. To generalize and perhaps oversimplify: in an earlier phase of imperialism, northern countries extracted natural resources and agricultural products—rubber, metals, and sugar, for example—from lands they conquered and colonized. Today, while still relying on Third World countries for agricultural and industrial labor, the wealthy countries also seek to extract something harder to measure and quantify, something that can look very much like love. Nannies like Josephine bring the distant families that employ them real maternal affection, no doubt enhanced by the heartbreaking absence of their own children in the poor countries they leave behind. Similarly, women who migrate from country to country to work as maids bring not only their muscle power but an attentiveness to detail and to the human relationships in the household that might otherwise have been invested in their own families. Sex workers offer the simulation of sexual and romantic love, or at least transient sexual companionship. It is as if the wealthy parts of the world are running short on precious emotional and sexual resources and have had to turn to poorer regions for fresh supplies.

There are plenty of historical precedents for this globalization of traditional female services. In the ancient Middle East, the women of populations defeated in war were routinely enslaved and hauled off to serve as household workers and concubines for the victors. Among the Africans brought to North America as slaves in the sixteenth through nineteenth centuries, about a third were women and children, and many of those women were pressed to be concubines, domestic servants, or both. Nineteenth-century Irishwomen—along with many rural Englishwomen—migrated to English towns and cities to work as domestics in the homes of the growing upper middle class. Services thought to be innately feminine—child care, housework, and sex—often win little recognition or pay. But they have always been sufficiently in demand to transport over long distances if necessary. What is new today is the sheer number of female migrants and the very long distances they travel. Immigration statistics show huge numbers of women in motion, typically from poor countries to rich. Although the gross statistics give little clue as to the jobs women eventually take, there are reasons to infer that much of their work is "caring work," performed either in private homes or in institutional settings such as hospitals, hospices, child-care centers, and nursing homes.

The statistics are, in many ways, frustrating. We have information on legal migrants but not on illegal migrants, who, experts tell us, travel in equal if not greater numbers. Furthermore, many Third World countries lack data for past years, which makes it hard to trace trends over time; or they use varying methods of gathering information, which makes it hard to compare one country with another. . . . From 1950 to 1970, for example, men predominated in labor migration to northern Europe from Turkey, Greece, and North Africa. Since then, women have been replacing men. In 1946, women were fewer than 3 percent of the Algerians and Moroccans living in France; by 1990, they were more than 40 percent. Overall, half of the world's 120 million legal and illegal migrants are now believed to be women.

Patterns of international migration vary from region to region, but women migrants from a surprising number of sending countries actually outnumber men, sometimes by a wide margin. For example, in the 1990s, women make up over half of Filipino migrants to all countries and 84 percent of Sri Lankan migrants to the Middle East. Indeed, by 1993 statistics, Sri Lankan women such as Josephine vastly outnumbered Sri Lankan men as migrant workers who'd left for Saudi Arabia, Kuwait, Lebanon, Oman, Bahrain, Jordan, and Qatar, as well as to all countries of the Far East, Africa, and Asia. About half of the migrants leaving Mexico, India, Korea, Malaysia, Cyprus, and Swaziland to work elsewhere are also women. Throughout the 1990s women outnumbered men among migrants to the United States, Canada, Sweden, the United Kingdom, Argentina, and Israel.

Most women, like men, migrate from the south to the north and from poor countries to rich ones. Typically, migrants go to the nearest comparatively rich country, preferably one whose language they speak or whose religion and culture they share. There are also local migratory flows: from northern to southern Thailand, for instance, or from East Germany to West. But of the regional or cross-regional flows, four stand out. One goes from Southeast Asia to the oil-rich Middle and Far East—from Bangladesh, Indonesia, the Philippines, and Sri Lanka to Bahrain, Oman, Kuwait, Saudi Arabia, Hong Kong, Malaysia, and Singapore. Another stream of migration goes from the former Soviet bloc to western Europe—from Russia, Romania, Bulgaria, and Albania to Scandinavia, Germany, France, Spain, Portugal, and England. A third goes from south to north in the Americas, including the stream from Mexico to the United States, which scholars say is the longest-running labor migration in the world. A fourth stream moves from Africa to various parts of Europe. France receives many female migrants from Morocco, Tunisia, and Algeria. Italy receives female workers from Ethiopia, Eritrea, and Cape Verde.

Female migrants overwhelmingly take up work as maids or domestics. As women have become an ever greater proportion of migrant workers, receiving countries reflect a dramatic influx of foreign-born domestics. In the United States, African-American women, who accounted for 60 percent of domestics in the 1940s, have been largely replaced by Latinas, many of them recent migrants from Mexico and Central America. In England, Asian migrant women have displaced the Irish and Portuguese domestics of the past. In French cities, North African women have replaced rural French girls. In western Germany, Turks and women from the former East Germany have replaced rural native-born women. Foreign females from countries outside the European Union made up only 6 percent of all domestic workers in 1984. By 1987, the percentage had jumped to 52, with most coming from the Philippines, Sri Lanka, Thailand, Argentina, Colombia, Brazil, El Salvador, and Peru.

The governments of some sending countries actively encourage women to migrate in search of domestic jobs, reasoning that migrant women are more likely than their male counterparts to send their hard-earned wages to their families rather than spending the money on themselves. In general, women send home anywhere from half to nearly all of what they earn. These remittances have a significant impact on the lives of children, parents, siblings, and wider networks of kin—as well as on cash-strapped Third World governments. Thus, before Josephine left for Athens, a program sponsored by the Sri Lankan government taught her how to use a microwave oven, a vacuum cleaner, and an electric mixer. As she awaited her flight, a song piped into the airport departure lounge extolled the opportunity to earn money abroad. The songwriter was in the pay of the Sri Lanka Bureau of Foreign Employment, an office devised to encourage women to migrate. The lyrics say:

After much hardship, such difficult times
How lucky I am to work in a foreign land.
As the gold gathers so do many greedy flies.
But our good government protects us from them.
After much hardship, such difficult times,
How lucky I am to work in a foreign land.
I promise to return home with treasures for everyone.

Why this transfer of women's traditional services from poor to rich parts of the world? The reasons are, in a crude way, easy to guess. Women in Western countries have increasingly taken on paid work, and hence need other—paid domestics and caretakers for children and elderly people—to replace them. For their part, women in poor countries have an obvious incentive to migrate: relative and absolute poverty. The "care deficit" that has emerged in the wealthier countries as women enter the workforce *pulls* migrants from the Third World and postcommunist nations; poverty *pushes* them.

In broad outline, this explanation holds true. Throughout western Europe, Taiwan, and Japan, but above all in the United States, England, and Sweden, women's employment has increased dramatically since the 1970s. In the United States, for example, the proportion of women in paid work rose from 15 percent of mothers of children six and under in 1950 to 65 percent today. Women now make up 46 percent of the U.S. labor force. Three-quarters of mothers of children eighteen and under and nearly two-thirds of mothers of children age one and younger now work for pay. Furthermore, according to a recent International Labor Organization study, working Americans averaged longer hours at work in the late 1990s than they did in the 1970s. By some measures, the number of hours spent at work have increased more for women than for men, and especially for women in managerial and professional jobs.

Meanwhile, over the last thirty years, as the rich countries have grown much richer, the poor countries have become—in both absolute and relative terms—poorer. Global inequalities in wages are particularly striking. In Hong Kong, for instance, the wages of a Filipina domestic are about fifteen times the amount she could make as a schoolteacher back in the Philippines. In addition, poor countries turning to the IMF or World Bank for loans are often forced to undertake measures of so-called structural adjustment, with disastrous results for the poor and especially for poor women and children. To qualify for loans, governments are usually required to devalue their currencies, which turns the hard currencies of rich countries into gold and the soft currencies of poor countries into straw. Structural adjustment programs also call for cuts in support for "noncompetitive industries," and for the reduction of public services such as health care and food subsidies for the poor. Citizens of poor countries, women as well as men, thus have a strong incentive to seek work in more fortunate parts of the world.

But it would be a mistake to attribute the globalization of women's work to a simple synergy of needs among women—one group, in the affluent countries, needing help and the other, in poor countries, needing jobs. For one thing, this formulation fails to account for the marked failure of First World governments to meet the needs created by its women's entry into the workforce. The downsized American—and to a lesser degree, western European—welfare state has become a "deadbeat dad." Unlike the rest of the industrialized world, the United States does not offer public child care for working mothers, nor does it ensure paid family and medical leave. Moreover, a series of state tax revolts in the 1980s reduced the number of hours public libraries were open and slashed school-enrichment and after-school programs. Europe did not experience anything comparable. Still, tens of millions of western European women are in the workforce who were not before—and there has been no proportionate expansion in public services.

Secondly, any view of the globalization of domestic work as simply an arrangement among women completely omits the role of men. Numerous studies, including some of our own, have shown that as American women took on paid employment, the men in their families did little to increase their contribution to the work of the home. For example, only one out of every five men among the working couples whom Hochschild interviewed for *The Second Shift* in the 1980s shared the work at home, and later studies suggest that while working mothers are doing somewhat less housework than their counterparts twenty years ago, most men are doing only a little more.

With divorce, men frequently abdicate their child-care responsibilities to their ex-wives. In most cultures of the First World outside the United States, powerful traditions even more firmly discourage husbands from doing "women's work." So, strictly speaking, the presence of immigrant nannies does not enable affluent women to enter the workforce; it enables affluent *men* to continue avoiding the second shift.

The men in wealthier countries are also, of course, directly responsible for the demand for immigrant sex workers — as well as for the sexual abuse of many migrant women who work as domestics. Why, we wondered, is there a particular demand for "imported" sexual partners? Part of the answer may lie in the fact that new immigrants often take up the least desirable work, and, thanks to the AIDS epidemic, prostitution has become a job that ever fewer women deliberately choose. But perhaps some of this demand . . . grows out of the erotic lure of the "exotic." Immigrant women may seem desirable sexual partners for the same reason that First World employers believe them to be especially gifted as caregivers: they are thought to embody the traditional feminine qualities of nurturance, docility, and eagerness to please. Some men feel nostalgic for these qualities, which they associate with a bygone way of life. Even as many wage-earning Western women assimilate to the competitive culture of "male" work and ask respect for making it in a man's world, some men seek in the "exotic Orient" or "hot-blooded tropics" a woman from the imagined past.

Of course, not all sex workers migrate voluntarily. An alarming number of women and girls are trafficked by smugglers and sold into bondage. Because trafficking is illegal and secret, the numbers are hard to know with any certainty. Kevin Bales estimates that in Thailand alone, a country of 60 million, half a million to a million women are prostitutes, and one out of every twenty of these is enslaved. . . . Many of these women are daughters whom northern hill-tribe families have sold to brothels in the cities of the south. Believing the promises of jobs and money, some begin the voyage willingly, only to discover days later that the "arrangers" are traffickers who steal their passports, define them as debtors, and enslave them as prostitutes. Other women and girls are kidnapped, or sold by their impoverished families, and then trafficked to brothels. Even worse fates befall women from neighboring Laos and Burma, who flee crushing poverty and repression at home only to fall into the hands of Thai slave traders.

If the factors that pull migrant women workers to affluent countries are not as simple as they at first appear, neither are the factors that push them. Certainly relative poverty plays a major role, but, interestingly, migrant women often do not come from the poorest classes of their societies. In fact, they are typically more affluent and better educated than male migrants. Many female migrants from the Philippines and Mexico, for example, have high school or college diplomas and have held middle-class—albeit low-paid—jobs back home. One study of Mexican migrants suggests that the trend is toward increasingly better-educated female migrants. Thirty years ago, most Mexican-born maids in the United States had been poorly educated maids in Mexico. Now a majority have high school degrees and have held clerical, retail, or professional jobs before leaving for the United States. Such women are likely to be enterprising and adventurous enough to resist the social pressures to stay home and accept their lot in life.

Noneconomic factors—or at least factors that are not immediately and directly economic—also influence a woman's decision to emigrate. By migrating, a woman may escape the expectation that she care for elderly family members, relinquish her paycheck to a husband or father, or defer to an abusive husband. Migration may also be a practical response to a failed marriage and the need to provide for children without male help. In the Philippines, . . . Rhacel Salazar Parrenas tells us, migration is sometimes called a "Philippine divorce." And there are forces at work that may be making the men of poor countries less desirable as husbands. Male unemployment runs high in the countries that supply female domestics to the First World. Unable to make a living, these men often grow demoralized and cease contributing to their families in other ways. Many female migrants tell of unemployed husbands who drink or gamble their remittances away. Notes one study of Sri Lankan women working as maids in the Persian Gulf: "It is not unusual . . . for the women to find upon their return that their Gulf wages by and large have been squandered on alcohol, gambling and other dubious undertakings while they were away."

To an extent then, the globalization of child care and housework brings the ambitious and independent women of the world together: the career-oriented upper-middle-class woman of an affluent nation and the striving woman from a crumbling Third World or postcommunist economy. Only it does not bring them together in the way that second-wave feminists in affluent countries once liked to imagine—as sisters and allies struggling to achieve common goals. Instead, they come together as mistress and maid, employer and employee, across a great divide of privilege and opportunity.

This trend toward global redivision of women's traditional work throws new light on the entire process of globalization. Conventionally, it is the poorer countries that are thought to be dependent on the richer ones—a dependency symbolized by the huge debt they owe to global financial institutions. What we explore in this book, however, is a dependency that works in the other direction, and it is a dependency of a particularly intimate kind. Increasingly often, as affluent and middle-class families in the First World come to depend on migrants from poorer regions to provide child care, homemaking, and sexual services, a global relationship arises that in some ways mirrors the traditional relationship between the sexes. The First World takes on a role like that of the old-fashioned male in the family—pampered, entitled, unable to cook, clean, or find his socks. Poor countries take on a role like that of the traditional woman within the family—patient, nurturing, and self-denying. A division of labor feminists critiqued when it was "local" has now, metaphorically speaking, gone global.

To press this metaphor a bit further, the resulting relationship is by no means a "marriage," in the sense of being openly acknowledged. In fact, it is striking how invisible the globalization of women's work remains, how little it is noted or discussed in the First World. Trend spotters have had almost nothing to say about the fact that increasing numbers of affluent First World children and elderly persons are tended by immigrant care workers or live in homes cleaned by immigrant maids. Even the political groups we might expect to be concerned about this trend—antiglobalization and feminist activists—often seem to have noticed only the most extravagant abuses, such as trafficking and female enslavement. So if a metaphorically gendered relationship has developed between rich and poor countries, it is less like a marriage and more like a secret affair.

But it is a "secret affair" conducted in plain view of the children. Little Isadora and the other children of the First World raised by "two mommies" may be learning more than their ABC's from a loving surrogate parent. In their own living rooms, they are learning a vast and tragic global politics. Children see. But they also learn how to disregard what they see. They learn how adults make the visible invisible. That is their "early childhood education." . . .

The globalization of women's traditional role poses important challenges to anyone concerned about gender and economic inequity. How can we improve the lives and opportunities of migrant women engaged in legal occupations such as nannies and maids? How can we prevent trafficking and enslavement? More basically, can we find a way to counterbalance the systematic transfer of caring work from poor countries to rich, and the inevitable trauma of the children left behind? . . .

Study and **Review** on **myanthrolab.com**

Review Questions

1. What kind of work do most female immigrants do when they move from poorer to richer countries?
2. What are the advantages of working in another country for women immigrants?
3. What are the negative aspects of the work in which female immigrants engage?
4. What are the four main "flows" of immigrants from poorer to richer countries?
5. What do the female immigrants and the women in wealthier societies have in common economically?
6. The authors argue that immigration has actually made rich countries dependent on poor countries. On what do they base their assertion?

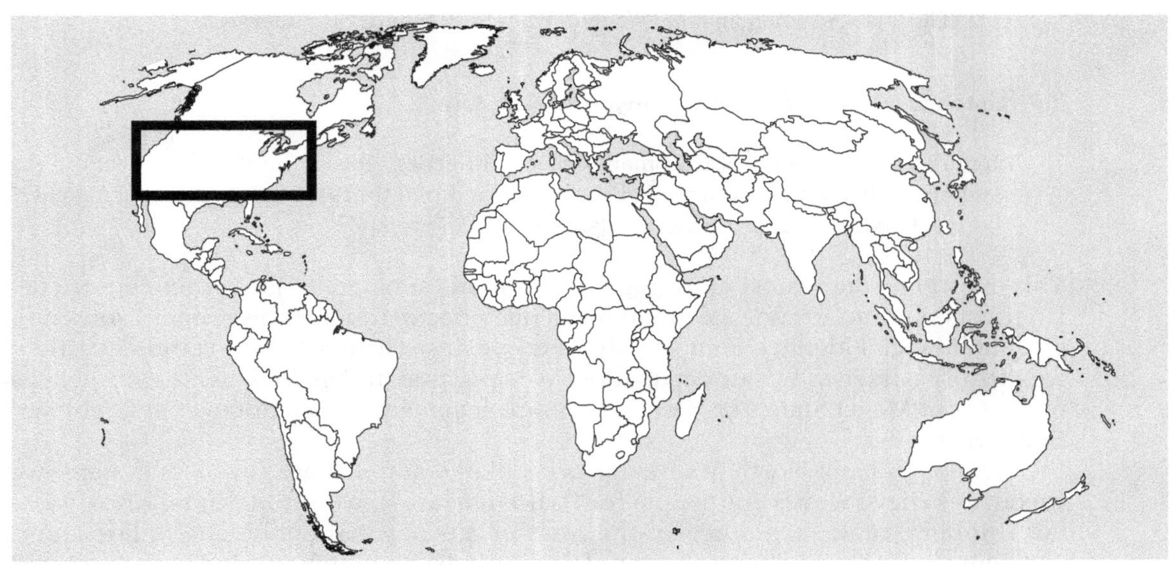

The Opt-Out Phenomenon: Women, Work, and Identity in America

Dianna Shandy and Karine Moe

*Young, successfully employed, college-educated women face a dilemma when they decide to have children. Can they continue to work full-time with the same intensity that up to then has brought them occupational success, or will they have to cut back? What will adjustments required by motherhood and family do to their occupational identity and ability to compete on an equal basis with men? In this article updated for the fourteenth edition of Conformity and Conflict, Dianna Shandy and Karine Moe discuss these and other questions concerning women's work and place in the home once they have children. Basing their comments on extensive interviews and focus groups as well as labor statistics, they argue that younger professional women, pushed by the stress of trying to do everything and pulled by the pleasure of being with their children, are beginning to choose home over work once they have a family. Despite doing so, they can often continue to hold their past occupational identity in the minds of those who know them.**

---

*Original article from Dianna J. Shandy and Karine S. Moe, "The Opt-Out Phenomenon: Women, Work, and Identity in America." Used by permission of the authors.

The Opt-Out Phenomenon: Women, Work, and Identity in America, original article from Dianna J. Shandy and Karine S. Moe, "The Opt-Out Phenomenon: Women, Work, and Identity in America." Used by permission of the authors.

From Chapter 22 of *Conformity and Conflict: Readings in Cultural Anthropology.* Fourteenth Edition. James Spradley, David W. McCurdy.

The Opt-Out Phenomenon: Women, Work, and Identity in America

Listen to the **Chapter Audio** on **myanthrolab.com**

> Jennifer, a tall, well-dressed woman in her mid-thirties, fingers the stem of her wine glass and braces herself for the question she will get a dozen times that night at a cocktail party her husband is holding for his clients: *"And what do you do?"*

This question, which most of us might write off as "small talk," is anything but trivial. It reflects the importance we attribute to one's occupation as the primary source of our public social identity. So normally when we answer the what-do-you-do question, we identify ourselves by our occupation. We might say things such as, "I am a college professor at Metro State," or "I'm a wealth management consultant over at Grant and Smith Securities."

Although most North Americans don't like to admit there is a class system (we prefer to believe we accept people for "who they are"), we actually, and often without thinking, rank each other on the basis of our occupational identity. For example, Jennifer's husband is president of an advertising company with both local and regional accounts. The clients at his cocktail party tend to be presidents, vice presidents, or division managers who work for the companies his firm promotes. They represent a more affluent class of people than, say, firefighters, fast food restaurant managers, or administrative assistants although some of these jobs, such as firefighting, confer prestige.

Occupational identity conveys more than just one's class, however. It implies relative status between individuals. When men and women work at the same jobs, their work signifies that they are approximately equal. This assertion gains credence not only from observations of contemporary U.S. society, but also from anthropological fieldwork and cross-cultural comparison. Take a well-known study by Ernestine Friedl, for example.[1] She points out that decades of ethnographic research in a variety of the world's societies have caused many anthropologists to conclude that males inherit a predisposition to dominate females everywhere. Friedl argues against this position by citing evidence about gender relations in four contrasting hunting and gathering societies. She asserts that control of publicly (beyond the family) shared resources, especially animal protein, determines the degree to which females are equal to males. First, she notes that among the Washo Indians (a foraging group that lived in the Sierra Nevada Mountains of southern California) both men and women foraged for edible plants and both caught rabbits and other small animals as a source of protein. The result was relative gender equality. Men and women were not segregated in daily activities. Both sexes could take lovers, dissolve marriages, and make decisions for the group. The Hadza of Tanzania, she points out, also display relative gender equality largely because men and women forage separately and work to meet their own individual needs for food.

On the other hand, the Tiwi living on islands off the North Coast of Australia show a more typical hunter-gatherer pattern. The men hunt and the women gather, and the male control of meat (protein), which is shared publicly by the whole group, results in domination over women. Men hunt and control the public distribution of meat; women gather only for family needs.

Finally, in the fourth case represented by the Inuit of the Arctic, males provide virtually all the food by hunting seals, walruses, whales, and fish. As a result, Inuit

[1]Enerstine Friedl, "Society and Sex Roles," *Human Nature*, April 1978.

women are "used, abused, and traded," as Friedl puts it. Friedl also notes that gender inequality continues in many agriculturally based societies where men control most of the food that is publicly exchanged. Anthropologists Jane Collier and Michelle Rosaldo have also argued that although women's roles as gatherers contributed significantly to the food supply, these contributions were symbolically less important than the men's hunting activities.[2] Friedl's argument appears to inform what is happening to U.S. women. Women have increasingly gained power and equality as they hold jobs once reserved for men. This has long been a goal for women in our society, and women in America now wield governmental and corporate power at levels never before seen in the history of this country. Women now have unprecedented access to education, jobs, and income.

And that's not all. A large part of the growth in the post–World War II U.S. economy can be attributed to the dramatic increase in the labor force participation by women, especially those who are married. For the first time in U.S. history, women have transitioned to making up half of all workers on U.S. payrolls. And this participation extends to management and leadership positions and the ownership of one-third of all U.S. businesses that employ a quarter of the workforce.

Going hand in hand with this surge in women's contributions to economic productivity, women are at least as well educated as men. Women make up a full 58 percent of the nation's college students and are, overall, the majority in graduate schools and professional schools. They are hired in equal numbers by the country's most prestigious law firms. The majority of veterinarians and accountants are women. Women physicians will soon dominate certain subspecialties within medicine.

In addition, although the number of women in the labor force has increased over the last few decades, fewer males have sought work. Labor economists note that if current trends continue, by 2020 only 70 percent of men will participate in the U.S. labor force, and by 2050, their participation will decline to 66 percent.

To be sure, a wage gap persists between males and females. However, when you look at specific niches within the population, a different picture emerges. Without children, men and women pursue their careers neck in neck in terms of pay when they work similar jobs for similar hours. In fact, the gender wage gap for childless people between the ages of 27 and 33 is practically zero. Does this all mean that gender bias is absent in the world of work in America today? No. Although gender discrimination at work continues, women have seen substantial gains in job equality over the past three or four decades.

Returning Home

And this brings us back to Jennifer's unease about the what-do-you-do question. Like an increasing number of young, married women with children, she decided to give up her career for life as an at-home mother. She did so despite the fact that her personal history fit the trend toward job equality and the growing public influence of women. She graduated from a prestigious eastern college with honors and gained her degree as an attorney at a "top 10" law school. She obtained a high-paying job in a firm specializing in mergers and acquisitions where she was in line to become a partner. Then

[2]Jane F. Collier and Michelle Z. Rosaldo, "Politics and Gender in Simple Societies," in Sherry B. Ortner and Harriet S. Whitehead (eds.), *On Sexual Meanings: The Cultural Construction of Gender and Sexuality* (Cambridge: Cambridge University Press, 1981).

something happened that changed her promising career: she had one, then two children. Now, as an at-home mom, she grapples with the issue of identity in settings such as business cocktail parties where occupational achievement outranks motherhood.

Jennifer's decision to leave her career is not unique. A study of well-educated women that we have been conducting reveals that an increasing number of young, professional women are leaving work to become "at-home moms." As we have discovered, this attorney turned at-home mother is emblematic of a growing number of American women today. In fact, the full-time labor force participation of married women with professional degrees and children under 18 fell from nearly two-thirds to just over a half between 1998 and 2005. From a labor market perspective, this is a significant and remarkable shift, with dramatic ramifications for economic growth. Having gained a foothold in formerly male-dominated positions, it becomes paradoxical that many highly educated, accomplished women are leaving their careers, often as a consequence of becoming mothers. This article is about why we think this is happening and at least partly, how women are managing to do this without losing status.

Who Drops Out

To better understand this conundrum, an anthropologist joined forces with a labor economist to look at national trends and learn more through interviews, surveys, and focus groups about what kinds of women leave work. We discovered from national labor force participation data that a surprising number of college-educated, especially professional, women were opting out of the labor force. From here we designed interviews and focus groups with women who were making or had made the decision to leave their jobs in order to stay home with their children, as well as those who were continuing to juggle home and office.

The first thing we discovered was that age counts. We learned that women in their twenties and thirties seemed to approach child birth, child rearing, and employment differently than their mother's and grandmother's generations. This older generation, the so-called Baby Boomers (women in their late forties to mid sixties) were the first large wave of women to compete for prominent positions in the labor force. They entered work with high expectations and demonstrated ability, and like today's younger women, soon found that work conflicted with marriage and the need to raise children. Overall their response has been to try to manage both work and family by trying to adjust to both, although with varying degrees of success. Nonetheless, these women were pioneering in their ability to anticipate and overcome obstacles and thereby created inroads for their daughters.

The second thing we discovered was that women in their early thirties to mid forties, usually labeled Gen Xers, benefited from the pioneering work of the earlier generation; however, they were the most likely to report having been "blindsided" by the realities of juggling career and children. Angie, a mother of two children in her mid thirties with an MBA typifies this group. When she considered her own expectations for combining work with motherhood said: "I thought women could do it all but just that my [own] mother did not do it well."

The third thing we discovered was that the youngest group of married and well-educated women with young children, women in their twenties and early thirties often called Millennials, seemed to be far more pragmatic than older women about the conflict between work and family. Accordingly, they were also the most creative in the strategies they had devised to manage this conflict. They were still gunning for top spots educationally, but they reported being more mindful about how they would negotiate career and family. We found that women in their twenties and early thirties were more likely than older women to have reduced their responsibilities at work for family reasons. For some this meant selecting a career that will be more flexible and amenable to the demands of child rearing. Others were planning to have careers and children sequentially. Still others planned to have children first and move into a career at some undefined future point when their children are older. But as we have noted above, many, faced with the need and desire to raise children, have left work behind, at least for the time being.

Finally, men rarely drop out of work to become at-home dads. Among married couples, when one parent leaves the labor force, 97 times out of 100 it is the woman who does so. The phenomenon of at-home dads is a growing trend, but when you look at the bigger picture of labor force participation, the number of men who do this is quite small. In this case couples bend to traditional gender roles—mom quits her job and dad presses even harder in his.

Before we go any further, we should note that by virtue of our focus on college-educated women for both our surveys and our interviews, we are *de facto* conducting a study of elite women. We realize that the notion of having a so-called choice not to work is available to only a narrow slice of American women, whereas many others need two incomes to keep their household afloat. Recent turmoil in the economy has brought this issue into even sharper focus. In this respect our study does not tell the story of all women.

However, we argue that it is important to focus on college-educated and therefore relatively elite women because their experiences have the potential to shape the lives of all American women. These women represent the potential leaders, the voices for change. If we don't have a critical mass of women executives, how can we expect the culture of companies to change? How can we expect laws to keep pace with women's lives if they aren't represented in Washington? Therefore, while at first glance middle- and upper-middle-class mothers are targeted most directly by our analysis, we believe the implications of our argument affect all women in America.

Why Do Women "Opt Out"?

So why do women "opt out" now when they have unprecedented access to education, jobs, and income, and potentially suffer the loss of their occupational identity? One suggested answer focuses solely on generation. It says that members of the younger generation, both men and women, are more likely to exit the workforce. Although we don't deny the importance of generation, we feel gender has to be part of the explanation too. In our research, we have grappled with the intersection of gender and generation to understand the outflow of professional women from the labor force. And we agree that younger women approach issues of work and family differently than older women. However, it is important to acknowledge that although gender and generation vie with one another for explanatory power, gender is crucial to what is happening here. Indeed, we believe that gender is more important than generation as a way to understand current intersections of gender, work, and identity in America today.

So if it is not just a generational difference, what are the gender-related factors that bear on women's decision to return home? Let's first look at the factors that are liable to *push* women to leave work.

What "Pushes" Women to Go Home?

There are several things that "push" women to leave the workforce. Let's look at a few of them.

The 100-Hour Couple

One of the most intriguing explanations for why women leave the workforce is the phenomenon of the 100-hour couple. Let's consider Valerie's situation. Valerie was an English and political science double major in college. A child of a single mother who single-handedly supported and raised five children, Valerie attended a state university and worked her way through school. She went on to attend law school and to work as a real estate attorney. She married her husband, also an attorney, who worked in banking. By the time they had their second child, their careers were at a zenith, with Jennifer and her husband each working an average of 75 hours a week. To meet their work obligations, they had a full-time and a part-time nanny. When they discovered they needed yet a third nanny to help out because of work obligations that increasingly spilled over into evenings and weekends, they decided to reevaluate their situation. They concluded that one of them had to reduce hours at work or quit his or her job altogether. They recognized that they could live on either Jennifer's or her husband's salary alone, although her husband's income was significantly larger than hers. Therefore, for financial as well as for other less tangible reasons that could not be tallied on a spreadsheet, Valerie decided to leave her job and to stay home with their children. Valerie described her decision in the following way:

> If we were financially able, one of us needed to quit our jobs. What was the point of having kids if we weren't spending time with them? My children were being raised by strangers—65 hours per week of child care. Deciding to quit my job and stay home with my children was the right thing to do.

Valerie's case illustrates some key points. As women's educational qualifications rise, so too have their occupational aspirations. It's not surprising that well-educated women gravitate toward high-powered, high-paying jobs and marry elite men who have done the same. Whereas previous generations saw a surplus of professional men relative to women, the educational gap has closed. Instead of the CEO marrying his secretary or the doctor marrying his nurse, the CEO is marrying the CFO and the doctor is marrying the doctor. With this larger pool of well-educated, well-employed women, we have transitioned to high-powered couples resulting in a rapid and significant increase in the percentage of high-earning couples that together work over 100 hours per week.

In Valerie's case, she and her husband surpassed 150-hour workweeks, but when we look across a larger sample of families, 100 hours is a threshold for couples who make a decision for one of them—and as pointed out, it is usually the woman—to alter their work situation.

Child Care

A key structural problem that mothers across socioeconomic groups face is child care. High-quality and affordable child care is hard to find, and even when found, it often has rigid drop off and pick up hours. Many child-care centers charge late parents by the minute and will call child protective services if parents do not arrive within an hour of closing time. Of course, these rules are structured so that the child-care workers can return home to care for their own children. Nevertheless, these constraints don't necessarily mesh with workplace demands for working late or getting a last-minute travel assignment. This dilemma is encapsulated in a shootout at an army base in Texas. Police Sergeant Kimberly Munley managed to shoot the gunman, but was herself shot in the process. When asked what her first thought was following the shooting, she replied that she wanted to grab her cell phone so she could call someone to pick up her kids from child care. Who cares for the children while the parents are at work is an enduring structural dilemma working parents face.

The Second Shift

Another factor pushing women out of the workforce is what sociologist Arlie Hochschild calls the second shift. Here she gives life to the old adage, "A man may work from sun to sun, but a woman's work is never done." The second shift refers to the work women do to maintain and sustain the household in addition to their paid employment. The second shift is commonly seen as a significant stressor for women across socioeconomic groups. It is well-documented that women shoulder a disproportionate percentage of housework. For example, one study reports that women do an average of 27 hours of housework a week, compared with 16 hours a week for men. Important here is that while women have made significant gains in the workplace itself, the sexual division of labor at home endures. A recent trend to hire household help is opening possibilities to redefine this aspect of women's lives, but even when families hire people to watch their children or clean their homes, women tend to take on the burden of managing the work that is done in the home and caring for the children.

Although it might strike many as a significant luxury to be able to afford to pay someone to clean their home and watch their children, in our interviews we found that hiring and supervising staff to care for the home and the children placed additional stress on women and was cited by them as part of the decision to quit their jobs. Women also mentioned moral and ethical concerns. Is it "right and fair" to hire women who often have to leave their own children behind to work these jobs? Then, too, was it advisable to hire nannies with lower educational levels to care for their children, and how does one manage the inevitabilities of sick children and/or sick child-care providers?

The women we interviewed did not just describe trying to balance the needs of their children and their jobs, but also the reality of their responsibility to manage their homes. For many the solution was to stay home full time.

The Glass Ceiling

Women mentioned a third factor that caused them to consider resigning their jobs. They talked about encountering a "glass ceiling" at work, meaning one that is a form of discrimination that limits a woman's advancement. They felt they were being blocked from moving upward in the institution because of some tacit or unwritten set of norms about women, especially married women with children. The women we interviewed were frustrated by seeing their counterparts without children (or with a spouse at home caring for their children and managing the household) advance more swiftly in their careers than they did. It seemed unfair because these coworkers did not have to take parental leave to care for children and were more available to work longer hours. One woman lamented that her peers who had not taken time off for children were now vice presidents sitting in corner offices. A lack of flexible work options forced many to choose resigning their jobs altogether or embarking on a "mommy track," which does not allow them to devote time to family for a period of their lives and then resume upward mobility in their careers on a par with their male colleagues who are parents.

One way to look at this is that women quit their jobs not because of their families but because the pressures and inflexibility of their work situations actually leave them no way to maintain both. This is why many women we spoke with take issue with the term *opting out*. Work conditions permitting, some of the women we interviewed would have preferred to *opt in*, albeit on terms that better allowed them to both keep their jobs and raise their children.

When we raised the possibility during a focus group of reducing their hours at the job while still remaining employed, one advertising executive summarized the opinion of many of her counterparts when she said, "Part-time is just a joke." Another woman with an MBA said, "My boss was reluctant to let me go part time at all. When I cut my hours, my boss said he'd pay me less per hour. After three months of fighting and going several levels above him [in the company], I was able to keep my same hourly wage."

We should point out that when viewed cross-culturally, different countries manage the intersection of parenting and labor force participation in other ways. When compared with other industrialized countries, the United States rarely accommodates the need for parents to have and care for children. One woman we interviewed who ironically worked for a children's museum took twelve weeks of unpaid leave when her first child was born. The only thing the museum guaranteed was that she would get her job back when she returned from leave. A *USA Today* article reported that the United States and Australia are the only industrialized countries that fail to provide paid leave for new mothers, although there are exceptions in some U.S. states. Australian mothers have it better, however, with one year of job-protected leave. The U.S. Family and Medical Leave Act provides for twelve weeks of job-protected leave, but it only covers those who work for larger companies. Out of 168 nations in a Harvard University study, 163 had some form of paid maternity leave, putting the United States in company with Lesotho, Papua New Guinea, and Swaziland. Sweden is one of the most progressive countries when it comes to parental leave: working parents are entitled to sixteen months paid leave per child. The cost is shared between the state and the employer. What makes Sweden's policy so notable, however, is that it stipulates that at least two months must be used by the "minority" parent, which usually means the dad.

Factors That "Pull" Women Home

Beyond understanding some of the reasons women are "pushed" out of the workforce, it is also important to understand what "pulls" them there.

Being with Their Children

One of the reasons women gave us for why they liked being "at home" revolved around being with their children. Take, for example, the case of Carol. Carol loves being home with her three kids—all in school now—and is thankful that she is able to do this. She loves spending time with the kids, talking with them, being the one they turn to with their questions. And she likes the freedom and flexibility. Last summer she drove across the country with her children to visit her mom for a month. Having the latitude to make this trip was especially meaningful to her when her mother died the following winter after a long battle with cancer.

Sara, a former dancer, introduces a long list of activities her children participate in by saying that Ryan and Aidan "get a lot of mommy time." She notes that she is able to do this because she has "a flexible enough schedule. I can just cart them wherever they need to go." She goes on to describe visits to grandparents in New Mexico and Florida. "When we go we stay for a week. So, before I quit working at General Mills I would max out my vacation." Having control over their time tended to be a central concern for many of these women.

Lower Stress

Many women seek to pursue a less hectic life. One woman's husband credits her with running "a great back office" such that the family spends their weekends together playing and not running errands. Most were tired of the "juggle and struggle" they encountered when they were still working. They had had to negotiate with their spouse over when, where, who, and how to cover child care. Another woman pointed out that staying at home "made my husband's life easier" and that "he enjoys his children more because he is not worrying about the day-to-day." And women freely point out that this arrangement also allows them to get their needs met by allowing them "time for themselves."

Sense of Responsibility

Women also discussed the moral importance and timing of their decision to head home. One attorney noted, "Conventional wisdom says we need to be there because we have infants. In hindsight, it's absolutely flipped. Now that the kids are getting older, it's more important for me to be there." Another bond trader noted that it was easier to hire someone to care for her children when they were "cute naughty" as toddlers, but now that they were not so cute as misbehaving adolescents she felt the need to be more in charge of her kids' care.

Nostalgia

We also found that a longing to reproduce what for them was a pleasant upbringing may pull many women home. Some had at-home mothers who were there for their kids with such amenities as milk and cookies after school. On the other hand, others may feel the need to redress the rejection they felt as latchkey kids when mothers were not there for them.

Group Support

It seems to be increasingly easier for young women to leave work as other like-minded women make the same choice. In one veterinarian turned at-home mom's words, "I run with a pack of smart women." The result is the formation of social networks of women with their children providing a sense of support, occasions for conversation about domestic matters, and opportunities for their children to play together. Although it's not fun to be an ex-veterinarian who stays home by herself with her kids, it is easier to do so when all your friends are doing it too.

Living within Our Means

Finally, the financial threshold for deciding that one parent will stay home with the kids is a lot lower than one might think. Some of the women we interviewed indicated that their family was making a deliberate choice to live within their means, as determined by one income. Although a somewhat counterintuitive point, having one parent "in reserve" who could join the labor force if the family hit tough financial times instead of taking out a mortgage that relied on both incomes can be a reason women may decide to opt out of the labor force.

Financial Costs

What happens when women give up their paychecks? As one woman aptly noted, "The paycheck gives you a tangible sense of value." Other women we interviewed described how their husband's work time, as the sole income earner, expands as his home effort decreases dramatically. Still other women lament the loss of what they called the "fuck you money," or the financial independence their own earnings afforded them and that potentially allowed them to leave their marriage if they ever felt they needed to. Still others argue that their power did not change because their husband's appreciation of their efforts at home. The threat that they might return to work and thus destroy the comfortable support system they provide moderates the increased power that husband might otherwise enjoy. When women leave their jobs for a period of time, they pay a significant financial penalty. Studies show that for every seven years a woman is out of the labor force, she suffers a ten-year penalty in terms of wages and advancement. Women also take significant financial risks when they become financially dependent on their husbands. It is clear that by leaving work and a paycheck, divorce or the death of a husband will likely have a greater impact on their lives.

Returning to Work

A lot has been written about the difficulty of reentering the workforce after significant absences. This is particularly true in a tight economic market. One problem is the limited shelf life of a professional degree. For example, a physician who does not practice for ten years would have to overcome significant hurdles to get back into clinical work. On the other hand, opportunities to work in the medical sector of the economy may still be available.

However, the chance for them to return to their original occupations did not seem to matter to some of our respondents. Many of the women we interviewed said they would prefer to change professions if they returned to work in the future. Some thought of starting their own businesses. Others described transitioning to a caregiving profession. Many of the bond traders, financial managers, and attorneys we interviewed indicated that when, and if, they returned to work they had their eyes on jobs such as elementary school teacher, social worker for the elderly, or advocate for patients in hospitals.

Maintaining Status

So how can Jennifer and many other young at-home mothers manage to maintain the prestige and power that accompanied the upscale jobs they once trained for and held? A traditional way more common in the past was to associate themselves with their husband's status. If she did so, Jennifer might have answered the what-do-you-do question by simply saying, "Oh, I am Paul's wife." But this kind of answer diminishes her past academic and occupational achievements. So she is more likely to mention what she used to do by saying "I am an attorney" or "I was an attorney with Brand and Cockrin, but I am home with the kids for a while."

Finally, if they remain outside the workplace for long, women may choose to maintain a sense of occupational worth by serving in "quasi-professional" settings such as membership on the boards of civic associations, positions with nonprofit organizations, and aides at their children's schools.

Finally, it is difficult at this point for us to predict what these young professionals, now turned full-time mothers, will do in the future as their children grow up and they are once again free to work. The move home may only be one phase in a life of shifting pressures, opportunities, and associated identities.

Study and **Review** on **myanthrolab.com**

Review Questions

1. What is the relationship between occupation, class, and social identity in the United States?
2. Shandy and Moe described Ernestine Friedl's work on the degree to which males dominate females. What is Friedl's main argument and what evidence does she use to support it?
3. At what age are women likely to move from work to home, according to Shandy and Moe?
4. What factors push women to "head home" instead of continuing to work?
5. What factors pull women to do so?
6. How do women who have left work to raise their children at home deal with the apparent loss of gender equality that comes with their domestic identity over their occupational one?

Kinship and Descent

PREVIEW

- What is descent, and why is it significant in organizing human relationships?
- What types of descent are found in human cultures?
- What kinds of kin groups do the various descent rules create?
- How do different unilineal descent rules affect people's interrelationships?
- How do kinship systems interrelate with other aspects of culture?
- How and why do kinship systems change?
- What terms do people use to classify their kin?
- How do kin terms reveal the type of kinship system people have?

A Color Engraving of A New England Dame School, 1713 The Dame School was one of few educational opportunities available for ordinary girls. *Bettmann/Corbis*

Listen to the Chapter Audio on myanthrolab.com

Read on myanthrolab.com

Whereas I, Joseph Mygatt, of Hartford upon the River and in the jurisdiction of Connecticut in New England, have in the behalf of my son Jacob and at his request made a motion to Mrs. Susanna Fitch, in reference to her daughter Sarah Whiting, that my said son Jacob might with her good liking have free liberty to endeavor the gaining of her said daughter Sarah's affection towards himself in a way of marriage: . . . I will pay thereupon unto my said son as his marriage portion the full sum of two hundred pounds sterling. . . . And I do further engage for the present to build a comfortable dwelling house for my said son and her daughter [Jacob's bride-to-be, Sarah] to live in by themselves. . . . And [I] also give them therewith near the said house one acre of ground planted with apple trees and other fruit trees, which said house, land, and trees shall be and remain to my said son as an addition for his marriage portion, before mentioned, and to his heirs and forever. . . . And I do further promise and engage that at the day of my death I shall and will leave unto him my said son and his heirs so much estate besides the dwelling house, ground, and trees. . . . I do hereby engage and bind over my dwelling house and all my lands and buildings in Hartford. . . . And I do further engage that my daughter Mary's portion of one hundred pounds being first paid to her, I will leave to my said son and his heirs forever my whole estate at the day of my death, he [Jacob, his son] paying to my wife during her natural life twelve pounds a year, and allowing to her a dwelling entire to herself in the two upper rooms and cellar belonging to my now dwelling house, with the going of half the poultry and a pig for her comfort in each year during her said life; also allowing her the use of half the household stuff during her life, which she shall have power to dispose of to Jacob or Mary at her death. . . . And lastly I do engage that the whole benefit of the Indian trade shall be to the sole advantage of my son Jacob, and do promise that I will during my life be assistant and helpful to my said son in the best ways I can, both in his trading with the Indians, his stilling, and otherwise, for his comfort and advantage.

Excerpts from "Marriage Settlement of Jacob Mygatt, of Hartford, Connecticut," cited in *Remarkable Prividences 1600–1700*, edited by John Demos. © 1972. Reprinted by permission of George Braziller.

This marriage contract for Jacob Mygatt and Sarah Whiting was written on November 27, 1654, in Hartford, Connecticut. It reveals a complex array of concerns common to all human societies: Among the people you live with, to whom do you owe the greatest loyalty and support? Who among them might you marry? What will happen to your dependents when you die? How will they support themselves? How will your property be divided and distributed, and to whom? Universally, these and other questions are resolved through kinship systems. This chapter compares the various ways that people define their relatives and reckon their kinship.

KINSHIP SYSTEMS

In all societies, people have ways of organizing their relationships with other people, especially their primary relationships with kin. As children, our earliest and most influential interactions are with our parents, siblings, and other relatives. We rely on our families for all of our survival needs. Our families feed us, clothe us, and provide our shelter. They also help us adjust to the world around us, teaching us the behavior and attitudes that our culture expects, and they provide emotional support in both good times and bad.

Many of our relatives continue as important economic and emotional supports throughout our lives. Even as adults, we can turn to our kin in networks of reciprocity, asking for aid in times of need. In turn, we may be asked to respond to their requests when they are in need. We may align ourselves with our relatives when they are engaged in disputes with others. We may expect loyalty from our kin when we are in conflict with neighbors or other community members. During personal or family crises, we may expect emotional support from our relatives. Together we celebrate happy occasions such as births and marriages, and we mourn the deaths of our kin.

In industrial societies, friends, colleagues, comembers of clubs, and other nonrelatives also function significantly to give us companionship and support. In most societies, however, kinship relations permeate people's daily lives and mold their identity and their sense of themselves. In societies or communities characterized by cohesive social systems, family members may be united in dense, complex networks. They may perform important functions in the absence of the formal institutions that regulate and organize economic, political, and religious life in industrial societies. People identify themselves not just as individuals, but as members of kinship groups.

A **kinship system** consists of connections between people by "blood," marriage, or adoption, and the beliefs and practices by which people regard and treat one another as relatives. The people may be genetically related (**consanguines,** "related by blood") or related by marriage (**affines**), or they may not be related at all. Many kin groups include adopted kin and **fictive kin,** unrelated individuals who are regarded and treated as relatives. Thus, the notion of kinship is essentially a social and symbolic idea, not based on universal objective criteria.

kinship system
System of determining who one's relatives are and what one 's relationship is to them.

consanguines
People related by blood.

affines
People related through marriage.

fictive kin
Unrelated individuals who are regarded and treated as relatives.

Among foragers, pastoralists, and horticulturalists, kinship relations were the primary regulators of social and economic life. Through kin relations, people organized their households, allocated work roles, controlled land and other property in common, made decisions affecting the group, and carried out ritual functions. In agrarian societies, kinship relations generally continued to be paramount in organizing and integrating communities, but new patterns of interaction also emerged. Gradually, as state societies developed, specialists and state institutions took over many of the functions carried out by kinship groups. The state regulated intergroup trade, established formal procedures for making decisions and settling disputes, and set up institutions to carry out some social functions, replacing the critical roles of kinship groups. In postindustrial societies, people may live apart from their relatives, and all of the functions of kin groups can be fulfilled through public or private institutions. Thus, fundamental differences exist between those societies where people's lives center around their kin and where social, economic, and political functions are integrated with kinship groups and those societies

Listen to the **Audio:** *Parents Increasingly Adopting Children of Another Race* on **myanthrolab.com**

This family reunion, held at Monticello in Virginia in July 2004, celebrates the kinship of descendants of Thomas Jefferson and the African slave Sally Hemings. Some relatives at this event met each other for the first time. Corbis/Susanna Raab/Sygma/Corbis

rules of descent
Social rules that stipulate the nature of relationships from one generation to another.

where ties among kin are looser and less intense and where formal institutions provide social, economic, and political functions.

Kinship systems are organized around rules of marriage and **rules of descent,** which stipulate the nature of relationships from one generation to another. Although the notion of kinship varies among societies, there are a limited number of ways in which people trace descent and organize kinship groups. Two fundamental organizing principles are bilateral descent and unilineal descent. In societies with **bilateral descent,** people think of themselves as related to both their mother's kin and their father's kin at the same time (*bilateral* means "two sides," from *bi* meaning "two" and *lateral* or "side"). In **unilineal descent** systems, people define themselves in relation to only one side, either their mother's or their father's (*unilineal* means "one line," from *uni* meaning "one" and *lineal* or "line").

What rule of descent is followed in your family? What is the name for the type of kin group formed by this rule?

Bilateral Descent

Organizing one's relatives according to the principle of bilateral descent creates a large, potentially limitless group of people to whom one may claim relationship. People usually do not interact with everyone in this large kinship group. Rather, they tend to know, socialize with, and depend on a smaller group of relatives within the wider network. This smaller group of bilateral relatives is called a **kindred** (see Figure 1).

Reckoning one's kin through bilateral descent is common in industrial societies, but it is also found in many foraging societies. Kindreds are adaptive in both kinds of cultures, but for different reasons. In foraging societies, bilateral descent allows people to make claims on a wide group of people for economic assistance and emotional support. This strategy is adaptive, especially when resources are scarce. In times of need, people may ask relatives for aid, based on the principle of reciprocity. At different times, people are both givers and receivers of support. They are at an advantage if they can call on the help of many others in times of need. They are also likely to be asked for help, but having diffuse reciprocal networks is an efficient and reliable adaptive strategy in the long run.

bilateral descent
Principle of descent in which people think of themselves related to both their mother's kin and their father's kin at the same time.

unilineal descent
Principle of descent in which people define themselves in relation to only one side, either their mother's side or their father's side.

kindred
Kinship group consisting of known bilateral relatives with whom people interact, socialize, and rely on for economic and emotional assistance.

Bilateral descent is also adaptive for people in industrial countries, where it functions to loosen kinship ties. Thus, the same system of descent can have different outcomes and serve different purposes, depending on people's needs as they adapt to specific ecological, social, and economic conditions. Although bilateral descent provides a large number of people with reciprocal obligations and responsibilities, it also creates a loosely organized kin group without definite social limits or boundaries. By loosening kinship ties, people establish greater individual autonomy, freeing themselves from claims that other people might make on them. Individuals and small family units can advance themselves economically, accumulate more wealth, and raise their standards of living if fewer people can make claims on them for support. Thus, capitalist societies favor bilateral descent because of the focus on individual achievement and accumulation of personal wealth. However, although autonomy and independence can free people from obligations, they may also result in social isolation and may limit the number of people from whom a person might seek aid in times of need.

The functions of bilateral descent are different in foraging and industrial societies because of both cultural context and cultural history. Although a particular cultural behavior may be adaptive, its advantage can be understood only within the society and

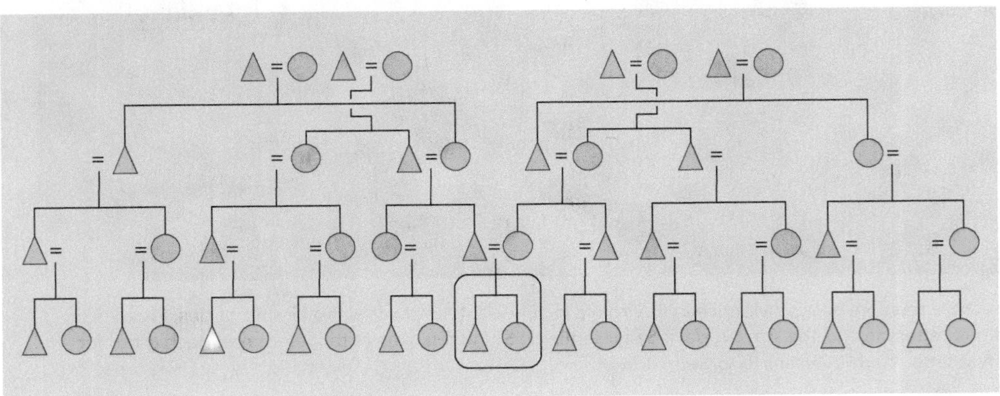

FIGURE 1
A Kindred. A group of people, traced through bilateral descent, related to the brother and sister shown at the bottom row, center.

Here, members of a G/wi band in Botswana gather around a cooking fire. Like other peoples of the Kalahari, the G/wi reckon their kinship bilaterally. Corbis/Peter Johnson/Corbis

circumstances. That is why a particular strategy (in this case, bilateral descent) can be advantageous in different societies for different reasons.

In historical context, bilateral kin groups in industrial societies reflected changing economic and social conditions favoring individual achievement and personal advancement. These conditions tended to weaken kin ties. Nevertheless, both the poor and the wealthy can benefit from membership in bilateral kin groups. Carol Stack's research in African American urban families (1975) and Rhoda Halperin's study of rural Kentuckians (1990) demonstrate that low-income people and people living in rural areas tend to maintain large networks of kin, which diversifies and widens their possibilities of support in times of need. The very wealthy, meanwhile, can shelter their money in trusts distributed among their kin (Marcus 1992). They also rely on one another for political support based on shared interests and goals.

The increasing prevalence of bilateral descent in the world today is partly an outgrowth of the adaptive functions of bilateral descent groups in industrial societies and partly a result of the globalization of culture based on Euro-American power and influence.

Unilineal Descent

Unilineal descent has two principal forms: matrilineal and patrilineal (see Figures 2 and 3). Other variants, discussed later in this chapter, are far less common. In both forms, kinship is traced through descendants on one side only, either through the mother or the

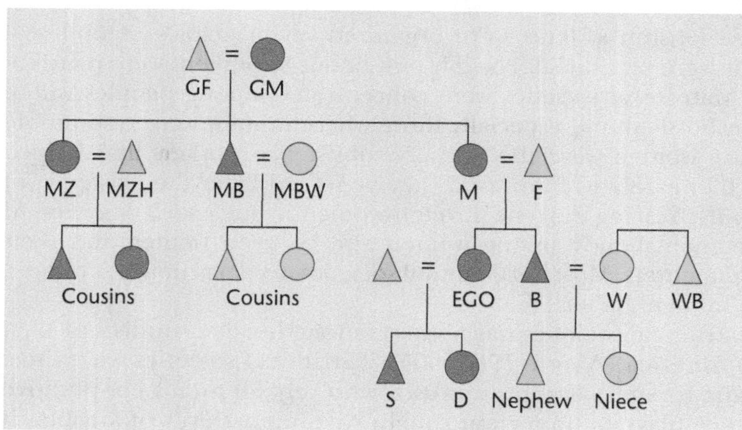

FIGURE 2

Matrilineal Descent. Brown triangles and circles are ego's kin group. Diagrams of kinship terminology systems use the following conventions: Circles represent females, triangles represent males, horizontal lines link siblings, vertical lines link generations, and equal signs link husband and wife. Abbreviations used to designate kin in a kin diagram are M = mother, F = father, Z = sister, B = brother, D = daughter, S = son, H = husband, and W = wife. Using combinations of these symbols, anthropologists can describe all kin relations in any kinship system.

FIGURE 3
Patrilineal Descent. Brown circles and triangles are in ego's kin group.

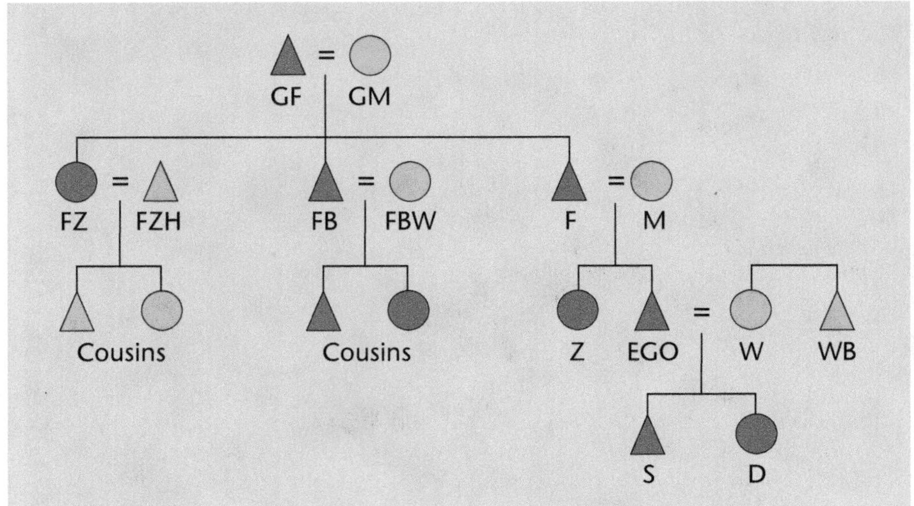

father. However, they differ in the side through which descent is traced or the side chosen for affiliations, or even whether both sides may be taken into account. In **matrilineal** societies, people reckon descent through their mothers. That is, children belong to the kinship group of their mother. In **patrilineal** societies, people reckon descent through their fathers, so that children belong to the kinship group of their father.

A kinship system consists of the beliefs and practices by which people regard and treat each other as relatives. The people may be genetically related (consanguines) or related by marriage (affines). They may also be unrelated, adopted, or fictive kin. Rules of descent stipulate the nature of kin relationships from one generation to another. Two ways that people trace their descent are bilateral descent (tracing relationships through both parents and both sets of their parents) and unilineal descent (tracing relationships through either the mother's kin or the father's kin). Bilateral descent groups are called kindreds.

MATRILINEAL AND PATRILINEAL SYSTEMS

If your kinship system were matrilineal, who would be in your kin group? Who would be your closest relatives if your kinship system were patrilineal?

Although people in unilineal systems belong to one particular line of descent, social bonds with people belonging to other kinship groups are also recognized. For example, in patrilineal systems, children belong to the father's kin group but still know that they are also related to people on the mother's side. Nevertheless, people feel the strongest ties to members of their own group, in this case, the father's.

Prevalence of Matrilineal and Patrilineal Descent

Of known cultures whose kinship systems were organized on principles of unilineal descent, the great majority were patrilineal. Possibly only about 15 percent were matrilineal (Aberle, 1961, 663). Matrilineal societies were concentrated among peoples whose economies were based on horticulture, especially those where women were responsible for the farmwork. Because women were the primary subsistence workers and helped one another with both child care and farmwork, they benefited from the existence of stable and cooperative units. Tracing descent through women in such societies stressed the communal and permanent bonds among women and between women and their children, especially their daughters. Most horticultural societies were patrilineal, however, even those that relied on women's labor.

matrilineal
Descent system in which kinship group membership and inheritance pass through the female line.

patrilineal
Descent system in which kinship group membership and inheritance pass through the male line.

The proportion of matrilineal societies was highest among horticulturalists of West Africa and native North America (Aberle 1961, 665). Patrilineal societies were most prevalent among nomadic foragers and pastoralists, who rely on men's cooperative labor. Although subsistence plays an important role in shaping patterns of kinship, it is not sufficient to explain these patterns. Exceptions to patterns show that other cultural variables are involved.

patriarchy
Social system in which men occupy positions of social, economic, and political power from which women are excluded.

Matrilineal and Patrilineal Societies Compared

A comparison of Figures 2 and 3 shows that the structure of matrilineal descent is the mirror image of the structure of patrilineal descent. In practice, however, there are several important differences between them, particularly in the kinds of bonds people maintain with their own kinship group after marriage. These differences stem from one main cause: In matrilineal societies, women bear their own lineal descendants; in patrilineal societies, women bear the lineal descendants of the men into whose group they marry.

In patrilineal systems, particularly those in which married couples live with the husband's family, women tend to leave their own kin group after marriage. Their separation is in part residential because they usually move to their husband's household, and in part structural and psychological. The intensity of a woman's separation from her own kin group and incorporation into her husband's group varies among patrilineal cultures. Separation is strongest in societies where men control descent, inheritance, and social power. Such societies are said to be patriarchal. In patriarchal societies, women typically lose much contact with and support from their own relatives. **Patriarchy**—rule or dominance by men in social, economic, and political life—is not the same as patrilineality—descent traced through men. One term refers to power and the other to descent.

In contrast, in patrilineal societies with greater gender equality, women may maintain strong emotional bonds with their families, especially with parents and siblings, even if they change residence after marriage. For instance, among the Tewa of New Mexico, daughters leave their natal family when they marry, but emotional ties to their kin remain strong. Women continue to visit their relatives often, to participate in family rituals and other important events, and to take part in discussions about matters of communal interest. In times of conflict with her husband or in-laws, a woman can also expect that her family members will be her allies.

In patrilineal systems, it is in the interests of kin groups to establish secure marital ties because a patrilineal descent group obtains its children through marriage. That is, through marriage, a man is able to claim the children his wife bears. For this reason, divorce tends to be difficult to obtain. The couple's relatives may exert pressure on both husband and wife to remain in an unhappy union. Even where divorce is possible, some social criticism attaches to the couple after divorce, especially to the wife.

In parts of rural India that are strongly patriarchal, once a woman marries and moves to her husband's household, she cannot expect emotional or financial support from her birth family. Alamy Limited/Vinod Alamy/Alamy

These conditions, common in patrilineal systems, are absent in matrilineal societies or appear in different form and function. Matrilineal kinship groups obtain new members (children) from women of their own group, so the marriage tie is often not as intense or secure. Divorce may be more easily obtained by either spouse and carries less social stigma, if any.

Although matrilineal societies have practices and attitudes that support women, none is matriarchal in the sense that some patrilineal societies are patriarchal. That is, there are no known examples of societies in which women exclusively control descent, inheritance, and social and political power. There are also no societies in which men's voices are silent and their interests are ignored.

In matrilineal systems, especially those in which married couples reside with the wife's kin, men often have split loyalties. Their identification with and integration into their wife's household may be rather loose, particularly in the early years of marriage. Men often maintain strong emotional, economic, and ritual ties to their family of birth. They may function as representatives of their natal family to outsiders and may have important decision-making roles within it.

inheritance rules
Rules for the passage of land, wealth, and other property from one generation to the next.

Influence and Inheritance in Unilineal Descent Groups

Matrilineal descent groups characteristically differ from patrilineal descent groups in several important ways (Schneider 1961). For instance, matrilineal descent groups depend for their continuity and operation on retaining control over both male and female members. In contrast, women are peripheral members of their own patrilineal descent groups because they bear children for their husbands' group. In matrilineal systems, women give birth and care for future members of their own kin groups. Men retain interests in their descent groups through ties that are not completely severed when they marry. They may continue to have some control over resources allotted to their kin group. They may be required to give economic support to their mothers and especially to their sisters. They may also play a role in the upbringing of their sisters' children, who, by virtue of descent, are members of their kin group (their own children belong to the kinship group of their wives, the children's mothers).

For example, among the Trobriand Islanders of Melanesia, men are responsible for supplying their sisters (and their sisters' husbands) with yams (Weiner 1976; 1988). Although men tend the yam gardens, the "owner" of the produce is the man's sister. A man begins planting a yam garden for his daughter with the understanding that one of her brothers will take over the responsibility and continue to supply her and her family with yams after she marries. A man also assumes the role of authority and disciplinarian to his sisters' children rather than to his own because his sisters' children are members of his own matrilineal kin group.

Inheritance rules are strongly related to rules of descent. In societies with matrilineal descent, for example, resources and property are inherited through women. However, men may still control the allocation and disposition of resources, so that inheritance passes from one man to another within the matrilineal kin group. In such societies, the role of the mother's brother is enhanced because inheritance passes from one's mother's brother to one's sister's son. For example, among the matrilineal peoples of the Pacific Northwest of North America, such as the Tlingit, resources that matrilineal kin groups own and men use are passed from a man to his sister's son rather than to his own son.

Thus, matrilineal descent groups do not require the statuses of father and husband. Because of the matrilineal descent rule, children belong to the kin group of their mother. Women do not need to be married, and the identity of the father is not relevant to descent. In contrast, in patrilineal systems, the statuses of father and husband are critical in the determination of descent and the legitimacy of the offspring. Marriage is necessary for men because a man as husband claims the status of father to his wife's children through marriage. Marriage is also necessary for women in patrilineal systems because, through marriage, a woman's child may claim membership in a kin group and thus be granted legitimacy.

These Trobriand Islanders are sorting yams from a patch that their father planted for their sister. A brother's responsibility is to supply his sister and her husband with yams. Anthro-Photo File/Bell/Anthro-Photo File

The institutionalization of strong, lasting, intense ties between husband and wife may not be compatible with the maintenance of matrilineal descent groups. In matrilineal societies, women's loyalties remain primarily with their own kin group and not with their husband. Men's loyalties, on the other hand, are split between the kin group of their wife and children and the kin group of their own family of descent. Men often are needed by their own kin group to perform economic, ritual, and political functions, and thus remain identified with and loyal to that group. In contrast, as noted earlier in this chapter, women in patrilineal societies may lose all or most attachments to their own kin group, and once married, they no longer have economic obligations to their family of origin.

The matrilineal Diné of the American Southwest recognize a man's continuing bonds and responsibilities to his natal family, especially to his mother

In Their Own VOICES

Wedding Songs from North India

The poignancy of women's separation from their kin is vividly dramatized in North India at the moment of departure, when a newly married woman first leaves her natal home in the company of her husband and his male kin. Both men and women are apt to shed tears at the sight of the heavily veiled young woman being carried to a waiting vehicle. The women of the bride's village sing "departure songs" at the doorway. Many of these songs are commentaries on the fragile position of a woman in her husband's household and on her relationships with her blood relatives and her in-laws.

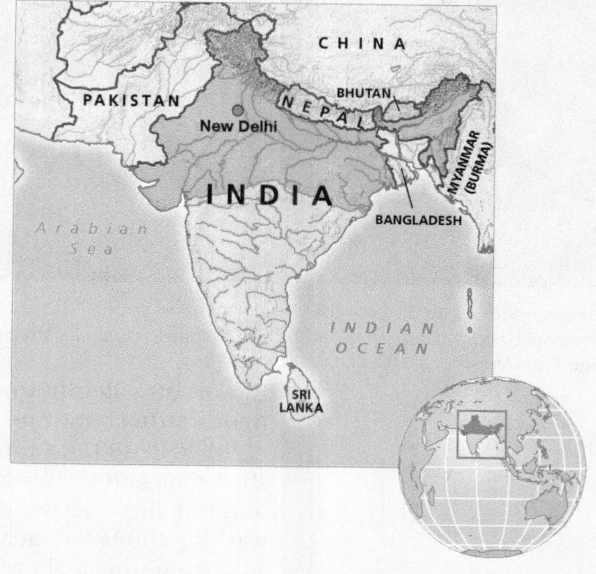

1. Refrain [bride's kin speaking]
   Dear girl, today you have left your father's house, today you have become "other".
   The streets in which you spent your childhood have today become "other".

[Bride speaking]
   My grandfather cries, my grandmother cries, the whole family cries.
   My younger brother cries, your sister born from the same mother has left and gone away.

[Verses are repeated with bride speaking, using different kin terms]

2. Two water pots are on my head.
   A beautiful golden pendant is on my forehead.
   Call me back quickly, Mother.
   Beg with folded hands.
   My heart is not here in my husband's mother's house.
   My heart is not here with this foreign man.
   Call me back quickly, Mother.
   Beg with folded hands.
   My friends still played with dolls together.
   But I went off to my in-law's house.
   Call me back quickly, Mother.
   Beg with folded hands.

[The first verse is repeated a number of times, changed only by the substitution of the names of other ornaments worn by married women.]

From Gloria Goodwin Raheja and Ann Grodzins Gold, *Listen to the Heron's Words: Reimagining Gender and Kinship in North India.*

CRITICAL THINKING QUESTION

What do these songs suggest about the positions of women in their husbands' households?

and sisters. His integration into his wife's household is gradual and limited. His role in decision making in his own household is only slowly recognized and remains limited in scope. In contrast, the patrilineal Yanomamo of the Amazonian rain forests of Brazil and Venezuela emphasize men's control over their own households, wives, and children.

The bonds that may develop between children and their father may compete with the authority of the children's matrilineal descent group. Thus, in matrilineal systems, fathers may develop strong, intense, and lasting emotional bonds with their children, but their authority over their children is usually weak. Instead, men in the mother's kinship group, especially the mother's brothers, tend to exert authority over the child. The Diné and the Trobriand Islanders exemplify this pattern. In both groups, men are affectionate toward their own children but are not authority figures for them.

In Japan, mothers encourage the development of strong, enduring emotional bonds, called *amae*, with their children, especially their sons. The Image Works/Jon Burbank/The Image Works

In matrilineal descent groups, the emotional investment of the father in his own children may be a source of strain because he owes his primary allegiance to the children of his own kin group, namely, his sister's children. In patrilineal descent groups, emotional ties between the mother and her children may be a source of strain. Because of children's early bonds with their mothers and a mother's affection for her children, children may not always identify with their father's group. Indeed, in strongly patrilineal societies, a mother and her children may form intense emotional ties as a buffer or refuge against the father's control. Nevertheless, these emotional ties do not directly threaten the father's dominant position as head of household.

In matrilineal societies, strong bonds between fathers and their children might threaten the mother's authority and the important position of other men in the children's matrilineal descent group. Men and women in the father's kinship group also play important roles, however. Among the Zuni of the American Southwest, for example, a baby's father's mother performs critical birth ceremonies honoring and protecting the child (Gill 1982). Immediately after a baby is born, its paternal grandmother comes to the home and recites protective prayers. She then bathes the baby, rubs ashes on its body, and remains with the mother and child for eight days. At sunrise on the eighth day, after washing the baby's head and sprinkling it with cornmeal, she takes the baby out to greet the rising sun, again reciting protective prayers.

Women also play an important role in funerals. At the end of life, the sister of a deceased's father has the responsibility of preparing the body for burial. She bathes the body, rubs cornmeal on it, and dresses it in new clothes, thus preparing the deceased for the journey to the afterworld.

The ritual participation of men's relatives dramatizes the connections between people and their paternal kin in a matrilineal system. Table 1 compares matrilineal and patrilineal descent groups in terms of the cultural and relational characteristics discussed in this section.

Other Forms of Unilineal Descent

double descent
Kinship principle in which people belong to kinship groups of both their mother and father.

Although most societies with unilineal descent trace kinship through either matrilineal or patrilineal principles, some societies reckon descent according to both patrilineal and matrilineal principles. In this system, called **double descent,** people belong to kinship groups of both mother and father. This system differs from bilateral descent because it is based on the existence of strongly delineated kinship groups. Some kinds of property

TABLE 1 A COMPARISON OF CULTURAL CHARACTERISTICS IN MATRILINEAL AND PATRILINEAL DESCENT

	Continuity	Status of Father and Husband	Strength of Marital Bond	Male Authority	Father–Child Relationship	Kin-Group Relationship
Matrilineal Descent Groups	Women bear their own descendants and are crucial members of their descent group.	Not required.	Weak	Weak in marital household, but often strong in sister's household.	Strong emotional bond, little authority.	Father's kin group retains important ceremonial functions.
Patrilineal Descent Groups	Women bear their husbands' descendants and are secondary members of their own descent group.	Required for legitimacy of offspring.	Strong	Strong in marital household.	Great authority.	Mother's kin group relinquishes attachments and obligations.

might be inherited along matrilineal lines and other kinds patrilineally. For example, the Yako of eastern Nigeria have a double descent system in which property is divided into patrilineal and matrilineal ownership (Fox 1984, 135). Patrilineal descent groups own farmland and grazing pastures, whereas matrilineal descent groups own cattle and other livestock. People inherit these two different kinds of resources, one permanent and inalienable and the other consumable, from each of their parents.

The Inca of Peru had a system of **parallel descent,** in which descent and inheritance followed gender-linked lines, so that men considered themselves descended from their fathers, and women considered themselves descended from their mothers (Silverblatt 1987). Inheritance of property and rights to use land typically followed these parallel lines as well. That is, men inherited from their fathers, and women inherited from their mothers. Parallel descent and inheritance created strong gender identity and solidarity. Principles of parallel descent made sibling bonds important in kinship unity. Inheritance could flow through men from a mother's brother to a sister's son and through women from a father's sister to a brother's daughter.

Finally, some peoples have systems of **ambilineal descent,** in which individuals may choose to affiliate with either their mother's kinship group or with their father's group. People make this decision based on a strategic consideration of the territory, wealth, and social prestige of each group they are eligible to join. In societies of the South Pacific where such systems operate, people can affiliate with only one group during their lifetime, but their offspring may choose a different affiliation. In societies with ambilineal descent, as in the Pacific Northwest of North America, a person could make claims to be a member of multiple descent groups. For example, among the Kwakwaka'wakw (or Kwakiutl) of British Columbia, people could inherit material and ceremonial wealth, as well as access to food resource sites, through claims to multiple kin groups.

parallel descent
Kinship principle in which descent and inheritance follow gender-linked lines so that men consider themselves descended from their fathers and women consider themselves descended from their mothers.

ambilineal descent
Principle of descent in which individuals may choose to affiliate with either their mother's or their father's kinship group.

lineage
A set of relatives tracing descent from a known common ancestor.

Unilineal descent rules include matrilineal (reckoned through one's mother's line), patrilineal (reckoned through one's father's line), ambilineal (reckoned through either parent's line), parallel descent (reckoned by women through their mothers and by men through their fathers), and double descent (reckoned through both one's mother's line and one's father's line). A patriarchy is any society, especially one organized by patrilineal descent, in which men have dominant power and authority. Inheritance rules generally follow principles of descent.

UNILINEAL DESCENT GROUPS

Unilineal descent systems usually organize people into more structured groupings than are formed by bilateral descent rules. Four kinds of unilineal descent groupings are lineages, clans, phratries, and moieties. Some cultures have all four types; others have only one or two. All have in common a focus on lineal descent, following either the mother's or the father's line, so that the specific descent group may be a matrilineage or patrilineage, or a matriclan or patriclan, respectively.

Lineages

The smallest kinship unit is a **lineage,** or a set of relatives tracing descent from a known common ancestor. In a matrilineal system, a matrilineage may consist of a female ancestor, her sons and daughters, her daughters' children, and her daughters' daughters' children. A patrilineage may consist of a male ancestor, his sons and daughters, his sons' children, and his sons' sons' children. The depth of lineages varies in different cultures. In some societies, people know the names of their lineage members for only a few generations, whereas people may have a known depth of nine or more generations in other societies. In some West African societies, the names and deeds of lineage members are memorized and passed on by word of mouth from generation to generation, in some cases covering 200 years or more. Written records create greater time depth. The Old Testament of the Bible, for example, contains a chronology of ancient patrilineages.

What do you know about the history of your descent group? How is this knowledge preserved?

exogamy
Marriage principle in which people cannot marry members of their own lineage or clan but instead must forge alliances with members of other groups.

endogamy
Marriage principle in which people marry members of their own group.

parallel cousin
A child of one's mother's sister or of one's father's brother.

cross-cousin
A child of one's mother's brother or of one's father's sister.

Among the Kwakwaka'wakw of British Columbia, lineages are named groupings that control access to resource sites such as ocean coastline, salmon streams, berry patches, and other foraging locations. Lineages also own ceremonial objects such as masks, crests, sacred songs, and dances. Each lineage has a founder shrouded in myth and a story of origin from an animal ancestor. Although membership in a lineage follows principles of descent, individuals can choose to affiliate with the group of their mother, father, or one of their grandparents. In the past, choices were made as they might best advance a person's social position. So, for instance, if one's maternal grandfather were a renowned chief, a person would choose to affiliate with his lineage. This is an example of the way that people can manipulate their positions in systems with ambilineal descent.

Siblings belong to the same patrilineage or matrilineage, depending on the descent rule in effect. New lineages are formed after the death of the senior parent. At that time, surviving sons in patrilineal systems and surviving daughters in matrilineal systems establish themselves as the heads of new groups. In societies where seniority contributes to one's social standing and prestige, sibling order determines the relative status of each new lineage. That is, an individual who is a member of the lineage of an elder son has higher status than an individual who is a member of the lineage of a younger son.

Exogamy and Endogamy

As mentioned previously, lineages have corporate functions in some societies. That is, they hold land in common, apportioning land and resources to member households. They may have formal procedures for selecting leaders and settling disputes among members or with members of other lineages. They also regulate marriage, forbidding unions between certain members. Most unilineal kin groups practice **exogamy,** or marrying out. In exogamy, people cannot marry members of their own lineage or clan but must forge alliances with members of other groups. Lineages and clans are usually exogamous.

A less common marriage rule is **endogamy,** or marrying in, as in parallel cousin marriage, for example. A **parallel cousin** is one's mother's sister's child or one's father's brother's child. In parallel cousin marriage, one of these sets of children would be one's preferred marriage partners—the mother's sister's children in a matrilineage and the father's brother's children in a patrilineage. Parallel cousin marriage is prevalent among Middle Eastern Arab societies with patrilineal descent. In patrilineal systems, brothers belong to the same patrilineage or patriclan, and descent is traced through men. Thus, through the endogamy rule, it is desirable for the children of brothers to marry. This "patrilateral" parallel cousin marriage conserves wealth within the patriclan. Thus, land, wealth, and resources stay within the kinship group rather than being dissipated or fragmented through inheritance among a wider group of claimants. Endogamous marriage patterns also solidify and strengthen bonds between brothers and avert conflicts over inheritance.

Does your kinship system distinguish between cross-cousins and parallel cousins?

The opposite of a parallel cousin is a **cross-cousin:** one's mother's brother's child or one's father's sister's child. In cross-cousin marriage, these children would be preferred as one's marriage partners. As in parallel cousin marriage, this form of endogamy functions to strengthen a unilineal descent group and to concentrate resources within it. Figure 4 shows the types of cousins. Notice that cross-cousins are related through

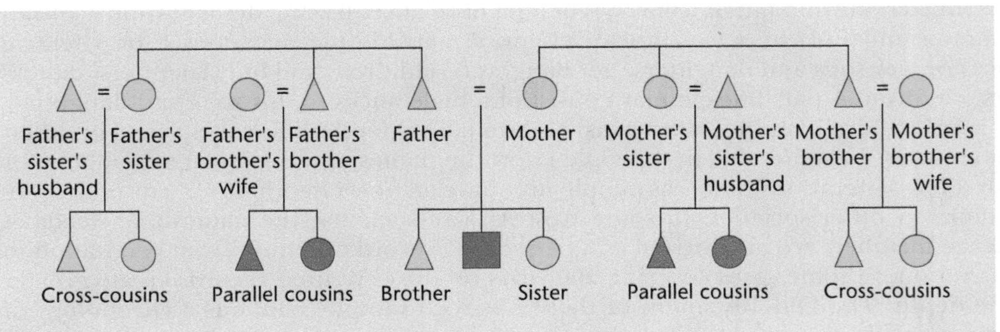

FIGURE 4
Distinctions between Parallel and Cross-Cousins

opposite-sex siblings (father's sister, mother's brother), whereas parallel cousins are related through same-sex siblings (father's brother, mother's sister).

Clans

Many cultures with unilineal descent organize their members into clans. **Clans** are named groups of people who believe that they are relatives, although they may not be able to trace all the actual relationships with clan members. Clans differ from lineages in this feature. That is, members of lineages can trace their exact relationship to all other members of the same lineage, but members of clans, which are much larger kin groups, can trace relationships only to close relatives.

Clans recruit new members through the birth of children. **Matriclans** obtain new members from women of their group (a child belongs to the clan of its mother), whereas **patriclans** recruit new members from men of their group (a child belongs to the clan of its father). Depending on the size of a society, clan size may range from several hundred members to many thousands. Although clan members cannot know all their relatives, because clans are named groups, members can always determine if strangers are related to them by asking them to identify their clan.

The conventions for naming clans vary cross-culturally. In some societies, clans are named after animals or plants; in others, they are named for locations. Where clans are named after animals, people often have beliefs about some mythic connection between the originators of the clan and the animal for which they are named. The origin myth might describe how the clan animal saved the human ancestors from some calamity or mated with the human ancestor to found the clan.

In some societies, clans are totemic. A **totem** is an animal or plant with a special spiritual connection to the members of its clan. There may be beliefs about descent from a totemic ancestor in the mythic past or sacred narratives recounting a bond between the totemic spirit and a human ancestor. Ritual prohibitions, or taboos, mark the relationship between clan animals and members of the kinship group. For example, people may not hunt or eat the animal that is their totem. By observing taboos, people express their respect for their ancestors. Totems also identify people in terms of their eligibility for marriage. In societies with clan exogamy, for example, two people with the same totem would not be allowed to marry.

clans
Named groups of people who believe that they are relatives even though they may not be able to trace their actual relationships with all members of their group.

matriclans
Clans formed through descent and inheritance from women of their group.

patriclans
Clans formed through descent and inheritance from men of their group.

totem
An animal or plant believed by a group of people to have been their primordial ancestor or protector.

Australian Aborigines believe that in mythic times, human ancestors had encounters with animals who endowed them with spiritual knowledge. The people honored these relationships by naming themselves after their animal protectors. The Image Works/Topham/The Image Works

Thus, clans, like lineages, not only establish and organize relatives but also regulate social relations, especially marriage. Clans usually are exogamous; that is, people cannot marry someone belonging to their own clan. Such a marriage would be considered incestuous. Marriage rules may also preclude people from marrying into the clan of either parent. For example, according to marriage restrictions among the matrilineal Diné, people cannot marry someone of their own clan or father's clan, even though people are not members of their fathers' groups by rules of matrilineal descent. An even wider proscription bars people from marrying anyone whose father is a member of one's own father's clan. These rules may be a reflection of an early Diné pattern of bilateral descent that prevailed before their arrival in the Southwest and the change from a nomadic foraging society to one based on semisedentary farming. According to bilateral principles, one's mother's and one's father's relatives are treated the same.

In some cultures, lineages and clans have corporate functions, owning or controlling land and resources in common. Lineages and clans have continuity independently of their specific membership at any one time. Their structures and functions are perpetual, and their membership is continually replenished with the births of new members. Lineages and clans also usually regulate marriage, favoring some unions or forbidding others between members of the same or related groups. Other social functions of unilinear kin groups vary from culture to culture, such as making communal decisions, settling disputes, selecting leaders, and performing ritual obligations.

The Diné talk about clan relations by saying that people are "born in" or "born to" their mothers' clan and "born for" their fathers' clan. Therefore, two people who are "born for" the same clan are not permitted to marry. According to the Diné view, such a marriage would be incestuous. The importance of Diné clan membership is also reflected in the etiquette of self-introductions. When introducing themselves to another person, the Diné first identify their mother's clan and then mention their father's clan. These identifications precede a statement of one's personal name. This practice reflects the importance of situating oneself within a network of kin. Kinship relationships are the most critical influences on one's social being.

Does your descent group have corporate functions?

In addition to social features, clans often have corporate functions. In some societies, these functions may be similar to those of lineages, whereas in others, they may be more highly structured and formalized. Clan members may hold land in common, apportioning fields or resource sites to their members individually or by household. Clan-held territory can be periodically reapportioned to adjust to changes in resources as well as to changes in the size of households.

Clans usually have structured means of decision making and problem solving. They have recognized leaders who may be informally selected by public opinion and consensus or formally chosen by representatives of households or lineages. Such leaders have various functions in different societies. In some, they may serve as spokespersons for their clan when interacting with similarly structured groups. They may meet with leaders of other clans to make decisions that affect the whole community, to resolve interclan disputes, and to act as a unified body when dealing with outsiders. Clan leaders may also adopt strategies to help foster community cohesion and cooperation by exhorting members to behave properly and to help one another.

In some societies, clans and lineages are organized in a complex hierarchical structure in which different levels of the hierarchy have different social or political functions. Several peoples in Sudan, for instance, were organized into clans composed of **segmentary lineages,** hierarchically ranked according to the number of generations they encompassed. The Nuer, for example, were organized into about twenty patrilineal clans (Evans-Pritchard 1955; Sahlins 1961). Each clan was subdivided into four levels of lineage segments. The first subdivision was into large units, called maximal lineages. Each maximal lineage was segmented into smaller groups, called major lineages, and these were divided into still smaller groups, called minor lineages. Finally, the smallest segment, referred to as a minimal lineage, consisted of a group of relatives descended from a common great-grandfather or great-great-grandfather. In other words, a minimal lineage had a depth of four or five generations. Members of these smallest segments interacted frequently, lived near one another, and shared resources in times of need. Seniority in a lineage conferred influence and prestige. Lineage segments could temporarily become allies in times of conflict, but there was

segmentary lineages
Lineages organized in a hierarchical structure, ranked according to the number of generations they encompass.

no established leadership beyond the smallest lineage and no permanent structure that united them. However, when disputes arose, the parties concerned could appeal for support to members of structurally similar units in wider and wider networks. Therefore, the segmentary system was a flexible solution to the problem of resolving disputes within and between the twenty clans.

CASE STUDY

A Patrilineal Society: The Ganda of Uganda

The Ganda are a horticultural people who live in small villages of between thirty and eighty homesteads. Homesteads contain several huts, and the Ganda use yards between huts for socializing and tending domesticated animals. Most households consist of husband and wife, although some men have more than one wife. Co-wives usually reside in the same household, each having her own bedroom, but women sometimes have separate huts within the homesteads. Some men establish residences for their several wives in separate villages. In any case, women leave their natal village when they marry to live with their husband. The marital bond tends to be unstable today, although in the past, men had greater authority and control over their wives (Southwold 1965, 105).

The people's principal subsistence crop is bananas or plaintains, but they also grow sweet potatoes, yams, peanuts, and a variety of leafy vegetables, roots, and fruits. Men clear the fields for planting, but women do most of the subsistence farmwork. In the past, men hunted and fished to supplement the diet, but today people keep domesticated animals. They also obtain money by growing cotton and coffee for the export market.

Ganda society is organized around membership in clans and lineages. Descent is patrilineal, so children belong to the lineage and clan of their father. Clans are exogamous, husband and wife belonging to different kinship groups. There currently are forty-eight named clans (Southwold 1965, 95). Each clan is associated with particular animals thought to have a special relationship to the members, who are not permitted to kill or eat their animal totem. Each clan is composed of several lineages, organized in a hierarchy of segments, or "segmentary lineages." There are four levels of segmentary organization: a clan; a segment of a clan, called a *ssiga;* a segment of a *ssiga,* called a *mutuba;* and a segment of a *mutuba,* the smallest segment, called a *lunyiriri.*

Watch the **Animation:** *Patrilineal Descent* on **myanthrolab.com**

In daily life, one's patrilineal kin are prominent in social interactions and share economic and personal responsibilities toward one another. People secure rights to use land and plant their gardens on the basis of membership in patrilineal clans. Men obtain these rights through descent from their fathers. Women obtain rights to gardens through marriage. That is, a woman plants her crops on her husband's land. After marriage, a man chooses his place of residence from among the villages in which he has rights through patrilineal affiliation, selecting acreage in clan-controlled territory.

Men prefer to marry women from villages other than their own to expand their network of relatives and allies. They also prefer to make a new homestead near more distant kin rather than live in their father's or their wife's father's village (Southwold 1965, 96). Ganda men wish to establish their independence from their fathers and also to avoid conflict with their brothers. Ties to other male relatives provide men with the aid and allegiance they expect from kin. Families may move to new villages if their needs or inclinations change.

Ganda clans have a number of corporate functions. Each clan and lineage has a leader who is responsible for administering his group. A council of the heads of subordinate lineage segments assists him. They settle disputes after hearing testimony from both sides. Decisions made by councils can be appealed to the council of the next higher segment in the lineage and clan hierarchy.

In the past, final appeals could be made to the highest authority or king, called *kabaka*. The corporate nature of clans is demonstrated in formal obligations that each clan owed to the *kabaka*. For example, clan members supplied bark cloth to the *kabaka* and herded his cattle. They also performed services for the *kabaka*'s mother, a person of great authority and prestige in her own right. And each clan provided boys to serve in the king's household.

Today the king's power has diminished, although he remains an honored and influential figure in Uganda. Clan councils and clan members supervise the activities of their group. If anyone commits an offense, the clan settles disputes and punishes its members. In the past, a clan could also suffer collective punishment, including the execution of all of its members, if one of its chiefs committed an offense against the *kabaka*.

Clans and lineage segments also own land in common. Each clan has an allotted territory in which its members have a right to live. Prominent members also have a right to be buried in clan territory. Residence on clan land is complicated because each clan owns territory in several areas. Therefore, people may make claims to diverse pieces of residential land, adjusting their needs to available acreage. People also base their decisions on the qualifications of political leaders who control each territory, choosing to affiliate where they might seek an advantage. Personal and political allegiance, then, contributes to settlement patterns as much as kinship connections do (Southwold 1965, 102).

In earlier times, clans controlled the distribution and inheritance of movable property from a deceased male clansman to his successor. The successor was formally chosen and ceremonially installed, taking the place of the deceased in kinship networks. He adopted the deceased's name and was called by kin terms appropriate to the deceased. He also received most of the dead man's property. Succession was inherited through kinship, but a man's eldest son was not eligible. In fact, there was a preference to bypass a man's sons altogether and instead choose a more distant patrilineal relative. This preferential pattern dispersed kinship ties and created linkages with more distant relatives, broadening one's alliances. The traditional rules of succession were changed in the late nineteenth century, so that a man's son could succeed him. Today, father to son inheritance is preferred. The practice of making wills setting out a person's wishes for the inheritance of his property has reduced clan power. Still, clan leaders influence the process through their prestige.

Collective principles underlying clan organization include the obligation to be hospitable to all members of one's clan. Men who move to new villages could expect to receive banana shoots from their resident clansmen to start their gardens. People are expected to be helpful to clansmen in economic difficulty or to help pay a fine for some offense that a clansman committed. Similarly, clansmen had the obligation of avenging an injured or murdered member of their group. Thus, clan membership remains fundamental in defining one's identity, organizing social relations, restricting marriage choices, and promoting ethics of hospitality and collective responsibility. **Read** the **Document** on **myanthrolab.com**

Phratries and Moieties

Clans may combine to form larger organized kinship units, such as phratries and moieties. **Phratries** are groups of linked clans that usually are exogamous: In a phratry, people cannot marry someone belonging to a clan associated with their own clan. The phratry may or may not be named. Unlike clans, phratries rarely have corporate functions. In a phratry system, there are always three or more linked groups.

Like phratries, **moieties** are groups of linked clans, but they differ in that there are only two of them. A moiety system divides a society into two halves (*moiety* comes from the French word meaning "half"). Thus, in such a system, all clans are apportioned into two groups. Like clans and phratries, moieties are usually exogamous, although people in some cultures can marry within their moiety even though they cannot marry within their clan. Moieties generally are named groups. They may or may not have corporate functions such as owning land, resource sites, and other property communally. In some societies, moieties may have ceremonial functions.

phratries
Groups of linked clans that are usually exogamous.

moieties
Groups of linked clans that divide a society into two halves, usually exogamous.

CASE STUDY

Two Matrilineal Societies: The Mohawks and the Trobriand Islanders

THE MOHAWKS

The Mohawks are one of the member nations of the Iroquois Confederacy. Organized on kinship principles of lineage, clan, and moiety (Bonvillain 2001, 69–70), Mohawk descent is reckoned matrilineally so that children belong to the lineage and clan of their mothers. Until about 200 years ago, the ideal was for members of a matrilineage to live together. A household typically consisted of an elder woman, her husband, their daughters and daughters' families, and the couple's unmarried sons. Each nuclear group of parents and children had its own quarters within a large house separated by bark partitions. If a woman survived to be elderly, she might live to have great-grandchildren and be the head of a lineage of four generations. In other cases, a lineage might have a three- or only a two-generation depth. The deeper the lineage, the more respected was its leading woman.

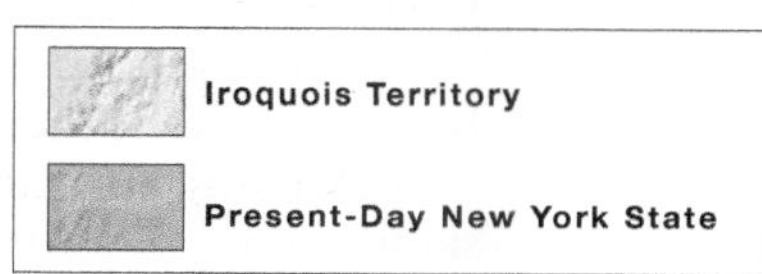

Mohawk society is divided into three matrilineal clans named after animals: Bear, Wolf, and Turtle. In former times, clans practiced exogamy, stipulating that people could not marry members of their own clan. These rules created linkages between kinship groups through marriage alliances. Today, restrictions on marriage choices have largely been abandoned. However, Mohawks who want their marriage ceremony performed in the indigenous Iroquois religion now known as the Longhouse Religion must belong to different clans.

Mohawk clans controlled and distributed farmland to their members. Land was held in common but was allocated and farmed by lineages working collectively. The leading woman of the matrilineage was said to own land, not as her personal property but as collective control. Women in the household were given portions of land that they planted and harvested. Finally, clans owned the large communal houses in which their members lived. Today, the corporate functions of clans have disappeared, and land is owned individually as a result of European and American influences. Most households consist of parents and children, although some grandparents may reside with the basic family group. Private property and individual economic pursuits have largely replaced the collective labor of clan relatives.

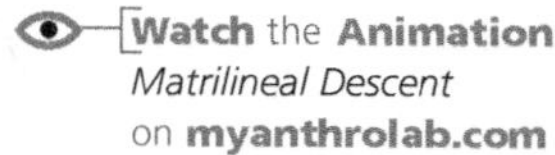

Watch the **Animation:** *Matrilineal Descent* on **myanthrolab.com**

Mohawk clans continue to have leaders, both women and men. Leading clan women, now usually referred to as clan mothers, are chosen informally through recognition of their intelligence, sound advice, and personal charisma. They lead by example and play a central role in protecting Mohawk lands, culture, and language. Clan mothers select the men who serve as clan chiefs. The women make their choices based on a man's intelligence, good judgment, even temper, and charisma. Clan chiefs represent their groups in community meetings and at meetings with representatives from the other Iroquois nations.

The Mohawk nation is divided into two moieties. The Wolf and Turtle clans form one moiety and the Bear Clan is the other. Like clans, moieties were formerly exogamous. They have mainly ceremonial functions, the most important of which is to prepare and conduct funerals for members of the opposite group. This custom reflects the Mohawk belief that people from the deceased's clan or moiety are too overcome by grief to be able to conduct a proper rite. Viewed as a feature of social structure, the reciprocal exchange of funerary duties symbolizes and enacts the mutual interdependence and unity of all members of the Mohawk nation.

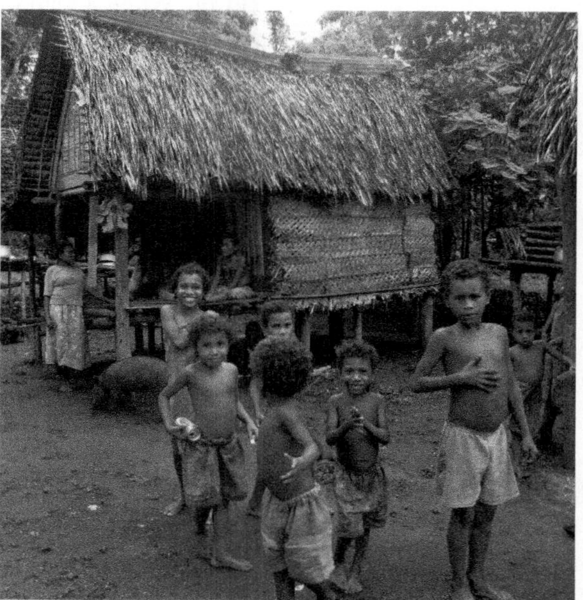

Children in the village of Kulukwekela on Kiriwina, the major island in the Trobriand Islands chain. Corbis/Ludo Kuipers/Corbis

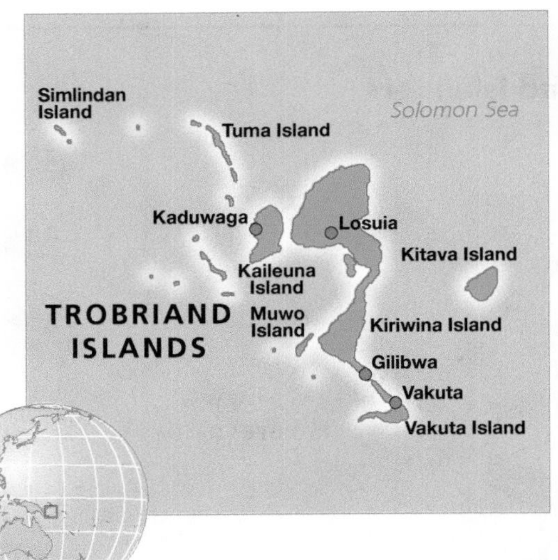

THE TROBRIAND ISLANDERS

The Trobriand Islanders, inhabiting a chain of islands off the coast of New Guinea, have a kinship system based on matrilineal descent, assigning children to the descent group of their mothers. Trobrianders are divided into four named exogamous clans, each associated with various plants, animals, and fish (Malinowski 1929). People belonging to the same clan consider themselves kin and believe that they share personality traits. However, clans do not function as corporate groups and have no collective obligations. Even though people of the same clan should not marry each other in principle, such unions do take place without serious negative consequences (Weiner 1976, 51). In place of the clan, the "dala" (what Malinowski referred to as a "sub-clan") is the unit that is the focus of social, economic, and political activities. Sexual relations within the dala are forbidden. Each dala has a sacred narrative of origin from a female ancestor who, along with her brother, emerged from inside the earth.

Each original pair then had to find land for themselves and their dala descendents. Currently, all land is owned by a particular dala, including a village, or more often a hamlet, surrounded by farmland. Each dala also owns protective magic that ensures the fertility of its fields. Malinowski reported that members of dalas have a right by descent to reside in the hamlet associated with their group. However, not all people live in their ancestral village. Couples, however, often reside in the dala settlement of the husband. The Trobriand system of residence in the husband's ancestral dala is sometimes referred to as "avunculocal," but, although men move to the place where their mother's brother resides, they do not actually move into his household but instead set up a separate dwelling for their own family. Although resident dala members do not live in the same household, they cooperate in economic and ceremonial activities.

In practice, however, most men remain in their father's hamlet, bringing their wife to live there. Weiner found that the only men who predictably moved to their mother's brother's hamlet were those who were positioned to become headman of the settlement (1976, 42). The difference in reports of residence patterns by Malinowski and Weiner (1976; 1988) may reflect either the contrast between idealized patterns and actual practices or changes over time, since Weiner's research took place fifty years after that of Malinowski. Weiner, though, does assert the absolute right of dala members to be buried in dala land regardless of where they resided during their lifetimes (1976, 43).

Trobriand men have to contribute to the support of their married sisters and sisters' children. When a man matures, he is allocated land to plant fields of yam, sweet potatoes, taro, bananas, and coconuts (Malinowski 1935). About 50 percent of the harvest is usually given as "urigubu" to his married sister's husband, but is intended for the support of the sister and her children. By principles of matrilineal descent, a man is not a member of the same kinship group as his own children but rather belongs to the group of his sister and her children. Urigubu symbolizes the claims that women have to the productive fields their dala controls, even though they do not live in those settlements. It further symbolizes the ties between sisters and brothers, that is, children of the same mother and members of the same kinship group. Sisters therefore have claims both to food and to the labor of their brothers. In this relationship, one sister is paired with one brother, not necessarily in order of seniority. If one sister has several brothers, the eldest is responsible for urigubu, although younger brothers are expected to contribute. If one brother has several sisters, he may rely on sisters' sons to help, but if none are old enough to do so, he will be responsible to provide for them all.

Each dala is ranked in relation to all others, not only to others within its own clan but to other dala in the three remaining clans as well. Each dala has a leader or "headman," usually the eldest male of the eldest lineage in the group. He is also generally the hamlet leader because his dala is localized in that settlement. Upon his death or retirement, the position of headman is passed to younger brothers in order of seniority or to a sister's son. Headmen allocate farmland to resident members of the dala and initiate the planting and harvesting cycles each year. They also have ceremonial duties to protect and enhance the fertility of their land. Finally, all the village households give them gifts of food, which are used as urigubu payments to the husband of the headman's sister and are redistributed to villagers and members of other communities in celebratory feasts.

Kinship plays a further role in territorial organization. The whole of Trobriand territory is divided into a number of districts (Malinowski 1929). Each district is led by a chief, the headman of the highest-ranking dala in that region. Chiefs are the only men allowed to have more than one wife. Typically, the chief's wives are sisters of the headmen of each village in his district. Because all men owe urigubu to their sisters' husbands, the headman of each village must deliver food to the district chief. The chief distributes this food to villages throughout his district in ceremonial feasts, thus enhancing his status through displays of generosity.

Men's power in Trobriand society is based on their control of land and of the statuses of hamlet headman and district chief. They exchange gifts of yams and ceremonial wealth. Women's power is based on their roles in the continuity of the dala and of dala identity. Through reproduction, women give birth to the future members of the dala and thus ensure its immortality. At the end of life, women's centrality is enacted through elaborate mortuary practices and exchanges of valuables (Weiner 1976; 1988). When a death occurs, rituals last for months. Exchanges of yams, products of male labor, are part of some of these rituals. But the most elaborate ceremonies focus on the exchange of women's valuables, such as skirts woven of banana leaves. One of the most prominent exchanges is that between a woman and the wife of the brother from whom she and her husband receive urigubu. Additional exchanges focus on other kinship relationships, including acknowledging the father and father's sister of the deceased. Although these individuals are not members of the deceased's dala, ceremonial gifts to them symbolize a wider unity of kin and community.

Mohawk and Trobriand kinship systems exemplify different types of matrilineal societies. In Mohawk society, women are central figures in kinship groups and in the economic and social activities of the household. Men and women share decision making and work out a consensus on public policy. In Trobriand society, men occupy major positions of prestige and productivity, whereas women preserve the continuity of kinship groups through birth and death. **Read** the **Document** on **myanthrolab.com**

REVIEW

Four levels of descent organization are lineages (relatives who trace descent from a known common ancestor), clans (groups of people who believe but do not know that they are relatives), phratries (groups of linked exogamous clans), and moieties (two groups of linked clans that divide the society). Depending on the unilineal descent rule in effect, a lineage may be a matrilineage or a patrilineage, and a clan may be a matriclan or a patriclan. Segmentary lineages are subdivisions of lineages that are hierarchically ranked. Most unilineal kin groups practice exogamy, or marrying outside of one's lineage or clan, which broadens kin ties. Clan membership and marriage eligibility are often defined through the use of totems and taboos. Forms of endogamy, or marrying in, are parallel cousin marriage (one's mother's sister's children or one's father's brother's children are preferred marriage partners) and cross-cousin marriage (one's mother's brother's children and father's sister's children are preferred). Endogamy keeps resources within a kin group rather than broadening kin ties.

PATTERNS OF RELATIONSHIPS

In addition to establishing structured groupings of relatives, kinship systems also define and enforce expected behaviors among kin. Members of every society share ideas about appropriate attitudes and actions between any set of individuals, especially relatives. For example, we may be taught to be respectful of our elders and gentle with younger siblings. We learn how to behave with our relatives, what to say to them, and what not to say to them. We learn our rights with respect to them, and we learn what obligations we owe them. We learn that we must behave with respect, deference, and obedience toward some relatives, whereas we can exert influence and authority over others. With some relatives, we learn to comply with their wishes and acknowledge their dominance in other ways. With others, we may joke, tease, and act informally.

As with other social rules, or norms, there is great cross-cultural variation in the types of behaviors prescribed between relatives, and there may be variation within a society as well. Factors of gender, age, and class may have effects on people's attitudes and actions.

Within the past century, the economies of preindustrial peoples worldwide changed from subsistence activities to wage work, and the production of food and goods for cash and export to national and international markets. How have these changes transformed people's kinship behavior and relationships?

avoidance relationships
Patterns of behavior between certain sets of kin that demonstrate respect and social distance.

joking relationships
Patterns of behavior between certain sets of kin that involve reciprocal joking, teasing, and playfulness, sometimes taking the form of flirtation and sexual innuendo.

The more homogeneous a society is, the more likely people will agree about appropriate behavior, whereas heterogeneous, or pluralistic, societies may have less consensus. Still, we can recognize general social values even if we do not behave in accordance with them as individuals.

Two common patterns that anthropologists observe in many cultures are avoidance relationships and joking relationships. The term "avoidance" is the one traditionally used in anthropology but it is perhaps somewhat misleading because the word usually implies a negative feeling (we avoid something that we don't like), but in kinship relationships, "respect" might be a better term, or what Gary Witherspoon (1972), writing about the Diné, refers to as "bashfulness." In some societies, **avoidance relationships** characterize the relationship between parents-in-law and their sons-in-law or daughters-in-law. For example, among the Diné, a man does not speak directly to his mother-in-law and avoids being alone with her. If he needs to make a request of her, he asks his wife to intercede on his behalf. He defers to his mother-in-law, complies with her wishes and requests, and makes himself helpful and cooperative.

This kind of behavior is fairly common between men and their mothers-in-law in matrilineal societies. In such societies, men usually leave their natal homes when they marry and take up residence with or near their wife's kin. Circumspect, deferential, and "bashful" behavior helps minimize potential conflict that may exist between a man and his mother-in-law in matrilocal households. A new husband does nothing that could be interpreted as a challenge to her authority or that of anyone else in the household. After many years in a stable marriage, a husband's behavior may be modified and he may begin to assert himself more with his wife's relatives. Eventually, he may take on leadership roles in the household.

Avoidance and respectful behavior on the part of a daughter-in-law toward her father-in-law is especially expected in patrilineal societies, where the married couple lives with the husband's kin. In this situation, a daughter-in-law lives in a household dominated by her father-in-law. Here, too, avoidance behavior mitigates any potential conflict. Rarely would a daughter-in-law have authority in such a household; rather, the potential conflict might concern the emotional allegiance of her husband, their son. The wife acts with deference and respect to avoid forcing the husband to choose sides between her and his parents. In strongly patriarchal societies, daughters-in-law are expected to be acutely aware of their subordinate status and act with extreme deference and obedience to their husbands' parents.

Do you have avoidance relationships and joking relationships among your kin?

The pattern of **joking relationships** between certain sets of relatives involves reciprocal joking, teasing, and playfulness. Joking may take the form of flirtation, sexual innuendo, and even explicit sexual remarks. This type of behavior is found most commonly between certain kinds of cousins, as between cross-cousins in societies in which cross-cousin marriage is preferred. Joking behavior may also be common between individuals and their spouses' same-sex sibling. For example, a woman may joke with her husband's brother, and a man may joke with his wife's sister. In many cultures, these in-laws are potential spouses. They may be preferred marriage partners in the event of the death of one's own husband or wife. So joking relationships between some types of relatives (cross-cousins, spouse's siblings) acknowledge the potential sexual or marital relationship that might be established between the individuals.

All societies identify specific behaviors as appropriate for specific sets of relatives. Two common patterns of relationship are avoidance relationships and joking relationships. In patrilineal societies, bashful behavior and avoidance are common for daughters-in-law toward their fathers-in-law, whereas these are seen with sons-in-law toward their mothers-in-law in matrilineal societies. In some cultures, avoidance may also be prescribed for siblings. In some societies, joking relationships are common among cross-cousins, spouse's siblings, or others who may be potential sexual or marital partners.

PATTERNS OF CHANGE

One would think that the way we reckon our kin would be a permanent feature of our culture. As you have read, however, even kinship systems respond to changes in the way people make their living or adapt to their environment. One pattern of change, for example, involves shifts from matrilineal descent to other rules of descent, based on changes in men's and women's subsistence roles. Forces of cultural contact and change also bring about changes in the way people reckon their kin, identify their kin group, and interact with relatives.

CULTURE CHANGE

CHEYENNE DESCENT

The Cheyenne currently reside on two reservations. The Northern Cheyenne live in Montana and the Southern Cheyenne share a reservation with the Arapaho in Oklahoma. These lands are the last refuge of people with a complex history, which reveals how changes in economic systems and adaptations to one's environment affect social life, even systems of descent (Eggan 1966).

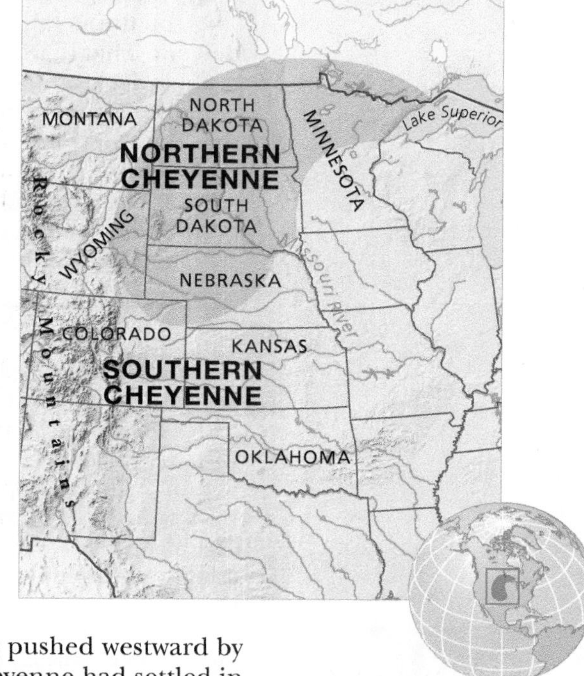

The Cheyenne originally lived in the woodlands surrounding the Great Lakes in what is now Minnesota. When the French explorer René-Robert Cavelier, Sieur de La Salle encountered them in 1680, the Cheyenne were living in small villages with perhaps 200 or 300 residents along the upper Mississippi River west of Lake Michigan and Lake Superior. Their economy was based on foraging. Women gathered wild rice that grew along the shores of lakes and in marshes, and many other plants, tubers, fruits, and nuts. Men caught fish in lakes and rivers, hunted deer and small animals in the dense woodlands, and caught waterbirds.

It is likely that their social systems revolved around families and kinship groups organized by principles of bilateral descent, consistent with the usual practice of foraging peoples in the northern woodlands. These patterns are adaptive for situations of resource flexibility and nomadic settlement.

The Cheyenne began to leave this region in the late seventeenth century because of conflict with neighbors who were being pushed westward by British and French traders and settlers. By the early 1700s, the Cheyenne had settled in eastern North Dakota in the northern prairies. There, borrowing from other native peoples in the region, they began to grow some of their own crops, especially corn, beans, squash, and tobacco. They also adopted the descent systems of the nearby Mandans and Hidatsas. Like them, the Cheyenne began to trace descent through matrilineal kinship ties in which children belong to the kin group and clan of their mother, and couples reside with the wife's family after marriage.

The Cheyenne soon began to trade buffalo hides and deerskins for manufactured goods with French merchants who had opened a post in southern Manitoba. Then, sometime after 1750, the Cheyenne obtained horses from other native peoples, such as the Crow. The horses made an enormous difference in the Cheyenne economy, enabling people to travel farther to hunt and trade and to more easily transport their possessions.

By the late 1700s, conditions on the prairies worsened. Native peoples from the East and Midwest were pushing into the central prairies because Europeans and American colonists were taking more and more land. As eastern peoples moved westward, they came into Cheyenne territory, competing for the region's natural resources. By the early nineteenth century, the Cheyenne were building settlements west of the Missouri River on the plains of South Dakota. They spread west and south, expanding their territory to the Rocky Mountains. There, the Cheyenne established a way of life different from the one they left behind on the prairies. They no longer lived in permanent villages, but moved their camps several times each year. They no longer planted crops. Instead, they hunted animals, especially buffalo, and gathered wild plants. They also more fully utilized horses for hunting and as beasts of burden (Jablow 1950).

As a consequence of the changes in their economy and settlement patterns, Cheyenne social systems were also transformed. The need to maximize alliances, to widen one's network of kin, and to be able to shift membership in local and territorial units, which their new way of life required, led to the disappearance of matrilineal clans and the reemergence of bilateral descent.

Nevertheless, the Cheyenne continued to live in groups of households of families linked by relationships through women, and couples continued to reside with the wife's family after marriage. Each nuclear family resided in its own lodge, but groups related through women generally built their dwellings near one another. Such residential groupings often consisted of an elder couple, their unmarried children, married daughters, and the daughters' husbands and children. These family groupings also shared resources and foraging tasks. Men hunted together and provisioned the coresidential group. Most of the men working together were unmarried brothers still living with their parents or the brothers-in-law brought in after marriage to daughters of the group. Women worked with their sisters and daughters, gathering wild foods and sharing cooking and child care.

A bilateral system allows for an emphasis on generations rather than on lines of descent. That is, whereas unilineal descent separates members of a generation according to their degrees of descent from specific ancestors, bilateral descent focuses on similarities among the members of each generation across lines of descent. The kinship terms that the Cheyenne used emphasized these generational relations, as well as the social equivalence of people. For example, kin terms made no distinction between siblings and cousins other than by relative age (Hoebel 1978), and only elder siblings were distinguished by gender. Rather than referring only to a small set of relatives, the Cheyenne system extended the concept of family to many people.

When studying changes in kinship systems, we can see how sensitive these systems are as indicators of cultural transformation. Principles of kinship reckoning are consistent with other cultural practices. When behavior changes, kinship systems respond by altering the way that kin groups are organized. Changes may come from internal dynamics within a society as people adjust to their environments and develop and transmit new ways of living. They may also come from external sources when societies come into contact with others, either learning and adopting new systems voluntarily or being forced to adapt to more powerful peoples.

REVIEW

Patterns of change in kinship systems are based on the functions of kin groups in relation to environmental adaptations. Foragers tend to develop bilateral descent rules, for example. Kinship also changes in response to cultural adaptations. For example, people may adopt the kinship system of another people with whom they come into contact.

KINSHIP TERMINOLOGY SYSTEMS

What are the names of the people you regard as members of your kindred? How are they related to you?

Cross-cultural comparisons of categories of kin terms (words used to identify relatives) can sometimes reveal basic similarities and differences in worldview and experience. For example, people's social relations can be inferred from their kin terms. North Americans generally use the following words for relatives: grandmother, grandfather, mother, father, aunt, uncle, sister, brother, cousin, daughter, son, niece, nephew, granddaughter, grandson. Analysis of these words reveals systematic meanings. First, North Americans distinguish between generations: grandmother/mother/daughter/granddaughter. Second, they note the sex of relatives: mother/father, sister/brother. Third, they distinguish between direct or lineal relatives and collateral relatives (those who may have a common ancestor but are not lineally related): mother/aunt, son/nephew. These three sets of contrasts—of generation, sex, and lineality—define the features of their kin that are meaningful to North Americans.

Other cultures may select other aspects of kinship relationships to emphasize, revealing different priorities through a different set of contrasts. Differences in kinship terminology are not merely linguistic; they reflect societal attitudes toward one's relatives. Individuals called by each kin term are understood to stand in particular social relationships and to have certain rights and obligations. The meanings of words, then, reflect one's social universe.

The Cheyenne, discussed in the Culture Change study, called siblings and cousins by the same kin term, using separate terms only for elder brother and elder sister. Younger siblings of both sexes were called by the same term, a fact that further indicates the importance of seniority in Cheyenne society. Relatives in one's parents' generation were called by terms that distinguished between paternal and maternal relatives and between the genders. The same term was used for one's father, father's brothers, and his male cousins, whereas another term was used for one's mother's brother and mother's male cousins. A parallel set of terms was used for female relatives. Grandparents were distinguished only by gender—one term for all the men and another for all the women. The terms used for one's children were extended to the children of one's same-sex siblings and cousins. So, for example, a woman used the same kin terms for her son and daughter and the children of her sisters and female cousins. A man used these terms for his son and daughter and for the children of his brothers and male cousins. A different set of names was used for children of one's opposite-sex siblings and cousins. On the generational level of one's grandchildren, all related children were called by the same term regardless of gender or relationship.

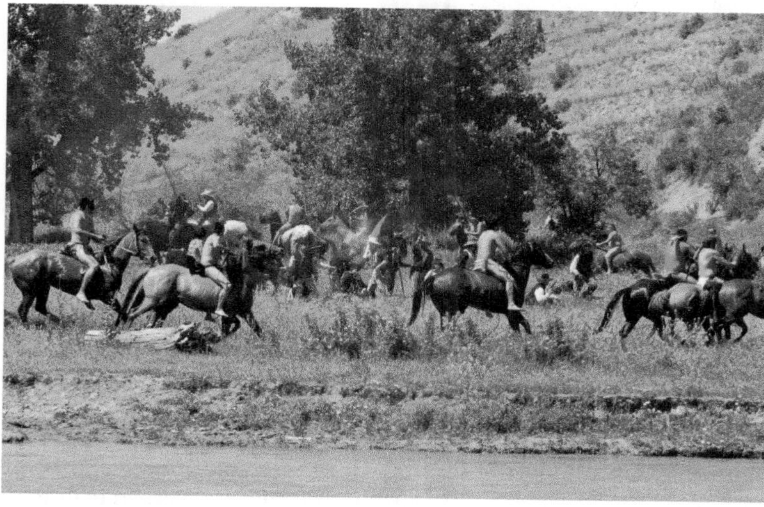

The Cheyenne used a system of naming relatives called the Iroquois system, which is based on the criteria of generation and age. Alamy Limited/allen russell/Alamy

The Cheyenne pattern of naming kin is an example of a type of **kinship terminology system** known as the Iroquois system. There are six types of terminological systems, and all people worldwide have a system of kin terms that fits one of these types, although there are sometimes minor variations within a system. Each type is named for the culture in which it was first described. Kinship terms are more than just words for people, however; they define types of relationships. The **Iroquois system,** for example, emphasizes the difference between one's parents' same-sex siblings (MZD, MZS, FBD, FBS) and parents' opposite-sex siblings (MBD, MBS, FZD, FZS). As Figure 5 shows, one's parents are classed with their siblings of the same sex, and parallel cousins are classed with one's own siblings. Separate names for cross-cousins identify them as potential marriage partners. Children of anyone whom one calls mother and father are called sister and brother.

The Eskimo and Hawaiian Systems

The Eskimo and Hawaiian types of kinship terminology systems make the fewest distinctions among kin. The **Eskimo system** focuses on distinctions between the nuclear family and all other types of relatives and on gender distinctions. This system is likely to be associated with bilateral descent and is prevalent in both industrial and foraging societies.

As Figure 6 shows, the Eskimo system has separate terms for mother, father, sister, and brother. Siblings of one's parents are distinguished by gender, but whether they are related through one's mother or one's father is ignored. Relatives of one's own generation outside of the nuclear family are all called by the same term: cousin. There are

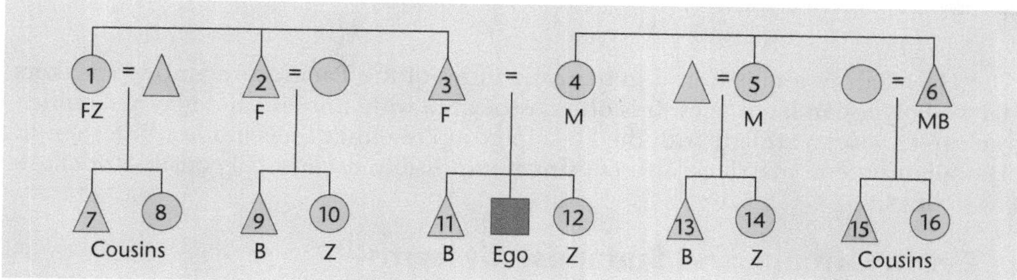

FIGURE 5

Iroquois Kinship System. According to the Iroquois system of kinship terminology, the father's brother (2) is called by the same term as the father (3); the mother's sister (5) is called by the same term as the mother (4); but the people numbered 1 and 6 have separate terms for themselves. Those people numbered 9–14 are all considered siblings, but 7, 8, 15, and 16 are cousins.

kinship terminology system
System of terms used to address and refer to relatives.

Iroquois system
Kin terms that emphasize the difference between one's parents' same-sex siblings and parents' opposite-sex siblings, classifying parallel cousins with one's own siblings.

Eskimo system
Kin terms making distinctions between the nuclear family and all other types of relatives and on gender.

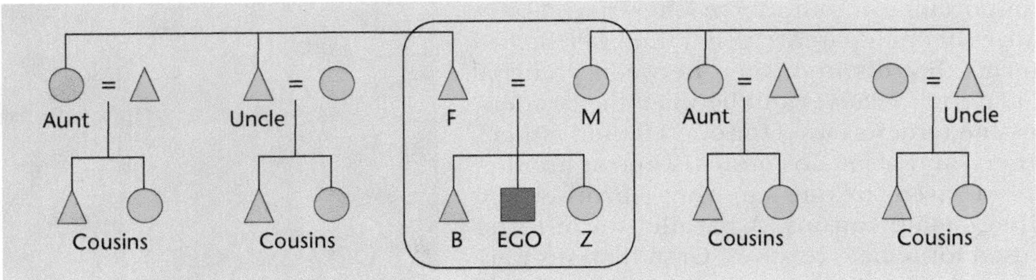

FIGURE 6
Eskimo Kinship System. The Eskimo system of kinship terminology emphasizes the nuclear family. Ego's father and mother are distinguished from ego's aunts and uncles, and siblings from cousins.

separate terms for one's own children and the children of one's siblings, based on gender: daughter, son; niece, nephew. And children of one's cousins are also called cousin, although some speakers may note different degrees of relationship.

The Eskimo system of terminology distinguishes among kin primarily by generation and gender. It highlights a distinction between the nuclear family and other relatives, but whether they are related through the mother or father is irrelevant. These terms are consistent with a social system that centers on the nuclear family as an independent, mobile, and potentially self-sustaining unit. As you may have noticed, this is the system generally used by North Americans.

The **Hawaiian system,** in contrast, has even fewer terms than the Eskimo system because it makes distinctions only of generation and gender. For this reason, it is sometimes referred to as a generational system. As Figure 7 shows, all male relatives of the parental generation are called father and all females are called mother. Similarly, all male relatives of one's own generation are called brother and all females of one's generation are called sister. Sons and daughters include one's children and the children of anyone that one calls brother or sister.

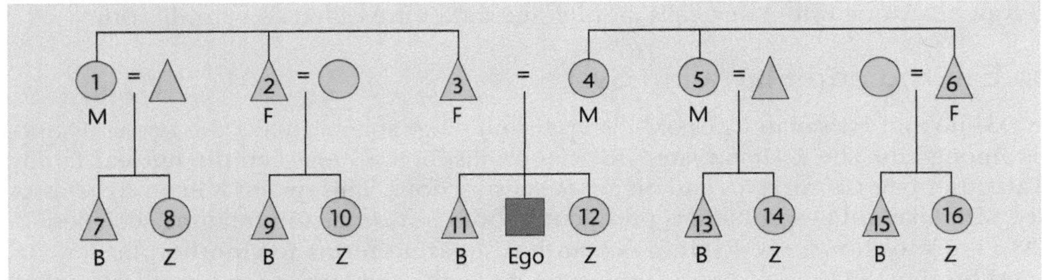

FIGURE 7
Hawaiian Kinship System. Ego calls the men numbered 2 and 6 by the same term as father (3) and the women numbered 1 and 5 by the same term as mother (4). All cousins of ego's own generation (7–16) are considered brothers and sisters.

The Hawaiian system is found in many societies of the Pacific and among speakers of Malayo-Polynesian languages. It is often associated with ambilineal descent, in which people can choose to affiliate with the kinship group of either their mother or father. In the Hawaiian system, marriage with cousins is impossible because all cousins are classified as siblings.

The Crow, Omaha, and Sudanese Systems

The Crow system is similar to the Iroquois system for the parental generation (see Figure 5). That is, father and father's brother are called by the same term and mother's brother is named separately; similarly, mother and mother's sister are called by the same term and father's sister is named separately. As Figure 8 shows, parallel cousins are called by sibling terms.

Hawaiian system
Kin terms making distinctions only of generation and gender.

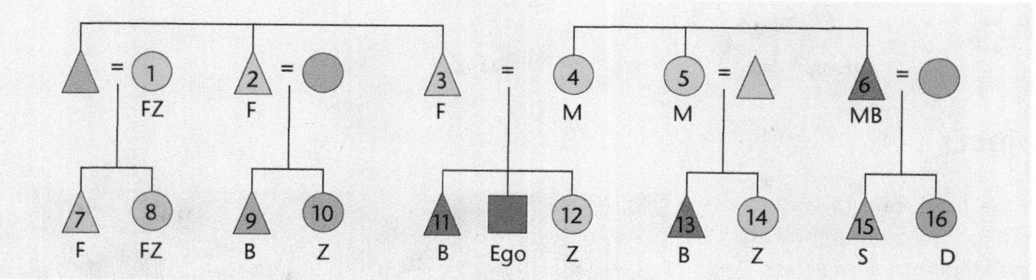

FIGURE 8

Crow Kinship System. The Crow system is the obverse of the Omaha system. Those numbered 4 and 5 are merged under a single term, as are 2 and 3. Ego's parallel cousins (9, 10, 13, and 14) are considered siblings, whereas the mother's brother's children are equated with the children of a male ego and his brother.

The **Crow system** is used by some matrilineal peoples. Its key feature is that it extends the terms for father and father's sister to include cross-cousins on the paternal side—that is, the children of father's sister—and then continues the terms for father and father's sister in the female paternal line. Thus, the children of the father's sister are called father and father's sister. The effect of the Crow system is that it distinguishes descendants in the female line on one's father's side.

The Crow system also extends the terms for son and daughter to include cross-cousins on the maternal side, the children of one's mother's brother. That is, the children of one's mother's brother are called son and daughter. So, although one's cross-cousins are of the same biological generation as oneself, these relatives are given terms otherwise applied to one's own children.

The **Omaha system** follows the same principles as the Crow system except that it applies the generational skewing pattern to the descendants of one's mother's brother instead of one's father's sister. The Omaha system is found in some patrilineal societies, where its purpose is to identify descendants of male members of the maternal side of the family.

Both the Crow and Omaha systems have a generational skewing pattern that focuses on lineal relatives not in one's own clan. So, in the matrilineal Crow system, the father's sister and her descendants are singled out because these are the people in one's father's clan. Similarly, in the patrilineal Omaha system, the mother's brother and his descendants are singled out because these are the people in one's mother's clan.

In the **Sudanese system,** which is rare, all kinship relationships are given separate terms. There are separate terms for members of the nuclear family, a distinctive word for mother's brother and another for father's brother, and separate words for mother's sister and for father's sister. Parallel cousins and cross-cousins are called by different terms. The Sudanese system allows individuals to negotiate their relationships with others and to affiliate with either side of their family, depending on their circumstances or personal inclinations.

Crow system
Kin terms used by some matrilineal peoples that extend the term for one's father and father's sister to include cross-cousins on the paternal side.

Omaha system
Kin terms used by some patrilineal peoples that extend the term for one's mother and mother's brother to include cross-cousins on the maternal side.

Sudanese system
Kin terms that give separate words for all kin relationships.

Kinship terminology system refers to how relatives are classified. It identifies a specific kind of relationship and the rights and obligations that that relationship entails. In the Eskimo system, which generally uses bilateral descent, the nuclear family is distinguished from other relatives. The Hawaiian system makes distinctions of gender and generation, and is often associated with ambilineal descent. The Iroquois system distinguishes between one's parent's same-sex and different-sex siblings and also between parallel cousins and cross-cousins. The Crow system, used in matrilineal societies, is similar to the Iroquois system except for the terminology referring to cousins. The Omaha system, found in patrilineal societies, is similar to the Crow system, with maternal cross-cousins called "mother" and "mother's brother" and paternal cross-cousins called "son" and "daughter." The Sudanese system is unique in that every individual has a distinct term. Differences in kin terms reflect differences in people's social systems.

ANTHROPOLOGY APPLIED

Linkages Genealogy Projects

When doing ethnography in the field, cultural anthropologists gather kinship data for the people they are among. Then they link these data into a local genealogy. This information tells anthropologists who people are and how they relate to one another. As you have seen from this chapter, understanding a society's kinship system is also a key to understanding how people organize their communities, subsistence activities, and leadership. Kin relations are the building blocks of human social organization. But what can ethnographic and historical genealogies of particular people tell us about what it takes to build self-sustaining human communities?

Linkages is an international network of researchers concerned with assessing how economic development and culture change affect populations. These researchers create database sets of recorded kinship data and track long-term changes. The researchers hope to show how knowledge of kinship must be taken into account when planning social policy and economic change. The knowledge gained from large-scale, long-term comparisons of kin networks may also help local communities participate more effectively in changes that affect their lives and cultural ecologies.

Corbis/Martin Harvey/Corbis

Bridgeman Art Library/USA/Giraudon/The Bridgeman Art Library

Corbis/Morton Beebe/Corbis

The data sets that Linkages maintains are diverse; among them are Alyawarra kin networks in Australia; kinship in Tlaxcala, Mexico; genealogies of U.S. presidents; Muslim elites in an Indonesian village; Old Testament patriarchs; Mbuti Pygmies of the Ituri Rainforest of Africa; genealogical censuses for band societies; and many others (for example, !Kung of Africa, Chechu of India, Ainu of Japan, Vedda and Semang of Indonesia, and Inuit of North America). Affiliates of Linkages around the world have established long-term field sites for tracking changes in kinship. Data are displayed in maps and graphs generated by special software, such as Large Network Analysis and Genealogical Information Manager. Studies on such a large scale have been made possible only though recent advances in computer technology and the Internet (http://eclectic.ss.uci.edu/~drwhite/linkages/linkages.html).

CRITICAL THINKING QUESTIONS

What do you know about your families' genealogies? How far back do they go? How might information about long-term changes in your networks of kin contribute to Linkages's goals?

Study and Review on myanthrolab.com

CHAPTER SUMMARY

Kinship Systems

- In every society, people have systems for tracing descent and organizing kinship groups to which they belong.

Bilateral Descent

- In many cultures, people consider themselves related to both their mother's and their father's families. In such systems of bilateral descent, the most significant kin group is that of the kindred, a loosely defined network of relatives who interact on a regular basis and acknowledge mutual rights and obligations. Systems of bilateral descent are commonly found in foraging societies and in modern industrial nations. Bilateral descent is adaptive in societies where mobility is a premium. In small-scale foraging societies, people can make claims in a wide network of kin in times of scarcity and need, whereas people in modern industrial countries can loosen their kin ties to promote their economic independence.

Matrilineal and Patrilineal Descent

- In unilineal descent, people acknowledge relationships on either only their mother's (matrilineal) or their father's (patrilineal) side. Unilineal descent is common in farming and pastoral societies. About 15 percent of unilineal groups are matrilineal; the remainder are patrilineal.
- A few societies have (or had) systems of double descent, in which people could belong to kinship groups of both their mother and father. In systems of parallel descent, men were considered descended from their fathers and women from their mothers. Finally, systems of ambilineal descent allow people to affiliate with either their mother's or their father's kin group.

Unilineal Descent Groups

- Unilineal descent systems usually organize people into structured groupings of related people. The smallest such unit is a lineage, a specific set of relatives that trace descent from a common ancestor. A matrilineage consists of a female ancestor, her children, her daughters' children, her daughters' daughters' children, and so on. A patrilineage consists of a male ancestor, his children, his sons' children, his sons' sons' children, and so on.
- Many cultures with the unilineal descent organize their members into clans, named groups of people who believe they are relatives but cannot trace their actual relationship with all members of their clan. Whereas members of lineages can prove their common descent from a specific ancestor, members of clans stipulate or claim relationship. Clans also often forbid marital or sexual unions between their own members. Clans also often have corporate functions such as holding land in common and apportioning fields or resource sites to their members. They may choose leaders who speak for their group and have methods of making decisions and settling disputes.
- Phratries are groupings of linked clans that serve primarily to regulate marriage by forbidding unions between members. Moieties are even larger groupings, dividing the society as a whole into two groups or halves. Typically, people cannot marry members of their own moiety. Moieties are usually named groups that may have corporate and ceremonial functions and control land, resource sites, and other property.

Patterns of Relationships

- Kinship groups sometimes have preferences for the kind of marriage that their members may make. Clans are often exogamous, their members marrying people of other groups. Endogamy, in contrast, is a preference for marriage with a member of one's own group. In some societies, there are preferences for marrying particular types of cousins, either cross-cousins or parallel cousins. Marriage patterns tend to be consistent with other rules that organize social groups.
- Members of every society share ideas about what is deemed appropriate between any set of relatives. Some societies highly structure behaviors between certain relatives. At one end of the behavioral spectrum, some people are in a "joking" relationship, allowing them to tease one another and make critical or sexual remarks, whereas at the other end, people may be in an "avoidance" relationship, barring them from teasing or criticizing but instead encouraging them to be "bashful," avoiding eye contact, and refraining from speaking directly to or even being alone with a dominant person.

Patterns of Change

- Kinship changes as a result of changes in people's economic systems. Globalization also causes people to change how they reckon their descent and their rules for inheritance and kin relations.

Kinship Terminology Systems

- Kinship terminologies are words that people use to refer to and address their relatives. Worldwide there are a small number of such sets of terminologies. Kinship terms are labels that symbolize relationships, including the rights and obligations that relatives have in relation to one another. The kinds of systems used reveal the kinds of distinctions that people make about which relatives are similar in status and relationship.

REVIEW QUESTIONS

1. What is bilateral descent? What are some cultural correlates of this descent rule in societies that practice it?
2. What are the two types of unilineal descent? With what kinds of societies is unilineal descent associated?
3. How would you compare and contrast the descent groups that are created by the application of descent rules? How are kindreds different from lineages?
4. What are the distinctions among lineages, clans, phratries, and moieties?
5. What patterns of relationships among kin group members do anthropologists observe?
6. How, and why, do kinship systems change?
7. What are the six methods of classifying relatives? What are the distinguishing characteristics of each?
8. How are kinship systems and rules of descent functionally interrelated with other social systems, such as economic and political systems?

MyAnthroLab Connections

Watch. Listen. View. Explore. Read. MyAnthroLab is designed just for you. Dynamic visual activities, videos, and readings found in the multimedia library will enhance your learning experience.

Resources from this chapter:

Watch on **myanthrolab.com**
- *Patrilineal Descent*
- *Matrilineal Descent*

Listen on **myanthrolab.com**
- *Parents Increasingly Adopting Children of Another Race*

Explore on **myanthrolab.com** In MySearchLab, enter the Anthropology database to find relevant and recent scholarly and popular press publications. For this chapter, enter the following keywords: kinship system, matrilineal, patriarchy, lineage, totem

Read the **Document**
- *Varieties of Marital Relationships* by Lewellyn Hendrix
- *Nandi: From Cattle-Keepers to Cash-Crop Farmers* by Regina Smith Ololer

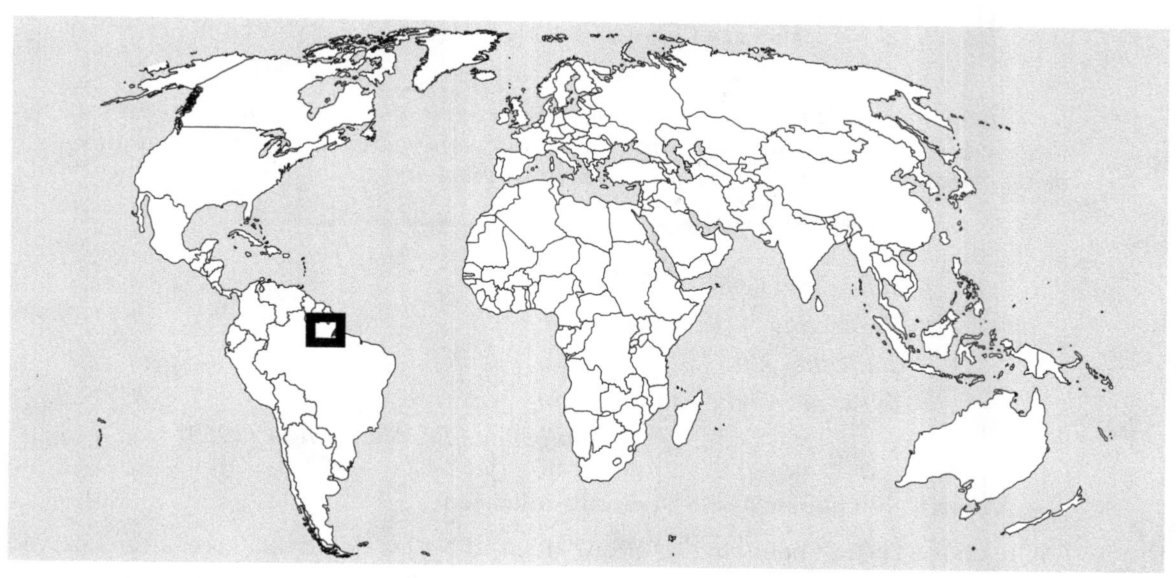

Mother's Love: Death without Weeping

Nancy Scheper-Hughes

Kinship systems are based on marriage and birth. Both, anthropologists assume, create ties that can link kin into close, cooperative, enduring structures. What happens to such ties, however, in the face of severe hardship imposed by grinding poverty and urban migration? Can we continue to assume, for example, that there will be a close bond between mother and child? This is the question pursued by Nancy Scheper-Hughes in the following article about the mother–infant relationship among poor women in a Brazilian shantytown. The author became interested in the question following a "baby die-off" in the town of Bom Jesus in 1965. She noticed that mothers seemed to take these events casually. After twenty-five years of research in the Alto do Cruzeiro shantytown there, she has come to see such indifference as a cultural response to high rates of infant death due to poverty and malnutrition. Mothers, and surrounding social institutions such as the Catholic church, expect babies to die easily. Mothers concentrate their support on babies who are "fighters" and let themselves grow attached to their children only when they are reasonably sure that the offspring will survive. The article also provides an excellent illustration of what happens to kinship systems in the face of poverty and social dislocation. Such conditions may easily result in the formation of woman-headed families and in a lack of the extended kinship networks so often found in more stable, rural societies.

In a current epilogue to this article, Scheper-Hughes notes that political changes in Brazil since the 1980s have led to improved health for mothers and babies. Mothers have *fewer babies and no longer give up on offspring who in the past would have seemed destined to die. Unfortunately, the rise of drugs and gangs along with vigilante death squads have become a major threat to survival and social life in Bom Jesus.**

I have seen death without weeping
The destiny of the Northeast is death
Cattle they kill
To the people they do something worse
—Anonymous Brazilian singer (1965)

Listen to the **Chapter Audio** on **myanthrolab.com**

"Why do the church bells ring so often?" I asked Nailza de Arruda soon after I moved into a corner of her tiny mud-walled hut near the top of the shantytown called the Alto do Cruzeiro (Crucifix Hill). I was then a Peace Corps volunteer and a community development/health worker. It was the dry and blazing hot summer of 1965, the months following the military coup in Brazil, and save for the rusty, clanging bells of N.S. das Dores Church, an eerie quiet had settled over the market town that I call Bom Jesus da Mata. Beneath the quiet, however, there was chaos and panic. "It's nothing," replied Nailza, "just another little angel gone to heaven."

Nailza had sent more than her share of little angels to heaven, and sometimes at night I could hear her engaged in a muffled but passionate discourse with one of them, two-year-old Joana. Joana's photograph, taken as she lay propped up in her tiny cardboard coffin, her eyes open, hung on a wall next to one of Nailza and Ze Antonio taken on the day they eloped.

Nailza could barely remember the other infants and babies who came and went in close succession. Most had died unnamed and were hastily baptized in their coffins. Few lived more than a month or two. Only Joana, properly baptized in church at the close of her first year and placed under the protection of a powerful saint, Joan of Arc, had been expected to live. And Nailza had dangerously allowed herself to love the little girl.

In addressing the dead child, Nailza's voice would range from tearful imploring to angry recrimination: "Why did you leave me? Was your patron saint so greedy that she could not allow me one child on this earth?" Ze Antonio advised me to ignore Nailza's odd behavior, which he understood as a kind of madness that, like the birth and death of children, came and went. Indeed, the premature birth of a stillborn son some months later "cured" Nailza of her "inappropriate" grief, and the day came when she removed Joana's photo and carefully packed it away.

More than fifteen years elapsed before I returned to the Alto do Cruzeiro, and it was anthropology that provided the vehicle of my return. Since 1982 I have returned several times in order to pursue a problem that first attracted my attention in the 1960s. My involvement with the people of the Alto do Cruzeiro now spans a quarter of a century and three generations of parenting in a community where mothers and daughters are often simultaneously pregnant.

*From "Death without Weeping," *Natural History,* October 1989. Copyright © 1989 by Nancy Scheper-Hughes, with an update in 2009. Reprinted by permission of the publisher.

The Alto do Cruzeiro is one of three shantytowns surrounding the large market town of Bom Jesus in the sugar plantation zone of Pernambuco in Northeast Brazil, one of the many zones of neglect that have emerged in the shadow of the now tarnished economic miracle of Brazil. For the women and children of the Alto do Cruzeiro the only miracle is that some of them have managed to stay alive at all.

The Northeast is a region of vast proportions (approximately twice the size of Texas) and of equally vast social and developmental problems. The nine states that make up the region are the poorest in the country and are representative of the Third World within a dynamic and rapidly industrializing nation. Despite waves of migrations from the interior to the teeming shantytowns of coastal cities, the majority still live in rural areas on farms and ranches, sugar plantations and mills.

Life expectancy in the Northeast is only forty years, largely because of the appallingly high rate of infant and child mortality. Approximately one million children in Brazil under the age of five die each year. The children of the Northeast, especially those born in shantytowns on the periphery of urban life, are at a very high risk of death. In these areas, children are born without the traditional protection of breast-feeding, subsistence gardens, stable marriages, and multiple adult caretakers that exists in the interior. In the hillside shantytowns that spring up around cities or, in this case, interior market towns, marriages are brittle, single parenting is the norm, and women are frequently forced into the shadow economy of domestic work in the homes of the rich or into unprotected and oftentimes "scab" wage labor on the surrounding sugar plantations, where they clear land for planting and weed for a pittance, sometimes less than a dollar a day. The women of the Alto may not bring their babies with them into the homes of the wealthy, where the often-sick infants are considered sources of contamination, and they cannot carry the little ones to the riverbanks where they wash clothes because the river is heavily infested with schistosomes and other deadly parasites. Nor can they carry their young children to the plantations, which are often several miles away. At wages of a dollar a day, the women of the Alto cannot hire baby sitters. Older children who are not in school will sometimes serve as somewhat indifferent caretakers. But any child not in school is also expected to find wage work. In most cases, babies are simply left at home alone, the door securely fastened. And so many also die alone and unattended.

Bom Jesus da Mata, centrally located in the plantation zone of Pernambuco, is within commuting distance of several sugar plantations and mills. Consequently, Bom Jesus has been a magnet for rural workers forced off their small subsistence plots by large landowners wanting to use every available piece of land for sugar cultivation. Initially, the rural migrants to Bom Jesus were squatters who were given tacit approval by the mayor to put up temporary straw huts on each of the three hills overlooking the town. The Alto do Cruzeiro is the oldest, the largest, and the poorest of the shantytowns. Over the past three decades many of the original migrants have become permanent residents, and the primitive and temporary straw huts have been replaced by small homes (usually of two rooms) made of wattle and daub, sometimes covered with plaster. The more affluent residents use bricks and tiles. In most Alto homes, dangerous kerosene lamps have been replaced by light bulbs. The once tattered rural garb, often fashioned from used sugar sacking, has likewise been replaced by store-bought clothes, often castoffs from a wealthy *patrão* (boss). The trappings are modern, but the hunger, sickness, and death that they conceal are traditional, deeply rooted in a history of feudalism, exploitation, and institutionalized dependency.

My research agenda never wavered. The questions I addressed first crystallized during a veritable "die-off" of Alto babies during a severe drought in 1965. The food and water shortages and the political and economic chaos occasioned by the military coup were reflected in the handwritten entries of births and deaths in the dusty, yellowed pages of the ledger books kept at the public registry office in Bom Jesus. More than 350 babies died in the Alto during 1965 alone—this from a shantytown population of little more than 5,000. But that wasn't what surprised me. There were reasons enough for the deaths in the miserable conditions of shantytown life. What puzzled me was the seeming indifference of Alto women to the death of their infants, and their willingness to attribute to their own tiny offspring an aversion to life that made their death seem wholly natural, indeed all but anticipated.

Although I found that it was possible, and hardly difficult, to rescue infants and toddlers from death by diarrhea and dehydration with a simple sugar, salt, and water solution (even bottled Coca-Cola worked fine), it was more difficult to enlist a mother herself in the rescue of a child she perceived as ill-fated for life or better off dead, or to convince her to take back into her threatened and besieged home a baby she had already come to think of as an angel rather than as a son or daughter.

I learned that the high expectancy of death, and the ability to face child death with stoicism and equanimity, produced patterns of nurturing that differentiated between those infants thought of as thrivers and survivors and those thought of as born already "wanting to die." The survivors were nurtured, while stigmatized, doomed infants were left to die, as mothers say, *a mingua,* "of neglect." Mothers stepped back and allowed nature to take its course. This pattern, which I call mortal selective neglect, is called passive infanticide by anthropologist Marvin Harris. The Alto situation, although culturally specific in the form that it takes, is not unique to Third World shantytown communities and may have its correlates in our own impoverished urban communities in some cases of "failure to thrive" infants.

I use as an example the story of Zezinho, the thirteen-month-old toddler of one of my neighbors, Lourdes. I became involved with Zezinho when I was called in to help Lourdes in the delivery of another child, this one a fair and robust little tyke with a lusty cry. I noted that while Lourdes showed great interest in the newborn, she totally ignored Zezinho who, wasted and severely malnourished, was curled up in a fetal position on a piece of urine- and feces-soaked cardboard placed under his mother's hammock. Eyes open and vacant, mouth slack, the little boy seemed doomed.

When I carried Zezinho up to the community day-care center at the top of the hill, the Alto women who took turns caring for one another's children (in order to free themselves for part-time work in the cane fields or washing clothes) laughed at my efforts to save Ze, agreeing with Lourdes that here was a baby without a ghost of a chance. Leave him alone, they cautioned. It makes no sense to fight with death. But I did do battle with Ze, and after several weeks of force-feeding (malnourished babies lose their interest in food), Ze began to succumb to my ministrations. He acquired some flesh across his taut chest bones, learned to sit up, and even tried to smile. When he seemed well enough, I returned him to Lourdes in her miserable scrap-material lean-to, but not without guilt about what I had done. I wondered whether returning Ze was at all fair to Lourdes and to his little brother. But I was busy and washed my hands of the matter. And Lourdes did seem more interested in Ze now that he was looking more human.

When I returned in 1982, there was Lourdes among the women who formed my sample of Alto mothers—still struggling to put together some semblance of life for a now grown Ze and her five other surviving children. Much was made of my reunion with Ze in 1982, and everyone enjoyed retelling the story of Ze's rescue and of how his mother had given him up for dead. Ze would laugh the loudest when told how

I had had to force-feed him like a fiesta turkey. There was no hint of guilt on the part of Lourdes and no resentment on the part of Ze. In fact, when questioned in private as to who was the best friend he ever had in life, Ze took a long drag on his cigarette and answered without a trace of irony, "Why my mother, of course!" "But of course," I replied.

Part of learning how to mother in the Alto do Cruzeiro is learning when to let go of a child who shows that it "wants" to die or that it has no "knack" or no "taste" for life. Another part is learning when it is safe to let oneself love a child. Frequent child death remains a powerful shaper of maternal thinking and practice. In the absence of firm expectation that a child will survive, mother love as we conceptualize it (whether in popular terms or in the psychobiological notion of maternal bonding) is attenuated and delayed with consequences for infant survival. In an environment already precarious to young life, the emotional detachment of mothers toward some of their babies contributes even further to the spiral of high mortality–high fertility in a kind of macabre lock-step dance of death.

The average woman of the Alto experiences 9.5 pregnancies, 3.5 child deaths, and 1.5 stillbirths. Seventy percent of all child deaths in the Alto occur in the first six months of life, and 82 percent by the end of the first year. Of all deaths in the community each year, about 45 percent are of children under the age of five.

Women of the Alto distinguish between child deaths understood as natural (caused by diarrhea and communicable diseases) and those resulting from sorcery, the evil eye, or other magical or supernatural afflictions. They also recognize a large category of infant deaths seen as fated and inevitable. These hopeless cases are classified by mothers under the folk terminology "child sickness" or "child attack." Women say that there are at least fourteen different types of hopeless child sickness, but most can be subsumed under two categories—chronic and acute. The chronic cases refer to infants who are born small and wasted. They are deathly pale, mothers say, as well as weak and passive. They demonstrate no vital force, no liveliness. They do not suck vigorously; they hardly cry. Such babies can be this way at birth or they can be born sound but soon show no resistance, no "fight" against the common crises of infancy: diarrhea, respiratory infections, tropical fevers.

The acute cases are those doomed infants who die suddenly and violently. They are taken by stealth overnight, often following convulsions that bring on head banging, shaking, grimacing, and shrieking. Women say it is horrible to look at such a baby. If the infant begins to foam at the mouth or gnash its teeth or go rigid with its eyes turned back inside its head, there is absolutely no hope. The infant is "put aside"—left alone—often on the floor in a back room, and allowed to die. These symptoms (which accompany high fevers, dehydration, third-stage malnutrition, and encephalitis) are equated by Alto women with madness, epilepsy, and worst of all, rabies, which is greatly feared and highly stigmatized.

Most of the infants presented to me as suffering from chronic child sickness were tiny, wasted famine victims, while those labeled as victims of acute child attack seemed to be infants suffering from the deliriums of high fever or the convulsions that can accompany electrolyte imbalance in dehydrated babies.

Local midwives and traditional healers, praying women, as they are called, advise Alto women on when to allow a baby to die. One midwife explained: "If I can see that a baby was born unfortuitously, I tell the mother that she need not wash the infant or give it a cleansing tea. I tell her just to dust the infant with baby powder and wait for it to die." Allowing nature to take its course is not seen as sinful by these often very devout Catholic women. Rather, it is understood as cooperating with God's plan.

Often I have been asked how consciously women of the Alto behave in this regard. I would have to say that consciousness is always shifting between allowed and disallowed levels of awareness. For example, I was awakened early one morning in 1987 by two neighborhood children who had been sent to fetch me to a hastily organized wake for a two-month-old infant whose mother I had unsuccessfully urged to breast-feed. The infant was being sustained on sugar water, which the mother referred to as *soro* (serum), using a medical term for the infant's starvation regime in light of his chronic diarrhea. I had cautioned the mother that an infant could not live on *soro* forever.

The two girls urged me to console the young mother by telling her that it was "too bad" that her infant was so weak that Jesus had to take him. They were coaching me in proper Alto etiquette. I agreed, of course, but asked, "And what do *you* think?" Xoxa, the eleven-year-old, looked down at her dusty flip-flops and blurted out, "Oh, Dona Nanci, that baby never got enough to eat, but you must never say that!" And so the death of hungry babies remains one of the best kept secrets of life in Bom Jesus da Mata.

Most victims are waked quickly and with a minimum of ceremony. No tears are shed, and the neighborhood children form a tiny procession, carrying the baby to the town graveyard where it will join a multitude of others. Although a few fresh flowers may be scattered over the tiny grave, no stone or wooden cross will mark the place, and the same spot will be reused within a few months' time. The mother will never visit the grave, which soon becomes an anonymous one.

What, then, can be said of these women? What emotions, what sentiments motivate them? How are they able to do what, in fact, must be done? What does mother love mean in this inhospitable context? Are grief, mourning, and melancholia present, although deeply repressed? If so, where shall we look for them? And if not, how are we to understand the moral visions and moral sensibilities that guide their actions?

I have been criticized more than once for presenting an unflattering portrait of poor Brazilian women, women who are, after all, themselves the victims of severe social and institutional neglect. I have described these women as allowing some of their children to die, as if this were an unnatural and inhuman act rather than, as I would assert, the way any one of us might act, reasonably and rationally, under similarly desperate conditions. Perhaps I have not emphasized enough the real pathogens in this environment of high risk: poverty, deprivation, sexism, chronic hunger, and economic exploitation. If mother love is, as many psychologists and some feminists believe, a seemingly natural and universal maternal script, what does it mean to women for whom scarcity, loss, sickness, and deprivation have made that love frantic and robbed them of their grief, seeming to turn their hearts to stone?

Throughout much of human history—as in a great deal of the impoverished Third World today—women have had to give birth and to nurture children under ecological conditions and social arrangements hostile to child survival, as well as to their own well-being. Under circumstances of high childhood mortality, patterns of selective neglect and passive infanticide may be seen as active survival strategies.

They also seem to be fairly common practices historically and across cultures. In societies characterized by high childhood mortality and by a correspondingly high (replacement) fertility, cultural practices of infant and child care tend to be organized primarily around survival goals. But what this means is a pragmatic recognition that not all of one's children can be expected to live. The nervousness about child survival in areas of northeast Brazil, northern India, or Bangladesh, where a 30 percent or 40 percent mortality rate in the first years of life is common, can lead to forms of delayed attachment and a casual or benign neglect that serves to weed out the worst bets so as to enhance the life chances of healthier siblings, including those yet to be born. Practices similar to those that I am describing have been recorded for parts of Africa, India, and Central America.

Life in the Alto do Cruzeiro resembles nothing so much as a battlefield or an emergency room in an overcrowded inner-city public hospital. Consequently, morality is guided by a kind of "lifeboat ethics," the morality of triage. The seemingly studied indifference toward the suffering of some of their infants, conveyed in such sayings as "little critters have no feelings," is understandable in light of these women's obligation to carry on with their reproductive and nurturing lives.

In their slowness to anthropomorphize and personalize their infants, everything is mobilized so as to prevent maternal overattachment and, therefore, grief at death. The bereaved mother is told not to cry, that her tears will dampen the wings of her little angel so that she cannot fly up to her heavenly home. Grief at the death of an angel is not only inappropriate, it is a symptom of madness and of a profound lack of faith.

Infant death becomes routine in an environment in which death is anticipated and bets are hedged. While the routinization of death in the context of shantytown life is not hard to understand, and quite possible to empathize with, its routinization in the formal institutions of public life in Bom Jesus is not as easy to accept uncritically. Here the social production of indifference takes on a different, even a malevolent, cast.

In a society where triplicates of every form are required for the most banal events (registering a car, for example), the registration of infant and child death is informal, incomplete, and rapid. It requires no documentation, takes less than five minutes, and demands no witnesses other than office clerks. No questions are asked concerning the circumstances of the death, and the cause of death is left blank, unquestioned and unexamined. A neighbor, grandmother, older sibling, or common-law husband may register the death. Since most infants die at home, there is no question of a medical record.

From the registry office, the parent proceeds to the town hall, where the mayor will give him or her a voucher for a free baby coffin. The full-time municipal coffinmaker cannot tell you exactly how many baby coffins are dispatched each week. It varies, he says, with the seasons. There are more needed during the drought months and during the big festivals of Carnaval and Christmas and São Joao's Day because people are too busy, he supposes, to take their babies to the clinic. Record keeping is sloppy.

Similarly, there is a failure on the part of city-employed doctors working at two free clinics to recognize the malnutrition of babies who are weighed, measured, and immunized without comment and as if they were not, in fact, anemic, stunted, fussy, and irritated starvation babies. At best the mothers are told to pick up free vitamins or a health "tonic" at the municipal chambers. At worst, clinic personnel will give tranquilizers and sleeping pills to quiet the hungry cries of "sick-to-death" Alto babies.

The church, too, contributes to the routinization of, and indifference toward, child death. Traditionally, the local Catholic church taught patience and resignation to domestic tragedies that were said to reveal the imponderable workings of God's will. If an infant died suddenly, it was because a particular saint had claimed the child. The infant would be an angel in the service of his or her heavenly patron. It would be wrong, a sign of a lack of faith, to weep for a child with such good fortune. The infant funeral was, in the past, an event celebrated with joy. Today, however, under the new regime of "liberation theology," the bells of N.S. das Dores parish church no longer peal for the death of Alto babies, and no priest accompanies the procession of angels to the cemetery where their bodies are disposed of casually and without ceremony. Children bury children in Bom Jesus da Mata. In this most Catholic of communities, the coffin is handed to the disabled and irritable municipal gravedigger, who often chides the children for one reason or another. It may be that the coffin is larger than expected and the gravedigger can find no appropriate space. The children do not wait for the gravedigger to complete his task. No prayers are recited and no sign of the cross made as the tiny coffin goes into its shallow grave.

When I asked the local priest, Padre Marcos, about the lack of church ceremony surrounding infant and childhood death today in Bom Jesus, he replied: "In the old days, child death was richly celebrated. But those were the baroque customs of a conservative church that wallowed in death and misery. The new church is a church of hope and joy. We no longer celebrate the death of child angels. We try to tell mothers that Jesus doesn't want all the dead babies they send him." Similarly, the new church has changed its baptismal customs, now often refusing to baptize dying babies brought to the back door of a church or rectory. The mothers are scolded by the church attendants and told to go home and take care of their sick babies. Baptism, they are told, is for the living; it is not to be confused with the sacrament of extreme unction, which is the anointing of the dying. And so it appears to the women of the Alto that even the church has turned away from them, denying the traditional comfort of folk Catholicism.

The contemporary Catholic church is caught in the clutches of a double bind. The new theology of liberation imagines a kingdom of God on earth based on justice and equality, a world without hunger, sickness, or childhood mortality. At the same time, the church has not changed its official position on sexuality and reproduction, including its sanctions against birth control, abortion, and sterilization. The padre of Bom Jesus da Mata recognizes this contradiction intuitively, although he shies away from discussions on the topic, saying that he prefers to leave questions of family planning to the discretion and the "good consciences" of his impoverished parishioners. But this, of course, sidesteps the extent to which those good consciences have been shaped by traditional church teachings in Bom Jesus, especially by his recent predecessors. Hence, we can begin to see that the seeming indifference of Alto mothers toward the death of some of their infants is but a pale reflection of the official indifference of church and state to the plight of poor women and children.

Nonetheless, the women of Bom Jesus are survivors. One woman, Biu, told me her life history, returning again and again to the themes of child death, her first husband's suicide, abandonment by her father and later by her second husband, and all the other losses and disappointments she had suffered in her long forty-five years. She concluded with great force, reflecting on the days of Carnaval '88 that were fast approaching:

> No, Dona Nanci, I won't cry, and I won't waste my life thinking about it from morning to night. . . . Can I argue with God for the state that I'm in? No! And so I'll dance and I'll jump and I'll play Carnaval! And yes, I'll laugh and people will wonder at a *pobre* like me who can have such a good time.

And no one did blame Biu for dancing in the streets during the four days of Carnaval—not even on Ash Wednesday, the day following Carnaval '88 when we all assembled hurriedly to assist in the burial of Mercea, Biu's beloved *casula,* her last-born daughter who had died at home of pneumonia during the festivities. The rest of the family barely had time to change out of their costumes. Severino, the child's uncle and godfather, sprinkled holy water over the little angel while he prayed: "Mercea, I don't know whether you were called, taken, or thrown out of this world. But look down at us from your heavenly home with tenderness, with pity, and with mercy." So be it.

Brief Epilogue

Many students write after reading this article asking me whether the situation has changed in the Alto do Cruzeiro. Is life better or worse for mothers and newborn babies? One of the advantages of long-term ethnographic research is seeing history in the making. I began my engagements with the people of the Alto in 1964 at the start of twenty years of military rule, a ruthless regime that produced deep impoverishment among those living in urban *favelas* and in rural areas. The scarcities and insecurities of that era contributed to the death of infants and small babies. By the time I completed my study of mother love and child death in the early 1990s Brazil was well on its way to democratization which ushered in many important changes, most notably a free, public, national health care system (SUS) which guaranteed poor women adequate pre- and post-natal care.

The decade of the 1990s witnessed what population experts call the demographic or epidemiologic transition. As both births and infant deaths declined, mothers began to treat their infants as potentially capable of survival and the old stance of maternal "watchful waiting" accompanied by "letting go" of infants thought of as having no "taste" or "talent" for life, was replaced by a maternal ethos of "holding on" and "holding dear" each infant. Today, young women of the Alto can expect to give birth to three or fewer babies and to see all of them live to adolescence. Many factors produced this reproductive transition: the "modernization" of Catholic beliefs about infant death; the under-the-counter availability of Cytotec, a risky "morning after" pill; the implementation under the national health care system (Serviço Único de Saúde) of local "health agents" who went door to door in poor communities, identifying and rescuing vulnerable infants, toddlers, and old people. The primary cause of the decline in infant mortality on the Alto do Cruzeiro, however, was the "simple" installation of water pipes reaching virtually all the homes in the shantytown with sufficient, clean water. Water = life! It is painful to consider how "culture," "belief," and even "maternal sentiments" follow basic changes in the material conditions—and therefore the possibilities—of everyday life.

Motherhood is not only a social and a cultural construction, but a constellation of embodied practices responding to the requirements and limitations of the political and economic conditions that determine the resilience or vulnerability of infants and their mothers. Today, new problems have beset the people of the Alto do Cruzeiro. Since the publication of "Death without Weeping" drugs and gangs have made their ugly mark on the community and death squads have sprung up to impose a kind of vigilante justice. These anti-social features of life in "Bom Jesus" take some of the pleasure away, as one sees the young men of the Alto who survived that dangerous first year of life, felled by bullets and knife wounds at the hands of gang leaders, *bandidos*, and local police in almost equal measure.

Study and **Review** on **myanthrolab.com**

Review Questions

1. What did Scheper-Hughes notice about mothers' reactions during the baby die-off of 1965 in Bom Jesus, Brazil?
2. How do poor Brazilian mothers react to their infants' illnesses and death? How do other institutions, such as the church, clinic, and civil authorities respond? Give examples.
3. How does Scheper-Hughes explain the apparent indifference of mothers to the death of their infants?
4. What does the indifference of mothers to the deaths of their children say about basic human nature, especially the mother–child bond?

Marriage and the Family

PREVIEW

- How do anthropologists define marriage and family?
- What are the characteristics of nuclear and extended families?
- How do residency patterns relate to other aspects of a culture?
- How do marriage rules extend kinship while observing incest taboos?
- What are some theories about the origins of the incest taboo?
- How is marriage a rite of passage?
- What are some social functions of marriage?
- What forms of marriage are known to exist?
- How is marriage a form of political alliance and economic exchange?

A bride and groom smile as they take part in a mass wedding ceremony in Baghdad's impoverished Sadr City 06 August 2005. The Iraqi Martyr Association for Humanitarian Services organized the mass wedding of 100 Shiite Muslim couples, giving each a 500 US dollar check as a wedding gift. *Ali al-Saadi/AFP/Getty Images/Newscom*

Listen to the Chapter Audio on myanthrolab.com

Read on myanthrolab.com

A woman had an only son who became grown up and had not been married yet. She wanted to find him a bride, but he always told her, "Later, not now...." One day his mother said to him, "Listen, my son, I've grown old and become tired of household work. You must get married before I die."

He said to her, "Well! Find me a good girl from a good house."

She ... found him a girl from one of the most notable houses in their town and he married her.

When the wedding [party] was over and after seven days or so, he went back to his shop to work, while his mother stayed with his wife. "Listen, in this house [you] don't open what is closed or close what is opened, nor uncover what is covered or cover what is uncovered, nor unwrap what is wrapped or wrap what is unwrapped, nor unfold what is folded or fold what is unfolded. Do you understand?"

The girl, his wife, said, "Yes."

Days passed with things like that. His mother is everything in the house; his wife works all day while his mother orders her around. When the man returns home, his mother would set the dinner for him and if he would say "[Let us] call [his wife] to eat with me," his mother would answer him, "This can't be. She is still new in the house. She would get bold with us. Wait for a few more days."

After a few more days her son would say, "Let her come and eat with me."

His mother would say, "She hasn't been broken to our house yet. She does not need to eat for she has been eating all day."

He would say to his mother, "May God extend his grace upon us. Let her eat as much as she wants," and [he] used to eat only until he was half-full and leave some of the best food to his wife. His mother would hide it and would give her only hard bread and water.

The girl grew sicker and weaker by the day. Whenever her husband asked her, "What is the matter with you?" she would answer, "Nothing."

One day he said to one of his friends at the store, "By God, my wife is becoming sick. Every day she is getting thinner and paler. I am afraid she doesn't want me. Ever since she set foot in my house, she doesn't speak to me, and she is always sad."

His friend said to him, "I'll tell you what to do to see whether she wants you and wants to stay in your house, or whether she hates you and would like to return to her father's house. After dinner swear by God that she joins you and your mother for the coffee, then break wind. If she laughs at you, she doesn't care for you and you should send her back to her father's home. If she doesn't, then she is ill."

That same day after the man ate his supper and thanked his God, he said to his mother, "Call [his wife] to have coffee with us." He swore by God, and his mother went to call her. As they were drinking their coffee, he broke wind. His mother laughed, but his wife didn't and kept on drinking until she finished her cup....

The following day he told his friend about what had happened. His friend said to him, "Your wife is hungry. Your mother is starving your wife."

He built a new house for his wife and moved out of the old one and got his mother a servant.

This narrative from Iraq tells of the conflict and tensions between a new bride and her mother-in-law. In the story, the young husband is beset with divided loyalties. His respect for his mother is tempered by his concern for his wife. The wife is obedient and deferential to the older woman. The narrative raises issues of power for women in patrilineal and patriarchal households. The mother tries to exert power over her daughter-in-law, but in the end she has less authority than her son because he is the man, the recognized head of the family. He chooses to protect his wife's interests and allies himself with her.

This Iraqi family unit was formed not only through rules of descent but also through marriage rules. The family unit at the household level consisted of a man, his widowed mother, his wife, any children borne by his wife, and the man's unmarried siblings. This chapter explores marriage and the family and how they interrelate with other elements of culture in a society.

Kinship systems and family arrangements are basic elements in all societies. They are among the topics of central concern in anthropology because they help structure people's daily lives and lay the foundations for how they are integrated into their communities. However, societies differ greatly in how families are formed, about who constitutes a family, and about the rights and obligations of family members toward one another. As we shall see, variations in family organization are not random but are consistent with economic and social needs. Thus, different types of families are preferred in different types of societies.

household
A group of people occupying a common dwelling.

family
A married couple or other group of adult kinfolk who cooperate economically and in the upbringing of children, and all or most of whom share a common dwelling.

DEFINING MARRIAGE AND FAMILY

People are social beings. We live together in groups, work with others, and form emotional bonds with other people. Although some individuals live alone at any given time in every society, most people live with others during all or most of their lives. Most people who live together are members of families. In everyday speech, we use the word *family* casually to refer to our relatives without specifying how we are related to these people. Even anthropologists do not agree on a single or concise definition of family.

Anthropologists tend to make a distinction between family and household, although the two words are often used interchangeably. A **household** refers to a group of people occupying a common dwelling. The Iraqi man, his wife, and his mother are members of a household. The term *homestead* refers to multiple dwellings occupied by related and interacting people.

Members of families are related either through descent (consanguines) or marriage (affines). For example, one's grandparents, parents, aunts and uncles, siblings, children, and cousins are all consanguineal relatives, whereas one's spouse and all the people called in-laws are affinal relatives. North Americans differ in the ways they apply the word*family* to many of these relatives. Some people use the word to encompass all their relations, but others restrict the term to refer to close relatives with whom they interact regularly.

A useful starting definition of **family** is one given by anthropologist Kathleen Gough (1975, 52). She defines the family as a "married couple or other group of adult kinfolk who co-operate economically and in the upbringing of children, and all or most of whom share a common dwelling." In this definition, a family is more than just a couple. Gough's definition includes several important features of family, stressing the cooperative links among members who share social and economic responsibilities. On this basis, the Iraqi man, his wife, and his mother constitute a family.

There are other definitions of family, however, and family members need not occupy the same household. Some members of polygynous families may occupy different households within an area. In addition, although marriage is the most common bond that creates families, marriage itself is not a required component of family. Heterosexual or gay couples who are not married also constitute families. The single-parent family of parent and child is perhaps the smallest family unit (Fox 1984).

Although issues of family composition, family life, and "family values" are controversial in the current climate of North American social and political discourse, the American Anthropological Association has taken a strong position supporting the legitimacy and viability

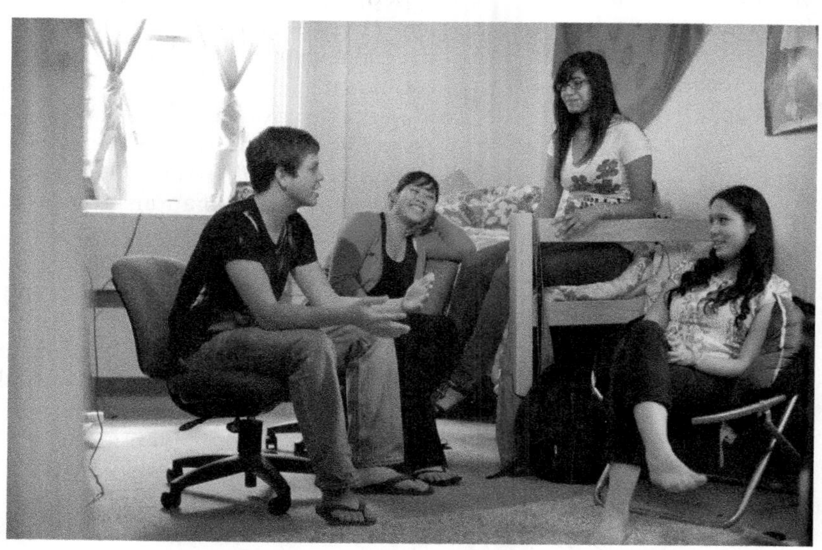

These roommates share a household. Unlike family households, roommates typically do not share all economic resources and have no expectations of mutual obligations or an enduring relationship. Alamy Limited/Blend Images/Alamy

These indigenous Mexican families in Tzintzuntzan are celebrating the Day of the Dead. Glow Images, Inc./Heeb Christian/Glow Images, Inc.

of all family types. In its statement, issued in 2003, the association said the following:

> More than a century of anthropological research on households, kinship relationships, and families, across cultures and through time, provide no support for the view that either civilization or viable social orders depend upon marriage as an exclusively heterosexual institution. Rather, a vast array of family types can contribute to stable and humane societies.

The family is a basic unit of economic cooperation and stability. Members of families usually perform at least somewhat different economic tasks, a pattern that highlights the interdependent relationships among family members. They also pool all or at least some of their resources for the survival of the group.

The family serves social needs as well, providing members with companionship, emotional support, and assistance. Families also function in the propagation and survival of society. They provide the context for biological reproduction and for the training and enculturation of children. Families function universally as vehicles for socialization into expected roles and goals of their own or adopted children. Children learn what is appropriate by observing adults and by overt learning and practicing of skills for roles they will assume as adult women and men. In the context of their families, children learn their gender identity and their role in households and communities. Through observation of social relations between their parents or among all adults in their households, they learn whether men and women have equal rights to contribute to discussions and decision making. They also deduce social rights through the ways that conflicts are resolved. Girls and boys also learn whether they can expect emotional and economic support from their natal kin groups once they reach adulthood and form their own families.

Watch the **Video:** *Swahili Naming Practices* on **myanthrolab.com**

Based on your experience in your family, what are some specific expressions of the functions of the family as a social institution?

In addition, families are decision-making groups. Members of families consult with one another, make decisions together, and may function as political units with others in their communities to establish and provide leadership. In some societies, positions of leadership are inherited within families. Everywhere, inheritance of property and the transmission of cultural knowledge take place within family units.

All societies contain units recognized as families, but there are differences in the ways in which families are formed. Throughout the world, most families are formed through marriage. *Marriage* is another word that we use casually with reference to a union between two people, but anthropologists have not settled on an uncontested definition of marriage. There is even some debate in the field about whether marriage and the family are universal constructs. Still, even if we accept that marriage is a recognized social status in most, if not all, cultures, there are differences in the ways that marriages are contracted and in the relationships between the spouses.

What do you think might be some sources of disagreements about the definitions of marriage and family?

Marriage is generally understood as a socially recognized, enduring, stable bond between two people who each have certain rights and obligations toward one another. These rights and obligations vary from culture to culture, but are likely to include some common features. For example, married partners have the right to expect to have a sexual relationship with each other, although the number of partners may vary. In plural marriages, for example, a person may have more than one spouse. In most societies, spouses have obligations to assist one another in rearing children and providing for their household. They share economic resources and provide shelter, clothing, and household equipment. Marriage also establishes bonds between groups of kin (the relatives of each spouse), who also have rights and obligations toward one another.

marriage
A socially recognized, stable, and enduring union between two adults who publicly acknowledge their rights and obligations and form a new alliance between kin groups.

Through marriage, men and their kinship groups may claim rights to children. For this reason, there is a fundamental difference in the emphasis on marriage in patrilineal groups, where descent and inheritance are traced through men, and matrilineal groups, where they are traced through women. In matrilineal societies, kinship groups obtain new members when the women of the group give birth to children. A mother's child automatically becomes a member of her own kin group, whether she is married or not. In contrast, patrilineal kinship units cannot obtain children from their own women because a child does not belong to its mother's kin group but to its father's. In this case, marriage serves the purpose of securing a stable relationship between men and women from outside their kin group. Marriage also provides for the establishment of what Kathleen Gough calls "social fatherhood." **Social fatherhood** may or may not be the same as biological paternity. One's social father is the man who fulfills the responsibilities of parenting, just as stepparents and adoptive parents are social parents.

REVIEW

A family is a group of people related by blood or by marriage who live together, raise children, and share economic and other social responsibilities. A household consists of relatives and, often, nonrelatives who live together and share economic responsibilities. In all societies, enculturation of children and the inheritance of property and status take place within families. In most societies, families are formed through marriage, a public acknowledgment of a couple's commitment and a new alliance between kin groups. Marriage enables men in patrilineal societies to add children to their kin group, whereas children in matrilineal societies are automatically in their mother's group. Marriage also allows for social fatherhood.

FAMILIES AND IDEAL TYPES

Anthropologists differentiate between one's family of orientation (the family one grows up in) and one's family of procreation (the family one founds as an adult). In addition, anthropologists have long used a classification of ideal family types that is generally descriptive of different family structures. Many real families diverge from these types in some way or to some degree. Nevertheless, the types are useful because they broadly correlate with other aspects of culture. The nuclear family, extended family, joint family, and single-parent family are some of these types.

Nuclear Families

Among nomadic foragers and members of industrial societies, most families are of the type that anthropologists call "nuclear." A **nuclear family** consists of one or both parents and their children, although another relative, such as a grandparent or an unmarried sibling of one of the parents, may reside in the same household for a time. The nuclear family is the characteristic family form of societies with bilateral descent, which, are typically either foraging or industrial societies.

A nuclear family structure provides certain benefits. For instance, it has the advantage of mobility. The relatively small number of people in a nuclear family unit can easily separate themselves from the larger community in which they live. In foraging societies, nuclear families aid in survival in conditions of scarcity. If there are insufficient resources to support a large group, nuclear families can go their own way, dispersing into a large territory and exploiting meager resources. In industrial societies, nuclear families allow for economic independence and promote the loosening or weakening of wider kinship bonds. This pattern is advantageous for societies where competition and individual advancement are goals.

social fatherhood
The status of a man who fulfills the responsibilities of parenting, a role that may or may not be the same as biological paternity.

nuclear family
Family consisting of parents and their children.

Comparatively, small families are an advantage for people in both foraging and industrial societies. Family size is limited among foragers in order not to exceed the carrying capacity of the environment. In addition, infants and young children need to be carried when traveling, which favors the spacing of births. Because foragers lack grains and animal milk as foods for babies, mothers nurse their children for as long as three or four years. Therefore, closely spaced children have a low chance of survival. As well, frequent pregnancies and deliveries have a negative impact on the health and long-term survival of mothers. In industrial societies, small nuclear families have the mobility necessary for leaving larger kin groups and moving from job to job and region to region. Distant relatives are unlikely to make claims for assistance, and if they do, families can easily avoid contact with them or deny their requests for aid. Small families are an advantage because dependent children are economic liabilities in industrial economies where work

This Japanese nuclear family is enjoying a day out. The Image Works/ Elizabeth Crews/The Image Works

This four-generation extended Polish family, grouped around their 96-year-old matriarch, is characterized by vertical ties between generations. The Image Works/David Grossman/The Image Works

requires strength, stamina, and skilled training and where laws forbid or restrict child laborers.

Nuclear families risk social isolation. Family reunions in industrial societies may be seen as equivalent to seasonal gatherings of larger kin units among nomadic foragers. **Single-parent families** in industrial societies are formed as the result of divorce or the death of a spouse and parent. Others develop when the parents do not marry or live together. In the United States, most single-parent households consist of mother and children. According to U.S. Census statistics for 2009, 12 percent of all households were headed by a single mother and 4 percent had a single father as head. Single-parent households, especially those headed by women, are more likely to have incomes near or below the poverty line. Their economic difficulties stem from a common problem of nuclear families: Economic independence accrues only to people with resources and jobs. For people with meager incomes, the isolation of single-parent families increases the difficulty of seeking support from kin. In contrast, in extended family systems, people who lose or lack a spouse can rely on a large network of relatives for assistance.

Extended and Joint Families

Family systems based on an extended family principle are more common worldwide. Extended family arrangements are especially prevalent in farming and pastoral economies. **Extended families** consist of three or more generations of people, extending the family vertically. Typically, an extended family unit is composed of an elder parent or couple, their unmarried children, some of the married children, and the children's spouses and children. Rules of descent determine which adult married children remain with the parents. That is, in patrilineal systems where descent and inheritance are traced through men, more often the sons remain with their parents, whereas daughters leave home after marriage to reside with their husbands' families. In matrilineal societies, daughters remain with their parents after marriage, but married sons leave to join their wives' families.

single-parent family
Family consisting of one parent (either mother or father) and her or his children.

extended family
Family formed with three or more generations—for example, parents, children, and grandparents.

CULTURE CHANGE

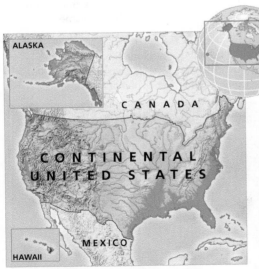

THE CHANGING AMERICAN FAMILY

Family types are responsive to changes in productive modes and general social values. In the United States, the percentage of family units conforming to the idealized model of husband, wife, and children has declined since the mid-twentieth century. The idealized nuclear family model is itself a product of economic needs and adjustments made during the nineteenth and twentieth centuries as capitalist and industrial production dominated North American society. Other kinds of family units have now become more common. The number of blended families, based on remarriages and the combining of children from previous marriages, has also increased.

Growing rates of divorce have also increased the number of single-parent households. As women have gained more economic independence, the financial need to remarry after divorce or the death of a spouse has declined. More people also never marry. Many households consist of a man and woman involved in a long-term relationship who choose not to marry. Such couples may or may not have children. Another less common but not unusual type of household consists of two people of the same gender who share a sexual relationship, economic responsibilities, and other attributes of family life such as child rearing.

Census statistics indicate changes in U.S. household composition, marital status, and numbers of children over the last several decades. Tables 1 through 4 present some of the relevant data.

As the figures in Table 1 indicate, the percentages of people "Never Married" and "Divorced" have risen between 1980 and 2009, whereas the percentage of people "Married" has declined.

View the **Slideshow:** *The Changing American Family* on **myanthrolab.com**

The size of families has also decreased between 1980 and 2009. More couples are having fewer children than in the past. Indeed, the number of childless couples has increased, as Table 2 demonstrates. Table 3 shows that the composition of households also changed from 1990 to 2009.

The number of cohabitating unmarried couples has also increased. In 1980, there were 1,589,000 such couples, but by 2000, there were 4,486,000 unmarried couples, and

TABLE 1 MARITAL STATUS OF THE U.S. POPULATION, 1980–2009 (AS PERCENTAGE OF TOTAL, BY SEX)

	1980		1990		2000		2009	
	Male	Female	Male	Female	Male	Female	Male	Female
Never Married	27.3	21.1	32.1	22.5	32.3	23.4	29.5	22.8
Married	67.1	64.3	60.9	62.4	59.7	60.7	58.9	56.0
Widowed	1.6	7.1	1.5	6.5	1.6	6.5	2.6	9.8
Divorced	4.0	7.6	5.5	8.5	6.4	9.3	9.0	11.4

Source: U.S. Census Bureau, *Statistical Abstract of the United States, 2001*, Table 49; *2011*, Table 56.

TABLE 2 NUMBER OF CHILDREN PER HOUSEHOLD

Number of Children	1980	1990	2000	2009
No children	48%	51%	52%	55%
One child	21	20	20	19
Two children	19	19	18	17
Three or more children	12	10	10	9

Source: U.S. Census Bureau, *Statistical Abstract of the United States, 2001*, Table 58; *2003*, Table 71; *2011*, Table 64.

TABLE 3 COMPOSITION OF HOUSEHOLDS

Type of Household	1990	2000	2009
Family Household	71%	69%	67%
Married couple family	56	53	50
Single father	3	4	4
Single mother	12	12	12
Nonfamily Household	29	31	33
Living alone	25	26	27
Males	10	11	12
Females	15	15	15

Source: U.S. Census Bureau, *Statistical Abstract of the United States, 2001*, Table 53; *2011*, Table 61.

TABLE 4 NUMBER OF PEOPLE PER FAMILY				
Size of Family	**1980**	**1990**	**2000**	**2009**
Two people	39%	42%	44%	33.4%
Three people	23	23	22	15.9
Four people	21	21	20	13.7
Five people	10	9	9	6.1
Six people	4	3	3	2.2
Seven or more people	3	2	2	1.3

Source: U.S. Census Bureau, *Statistical Abstract of the United States, 2003,* Table 67; *2011,* Table 62.

the number rose to 6,214,000 by 2008 (U.S. Census Bureau, *Statistical Abstract of the United States, 2001,* Table 52; *2009,* Table 63).

Finally, as Table 4 indicates, the number of people per family has declined since 1980.

More families with children consist of single parents. In 1990, 71.9 percent of all families with children contained two parents; by 2005, the percentage had dropped to 67.4 percent. In 2005, mothers headed 26.4 percent of all families with children, whereas fathers headed 6.2 percent (U.S. Census Bureau, *Statistical Abstract of the United States, 2011,* Table 63). In addition, although the actual numbers remain small, the growth of stay-at-home fathers reflects changes in gender expectations. In 2009, of all married couple families with children under 15 years old, 22.6 percent had stay-at-home mothers while 0.7 percent had stay-at-home fathers. This represents a more than doubling of stay-at-home fathers since 1995 and a decline in the numbers of stay-at-home mothers (U.S. Census Bureau, *Statistical Abstract of the United States, 2011,* Table 68).

Census figures also indicate a sharp increase in the number of same-sex households between 1990 and 2009. This may reflect both real growth in same-sex households and a greater likelihood that their members self-report. In 2006, 776,943 households consisted of same-sex partners. Of these, 413,095 were male couples and 363,848 were female couples (U.S. Census Bureau, *Statistical Abstract of the United States, 2006,* Table 62). Taking a different perspective on the data, in 2009 of all households with unmarried partners, 0.24 percent consisted of two men while 0.26 percent consisted of two women (U.S. Census Bureau, *Statistical Abstract of the United States, 2011,* Table 63).

Although same-sex marriages are legal in Massachusetts, Connecticut, Iowa, Vermont, New Hampshire, and New York State, the U.S. Census Bureau reclassifies legally married same-sex couples as "unmarried, same-sex partners" in compliance with the Defense of Marriage Act.

Data for 2009 reveal that 69.8 percent of all children live with two parents (U.S. Census Bureau, *Statistical Abstract of the United States, 2009,* Table 69). Although this is a decline from the 85 percent in 1970, it is still a sizable majority. In 2009, 22.8 percent of children lived with their mother only (up from 11 percent in 1970) while 3.4 percent lived only with their father. Comparative evidence shows that the figures on children and household composition have remained fairly steady since 1990, indicating that the familial effects of social changes in the 1960s and 1970s have leveled off. Only 4.0 percent of the nation's children live in households without either parent, and about 2 percent are living with their grandparents only. There are marked disparities in children's experiences for different racial and ethnic groupings; for example, 85.2 percent of Asian children, 75.8 percent of non-Hispanic white children, 68.7 percent of Hispanic children, but only 38.1 percent of African American children live with two parents.

All of these data are consistent with quantitative and qualitative studies soliciting Americans' attitudes toward marriage and family life. Several large-scale research projects from the 1960s through the late 1990s reveal that, although most Americans "... value marriage, children, and family life, these institutions are now much more voluntary and less obligatory... leading to more individual freedom in these areas" (Thornton and Young-DeMarco 2001, 1031). Examples of these shifts include more acceptance of divorce, of unmarried couples living together, and of unmarried women having children.

A family that is extended laterally rather than vertically is referred to as a joint family, which is much less common. A **joint family** typically consists of siblings who combine their families to share work and resources, such as two or three brothers, their wives, and their children.

Extended and joint family systems have the advantage of establishing a more or less stable group of people who can share resources, household tasks, and subsistence work, and provide emotional support and material aid. However, because many people live together, conflicts may develop. Intergenerational tensions may arise because of the authority of the eldest couple over their adult children, or sibling rivalry may develop in a joint family compound. Conflicts over authority, inheritance, and loyalty are common. In addition, extended and joint family systems may lead to social difficulties for in-marrying spouses. Women moving in with their husbands' kin, for example, may face demanding mothers-in-law. Economic cooperation and interdependence is a prominent feature of extended and joint families. For this reason, people in industrial societies may form this type of family unit on a temporary or permanent basis when they are unemployed or otherwise lack resources. For example, according to the U.S. Census Bureau, in the current economic crisis experienced by many American families, the number of "multifamily households" rose sharply, by 11.7 percent from 2008 to 2010. In 2010, there were 15.5 million such households, accounting for 13.2 percent of all households and including 54 million people (Luo 2010). However, this dramatic increase does not reflect the full scope of the problem since the Census Bureau defines a multifamily household as one consisting of at least two nuclear families, excluding arrangements when adult siblings reside together or a childless adult moves in with his or her parents.

Which ideal type best characterizes your family? What are some benefits and challenges of life in this type of family in relation to the larger culture?

Ideal family types include nuclear, single-parent, extended, and joint families. A nuclear family consists of parents and their offspring and occasionally another relative. Single-parent families have a mother or a father and children. Women head most single-parent families. Extended families consist of parents, their unmarried children, married children and their spouses, and their grandchildren. Joint families extend the family unit horizontally among siblings rather than vertically across generations.

ENDOGAMY, EXOGAMY, AND THE INCEST TABOO

Marriage serves as a means of extending kinship within a particular group (*endogamy*) or extending kinship to other groups (*exogamy*). All societies ban marriage—and condemn sexual relations—within the nuclear family, particularly between parents and children and also, with very few exceptions, between brothers and sisters. This ban is referred to as the **incest taboo.** The incest taboo is essentially a rule of nuclear family exogamy, forcing people to marry outside their families. The incest taboo is universal, but beyond the nuclear family the "forbidden" relatives are different in different societies. For example, one set of cousins is preferred for marriage in some societies, whereas other sets of cousins are forbidden under the incest taboo.

Effects of Exogamy on Social Organization

The marriage rules of endogamy and exogamy are predicated on the incest taboo. Both exogamy and endogamy reflect and reinforce the structure and organization of a society. For example, village exogamy is the norm in societies in which people contract marriages with residents of other villages. Through intervillage marriages, people create alliances over a broader geographic area, thereby widening their networks of allies and supporters. In areas of frequent warfare, such marriages also give some protection against raids because people are less likely to attack villages where they have relatives.

In addition, some stratified societies practice exogamy, stipulating that members of identifiable social groups or strata need to marry outside their own group or **class,** a social grouping whose membership is usually based on a combination of birth and achievement. For example, the Natchez of the south-central United States were divided into two major classes—nobles and commoners. These groups had different, unequal access to resources, services, and power. The nobility consisted of three graded ranks: Suns, Nobles,

joint family
Family consisting of siblings with their spouses and children, sharing work and resources.

incest taboo
A ban on sexual relations or marriage between parents and their children or between siblings.

class
Social grouping usually determined on the basis of a combination of birth and achievement.

CONTROVERSIES

Explaining the Incest Taboo

The origins of the incest taboo are much debated. One theory proposes that the incest taboo arose out of an instinctive aversion toward sexual relations within the nuclear family. However, incest occurs fairly widely in human societies, so avoiding it is not instinctual. Another biological theory suggests that the incest taboo is a learned, cultural response to the possible biological consequences of inbreeding, which can increase the incidence of undesirable or harmful (as well as desirable and beneficial) genetic traits in a population. This theory assumes that ancestral humans understood the relationship between mating and the variability of traits in their population, and that this cultural adaptation then spread to all human societies through diffusion or contact to become a universal element of culture or, alternatively, that human societies in different areas independently invented an incest taboo.

A theory championed by anthropologist Bronislaw Malinowski, based on the work of Sigmund Freud, focused on the origin of the incest taboo as a response to the need to lessen sexual competition within the nuclear family unit. This psychological theory might account in part for the ban on sexual relations between parents and their children, which would strain the marriage bond between husband and wife. However, it does not explain the near-universal prohibition on marriage between siblings. Sibling marriage occurred among the monarchs of ancient Peru, Egypt, and Hawaii but was not defined as incest. Marriage between a brother and sister at the highest level of the state consolidated power and minimized struggles over succession. However, sibling marriage was not permitted among ordinary citizens.

Many anthropologists favor understanding the incest taboo as a means of ensuring survival by forcing people to make alliances with others outside the nuclear family. This "marry out or die out" theory emphasizes that marriage within a small unit will over time lead to the isolation and genetic homogeneity of the group, which makes the unit more vulnerable to population loss or even extinction. Mating outside the nuclear family reduces this risk and also creates social alliances and bonds of reciprocity with other people that can be critical in times of scarcity and other dangers to survival.

We may never know why the incest taboo started, but the fact that it is universal indicates its importance. All these theories add interesting dimensions and clues to the debate.

CRITICAL THINKING QUESTION

Which theory or combination of theories about the origin of the incest taboo do you favor, and why?

and Honored Persons. Descent was matrilineal. The chief was the highest-ranked member of the highest-ranked matrilineage, the Suns. The Suns were never able to consolidate their power and wealth, however, because the Natchez social system required that all members of the nobility practice class exogamy. That is, they had to marry commoners. The Sun matrilineage was perpetuated through children of Sun women who were Suns themselves, but children of Sun men, including children of the Great Sun, were not members of that chiefly lineage. The children and more distant relatives of Sun men became Nobles and Honored Persons, whose male children were commoners through membership in their mothers' lineage. On the other hand, children of male commoners became members of the nobility if their fathers married noble women. Commoners could also raise their status through exemplary services to the nation, such as serving in the military, which raised wives' status as well (Bonvillain 2001, 132–33).

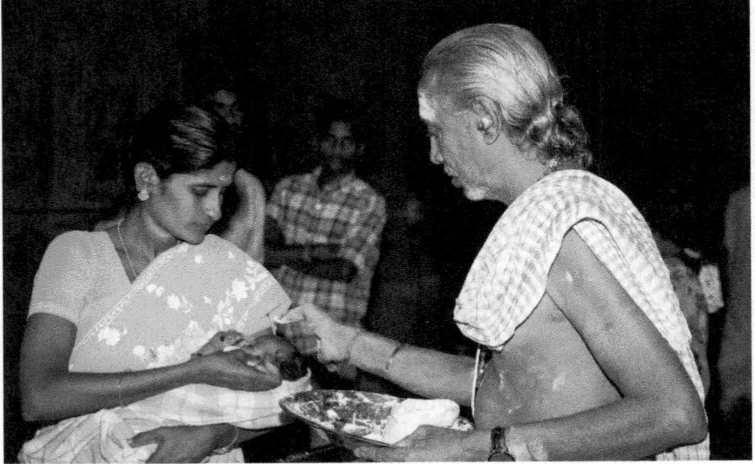

Brahmans, like the one in this photograph, are the highest of four main castes identified in ancient Hindu sacred writings. Alamy Limited/Melvyn Longhurst/Alamy

Effects of Endogamy on Social Organization

Many stratified societies also practice endogamy, in which people marry within their class or rank to maintain social, economic, and political distinctions. Endogamous marriages solidify and preserve the privilege of elites by consolidating wealth and power. Recall the examples of parallel cousin marriage and cross-cousin marriage.

A strong form of endogamy occurs in caste systems. **Caste** is an ascribed social category identifying a group by status or by occupation. At birth, people automatically become members of the caste of their parents and remain in that caste throughout life. In India, for example, people traditionally must marry other members of their own caste. Caste exogamy (marrying someone of another caste) is, in principle, forbidden, although it does occur.

Increases in rates of multiracial marriage and in numbers of mixed-race children in many parts of the world can be seen as an extension of the process of globalization. In many countries, including the United States, interethnic marriage also contributes to the spread of English.

Informal class endogamy is widespread in stratified societies, simply because people with similar backgrounds tend to associate with one another and marry within their group. Members of the same class tend to socialize together, attend the same schools, live in the same neighborhoods, perform the same social activities, and so on. Therefore, even in the absence of a strong marriage rule, proximity and informal sanctions against marrying down tend to lead to class endogamy. Other marriage preferences that follow informal social norms include the tendency for people in pluralistic societies to marry within their own racial or ethnic group and to choose partners who speak the same language and observe the same religion.

The universal incest taboo is a general ban against sexual relations between individuals within a nuclear family. Explanations for its origins include biological and psychological explanations and hypotheses based on cultural adaptations to survival factors. Marriage rules affect the organization of a society. Examples of impacts of endogamy on social systems include the caste system of India, alliances created through cross-cousin marriage, and class systems with preferential marriage based on shared membership in a social, racial, or ethnic group.

FORMS OF MARRIAGE

Marriage rules define the forms that marriages can take, and these forms vary. For example, norms concerning the number of spouses that can constitute the marital unit differ in different societies. In most societies, marriage is a union between two people—**monogamy.** However, in some societies the marital unit may consist of three or more people—**polygamy,** or plural marriage. Monogamy is the most common form of union today, even in societies where plural marriages are possible. Societies that permit remarriage after the death of a spouse or divorce practice **serial monogamy,** meaning that a person can be married to only one person at a time, although individuals may have two or more spouses during their lifetime.

Polygyny and Polyandry

There are two forms of polygamy. **Polygyny** is marriage between a man and two or more women, and **polyandry** is marriage between a woman and two or more men. Polygyny is far more common than polyandry as a form of plural marriage, but most couples live in monogamous unions, even in societies where plural marriages are possible. A common type of polygyny is a pattern in which a man marries two or more sisters, usually wedding one first and the other years later. This system is called **sororal polygyny.** Sororal polygyny has the advantage of minimizing potential conflicts between wives because the women have close emotional and supportive bonds as sisters. When co-wives are not related, they may have tensions between them, each vying for favoritism from their common husband to benefit themselves and their children. Different societies favor different kinds of residence patterns for plural marriages. In some, the entire unit of husband and several wives lives together in one dwelling. In others, each wife of a polygynous homestead has a separate hut for herself and her children.

Polyandry may also take several forms. In some cases, a woman may marry unrelated men whereas, in others, several brothers may be married to the same woman, a form called fraternal polyandry. The best documented examples of polyandry occur in South Asia, especially in India, Tibet, and Nepal. Polyandry has also been reported elsewhere in the past, including among the Inuit of Arctic Canada and the Iroquois of New York State.

caste
Social grouping whose membership is determined at birth and is generally inflexible.

monogamy
Marriage rule that stipulates a union between two people.

polygamy
Marriage in which the marital unit consists of three or more people.

serial monogamy
Marriage pattern that stipulates that a person can be married to only one person at a time, although individuals may have two or more spouses during their lifetime. Subsequent marriages may be formed after the death of one spouse or after divorce.

polygyny
Marriage between a man and two or more women.

polyandry
Marriage between a woman and two or more men.

sororal polygyny
Marriage between a man and two or more women who are sisters.

In this West African family, each co-wife has her own hut, which she occupies with her children. The Image Works/Lauren Goodsmith/The Image Works

Polyandrous marriages may occur in societies where there are shortages of women. For example, in some communities in the Indian Himalayas and Chinese Tibet, such as the Nyinba and the Pahari, brothers may jointly contract for a wife. This fraternal polyandry permits all men to be married, and also promotes economic cooperation among brothers for their mutual benefit. Rather than fragmenting a family's property through inheritance by numerous and possibly conflicting heirs, polyandrous unions solidify wealth, property, and social status and raise people's overall standard of living (Levine 1988). However, the shortage of women in Nyinba society derives from social attitudes that devalue females. Because sons are preferred, they are better fed and cared for than are daughters. The neglect of females leads to higher rates of infant and child mortality, resulting in a gender imbalance. Currently, in traditional Nyinba communities, the sex ratio is 118 men to 100 women (Stone 2006, 201). Polyandry permits all men to marry while at the same time limiting population growth, an adaptive strategy in a region of scarce resources.

Finally, Nyinba men are often away from their households pursuing economic activities. Men's work includes herding their households' animals, especially goats and sheep. They are also involved in trading grains and other products, traveling from Tibet into northern India (Stone 2006, 195). Polyandry ensures that households will likely have at least one man at home to accomplish male economic tasks.

Fraternal polyandrous marriages were also common in villages of the Lahaul Valley in India, close to its border with Tibet. Such arrangements solved the problem of splintering small family farms among brothers and instead allowed the continued consolidation of scant acreage. In addition, in the words of a 60-year old man living in a polyandrous household, "If you marry a different woman, then there are more chances of family disputes. Family property is divided, and problems arise" (Polgreen 2010). Finally, polyandry helps to limit population growth, an economic necessity in an environment of scarce farmland. Familial relationships were also regulated by kinship practices in which children used the term meaning "father" for the eldest brother married to their mother. The other brothers were called "uncle." Although descent followed patrilineal principles, women had high status in their households.

Watch the **Video:** *African Polygamist Wives* on **myanthrolab.com**

Explanations of Polygyny

Polygyny develops in different societies for different reasons. Care must therefore be taken in interpreting its meanings and functions depending on the cultural and historical contexts in which polygyny occurs. In communities where women significantly outnumber men, polygyny helps correct imbalances in the sex ratio. Among the Innu of eastern Canada in earlier centuries, for example, polygyny, limited to two or three wives, ensured marriage for all women in a society with a scarcity of men. Male mortality rates were comparatively higher than female mortality rates because of the dangers for men in hunting and warfare. After lecturing the Innu about the evils of plural marriage, the seventeenth-century French Jesuit missionary Paul LeJeune observed: "Since I have been preaching among them that a man should not have more than one wife, I have not been well received by the women; for, since they are more numerous than the men, if a man can only marry one of them, the others will have to suffer. Therefore this doctrine is not to their liking" (Thwaites 1906, vol. 12, 165). In the case of the Innu, polygyny prevented population decline by maintaining an effective rate of reproduction.

Polygyny occurs in some strongly patriarchal societies in which women are viewed as property and a source of status. Men who can afford to support a greater number of wives and dependents are seen to have greater wealth, power, and prestige in their communities. Historically, hereditary high chiefs of polygynous Central African kingdoms boasted hundreds of wives and concubines. In pre-Communist imperial China, wealthy men measured their status and good fortune in the number of wives they accumulated. Daughters became mediums of exchange between men seeking to form alliances with each other.

Polygyny also develops as an adaptation to economic needs or goals because of the important economic roles women serve. For example, as the economy of the Plains Indians shifted to dependence on the buffalo by the middle of the nineteenth century, men wanted to obtain the economic services of more than one wife because women were responsible for tanning the buffalo hides and thus turning a raw product into a marketable item. To advance themselves in trade networks that were supplied by the labor of women, men wanted several wives.

In some farming societies, polygyny serves the purpose of supplying additional labor of women and their children. For example, among the Tswana and Herero, two cattle-herding and horticultural societies of southern Africa, men with more than one wife were able to accumulate greater farm surpluses because of women's key roles as subsistence farmers. Also, the more wives a man had, the more children he acquired. His children raised his social standing because they contributed to the growth of his patrilineage and patriclan. A man's sons helped care for his cattle, and his daughters brought cattle to the family as wedding gifts from their husbands' kin.

Men living in foraging societies may reap benefits from the labor of more than one wife. Among the Tiwi of Australia, men want to have several wives because the Aboriginal foraging economy centers on the collection of wild plant resources, work that women generally do. As one Tiwi reported, "If I had only one or two wives I would starve, but with my present ten or twelve wives I can send them out in all directions in the morning and at least two or three of them are likely to bring something back with them at the end of the day, and then we can all eat" (Hart and Pilling 1960, 34).

Tiwi husbands benefit from polygyny both economically and socially. A man with several wives can accumulate enough food surplus to give to others, raising his prestige by his generosity. Australian Aborigine men also value their wives because of their desire to have many children, a condition of marriage. The Tiwi traditionally practiced reciprocal polygyny, with men sometimes agreeing to marry each other's sisters or each other's daughters.

The shared practice of polygyny fostered the rapid spread of patriarchal Arab culture and Islam to African nations. It is well known that culture change occurs more rapidly and more completely when peoples in contact share basic cultural characteristics such as forms of marriage and family.

Specialized Adaptive Forms of Marriage

Cultures demonstrate a great deal of variety in the ways that people think of sexual relations, marriage, and family. Marriage might even be entirely symbolic and not involve procreation. Yet, even in rare forms of marriage, principles of descent, patterns of residence and household composition, and ways of establishing bonds with others form systems of relationships and meaning that integrate individuals into families and communities. So, although these forms of marriage were restricted to only a few societies, they shed light on the various social and economic functions of marriage.

In some African societies with patrilineal descent, marriages can be contracted in ways that emphasize the importance of descent and the continuity of patrilineal kin groups. Among the Nuer, for example, if a married man died without sons, one of his younger brothers married his widow. The children of the new couple, though, were considered heirs of the deceased (Evans-Pritchard 1955). Nuer **ghost marriage** thus permitted an elder brother to maintain his patrilineage even after his death. In Nuer society, seniority in a lineage was an important criterion for determining relative social status, so allowing descent to follow from an elder sibling, dead or alive, was a strategic practice. In this way, children born to the younger brother but claimed by the dead older brother would have seniority over members of junior lineages.

Another Nuer marital option was allowed when a lineage failed to produce a male heir. In that event, a woman in the lineage could take the role of husband and be married to another woman. The woman who became a husband refrained from having sex because husbands cannot conceive. The "wife" conceived by having sex with a chosen man from any lineage other than her own. The children borne to the "wife" belonged to the "husband's" lineage, thus supplying the line with heirs (Evans-Pritchard 1955, 108).

In marriages between women, the woman who acted as husband was transformed into a legal man. As a "man," she could receive bridal payments given in marriages for her kinswomen, and she could inherit cattle from her father. She could also be compensated with cattle if her "wife" had an adulterous affair without her consent. Nuer practices of marriage between women and "ghost marriage" both create social fatherhood for the purpose of securing the continuation of patrilineages.

ghost marriage
Marriage practice among the Nuer of Sudan in which a widow marries her dead husband's brother and in which the children ensuing from the second marriage are said to be the children of the first, dead husband.

In another rare form, the matrilineal Kwakwaka'wakw (Kwakiutl) of British Columbia developed a marriage option that created daughters for men who had none. Such a strategy was necessary because status, wealth, and named titles were transmitted from men to men through women. In practice, men needed daughters because wealth and titles passed from a father to his daughter's children. To accommodate men who had no daughters, several types of marriage could be arranged. According to George Hunt, a Kwakiutl chief, a man "turned the left side of his son's body into a woman and gave ['her'] the name belonging to the oldest daughter of his line" (quoted in Boas 1966, 55). Then another man proposed marriage to the first man's "daughter." After they were married, the first man was able to acquire the titles belonging to "her" lineage and could pass these on to children whom he had with a subsequent wife. If a man had no children at all, according to Hunt, "the father may call his foot or one side of his body, his daughter. The marriage ceremony is performed as though these were the women married, and the names are transferred in the usual manner." This was called "taking hold of the foot" (Boas 1897, 359). These marital options allowed for the transmission of wealth and status in a society where men controlled wealth but the wealth passed through women.

The Nayar, a matrilineal people living in Kerala, South India, had concepts of marriage that differ from most peoples' (Gough 1961; Mencher 1965). Although contemporary Nayar no longer practice these marriage options, they demonstrate possible societal options. Nayar kinship centers on matrilineal relatives, organized into matrilineal descent and residence groups called *taravad*. The *taravad* consists of sisters and brothers, the sisters' children, the sisters' daughters' children, and so on, all descended from a female ancestor. They hold land and other property in common, managed by the senior man. They also care collectively for children born to their female members. In the past, shortly before a girl reached puberty, she was married to a man chosen by her family. After the marriage ceremony, the couple stayed together for three days. If they wanted, they were permitted to have sexual intercourse but that was not a requirement. On the fourth day, they separated and need not ever see each other again. The man and woman had no social or economic responsibilities toward one another and did not live together. However, the bond between them was symbolized when the man died because the woman honored him in mourning ceremonies.

Thereafter, the man and woman had a succession of lovers over the years. These unions were referred to as "joining together" (Stone 2006, 143). A lover acknowledged and legitimized his sexual relationship with a particular woman by giving her gifts three times a year for as long as the liaison lasted. Children produced from these unions belonged to the *taravad* of the mother, and her family took responsibility for the economic care of children. Fathers had no economic obligations for their children, but establishment of paternity was critical to the social standing of mother and child. Her "husbands" publicly declared themselves possible fathers of a child by giving gifts to the mother and to the midwife who assisted in the birth.

Today, distinctive Nayar marriage practices have largely disappeared, replaced by monogamous marriages and nuclear family residence patterns. Although matrilineal kinship groups continue to delineate relationships for some people, the Nayar have shifted toward patrilineal preferences consistent with the loss of property rights previously held by matrilineal groups because contemporary wage work, especially performed by men, has led to the separateness and mobility of the family unit.

The Na, an ethnic group of Yunnan province in southern China, do not recognize marital ties or obligations at all (Hua 2001). Households consist of siblings and the children of female members. Men or women can propose sexual encounters, termed "visits," but they always take place at night in the woman's house. They have no mutual obligations or rights and do not expect to have exclusive sexual access to one another. Nor do they contribute to a joint household. Children belong to the kin group of the mother, but they do not acknowledge paternity or social fatherhood. Instead, children are raised by their mother and her male and female kin.

Same-Sex Marriage

Although most marriages in most cultures are unions between men and women, some societies allow marriage between individuals of the same sex. This is not the same as the **same-sex marriages** practiced by the Nuer, in which a woman is legally defined as a man for purposes of marriage to another woman. In this case, the couple does not have sexual relations. Rather, the female wife has sex with a man in order to bear children for her female husband.

same-sex marriage
Marriage between two men or two women.

In May 2004, Massachusetts became the first state to legalize gay marriage. Other states permitting same-sex marriage include Vermont, Iowa, New Hampshire, the District of Columbia, and New York State. Pictured here is a couple preparing to marry in New York City in 2011. Newscom/SIPA USA/SIPA/Newscom

Same-sex marriage was an option in many Native American societies as late as the early decades of the twentieth century. Especially in cultures of the Great Plains, the Southwest, and California, two women or two men might marry, have sexual relations, and share household and family responsibilities. These people, now often referred to as "Two-Spirits," were publicly recognized as forming legitimate couples.

In North America today, growing numbers of lesbian and gay couples advocate for the right to marry in ceremonies that have legal standing. Advocates note that same-sex couples fulfill all of the same obligations and responsibilities toward one another as do heterosexual couples. They share their resources, make joint decisions, and make commitments to exclusive sexual relationships. Many also raise children together. Opponents of lesbian and gay marriage claim that the traditional cultural concept of marriage, based on religious precepts, applies only to the union of one man and one woman. Growing tolerance for homosexual marriages in the United States and Canada is a measure of social and culture change. In the United States, Vermont was the first state to permit the legal recognition of civil unions between homosexuals, so long as they did not call it "marriage." In 2004, Massachusetts became the first state to legalize same-sex marriage, not simply to recognize same-sex civil unions, followed in 2008 by California and Connecticut. However, in 2008, voters in California approved a ballot initiative banning same-sex marriages. Then in 2009, Vermont, Iowa, and Maine recognized same-sex marriages but Maine voters rejected the law in 2010 and in 2010, same-sex marriage was legalized in New Hampshire and the District of Columbia. Finally, in 2011, the New York State legislature enacted a bill to legalize same-sex marriage, as did the Tribal Council of the Suquamish Tribe in the state of Washington. The inconsistencies in legislative action and voter responses demonstrate that the issue remains deeply controversial. In 2003, the Supreme Court of Canada ruled that Canadian marriage laws allow homosexuals to wed. Belgium, the Netherlands, Norway, Spain, South Africa, Sweden, and Argentina also allow same-sex couples to marry.

REVIEW

Monogamy is the marriage of one man and one woman, either for life or for a given time (serial monogamy). Polygamy, or plural marriage, can be in two forms: polygyny or polyandry. Polygyny is marriage between one man and two or more women. Marriage between a man and two or more sisters is called sororal polygyny. Explanations for the development of polygyny relate to population sex ratios, the status of women, and economic adaptations. Polyandry, marriage between one woman and two or more men, often brothers, is rarer. Other rare forms of marriage include ghost marriages, foot marriages, and same-sex marriages.

MARRIAGE AS ALLIANCE AND ECONOMIC EXCHANGE

The relationship established through marriage is not only social but economic as well. Each spouse usually has certain obligations to the other and to their children to supply basic needs such as food, clothing, and shelter. The economic factor in marriage may also be expressed through exchanges of goods and services prior to, during, or after marriage rites. In most Native American cultures, for instance, gifts were mutually exchanged before and during a marriage ceremony. Relatives of the bride and groom gave each other foods,

Some of these Botswana cattle may become bridewealth for sons from the owner's family to give to the parents of their prospective wives.
Corbis/Peter Johnson/Corbis

clothing, and ornaments as a sign of their mutual respect and support. The reciprocal exchange of gifts is common in egalitarian societies in which the families of bride and groom demonstrate an equality of relationship and obligation.

Bridewealth and Brideservice

In some places, substantial gifts and/or services may be given, not mutually by both sides, but more often by one side to the other. In patrilineal societies, for example, **bridewealth** is given from the husband's group to that of the wife. Among the Nuer and most of the cattle-herding societies of eastern Africa, bridewealth was primarily in the form of cattle. In the plains of North America, people gave horses as bridewealth. The number of cattle or horses given was taken to be a reflection of the wealth and prestige of the husband's kin and an indication of the esteem in which they held the bride and her family. Offering too little, then, could be an insult.

In societies where a married couple lived with the husband's kin, the transfer of goods from the husband's group to that of the wife was symbolic compensation for the woman's loss to her family. Bridewealth was also recognition that, after the wedding, the husband's family benefited from the bride's labor while her own kin would be deprived of it. In addition, bridewealth was a means of legitimizing the couple's children and their membership in the husband's patrilineal group since patrilineal kinship groups obtain new members by monopolizing the reproductive potential of women who their men marry. Bridewealth typically was returned if a couple divorced, so the wife's kin often had a large stake in discouraging the dissolution of the marriage.

Patterns and amounts of bridewealth payments may change as societies undergo economic and social transformations. For example, among the Nuer of the Southern Sudan, the number of cattle expected as gifts from the husband's family to that of the wife has fluctuated in the last 50 years in response to conditions that affected the size of herds. When drought or cattle diseases decimated herds, the number of cattle given as bridewealth declined. During the first civil war in Sudan, which lasted from 1963 until 1972, bridewealth rates also declined sharply (Hutchinson 1996, 81). Thereafter, the expected number of cattle increased in the 1980s during a period of relative stability.

A second change in bridewealth practices among the Nuer was the introduction of money. Although some families are willing to accept some money, cattle remain the preferred tokens of bridewealth. As the Nuer say, "Money has no blood" (Hutchinson 1996, 74).

Finally, some young Nuer men now attempt to free themselves from family ties by purchasing cattle for their own bridewealth payments with funds that they have earned from work. This is a significant break with past practices where the circulation of cattle among families in bridewealth payments secured and symbolized larger social bonds, linking individuals to the support networks of their kin who contributed cattle for their bridewealth payments and linking families to other kinship groups.

In another form of gift giving related to marriage, called **brideservice,** men are obligated to perform services for their wife's parents. A period of brideservice may predate the marriage ceremony, or the period may extend for many years after marriage. During this period, the future or newly married husband contributes his labor to his parents-in-law. Depending on the subsistence strategies employed, he may give all or a portion of animals he has caught and help with planting and harvesting crops. In addition, the husband may help construct his parents-in-law's dwellings, fetch wood or water, and perform other domestic tasks.

bridewealth
Presents given by the husband's family to the wife's kin before, during, or after the wedding ceremony.

brideservice
A period of months or years before or after marriage during which the husband performs labor for his wife's parents.

groom-service
Obligation for a future bride to perform service for her future husband and his family.

Groom-Service and Groom-Wealth

Although less common than brideservice and bridewealth, in some societies, a future bride is obligated to perform service for her future husband and his family. Such **groom-service** might include preparation of food or production of household items deemed expected of the work of wives. A bride might go to stay at her future in-laws' dwelling to perform these services and remain there until they are completed

Instead of, or in addition to, rendering service, the bride's parents and relatives may donate goods to the groom's parents and relatives. **Groom-wealth** might include clothing, ornaments, and household supplies. The gifts given are then distributed among the relevant kin.

From the parents' perspective, both brideservice and groom-service provide demonstrations of the "suitability" of a future son-in-law or daughter-in-law as a "marriage partner and a household member" (Huber, Danaher, and Breedlove 2011, 5). These are also opportunities for the groom or bride to demonstrate and practice the skills that will be expected of them in their roles as husband or wife.

groom-wealth
Gifts such as clothing, ornaments, and household supplies given by the parents and relatives of the bride to the parents and relatives of the groom.

dowry
Gifts given by the wife's family to the married couple or to the husband's kin before, during, or after the wedding ceremony.

Dowry

In some societies, the bride's family gives goods of value to the bride, although these gifts do not usually remain as the property of the bride but rather are given to the newly married couple and/or to the husband's kin prior to or upon the marriage. This type of exchange is called **dowry.** Dowries are prevalent in some patriarchal cultures that stress the prestige of men and their families. In theory, dowries are a kind of insurance that protects the interests of a wife in a patrilineal and patriarchal society. In practice, however, dowry wealth is often appropriated by the husband and his family.

CULTURE CHANGE

DOWRY IN INDIA

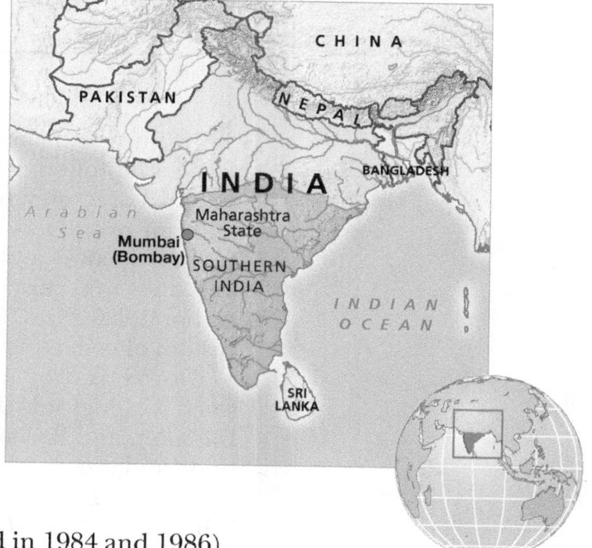

Dowry was the traditional marital exchange in India. A woman's family had to present wealth in jewelry, fine cloth, and money to the husband's family before the marriage took place. The amount of wealth given was an indication of both the bride's status and the esteem of the husband's kin. Wealthy parents gave a lot of property, but even poor families tried to collect as many valuables as they could so as not to shame their daughter and themselves.

The economic burden of dowry contributed to a preference for sons over daughters because girls were a financial liability whereas boys brought in dowry wealth when they married. Thus, the custom of dowry contributed to female infanticide and the neglect of the health of daughters in India and Bangladesh. However, dowry was not the only factor involved in preferences for sons and the consequences of such preferences. Rather, a constellation of behaviors and attitudes place value on men and undermine the worth of women: kinship based on patrilineal descent and inheritance, subsistence strategies emphasizing intensive agriculture done primarily by men, and male control over land.

Although outlawed by the Dowry Prohibition Act (1961, amended in 1984 and 1986), a husband's family often still demands specific amounts of cash or goods to contract a marriage (Ghadially and Kumar 1988, 175). Young men of high status, good education, and favorable employment prospects command large sums. Dowry demands are often made after a marriage is contracted and even after a wedding.

The deaths of young wives whose families have not satisfied the dowry demands of their in-laws have led to controversy. Of a registered 179 "unnatural deaths" of young married women in Delhi between 1981 and 1982, 12 percent to 16 percent were reportedly dowry-related (Ghadially and Kumar 1988, 167). In two-thirds of these cases, young women committed suicide; their in-laws murdered the remaining third. The families involved were of all social classes, educational levels, and occupations.

Ghadially and Kumar (1988) also report that, in the Indian state of Maharashtra, dowry deaths rose from 120 in 1984 to 211 in 1985, an increase of 64 percent. By the mid-1990s, dowry deaths, including bride burnings, had climbed to an estimated 5,800 incidents a year. Many "unnatural deaths" of women are classified as "kitchen/cooking accidents" and "stove bursts," a common method of killing unprofitable daughters-in-law. Retaliation against wives whose families fail to meet dowry demands takes many forms, from verbal abuse to beatings, burns, hanging, poisoning, and strangulation.

A disturbing finding in studies of dowry abuse and death is that the wife's parents are sometimes aware of the violence perpetrated against their daughter but tell her to endure her situation rather than stir controversy that would sully her family's reputation.

Dowry and the related mistreatment and deaths of women gave impetus to the birth of the feminist movement in India. Beginning in 1979, women's groups staged public protests to publicize the issue of dowry harassment. As a result, many families of abused daughters came forward to give testimony and ask for redress. In 1980, the government mandated police investigation of the death of any woman who had been married less than five years at the time of her death. In 1983, legislation made "cruelty to a wife a cognizable, non-bailable offense" and stipulated that "cruelty" included both mental and physical harassment (Kumar 1995, 68). Cases reported as suicides (frequently involving death by dousing and burning) could be investigated as "abetment to suicide," shifting the burden of proof to the woman's husband and his family, and women who died within seven years of marriage had to have autopsies.

The latest studies, however, indicate increases in dowry demands. For example, the All India Democratic Women's Association surveyed 10,000 people in eighteen of India's twenty-six states and found "an across-the-board increase in dowry demands" (Brooke 2003). Government statistics report that, in 2001, husbands or in-laws angry over small dowries killed nearly 7,000 women. In 2003, a well-publicized case brought the issue of dowry demands to national attention. A bride called police on her wedding day when her father refused to pay her in-laws an additional $25,000 they demanded, and a scuffle broke out. The husband eventually served fourteen days in jail for violating laws against dowry (Brooke 2003). Government statistics indicate that dowry deaths rose 46 percent from 1995 to 2005 (Government of India 2006, 171).

In Europe, from medieval times until well into the nineteenth century, well-to-do families bestowed dowries on their daughters when they married. The ability to give large amounts of money, property, and annual incomes was a sign of a family's wealth, enhancing their prestige as well. In turn, fathers who could afford handsome dowries could bargain for wealthy and powerful sons-in-law. Through marriage exchanges of dowries for husbands with property and status, men acquired a host of affinal relatives as personal and political allies. The legacy of the European dowry system is preserved today in the custom of collecting fine clothes and linens in a bridal hope chest.

Dowry as property given by the bride's parents is the most common form, but in some societies it is the groom's parents who transfer wealth to the new couple (Huber, Danaher, and Breedlove 2011, 6). In others, both sets of relatives give property to the bride and groom.

Marriages are economic transactions, but they are also occasions for celebration. What is celebrated is not simply the union of two people, but the alliances formed between two families, lineages, or clans. When marriage takes place between a man and a woman who come from different villages, the wedding may symbolize extended networks and alliances between two communities.

REVIEW

As well as creating alliances among families and larger social units, marriage has important economic functions, and economic exchange is a common feature of marriage arrangements. Gifts are exchanged in many societies to represent the new economic obligations the spouses now have to one another and their in-laws. Bridewealth, found in patrilineal societies, consists of forms of wealth or objects of value given to the bride's family by the groom's family. Brideservice consists of work that the groom does for his in-laws. In the dowry system, the family of the bride pays or promises to pay wealth to the family of the groom in exchange for the marriage of their daughter.

CASE STUDY

A Wedding in Nepal

In larger communities and settled populations, especially where lineages are important kinship, economic, and political units, marriages may be complex, lengthy procedures. Among the Lohorung Rai of eastern Nepal, marriage involves a ten-step process (Hardman 2000). The most complex aspect of the marriage is the negotiation between the families of the intended husband and wife. These negotiations underscore the social and economic as well as spiritual alliances created between two families, their clans, and their villages.

Most Lohorung Rai marriages are arranged when the boy and girl are young, beginning with a gift of liquor brought from the boy's kin to the girl's parents. The boy's emissaries recount his good qualities and those of his family. The girl's family often refuse the initial request, returning the gift to the boy's relatives, and several trips may be needed before the girl's parents drink the liquor and tell the boy's relatives how much meat they will need to distribute to their kin.

At this Nepalese wedding, the bride's relatives accept gifts of gold, clothing, and jewelry that symbolize the marriage. Corbis/John Van Hasselt/Corbis

Subsequently, the boy's kin bring more gifts to those of the girl. Eventually, they present the final gift of a live pig, some rice, and liquor to the girl's kin. This final gift, referred to as a "ransom," marks the formal betrothal of the couple and commits the families to the marriage. The wedding, lasting all night, takes place at the bride's home. The groom proceeds there accompanied by his cousin (father's sister's son). The rite not only celebrates a marriage but also marks the transition of a male from boyhood to manhood.

After the wedding, the bride accompanies her husband to his parents' home, but the following day she returns to her own parents' home, bringing additional gifts from her husband's family. She returns to her husband's home sixteen days later but remains for only a few days, not finally taking up residence there for perhaps a year. Several years later, usually after the birth of her first child, she returns to her parents' home for a final rite of separation, receiving gifts from her brothers.

The lengthy and complex Lohorung Rai marriage process not only solidifies an alliance between two families but also symbolizes and enacts the difficulty of a young woman's separation from her family in a society where postmarital residence is in the husband's locality and usually involves village exogamy. The woman's family demonstrates their reluctance to lose her by hesitating to accept the initial gifts, and she shows her reluctance to leave by repeatedly returning to her parents' home. Read the Document on myanthrolab.com

MARRIAGE AS A RITE OF PASSAGE

For individuals, families, kin groups, and communities, marriages are crucial rites of passage. Because of the importance of the alliances formed by marriage, one's parents or other relatives arrange marriages, especially first marriages, in many societies. A proposal of marriage may be made from one side or the other, although it is more common

In Their Own VOICES

"I Hear That I'm Going to Get Married!"

Florence Edenshaw Davidson, a Haida woman from Vancouver Island, British Columbia, Canada, was 14 when her parents told her that she would be married to Robert Davidson. As was proper in this matrilineal society, Robert's kin made the proposal to Florence's parents. Her father deferred to his wife's brother (Florence's mother's brother), who was a senior member of Florence's matriclan. These are Florence's recollections about how she came to be married to her husband.

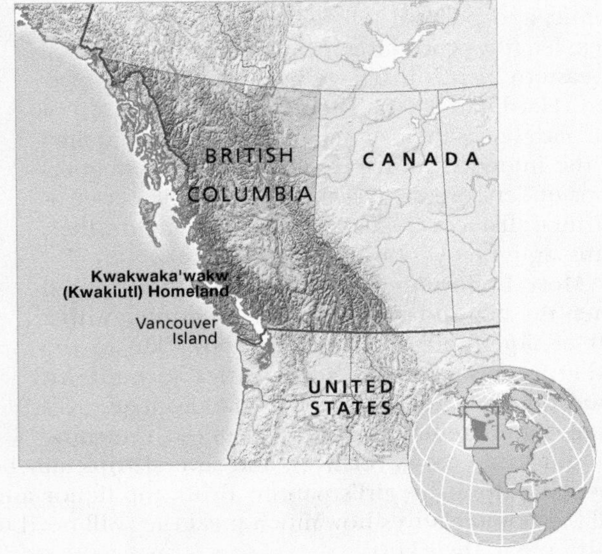

I was still going to school yet when several people came into my dad's house to propose for my husband-to-be. I was wondering what was going on when all these people came in. The women all belonged to C'al'lanas, my husband's tribe [lineage], and the men all belonged to my husband's dad's tribe, Stl'ang'lanas, except for my husband's brother. They were all streaming in and I didn't know what was going on....

"Don't say anything when I tell you something," my mother said to me. "Those who came in last week proposed to you." I didn't know what to say. Propose! Why? I thought. I was just a kid yet. I didn't know what to say and mother advised me not to say anything about the proposal because they were high-class [y'a Yet] people....

"They want you to marry Robert Davidson." "Did you say yes?" I asked her. "No, your dad sent them to your uncle [Florence's mother's brother]. Your dad says he's got nothing to do with it; it has to go through your uncle. You have more respect for your uncle than for us," she told me. "That's the only brother I have." "You're going to make me marry," I said. "Yes, you're going to marry him." "I'm not going to marry him," I said. "Don't say that, Florence, he's a real prince [y'a Yet]."

It bothered me so much.... Every day I bothered my mother. "I'm not going to marry that old man. I'm not. If you make me marry him, summertime I'll run away. You won't see me again." My mother didn't say anything.... My dad didn't say a word to me about it. Finally, my mother said, "Don't say anything dear. Your uncle thinks it's best for you to marry him. He's a prince. He's going to respect you all your life and if you don't want to marry him you're going to feel bad all your life. He belongs to clever people; you're not going to be hard up for anything. We need a young man's help, too. You must remember that. We belong to chiefs too and you're not supposed to talk any old way. You have to respect yourself more than what you worry about." ... I made up my mind not to say anything much as I disliked it.

From Margaret Blackman, *During My Time: Florence Edenshaw Davidson, a Haida Woman*, pp. 95–96. © 1982. Reprinted by permission of the University of Washington Press.

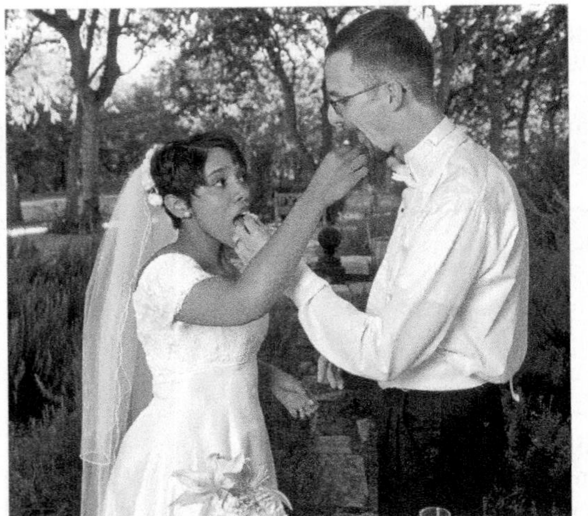

worldwide for the future husband's kin to approach the family of the intended wife. This is true whether the people follow patrilineal or matrilineal rules of descent.

A proposal of marriage may be a simple, short process, or it may be a long, drawn-out, ritualized exchange of greetings, proposals, counterproposals, and gift exchanges before the hoped-for marriage is finally settled upon. Among the Lohorung Rai of Nepal, for example, the marriage proposal process may take many years to accomplish. After the husband's family makes the initial contact, numerous exchanges of refusal and counterproposal follow before a final date is set for the wedding.

Arranged marriages symbolically emphasize the fact that such unions are not simply relationships between a woman and a man but are more

This couple married through mutual consent after declaring their love for one another, and their families were the last to know about their plans. The Image Works/Bob Daemmrich/The Image Works

And these are the recollections of James Sewid, a Kwakwaka'wakw man from Alert Bay, British Columbia. He, too, was married when he was nearly 14 to a girl he knew only by sight.

And that's when the big day came.... I had been out late that night to a dance with my friends and when I came in I lay down on the couch. That was when I heard Jim and Mary Bell talking about me to Ed and Rachel Whanock and my mother and stepfather. One of them was saying, "You might as well go and see her parents because I think he should get married because we don't want him running around like this."... I lay there and pretended that I was sleeping and pretty soon my grandparents walked out. So as soon as they had gone I got up and said to my stepfather, "Let's go take a walk. It's pretty warm in here."... When we got outside... I asked him, "What was going on in there? I heard the people talking about me." "Well," he said, "you're going to get married." "Well," I said, "I can't get married! I'm too young!" "Oh that's all right," he said. "We'll look after you. I think it is the best way for you, to get married now, because if you're not going to get married now you might go haywire." "Well," I said, "who is this girl anyway?" And just then we happened to be passing by the house where Moses Alfred lived, and David said, "It is the girl that lives here." I didn't know what to say. I used to see her around the village but I didn't know her.

Well, it was the Indian custom for someone to go to the parents of the girl and ask their consent. That is where my grandparents had gone that night when they walked out of the house. So I just waited for the answer that this girl's parents would give to the old people who went to talk with them. I was careful after that not to listen anymore because I didn't like to butt in on what was going on. A few days after that I was alone with my mother.... I said to her, "I hear that I'm going to get married. You know that I'm too young to get married." "Oh, no!" she said. "Don't talk like that. We want you to get married. You are going to marry Flora Alfred. It has already been arranged with her parents and it's all right. Now you have to go and see the minister so it can be announced in the church and published in the band." "Well," I said, "I don't think I should get married. It isn't that I don't want to get married, but what am I going to do if I have children?" "Well," my mother said, "we'll look after you some."

After that I went to see my old grandmother, Lucy. She had already heard about it. I went in and sat down and said, "Well, they say I'm going to get married." "Yes," she said, "I heard about that and I think it's a wonderful thing. I would really like to see it. I want to see you get married and have children before I die.... " Well, that is what made me kind of give in. I didn't want to get married but of course... I had no business to try and argue or anything like that because I knew that the older people knew what was right for me; that's what I figured. I never did like to argue with anybody that was older than me but I always liked to respect what they said to me.

From James Spradley, *Guests Never Leave Hungry: The Autobiography of James Sewid, a Kwakiutl Indian*, pp. 66–67.

Although both Florence and James voiced reservations about their arranged marriages, especially concerning their young age and fears about taking on adult responsibilities, they gave up in the interests of their families. As it turned out, they both had long and loving relationships with their spouses.

CRITICAL THINKING QUESTIONS

Would you be willing to have your family arrange your marriage? Why, or why not?

fundamentally alliances between families. Each side measures their own worthiness in relation to the social standing and resources of the other side. Their willingness to promote a marital union is an indication of their trust in their future affines.

Weddings are rites of passage in which the participants change their status from single to married. In societies without arranged marriages, preparation for marriage usually involves some form of **courtship,** in which a couple tests their attraction and compatibility as well as the acceptability of their union to others who are important in their lives. Mate selection is the common goal of courtship, and weddings mark the passage from courtship to marriage. The bases on which people choose their mates may include personal compatibility, desired personality traits, likelihood of reliability and economic contributions, and physical attraction. In most societies, the Western concept of romantic love is not a prerequisite for courtship or marriage, although these feelings may develop when people begin to live together, adjusting to one another and sharing their lives.

In foraging and horticultural societies, a wedding ceremony is usually a simple affair. Among the Mohawk, a young man's family traditionally proposed a marriage to the family of the intended bride, or a couple announced their plans to marry. Before the

Listen to the **Audio:** *Matched by Mom: Arranged Marriage in America* on **myanthrolab.com**

arranged marriages
Marriages that are arranged by the parents or other relatives of the bride and groom.

courtship
Period prior to marriage when a couple tests attraction to and compatibility with each other.

wedding, the couple separately presented gifts to their future mothers-in-law. The future husband gave his bride's mother a gift of deer meat, and the future bride gave her husband's mother a gift of cornbread. These presents were symbolic of the economic roles of men as hunters and women as farmers, thus representing the interdependence of spouses and households.

A Mohawk wedding involved a feast sponsored by the bride's family for relatives, clan members, and villagers. The father of the bride made a formal announcement of the couple's marriage and bestowed the family's approval. Then followed speeches from a number of respected elder guests who exhorted the couple to behave properly, responsibly, and kindly to each other.

In contrast, in societies where the accumulation of wealth is valued, typically in agrarian or industrial societies, weddings may be elaborate affairs, attended by hundreds of people. These rituals include displays of family wealth and transfers of gifts and property to the couple and/or to their relatives.

REVIEW

Weddings are rites of passage that publicly confirm the changes in marital and kinship status of the participants. Societies that place high value on kinship and community relations often have arranged marriages. In others, individuals choose their own marriage partners. Weddings also extend the alliance and economic transaction functions of marriage.

PATTERNS OF RESIDENCE AFTER MARRIAGE

The elaborate Nepalese wedding process described in the Case Study is partly a result of postmarital residence patterns that call for a bride to separate herself from her relatives. In all societies, newly married couples follow norms dictating where they should live. They may live with or near the husband's or the wife's family; they may alternate their residences between families; or they may establish a place of their own apart from any of their relatives. Their choice may depend on factors such as the amount of resources available or the composition of existing households. Societies vary in the patterns of postmarital residence that they encourage. Particular postmarital **residence rules** are often associated with different descent systems and specific economic strategies.

residence rules
Rules that stipulate where a couple will reside after their marriage.

matrilocal residence
Pattern for residence after marriage in which the couple lives with or near the wife's family.

uxorilocal
Living with or near the wife's parents.

patrilocal residence
Pattern of residence after marriage in which the couple lives with or near the husband's relatives.

virilocal
Living with or near the husband's parents.

avunculocal residence
Patterns of residence after marriage in which the couple lives with or near the husband's mother's brother.

Matrilocal and Patrilocal Residence

Arrangements in which a married couple lives with or near the wife's family are termed **matrilocal residence.** Usually (but not always), matrilocal residence is associated with matrilineal descent. That is, societies that reckon descent matrilineally usually prefer that couples live with the wife's family. Because children resulting from marriage belong to the lineage of the mother, matrilocal residence ensures that kin group members remain together. Matrilocal households typically consist of an elder couple, their daughters, their daughters' husbands and children, and their unmarried sons. Married sons live with their wives' kin. This kind of residence pattern is also called **uxorilocal**—living with the wife's family.

Patrilocal residence refers to arrangements in which a married couple lives with or near the husband's family. Patrilocal residence usually occurs in societies that reckon descent patrilineally. Because children resulting from marriage belong to the father's lineage, patrilocal residence creates stable, interacting groups of patrilineally related kin. Patrilocal households, therefore, consist of an elder couple, their sons, their sons' wives and children, and their unmarried daughters. Married daughters live with their husbands' relatives. This kind of residence pattern is also called **virilocal**—living with the husband's family.

Avunculocal Residence

In some societies with matrilineal descent and inheritance, an arrangement called **avunculocal residence** is preferred (from the Latin word *avunculus* meaning "mother's brother" and origin of the English word *uncle*). In these cases, a married couple lives with the husband's mother's brother. Avunculocal residence is found in societies where inheritance follows matrilineal descent but in which men hold wealth, property, and social status.

According to rules of matrilineal descent, a man's wealth and status cannot be passed to his own son because his son is a member of his wife's kinship group, not his own. Wealth, therefore, passes from a man to his sister's son. From the inheritor's point of view, a man gains wealth and status from his mother's brother. Avunculocal residence establishes a residential and emotional bond between a man and the person from whom he will inherit.

bilocal residence
Patterns of residence after marriage in which the couple alternates between living with the wife's kin and the husband's kin.

neolocal residence
Pattern of residence after marriage in which the couple establishes a new, independent household separate from their relatives.

Bilocal and Neolocal Residence

In **bilocal residence,** married couples live alternately with the husband's and the wife's families. Bilocality has the advantage of flexibility, adapting residence to economic and resource conditions. When resources are scarce, couples can make adjustments by relocating from one household to another. Bilocal patterns are also adaptive in realigning living arrangements depending on the composition of households. That is, if households grow too large by the addition of in-marrying spouses and their children, then some people can leave and align themselves with their spouse's kin.

In societies with **neolocal residence,** a married couple establishes a new household independently of the residence of either the husband's or the wife's kin. Such systems typically are found in industrial and postindustrial societies, where couples tend to form new households immediately after marriage or within a year or two. Neolocal residence has the feature of independence, another reflection of the loosening of kinship bonds advantageous in capitalist economies. Neolocal residence separates people from larger kinship groups, allowing them to ignore claims from relatives who might want to share their resources.

Correlates of Residence Patterns

Among foragers, postmarital residence tends to be fairly diverse. Although couples generally live with relatives, the choice of the wife's or husband's family depends on the composition of the households, the availability of resources, and personal preferences. According to Kathleen Gough (1975), approximately 60 percent of foraging societies tended to live patrilocally, whereas 16 percent to 17 percent preferred matrilocal residence. An additional 15 percent to 17 percent were bilocal, choosing location with the family of either spouse. In farming societies with unilineal descent systems, postmarital residence tends to be consistent with principles of descent. Societies with matrilineal descent usually prefer matrilocal residence, whereas those with patrilineal descent prefer patrilocal residence. In societies whose economies are based on intensive agriculture, descent is nearly always patrilineal,

What residence rule is observed in your culture? Are there different historical patterns in residence that relate to people's cultures of origin?

Like the Yanomamo of the Amazon, the Dani of the New Guinea highlands were patrilineal horticulturalists who engaged in frequent internal warfare. Anthro-Photo File/Adrian Arbib/Anthro-Photo File

internal warfare
Warfare between closely situated villages or communities.

external warfare
Warfare that takes place at some distance from home communities, requiring warriors' absence from their homes for extended periods of time.

and residence is nearly always patrilocal. The patterns are consistent with men's primary responsibility for farming and their control over the allocation and use of land.

Residence patterns have been observed to correlate with other cultural patterns. For example, in a classic study, anthropologists found that in societies with frequent **internal warfare,** household groups are likely to be organized patrilocally (Ember and Ember 1971). Internal warfare is characterized by frequent raiding among neighboring or nearby settlements. Because men act as warriors who defend their households and communities against the threat of attack by others, living near male relatives they trust is advantageous for them. In contrast, **external warfare,** fought against people from other societies, does not favor a particular residence rule, though external warfare that takes warriors away from home for extended periods may shift economic burdens to women in a way that favors matrilocal residence.

The Iroquois of North America and the Yanomamo of South America provide contrasting examples of the connection between types of warfare and postmarital residence patterns. Iroquois society was based on matrilineal descent, with people organized into matriclans. Iroquois economy centered on horticulture, an occupation for women, supplemented by hunting and fishing, performed by men. By the seventeenth and eighteenth centuries, men were involved in frequent and prolonged external warfare with Europeans and with other native peoples, spending many months away from home. Matrilocal residence, the traditional preferred pattern, was strengthened by men's absence from home communities. In contrast, the Yanomamo reckon descent patrilineally. They are horticulturalists whose subsistence is provided almost entirely by men. Yanomamo men engage in frequent internal warfare, raiding neighboring villages and defending their own homes against attacks by others. Consistent with the Embers's predictions, postmarital residence is strongly patrilocal.

REVIEW

Residence rules tend to ensure that people belonging to the same kin group remain close to one another. Matrilocal patterns, in which the couple lives with or near the wife's parents, are common in matrilineal societies. Patrilocal patterns, in which the couple lives with or near the husband's parents, is common in patrilineal societies. In avunculocal residence, the couple moves in with the husband's mother's brother. Bilocal residency allows the couple to live with either the husband's or wife's family, depending on the resources available. Neolocal residency allows the couple to establish their own independent household.

CASE STUDY

Residence in Rural North India and Western Borneo

RURAL NORTH INDIA

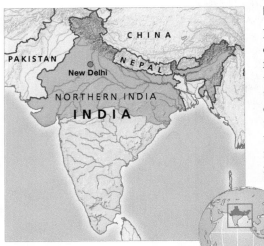

Households consist of large extended or joint families. Village economies center on farming, although villagers may have other occupations. Descent follows patrilineal principles; that is, people belong to the kinship group of their father. Parents arrange marriages. Men typically marry in their early twenties to women in their teens. Girls may be betrothed as young children. Postmarital residence is generally patrilocal. Residential groups, therefore, consist of a couple, their sons and sons' families, and their unmarried daughters. Women move to their husbands' homes upon marriage and have infrequent contact with their own kin. Because girls usually marry shortly after puberty, a wife's subordination is based on age as well as gender. She is thus easily dominated by her husband and especially by his mother. As many researchers have noted, Indian wives often experience their greatest difficulties from their mothers-in-law rather than their husbands (Chitnis 1988).

The domination by mothers-in-law is due, in part, to the uncertain quality of relationships between spouses. Rarely are newlywed couples acquainted before marriage, and unions are arranged without consent from either the bride or the groom. Once married, couples have little interaction. The husband is himself young and lives under his father's authority. As a subordinate in his father's household, he takes care not to shift away from his first allegiance to his parents. Because wives are perceived as potentially destabilizing to established familial order, married sons refrain from showing too much affection or even concern for them, especially early in their married life. Couples rarely interact publicly or have extended conversation when other family members are present. A wife thus spends most of her time with other women in the household. These women, unmarried daughters and in-marrying wives, are all under the supervision of the elder woman. A new daughter-in-law is typically met with some hostility by her husband's mother and sisters. As a result, authoritative statuses are immediately established and reinforced.

WESTERN BORNEO

Iban of Western Borneo

The Iban are rice farmers living along rivers in Western Borneo, especially in the province of Sarawak, Malaysia. Their social system centers on an autonomous unit called a "bilek" or family whose members are related through bilateral ties. The bilek controls land collectively and owns ritual property. Members of the family work cooperatively in economic tasks, especially but not limited to farming the rice fields that supply their basic subsistence. The bilek also owns and occupies a section of the longhouse dwelling that typifies Iban society. An Iban settlement contains one longhouse that is structurally divided into several apartment-like units. Most longhouses contain between ten and twenty bilek units (Freeman 1970, 184).

A bilek itself consists of three generations: an elder couple, one of their married sons or daughters, his or her spouse and children, and the elder couple's unmarried children. Siblings have equal rights as to who will remain with their parents. The Iban show no preference based on gender or seniority. Decisions about where a new couple resides are made on the basis of personal choice and negotiation about access to resources. The son or daughter who remains has full rights to bilek land and other property, whereas sons or daughters who leave to reside with the families of their spouses give up their ancestral rights and instead gain access to the land and property of their spouse's family. That is, residence, not genealogy alone, confers social, economic, and ritual rights.

When more than one sibling and spouse claim the natal bilek unit, one of the siblings will eventually leave and set up his own bilek unit (with spouse and children), beginning the process of descent and affiliation anew. Looked at as a structure over time, the bilek family persists, but its members change as generations succeed generations and as siblings unite and then separate to form their own families.

The separate families that together occupy a longhouse form a community distinct from similar communities. Longhouses are dispersed at irregular intervals along river banks (Freeman 1970, 184). They are the residential bases of a community. The residents have ritual responsibilities toward one another and ensure their collective well-being through the proper performance of rituals. Each longhouse has a headman who can help resolve disputes and advise residents on appropriate behavior in keeping with customs and beliefs. When a headman dies or retires, any male resident of the longhouse can succeed him. The choice is made by community consensus.

A few closely related families form the core of the longhouse. The other resident families can claim ties to one of the core groups through either blood or marriage. Indeed, although marriages between siblings are banned, marriage between first or second cousins is preferred because it "…constantly reinforces the network of cognatic ties linking individual Iban, and kin" (Freeman 1970, 190). However, people are free to choose their own spouse. Relationships between husband and wife are based on mutual respect and equality. Although

levirate
Marriage preference rule in which a widow marries her deceased husband's brother.

sororate
Marriage between a widower and his deceased wife's sister.

women's and men's economic and ritual roles are distinct, they treat each other and are viewed by others as equals.

Finally, the core group of families in each longhouse generally remains stable until the death of an elder couple leads to fragmentation. However, other families may move to another longhouse in cases of serious conflict. Because people have consanguineous or affinal ties to many other communities, relocation is usually easy.

Today, the Iban (also known as "Dayak") are an indigenous minority within Malaysia, dominated by ethnic Malays who differ in their language, religion, and cultural practices. Many Iban have been educated in British and American schools. They have used their education to advance the rights of their people. Nearly half of the 1.4 million inhabitants of Sarawak are Iban. Another quarter are Moslem Malays, and most of the remainder are ethnic Chinese (Crossette 1987). According to Iban anthropologist James Masing, the Iban are attempting to strengthen their own communities and identities: "Our priority now is to organize the Dayak community and make them a strong political force" (Crossette 1987). Read the Document on myanthrolab.com

WIDOWHOOD AND DIVORCE

All societies have strategies intended to preserve kin ties, marriage bonds, and household units. All cultures have patterns of beliefs and behaviors for dealing with widows and orphans, for example, and for regulating divorce and remarriage. These cultural patterns reveal the underlying principles of kinship, marriage, and family that are most important in a society. For example, the importance of family alliances is highlighted by marriage preference patterns that anthropologists refer to as "levirate" and "sororate."

The Levirate and Sororate

In the levirate and sororate marriage patterns, if a spouse dies, the deceased's family of origin supplies a younger sibling to marry the surviving spouse. So, for example, in the **levirate,** if a husband dies, his (usually younger) brother will marry the surviving widow. In the **sororate,** a younger sister of a deceased wife will marry the surviving widower. These kinds of marriages symbolically stress family alliances because they say in effect that once two families are joined through marriage, maintaining the established alliance is in the families' interests. Because the death of a husband or wife potentially disrupts the bond between families, a sibling of the deceased spouse perpetuates the alliance by marrying the survivor. The "ghost marriage" of the Nuer is a type of levirate because a younger brother marries the widow of his elder brother. It differs from the more common pattern only in that children of the subsequent union are considered the offspring of the dead brother.

In Saudi culture, children belong to the father, his patrilineage, and his patriclan. The Image Works/Peter Sanders/HAGA/The Image Works

Divorce

Societies vary in their views about the dissolution of marriages. In some societies, divorce is a common outcome of an unhappy union, whereas in others, it rarely occurs because of social or religious restrictions. In some societies, either husband or wife may seek divorce; in others, only one of the parties (usually the husband) may initiate a breakup of the marriage. The ways in which marriages are dissolved also vary across cultures.

In general, matrilineal societies have more lenient attitudes toward divorce than do patrilineal societies because of the differences in principles of descent and the resulting claims that kinship groups have over children. Nearly universally (although there are exceptions), young children continue to live with their mothers after a divorce. Because children belong to the kin group of their mother in matrilineal societies, divorce does not cause a contradiction between location and kinship. In contrast, the dissolution of a marriage in patrilineal societies causes a problem because patrilineal descent groups are able to make claims over children produced by the wives of their male members through marriage. In addition, patrilineal societies generally exert more control over women's sexual behavior than do matrilineal societies because they need to establish paternity to ensure a child's legitimate place in the father's kinship group.

Foraging and horticultural societies often have flexible attitudes toward divorce, regardless of the type of descent system in their culture. In native North America, for example, with few exceptions, either husband or wife could initiate a breakup of their marriage. Divorce was fairly common, especially in the early years of a marriage and especially if the couple had no children. Acceptable grounds for divorce included adultery, failure to provide or fulfill domestic obligations, or simply personal incompatibility. Few societies had formal procedures for divorce. Rather, the couple would separate, each returning to his or her natal family, or the in-marrying spouse would leave. A divorce could be the result of a joint decision by husband and wife, or one or the other could initiate it.

In some Native American societies, there were publicly recognized ways to signal one's wishes for divorce. For example, among both the Mohawk and the Diné, two matrilineal, matrilocal societies, if a woman wanted a divorce, she might remove her husband's personal belongings from the house when he was away and place them outside. When the husband returned, he would collect his belongings and go back to the home of his mother or sister. If the husband initiated the divorce, he would simply take his possessions and leave. No social stigma was attached to either husband or wife after a divorce.

Among the Lakota and some other peoples of the Great Plains, both parties could jointly agree upon a divorce. However, a man had a public way of signaling his wishes to end their marriage that was not available to a woman. He would beat a drum at a warrior society dance and proclaim that he wished to "throw away [his] wife" (Hassrick 1964, 130). Through this strategy, a man not only ended his marriage but publicly humiliated his wife as well. Although men did not suffer social criticism if their marriages ended, divorced women were shamed.

There are economic deterrents to divorce. For example, exchanges of bridewealth tend to lessen rates of divorce. The husband's kinship group does not favor divorce because a couple's children, although belonging to the husband's kin group in patrilineal societies, usually stay with their mother and therefore leave the husband's household if divorce occurs. A wife's family may also be reluctant to sanction a divorce because when couples break up, the wife's kin must return the goods that they received as bridewealth. Therefore, they may pressure an unhappy wife to remain with her husband. Conflicts over bridewealth and its return in cases of divorce may not only result in the end of family alliances but lead to interfamilial tension and conflict.

In extreme patriarchal societies, such as in some villages in India, in prerevolutionary China, and in many Middle Eastern nations, women rarely have the right to divorce, whereas men are free to break up their marriages, usually on grounds of their wives' disobedience, laziness, or adultery. In some societies, a woman's failure to produce sons might also be a cause for divorce. In such cases, great social criticism is heaped on a divorced woman and on her family as well, although little if any criticism is leveled at the husband.

In some cultures, religious beliefs are used to strongly condemn and even outlaw divorce. Today, Roman Catholicism, Islam, and Orthodox Judaism place barriers to the breakup of marriages. In these belief systems, people have no right to dissolve a union because a marriage was sanctified in the wedding ceremony. In strict Islamic and Orthodox Jewish communities, it is very difficult for women to initiate divorce, but men may seek divorce in religious councils if they cite acceptable grounds.

REVIEW

The levirate and the sororate marriage patterns maintain alliances between families after the death of a spouse. Marriage is not only a relationship but also an economic obligation to the other party. Patrilineal societies generally have more strict rules concerning divorce than do matrilineal societies.

CASE STUDY

Marriage and Divorce among the Kpelle of Liberia

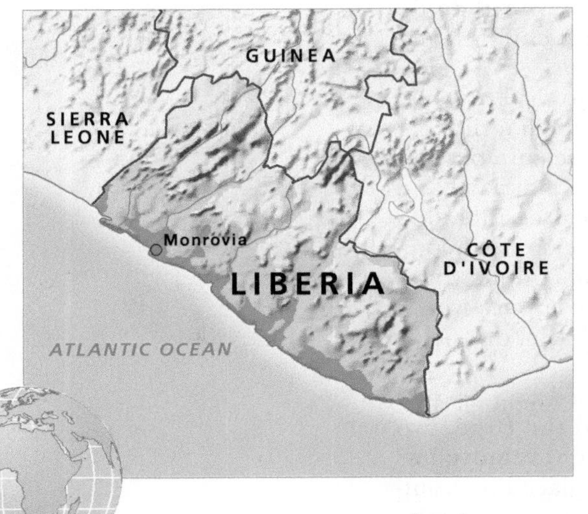

Marriage patterns among the Kpelle, a farming society, provide several options of payment and service that lead to differences in the strength of bonds between couples and the rights that a man exercises over his children (Gibbs 1965). The idea and standard form of marriage involves transfer of bridewealth from a husband's kin group to that of his wife. It permits a husband and his lineage to claim children produced by the marriage. A second form involves performance of brideservice rather than payment of bridewealth. In this type of marriage, a couple resides with the wife's family for a fixed time agreed upon by the parties concerned. During this period, the husband performs labor for his in-laws. Children born to the couple during the years of service belong to the wife's lineage rather than to the husband's. Once the period of brideservice is completed, the children become members of the father's patrilineage.

A third marital option is "male concubinage." In this option, the status of the couple is ambiguous. It involves an economic and sexual union between a poor man and one of the wives of a chief or wealthy man. Although the woman remains the legal wife of the patron, her relationship with the client is publicly recognized and sanctioned. Such a marriage enables a poor man who would otherwise have few marital prospects to marry and ally himself with the wealthy person. A wealthy man who is either already a chief or wishes to become one can gain the political support of a dependent client. Because the client and the patron's wife farm land the patron controls, the latter obtains products of their labor that he can sell for cash or distribute to others and thereby gain their support as well. Finally, because the woman remains the legal wife of the patron, children born to the client couple belong to the patron's lineage rather than to that of their biological father.

Kpelle marriages, then, are basically differentiated in terms of the legal status of women and the rights that husbands and their lineages may claim over a woman's children. If a woman is a full legal wife, that is, in a standard marriage with payment of bridewealth, her children belong to her husband's patrilineage. If a woman's legal status is in transition, as during the period of brideservice, her children belong to her patrilineage and her husband cannot claim them. And if the woman is the legal wife of a patron even though she lives with another man, her children belong to the patron.

Although marriage is the usual and preferred state for adults, rates of divorce are "moderately high" (Gibbs 1965). Divorces are granted by formal courts under the jurisdiction of local chiefs. Proceedings involve public hearings to determine the party at fault. Women usually initiate divorce, in part because the initiator usually ascribes blame, and men are reluctant to be publicly criticized for ending their marriages. Even though women are characteristically blamed for failed marriages, their request for divorce is usually granted. A man who wishes a divorce may mistreat his wife, so that she will seek a formal divorce in court. In this manipulative manner, he obtains his objective but is not publicly faulted.

Kpelle divorce benefits both wife and husband in an unhappy marriage. A wife who seeks to divorce is given her freedom and thus is personally satisfied. A husband, whether or not he wants to be divorced, receives the return of bridewealth that he had given to his wife's kin when he married, and retains rights as father to his children, including the privilege of receiving bridewealth for his daughters when they marry.

This description of Kpelle practices remains accurate for those in relatively isolated villages. However, in areas where economic transformations have affected subsistence patterns, marriage and divorce have also changed. In traditional villages, household farming, especially of rice, is the basis of subsistence. In villages close to main roads or larger towns, some people also produce cash crops, whereas others work in towns and cities. Both cash crops and wage work provide money to purchase food and other goods previously produced in the household. These changes have affected bridewealth payments. Previously, a prospective husband and his family often needed to spend years accumulating the goods or funds needed for bridewealth. If they did not have the funds themselves, they needed to borrow from others, thus becoming clients financially and socially of people more prosperous than themselves. Men are now often able to amass bridewealth while they are relatively young and are therefore less dependent on other members of their families, including their parents. This has loosened family ties.

Women can also benefit from changed circumstances. Young women can postpone marriage and maintain their independence by selling crops they have grown or other goods in markets in towns, or through wage work, even though women have fewer jobs available than do men. Older women who are divorced or widowed can decide not to remarry if they have independent sources of income. Studies conducted in the 1970s document the beginnings of trends still operative today; for example, women residing in "modern towns" are more likely to "marry later, divorce more often, and remarry less frequently" than women living in traditional villages (Bledsoe 1976, 380).

Conversations with Kpelle living in small villages or larger towns revealed complicated attitudes toward marriage and divorce. Although young men and women favored the severing of responsibilities toward their elders, exemplified for men by amassing their own bridewealth payments and for women by postponing marriage, older men and women regretted the breakdown of family obligations that had kept younger people dependent on them. In Bledsoe's view, ". . . the distinction between the old and the young is probably more important in understanding individuals' goals and strategies in African societies, than the distinction between men and women" (1976, 387). Men and women have, however, used different strategies to reach their goals. **Read** the **Document** on **myanthrolab.com**

ANTHROPOLOGY APPLIED

Anthropologists as Expert Witnesses

Testifying in court is not associated with cultural anthropology. However, cultural anthropologists are often called to testify in cases involving possible cultural misunderstandings on issues ranging from landownership to family law and child custody. They also testify as expert witnesses in cases about tribal rights, criminal investigation, and forensic science.

In her article "Infighting in San Francisco: Anthropology in Family Court, Or: A Study in Cultural Misunderstanding," anthropologist Barbara Jones (1998) outlines a custody dispute in which she was an expert witness. The dispute was between a mother seeking custody and the father, with whom the child was living. The mother had remarried a fourth time, was pregnant, and planned to leave the country. The father was single but closely tied to an extended family network. A psychologist, hired by the court and assumed to be unbiased, examined both households and concluded that the mother should have sole custody of the child. Jones believed that the psychologist did not understand the benefits that the father and his extended family could offer the child.

Corbis/Reuters/Corbis

Corbis/Tony Savino/Sygma/Corbis

She told the court that the child had been interacting almost daily with loving grandparents, cousins, aunts, and uncles. The father had also hired a full-time nanny to care for his daughter while he worked. Contrary to the psychologist, Jones concluded that the father's extended family provided greater benefits to the child than the mother's situation would allow.

CRITICAL THINKING QUESTION

What perspectives do anthropologists have that might make them valuable contributors to legal cases?

Study and Review on myanthrolab.com

CHAPTER SUMMARY

Defining Marriage and Family

- Families serve economic and social functions. Members of families usually reside together and provide for biological reproduction and the training and enculturation of children. Families provide people with companionship, emotional support, and assistance, and are the basic unit of economic cooperation and interdependence. Families, particularly households, work together to complete the daily tasks necessary for survival. They are also decision-making groups. In many societies, families perform religious functions and rituals that celebrate significant events in members' lives.

- Marriage is the most common way in which families are formed. Marriage is a socially recognized, enduring, stable bond between people who each have certain rights and obligations with respect to one another. Husbands and wives can expect to have an exclusive sexual relationship and assist one another in raising children and in provisioning their household. Through the marriage bond, men are able to claim "social fatherhood" by establishing themselves as the husband of the mother.

Families and Ideal Types

- Although the family is a universal cultural construct, the types of families found in different kinds of societies vary. Nuclear families consist of parents and their children, whereas extended families usually contain at least three generations. Nuclear families are often found in industrial societies, which stress economic independence, and in many foraging societies, because they are adaptive to survival when resources are scarce.
- Extended families are more common in farming and pastoral societies. They have the advantage of perpetuating the social unit, sharing resources and work, and providing emotional support and material aid.
- Family types are responsive to changes in productive modes and general social values. In many countries, the idealized model of husband, wife, and children has declined, as has the number of children per household.

Endogamy, Exogamy, and the Incest Taboo

- The incest taboo universally forbids marriage between parents and their children and between siblings. In some societies, it also forbids marriage between other relatives.
- Theories about the origin of the incest taboo include an instinctual revulsion and aversion toward sexual relations within the nuclear family, the biological consequences of inbreeding, a reduction in the fitness of a population through genetic homogeneity, a response to the need to diminish sexual competition within the nuclear family unit, and a means of forcing people to make alliances with others.

Forms of Marriage

- Different societies allow people to have different numbers of spouses at any one time. Marriage between one man and one woman is called monogamy; marriage between more than two people is called polygamy. Polygyny is the marriage between one man and two or more women. Polyandry is the marriage between one woman and two or more men.

Marriage as Alliance and Economic Exchange

- Marriage often involves an economic exchange. Bridewealth is a gift a husband or his family gives to the family of his intended wife. Similarly, groom-wealth is given by a wife or her family to the family of her intended husband. Brideservice or groom-service requires the husband or wife to perform some services for the parents of his or her spouse. Dowry is the economic goods or wealth the bride's family gives to the new couple or to the husband's kin.

Marriage as a Rite of Passage

- Marriages may be arranged by parents or by the couple themselves through courtship. The marriage ceremony publicly sanctions marriage and symbolizes the rights and duties of couples to each other and to their families.

Patterns of Residence after Marriage

- In some societies, a married couple resides with or near the husband's relatives (patrilocal residence). In others, they reside with or near the wife's kin (matrilocal residence). In bilocal residence, married couples live alternately with the husband's and the wife's families. In societies with matrilineal descent and inheritance, a couple may live with the husband's mother's brother (avunculocal residence). In neolocal residence, couples establish a new household, separate from either group of kin.

Widowhood and Divorce

- Marriage preference patterns, called levirate and sororate, emphasize marriage as an alliance between families. In the levirate, a deceased husband's brother (usually younger) marries the surviving widow; in the sororate, a younger sister of the deceased wife marries the surviving widower.

REVIEW QUESTIONS

1. What definition of marriage would cover all the marriage types discussed in this chapter?
2. How is subsistence related to family forms? How can changes in marriage and family reflect adaptations to changes in subsistence?
3. How do endogamy and exogamy affect a society's social organization?
4. What are some hypotheses about the origins of the incest taboo?
5. What are the benefits of polygamous marriages? What are the drawbacks?
6. What are common forms of political and economic exchange in marriage, and what types of kinships are associated with those forms?
7. How are postmarital residence patterns related to kinship? How are residence rules related to women's and men's status in a society?
8. What are some reasons that marriages are arranged? Why is divorce discouraged in arranged marriages?
9. How are levirate and sororate different? Why do societies have these practices?

MyAnthroLab Connections

Watch. Listen. View. Explore. Read. MyAnthroLab is designed just for you. Dynamic visual activities, videos, and readings found in the multimedia library will enhance your learning experience.

Resources from this chapter:

Watch on **myanthrolab.com**
- *Swahili Naming Practices*
- *Africa Polygamist Wives*

Listen on **myanthrolab.com**
- *Matched by Mom: Arranged Marriage in America*

View on **myanthrolab.com**
- *The Changing American Family*

Explore on **myanthrolab.com** In MySearchLab, enter the Anthropology database to find relevant and recent scholarly and popular press publications. For this chapter, enter the following keywords: caste, extended family, nuclear family, courtship

Read the **Document**
- *Konda Valley Dani: Marriage, Politics, and War* by Denise O'Brien
- *Nayars: Tradition and Change in Marriage and Family* by N. Prabha Unnithan

Polyandry: When Brothers Take a Wife

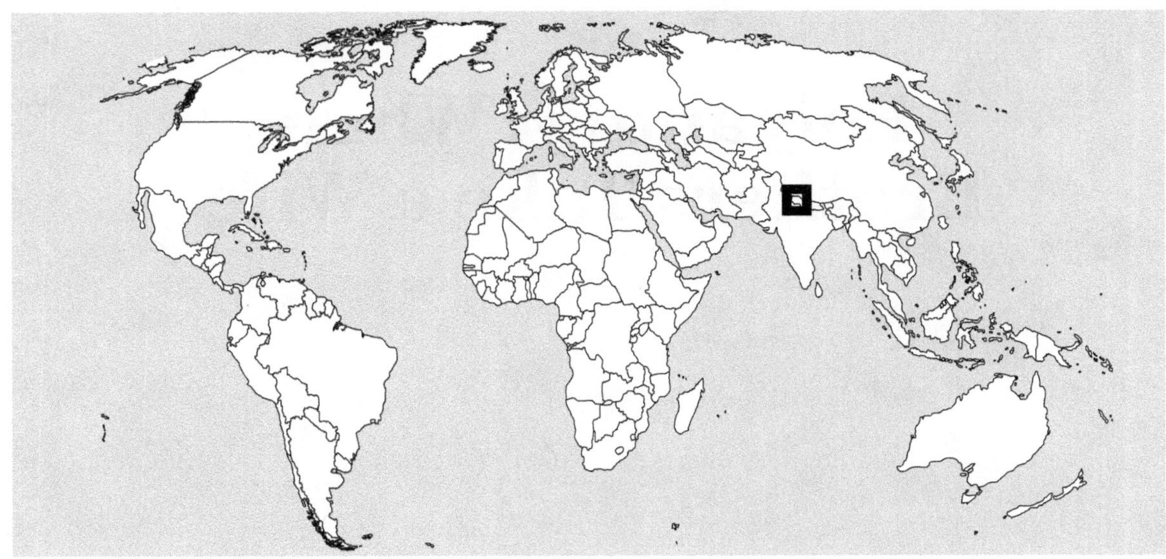

Polyandry: When Brothers Take a Wife

Melvyn C. Goldstein

*Many of the world's societies permit polygamy, the marriage of an individual to more than one spouse. The most common form of polygamy is polygyny, an arrangement in which a man marries more than one wife. Polygyny may exist for many reasons, not the least of which is its relationship to the substantial economic contributions of women. But there is a second kind of polygamy called polyandry, organized around the marriage of a woman to more than one husband, and its causes may seem less clear. In this article, Melvyn Goldstein describes the fraternal polyandry practiced by Tibetans living in Northern Nepal and seeks to explain why, despite having a choice of marriage forms including monogamy and polygyny, men and women often choose this rare form of marriage. He argues that, by marrying a single wife, a group of brothers can more easily preserve their family resources, whereas monogamous or polygynous marriage usually costs a man his inheritance and requires him to make a fresh start.**

Listen to the **Chapter Audio** on **myanthrolab.com**

Eager to reach home. Dorje drives his yaks hard over the seventeen-thousand-foot mountain pass, stopping only once to rest. He and his two older brothers, Pema and Sonam, are

*From Melvyn C. Goldstein, "When a Brother Takes a Wife," *Natural History,* March 1987. Reprinted from *Natural History* March 1987; copyright © Natural History Magazine, Inc., 1987.

jointly marrying a woman from the next village in a few weeks, and he has to help with the preparations.

Dorje, Pema, and Sonam are Tibetans living in Limi, a two-hundred-square-mile area in the northwest corner of Nepal, across the border from Tibet. The form of marriage they are about to enter—fraternal polyandry in anthropological parlance—is one of the world's rarest forms of marriage but is not uncommon in Tibetan society, where it has been practiced from time immemorial. For many Tibetan social strata, it traditionally represented the ideal form of marriage and family.

The mechanics of fraternal polyandry are simple. Two, three, four, or more brothers jointly take a wife, who leaves her home to come and live with them. Traditionally, marriage was arranged by parents, with children, particularly females, having little or no say. This is changing somewhat nowadays, but it is still unusual for children to marry without their parents' consent. Marriage ceremonies vary by income and region and range from all the brothers sitting together as grooms to only the eldest one formally doing so. The age of the brothers plays an important role in determining this: very young brothers almost never participate in actual marriage ceremonies, although they typically join the marriage when they reach their midteens.

The eldest brother is normally dominant in terms of authority, that is, in managing the household, but all the brothers share the work and participate as sexual partners. Tibetan males and females do not find the sexual aspect of sharing a spouse the least bit unusual, repulsive, or scandalous, and the norm is for the wife to treat all the brothers the same.

Offspring are treated similarly. There is no attempt to link children biologically to particular brothers, and a brother shows no favoritism toward his child even if he knows he is the real father because, for example, his other brothers were away at the time the wife became pregnant. The children, in turn, consider all of the brothers as their fathers and treat them equally, even if they also know who is their real father. In some regions children use the term "father" for the eldest brother and "father's brother" for the others, while in other areas they call all the brothers by one term, modifying this by the use of "elder" and "younger."

Unlike our own society, where monogamy is the only form of marriage permitted, Tibetan society allows a variety of marriage types, including monogamy, fraternal polyandry, and polygyny. Fraternal polyandry and monogamy are the most common forms of marriage, while polygyny typically occurs in cases where the first wife is barren. The widespread practice of fraternal polyandry, therefore, is not the outcome of a law requiring brothers to marry jointly. There is choice, and in fact, divorce traditionally was relatively simple in Tibetan society. If a brother in a polyandrous marriage became dissatisfied and wanted to separate, he simply left the main house and set up his own household. In such cases, all the children stayed in the main household with the remaining brother(s), even if the departing brother was known to be the real father of one or more of the children.

The Tibetans' own explanation for choosing fraternal polyandry is materialistic. For example, when I asked Dorje why he decided to marry with his two brothers rather than take his own wife, he thought for a moment, then said it prevented the division of his family's farm (and animals) and thus facilitated all of them achieving a higher standard of living. And when I later asked Dorje's bride whether it wasn't difficult for her to cope with three brothers as husbands, she laughed and echoed the rationale of avoiding fragmentation of the family and land, adding that she expected to be better off economically, since she would have three husbands working for her and her children.

Exotic as it may seem to Westerners, Tibetan fraternal polyandry is thus in many ways analogous to the way primogeniture functioned in nineteenth-century England. Primogeniture dictated that the eldest son inherited the family estate, while younger sons had to leave home and seek their own employment—for example, in the military or the clergy. Primogeniture maintained family estates intact over generations by permitting only one heir per generation. Fraternal polyandry also accomplishes this but does so by keeping all the brothers together with just one wife so that there is only one *set* of heirs per generation.

While Tibetans believe that in this way fraternal polyandry reduces the risk of family fission, monogamous marriages among brothers need not necessarily precipitate the division of the family estate: brothers could continue to live together, and the family land could continue to be worked jointly. When I asked Tibetans about this, however, they invariably responded that such joint families are unstable because each wife is primarily oriented to her own children and interested in their success and well-being over that of the children of the other wives. For example, if the youngest brother's wife had three sons while the eldest brother's wife had only one daughter, the wife of the youngest brother might begin to demand more resources for her children since, as males, they represent the future of the family. Thus the children from different wives in the same generation are competing sets of heirs, and this makes such families inherently unstable. Tibetans perceive that conflict will spread from the wives to their husbands and consider this likely to cause family fission. Consequently, it is almost never done.

Although Tibetans see an economic advantage to fraternal polyandry, they do not value the sharing of a wife as an end in itself. On the contrary, they articulate a number of problems inherent in the practice. For example, because authority is customarily exercised by the eldest brother, his younger male siblings have to subordinate themselves with little hope of changing their status within the family. When these younger brothers are aggressive and individualistic, tensions and difficulties often occur despite there being only one set of heirs.

In addition, tension and conflict may arise in polyandrous families because of sexual favoritism. The bride normally sleeps with the eldest brother, and the two have the responsibility to see to it that the other males have opportunities for sexual access. Since the Tibetan subsistence economy requires males to travel a lot, the temporary absence of one or more brothers facilitates this, but there are also other rotation practices. The cultural ideal unambiguously calls for the wife to show equal affection and sexuality to each of the brothers (and vice versa), but deviations from this ideal occur, especially when there is a sizable difference in age between the partners in the marriage.

Dorje's family represents just such a potential situation. He is fifteen years old and his two older brothers are twenty-five and twenty-two years old. The new bride is twenty-three years old, eight years Dorje's senior. Sometimes such a bride finds the youngest husband immature and adolescent and does not treat him with equal affection; alternatively, she may find his youth attractive and lavish special attention on him. Apart from that consideration, when a younger male like Dorje grows up, he may consider his wife "ancient" and prefer the company of a woman his own age or younger. Consequently, although men and women do not find the idea of sharing a bride or a bridegroom repulsive, individual likes and dislikes can cause familial discord.

Two reasons have commonly been offered for the perpetuation of fraternal polyandry in Tibet: that Tibetans practice female infanticide and therefore have to marry polyandrously, owing to a shortage of females; and that Tibet, lying at extremely high altitudes, is so barren and bleak that Tibetans would starve without resort to this mechanism. A Jesuit who lived in Tibet during the eighteenth century articulated this second view: "One reason for this most odious custom is the sterility of the soil, and the small amount of land that can be cultivated owing to the lack of water. The crops may suffice if the brothers all live together, but if they form separate families they would be reduced to beggary."

Both explanations are wrong, however. Not only has there never been institutionalized female infanticide in Tibet, but Tibetan society gives females considerable rights, including inheriting the family estate in the absence of brothers. In such cases, the woman takes a bridegroom who comes to live in her family and adopts her family's name and identity. Moreover, there is no demographic evidence of a shortage of females. In Limi, for example, there were (in 1974) sixty females and fifty-three males in the fifteen- to thirty-five-year age category, and many adult females were unmarried.

The second reason is incorrect because the climate in Tibet is extremely harsh, and ecological factors do play a major role in perpetuating polyandry, but polyandry is not a means of preventing starvation. It is characteristic, not of the poorest segments of the society, but rather of the peasant landowning families.

In the old society, the landless poor could not realistically aspire to prosperity, but they did not fear starvation. There was a persistent labor shortage throughout Tibet, and very poor families with little or no land and few animals could subsist through agricultural labor, tenant farming, craft occupations such as carpentry, or by working as servants. Although the per-person family income could increase somewhat if brothers married polyandrously and pooled their wages, in the absence of inheritable land, the advantage of fraternal polyandry was not generally sufficient to prevent them from setting up their own households. A more skilled or energetic younger brother could do as well or better alone, since he would completely control his income and would not have to share it with his siblings. Consequently, while there was and is some polyandry among the poor, it is much less frequent and more prone to result in divorce and family fission.

An alternative reason for the persistence of fraternal polyandry is that it reduces population growth (and thereby reduces the pressure on resources) by relegating some females to lifetime spinsterhood (see Figure 1). Fraternal polyandrous marriages in Limi (in 1974) averaged 2.35 men per woman, and not surprisingly, 31 percent of the females of child-bearing age (twenty to forty-nine) were unmarried. These spinsters either continued to live at home, set up their own households, or worked as servants for other families. They could also become Buddhist nuns. Being unmarried is not synonymous with exclusion from the reproductive pool. Discreet extramarital relationships are tolerated, and actually half of the adult unmarried women in Limi had one or more children. They raised these children as single mothers, working for wages or weaving cloth and blankets for sale. As a group, however, the unmarried women had far fewer offspring than the married women, averaging only 0.7 children per woman, compared with 3.3 for married women, whether polyandrous, monogamous, or polygynous. When polyandry helps regulate population, this function of polyandry is not consciously perceived by Tibetans and is not the reason they consistently choose it.

If neither a shortage of females nor the fear of starvation perpetuates fraternal polyandry, what motivates brothers, particularly younger brothers, to opt for this system of marriage? From the perspective of the younger brother in a landholding family,

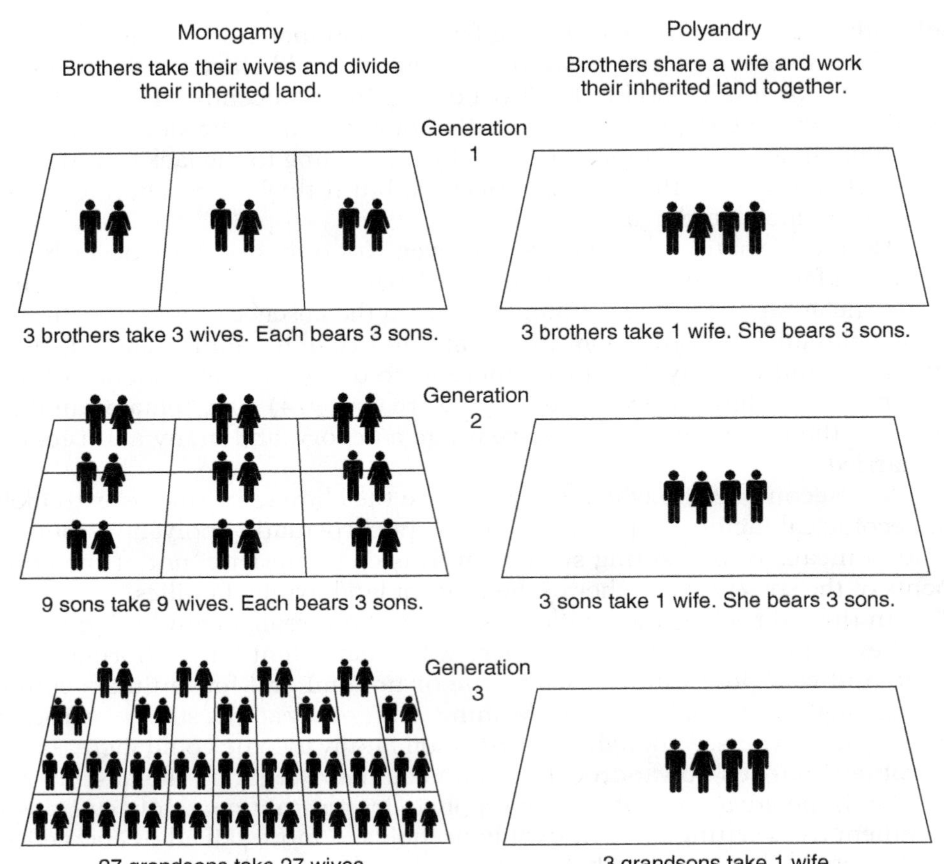
Monogamy
Brothers take their wives and divide their inherited land.
Polyandry
Brothers share a wife and work their inherited land together.
Generation 1
3 brothers take 3 wives. Each bears 3 sons.
3 brothers take 1 wife. She bears 3 sons.
Generation 2
9 sons take 9 wives. Each bears 3 sons.
3 sons take 1 wife. She bears 3 sons.
Generation 3
27 grandsons take 27 wives.
3 grandsons take 1 wife.

FIGURE 1 Family Planning in Tibet
An economic rationale for fraternal polyandry is outlined in the diagram above, which emphasizes only the male offspring in each generation. If every wife is assumed to bear three sons, a family splitting up into monogamous households would rapidly multiply and fragment the family land. In this case, a rule of inheritance, such as primogeniture, could retain the family land intact, but only at the cost of creating many landless male offspring. In contrast, the family practicing fraternal polyandry maintains a steady ratio of persons to land.

the main incentive is the attainment or maintenance of the good life. With polyandry, he can expect a more secure and higher standard of living, with access not only to his family's land and animals but also to its inherited collection of clothes, jewelry, rugs, saddles, and horses. In addition, he will experience less work pressure and much greater security because all responsibility does not fall on one "father." For Tibetan brothers, the question is whether to trade off the greater personal freedom inherent in monogamy for the real or potential economic security, affluence, and social prestige associated with life in a larger, labor-rich polyandrous family.

A brother thinking of separating from his polyandrous marriage and taking his own wife would face various disadvantages. Although in the majority of Tibetan regions all brothers theoretically have rights to their family's estate, in reality Tibetans are reluctant to divide their land into small fragments. Generally, a younger brother who insists on leaving the family will receive only a small plot of land, if that. Because of its power and wealth, the rest of the family usually can block any attempt of the younger brother to increase his share of land through litigation. Moreover, a younger brother may not even get a house and cannot expect to receive much above the minimum in terms of movable possessions, such as furniture, pots, and pans. Thus a brother contemplating going it on his own must plan on achieving economic security and the good life not through inheritance but through his own work.

The obvious solution for younger brothers—creating new fields from virgin land—is generally not a feasible option. Most Tibetan populations live at high altitudes (above 12,000 feet), where arable land is extremely scarce. For example, in Dorje's village, agriculture ranges only from about 12,900 feet, the lowest point in the area, to 13,300 feet. Above that altitude, early frost and snow destroy the staple barley crop. Furthermore, because of the low rainfall caused by the Himalayan rain shadow, many areas in Tibet and northern Nepal that are within the appropriate altitude range for agriculture have no reliable sources of irrigation. In the end, although there is plenty of unused land in such areas, most of it is either too high or too arid.

Even where unused land capable of being farmed exists, clearing the land and building the substantial terraces necessary for irrigation constitute a great undertaking. Each plot has to be completely dug out to a depth of two to two and a half feet so that the large rocks and boulders can be removed. At best, a man might be able to bring a few new fields under cultivation in the first years after separating from his brothers, but he could not expect to acquire substantial amounts of arable land this way.

In addition, because of the limited farmland, the Tibetan subsistence economy characteristically includes a strong emphasis on animal husbandry. Tibetan farmers regularly maintain cattle, yaks, goats, and sheep, grazing them in the areas too high for agriculture. These herds produce wool, milk, cheese, butter, meat, and skins. To obtain these resources, however, shepherds must accompany the animals on a daily basis. When first setting up a monogamous household, a younger brother like Dorje would find it difficult to both farm and manage animals.

In traditional Tibetan society, there was an even more critical factor that operated to perpetuate fraternal polyandry—a form of hereditary servitude somewhat analogous to serfdom in Europe. Peasants were tied to large estates held by aristocrats, monasteries, and the Lhasa government. They were allowed the use of some farmland to produce their own subsistence but were required to provide taxes in kind and corvée (free labor) to their lords. The corvée was a substantial hardship, since a peasant household was in many cases required to furnish the lord with one laborer daily for most of the year and more on specific occasions such as the harvest. This enforced labor, along with the lack of new land and the ecological pressure to pursue both agriculture and animal husbandry, made polyandrous families particularly beneficial. The polyandrous family allowed an internal division of adult labor, maximizing economic advantage. For example, while the wife worked the family fields, one brother could perform the lord's corvée, another could look after the animals, and a third could engage in trade.

Although social scientists often discount other people's explanations of why they do things, in the case of Tibetan fraternal polyandry, such explanations are very close to the truth. The custom, however, is very sensitive to changes in its political and economic milieu and, not surprisingly, is in decline in most Tibetan areas. Made less important by the elimination of the traditional serf-based economy, it is disparaged by the dominant non-Tibetan leaders of India, China, and Nepal. New opportunities for economic and social mobility in these countries, such as the tourist trade and government employment, are also eroding the rationale for polyandry, and so it may vanish within the next generation.

Study and **Review** on **myanthrolab.com**

Review Questions

1. What is fraternal polyandry, and how does this form of marriage manage potential conflict over sex, children, and inheritance?
2. Why do many Tibetans choose polyandry over monogamous or polygynous marriage?
3. According to Tibetans, what are some of the disadvantages of polyandry?
4. What is wrong with the theory that Tibetan polyandry is caused either by a shortage of women due to infanticide or is a way to prevent famine by limiting population and land pressure?
5. Why might Tibetan polyandry disappear under modern conditions?

Economic Systems

PREVIEW

- What is an economic system? How is it integrated into a culture?
- What are the different types of economic exchange?
- How do different economic systems allocate land and resources?
- How is surplus related to the different subsistence modes?
- How is specialization related to the different subsistence modes?
- Why is the theory of surplus value in a capitalist economy important?
- How has industrialization affected economies and cultures?
- What are the characteristics of postindustrial societies and of today's global economy?

A villager plants manioc (a woody root which is a large source of carbohydrates) after slash & burn of a rainforest near Mantadia National Park, Madagascar. *NHPA/SuperStock*

((•– Listen to the Chapter Audio on myanthrolab.com

Read on myanthrolab.com

Three men went into the forest: one was the Cultivator, the other the Trapper, the third the Gatherer-of-Honey. Arriving in the forest, they asked themselves: "how shall we build our houses?" They said: "you, the Cultivator, build your house than the middle of the three hills." The Trapper built his house on a hill, the Gatherer-of-Honey built his on a hill. No sooner had they finished building their houses than the Cultivator had already finished growing plants behind his house. The Trapper asked the Gatherer-of-Honey to make a blood pact with him, stating that they should not make such a pact with the Cultivator. Having finished making friendship, and having killed game, the Trapper went with the meat to his friend. They did not show it to the Cultivator. The following day, the Gatherer-of-Honey passed with a jar of honey to bring to his friend the Trapper. They did not give anything to the Cultivator. And so it was every day; they made things pass at the entrance of the village of this one, the Cultivator. He said to himself that his children alone would die of hunger.

This Harvester, this Cultivator, went to sow discord between the two friends. He called in a loud voice, "you man of the rodents Mikii, you the Trapper, it is you will kill my children, never again bring rodent Mikii here at my house." The Cultivator also set out to the village of the Gatherer-of-Honey calling, "you Gatherer-of-Honey, it is the flies that you bring here that cause my children to be sick; also it is my rodents Mikii, which you eat, that makes you fatter." On his side, the Trapper reflected much, stating that so then his friend had just insulted him; on his side the Gatherer-of-Honey also thought that his friend had just insulted him. Having heard that, the Trapper and the Gatherer-of-Honey . . . met in the valley at the Cultivator's. Arriving there, they questioned each other.

One said, "you yelled to me that it was my rodents Mikii who are the reason why your children have caught the kwashiorkor, yes my rodents Mikii!" And the other said, "you yelled that because of me your children have their throat obstructed by larvas of bee." The one denied and the other denied, both at the same time. At this time, the Cultivator . . . took to dancing and singing:

I, the instigator Cultivator.
I just finished placing in discord those who are two.

The two friends understood, having heard the manner in which this Cultivator had placed them in discord, one against the other. Having considered that, they made a pact of friendship with the Cultivator. As such, the three became friends among each other; and they began to give meat, honey, and agricultural products, all of them giving to one another mutually.

That is why a man should never refuse the mark of friendship because the mark of friendship is a thing capable of saving the family group.

In this narrative, the Nyanga of Central Africa dramatize the three significant elements in their economic system: hunting, gathering, and farming. They express the interdependence of these subsistence strategies and the importance of trade and exchange in binding a community together.

This chapter analyzes economic systems involving issues of the production, distribution, and consumption of foodstuffs and other goods and services. As you will learn, cultural features, such as population growth, emphasis on accumulating wealth, and status differences within a community are interrelated with others aspects of economic systems.

ANALYZING ECONOMIC SYSTEMS

consumption
The use of subsistence resources, including outcomes of production.

economic system
Cultural methods of allocating natural resources, the means of exploiting the resources through technology, the organization of work, and the production, distribution, consumption, and exchange of goods and services.

Societies organize subsistence strategies to utilize their land and resources efficiently. Available land must be distributed among members of the community. People need to agree about methods of exploiting their resources so that everyone has at least a minimal share to survive. People also need to know how to organize their work, taking account of differences in age, gender, and skill, as well as whatever other social variables are considered significant (such as class, race, or ethnicity). Societies must also have methods of distributing food, goods, and services within and among their communities. Rarely do people consume all and only what they produce individually. Instead, they share with others or exchange their products or services for other products or services. Patterns of **consumption,** therefore, are also affected by cultural norms. In some communities, all members have similar opportunities to consume or avail themselves of resources and goods and services. In other communities, though, levels of consumption may vary considerably. Taken together, these various factors constitute an **economic system.**

Anthropologists understand economies and economic systems holistically. They try to situate features of land, resource use, and labor organization in the context of people's adaptation to their environment. They also try to delineate the ways that land, resources, and labor are interrelated with other features of culture, including social and political systems. Put another way, economic systems consist of practices that organize people's activities of production, distribution, and consumption.

Subsistence strategies constitute an important but not exclusive factor in economic systems. Food-obtaining techniques are central to economies, but other factors, such as production of utilitarian and luxury goods, distribution and exchange of products, and specialization of work and services, are also important aspects of economic systems. Thus, for example, different modes of subsistence generally are correlated with different principles on which economic systems are organized. Subsistence strategies that focus on foraging, pastoralism, or farming tend to have different ways of allocating land and resources, organizing labor, producing goods, and distributing or exchanging products and services.

Allocating Land and Resources

What do you own, and how did you come to own it? Do you control the redistribution of what you own?

Different subsistence modes tend to foster different attitudes about land rights and access to natural resources. Foragers' concepts of open access to the lands and resources in their territories and to the lands' resources are especially useful for nomadic peoples, who rely on their ability to exploit available resources seasonally. Despite this general principle, some foraging and nomadic peoples do have territorial concepts that assign lands or resources to groups identifiable on the basis of kinship or community membership. Foragers' occupation of territory is usually occasional and temporary rather than permanent. Pastoral peoples may also extend rights to exploit all available land in their territory to graze their herds. However, some pastoral societies limit access to land to particular groups on either a seasonal or permanent basis. Farming peoples need to make claims to specific parcels of land that they cultivate. Among some farming peoples, land is permanently owned by an individual. In others, land may be reallocated from time to time, depending on inheritance rules and the size and composition of households living in the same area. Finally, in industrial and postindustrial societies, individuals, groups, and states own land and resources and other means of subsistence and production.

In Vietnam, rice farming has become women's work as men have left farming for wage jobs. Here, peasants near Danang irrigate their fields with wooden paddlewheels. Superstock/age fotostock/SuperStock

As a way of allocating resources, ownership varies in different types of societies. Ownership may be vested in a community as a whole or in individuals. Among nomadic foraging peoples, individuals

production
System of extracting resources and utilizing labor and technology to obtain foods, goods, and services.

specialization of labor
System of allocating work in which different people perform different tasks.

rarely have rights to exclusive ownership and control of land and resources. Ownership of land tends to be most formalized among farming peoples, who expend a great deal of labor readying their fields for planting and need specific acreage to produce sufficient food.

Producing Goods

In addition to subsistence products, people also need other goods to ensure their survival and well-being. Systems of **production** provide clothing, shelter, tools, utensils, and weapons. People also want decorative items to adorn their bodies and their residences. Their religious practices require ritual objects, costumes, and other paraphernalia for ceremonial use. In some societies, people within a household may make all of the various types of equipment that their family requires. In others, some people develop the skills and arts that enable them to become part-time or full-time specialists in the production of specific types of goods. Specialists engage in some types of exchange in which they either sell their products or exchange them for other goods and services.

Different types of subsistence strategies are more or less likely to produce surpluses. When surpluses arise, societies use different ways to dispose of them. Sometimes people keep surpluses on hand for use when supplies are low. At other times and in other circumstances, surpluses may be traded or sold so that the producers can obtain goods or services that they require but do not make themselves. Surpluses, therefore, are tied to patterns of distribution and exchange. In general, nomadic peoples obtain little in the way of surplus goods because of the inconvenience of carrying more than basic necessities when moving from one camp to another. Sedentary peoples, in contrast, prefer producing a certain amount of surplus to protect themselves against lean years.

In addition, surpluses serve social functions. Surplus farm produce or manufactured goods can be distributed by the wealthy to those less fortunate, stabilizing social networks and enhancing the prestige of the givers. Surplus goods can be distributed in ritual contexts, such as celebrations of births, marriages, and funerals. Finally, in state societies, surplus wealth may be appropriated through taxation to support the various functions of government and public services.

Watch the **Video:** *Specialization* on **myanthrolab.com**

Organizing Labor

Societies allocate the labor of their members to productive tasks through division of labor. Work roles are assigned minimally on the basis of age and gender. In addition, certain individuals may specialize in craft production or other arts and skills. Men and women may be assigned different but complementary tasks. Elderly people usually retire from direct productive work, depending on the ability of the family or society to support them, although their advice may be sought because of their knowledge and experience. Young children are assigned household and subsistence tasks consistent with their physical and cognitive maturation as well as the type of economy. Whereas farm families depend on children's labor, children in industrial societies typically are prevented from competing with their parents for jobs and wages. These norms often are codified as laws. The legal age of work in the United States, for example, is 14. Nevertheless, children are widely exploited as sources of labor in the world today.

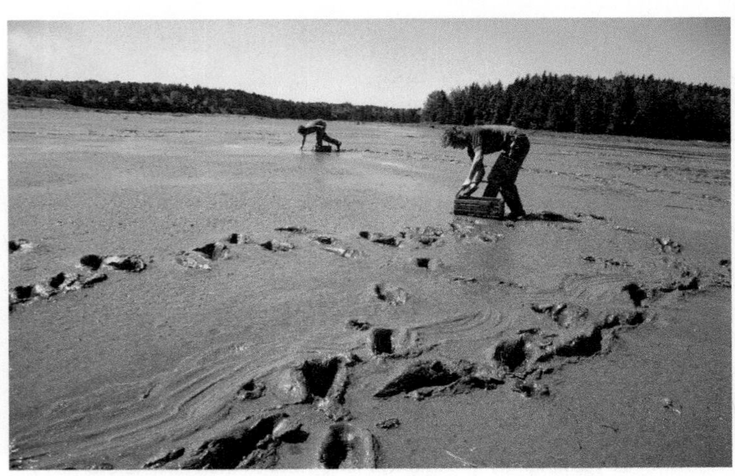

These clam diggers belong to a maritime community in New England and are among the few who are granted commercial licenses each year to exploit this easily overburdened resource. PhotoLibrary/David Cavagnaro/Peter Arnold/PhotoLibrary New York

Labor and Specialization. **Specialization of labor** based on skill, talent, or training is a common feature of many societies. All societies have some degree of labor specialization within households as well. In addition, communities may value individuals skilled at making certain kinds of tools, utensils, or crafts. Others may seek to acquire their high-quality, unique, or effective products or services. In some societies, part-time specialists accumulate income from their work. The more skilled the artisans, the more compensation they may receive because others especially prize their work. In other societies, labor specialization involves full-time specialists. These people do not participate in direct subsistence activities but instead exchange their labor and skill for food and goods obtained through the labor of others. Depending on the system of exchange and relationships between people, these products may be given away, exchanged, traded, purchased, or sold.

CASE STUDY

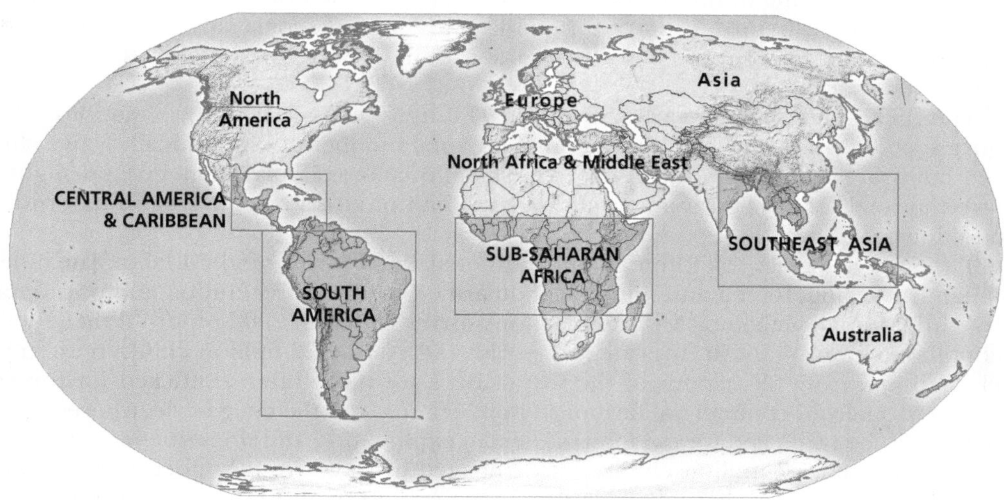

Child Laborers Today

The exploitation of child labor is an international concern. According to a report issued in 2006 by the International Labour Organization (ILO), children who work are divided into four categories: "children at work in economic activity," "child laborers," "children in hazardous work," and "children in unconditional worst forms of child labor." "Children at work in economic activity" is a broad category that encompasses most productive activities that children perform, including all market production (paid work) and some types of nonmarket production (unpaid work), such as producing goods for one's own use. Work may be in the formal sector (especially factory work) or the informal sector (street vendors, construction) and may involve legal or illegal activities.

"Children at work in economic activity" includes children who work in a market-oriented establishment that a relative in the same household operates. It also includes children who are domestic workers in someone else's household, but it excludes children who do the same chores in their own households without pay. The ILO estimates that some 317 million children between the ages of 5 and 17 "work in economic activity." Of these, about 196 million are under the age of 14.

Boys and girls are equally likely to be engaged in economic activities. For children younger than 14, there are no significant gender differences; however, for children ages 15 through 17, more boys than girls are engaged in economic activities, perhaps because many girls in developing countries are married or doing unpaid work in their own households by age 15.

The largest numbers of children engaged in economic activity are found in the Asia-Pacific region (127.3 million), followed by sub-Saharan Africa (48 million) and Latin America and the Caribbean (17.4 million). In terms of the ratio of working to nonworking children, sub-Saharan Africa has the highest ratio of child workers. There, about 29 percent of children younger than 15 are engaged in economic activities. In developed countries, only about 2 percent of children below the age of 15 are economically active.

The second ILO category, "child laborers," refers to child workers under the internationally agreed minimum ages for specific kinds of work, but any working child younger than 12 or 13 is considered a laborer. Children between the ages of 12 and 14 may also be classified as "child laborers" if they do light work for more than 14 hours per week. The ILO defines "light work" as work that is not harmful to children's physical development and health and does not interfere with their education. By this definition, an estimated 166 million child laborers are under age 15. Here, too, boys are more likely than girls to be child laborers, particularly in the older age group (15 to 17), where 57 percent are boys.

The third ILO category, children engaged in "hazardous work," is defined as "any activity or occupation that has, or leads to, adverse effects on the child's safety, health (physical or mental), and moral development." Hazardous work may also refer to excessive workloads or long or intense periods of work, even if the work itself is not hazardous. Some examples of hazardous work for children are mining, construction, working with heavy machinery, exposure to pesticides, and work underwater, at dangerous heights, or in confined spaces.

The ILO estimates that nearly 126 million children work in hazardous situations. This figure accounts for somewhat less than half the total number of economically active children but more than two-thirds of the world's child laborers. For all age groups, slightly more than half of boys and somewhat less than half of girls were working in hazardous conditions.

The final category, "children in unconditional worst forms of child labor," includes human trafficking, forced and bonded labor, armed conflict, prostitution and pornography, and criminal activities. A United Nations survey issued in 2002 reported that about 8.4 million children are in this category worldwide. About 1.2 million children are trafficked to and from all regions of the world. Boys are more often trafficked for forced labor (especially in commercial farming), petty crimes, and the drug trade, whereas girls are likely to be trafficked for commercial sexual exploitation and domestic service.

An estimated 5.7 million children are engaged in forced and bonded labor. About 5.5 million of these reside in the Asia-Pacific region, although Africa and Latin America also have many. Some 300,000 children, mostly boys, are forced to serve in wars, mostly in Africa and the Asia-Pacific region. About 1.8 million children in all regions of the world are engaged in prostitution and pornography. Both tourists and domestic clients exploit child prostitutes. Finally, about 600,000 children are engaged in illicit activities, including petty crimes and especially the production and trafficking of drugs.

Rates of child labor reported in 2006 indicate declines of about 11 percent worldwide from previous surveys. The decline was sharpest in Latin America, with somewhat narrower decreases in Asia and no decrease in sub-Saharan Africa. ILO officials attribute the worldwide decline to efforts by the United Nations and member countries to address the problems of child laborers. The lack of decline in sub-Saharan Africa, however, can be attributed to the devastating effects of HIV/AIDS on the adult population, forcing children to support their families. Read the Document on myanthrolab.com

Labor and Social Status. The relationship between labor and social status is reflected in relative contributions to subsistence, which affect social prestige and influence. For example, in societies where men have higher social status than women and perform most of the subsistence work, their higher social standing may be attributed to their contributions to their households as producers. In contrast, women's lesser social standing may result from their relatively minor contributions to the food supply. Performing a major share of productive work does not necessarily translate into social prestige or power, as in the case of slavery. In the Caribbean and the southern United States, for instance, African slaves in the eighteenth and first half of the nineteenth centuries were the primary subsistence workers and also produced most of the crops intended for external trade. However, they clearly did not benefit from their labor in terms of greater social prestige. The determinants of social power stem more from control over labor and the right or authority to exert control, manage productive forces, and distribute the products. For example, monarchs, nobles, and other members of elite classes control and benefit from the labor of others. Finally, in many large-scale industrial societies, some people accumulate wealth and power from the labor of others and do little or no productive work themselves.

Distributing and Exchanging Products and Services

Once goods, whether foodstuffs or manufactures, are produced, they enter into patterns of distribution and consumption. Because societies are organized on principles of interdependence in cooperation and competition, individuals must always be connected to others in networks of distribution. Systems of exchange include reciprocity, defined as giving and taking "in kind" between individuals and families, as in simple spontaneous gift exchange or in the exchange of services rendered during different phases of the life cycle; for example, as parents aid and support their young children, adult children may aid and support their elderly parents. Reciprocity can be far from simple, however. Networks of reciprocal relations may be complex and of long standing. For example, in the Trobriand Islands of Melanesia, complicated patterns of interisland trade linked people through the exchange of ritual items (necklaces and armbands), as well as food and other goods.

generalized reciprocity
The exchange of goods and services without keeping track of their exact value, but often with the expectation that their value will balance out over time.

balanced reciprocity
Exchange of goods and services of a specified value at a specified time and place.

potlatch
Ceremonial feast, characteristic of indigenous Pacific Northwest coast societies, during which hosts distributed to guests a great deal of food and goods that had been accumulated over many months or years.

Types of Reciprocity. Members of families and households may be intertwined in recurring series of exchanges, a type of distribution called generalized reciprocity. In **generalized reciprocity,** goods and services are exchanged, but the value of the products or services given and received is not exactly or objectively calculated. There may be an expectation that goods and services will be given and received frequently and will have approximately equivalent worth, but the frequency and the amount of value are not specified. Many exchanges between parents and children, for example, are examples of generalized reciprocity. Distribution of food in some societies likewise involves principles of generalized reciprocity, as in the exchanges of foraging peoples such as the Inuit and Ju/'hoansi. Through generalized reciprocity, all families become both givers and receivers of food over time.

Some exchanges are characterized by **balanced reciprocity,** in which exchanges more closely specify the value and the time at which an exchange will take place. The mutual giving and receiving of gifts at birthdays or religious holidays and the informal exchanges of clothing or objects are examples of balanced reciprocity. Balanced reciprocity characterizes exchanges between people of equal social status who are not kin.

CASE STUDY

The Potlatch: An Example of Economic and Social Reciprocity

An example of a complex system of reciprocity, called the **potlatch,** was prevalent in indigenous societies of the Pacific Northwest coast. The Kwakwaka'wakw (known previously as the Kwakiutl) now live on reserves and in communities in British Columbia, Canada. They formerly were a cultural and linguistic group made up of approximately thirty independent "tribes" that each occupied a separate territory. They were foragers, but not nomadic. An abundance of wild resources, especially fish and other sea products, land animals, plants, fruits, and berries allowed the Kwakwaka'wakw to live in permanent villages containing hundreds of residents.

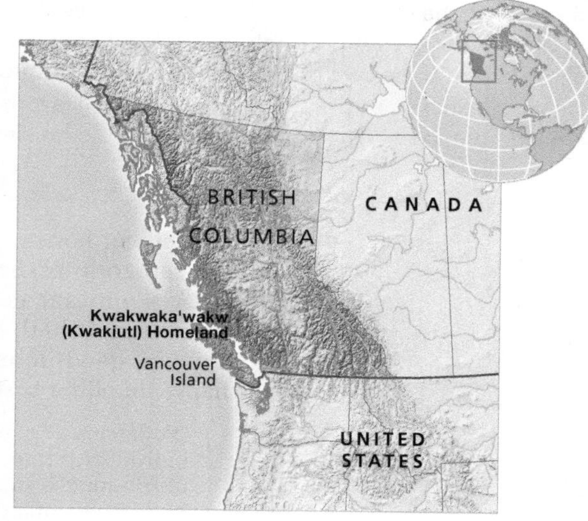

People of highest status constituted the informal leadership of kin groups and villages. Chiefs received portions of animal, fish, and plant products obtained by members of their group and were usually exempt from subsistence tasks. Chiefs organized cooperative activities, such as house building, but individuals acting alone did most hunting and fishing. Chiefs were also representatives of their lineages in the system of potlatching or feasting that served to validate people's social standing.

Potlatches (from the Chinookan word for "to give") were feasts to which relatives, community members, and high-ranking chiefs were invited. They were held to celebrate life-cycle transitions (birth, naming, puberty, marriage, death), the building of new houses, and the naming of new chiefs. As part of the potlatch, the host, who had accumulated goods over many months or even years, gave food and gifts to the invited guests. High-ranking chiefs also received gifts such as bowls, dishes, and ceremonial objects. The host sought to distribute more wealth than other hosts had given out at potlatches. By doing this, the host raised and secured his social standing. Then

In Their Own VOICES

"Free to Do as You Like"

In this excerpt from his autobiographical novel, Fragments of Memory: A Story of a Syrian Family, Hanna Mina describes the plight of sharecroppers in his homeland, bound to and dependent on landlords who extract most of the profits from the farmers.

Ever since February, Mother had been gathering the hen eggs with great care. We were living and working as day laborers in a field belonging to the village *mukhtar* [headman]. It was a small field, empty except for mulberry trees. Our only duty was raising silkworms during the silk season. It was a raw deal that Father had contracted with the *mukhtar*. . . . He didn't succeed here either but he was forced into it. . . . He had to find shelter somewhere, so he agreed to take the abandoned field. The *mukhtar* opened a page for us in his debt ledger. The first thing he put down in it, against the account of the silk harvest, was five kilos of mixed sorghum and barley, a few meters of unbleached cotton and a few articles like salt, oil, kerosene and soap. He also advised Father to be a faithful share cropper who knows his obligations and pays his debts. Father raised his hand to his forehead and then placing it over his heart said, "At your service, Mr. Elias!" . . .

Our house was a rectangle built of unbaked clay bricks, divided into two parts by a wall. One part was for animals, the other for living in. Since we possessed no animals, that part remained empty. Hens that relatives had generously bestowed upon Mother ran around and pecked there. In one corner we piled up firewood and dung, and in another near a small window high in the wall was a hearth made of stones and clay.

Father began, with the help of the family, the cultivation of the land and the care of the mulberry trees by borrowing a neighbor's animal. Before the work was finished, a messenger arrived from the *mukhtar* asking for Father. So he went only to be told that he must work in his fields first and that Mother must work in the *mukhtar's* house. Father raised his hand to his forehead, lowered it and placing it over his heart said, "At your service, Mr. Elias!"

Although the parents worked hard as sharecroppers, their precarious situation worsened because synthetic silk made in India undersold natural silk. The landlord shut down silkworm production, forcing sharecroppers to leave.

So we bundled up the belongings we had left, and our parents went to inform the *mukhtar* that we were leaving.

We could have left covertly at night or in the early morning without our departure arousing anyone's attention or interest.

subsequent hosts who had been guests at one potlatch would attempt to match or outdo the generosity of the previous host to validate or raise his own social status.

A significant goal in potlatching, therefore, was for one to give more than one received, but both economic and social goods were being negotiated. Hosts gave away material goods in exchange for greater social prestige. Helen Codere (1950) gives perhaps one of the best definitions of the potlatch:

> "Potlatching" is more than any single potlatch. The public distribution of property by an individual is a recurrent climax in an endless series of cycles of accumulating property—distributing it in a potlatch—being given property—again accumulating and preparing. The whole potlatch system is a composition of these numerous individual potlatch cycles.

In addition to its social and symbolic value, the potlatch cycle thus served economic functions. In days of feasting, food was distributed along with blankets and other surplus wealth. People of high status could recirculate these goods when they hosted potlatches, but lower-ranking people used them in their domestic consumption. This system of exchange maintained the entire society. Read the Document on myanthrolab.com

In this 1960s photograph, a family and their neighbors in Balakan, Azerbaijan, reel silk by hand from silkworm cocoons they have harvested from their mulberry trees. Craft specialization in transitional economies is risky for landless families because their income is dependent on a stable market in which to sell their product—but market forces are beyond their control. Azerbaijan International/Azerbaijan International

The surrounding houses were empty, the mulberry groves were being cut down and burned or their trunks gathered for wood. The paths were filled with columns of travelers on the backs of animals or in carts drawn by donkeys or cows. The fathers who lacked these means carried their things on their backs, dragging their children along, fleeing from hunger, fear, and thieves, traveling together to be safe from highway robbers who lay in wait for them in the valleys and the foothills of the mountains.

It was possible for us, in this state of collective emigration, this mutual dissolution of contracts to forsake our mud hut and the mulberry grove, empty except for the whistling wind, and flee the whole village without letting anyone know and without anyone asking about us. But our oldest sister was with the *mukhtar.* Considering her to be payment for the debt, he had tightened his watch over her since learning that Father had returned and that we were on the point of leaving since it had become impossible for us to stay on.

Father's lengthy beseeching diatribe, Mother's tearful entreaties, and requests from those who were acquainted with our circumstances and sympathized with us, were of no avail. The *mukhtar* spurned them all. He would not give us anything to eat and could not cope with us remaining hungry. We were of no use to him as *fellahin* [peasant farmers]. So he made it known that we were free to leave, but as far as our sister was concerned, he would keep her until we paid our debt.

"You're free to do as you like!" said the *mukhtar.* The landowners had said that before him, and he said it to other *fellahin* beside us. The sweet word "freedom" had become frightening, meaning no money, no food and no concern for the unpredictable destiny of the families who had lived on raising silkworms. The arrival of artificial silk was finishing off them and the silkworms together.

Therefore the word "free" became an odious term to the *fellahin,* who came from their fields seeking aid from the owners of the fields. As a consequence, they rejected this term, bringing up the matter of their servitude being in exchange for certain conditions, among which was the stipulation that they should be sustained until winter was over and the growing season arrived.

From Hanna Mina, *Fragments of Memory: A Story of a Syrian Family,* pp. 19–20, 88–89. © 1993. Reprinted by permission of the Center for Middle Eastern Studies, the University of Texas at Austin.

CRITICAL THINKING QUESTIONS

Why were Hanna and his family not really free to do as they wanted? What patterns in agricultural societies lead to social inequality?

Balanced and generalized reciprocity are similar in their social basis and principle of equivalence; for example, items or services given or received are roughly equal in value. Furthermore, in addition to distributing food and material items, reciprocal exchanges are symbolic affirmations of social relationships. By exchanging goods and services, people enact their mutual interdependence.

A third type of reciprocity, **negative reciprocity,** characterizes exchanges in which some parties receive more than they have given. Negative reciprocity is rarely found within families or among members of small communities but is typical of trade or market exchanges in which the goal is profit. Negative reciprocity is common between strangers or enemies. However, negative reciprocity may occur among people in the same community who operate on the principle of competition. Trade exchanges called barter may be based on negative reciprocity. In **barter,** people trade a product they have in excess to obtain an item they need but do not produce themselves. Capitalist economic systems are based on negative reciprocity. For example, manufacturers and providers of services strive to sell their goods at prices that exceed the costs of producing those goods, earning them a profit and increasing their wealth.

negative reciprocity
Exchange of goods and services in which each party seeks to benefit at the expense of the other, thus making a profit.

barter
An exchange of products in which one person gives one type of product in exchange for another type of product.

Have you ever bartered services or products?

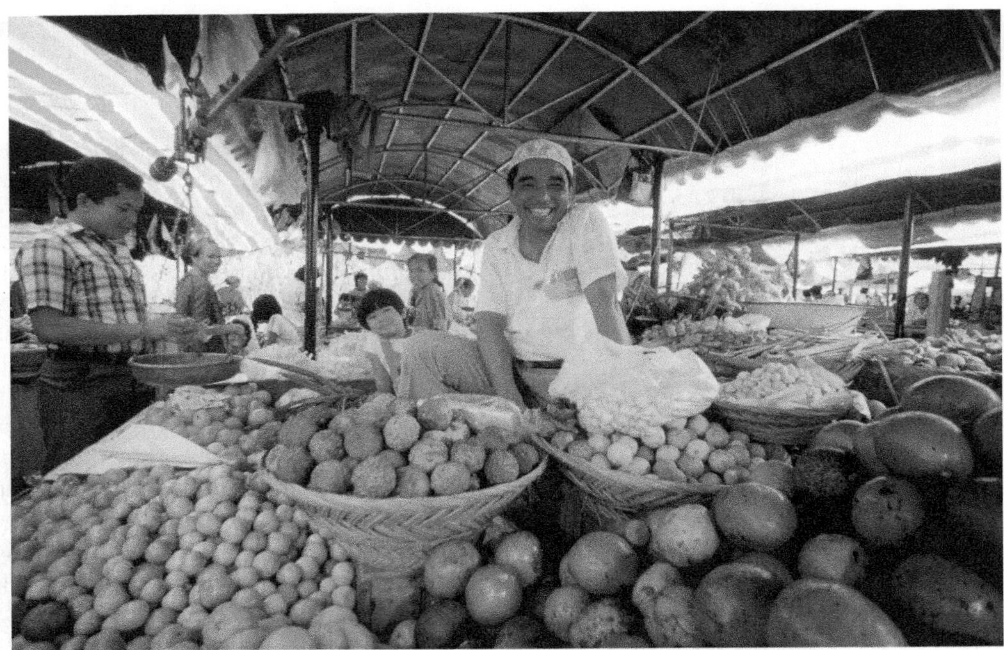

In Sumatra, horticulturalists still barter for manufactured goods, especially hunting tools, or even for tourists' personal objects. Corbis/Owen Franken/Documentary Value/Corbis

Redistributive Networks. The Pacific Northwest potlatch is an example of a system of redistribution. In **redistributive networks,** an organizer collects produce and other goods and then distributes them to community members or guests at a large public gathering. The occasions for redistribution are many. Ceremonial events, especially those marking rites of passage (birth, marriage, death), may provide the context for redistribution by the host to the guests, as in the potlatch. Political events, such as installations of chiefs in Melanesia and Polynesia, are occasions for redistribution as the new leaders or their relatives provide giveaways displaying their generosity and at the same time attracting loyal followers. In some early states that had agriculture as an economic base, such as the Inca, central governments collected surplus produce and other goods, stored them in granaries and warehouses, and distributed them to needy people in times of poor harvests or other catastrophe.

In contemporary societies, state governments organize networks of redistribution. One of the state's functions is to collect taxes, now paid in money, from its citizens to fund and support public projects and programs. In theory, the value of these monies is returned to citizens in public services such as road construction, water supplies, schools, justice systems, and defense. In practice, however, systems of redistribution based on taxation are often flawed or work imperfectly as leveling mechanisms. For example, in the United States, the progressive income tax was developed to allocate people's tax burdens more equitably so that wealthier people paid a higher percentage of their income in taxes than poorer people. The wealthiest people have many ways to reduce their tax liability, however, so poorer people shoulder a disproportionately higher tax burden. Conflicts over tax rates for wealthy people current in the United States are examples of how complex and contentious issues of redistribution can be.

redistributive networks
Economic systems in which an organizer amasses food and other goods and then distributes to community members or guests at large public gatherings.

trade
System of exchange in which goods are exchanged for either other goods or money.

Markets and Trade. Another form of redistribution is **trade,** in the form of either barter or market exchange. As defined previously, barter is the exchange of goods between individuals, each one supplying the other with produce, crafts, or other items. People who engage in barter usually know one another. In some cases, they may establish relatively formalized and permanent trading relationships, visiting one another's communities from time to time and exchanging their goods. Market exchange, on the other hand, is usually impersonal and is based, in principle, on fixed prices for goods. However, people buying and selling in local and regional markets in many societies frequently haggle over prices in an attempt to reach a compromise between the seller's desire to get as much as possible for the goods and the buyer's desire to pay as little as possible.

In West African societies, local and regional markets function to redistribute farm products and crafts among villagers who themselves lack mobility to obtain a variety of goods. For example, among the Igbos of Nigeria, women are the principal local traders, bringing their own and their husbands' products to market (Njoku 1990). Some women are part-time traders, combining their own farm labor and their commercial activities. Part-time traders usually live in rural areas where they have access to land. Other women are full-time specialists, working in markets in urban areas. They are buyers and sellers, purchasing farm goods and other products from people in rural areas and then selling them in town markets. Some urban traders employ assistants to travel to the villages to buy produce. Finally, foreign goods enter local and urban markets through the work of large-scale importers and exporters. Most of these traders are men.

The modern Igbo system of market exchange is partially financed by credit associations. Some of these are based on kinship, whereas others bring together unrelated traders who form credit unions (Njoku 1990, 106–07). In one type of savings club, each member contributes a fixed amount of money at specific times (for example, on market day). Then the full amount of money collected each time is given to each member of the club in rotation. In addition, money is available to members for emergencies. Some savings clubs lend money to members, charging rates of interest for a fixed loan. Women traders sometimes organize together to protect their rights and to support one another with loans and credit.

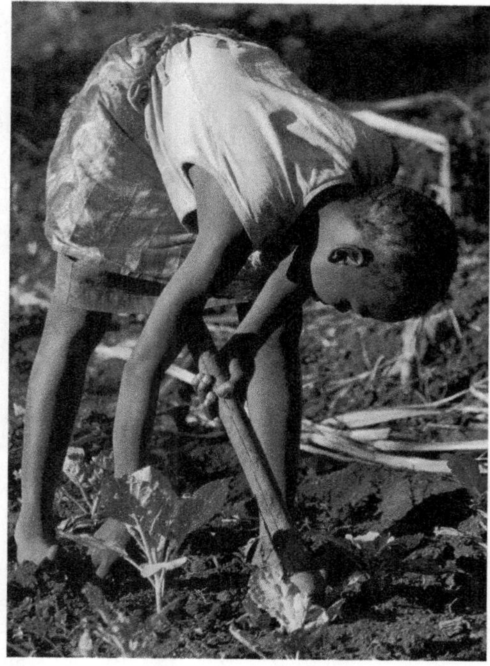

Many subsistence farmers in Africa use simple technologies to cultivate their fields. Here, a girl in Zimbabwe uses a digging stick to plant and weed her crops. Corbis/Bojan Brecelj/Corbis

An economic system involves interdependent systems of production, consumption, allocation of land and resources, organization and specialization of labor, and exchange. In systems of exchange-based generalized reciprocity, people exchange goods and services of unequal or unfixed value. In balanced reciprocity, equal exchanges are sought. In negative reciprocity, people expect to get more than they give. Systems of exchange also include redistributive networks, barter, trade, and market transactions.

MARKET ECONOMIES AND CAPITALISM

A **market economy** is a system of allocating goods and services and determining prices on the basis of market forces, such as supply and demand. Thus, items in short supply and with high demand cost more to buy. In contemporary societies, buying and selling of goods and services is negotiated through a system of money exchange. Money, whether in the form of paper, coin, precious metals, gems, or other material objects, is endowed with a specific value. Societies might have special-purpose money, such as cowrie shells, of fixed value that can be exchanged only for certain commodities, or tokens or tickets good only for a particular event on a particular day. In contrast, market economies rely on all-purpose money that can be exchanged for any product or service at any time. This money is portable, durable, divisible, abstract, and universal. Its value is calculated independently of any particular exchange, therefore, and can be used as a measure of worth in any exchange of goods, services, and labor. Money can even be used to "commodify" (make into a **commodity** to be bought and sold) essentially noneconomic things, such as people, their talents, and events in their lives. Market economies are based on these principles of measurement of the value of goods and services. Markets as physical places for the exchange of products, such as in local or regional markets, may exist in societies with all kinds of subsistence strategies, even including foraging, simple farming, or pastoralism.

Capitalism is both an economic system based on money and markets and an ideology based on the private and corporate ownership of the means of production and

market economy
Economic system in which products are traded in impersonal exchanges between buyers and sellers using an all-purpose currency.

commodity
A product that can be sold or traded in return for money or other products.

capitalism
An economic mode of production in which the goal is to amass wealth in the form of money to gain control over the means of production and then use this control to accumulate even greater wealth.

Here, a Senegalese woman wears a traditional headpiece made of cowrie shells. For centuries, West Africans used cowrie shells from the Indian Ocean as currency. Corbis/ Philippe Lissac/Godong/Corbis

distribution. Means of production include land, money, factories, and the like, collectively called **capital.** Economies based on capitalism must grow to survive, and growth is based on profits from buying and selling in diverse markets. The greatest profits are made in free markets that are unrestricted by industries or governments, and the greatest growth occurs as profits are accumulated and reinvested in businesses. Thus, capitalist economies favor business interests and state expansion for the purposes of acquiring new capital, including land, raw materials, and inexpensive labor.

Capitalism as an ideology-based economic system arose in Europe beginning in the sixteenth century, based on the principles of private property, individual rights, free trade, profit, and the amassing of wealth. By amassing wealth in the form of money, some people are able to gain control of the means of production and can then use this control to accumulate even greater wealth. The capitalist mode of production differs in many significant ways from modes of production in traditional indigenous societies. In contrast to economic relations in kin- and community-based societies, capitalist economic relations are impersonal and institutionalized. According to Karl Marx, these relations are facilitated through the exchange of money, which, although seemingly abstract and neutral, "... actually conceals, instead of disclosing, the social character of private labor, and the social relations between individual producers" (1967, 76).

Today, farm products enter into complex systems of and delivery to national and worldwide markets. Some of the profits reaped from sale of produce are reinvested in newer technologies that permit the production of even greater surpluses, a cycle of profit and growth consistent with the principles of capitalist economic production.

Capitalist production is characterized by the following three fundamental attributes (Plattner 1989):

1. Workers do not control the means of production; they cannot by themselves produce the goods they need for survival. In contrast to subsistence farmers and artisans, workers in capitalist production are dependent on the owners of factories or industries that organize and produce goods and services.
2. Workers gain access to the means of production only through working for wages. According to the classic Marxist paradigm, because of this relationship, capitalist societies are divided into two basic classes: owners of the means of production (capitalists) and workers (proletariat). While some discussions of capitalism describe workers as "free" in the sense that they can sell their labor independently of kinship or other constraints, they are not free in that their lack of capital forces them to work for wages.
3. Workers produce value that is greater than the wage paid to them. This **surplus value** is retained by the owners of capital and contributes to their profit (above the costs of maintaining the means of production). In contrast to economic systems that strive for balance and stability in labor output and the benefits reaped, capitalist systems strive for continual increases in profits and rates of growth. Capitalists raise profits by increasing the scale of production, purchasing more machinery, increasing the efficiency of production, investing in new technology, finding inexpensive labor, and increasing labor output.

Cultural beliefs and values support the principles and practices by which economic systems operate. Ideological constructs that support capitalism include the idea that benefits accruing to owners are "natural" and legitimate. Owners deserve their wealth because they plan ahead, take risks, make sacrifices, and work hard. In contrast, people who are poor are seen as undeserving. Poverty, which actually results from fundamental social and economic inequalities, is presented as the consequence of an individual's personal failings—lack of intelligence, laziness, or even moral deficiencies. Through formal and informal enculturation and the reinforcement of political and religious beliefs, most members of capitalist societies learn to accept their "proper" roles without

capital
Land, money, factories, and the like that support and supply the materials needed for production.

surplus value
The amount of value that workers produce in capitalist production that is greater than the wage paid to them.

What values, beliefs, and practices support the type of economic system in which Tokyo thrives? The Image Works/Fujifotos/The Image Works

question. Members of elite classes expect to be privileged, to have wealth, and to exert social and political power; in turn, members of lower classes accept their comparative disadvantage.

REVIEW

A market economy is based on supply and demand and the use of money and other capital as mediums of exchange. A good, service, idea, or even a person is treated as a commodity to be bought and sold. In capitalism, workers are dependent on owners to organize and produce goods and services, sell their labor for wages or salaries, and produce a surplus value that the owners retain as profit. Capitalism is based on private property and profits from the buying and selling of commodities in free markets.

IMPACTS OF COLONIAL EXPANSION, INDUSTRIALISM, AND GLOBALIZATION

The growth of capitalism depended on the exploitation of land, labor, natural resources, and raw materials. Beginning in the fifteenth century, European explorers, traders, soldiers, missionaries, and settlers traveled throughout the world in an effort to acquire new territories, resources, markets, and souls. Each colonial power had its specific goals but all shared a common purpose and worldview, namely, to expand their national wealth and power. In the process, they had to control and conquer other lands and peoples.

Through **colonialism,** conquered or dominated peoples were incorporated into European economic systems as extractors of resources. In North America, native peoples became enmeshed in trading networks directed by Dutch, French, British, and Russian merchants, delivering animal furs in exchange for manufactured goods. In Mexico, Central and South America, and the Caribbean, indigenous peoples were forced to work on plantations and in mines operated by Spanish and Portuguese owners. In Africa, people were extracted as resources to be bought and sold along with gold and ivory. Many millions of other people died from warfare, overwork, and disease as the direct and indirect casualties of European colonial expansion.

colonialism
Policies in which countries establish colonies in distant places to exploit their resources and labor, and possibly to establish settlements of their own citizens abroad.

In Asia, European expeditions met powerful, centralized, and well-organized states that they were not able to defeat militarily. Instead, Europeans developed trading

The Europeans needed to develop markets to sell goods manufactured in Europe and to expand markets for materials extracted from their colonies. This dynamic produced the complex economic system that we refer to as globalization.

networks that brought resources and products to Asia from colonies in other parts of the world. In exchange, they obtained Asian luxury items to sell in Europe. Some indigenous peoples in all parts of the world readily and even enthusiastically welcomed European traders, wanting to acquire manufactured goods and luxury items. They willingly supplied the merchants with the resources, products, and people so much sought after in European and world markets. The participation of many other indigenous peoples was not voluntary, however.

European economic expansion was closely connected with nation building. Governments controlled much of the trade, directly or through state-appointed merchant organizations, and pursued policies of political and military intervention to promote and protect their economic interests. These policies often led to military invasions and wars of conquest, followed by the establishment of direct colonial rule. Far-flung empires were established, with European powers competing to acquire colonial possessions. The French and British claimed much of North America, for example; the British claimed India while the Spanish took most of South America and many European powers competed for control of territories in Africa.

As colonial control spread throughout the world, capitalism and market economies were introduced to peoples whose subsistence strategies were based on foraging, pastoralism, and horticulture. Because economic systems are integrated with other aspects of culture, changes in work and landholding practices caused by colonialism and trade stimulated political, social, and ideological transformations as well. These processes of globalization increased cultural connections throughout the world.

Colonialism and the Exploitation of Labor

Slavery was the most extreme form of colonial exploitation of labor of indigenous peoples. Slavery deprived the victims of all rights to determine their own labor, forced them to produce goods directed by their owners, and expropriated all their products to be distributed and consumed according to the wishes of their masters. In the eighteenth and first half of the nineteenth centuries in the Caribbean and southern United States, the economic value produced by slaves fueled the growing wealth of these regions but did not benefit the workers themselves. From the beginning of the slave trade in the fifteenth century until its end in the nineteenth century, some 10 million Africans were forcibly sent to the Americas (Wolf 1982). Although the vast majority of slaves in the Americas were taken from Africa, peoples indigenous to the Americas were also systematically enslaved. For example, in the mid-eighteenth century, the Spanish colonizers of what became California rounded up native inhabitants and forced them to live and work at mission sites, growing grains, fruits, and vegetables for the consumption of the Spanish settlers (Jackson and Castillo 1995). They also raised livestock and produced textiles intended for local and regional sale. When the United States government took control of California, it disbanded the missions, but the practice of kidnapping and enslaving native children and adults continued. By the time the practice ended in 1867, more than 4,000 Indian children had been taken (Castillo 1978, 109).

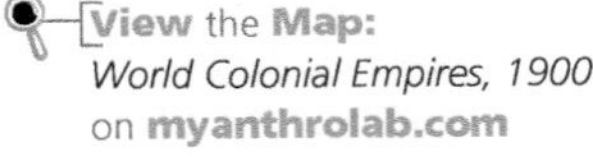
View the Map: *World Colonial Empires, 1900* on myanthrolab.com

Spanish and Portuguese settlers used forced native labor to work on plantations in Central and South America prior to the importation of slaves from Africa. Native workers also mined silver, gold, and other metals. In Australia, New Zealand, and the Pacific islands, colonial regimes forced indigenous peoples to work on plantations under European control.

Another means of controlling indigenous labor was the imposition of colonial taxes, for example, mandatory **poll taxes,** or head taxes. Because taxes had to be paid in cash, people were compelled to seek wage employment in the European-controlled economic sectors in their countries—in mines, plantations, or service and construction jobs—or they grew crops for cash, removing land from subsistence farming. Their crops thus entered national and international markets under the control and distribution of colonial powers.

Ideologies that supported these practices focused on perceived benefits to the native peoples. In the words of a member of the British Parliament, speaking in 1906, "Under all circumstances the progress of natives toward civilization is only secured when they shall be convinced of the necessity and dignity of labor; and therefore I think that everything we reasonably do to encourage the natives to work is highly desirable" (Joseph Chamberlain, quoted in Wellington 1967, 250). In 1934, another British official stated,

poll taxes
Taxes levied on households.

"As the natives were often reluctant to leave their homes, a little gentle pressure was brought to bear upon them with the introduction of a poll tax. This measure quite effectively stimulated their desire for earning the white man's money" (Eiselen 1934, 71). Comments such as these show how colonial powers were able to rationalize the economic exploitation of colonized peoples.

industrialism
The use of machines to produce products and foods.

Industrial Economies

Colonialism led to the spread of capitalism and market-based economies, which increasingly relied on the mass production of commodities. Merchants, desiring to increase their profits and to find new markets for their goods, promoted the invention of new technologies that would increase productivity. Demand for mass-produced goods also encouraged new technologies and the development of the factory system, a hallmark of **industrialism,** the use of machinery to produce goods. In Europe and the United States in the late eighteenth century, innovations in production began a process that transformed agricultural societies into industrial nations.

Industrial production began in Great Britain as an outgrowth of cottage piecework in the making of textiles and clothing. Women traditionally wove woolen cloth and made garments for their families, in keeping with a domestic division of labor between men and women in a farm household. Gradually, women began to produce surplus cloth and garments for sale to merchants, who bought up the products and sold them in regional and then national markets. Initially, women were paid to produce the cloth and garments in their homes. Eventually, cottage piecework shifted to factories, whose owners hired workers and directed their labor on site, away from homes and household duties. In some cases, entire families were hired to work in the factories. However, to fulfill domestic and child-care responsibilities, many married women dropped out of the labor force.

By 1820, manufacturing incorporated complex machinery and new sources of energy. These innovations enabled workers to create more products in the same amount of time, and machine production replaced handwork. Labor patterns shifted. The employment of children became inefficient because they could not operate heavy or complicated equipment. In addition, public disclosure of children's illnesses and injuries caused by long working hours and unsafe conditions led to demands for legal protections against the abuse of children. Consequently, men and young women remained the primary factory employees.

Workers in a silk factory in Mysore, India. Alamy Limited/Stuart Forster India/Alamy

industrial agriculture
Application of industrial technology and chemicals to farming for increased productivity.

In the United States, one of the first industries to develop was textile manufacturing. In Massachusetts mill towns, for example, young women from farm families worked to help their families buy a growing number of commodities, such as shoes, household utensils, and tools. Unmarried daughters were available for factory jobs because their labor was not as critical to agricultural production on the family farm as that of sons.

By the use of machines and powerful energy sources (coal, steam, electricity) to produce goods, industrial processes have vastly increased the efficiency and growth of commodity production. Increased production makes higher levels of consumption possible, and consumption creates demand, which, in turn, fuels more production. That is, the more goods that are produced, the greater the demand; and the greater the demand, the more goods are produced. Our attitudes about consumption are shaped by this cycle, which reflects the needs of a capitalist economy. We are given every incentive to consume and to believe that we need to consume more. In other words, demand is artificially created and maintained through an ideology that promotes the acquisition of material goods as the means of achieving pleasure and progress.

What do you think about your role as a consumer in a capitalist economy?

Industrial Agriculture

Industrial agriculture is characterized by six general features (Bartlett 1989): (1) increased use of complex technology, leading to increased replacement of human labor with machinery and increased use of fossil fuels as sources of energy in production; (2) increased role of state agencies in farm production policies; (3) a tendency toward competition among producers; (4) specialization of crop production; (5) overproduction of farm products; and (6) increased interdependence between farm units and the corporations that control machinery, sales, processing, and transport.

Mechanization has become part of nearly all agricultural processes, from planting to weeding and harvesting. Many small farmers cannot afford to invest in all of the new machinery available and, therefore, are threatened by large, corporate-run farms, or agribusinesses. Chemicals are also increasingly expensive, putting a strain on the budgets of small farmers. They pose a threat as well in the contamination of water and the destruction of ecosystems. Chemical use also harms farmworkers. A study carried out in the 1980s showed that corn farmers in Iowa and Nebraska had a 44 percent to 63 percent greater risk of leukemia than the general population (Bartlett 1989). Furthermore, agricultural chemicals are potentially harmful to anyone who consumes food treated with chemicals. The industrial conditions under which poultry and livestock are grown and slaughtered can result in outbreaks of illness from dangerous bacteria like *Salmonella* and *Escherichia coli*. The use of antibiotics in the poultry and livestock industries contributes to the emergence of immune strains of those same bacteria (ibid.).

Does your local store sell irradiated or genetically engineered foods? Do you think these foods should be labeled accordingly?

Genetic engineering and irradiation of foods have become standard, but controversial, processes. Genetic engineering modifies the genetic codes inherent in the foods to produce strains that have particular market advantages, such as more even textures or tougher skins on fruits and vegetables so that they will not be bruised in transport from fields to stores. According to the Centers for Disease Control, ionizing irradiation eliminates disease-causing bacteria and parasites. Although some people favor these processes, others fear potential danger because of the manipulation of genetic codes for foodstuffs and the introduction of possibly harmful substances.

Energy usage has increased significantly in industrial agriculture. For example, although 2.2 pounds (1 kilogram) of a breakfast cereal provides 3,600 calories of food energy, 15,675 calories are required to produce and transport that 1 kilogram (Bartlett 1989). The processes involved in growing, packaging, processing, and transporting food, in other words, expend far more energy than the food provides in calories.

Industrial production of farming has led to a decline in the number of varieties of crops. For example, by the 1990s, "... only six varieties of corn accounted for 46 percent of the crop, nine varieties of wheat made up half of the wheat crop, and two types of peas made up 96 percent of the pea crop" (Union of Concerned Scientists 2008). In addition, as an example of the influence of market forces, more than half of the land throughout the entire world that is planted with potatoes is devoted to growing only one variety of potato, the one utilized by McDonald's. The declining number of varieties of foods has a nutritional cost in narrowing the range of vitamins, minerals, and other dietary essentials available. In addition, it makes large segments of the productive system vulnerable to pests

Industrial agriculture, using complex machinery, increasingly replaces labor-intensive production techniques used by family farmers. Fotolia LLC/Sly/Fotolia

that might destroy specific crops. Increased pesticide use is then a technological response that also carries dangers to the consumers and the environment.

The U.S. government influences agricultural production by implementing tax laws that favor capital investment over labor. Tax benefits are provided for investments in farming technology and research. The government also directly subsidizes agricultural research that leads to increased mechanization, genetic engineering of plants, and other scientific processes. And government programs subsidize the production (and overproduction) of particular crops. Intense capital investment and competition have led to a sharp drop in the number of farms in the United States. Government programs also encourage the integration of plant and animal production. For example, most of the corn grown in the United States goes to feed livestock. Thus, promoting the consumption of meat also aids farmers who grow corn.

Practices involved in industrial agriculture also lead to health risks for consumers, especially due to high levels of chemicals, fertilizers, and contamination of food. Recent food recalls in the United States of eggs, tomatoes, and spinach are just some of the latest examples of the risks engendered by the drive to produce huge quantities of foods without careful oversight. Some of these contaminated foods led to hospitalizations and even deaths of consumers. And as Eric Schlosser (2008) demonstrates in *Fast Food Nation,* diets around the world have become more limited and less nutritious because of the concentration of foods grown for multinational companies.

In many parts of the world, industrial agriculture undermines the stability of subsistence farming. In Africa and Latin America, household farming for subsistence has become precarious, as owners of large plantations have succeeded in putting pressure on local farmers to sell their land. Smallholders are caught in the bind of needing cash to buy clothing, household goods, equipment, and food. As their household economies become insecure, people need to obtain cash either through employment or sale of their land. Employment is difficult to find in rural communities, so many people opt to leave their homes, temporarily or permanently, and migrate to towns and cities to find jobs. However, rampant urban growth, especially in developing regions of the world, has led to the spread of slums, deteriorating health conditions, and increasing rates of urban crime.

CULTURE CHANGE

DEFORESTATION, ENVIRONMENTAL CHANGE, AND RESOURCE SUSTAINABILITY

Throughout human history, economic activities that people have undertaken to survive have affected their environments and resources. Even foraging peoples affect the resources they use by selectively gathering or hunting different species of plants or animals in different locations at different times of the year. Farmers have more sustained techniques of environmental modification. Swidden farming utilizes slash-and-burn strategies to clear fields and enrich the soil. Intensive agriculturalists modify the land even more to extract ever-increasing yields from it. Environmental change resulting from human occupation is, therefore, nothing new. However, the scope and rapidity of change today are unprecedented and frequently negative, destroying environmental equilibrium and resources, threatening the survival of indigenous communities, and potentially leading to worldwide shortages of food and other resources. For example, Michael Williams (2003) reports that the rate of global loss of forest cover was only 1.94 percent per year between 1700 and 1849, jumping to 11.52 percent per year by 1950, and increasing again to 15.10 percent per year in 1995 (2003, 396). Until the early twentieth century, most

Clear-cutting for commercial timber results in deforestation that can have widespread environmental and economic consequences. Shutterstock/ Frontpage/Shutterstock

forest loss occurred in temperate climates, but since then, the decline in tropical regions has far outpaced temperate losses.

Many factors contribute to environmental degradation. The sheer growth in human populations puts added stress on land and resources. The intensification of industrial agriculture, turning vast amounts of acreage over to production of foods and other crops, has led to the loss both of land for subsistence farming and of animal and plant species. Oil, mineral, and timber companies are also major contributors to environmental exploitation, particularly to deforestation and water pollution.

The effects of these processes are especially evident in tropical countries that have been used for centuries as sites of resource extraction. The desire for their products has grown since the mid-twentieth century as consumer demands have broadened and deepened. Consumerism in the United States was the principal catalyst for this increase, but more recently, worldwide consumption is responsible for the exploitation of tropical resources. Richard Tucker (2007) identifies the production of sugarcane and bananas in the Caribbean, coffee in South America, rubber and timber extraction in the tropical rain forests, and cattle ranching in Latin America as the major culprits. Throughout much of the twentieth century, multinational corporations exploited tropical resources with few or no environmental safeguards. Middle-class and elite affluence accelerated during this period without concern for ecological consequences in distant lands (Tucker 2007, 218).

By the 1970s, unrestrained deforestation led to the strengthening of conservation groups, whose alarm began to reach a worldwide audience. Governments in many newly independent tropical countries also used conservation rhetoric as an argument to manage their own resources. However, postcolonial governments have often formulated policies that, although sounding protective, in fact exploit resources to the point of causing ecological damage. For example, the Indonesian government has promoted the policy of turning natural forests into forest plantations that produce specific types of trees for timber exports (Peluso 1992, 5). However, the government allows multinational corporations that have little regard for sustainability to extract these woods even though international conventions outlaw trade in woods that have not been "sustainably harvested" (Intrator 2007, 27). The land rights of indigenous peoples and their access to forest resources are routinely ignored. Indonesian government agencies that control the extraction of forest resources allot contracts to companies and receive revenue from their operations. Local residents have no say in this system (Peluso 1992, 10). In Indonesia, and in Central and South America, state forest management is often linked to national development plans that view indigenous subsistence strategies as obstacles to affluence. However, indigenous communities continue to occupy some of these forests. On the Indonesian island of Java alone, 6,000 "forest villages" are located in or adjacent to state forests (Peluso 1992, 23).

The Amazonian region has become representative of global deforestation. The Amazon basin encompasses parts of Brazil, Peru, Bolivia, Colombia, Ecuador, and Venezuela (in descending order of acreage). Deforestation in the region has multiple interrelated causes. In Brazil, colonial settlement began the destructive process along coastal forests to establish plantations for sugar, cotton, cocoa, and coffee in the 1500s (Williams 2003, 464). In the latter half of the twentieth century, peasants seeking land for farming and cattle ranching invaded the Amazon. Here, as elsewhere, rural poverty and deforestation are intertwined. Governments encouraged settlement and economic development to improve the standards of living of some of their poorest citizens.

Timber companies are also responsible for forest loss in the Amazon. Between 1970 and 1990, between 8.2 percent and 9.6 percent of the forested area there had been cut (Williams 2003, 480). Rates of clearing continue to destroy the Amazon forests with no effective safeguards. For example, in the Madre de Dios region of Amazonian Peru, stands of big-leaf mahogany are rapidly disappearing. This wood is a highly popular variety for the manufacture of furniture in particular. Approximately 80 percent of Peruvian mahogany is destined for U.S. markets (Intrator 2006, 27). By 2005, there was a loss of about 50 percent of the range of mahogany in Peru, with another 28 percent decrease predicted by 2015. Although Peruvian and international laws forbid trading in mahogany that is not sustainably harvested, little actual oversight takes place. According to the text of a cable sent in 2006 by United States embassy in Peru, and released by WikiLeaks in 2011, the U.S. ambassador estimated that about 70 to 90 percent of Peruvian mahogany exports were illegal (Dudenhoefer 2011, 30). Loggers continue to illegally enter the region, set up camps, build roads, and cut trees. In addition to the environmental destruction, their activities infringe on the territories and livelihoods of at least eleven groups of indigenous peoples who inhabit the region.

Deforestation also contributes to climate change. Loss of trees leads to declines in rainfall, causing droughts and land erosion. Forest clearing also releases carbon into the atmosphere, which increases temperatures (Williams 2003, 430–34).

In some tropical countries, indigenous resistance to state control is manifested both in acts of sabotage and in the growth of organizations to promote sustainable resource management. As a result, governments have begun to work with local communities to develop systems of "social forestry" that take into account local knowledge and needs for sustainable development. However, indigenous communities have only limited participation in planning and implementing these programs.

Opposition to central state management of resources is not simply because of opposition to development. Indeed, indigenous communities may favor development to improve their standards of living (Kirsch 2006; 2007). However, they may want guarantees that their resources, particularly the quality of the land and water, are sustained rather than degraded. For example, complex issues of development and sustainability have arisen in Papua New Guinea in communities near the Ok Tedi gold and copper mine that began operating in 1984. By the late 1980s, particulate pollution from the mine was destroying trees and gardens. By 2007, more than one billion metric tons of finely ground metal tailings had been released into the Ok Tedi River (Kirsch 2007, 305). The affected area of rain forest currently comprises more than 579 square miles and is expected to more than double (Kirsch 2007, 308). The government of Papua New Guinea supports the operation of the mine, the source of 18 percent of the country's foreign exchange revenue (Kirsch 2007, 309).

The Yonggum people, indigenous inhabitants of the region, protested against the mining company because of the harm done to their subsistence. Their goal is containment and proper disposal of mine tailings, not closure of the mine, because they favor the jobs and revenues the mine can provide. The Yonggum understand the struggle in terms of principles of reciprocity and responsibility and the dire consequences of failed relationships (Kirsch 2006, 25). For them, the rain forest is a world full of communication between themselves and the animals with which they share it. Indeed, they believe people can assume the shape and knowledge of animals (ibid.). The Yonggum's concepts of sustainability, therefore, are intertwined with social and religious practices and values.

Conflicts between state agencies and indigenous peoples also occur over traditional subsistence practices. For example, for centuries, subsistence farmers have used fire to clear fields for planting and to control invasive species. These practices are particularly effective in the African savanna, but in Zambia, for instance, the state views fire as destructive, an attitude it inherited from colonial authorities (Eriksen 2007). In tropical and savanna drylands, however, fire and other natural factors such as drought actually support and encourage the coexistence of multiple types of vegetation. By shaping their natural environment through fire, Zambians increase their subsistence base, providing land for planting, vegetation for animals, and weed control (Eriksen 2007, 23).

In some regions, reviving indigenous practices can reclaim lands that have been deforested and eroded. For example, Mixtec farmers in Oaxaca, Mexico, are slowly reclaiming their land by planting trees, building terraces of stone walls on the hillsides, and digging ditches along the slopes of the hills to capture rainwater. They are also planting corn, beans, and squash together in native fashion, a practice that improves the nutrient content of the soil and reduces insect pests. Since beginning this project, the Mixtec have tripled or quadrupled their yield (Malkin 2008).

In the Guatemala highlands, indigenous Kiche Maya people have sustained their forests by using traditional methods of control, in contrast to an estimated 75 percent loss of forest cover in the country as a whole (Camp 2008, 28). The Kiche Maya rely on their forests for growing crops in clearings and using woods to make household goods and crafts. One of their principal means of control is community and collective responsibility for the forests.

Even though most of the forested lands have been divided into small parcels owned by individual families, their use is overseen by community boards that have the authority to grant or reject permission to cut down trees or clear fields. In addition, fields are not permitted near watercourses. And when harmful insects infest the forest, rather than using toxic chemicals, several hundred people work together to crush the beetles. Village and regional boards also can fine people who violate community regulations or pollute water sources.

An important and frequently overlooked issue in environmental degradation is access to potable water. As industrial development, resource extraction, and mining move further into forests, waterways become polluted from runoff and waste products. Indigenous strategies for sustainable supplies of clean water are defenseless against these new pollutants (Lutz 2006), which threaten the health of the people and their subsistence in their own lands.

The World Summit on Sustainable Development, held in 2002, affirmed international conventions linking "environmental degradation, poverty reduction, indigenous rights, and access to education, health services and employment" (Carter 2008, 63). To make these linkages real, governments committed themselves to working with local communities when planning and implementing development schemes. Anthropologists and other social scientists can participate by carrying out research in communities affected by the environmental and economic consequences of development projects. This research can reveal how indigenous peoples see the projects and advocate for their concerns, so that local participation is meaningful and effective (Carter 2008, 64).

In many countries, indigenous peoples are working out agreements with governments to gain recognition of rights to resources and to continue and develop sustainable economies. These initiatives are especially significant in Bolivia, Peru, and Colombia, where indigenous lands are being demarcated and protected (Aylwin 2007, 14–15). Although the pace of demarcation is not always swift, the policies at least establish principles that can form the basis of meaningful negotiation and action.

Social Consequences of Capitalism and Industrialism

Listen to the Audio: *Economists Explain how to Save Capitalism* on myanthrolab.com

Social inequalities increase in capitalist economies based on industrialism. This raises the question of whose needs are satisfied by socioeconomic systems. Unlike in foraging, pastoral, or horticultural economies, the needs of some people in a capitalist economy are satisfied much more than those of others. Another question is to what extent the general affluence of capitalist economies compared to other kinds of economies gives people more leisure and security, as is commonly believed. Anthropologists have tried to answer this question. For example, in a comparison of middle-class French people and members of the Machiguenga society in Peru, Allen Johnson (1978) points out that horticulturalists like the Machiguenga spend less time in subsistence work and have more leisure time than workers in modern industrial nations. Johnson compared the ways in which French and Machiguenga people spend their time in production (of goods and services), in consumption (using consumption goods, as in eating and leisure activities), and free time (idleness, rest, and chatting). Johnson found that French men spent more time in production than any other group, while Machiguenga women spent the least time producing. Machiguenga men and French women spent about the same amount of time in production, less than French men but more than Machiguenga women. In addition, French people spent far more time in consumption than the Machiguenga, about three to five times as much, in fact. In contrast, the Machiguenga had much more leisure time than did the French.

Western consumerism has infiltrated developing countries (Dannaeuser 1989). In Latin America, Asia, and Africa, Western-style shopping malls satisfy the demands of the rising numbers of the middle class. Products with the greatest demand include home appliances, TVs, computers, and other electronic equipment.

Johnson and others have also pointed out that people's ideas about their needs and satisfactions are subjective and culturally constructed. For example, although North Americans and Europeans consume more goods and services than any other group, they often feel a shortage of time. Consumption provides pleasure and excitement, but people sometimes do not enjoy it because they feel pressed for time, needing to keep busy schedules, and cram as much as possible into a day. Time itself is treated as a commodity. In English, metaphors for time as a commodity include "spending time," "saving time," "having time for [something]" (Lakoff and Johnson 1980).

consumerism
Culture of consumption of goods and services.

Consumerism, which is the culture of consumption, has grown among all economic classes in all parts of the world. The expansion of consumer credit enables people without cash on hand to accumulate household and personal possessions that represent a lifestyle above their means. The extent of consumer debt in the United States and elsewhere reveals the power of culturally constructed demand, including the desire to display the trappings of wealth and prestige. For example, American households carry about $8,000 in credit card debt annually. According to the Federal Reserve, U.S. consumer debt in February 2011 stood at $2.4 trillion, or more than $20,000 per household, not including mortgage debt (Federal Reserve 2011). Consumer debt grew at a rate of 5.5 percent annually. The U.S. national debt is currently the highest in history and continues to increase.

By creating a perception of need, these advertisements in Vietnam contribute to overspending and debt. Corbis/Steve Raymer/Corbis

An important difference in consumer spending between the developed and developing countries is the fact that the developed countries have a strong domestic industrial base, whereas most of the developing world lacks national industries. Therefore, spending in the developing world pays primarily for imported goods, which tend to be more expensive. Developing countries often lack the capital and infrastructure to build strong domestic industries, and so become dependent on other nations for production and distribution of products to their citizens. Local economies may be undermined as a result, as rural subsistence farmers and artisans are put out of business by imported and mass-produced goods.

In a new trend, service jobs are now being exported, or outsourced, from countries like the United States to countries in the developing world, where labor costs are less. As service industries and information technologies increase, heavy industry declines, prompting some analysts to refer to Western nations as "postindustrial."

In the past 100 years, a dramatic shift has taken place in the types of work that people do. A century ago, the vast majority of people in the world worked in the agricultural sector, either owning or working on a farm. Today, only a small fraction of the population in many countries works in agriculture, as Tables 1 and 2 show.

In Table 1, "agriculture" includes all farming for commercial purposes as well as full-time subsistence farmers; "industry" refers to heavy industry; and "services" includes secretarial, sales, and information occupations. The figures show that (1) participation in farming is lowest in the wealthiest regions with the highest standards of living—developed economies and Europe; (2) conversely, participation in farming is highest in the poorest regions—Africa and Asia; (3) levels of industrial production are in an

TABLE 1 PERCENT OF POPULATION INVOLVED IN THREE ECONOMIC SECTORS, 2007

	Agriculture	Industry	Services
World	34.4	22.7	42.9
Developed economies and European Union	3.9	25.0	71.1
Central, South Europe (non-EU)	19.5	25.4	55.1
East Asia	38.6	27.0	34.4
Southeast Asia and Pacific	44.8	18.8	36.4
South Asia	48.2	21.8	30.0
Latin America and Caribbean	17.1	22.6	60.3
Middle East	17.3	24.8	57.9
North Africa	33.1	22.7	44.2
Sub-Saharan Africa	62.5	10.1	27.4

Source: International Labour Organization, Global Employment Trends, Econometric Models, December 2008.

TABLE 2 PERCENTAGE OF GROSS DOMESTIC PRODUCT (GDP) IN THREE ECONCOMIC SECTORS

Continent	Country	%GDP Agriculture	%GDP Industrial	%GDP Service	Poverty Rate
Africa	Chad	40	14	46	64
Africa	Egypt	17	32	51	23
Africa	Liberia	60	10	30	80
Africa	Rwanda	40	20	40	70
Africa	Zimbabwe	28	32	40	60
Asia	Bangladesh	30	18	52	36
Asia	India	25	24	51	35
Asia	Mongolia	36	22	42	40
Asia	Vietnam	25	35	40	47
Europe	Belgium	1	26	73	4
Europe	Poland	4	37	59	18
Europe	Romania	14	33	53	45
Europe	Ukraine	12	26	62	50
North America	Costa Rica	12	31	57	21
North America	El Salvador	12	28	60	48
North America	Haiti	32	20	48	80
North America	Mexico	5	27	68	27
North America	United States	2	18	80	13
South America	Brazil	9	29	62	17
South America	Chile	8	38	54	22
South America	Colombia	19	26	55	55
South America	Ecuador	14	36	50	50
South America	Paraguay	28	21	51	36

Source: National Council of Economic Education, 2008. www.econedlink.org. For more information, visit www.councilforeconed.org or call 1-800-338-1192.

inverse relationship with farming—where farming is high, industrial production is low, and where farming is low, industrial production is high; and (4) service employment is highest in the wealthiest regions. Table 2 indicates that countries deriving greater percentages of their gross domestic product from agriculture tend to have higher rates of poverty. Of course, government policies also influence poverty rates.

REVIEW

Native peoples across the world became enmeshed with European market economies beginning in the fifteenth century. Through colonialism and trade, the exploitation of native lands, resources, labor, and coercive practices such as poll taxes and the mission system, capitalist and industrial economies gradually came to dominate the growing present-day global economy. Industrial agriculture and manufacturing have replaced foraging, horticulturalism, and pastoralism in most regions of the world. Industrialism increases efficiency and productivity through the use of machines and automation. Increases in production lead to greater wealth, and increases in consumption and consumerism further stimulate economic growth. Over the past 100 years, service industries have replaced agriculture and industrial manufacturing as the dominant economic sector in wealthy postindustrial societies.

COMPARING SUBSISTENCE STRATEGIES

We tend to think that, because of its ability to feed so many billions of people, modern industrial agriculture is superior to all earlier subsistence strategies. However, other strategies have their advantages as well as disadvantages. Foragers do not have exclusive ownership of land and resources. Division of labor is based on age and gender, though men and women often share the same tasks. Labor specialization in foraging societies is at the household level, with individuals doing craftwork for the family. Among nomadic foragers, surpluses, when they occur, are consumed and shared with the group to reinforce social ties.

Foraging societies had the advantage of access to a complex and varied diet from resources growing wild in different ecological niches. For example, the Ju/'hoansi ate about 100 kinds of plants, fruits, and nuts in a yearly foraging cycle. Offsetting this advantage, however, was their vulnerability to malnutrition or starvation in years of severe drought or other environmental disaster. Moreover, foragers' dietary variety usually came at a price—the need to move constantly. Nomadism puts a premium on good health because it is hard for the frail, sick, and elderly to relocate frequently. It also puts a burden on pregnant women and parents with young children. The need for mobility also prevents the accumulation of surpluses of clothing, shelter, and tools and utensils.

The physical activity required by a nomadic lifestyle has health benefits of its own. The kinds of infectious diseases that plague people living in close quarters in settled communities were rare or absent among nomadic peoples. As they moved, they left behind their garbage and bodily waste—another source of disease. The small community size characteristic of foraging societies had the advantage of minimizing pressure on resources and reducing interpersonal tensions. The need to limit household size, however, may have been a burden because of the need for aggressive birth control.

Pastoralists put more stake in the idea of land and animal ownership. Grazing land may be owned by a collective (a family or group), with individuals owning or having rights to the animals. Wealth and prestige are counted by the size of one's herd, so marked social differences may develop. Division of labor is variable, but everyone's work addresses the care and herding of the animals and secondary production using animal products.

In horticultural societies, families or kin groups own and allocate land. Men clear fields, cut trees, and burn brush. The division of labor for other subsistence tasks varies from society to society. Part-time artisans are paid in goods or food. Horticultural surpluses are stored against famines and disasters and are redistributed to those in need.

Horticulture solves some of the problems of foraging. Farming provides people with a stable source of food. Rather than relying on the fluctuating bounty of nature, people grow their own crops. The security of horticulturalists is not absolute, however, because drought, insect infestation, flooding, or other natural disasters may wipe out a season's produce. For these reasons, horticulturists try to obtain surpluses to rely on in bad years. Pastoralists solve the uncertain success of hunting by maintaining their own herds of animals. In contrast, hunters and fishers may or may not find the game they seek. However, pastoralists must invest more labor and resources in maintaining their herds than foragers do in hunting.

In most agricultural societies, individuals own and control land. Surpluses are more common and may be hoarded or used to pay tribute or taxes to state governments, which redistribute surpluses to those in need. Surpluses also support full-time specialists, who do nonagricultural work in arts, crafts, occupations, and professions.

Intensive agriculturists solve many of the problems engendered by other subsistence strategies, but they also create additional difficulties. They solve the problems of nomadism by establishing sedentary communities, but settled life also has problems. Sedentary farmers usually have a much less varied diet than foragers or people who utilize a mixed horticultural and foraging strategy. The more limited variety of crops and foods potentially leads to the kinds of diseases that result from the lack of certain nutrients. Sedentary communities are also more vulnerable to epidemic diseases. With many people confined to one place, their communities are subject to festering tensions or open conflicts between groups and individuals. Agriculturists do, however, have a striking advantage in that they are able to use increasing numbers of people to produce larger surpluses and, therefore, they have access to a secure supply of food except in times of natural catastrophe. This often comes at the cost of backbreaking labor, however. Agriculturists work harder and longer than do horticulturists, pastoralists, or foragers.

ANTHROPOLOGY APPLIED

Economic Anthropologists and Consumer Behavior

Methods of cultural anthropology include ethnographic observation, interviews, and recording qualitative (as well as quantitative) information about human behavior. Anthropologists are also trained in cross-cultural research. For these reasons, companies hire anthropologists to do consumer research, especially to reveal the cultural and social patterns that shape consumer behavior.

People's cultural identities, beliefs, and values, as well as their environmental influences, shape their economic behavior. Anthropologists can see through the "other's" eyes to find insights that companies can use to increase their sales. Anthropologists also analyze brands, conduct focus groups, and write employee and customer ethnographies.

For example, economic anthropologists might help a company test a new product, enter a new market by appealing to an ethnic group or other demographic, decide on the right interface for selling products online, analyze a wedding registry for consumer preferences, observe shoppers in a new setting, gather information on customer satisfaction or loyalty, predict trends in technologies for the home, or identify how people make shopping decisions, such as whether to buy organic produce (http://www.ethno-insight.com/). Anthropologists also do market research for pharmaceutical firms, professional sports teams, and companies like Pizza Hut and Coca-Cola (http://www.ethnographic-solutions.com/).

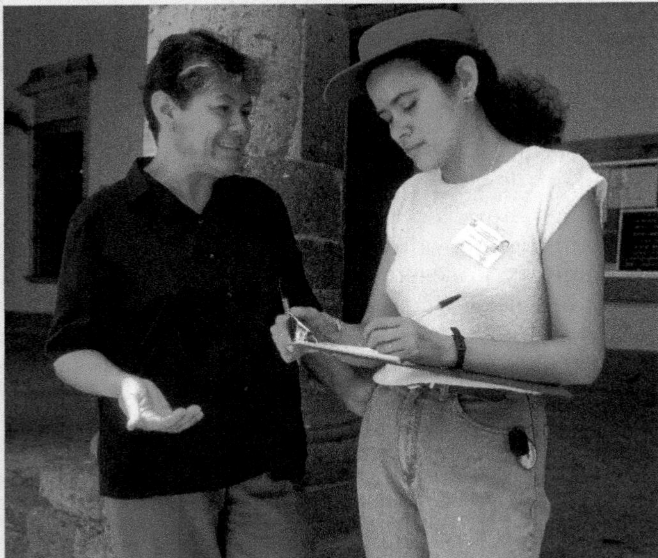
Newscom/JACQUELINE CASTELLON Notimex/Newscom

Alamy Limited/Robert Fried/Alamy

Anthropologists who work for corporations are also concerned with the cultural, material, and health and safety impacts that products and services have on consumers, company employees, and communities. In addition, they analyze the sustainability of economic growth and development in relation to people's physical, social, and cultural environments.

CRITICAL THINKING QUESTION

In applied anthropology, what might be some concerns in balancing the goals of corporations with anthropological perspectives?

The relaxation of population-control mechanisms in some agricultural societies results in rapid population growth and problems of overpopulation. As a consequence, more labor is available, but more labor is also required to feed larger populations. This process leads to greater burdens on the land and creates needs for more land for farming and living space. In addition, numerous pregnancies and births create burdens on mothers' health and increase the risks of maternal death.

Industrial agriculture solves some problems of supply. Through industrial techniques, farm output has increased enormously. There is now the ability to feed everyone in every country, but many people continue to go hungry and to die of malnutrition because of the uneven distribution of food. The complex reasons are partly economic and partly political. But industrial agriculture has also created unforeseen problems in its overreliance on harmful chemicals in food growing and processing.

Modes of subsistence can be compared and contrasted in terms of how they affect the quality of human life in relation to security, food supply, diet, living space, living conditions, labor burdens, health risks, and life expectancies.

Study and Review on myanthrolab.com

CHAPTER SUMMARY

Analyzing Economic Systems

- Economic systems include strategies for allocating land, resources, and labor. People everywhere need to produce, distribute, and consume foods and other goods. They obtain their resources from their land through various modes of production. Different cultures allocate land and resources in different ways.
- Societies need to allocate the labor of their members to productive tasks. Work roles are often assigned to people on the basis of age and gender. How gender affects work roles varies in different cultures.
- Economic exchanges occur among family members, friends, traders, and other members of communities. Exchanges between family members or other familiars are usually of the type called generalized reciprocity, where no immediate return is expected, whereas exchanges between other members of communities are called balanced reciprocity, where there is usually a mutual exchange of goods. Exchanges between strangers, especially in the marketplace, are characterized by negative reciprocity, where all parties try to receive more value than they give.
- Systems of exchange also include redistributive networks, barter, trade, and market transactions.

Market Economies and Capitalism

- Market economies are based on the buying and selling of commodities of fixed value, depending on supply and demand and using standardized mediums of exchange.
- Capitalist economic production is based on the desire by owners of the means of production to increase their profit. In capitalist production, workers must sell their labor for a wage to owners of institutions that produce goods and services. Workers produce "surplus value": The value of the goods they produce by their labor is greater than the wage paid to them. This surplus value becomes profit for the owners. Capitalist economic systems are geared toward an ever-increasing rate of profit. Unlike traditional indigenous subsistence economies, capitalist production is inherently unstable.

Impacts of Colonial Expansion, Industrialism, and Globalization

- In the fifteenth century, European powers began a process of economic and colonial expansion aimed at expropriating resources and labor from indigenous lands and peoples. In this process of globalization, which was not confined to Europeans, resources and trade items were incorporated into a worldwide economic system that led to the growth and concentration of wealth in Europe. This wealth and desire for even greater profits motivated the development of industrialization.
- In complex agrarian and industrial societies, systems of distribution have developed to circulate foods and other goods from direct producers to those who do not produce food. Members of elite classes in particular benefit from the distribution of goods. Some segments of society are not able to control at least some of the products of their labor.
- Postindustrial societies increasingly rely on consumerism and the provision of information and services to the global economy rather than goods.

Comparing Subsistence Strategies

- In most foraging societies, all members of the community generally have access to land and resources. In pastoral societies, individuals or families control or own land and especially animals. In horticultural and agricultural societies, individuals or family groups own land. Intensive farming increases the need to retain permanent and individual control of land.
- In foraging, pastoral, and horticultural societies, most people, given characteristics of gender and age, perform similar subsistence work. However, in complex agricultural and industrial societies, economic life is characterized by labor specialization. In the past century, the percentage of people engaged in producing food has declined everywhere.

REVIEW QUESTIONS

1. What social behaviors are part of any society's economic system? How do anthropologists view economic systems?
2. How do systems of exchange relate to modes of subsistence?
3. What are the different types of reciprocity? Why is balanced reciprocity seen in foraging groups? How is the potlatch an example of negative reciprocity?
4. How do foragers, pastoralists, horticulturalists, and agriculturalists allocate land and labor?
5. How are economic concepts, such as ownership, integrated with other cultural systems, such as kinship, social status, political power, and ideology?
6. What is a market economy? How does capitalism affect production, distribution, and consumption?
7. Which changes in economic systems lead to social inequality?
8. How were indigenous peoples brought into European economies? How did colonialism affect those peoples and their economies?
9. Why do capitalist economies depend on ever-increasing consumerism?

MyAnthroLab Connections

Watch. Listen. View. Explore. Read. MyAnthroLab is designed just for you. Dynamic visual activities, videos, and readings found in the multimedia library will enhance your learning experience.

Resources from this chapter:

Watch on **myanthrolab.com**
- *Specialization*

Listen on **myanthrolab.com**
- *Economists Explain How to Save Capitalism*

View on **myanthrolab.com**
- *World Colonial Empires, 1900*

Explore on **myanthrolab.com** In MySearchLab, enter the Anthropology database to find relevant and recent scholarly and popular press publications. For this chapter, enter the following keywords: subsistence strategies, colonialism, reciprocity

Read the **Document**
- *Variation in Economy* by Richard E. Blanton
- *Miskito: Adaptations to Colonial Empires* by Mary W. Helms

Life without Chiefs

From Chapter 26 of *Conformity and Conflict: Readings in Cultural Anthropology.* Fourteenth Edition. James Spradley, David W. McCurdy.

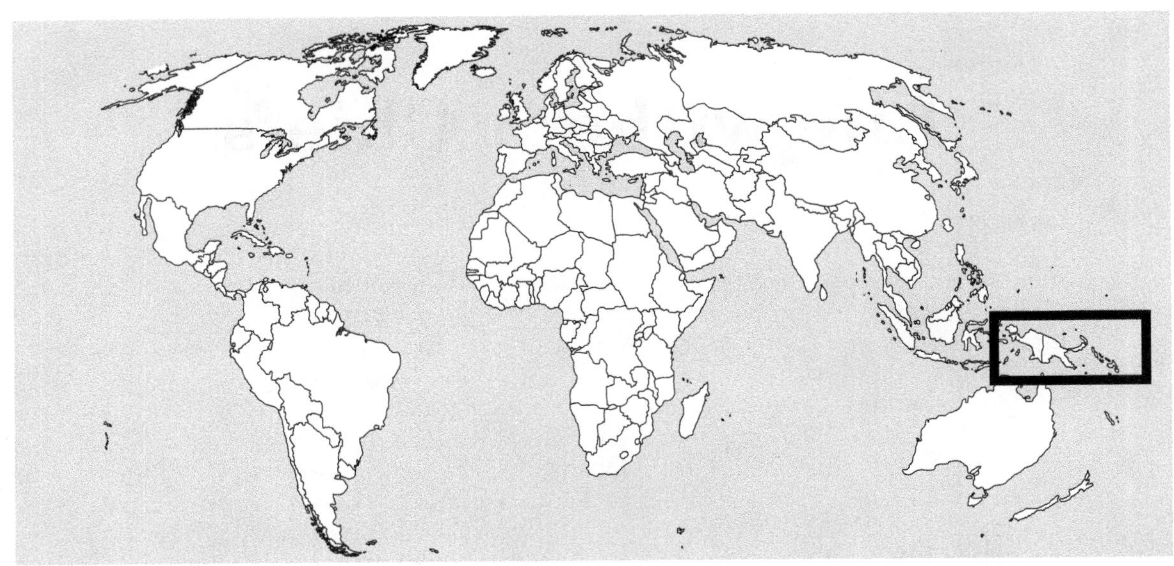

Life without Chiefs

Marvin Harris

*It may come as a surprise to most Americans, but there were, and in a few cases still are, societies in the world that lack formal political structure. Instead of presidents, mayors, senators, and directors of homeland security, there are headmen, big men, and chiefs who lead by their ability to persuade and impress without the authority to make people act. In this article, Marvin Harris traces the evolution of political leadership, associating headmen with small hunting and gathering societies marked by reciprocal exchange, and big men with slightly larger horticultural societies that employ redistributive exchange. Chiefs also occupied the center of redistribution systems but their societies were larger and chiefs could inherit their positions. He concludes that human biological inheritance was shaped by a hunter-gatherer existence; there is nothing inherited about the political formalism and social inequality that characterize large state societies.**

Listen to the **Chapter Audio** on **myanthrolab.com**

Can humans exist without some people ruling and others being ruled? To look at the modern world, you wouldn't think so. Democratic states may have done away with emperors and kings, but they have hardly dispensed with gross inequalities in wealth, rank, and power.

However, humanity hasn't always lived this way. For about 98 percent of our existence as a species (and for four million years before then), our ancestors lived in small, largely nomadic hunting-and-gathering bands containing about 30 to 50 people apiece. It was in this social context that human nature evolved. It has been only about ten thousand years since people began to settle down into villages, some of which eventually grew into cities. And it has been only in the last two thousand years that the majority of people in the world have not lived in hunting-and-gathering societies. This brief period of time is not nearly sufficient for noticeable evolution to have taken place. Thus, the few remaining foraging societies are the closest analogues we have to the "natural" state of humanity.

To judge from surviving examples of hunting-and-gathering bands and villages, our kind got along quite well for the greater part of prehistory without so much as a paramount chief. In fact, for tens of thousands of years, life went on without kings, queens, prime ministers, presidents, parliaments, congresses, cabinets, governors, and mayors—not to mention the police officers, sheriffs, marshals, generals, lawyers, bailiffs, judges, district attorneys, court clerks, patrol cars, paddy wagons, jails, and penitentiaries that help keep them in power. How in the world did our ancestors ever manage to leave home without them?

Small populations provide part of the answer. With 50 people per band or 150 per village, everybody knew everybody else intimately. People gave with the expectation of taking and took with the expectation of giving. Because chance played a great role in the capture of animals, collection of wild foodstuffs, and success of rudimentary forms of agriculture, the individuals who had the luck of the catch on one day needed a handout on the next. So the best way for them to provide for their inevitable rainy day was to be generous. As expressed by anthropologist Richard Gould, "The greater the amount of risk, the greater the extent of sharing." Reciprocity is a small society's bank.

In reciprocal exchange, people do not specify how much or exactly what they expect to get back or when they expect to get it. That would besmirch the quality of that transaction and make it similar to mere barter or to buying and selling. The distinction lingers on in societies dominated by other forms of exchange, even capitalist ones. For we do carry out a give-and-take among close kin and friends that is informal, uncalculating, and imbued with a spirit of generosity. Teenagers do not pay cash for their meals at home or for the use of the family car, wives do not bill their husbands for cooking a meal, and friends give each other birthday gifts and Christmas presents. But much of this is marred by the expectation that our generosity will be acknowledged with expression of thanks.

Where reciprocity really prevails in daily life, etiquette requires that generosity be taken for granted. As Robert Dentan discovered during his fieldwork among the Semai of Central Malaysia, no one ever says "thank you" for the meat received from another hunter. Having struggled all day to lug the carcass of a pig home through the jungle heat, the hunter allows his prize to be cut up into exactly equal portions, which he then gives away to the entire group. Dentan explains that to express gratitude for the portion received indicates that you are the kind of ungenerous person who calculates how much you give and take: "In this context, saying 'thank you' is very rude, for it suggests, first, that one has calculated the amount of a gift and, second, that one did not expect the donor to be so generous." To call attention to one's generosity is to indicate that others are in debt to you and that you expect them to repay you. It is repugnant to egalitarian peoples even to suggest that they have been treated generously.

Canadian anthropologist Richard Lee tells how, through a revealing incident, he learned about this aspect of reciprocity. To please the !Kung, the "bushmen" of the Kalahari desert, he decided to buy a large ox and have it slaughtered as a present. After days of searching Bantu agricultural villages for the largest and fattest ox in the region, he acquired what appeared to be a perfect specimen. But his friends took him aside and assured him that he had been duped into buying an absolutely worthless animal. "Of course, we will eat it," they said, "but it won't fill us up—we will eat and go home to bed with stomachs rumbling." Yet, when Lee's ox was slaughtered, it turned out to be covered with a thick layer of fat. Later, his friends explained why they had said his gift was valueless, even though they knew better than he what lay under the animal's skin.

"Yes, when a young man kills much meat he comes to think of himself as a chief or a big man, and he thinks of the rest of us as his servants or inferiors. We can't accept this. We refuse one who boasts, for someday his pride will make him kill somebody. So we always speak of his meat as worthless. This way we cool his heart and make him gentle."

Lee watched small groups of men and women returning home every evening with the animals and wild fruits and plants that they had killed or collected. They shared everything equally, even with campmates who had stayed behind and spent the day sleeping or taking care of their tools and weapons.

"Not only do families pool that day's production, but the entire camp—residents and visitors alike—shares equally in the total quantity of food available," Lee observed. "The evening meal of any one family is made up of portions of food from each of the other families resident. There is a constant flow of nuts, berries, roots, and melons from one family fire-place to another, until each person has received an equitable portion. The following morning a different combination of foragers moves out of camp, and when they return late in the day, the distribution of foodstuffs is repeated."

In small, prestate societies, it was in everybody's best interest to maintain each other's freedom of access to the natural habitat. Suppose a !Kung with a lust for power were to get up and tell his campmates, "From now on, all this land and everything on it belongs to me. I'll let you use it but only with my permission and on the condition that I get first choice of anything you capture, collect, or grow." His campmates, thinking that he had certainly gone crazy, would pack up their few belongings, take a long walk, make a new camp, and resume their usual life of egalitarian reciprocity. The man who would be king would be left by himself to exercise a useless sovereignty.

The Headman: Leadership, Not Power

To the extent that political leadership exists at all among band-and-village societies, it is exercised by individuals called headmen. These headmen, however, lack the power to compel others to obey their orders. How can a leader be powerless and still lead?

The political power of genuine rulers depends on their ability to expel or exterminate disobedient individuals and groups. When a headman gives a command, however, he has no certain physical means of punishing those who disobey. So, if he wants to stay in "office," he gives few commands. Among the Eskimo, for instance, a group will follow an outstanding hunter and defer to his opinion with respect to choice of hunting spots. But in all other matters, the leader's opinion carries no more weight than any other man's. Similarly, among the !Kung, each band has its recognized leaders, most of whom are males. These men speak out more than others and are listened to with a bit more deference. But they have no formal authority and can only persuade, never command. When Lee asked the !Kung whether they had headmen—meaning powerful chiefs—they told him, "Of course we have headmen! In fact, we are all headmen. Each one of us is headman over himself."

Headmanship can be a frustrating and irksome job. Among Indian groups such as the Mehinacu of Brazil's Zingu National Park, headmen behave something like zealous scoutmasters on overnight cookouts. The first one up in the morning, the headman tries to rouse his companions by standing in the middle of the village plaza and shouting to them. If something needs to be done, it is the headman who starts doing it, and it is the headman who works harder than anyone else. He sets an example not only for hard work but also for generosity: After a fishing or hunting expedition, he gives away more of his catch than anyone else does. In trading with other groups, he must be careful not to keep the best items for himself.

In the evening, the headman stands in the center of the plaza and exhorts his people to be good. He calls upon them to control their sexual appetites, work hard in their gardens, and take frequent baths in the river. He tells them not to sleep during the day or bear grudges against each other.

Coping with Freeloaders

During the reign of reciprocal exchange and egalitarian headmen, no individual, family, or group smaller than the band or village itself could control access to natural resources. Rivers, lakes, beaches, oceans, plants and animals, the soil and subsoil were all communal property.

Among the !Kung, a core of people born in a particular territory say that they "own" the water holes and hunting rights, but this has no effect on the people who happen to be visiting and living with them at any given time. Since !Kung from neighboring bands are related through marriage, they often visit each other for months at a time and have free use of whatever resources they need without having to ask permission. Though people from distant bands must make a request to use another band's territory, the "owners" seldom refuse them.

The absence of private possession in land and other vital resources means that a form of communism probably existed among prehistoric hunting and collecting bands and small villages. Perhaps I should emphasize that this did not rule out the existence of private property. People in simple band-and-village societies own personal effects such as weapons, clothing, containers, ornaments, and tools. But why should anyone want to steal such objects? People who have a bush camp and move about a lot have no use for extra possessions. And since the group is small enough that everybody knows everybody else, stolen items cannot be used anonymously. If you want something, better to ask for it openly, since by the rules of reciprocity such requests cannot be denied.

I don't want to create the impression that life within egalitarian band-and-village societies unfolded entirely without disputes over possessions. As in every social group, nonconformists and malcontents tried to use the system for their own advantage. Inevitably there were freeloaders, individuals who consistently took more than they gave and lay back in their hammocks while others did the work. Despite the absence of a criminal justice system, such behavior eventually was punished. A widespread belief among band-and-village peoples attributes death and misfortune to the malevolent conspiracy of sorcerers. The task of identifying these evildoers falls to a group's shamans, who remain responsive to public opinion during their divinatory trances. Well-liked individuals who enjoy strong support from their families need not fear the shaman. But quarrelsome, stingy people who do not give as well as take had better watch out.

From Headman to Big Man

Reciprocity was not the only form of exchange practiced by egalitarian band-and-village peoples. Our kind long ago found other ways to give and take. Among them the form of exchange known as redistribution played a crucial role in creating distinctions of rank during the evolution of chiefdoms and states.

Redistribution occurs when people turn over food and other valuables to a prestigious figure such as a headman, to be pooled, divided into separate portions, and given out again. The primordial form of redistribution was probably keyed to seasonal hunts and harvests, when more food than usual became available.

True to their calling, headmen-redistributors not only work harder than their followers but also give more generously and reserve smaller and less desirable portions for themselves than for anyone else. Initially, therefore, redistribution strictly reinforced the political and economic equality associated with reciprocal exchange. The redistributors were compensated purely with admiration and in proportion to their success in giving bigger feasts, in personally contributing more than anybody else, and in asking little or nothing for their effort, all of which initially seemed an innocent extension of the basic principle of reciprocity.

But how little our ancestors understood what they were getting themselves into! For if it is a good thing to have a headman give feasts, why not have several headmen give feasts? Or, better yet, why not let success in organizing and giving feasts be the measure of one's legitimacy as a headman? Soon, where conditions permit, there are several would-be headmen vying with each other to hold the most lavish feasts and redistribute the most food and other valuables. In this fashion there evolved the nemesis that Richard Lee's !Kung informants had warned about: the youth who wants to be a "big man."

A classic anthropological study of big men was carried out by Douglas Oliver among the Siuai, a village people who live on the South Pacific island of Bougainville, in the Solomon Islands. In the Siuai language, big men were known as *mumis.* Every Siuai boy's highest ambition was to become a *mumi.* He began by getting married, working hard, and restricting his own consumption of meats and coconuts. His wife and parents, impressed with the seriousness of his intentions, vowed to help him prepare for his first feast. Soon his circle of supporters widened and he began to construct a clubhouse in which his male followers could lounge about and guests could be entertained and fed. He gave a feast at the consecration of the clubhouse; if this was a success, the circle of people willing to work for him grew larger still, and he began to hear himself spoken of as a mumi. Larger and larger feasts meant that the mumi's demands on his supporters became more irksome. Although they grumbled about how hard they had to work, they remained loyal as long as their mumi continued to maintain and increase his renown as a "great provider."

Finally the time came for the new mumi to challenge the older ones. He did this at a *muminai* feast, where both sides kept a tally of all the pigs, coconut pies, and sago-almond puddings given away by the host mumi and his followers to the guest mumi and his followers. If the guests could not reciprocate with a feast as lavish as that of the challengers, their mumi suffered a great social humiliation, and his fall from mumihood was immediate.

At the end of a successful feast, the greatest of mumis still faced a lifetime of personal toil and dependence on the moods and inclinations of his followers. Mumihood did not confer the power to coerce others into doing one's bidding, nor did it elevate one's standard of living above anyone else's. In fact, because giving things away was the essence of mumihood, great mumis consumed less meat and other delicacies than ordinary men. Among the Kaoka, another Solomon Islands group, there is the saying, "The giver of the feast takes the bones and the stale cakes; the meat and the fat go to the others." At one great feast attended by 1,100 people, the host mumi, whose name was Soni, gave away thirty-two pigs and a large quantity of sago-almond puddings. Soni himself and some of his closest followers went hungry. "We shall eat Soni's renown," they said.

From Big Man to Chief

The slide (or ascent?) toward social stratification gained momentum wherever extra food produced by the inspired diligence of redistributors could be stored while awaiting muminai feasts, potlatches, and other occasions of redistribution. The more concentrated and abundant the harvest and the less perishable the crop, the greater its potential for endowing the big man with power. Though others would possess some stored-up foods of their own, the redistributor's stores would be the largest. In times of scarcity, people would come to him, expecting to be fed; in return, he could call upon those who had special skills to make cloth, pots, canoes, or a fine house for his own use. Eventually, the redistributor no longer needed to work in the fields to gain and surpass big-man status. Management of the harvest surpluses, a portion of which continued to be given to him for use in communal feasts and other communal projects (such as trading expeditions and warfare), was sufficient to validate his status. And, increasingly, people viewed this status as an office, a sacred trust, passed on from one generation to the next according to the rules of hereditary succession. His dominion was no longer a small, autonomous village but a large political community. The big man had become a chief.

Returning to the South Pacific and the Trobriand Islands, one can catch a glimpse of how these pieces of encroaching stratification fell into place. The Trobrianders had hereditary chiefs who held sway over more than a dozen villages containing several thousand people. Only chiefs could wear certain shell ornaments as the insignia of high rank, and it was forbidden for commoners to stand or sit in a position that put a chief's head at a lower elevation. British anthropologist Bronislaw Malinowski tells of seeing all the people present in the village of Bwoytalu drop from their verandas "as if blown down by a hurricane" at the sound of a drawn-out cry warning that an important chief was approaching.

Yams were the Trobrianders' staff of life; the chiefs validated their status by storing and redistributing copious quantities of them acquired through donations from their brothers-in-law at harvest time. Similar "gifts" were received by husbands who were commoners, but chiefs were polygymous and, having as many as a dozen wives, received many more yams than anyone else. Chiefs placed their yam supply on display racks specifically built for this purpose next to their houses. Commoners did the same, but a chief's yam racks towered over all the others.

This same pattern recurs, with minor variations, on several continents. Striking parallels were seen, for example, twelve thousand miles away from the Trobrianders, among chiefdoms that flourished throughout the southeastern region of the United States—specifically among the Cherokee, former inhabitants of Tennessee, as described by the eighteenth-century naturalist William Bartram.

At the center of the principal Cherokee settlements stood a large circular house where a council of chiefs discussed issues involving their villages and where redistributive feasts were held. The council of chiefs had a paramount who was the principal figure in the Cherokee redistributive network. At the harvest time a large crib, identified as the "chief's granary," was erected in each field. "To this," explained Bartram, "each family carries and deposits a certain quantity according to his ability or inclination, or none at all if he so chooses." The chief's granaries functioned as a public treasury in case of crop failure, a source of food for strangers or travelers, and as military store. Although every citizen enjoyed free access to the store, commoners had to acknowledge that it really belonged to the supreme chief, who had "an exclusive right and ability . . . to distribute comfort and blessings to the necessitous."

Supported by voluntary donations, chiefs could now enjoy lifestyles that set them increasingly apart from their followers. They could build bigger and finer houses for themselves, eat and dress more sumptuously, and enjoy the sexual favors and personal services of several wives. Despite these harbingers, people in chiefdoms voluntarily invested unprecedented amounts of labor on behalf of communal projects. They dug moats, threw up defensive earthen embankments, and erected great log palisades around their villages. They heaped up small mountains of rubble and soil to form platforms and mounds on top of which they built temples and big houses for their chief. Working in teams and using nothing but levers and rollers, they moved rocks weighing fifty tons or more and set them in precise lines and perfect circles, forming sacred precincts for communal rituals marking the change of seasons.

If this seems remarkable, remember that donated labor created the megalithic alignments of Stonehenge and Carnac, put up the great statues on Easter Island, shaped the huge stone heads of the Olmec in Vera Cruz, dotted Polynesia with ritual precincts set on great stone platforms, and filled the Ohio, Tennessee, and Mississippi valleys with hundreds of large mounds. Not until it was too late did people realize that their beautiful chiefs were about to keep the meat and fat for themselves while giving nothing but bones and stale cakes to their followers.

In the End

As we know, chiefdoms would eventually evolve into states, states into empires. From peaceful origins, humans created and mounted a wild beast that ate continents. Now that beast has taken us to the brink of global annihilation.

Will nature's experiment with mind and culture end in nuclear war? No one knows the answer. But I believe it is essential that we understand our past before we can create the best possible future. Once we are clear about the roots of human nature, for example, we can refute, once and for all, the notion that it is a biological imperative for our kind to form hierarchical groups. An observer viewing human life shortly after cultural takeoff would easily have concluded that our species was destined to be irredeemably egalitarian except for distinctions of sex and age. That someday the world would be divided into aristocrats and commoners, masters and slaves, billionaires and homeless beggars would have seemed wholly contrary to human nature as evidenced in the affairs of every human society then on Earth.

Of course, we can no more reverse the course of thousands of years of cultural evolution than our egalitarian ancestors could have designed and built the space shuttle. Yet, in striving for the preservation of mind and culture on Earth, it is vital that we recognize the significance of cultural takeoff and the great difference between biological and cultural evolution. We must rid ourselves of the notion that we are an innately aggressive species for whom war is inevitable. We must reject as unscientific claims that there are superior and inferior races and that the hierarchical divisions within and between societies are the consequences of natural selection rather than of a long process of cultural evolution. We must struggle to gain control over cultural selection through objective studies of the human condition and the recurrent process of history. Not only a more just society, but our very survival as a species may depend on it.

Review Questions

1. What is the difference among headmen, big men, and chiefs according to Harris?
2. What does Harris see as the connection between forms of leadership and modes of economic exchange? How does this connection work?
3. Harris makes a distinction between biological evolution and cultural evolution. What is the distinction and how does he apply it to types of leadership?

Political Systems

PREVIEW

- What do political anthropologists study?
- What are the five main types of political organization in human societies? How are they different?
- Why and how do political systems change?
- What are the origins and characteristics of states?

The Bear Hunt drawing by 'Making Medicine' a Cheyenne North American Plains Indian prisoner at Fort Marion Florida August 1875. *World History Archive/Alamy*

Listen to the Chapter Audio on myanthrolab.com

Read on myanthrolab.com

Long ago, a girl named Short Woman lived with her parents and her brother on the plains at a distance from a large Cheyenne camp. One day the father, named Bull Looks Back, killed his wife and deserted his two young children. The children wandered about for a time trying to find the main camp to seek shelter and food. Finally, they came upon the camp and entered a lodge. There they were told that they were the children of Bull Looks Back, who was then also in the camp. When the father heard that his children had arrived, he said aloud: "Those monstrous children of mine killed their own mother and ate her flesh. That is why I left them. They should be staked to the ground and abandoned."

And so the people did as he said. The girl and boy were bound by leather ropes and left to die on the plains. But a dog approached at nightfall and chewed on the straps binding the girl. When she got free, she untied her brother and both ran swiftly away. They were met by a stranger who told them that the girl had a power to kill buffalo by looking at them. At first she did not believe the stranger's words, but when a large herd of buffalo appeared, she looked up and they all fell dead.

After she butchered the animals, the girl told a crow to carry some meat to the Cheyenne camp where she and her brother had been abandoned. She said to the crow: "Tell those people the meat is from the children they left on the plains to die." The people then understood that the children were alive and that the girl had special powers.

Then the girl sent for the people to come to her. She told them, "We are going to make chiefs. You know I have been accused of killing my mother. That is not true. Now, we shall make chiefs, and hereafter we shall have a rule that if anyone kills a fellow tribesmember they shall be ordered away from one to five years, whatever the people shall decide."

The girl chose the first chiefs. She told them, "You will swear that you will be honest and care for all the tribe."

The girl told the chiefs how they should act and gave them a pipe of peace to smoke. She taught them songs and prayers to guide and protect them. Then she said, "My brother and I will leave this earth. We may go up into the heavens. Yet I shall always be working for the people. I may be a star."

In this narrative, the Cheyenne of the American Plains tell the story of the founding of their system of tribal governance. It tells of the creation of the Council of 44, chosen from the ten Cheyenne bands (Hoebel 1978). Members served ten-year terms. They met only during the summer, when the Cheyenne nation gathered for communal buffalo hunts. Council members settled internal disputes and organized the hunts. The members of the council were selected because they were men of judgment and good character. The story also relates that wrongdoers were banished from their communities, a punishment that might have severe consequences because other bands would be reluctant to take in strangers or people suspected of antisocial behavior. Systems of leadership and decision making are mechanisms that help unify and integrate community members into a cohesive society.

POLITICAL ANTHROPOLOGY

In every society—indeed, in every social group—actions need to be planned, decisions need to be made, and procedures for organizing group activities need to be drawn up. Societies differ in the ways in which people organize their interactions and integrate themselves into a cohesive community. In every society and in every social group, different people have different roles to play. Some people have more influence than others when group decisions have to be made and assume leadership responsibilities when actions have to be undertaken. These features of society are some of the components of each group's **political organization.** Political systems include procedures for making decisions, organizing group actions, choosing leaders, and settling disputes both within the group and with other groups. All societies have some form of political organization, but not all have formal governments familiar to people living in modern states.

Political anthropology studies these cultural dynamics. Political anthropologists focus on the mechanisms people use to solve the basic problems that confront them as a group. Although every person has individual interests and needs, social groups are formed on principles of cohesion, sharing, and reciprocity. People know that no matter what their individual inclinations, they need to adjust their actions in ways that enable their group to survive and thrive. Political anthropologists are concerned with understanding these mechanisms and with analyzing how they develop and are implemented. They are interested in understanding differences in the degree of influence, authority, or power that leaders may wield in different types of society. Of course, not everyone in any community agrees with group goals or conforms to group wishes. So political anthropologists also study the ways that community decisions are reached and conflicts are resolved. In this chapter, we examine questions of community organization and leadership.

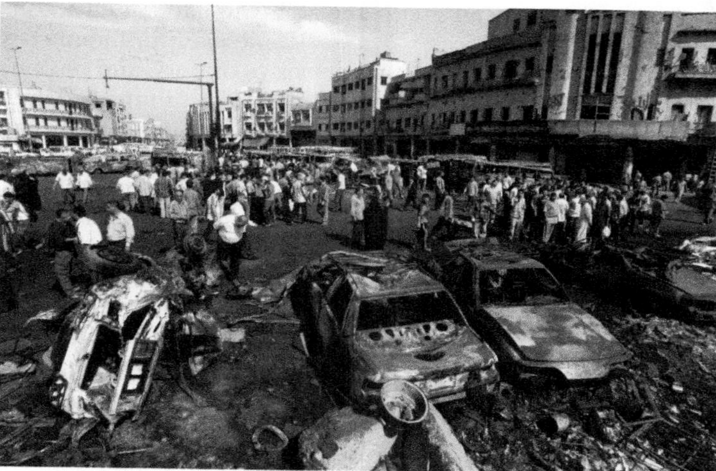

Political disputes may erupt in violence when negotiations fail to resolve underlying conflicts. Car bombs, such as this one on April 18, 2007, in Baghdad, Iraq, are deadly symptoms of such unresolved conflicts.
Corbis/Ali Abbas/epa/Corbis

Political anthropology studies political organization—the roles and processes that societies have for making decisions, mobilizing action, choosing leaders, settling disputes, and enforcing social norms.

REVIEW

TYPES OF POLITICAL ORGANIZATION

It has become commonplace in anthropological discussions of political organization to describe political systems in a four-part typology of band, tribe, chiefdom, and state. This typology, introduced by Elman Service (1962), is based on distinguishing different kinds of sociopolitical organization in terms of types of leadership, societal integration and cohesion, decision-making mechanisms, and degree of control over people. Although the typology might make too sharp distinctions among societies, it is a useful tool in discussing cultural differences. It is important to remember, though, that few societies are ideal "types"; rather, there are features within them that overlap from one set in the typology to another. It is best to think of the types as constellations of varying features rather than as overgeneralized, absolute cases. It is especially important to note that listing or discussing these types in a particular order (bands, tribes, chiefdoms, states) does not in any way imply an underlying sense of progress or evolution. No system is inherently better or worse than any other; rather, each develops its cultural practices in adaptation to its ecological setting, to its population dynamics, and to other societal norms. Each develops mechanisms that allow its members to coordinate group activities, make decisions, select leaders, and resolve conflicts.

The different sociopolitical types of societies tend to co-occur with particular kinds of subsistence activities, economic modes, settlement patterns, and kinship systems. In the discussions that follow, such linkages among political systems and economic and social features will be examined.

Before turning to this discussion, however, we should clarify distinctions among terms that may be used loosely in colloquial speech but that have particular meaning in the study of political organization. These are: influence, authority, and power. **Influence** is

political organization
The ways in which societies are organized to plan group activities, make decisions affecting members of the group, select leadership, and settle disputes both within the group and with other groups.

political anthropology
The study of the ways that communities plan group actions, make decisions affecting the group, select leadership, and resolve conflicts and disputes both within the group and with other groups.

influence
Ability to have an effect on the activities of others and on the decisions taken by others. Influence is based on an individual's personal characteristics of intelligence, skill, oratory, and charisma.

authority
Ability to affect the activities and decisions of others based not only on one's personal characteristics but also because of one's social role.

power
Ability to force other people to comply with one's wishes, follow one's advice, and accede to one's demands, based in part on the possibility of using coercive measures to gain compliance.

bands
Small, loosely organized groups of people held together by informal means.

the ability to have an effect on the activities of others and on the decisions taken by others. People exert influence based on their personal characteristics of intelligence, skill, persuasive oratory, and personal charisma. Other people voluntarily ask them for advice because of their sound judgment and their proven success. **Authority** derives from a combination of personal characteristics and social status. That is, a person has authority over the actions of others in part because of their intelligence and other personal characteristics but also because of the social role that they occupy. For example, in terms of kinship, parents generally have authority over their children, and in our society, people may have authority because of the institutional role that they occupy, as do, for example, teachers vis-à-vis students, doctors vis-à-vis patients, and so on. Finally, **power** is the ability to force other people to comply with one's wishes, follow one's advice, or accede to one's demands. Unlike influence and authority, power is coercive. That is, a person who does not comply may be punished by various means or physically forced to obey whatever rules are in effect or demands are made. In societies where power is wielded, people usually comply, though they may not do so voluntarily but rather because they want to avoid the consequences of refusal or resistance.

Bands

Bands are generally small, loosely organized groups of people. Their leaders are selected on the basis of personal qualities and skills. They lead by example and influence but lack authority to enforce their opinions on the community. Decision making is relatively informal and open to the participation of all competent members. Until a few centuries ago, band societies could be found in many parts of the world, but, by the middle of the twentieth century, the remaining band societies were located only in marginal areas of the world, such as the Arctic, the desert regions of Africa and Australia, and the dense forests of South America (see Table 1). Bands generally have (and had) relatively small populations. The smallest groups have perhaps only twenty-five to fifty people, whereas larger bands might have as many as several hundred members. Individual settlements were generally dispersed throughout a wide territory; consequently, population densities were low.

Most bands relied on foraging as their primary, if not exclusive, subsistence strategy. Consistent with foraging, bands were nomadic, utilizing various resource sites within a familiar territory. Today, some bands are seminomadic, moving their settlements between several relatively fixed locations on a yearly basis. Bands are often no more than

TABLE 1 EXAMPLES OF BAND SOCIETIES

Americas	Europe	Africa	Asia	Pacific
Netsilik of Arctic Circle	Lapp (Saami) of northern Scandinavia	Mbuti (Pygmies) of Congo Basin	Ainu of Japan	Tiwi of Australia
Inuit of eastern Canada			Chenchu of India	
Apache (historical) of western United States		Ju'/hoansi of Botswana	Semang (Negritos) of Malaysia	
Mi'kmaq of Nova Scotia			Vedda of Sri Lanka	
Ojibwe of Great Lakes region, United States and Canada				
Yahgun of Tierra del Fuego				

territorial units, occupying common territory that may be well defined or that may be only vaguely delineated in relation to other comparable groups.

Bands are held together by informal means. Families or households are the significant units of the band. Membership within one band rather than another is generally based on kinship ties, through either descent or marriage, to other people in the group. Choice of band membership may also be based on loyalty to and approval of the band's leader. But band leadership is also informal. It is based on the personal abilities of the leader, including intelligence, subsistence skills, charismatic personality traits, and in some cases spiritual knowledge. The leader contributes as much as, and in some cases more than, anyone else to the band's subsistence. He (or she, although most leaders of bands are men) lives no differently than other members of the band and receives no financial economic rewards.

The reward of leadership is prestige. Leadership also carries with it greater responsibilities because the leader is thought to be responsible for the well-being of the group. Although the band's success increases the prestige of its leader, the band's failure is similarly attributed to the leader's weakness or faults. A leader who proves unsuccessful risks losing his position. The band members will simply choose another among themselves to be the leader or will leave the settlement and relocate to another group. Band leaders, therefore, have only influence, not power. That is, they can use their oratorical skills to persuade people to remain with them and to follow their advice, but they have no means of enforcing their decisions. In fact, in many band societies, leaders who even attempt to control the actions of others would immediately disqualify themselves as leaders. Authority roles tend to be limited to the family, and even in that context, the authority of parents over adult children or of one spouse over the other is generally weak.

Other features of band societies are not necessarily components of a sociopolitical system but derive from the kind of subsistence and production generally found in bands. So, for example, the small size of settlements follows from the principle of carrying capacity—that is, the number of people that can be supported by the land and its resources. In addition, notions of private property are generally weak or absent. Land is never individually owned but is understood to be the common domain of band members. In some bands, specific resources or resource sites may be controlled by kinship groups but never by individuals. People in band societies do not accumulate significant surpluses of resources or personal possessions. These concepts about land and property derive from a foraging economic system and a nomadic or seminomadic settlement pattern. Band societies, and foraging societies generally, are usually egalitarian in their social system. Their egalitarian ethics are reflected in people's equal access to resources, equal potential access to prestige, and generally equal gender relations.

CASE STUDY

A Band Society: The Tiwi of Northern Australia

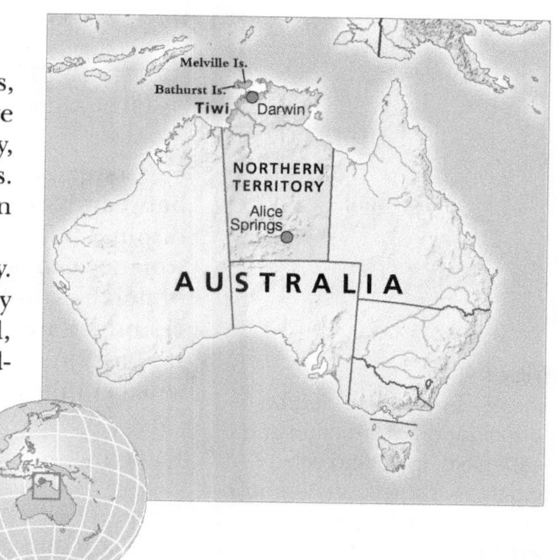

The Tiwi are indigenous foragers living on Bathurst and Melville islands, off northern Australia. Both islands have rivers, marshlands, extensive coastlines, dense forests, and abundant natural resources. Until recently, the Tiwi obtained their food by hunting, fishing, and gathering wild plants. Most of their diet was derived from the vegetable foods that the women gathered. Men did most of the hunting and fishing.

Tiwi camps consisted of a number of related families or one large family. If the camp contained more than one family unit, the groups were usually related through men. During the rainy season, November through April, people needed protection against the heavy rains. They built small dwellings made of wooden poles covered with bark. In the dry season, May through October, dwellings were made with leaf-covered branches tied together to give shade.

Households were the basic social units. Households hunted and gathered food for their group together. Households and camps were linked informally into larger units or bands of about 100 members, although people did not necessarily identify with the same band from year to year, and households within a band might disperse to exploit seasonal resources.

Band membership and residence overlapped. Every adult owned land, usually where they were born and lived. But land was not divided into individual parcels. Rather, a particular area, now referred to as a "country," was owned collectively (Goodale 1971). All of the owners of a particular country were communally responsible for its well-being, including its physical and spiritual protection. Women and men inherited landholding rights from their fathers. People could hold land through their fathers in several countries if the father had lived and was buried in a place other than his own land. Since 1976, when Tiwi were officially recognized as the legal owners of their land, the Tiwi Land Council regulates and registers the owners of countries and holds them responsible for protecting the land.

The Tiwi kinship system is based on membership in matrilineal clans. All clans are linked into four larger units, or phratries, that are exogamous—that is, a person cannot marry someone belonging to a clan in one's own phratry. Clans and kinship groups generally have informal leaders. These people, usually men, have influence in their families and communities because of their intelligence, skills, and sound judgment. Although every man in theory can aspire to high status, men with large families have advantages because of the loyalty and support of their kin.

Men enlarged their families, and, therefore, their influence, by marrying more than one wife. Prestige and leadership were thus intertwined with marriage customs. In traditional Tiwi society, all females had to be married from birth to death. Girls were betrothed immediately upon their birth, sometimes even before birth. Fathers arranged their daughters' marriages to men with whom they wished to form an alliance. The men were usually in their twenties or thirties and had shown promise by their hunting skills and personality. The actual marriage ceremony did not take place until the girl reached puberty, but the future son-in-law supplied his future in-laws with meat, rendered other aid, and acknowledged his father-in-law's influence. Fathers were also guaranteed support in their old age. Thus, fathers used their daughters to gain economic support and social prestige.

Given the age difference between a wife and her first husband, women were usually widowed one or more times. Immediate remarriage was expected. Often, a middle-aged or elderly widow would marry a much younger man who had been unable to contract a favorable marriage. An older woman's extensive kinship relations could help her young husband. Eventually, he could marry other women and form alliances with their fathers.

Tiwi women also could aspire to positions of influence and prestige in their families and communities. A woman gained prestige and authority as she aged and accumulated a large family. So men's and women's leadership intertwined. No one wielded absolute control over anyone else, however, and no one's position of authority was automatic. Rather, leadership and influence were available to all community members and could be manipulated by the most skilled and intelligent. Read the **Document** on **myanthrolab.com**

Comparatively, there is little violence in band societies. Because of the informal links between band members and the instability of group composition, people can react to disputes by leaving the band and joining another. Tensions that might otherwise erupt in violence can be relieved by the departure of a party to a dispute. Violence between bands in neighboring territories is also infrequent because there is little to fight over. Land and resources are not owned and surpluses are not amassed, so conflicts over property have no basis. As well, because bands are widely dispersed within a large territory, even personal conflicts with neighbors are unlikely to arise.

tribes
Societies with some degree of formalization of structure and leadership, including village and intervillage councils whose members regularly meet to settle disputes and plan community activities.

Tribes

Tribes differ from bands in the degree of structure and organization contributing to group cohesion and community integration. Tribal societies may have more formalized organizational procedures than those found in bands. For example, they may have highly structured councils with greater authority whose members meet and deliberate regularly. In addition to their roles as influential advisory bodies, councils may have some coercive powers in some contexts. Tribal chiefs with enforcement powers may be selected in more formal ways than the casual and informal recognition of band leaders. However, the powers of tribal chiefs and councils are limited by the underlying egalitarian social ethics prevalent in most tribal societies. Often there are structured ways to ignore or depose leaders who try to exert too much authority. Like leveling mechanisms that prevent overcentralization of wealth, structured ways to ignore or depose leaders are leveling mechanisms that prevent overcentralization of power. Examples of tribes are given in Table 2.

A number of cultural correlates tend to be associated with tribes, although subsistence patterns vary considerably. Some tribes have economies based on foraging, some on pastoralism, and still others on horticulture. Many tribal societies have mixed economies, combining resources derived from foraging, farming, and animal herding.

By 1900, Mi'kmaq families in Nova Scotia like this one had transformed many traditional practices. Nova Scotia Museum/Courtesy of the Nova Scotia Museum – Ethnology Collection

Settlement patterns and sizes vary as well. Some tribal groups are fully sedentary, remaining in stable villages for many years. Farmers are especially likely to be sedentary, locating near their fields. Some farmers, though, shift locations, alternating between two or more residences each year. Foragers and pastoralists are less likely to remain in stable settlements due to the necessity of gathering wild plants, hunting animals, or finding grazing land for their animals. Sedentary villages may consist of many hundreds of people, whereas less permanent settlements tend to be much smaller.

Watch the **Video:** *Living with the Darhad—Rechinlhumble* on **myanthrolab.com**

Regardless of size, tribal societies often have mechanisms to unite the group at certain times of the year or at regular intervals. At those times, larger concentrations of people congregate to socialize, discuss issues of common interest, trade with one another, and celebrate religious occasions through group ritual. For example, the Cheyenne communal buffalo hunts referred to in the opening narrative took place every year in the summer and brought together large groups of people to hunt, perform rituals, socialize, plan group actions, and exchange products and gifts.

TABLE 2 EXAMPLES OF TRIBAL SOCIETIES

Americas	Europe	Africa	Asia	Pacific
Penare of Venezuela	Scottish clans (historical)	Berbers of the western Sahara	Bani Khalid of Saudi Arabia	Dani of New Guinea
Kayapo and Yanomamo of Brazil	Druids of France (historical)	Kababish of northern Sudan	Munda of India	Marquesans (Polynesian island group)
Blackfeet of Montana	Celts of Eastern Europe (historical)	Samburu and Maasai of Kenya	Hmong of Southeast Asia	
Hidatsa of North Dakota		Amhara of Ethiopia	Miao of China	
Cheyenne of the Great Plains		Igbo of Nigeria		
Passamaquoddy of Maine				

associations
Sociopolitical groups that link people in a community on the basis of shared interests and skills.

age grade (age set)
A sociopolitical association of people of more or less similar age who are given specific social functions.

confederacy
A form of political organization in which tribes and bands join together under common leadership to face an external threat.

Intergroup trade is common in tribal societies. People exchange foods and specialized handcrafts with others to obtain resources not found in their own territories or not produced by their own artisans. Well-established trading networks can carry resources and other goods over many hundreds if not thousands of miles, either through long-distance trade or through local and regional exchanges.

Concepts of territoriality and private property tend to be more significant in tribal than in band societies. Farming and pastoral people delineate commonly recognized boundaries encompassing their territories. Status differentiation based on wealth occurs in some tribal cultures. However, great imbalances in wealth and standards of living do not develop because the values of generosity and hospitality counter tendencies toward accumulation. People aspiring to positions of prestige and influence must cooperate with others and generously give away whatever surpluses they may have. People are especially obligated to help and support their kin materially as well as emotionally. In tribal societies, networks of kin are the primary arena of social action and social responsibility.

Kinship relations in tribal societies are usually organized according to some unilineal principle, either patrilineal or matrilineal. However, some tribal societies reckon descent bilaterally. Where they exist, unilineal kinship groups, such as patriclans, are often corporate political bodies, controlling access to land and resources. Kinship groups may become differentiated on the basis of the amount or value of the resources they control. Some social inequality may arise as members of some kin groups have higher status than members of other groups. Although kinship is the most important factor in organizing social interactions and responsibilities, many tribal societies also develop non-kin sociopolitical **associations** that link people in a community on the basis of shared interests and skills. These associations may have social, economic, ritual, or military functions. Membership may be voluntary or it may be assigned on the basis of specific criteria. Membership may also be temporary or permanent. By drawing members from diverse kinship groups, associations integrate or ally people on a basis other than kinship and descent. Modern state societies also have such associations, such as political clubs, religious groups, and hobby groups.

Some tribal societies have a system of age grades or age sets, associations of people of a similar age. An **age grade** (or **age set**) is an assigned sociopolitical association—a grouping of people of more or less similar ages who are given specific social functions. Members of the same age grade consider themselves to have a kin-like relationship. They are expected to aid one another in times of need, to share resources when necessary, and to give one another emotional support. When disputes arise between members of different age grades, the members of each are expected to rally behind their own. Although their functions are very different, modern state societies also have age groups, as in school categories, for example, freshmen, seniors, or the Class of 2013.

Confederacies

In some tribal societies, formal systems of leadership and decision making may develop that link separate tribes into political systems aimed at coordinating activities and arriving at decisions that affect all members. People may choose leaders and then set and follow procedures for decision making. In such societies, intertribal unity is an important goal and an important factor in the people's survival. A well-organized political apparatus may develop in response to perceived external threats. A form of political organization in which tribes and bands join together under common leadership to face an external threat is referred to as a **confederacy.** A prime example is the Iroquois, a group of five distinct but closely related indigenous nations living in what is now New York State, Vermont, and the Canadian provinces of Québec and Ontario. The Iroquois developed a highly structured confederacy that created internal unity and protection from external threats.

The five nations that came to be known as the Iroquois (Mohawk, Oneida, Onondaga, Cayuga, and Seneca) came together in a league or confederacy to preserve peace among members and to act as a unified body in dealing with other nations, either in peace or war. On the whole, these goals were achieved, although internal conflicts were not unknown. The founding of the Iroquois Confederacy predated the arrival of Europeans in North America. Although some historians and anthropologists assume a fourteenth- or fifteenth-century origin, Iroquois datekeepers contend that the confederacy began much earlier. Using the arguments of the datekeepers, archaeological data, astronomical data of the eclipses, and historical sources, researchers have dated the League's origin to 1142 (Mann and Fields 1997).

Employing the kinship metaphor of family, the confederacy was symbolized as a great longhouse, stretching from east to west across Iroquois territory. In this longhouse, the Mohawk were referred to as "Keepers of the Eastern Door" and the Seneca were "Keepers of the Western Door," reflecting their geographic locations as the easternmost and westernmost nations. Leadership was vested in clan heads, their advisers, and respected elders. Clan chiefs were men chosen by leading women of their group. Chiefs ideally retained their office for life, but if a chief's behavior was deemed inappropriate or contradicted local opinions, he could be demoted and replaced by another of his clan. Each chief had assistants or advisers, men and women who also could be demoted if their behavior was considered unacceptable.

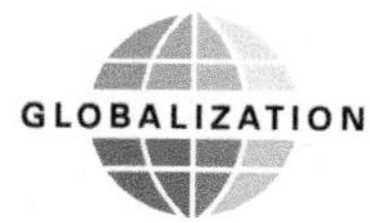

Many indigenous peoples established confederacies prior to the globalization stimulated by the colonial era. The earliest written records report confederations for commerce and war. However, many confederacies sprang up as defensive measures against the spread of European dominance and control. Today, independent states in Central America, the Caribbean, and West Africa, for example, have established political confederacies to further regional economic interests.

CASE STUDY

Age-Linked Associations in Tribal Societies: The Hidatsa and the Maasai

The Hidatsa were a farming people who resided in present-day central North Dakota. Their kinship system was organized around matrilineal clans and moieties. Membership in households revolved around a stable core of lineally related women. Kinship informed most daily interactions, but non-kin associations also figured prominently in village life.

Most adults belonged to age-grade societies that had social, economic, and ceremonial functions. Both men and women began their participation in the age-grade system in their early teens and proceeded from one age grade to the next until they retired in old age. The age-grade system united individuals across families, clans, and moieties. Members aided one another and presented food and gifts to relatives of a deceased age-mate. Certain women's and men's societies were linked as "friends," and their members gave reciprocal aid and assisted in rituals and feasts.

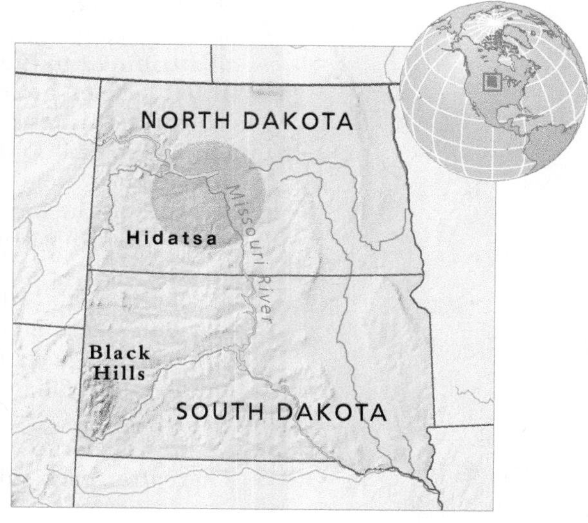

People advancing to an appropriate age group because of their age and achievements collectively purchased membership in it. The relationship between the buyers and sellers was phrased as one between parent and child (mother/daughter, father/son). Purchase of membership included transfer of spirit powers and sacred objects associated with the group. Women gained spirit powers directly from the previous holders, but men needed the assistance of their wives to finalize the transfer. As part of the ritual of purchase, wives of the buyers invited the sellers to have sexual intercourse with them in the belief that the elder men passed their spirit power to the woman in the sex act and that she later transferred it to her husband when they had intercourse.

Twelve age-grade societies existed for men and four for women. Most of the male societies were connected to military participation. The Black Mouths, one of the major male associations, served as police, enforcing decisions of the village council of elders. Black Mouths also attempted to arbitrate disputes and dissuade victims of assaults or the kin of a murdered relative from exacting blood revenge. Because of the Black Mouths' community control functions, the Hidatsa considered it crucial that men not be advanced to the society until they were mature and showed sound judgment. Consequently, most Black Mouths were between 30 and 45 years old (Bowers 1992).

Members of the most senior male age grade, called the Bull Society, formed the council of elders, who made decisions about community matters and chose village leaders. The Bull Society also had the important task of performing "buffalo calling" rituals of renewal and thanksgiving for the buffalos.

The most prominent of the women's associations were the Goose Society and the White Buffalo Cow Society. The Goose Society was composed of mature women, usually between ages 30 and 40. Members performed planting rites in the spring when the first waterbirds appeared, celebrating the renewal of the earth and the fertility of crops. They also performed dances during the summer whenever villagers so requested. Their aid was sought during droughts to bring rain and protect crops. The Goose Society also performed rituals at the time of the fall migration of waterbirds in thanks for successful harvests. The eldest women's association was the White Buffalo Cow Society. When the people moved to their winter settlements, members performed rituals to attract buffalo near the camps, so that they could be caught easily during that difficult season.

Each Hidatsa village had a council composed of mature men who were beyond the age of membership in the Black Mouth Society. Anyone could speak at council meetings, but the influence of the participants varied with their ages and achievements. Still, consensus was the paramount goal. Representatives of all households in the village were asked to express their opinions before important decisions were made. For decisions to have weight, approval by all households was critical. If a unanimous decision could not be reached, the matter was dropped.

Village councils chose a mature man to be the village leader, alternating between a summer and a winter incumbent. Fortunate occurrences during any leader's term of office, such as successful buffalo hunts, victorious raids, the appearance of buffalo near the camp in winter, and the good health and fortune of the community, were all attributed to the leader's practical and spiritual abilities. Failures were attributed to his lack of power. Generosity, intelligence, even temper, and compassion were critical requisites for being chosen for leadership. Spirit power was also a necessary adjunct to civil and military success. However, as one assumed greater responsibilities, spirit powers eventually waned. In fact, the more responsibilities one had, the greater was the loss of spirit power. These beliefs limited people's remaining in office for any length of time. Power sharing thus reflected the egalitarian basis of Hidatsa society.

The Maasai, cattle herders living in Kenya and Tanzania, have a system of age sets that organize military, political, and ritual life for men (Spencer 1988). Passing from one named age set to another is automatic upon reaching the proper age and achievements. Men collectively move from one group to the next from the time they are teenagers.

Boys undergo ritual circumcision in preparation for entering the youngest age set. Thereafter, each subsequent "graduation" to the next age set requires a ritual of initiation. The first age set is that of the warriors or "murran." As murran, young men learn the skills of warfare and cattle raiding. They live together in a murran village where they form close, lifelong bonds. They learn to depend on and help one another. Murran may wear distinctive clothing and adornments, emphasizing their youthfulness and vigor (Spencer 1993, 141). The murran stage usually lasts about fifteen years. Then the murran participate in a ceremony of transition to the next group where they retire from active military engagement. They are then eligible to marry. Because of the delay in marriage, Maasai husbands are markedly older than their wives, who tend to marry in their teenage years.

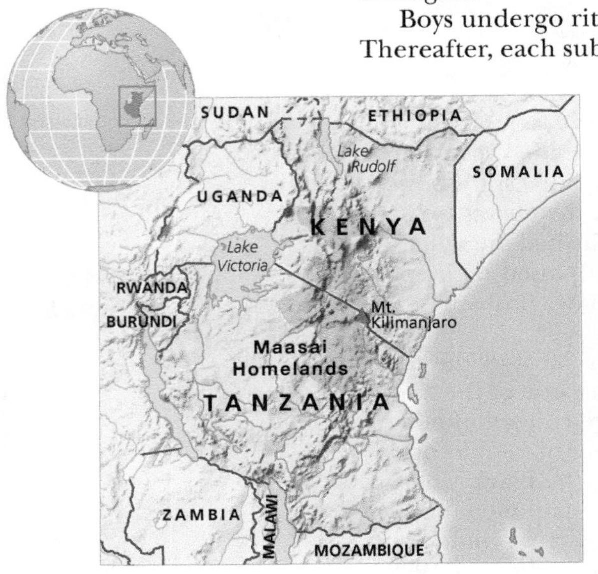

The third stage of a Maasai male's life cycle comprises the elders who function as village political and religious advisers and leaders. Their interests contrast with those of the murran. In fact, Maasai society is organized around a gerontocracy, with leadership and power vested in elders who advance their group interests

(Spencer 1993). The system of age sets, with its restrictions on marriage for young men, means that elders can live polygynously, marrying several women and thereby creating alliances with their wives' families that contribute to their political support. The power of individual elders wanes when the next set of murran advance into elderhood, pushing the previous elders into retirement.

In recent years, the Maasai age-set system has changed significantly because the governments of Kenya and Tanzania have banned cattle raiding and warfare, the traditional functions of the murran. Young men in the murran set have difficult adjustments to make. Many young Maasai men do not become murran, and some who do never reside in separate murran villages (Spencer 1993, 150). However, by tradition, they are too old to live with their mothers but not yet considered eligible to marry. Tension between young men and elders remains because the elders control property, especially cattle, which constitute the bridewealth necessary to solidify a marriage.

Although Maasai women do not belong to age sets, women function prominently in their relationships with men. Mothers of murran often accompany their sons to the murran villages, supporting and enhancing their sons' reputations. Principles of seniority order the status of women as well as men. Older women, especially the mothers of sons, gain prestige and authority, not only among women but also in the community at large. Women may act collectively to humiliate an elder man who violates social, and especially sexual, norms and may destroy his property (Spencer 1993, 154). Women, therefore, play roles as spectators of and commentators on the behavior of the murran and the elders. **Read** the **Document** on **myanthrolab.com**

Political integration and expression of public opinion took place in councils that were structured by territory and by social identity. Three types of councils were held in villages: those of the elder men (including but not limited to clan chiefs), those of women, and those of young men. Members of each council deliberated together and eventually came to a unanimous opinion concerning the matter at hand. Then each group chose a speaker, who presented the group's decisions in a unified meeting. Chiefs delegated one of their members to speak for them; women and young men appointed representatives who made their opinions publicly known. These representatives were often chosen among prominent senior men, but a woman or a young man was the selected delegate in some cases. If decisions varied, further discussion was necessary in *caucus* (a word of Native American origin referring to a meeting for the purpose of achieving consensus). The process of deliberation and consensus was repeated in tribal (or national) and confederacy forums, finally arriving at a universally accepted position.

Chiefdoms

Chiefdoms are stratified societies organized by kinship, although the degree of difference among the various strata varies cross-culturally (see Table 3). They have structured methods of choosing leaders from within kin groups. These leaders, or chiefs, perform both political and economic functions. Chiefs and their families have higher status than other people. In some chiefdoms, they are not markedly distinguished from other people except in their social prestige, whereas in other chiefdoms, higher-status people have economic, social, and political privileges. In all cases, however, higher-status chiefs and their families have authority but not power. That is, because of their position, chiefs have some ability to control economic production and labor and the distribution of resources. However, their position and influence depend on the voluntary compliance of members of their kin groups and communities. Chiefs cannot coerce other people, whether relatives or nonrelatives, to do their bidding. They can only advise, cajole, encourage, and request the labor and support of others, and they lead more by example and goodwill than by control.

chiefdoms
Stratified societies organized by kinship.

TABLE 3 EXAMPLES OF CHIEFDOMS

Americas	Europe	Africa	Asia	Pacific
Timucuan of Florida	Mycenae of Middle Bronze Age, Greece	Ashanti of Ghana	Buyeo of Manchuria (prior to Chinese conquest)	Trobriand Islanders (Boyowans)
Natchez of the Mississippi Valley		Bamileke of Cameroon		Tongan Islanders
Olmecs of Mexico (historical)		Zulu of South Africa		Maoris of New Zealand
Kwakwaka'wakw of British Columbia				Tikopians and Tahitians of Polynesia

Despite the marked stratification in chiefdom societies, ethics of egalitarian relationships underlie daily interactions and community activities. Although the chief and chief's family are privileged, notions of equality and the responsibility of kinspeople to one another remain strong. These ethics are demonstrated in the redistributive networks and functions of the chief. Chiefs know very well that they owe their position to the voluntary loyalty of their kin and others in the community. They solidify their support through their generosity, through attending to emergency needs of members of their community, and by showing respect and consideration to others. In essence, then, chiefs are embedded in kinship networks and are burdened with the responsibilities and obligations that come from expectations of reciprocity and fair treatment.

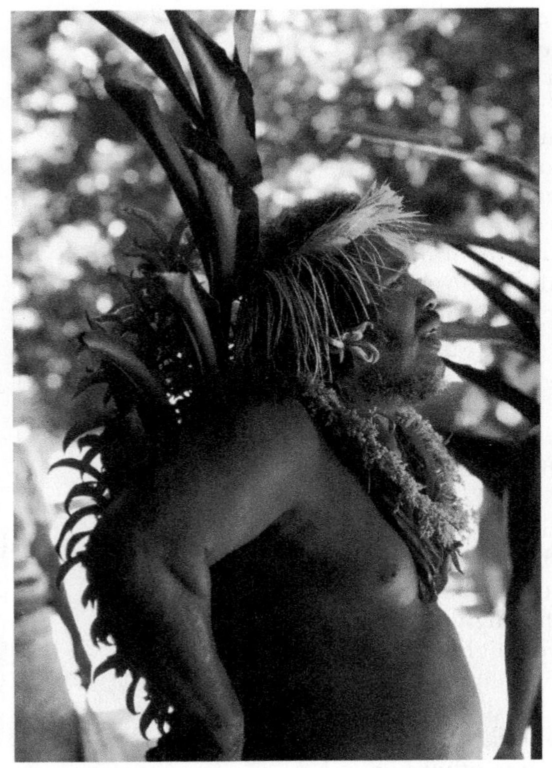

Tikopian society is ranked, with chiefs having the highest status. Chiefs of patrilineages (*maru*) are elders directly descended from lineage ancestors, whereas clan chiefs (*ariki*) are descended from the common ancestor of the lineages (Firth 1970). PhotoLibrary/ K. Hympendahl/Peter Arnold, Inc./PhotoLibrary New York

In contrast to band and tribal societies where leadership is diffuse and spontaneous, chiefdoms have some centralization of authority. However, this centralization does not extend to the whole society but, rather, to local kinship groups such as lineages and clans. There are, therefore, many chiefs in a chiefdom, not one paramount leader, and each chief owes primary allegiance to his or her kin group. Chiefs usually are chosen by seniority. In some, the eldest child of either gender ascends to the position of chief when the incumbent dies. In other chiefdoms, succession is not automatic. A person aspiring to the position of chief needs the requisite skills, intelligence, and personality traits as well as the support of kin. In some parts of the world, particularly in Melanesia and Polynesia, chiefs are sometimes referred to in the anthropological literature as "Big Men." A Big Man earns his prestige and status by maneuvering within his kin group, displaying generosity by sponsoring pig feasts and other redistributions, and forming strategic alliances with other high-status and influential people.

With only a few exceptions, chiefdom economies are based on farming, either horticulture (gardens and groves) or agriculture (fields). The aboriginal chiefdoms of the Pacific Northwest in Canada and the United States were exceptional because their economies were based on foraging. However, like the farming chiefdoms, they were able to amass a surplus because of the abundance of natural resources in their environment. This points out an important characteristic of chiefdoms: They are surplus-producing economies, able to extract or produce more than enough food for their subsistence.

The distribution of surplus goods, both in food and material items, is the special prerogative of chiefs in such societies. As heads of their lineages and clans, chiefs redistribute resources among their members and throughout their local communities. They arrange and host feasts periodically, celebrating harvests, successful hunts, and ceremonial events such as marriages or deaths. They might also host feasts that celebrate victorious raids or sporting competitions. In preparation for feasts, chiefs encourage their kinspeople to work hard to produce surplus crops and to amass large stores of foods. Then entire communities and sometimes neighboring villages as well are invited to the feasts. The visitors receive part of the bounty of goods produced and collected by the host lineage or clan. They thus benefit economically and also bear witness to the generosity of the chief. The potlatch is a classic example of the redistributive functions of chiefs and the complex meanings of the feasts that they sponsor.

Because of their role at the center of redistributive networks, chiefs and their close kin have access to strategic resources not available to other people. In some chiefdoms, the chief and chiefly families do not benefit at all economically from their position. They work just as hard as other members of the community. In other chiefdoms, the chiefs and their kin are able to retain a disproportionate amount of surplus brought in for feasting occasions. They use this surplus, of both foods and goods, for their own economic and social benefits. Their standard of living is higher or more elaborate than that of other people in the community. Their houses are larger, their clothing and ornaments finer, and their foods more exotic. In addition to economic benefits, chiefs and their kin use their access to strategic resources to attract followers. Through their redistribution of goods and their generosity in both formal and informal contexts, chiefs secure the loyalty of their followers.

Although chiefs and their families are privileged economically and socially, their position is inherently unstable. Chiefs may compete with one another for followers in attempts to solidify and expand their spheres of influence. These underlying tensions create competition because each chief and chiefly lineage continuously has to reinforce their position in the face of competitors.

A number of other cultural correlates are associated with chiefdom societies. Concepts of territoriality and landownership tend to be well developed. The boundaries between neighboring chiefdoms are usually marked and recognized by both residents and outsiders. Ownership or control of other resources is also strongly identified. Some property might be deemed private and individual, and other types might be considered a communal heritage of kinship groups as collective bodies. Where property is held communally, the chief becomes its guardian and titular owner (owner by title). Most chiefdoms have fully sedentary settlements with economies based on farming or pastoralism. Populations tend to be larger than in band or tribal societies. Methods of economic production allow for the accumulation of surpluses that can be used to support a growing population.

People in chiefdoms tend to have a strong sense of belonging not only to their own kinship group but to wider political and social associations as well. This sense of identity may promote rivalry and competition. Rivalry may be friendly, expressed in competitive sporting events, or, in some cases, lead to raiding and warfare. Warfare tends to occur more frequently in chiefdoms than in band and tribal societies. The goals of warfare may involve factors relatively rare or unknown in band or tribal warfare, such as the goal of economic gain by looting or confiscating enemy property. Warfare may also include raiding for captives. Warfare in chiefdoms also tends to be more deadly than in band or tribal groups, as killing one's enemies becomes a goal.

An important function of the chief is as a mediator in disputes. Conflicts within a lineage or clan are often brought to the chief for advice and mediation. Some chiefdoms have councils of leaders that intervene to settle disputes between people belonging to different kinship groups. Ultimately, the chief or the

Maori men performing a traditional dance for war. Corbis/Bettmann/Corbis

In Their Own VOICES

Constitution of the Iroquois Confederacy

The Iroquois Confederacy was founded by two great leaders as an organization dedicated to establishing peace among the five original member nations—the Mohawk, Oneida, Onondaga, Cayuga, and Seneca. The two leaders, one known as the Peacemaker and the other named Hayonhwatha, devised the plan and then brought it to the council of each nation for consideration. The following is an excerpt from the founding narrative of the Iroquois.

The Peacemaker then said, "My junior brother, your mind being cleared and you being competent to judge, we now shall make our laws and when all are made we shall call the organization we have formed the Great Peace. It shall be the power to abolish war and robbery between brothers and bring peace and quietness."

Hayonhwatha [Hiawatha, a historical figure but not the subject of the poem by Henry Wadsworth Longfellow] then said, "What you have said is good, I do agree."

Then the Peacemaker said, "My younger brother, we shall now propose to the Mohawk council the plan we have made. We shall tell our plan for a confederation and the building of a house of peace. It will be necessary for us to know its opinion and have its consent to proceed."

The plan was talked about in the council and the Peacemaker spoke of establishing a union of all the nations. He told them that all the chiefs must be virtuous men and be very patient. Then the speaker of the Mohawk council said, "You two, the Peacemaker and Hayonhwatha, shall send messengers to the Oneida and they shall consider the plan."

When the tomorrow of the next year had come, there came the answer of the Oneida council, "We will join the confederation."

So then the Mohawks sent two messengers to Onondaga asking that the nation consider the proposals of the Peacemaker. The next year when the midday came and the Onondaga council sent messengers who said, "We have decided that it would be a good plan to build the fire and set about it with you." So then at the same time the Peacemaker and Hayonhwatha sent messengers to the Cayuga nation and the answer was sent back. The next year at midsummer the Cayugas sent their answer and they said, "We do agree with the Peacemaker and Hayonhwatha."

Now the Senecas were divided and were not agreed because there had been trouble between their war chiefs, but messengers were sent to them but the Senecas could not agree to listen and requested the messengers to return the next year. So when the messengers returned the councils did listen and considered the proposals. After a year had passed they sent messengers to say that they had agreed to enter into the confederacy.

The Peacemaker requested some of the Mohawk chiefs to call a council, so messengers were sent out among the people and the council was convened.

The Peacemaker said, "I, with my co-worker, have a desire to now report what we have done on five successive midsummer days, of five successive years. We have obtained the consent of five nations. These are the Mohawks, the Oneidas, the Onondagas, the Cayugas and the Senecas. Our desire is

council has only an advisory function, lacking the ability or power to force their decisions on adversaries in a dispute.

Chiefs and their families may be associated with ritual and spirit power. They may function as leaders of ceremonies that help bind members of the community together. In some chiefdoms, the chief may be thought to possess special spirit powers or even to be a descendant of divine beings. Religious beliefs, therefore, can be seen to enhance the status and authority of the chief. Among the Maori of New Zealand, for example, *mana* is a kind of power and knowledge derived from the spirit world that can be controlled and manipulated by human beings and human action (Mataira 2000). People demonstrate their control of *mana* by success and achievements. Chiefs, who have the highest status and greatest success, are assumed also to have greater control of *mana*.

In some chiefdoms of Polynesia, including Tikopia and Tahiti, contact with a chief's powerful *mana* could cause harm to an ordinary person. Commoners, therefore, were not permitted to approach a chief too closely, to look at him directly, or to speak to him without an intermediary. Such beliefs isolated the chief from ordinary people. Although separation between chiefs and commoners was phrased as being necessary for the protection of the commoners' well-being, the chief was protected from contact with and the demands of ordinary people. Through these processes, religious beliefs served to mystify the person of the chief and to render his actions and statements beyond the questioning of common people.

to form a compact for a union of our nations. Our next step is to seek out Adodarhoh [an Onondaga chief]. It is he who has always set at naught all plans for the establishment of the Great Peace.

Now the Peacemaker addressed the council and he said, "I am the Peacemaker and with me is my younger brother. We two now lay before you the laws by which to frame the Ka-ya-neh-renh-ko-wa or the Great Peace. The titles shall be vested in certain women and the names shall be held in their maternal families forever." All the laws were then recited and Hayonhwatha confirmed them.

Therefore the council adopted the plan.

Then the Peacemaker himself sang and walked before the door of Adodarhoh's house. When he finished his song he walked toward Adodarhoh and held out his hand to rub it on his body and to know its inherent strength and life. Then Adodarhoh was made straight and his mind became healthy.

The Peacemaker addressed the three nations. He said, "We have now overcome a great obstacle. It has long stood in the way of peace. Now indeed may we establish the Great Peace."

"Before we do firmly establish our union each nation must appoint a certain number of its wisest and purest men who shall be rulers, Rodiyaner. They shall be the advisers of the people and make the new rules that may be needful. These men shall be selected and confirmed by their female relations in whose lines the titles shall be hereditary."

So then the women of the Mohawks brought forward nine chiefs who should become Rodiyaner and one man as war chief.

So then the women of the Oneidas brought forward nine chiefs who should become Rodiyaner, and one man who should be war chief.

So then the Onondaga women brought forward fourteen chiefs who should become Rodiyaner, and one man who should be war chief.

The Peacemaker then said: "Now, today in the presence of this great multitude I disrobe you and you are not now covered by your old names. I now give you names much greater." Then calling each chief to him he said: "I now place antlers on your head as an emblem of your power. Your old garments are torn off and better robes are given you. Now you are Royaner, each of you. You must be patient and henceforth work in unity. Never consider your own interests but work to benefit the people and for the generations not yet born. You have pledged yourselves to govern yourselves by the laws of the Great Peace. All your authority shall come from it."

Then did the Peacemaker repeat all the rules which he with Hayonhwatha had devised for the establishment of the Great Peace. Then in the councils of all the Five Nations he repeated them and the Confederacy was established.

From Arthur C. Parker, *Parker on the Iroquois: The Constitution of the Five Nations*, edited and with an introduction by William N. Fenton, pp. 24–29.

CRITICAL THINKING QUESTION

What principles of leadership and decision making guided the creation of the Iroquois Confederacy and the Great Peace?

Tongan chiefs often embraced the new opportunities for acquiring wealth and power made available through European trade. The Tongans were not passive victims of colonization but active participants in a new kind of society. The Image Works/Mary Evans Picture Library/The Image Works

CULTURE CHANGE

GLOBALIZATION AND THE TRANSFORMATION OF A TONGAN CHIEFDOM INTO AN ISLAND STATE

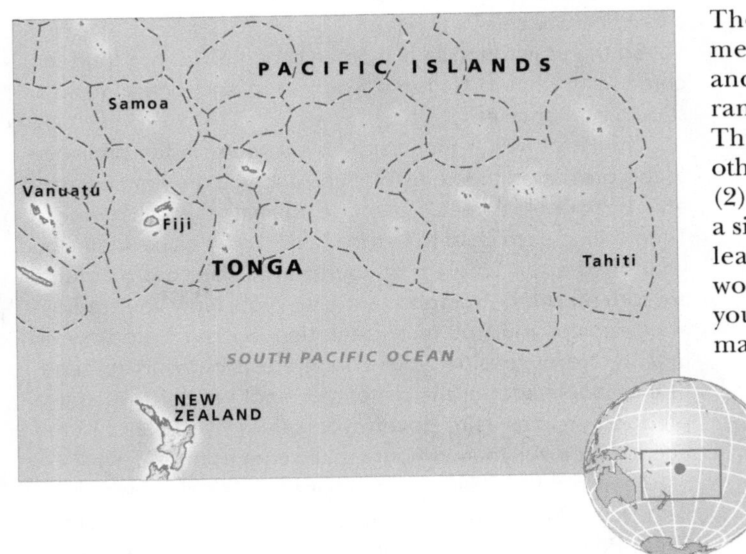

The Tongans are islanders of the South Pacific. In former times, they were organized into a highly stratified and complex chiefdom. Their social system was based on ranking in which no two individuals were of equal rank. Three principles determined an individual's status relative to others: (1) seniority—an older person outranked a younger; (2) gender—a man outranked a woman; and (3) sisterhood—a sister outranked her brother (Gailey 1987b). This could lead to variable ranking between, for example, an older woman and a younger man or an older brother and a younger sister. Actual determination of rank was open to maneuvering and personal claims.

The Tongan system divided the populace into two primary social strata: chiefs and non-chiefs. These two groups had different relationships to land and different roles in subsistence. Land was controlled by paramount chiefs, who then allocated portions to lower or district chiefs. Chiefs were guardians of the land.

Chiefs had prestigious titles through membership in high-ranking lineages. Succession to a title was ideally awarded to a chief's oldest son, but other men could make rival claims based on kinship with the previous chief's sister and on their wealth, ability, and charisma. Descent through a sister was especially important if the prior chief had no surviving children. Because sisters were of higher status than brothers, a chief's sister's son outranked his brother's sons. But claims through sisterhood could be made even against a chief's own sons, particularly if the sister were senior to the deceased chief.

Chiefly people obtained food and goods from the work of others. Chiefs commanded collective labor by men, who farmed the chief's fields, and by women, who produced mats, bark cloth, and other valuables. Although most rights and obligations in Tongan society stemmed from kinship relations, the right of chiefly people to obtain support from commoner households reflected their dominance over non-kin.

Two groups functioned as buffers between chiefs and commoners. *Matapules* included artisans, warriors, administrators, and attendants to chiefs. They were internally ranked, depending on what job each performed. Attendants and administrators oversaw cooperative work for the chiefs and summoned assemblies of commoners to advise them of chiefs' directives. *Mu'as* were offspring and descendants of intermarriages between chiefs' families. They watched over young members of chiefs' families to ensure that the youths conformed to norms of public etiquette and morality. Although high rank brought privileges, it also incurred obligations to act in a suitable manner.

Chiefly people used marital alliances to consolidate high rank. At the highest levels, among paramount chiefs, marriage between a brother and sister was the most direct form of exclusion of counterclaims. This violation of the usual incest prohibitions set the chiefs apart from the rest of the population, but it also solidified alliances and consolidated wealth. Another strategy that the most powerful chiefs used to secure their dominance and exclude rivals was to marry their sisters to foreigners. By such marriages, the chiefs simultaneously forged alliances with other leaders and eliminated competition from their sisters' sons, who instead became chiefs in their fathers' communities.

Seeds of political and social transformation were inherent in the Tongan chiefdom, as chiefs vied for power and control. However, contact with Europeans accelerated change and channeled cultural shifts in particular directions. Among the consequences, men's authority over women's social, economic, and political claims increased.

Tongans first encountered European traders and explorers in the seventeenth century. Chiefs were keenly interested in trade with the British. They especially

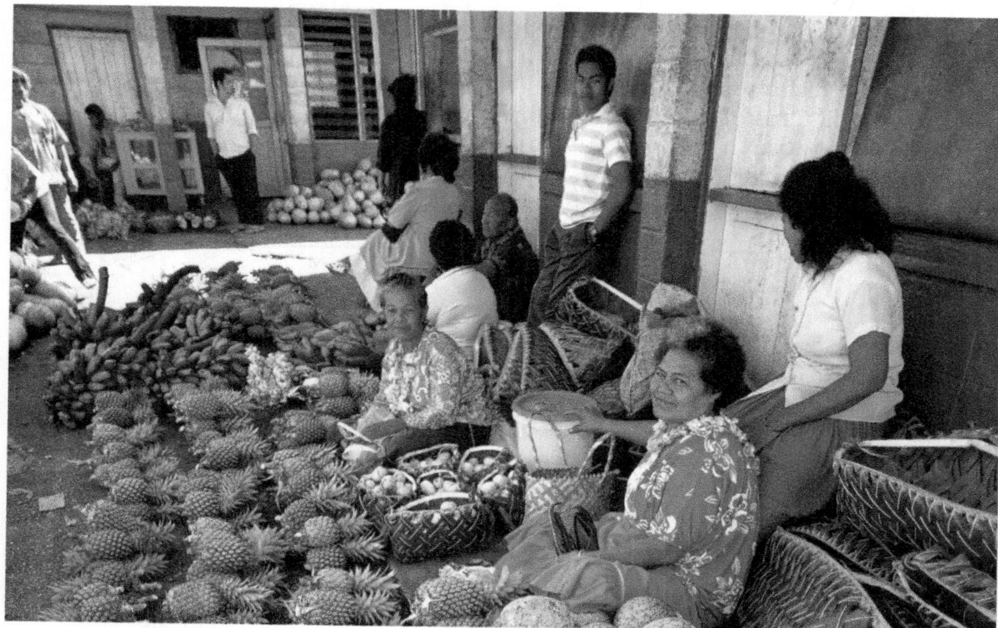

Market place in Talamahu, Tonga. Alamy Limited/FB-Fischer/imagebroker/Alamy

wanted to obtain firearms. Guns intensified Tongan disputes over succession to chiefly titles, disputes that sometimes led to warfare. By the mid-nineteenth century, reasons for warfare widened to include quests for land (Gailey 1987b). These struggles transformed the Tongan political system from a chiefdom into a **kingdom,** which became institutionalized in 1845, when a paramount chief named Taufa'ahau assumed the title of king.

Coconut oil, traditionally processed by women, was an important trade item because Europeans used it to light lamps and manufacture soap. Women's production of coconut oil increased to fill demand, and their importance in commerce enhanced their status (Gailey 1980). The economic value of coconut oil was consistent with Tongan systems that privileged products made by women, collectively called *koloa,* over products made by men, called *nguae* (Gailey 1987b). However, after the mid-nineteenth century, the market for coconut oil declined. Instead, Europeans wanted copra (dried coconut meat), which was traditionally processed by men. The shift to trade in copra began a realignment of Tongan beliefs about the inherent value of women's and men's products.

As copra production increased, men spent less time doing other subsistence and domestic tasks. Women had to engage in work that carried low status, such as farming and cooking, rather than producing *koloa,* valuables used in social, economic, political, and ritual contexts. Women also occasionally helped in copra production (men's work) to amass a greater supply. Although this increased the household incomes of women, it further altered the traditional division of labor.

Watch the **Animation:** *Trends in Political Organization* on **myanthrolab.com**

Women's work was also affected by the importation of European manufactured cotton and wool cloth, replacing traditional bark cloth, one of the most highly valued *koloa* items. Because cotton cloth was purchased with cash, men's access to money from copra production changed Tongan concepts of value. A dual process of material replacement and ideological change thus undermined women's wealth.

Economic changes and political changes went hand in hand. Codification of laws and enactment of a constitution in the mid-nineteenth century solidified the state's power and men's authority over women. New laws also granted land-use rights individually to men as heads of their households. After the establishment of the Tongan kingdom, Tongan land was owned by the king, who allocated its use to men. Inheritance of land rights passed patrilineally from father to son. Laws abolished the traditional right, called *fahu,* of a sister to the labor and products of her brother and his children. This shift resulted in women's dependence on their husbands, because other means of support

kingdom
A centralized political organization with the king as the paramount leader.

were eliminated. In addition, a woman could no longer inherit chiefly titles from her father unless she was the firstborn child with no brothers. Even in this case, if her father had a brother, his claim took precedence.

Thus, historical transformations stemming from both internal competition and external pressures from British colonial authorities benefited men of the chiefly stratum. Women lost rights relative to chiefly men, and the economic and political autonomy of non-chiefly people of both genders declined.

REVIEW

Foraging societies tended to form small, mobile, loosely defined bands. Leadership was informal, temporary, and consensual in bands. The political organization of tribes, whether horticultural, agricultural, or pastoral, was based on kin groups such as clans, which might be ranked. Tribal people also formed groups that crosscut kin ties, based on associations such as warrior societies or age grades. Confederacies were bands and tribes that joined together for mutual benefit. Chiefdoms were stratified societies based on kinship and the inheritance of social status. Chiefs were chosen more formally and served as the heads of redistributive networks. Chiefdoms became kingdoms when power and authority came to be inherited through a single paramount chief.

CHARACTERISTICS OF STATE SOCIETIES

Imperialism is the empire-building process by which expanding state societies gain more land and resources and control more labor, either directly through conquest or indirectly through power and influence. Imperialism has been a major contributing factor in the process of globalization that we see today.

states
Highly organized, centralized political systems with a hierarchical structure of authority.

republics
State societies with elected rather than inherited leadership.

primogeniture
A system of inheritance of leadership in which the eldest child (usually the eldest son) automatically inherits the position of leadership from his or her parent.

empires
States expanded into larger units through conquest and the occupation or annexation of new territories.

States are centralized social and political systems with formal governments organized into a hierarchical structure of authority. Ultimate authority and power rest with the head of state, whether called a president, a king, or an emperor. The head of state delegates responsibilities to advisers and assistants. State government systems include procedures for formally selecting leaders. In **republics,** presidents and prime ministers are elected by some segment of the citizenry for a set period of time. In some republics, officeholders may seek reelection for an additional term or terms, whereas in others, they are barred from succeeding themselves. Factors of age and gender may affect a person's right to vote.

In kingdoms, or monarchies, the successor to the king or queen is chosen by traditional patterns of inheritance, usually **primogeniture.** The eldest child, or more often the eldest son, automatically becomes the next monarch upon the death of the previous holder of that title. Monarchies and republics also differ in that the kings or queens in monarchies, once installed, remain in the position until death or voluntary abdication.

Based on principles of sovereignty, or the right to self-rule, state systems usually demarcate their territory and divide it into jurisdictions or districts and subdistricts. The size and complexity of these units vary considerably, but often each unit has some degree of independence and coordination of functions. Each territorial unit is administered by officials chosen locally or delegated by central authorities. These officials are in charge of implementing government policies in their regions, acting as conduits for central powers and sometimes as intermediaries between local residents and state officials. The larger the unit over which they have control, the greater their power and prestige. Thus, states are based on political unification, often with a national identity, and the centralization and delegation of power within a sovereign territory. Expanding state societies become **empires,** enlarging their territory and power through conquest.

State societies have much larger populations than bands, tribes, or chiefdoms, and continuous population growth leads to the development of labor specialization. Unlike other types of societies where all members, given characteristics of age and gender, perform at least some direct subsistence work, many people in state societies do not engage in economic production. Some people work as artisans and craft specialists making pottery, baskets, clothing, woodwork, and all manner of necessary tools, equipment, and utensils. Other people obtain these goods either in exchange for money or for barter with foods and other resources.

In addition, state societies have the need for many different kinds of officials and bureaucrats who help organize and run projects that involve many people. Some of these are public works projects, such as construction and maintenance of roads, water delivery systems, and other infrastructure. Some bureaucrats keep track of the populace, taking census and collecting tribute or taxes. Other people work for the state as members of a police force that controls the resident population, or as a military force that defends the state from its enemies and conducts offensive warfare to expand the borders or influence of the state. Still other specialists work in commerce, facilitating the flow of raw materials, foods, and manufactured goods from one area of the state to another, as well as to other states. And some members of society are full-time religious practitioners, conducting private and public rituals. Finally, some segments of the state society do no work at all but are fully supported by the labor of others.

Labor specialization intersects with systems of social stratification. All states are hierarchically stratified societies in which some people have greater access than other people to property of all kinds and to other strategic social and economic resources. States are divided into at least two strata: elites and commoners. Elites make up a minority of the population but reap disproportionate wealth and disproportionately occupy positions of social prestige and political power (Mills 1956). Elites have important economic functions in society but rarely enter the labor force as workers. They are sustained directly or indirectly by the tribute, rents, and taxes that commoners pay. For example, elites may own land that peasant workers farm, receiving part of the harvest as tribute.

How is the society of the United States stratified? What ideologies support your status in this system?

State societies develop urban areas where populations are concentrated. These urban centers become the seats of centralized government functions. Cities include structures of great size and opulence such as palaces and other residences of leaders, monumental buildings for governmental, administrative or religious functions, and the homes of wealthy elites. The monumental architecture characteristic of urban centers is a visual celebration of the power and wealth of the state.

Because of the complexity of governmental and economic functions, state societies usually develop some form of recordkeeping related to both labor specialization and the need to keep track of the flow of goods locally, regionally, nationally, and even internationally. Systems of writing and notation are also utilized by the state to document the tribute or taxes owed and paid by the populace as well as for many other bureaucratic functions.

Just as in chiefdoms, where chiefs manage and organize redistributive networks, elites in state societies control the production and distribution of foods and other resources for consumption. However, unlike chiefs, elites retain the majority of surplus, improving their standard of living as a class, whereas other people live in situations of comparative disadvantage. The degree of inequality between elites and commoners varies among states. The greater the disparity in wealth, the greater the likelihood that elites will exert control over commoner classes, as commoners may come to resent the fact that the elite lifestyle is supported by their own labor. Therefore ideologies arise in state societies that legitimate the status and privileges that elites receive.

Watch the **Video:** *Types of Government* on **myanthrolab.com**

In addition to ideological control, state societies have mechanisms of force that can be brought to bear on an unruly populace. Laws are codified and standardized that regulate behavior and declare certain actions criminal offenses punishable by state authorities. Court systems determine the guilt or innocence of individuals accused of crimes and punish those deemed guilty. A police force is used as an agent of **social control,** an informal or formal mechanism in society through which people's actions are controlled and social norms or laws are enforced. In the codification of rules of conduct and in the punishment of wrongdoing, the state replaces kinship groups as the regulators of social behavior. These and other characteristics of state societies are itemized in Figure 1.

In bands, tribes, and chiefdoms, social relations are enmeshed in networks of kin. People's behavior conforms to the principles of reciprocity and ethical standards valued among relatives. In state societies, however, kinship groups lose their control over members and are replaced by mechanisms of the state. Anonymous and depersonalized procedures and personnel replace individual and personalized loyalties and affections. The loosening of the bonds of kinship is a slow process that is never complete, for people in all societies have responsibilities and loyalties to their kin, as well as to other people and other entities. In state societies, powerful extended family systems continue to thrive, especially among the ruling classes. Networks of kin among the elites help solidify their power and maintain their distinctiveness.

social control
Informal and formal mechanisms in society through which people's actions are controlled and social norms or laws are enforced.

The state, through its police force and court system, supervises decision making and sanctioning. Individuals are deemed solely responsible for their actions, whereas kin groups

FIGURE 1
Features of State Society

• Centralized government
• Hierarchical structure of authority
• Bureaucratic administrative functions
• State control of redistributive services
• Territorial districts
• Labor specialization
• Social stratification, class and status differentiation
• Urbanization, monumental architecture
• State control of law and punishment
• State monopoly over military force, used internally as police and externally as an army
• Regulation of social relations, marriage, and family
• Delineation of rights and obligations of citizenship
• Integrative networks of communication and transportation
• Ideological support through religious and social ideologies

are collectively responsible for the behavior of their members in bands and tribal societies. State governments assume the right to enforce decisions that they make in the name of the society at large. These decisions affect internal functioning, law and order, and procedures that regulate many of the activities of private citizens. Other decisions affect external relations with other societies. The existence of capital punishment is an example of the state's monopoly on power. It demonstrates that only the state can legally kill.

terrorism
Acts of violence perpetrated by private citizens against groups within their own country or against a foreign country without the cover and sanction of a state-declared war.

How is terrorism a factor in the maintenance and expansion of modern states today?

In external relations, the state also monopolizes rights to conduct warfare against others. Private citizens cannot legitimately take up arms against a foreign country without the cover and sanction of a state-declared war. In fact, we now label such behavior **terrorism.** According to the U.S. Federal Bureau of Investigation, terrorism is "the unlawful use of force against persons or property to intimidate or coerce a government, the civilian population or any segment thereof, in the furtherance of political or social objectives" (U.S. Department of Justice 1999). From their origin and throughout their history, states have specialized in warfare. Unlike band and tribal societies, where raiding and warfare were carried out for personal honor, revenge, prestige, or ritual goals, wars in state societies are undertaken to conquer neighboring peoples and to incorporate them and their territories into the expanding state population.

All the characteristics of a state society described in this section can be seen in the Inca Empire of South America. Here, the ruins of Machu Picchu mark one of the last sacred outposts of the Inca. Getty Images/Philippe Colombi/ Photodisc/Getty Images

The state also regulates social relations concerning marriage and the family. Through religious sanction and state rules, the state determines eligibility for marriage, grounds for divorce, and the legitimacy of children. The state thus intervenes in personal and familial relations and decisions. States also determine procedures for extending citizenship to new members and regulating their rights and obligations. People may be assigned particular work to perform and tribute or taxes to be paid. Privileges of citizens may include the right to some level of support in times of need, protection against foreign invaders or domestic disorder, and access to training or education. Obligations of citizens to the state may include contributing to communal efforts and obeying

CONTROVERSIES

Origins of the State

Many theories have been suggested for the origin of the state. One of the most widely accepted theories is that offered by Robert Carneiro (1970). According to Carneiro, a critical factor in state development is what he calls *environmental circumscription*. Under certain circumstances, economies expand and intensify production in territories that are limited by natural barriers, such as mountains, oceans, or deserts. The problem people face in such circumstances is the natural limitation on access to more land as populations increase. This theory of state origins is related to theories about the interrelationship between population growth and economic production. Surplus food and population growth are intertwined. As people produce more food, they can support larger families and communities. As more people are available to work, they can produce even larger surpluses, leading to more population growth. This cycle of rising economic production and population can continue until it threatens to surpass the carrying capacity of the land. At that point, they must develop new methods of increasing production and obtain additional land.

Where people have enough land, they can convert it into fields. But, according to Carneiro, when natural surroundings curtail access to additional land, competition among neighboring peoples may lead to raiding and warfare. Unlike warfare in band, tribal, and even chiefdom societies, warfare in developing state societies is aimed at confiscating land and controlling its inhabitants. These inhabitants may be forced out of their original territory or reduced to the status of captives, slaves, or indentured workers.

The processes that lead to increased production, population growth, and the need for new land are never-ending. State societies, therefore, are unstable. As populations grow, land shortages intensify, leading to renewed cycles of expansion, competition, and war. The more intense and rapid these cycles are, the greater the need for centralization and control over economic and political functions. Successful states continue to expand beyond their original boundaries as they move into the territories of smaller independent societies. As they do so, they confiscate land and disrupt the inhabitants' lives by incorporating them into the expanding state society under the control of the central authorities. Such expanding states may become *empires*.

Carneiro's theory of state origins also addresses the fact that states have been established in areas without environmental circumscription. According to Carneiro, states may arise where natural resources are concentrated in a relatively small area, and where land elsewhere is poor. Therefore, people congregate, and populations grow in these small areas of resource abundance. High population densities may also lead to the development of state societies without environmental circumscription.

An earlier theory about state origins is the *hydraulic hypothesis*, proposed by Karl Wittfogel (1957). According to this theory, states originated in certain environments near rivers when institutions arose to organize the construction of large-scale irrigation systems. Wittfogel, therefore, saw state organization as responding to the internal need for increasing agricultural production as populations increased. Whereas Carneiro emphasizes the political and military pursuit of wealth, Wittfogel stresses the structural bureaucratic mechanisms that help organize communal activities in large populations. These theories emphasize different aspects of state functioning. However, the hydraulic hypothesis does not account for the existence of either productive irrigation without state control—for example, in early Mesopotamia and Peru (Adams 1982)—or state bureaucracies before the development of large irrigation systems (Johnson 1973).

CRITICAL THINKING QUESTIONS

How does Carneiro's theory interrelate population and environment? How does the hydraulic hypothesis explain the emergence of states?

authorities. In some early states, officials organized a complex system of public warehouses that kept stores of foods and other necessities to dispense to the populace if crops failed. States vary considerably in their provisions for social welfare.

States are integrated through networks of communication and transportation. The larger the population and territory, the more likely that complex systems of record keeping and notation will develop. Specialist bureaucrats are trained to keep track of the settlements and movements of populations within the territory, tribute and taxes collected, public labor organized and expended, and services required and rendered. Routes of trade and commerce also link urban centers with one another and rural villages to regional and urban markets. Networks of long-distance trade transport products and resources throughout the state. Regional specializations, therefore, develop, enabling each locality to become efficient producers of foods and other goods in their territory.

theocracies
Societies ruled by religious leaders, in which the social order is upheld through beliefs in its divine origin or sanction.

State systems are often supported by religious ideology. A unifying state religion may develop that legitimates and rationalizes the system, including its social inequalities. A trained and specialized priesthood may ally itself with civil authorities, both groups benefiting from their consolidation of power. Religious specialists may define right and wrong, encourage obedience to authority, and claim divine origin or sanction for the political system. Many early states were **theocracies,** ruled by religious leaders or by rulers thought to be divine or divinely sanctioned to rule.

REVIEW

States are centralized social and political systems with hierarchical formal governments that replace or supersede kin groups in many social functions. Theories of the origins of states include environmental conscription, in which states arose through a mutually reinforcing spiral of economic production and population growth within a territory, and the hydraulic hypothesis, in which states developed to ensure the regulation of intensive agriculture through irrigation. State societies are stratified, with ruling elites exercising power and authority. States enforce formal systems of social control and regulate warfare. Terrorism includes acts of war that are not state sanctioned. State systems are justified through ideologies and religious teachings. Many early states were theocracies.

CASE STUDY

The Inca of Peru and Ecuador

The Incas developed a complex, multiethnic, centralized agricultural empire, growing out of indigenous Andean cultures centered around Cuzco, Peru. The Incas were members of two dominant kinship groups that gradually increased their wealth and power over others, eventually transforming Andean cultures into a hierarchical state society. The Inca state expanded in the fifteenth century to encompass an estimated 6 million people living in what are now Peru and Ecuador. The empire grew by incorporating and transforming local cultures. The social and political features of Inca society are consistent with the general patterns of agricultural societies. Villages, towns, and cities were permanent and varied in size, depending on their location and importance to the Inca Empire. Major cities contained thousands of inhabitants. Social and economic roles were highly differentiated and specialized. People were also segmented according to social status and power.

The Inca state was headed by a supreme ruler, or emperor, who maintained his power through a complex network of agents, bureaucrats, armies, and priests. These people ensured that local communities fulfilled elite demands. Administrative power was exclusively a male domain. The emperor chose most of his closest advisers and aides from among the men in his lineage. Succession to the throne was not rigid, but the emperor usually selected one of his sons to be his successor.

The ruler's wife, known as *coya,* or "queen," was his own sister. Marriage between a brother and sister at the highest level of state consolidated power and minimized struggles over succession. Marriage between siblings was absolutely forbidden to all except the emperor and *coya*. The *coya* had both economic and administrative influence. She owned land and could dispose of its produce, but she redistributed some of the surplus delivered to her, holding huge public feasts as demonstrations of her generosity. *Coyas* had special lands that they used to grow new crops (Silverblatt 1978). Also, they occasionally governed from Cuzco in the absence of their husbands.

Local kinship groups called *ayllus* controlled Andean land. An *ayllu* consisted of people living within a particular territory. It was a corporate entity and allocated land to households. *Ayllu* leaders periodically reassigned allotments to adjust to changes in household composition. Land was apportioned to male heads of households on the basis of family size. Each married man received one measure (*tupu*) of land for himself and his wife. He received an additional *tupu* for each of his sons, one-half *tupu* for each daughter. When a son married, he was allotted the portion of land originally given to his father on his behalf. In most cases daughters relinquished their share of land upon marriage (Silverblatt 1978; 1980).

Both men and women, working singly or together, performed agricultural work. They cultivated more than forty species of plants (Rowe 1950), depending on altitude, climate, and topography. Basic crops were potatoes, maize, grains, berries, chilies, squash, beans, peanuts, tomatoes, and coca. People also kept domesticated animals, especially llamas, alpacas, dogs, guinea pigs, and ducks. Guinea pigs supplied most of their meat. Foraging and hunting were relatively unimportant.

Communal rights to resources within an *ayllu* were recognized and enacted through redistribution of foods and goods to community members. A family or individual in need received aid from others. This system of redistribution was based on egalitarian ethics and limited individuals' accumulation of wealth.

However, although all people had rights to resources and sustenance, some individuals were of higher social status than others. These people, known as *curacas*, constituted a governing body (Silverblatt 1980, 153). Although there were women *curacas*, it is uncertain whether they had only economic privileges or whether they also had decision-making and leadership roles (Silverblatt 1987, 16–18). In return for goods received from common people, *curacas* were obligated to be generous to those in need.

Common people also had to perform other kinds of labor, known as *mita* service. Men were enlisted to construct and maintain public works projects, such as palaces, temples, forts, irrigation systems, and roads. Some men were conscripted into army units. Others were trained from childhood to serve as runners in an elaborate postal system, carrying messages throughout the empire. Women were compelled to spin and weave cotton and wool cloth.

Households, not individuals, paid tribute in labor or goods to the Inca elite. Each household had collective responsibility to fulfill its obligations. Work was assigned within a household depending on individuals' availability and skills. Although men and women performed different kinds of work, flexibility was possible when people were called to state service or when illness or absence required a shift in tasks.

Although Inca society was highly stratified and power rested exclusively with the upper class, chiefly generosity was expected. To ensure basic survival, the state maintained granaries and warehouses from which *curacas* could obtain supplies for *ayllus* in times of famine. These goods were derived from surpluses originally taken by elites from the labor of commoners. The Inca system reveals the ethics of reciprocity underlying social relationships and uniting people in kin-based societies. As in other state societies, these ethics were kept alive even as the Inca extended their empire. Read the **Document** on **myanthrolab.com**

POLITICAL CHANGE AND STATE SOCIETIES

State societies are the largest, most complex, and highly centralized political systems. The first states arose in the Middle East in Mesopotamia around 8,000 years ago. Other states developed slightly later in the Nile region of Egypt. States also arose independently in the Indus River valley of India, in China, in Mesoamerica (Mexico and Guatemala), and in the Andes of Peru. Today, state societies exist everywhere, replacing other kinds of society and dominating the world scene.

Political systems are subject to change through varied internal processes. State societies, for example, change through the growth of disagreements among various segments of society, possibly leading to **factionalism,** the tendency for groups to split into opposing parties over political issues. Disagreements about community actions occur in all societies, but they can lead to entrenched factionalism as various interest groups vie for control of decision-making and leadership roles. If a powerful faction can assert its will, this

factionalism
The tendency for groups to split into opposing parties over political issues, often a cause of violence and a threat to political unity.

can lead to fundamental social changes as one group and their interests dominate the political process and the ideological beliefs that support it.

In states with a history of internal colonization, indigenous peoples may disagree about how best to react to the policies of dominant governments. For example, in the early 1900s, two contentious factions developed in the Hopi community of Oraibi in Arizona over whether to participate in federal educational programs for Hopi children. Some people believed that knowledge of the English language and American culture would benefit the Hopi, but others feared that any but the most tangential contacts with American culture would lead to the destruction of Hopi lifeways.

Conflicts between these two factions grew increasingly bitter, eventually spilling into other issues and even dividing family groups. Finally, in 1906, the Hopi in Oraibi decided that they could not all live together in the same community. Using the quasi-ritualistic means of a "tug-of-war" across a line etched in the dirt, the two sides dramatized their inability to coexist. The group who lost (called the "Hostiles," because of their opposition to American assimilationist policies) was forced to leave, later founding a new village, Hotevilla. The faction known as the "Friendlies" remained at Oraibi and continued their more accommodating approach toward American cultural innovations (Titiev 1992). Today, the two groups have achieved more cooperation toward community goals, although disagreements reemerge from time to time about policies affecting internal development and direction, as well as about attitudes toward outsiders.

In societies (such as the Hopi) where people are linked with many others through ties of kinship, marriage, and social association, factionalism may be disruptive but rarely leads to violence within communities. In state societies, however, factionalism may lead to armed conflict. In our contemporary world, we find many examples of internal disputes escalating into civil war. In many of these cases, ethnic or religious differences become highlighted, although the fundamental issues in contention are usually economic inequalities and/or political power struggles. For example, the breakup of the former Yugoslavia in 1992 was exacerbated by dredging up ethnic and religious rivalries of centuries past. The genocidal campaigns in Rwanda in 1994 also turned on ethnic differences, although political and economic rights and privileges underlay the ethnic conflicts. Finally, the fighting between Shiite and Sunni groups in Iraq and between various Palestinian factions in the occupied territories of Israel/Palestine are additional manifestations of the tenuous nature of some modern states and the tendencies for disagreements over political and economic policies to erupt in violence in such circumstances.

King Mohammed VI of Morocco addressing the United Nations General Assembly in 2004. He began his reign in 1999 pledging political and economic reforms. Corbis/JEFF CHRISTENSEN/Reuters/Corbis

In large stratified societies, political change can come about as a result of rebellion and revolution. These are complex processes that take different forms in different contexts. In colonial situations, residents of the colonies may eventually decide that they no longer want to live under foreign domination. They may rebel in wars of independence to oust their rulers. A successful rebellion may enable indigenous people to return to some form of traditional life. Or the colonists themselves may rebel against their country of origin to set up an independent nation. For example, the American Revolution was a revolution in its focus on eliminating what had come to be seen as a foreign, distant power controlling people in the colonies. It was revolutionary in its transformation from a monarchy to a republic with ultimate power in the hands of elected officials. The French Revolution of 1789 had the additional goal of overturning a whole social system, eliminating the class privileges of wealthy and aristocratic elites. These goals were never fully met, demonstrating how difficult it is to break completely with the past.

In the twentieth century, new movements for social and political change occurred in many places in the world. The Mexican Revolution of 1910 and the Russian Revolution of 1917 were attempts to change the stratified social systems that created economic and political inequalities. Following the end of World War II, many countries in Africa that European states had colonized gained their independence. These movements were successful because of both internal resistance to colonial control and external pressure from growing international anticolonialism.

More recently, movements for democratic change have also taken root worldwide as people in stratified societies with great imbalances in wealth and power have attempted to claim a more equitable share of their country's resources. Elites do not give up their power and privilege easily, however. They may resist openly by using the police force at their disposal to put down revolutionary movements or by using the legal apparatus to arrest and punish leaders and participants. They may also resist by ideological means, claiming the moral authority and legitimacy of the prevailing system. In the end, movements for social and political change succeed when supported by a large and dedicated segment of the population. The civil rights movement in the United States in the 1950s and 1960s and the antiapartheid struggles in South Africa in the 1970s and 1980s eventually won fundamental political transformations, despite strenuous opposition from those in power, because people in those countries, and their supporters, finally refused to acquiesce to their disenfranchisement and lack of opportunity.

Today, the crises in the Middle East have spawned movements for social and political change within many countries in the region. Middle Eastern monarchs have implemented or begun to talk about steps toward democratization of their political processes. For example, King Mohammed VI of Morocco, installed in 1999, has broadened citizens' access to political participation and given more power to elected representatives in an attempt to respond to people's desire for a voice in their own society. And King Fahd bin Abdul Aziz of Saudi Arabia, head of one of the most autocratic governments in the world, has hinted at the possibility of reforms to allow more popular participation, although no actual changes have been implemented. These governments are responding to forces of globalization that have begun to affect their own citizenry and, perhaps, to fears of the spread of Islamic fundamentalism, which feeds on deep popular resentment within Middle Eastern countries. And, most recently, populist movements for political change have forced presidents to resign in Tunisia and Egypt. Most remarkably, in February 2011, Hosni Mubarak of Egypt was forced to leave office after a thirty-year presidency, ousted by generally peaceful public demonstrations that lasted only eighteen days, with the participation of men and women from all classes, religions, and occupations. Interim governments in both Egypt and Tunisia are promising reforms of political institutions, but time will tell whether fundamental changes take place. These movements for change are spreading and threatening to destabilize other countries in the region as well, as evidenced by the overthrow of Muammar Gaddafi in Libya and mass demonstrations against the government of Syria.

Some political anthropologists trace the spread of Euro-American political concepts and institutions. These concepts, such as democracy, and institutional behaviors, such as elections, tend to accompany the economic influences of those regions on world cultures. Political ideas and behaviors also may be forced on other people through conquest or other dominating influence.

Internal patterns of change in political systems include factionalism, in which groups split over issues and vie for power, as well as revolution, in which citizens rebel against their rulers.

ANTHROPOLOGY APPLIED

Anthropologists and the NGOs

NGOs—nongovernmental organizations—include charities, research institutes, churches, professional associations, and advocacy or lobby groups. These private organizations may be international, national, or community-based. They often work with governments and with international umbrella organizations such as the United Nations. NGOs may defend a particular cause, such as land rights or refugee resettlement, or design and implement large economic development programs. Most NGOs serve people in disadvantaged or developing countries, based on values of social justice (http://library.duke.edu/research/subject/guides/ngo_guide/).

Oxfam, CARE, and Save the Children are international public charities. Private-sector NGOs include the Mennonite Central Committee and World Vision, a Christian relief organization. Partners in Health (PIH) is a Boston-based international professional organization that serves people in poor countries. PIH medical teams, working with anthropologists and local community leaders, treat people with HIV in Haiti and people with drug-resistant tuberculosis in Peru (Castro 2004).

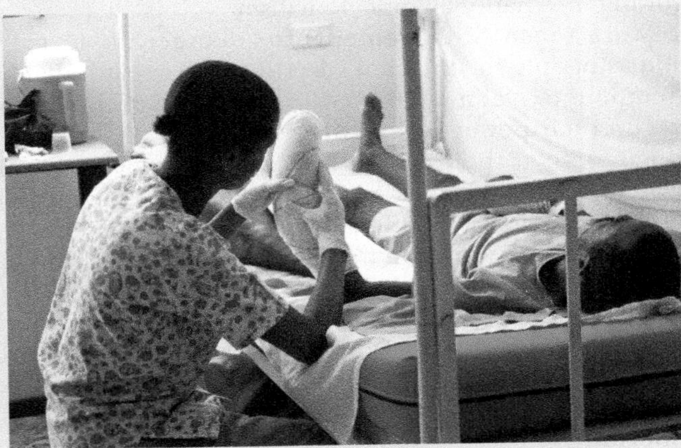

Corbis/Jean-Marc Bernard/Realis Agence/Corbis

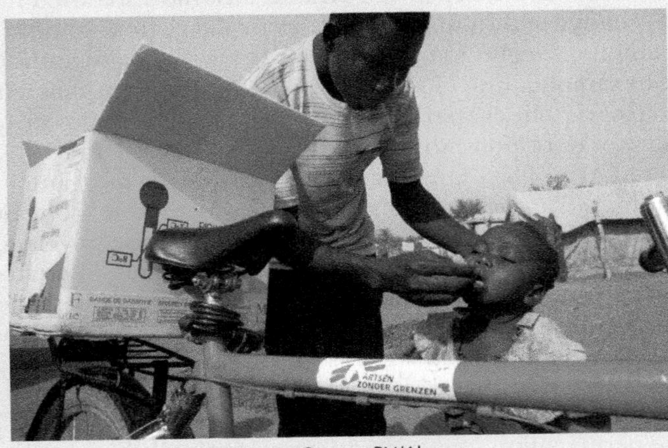

Alamy Limited/Ton Koene/Picture Contact BV/Alamy

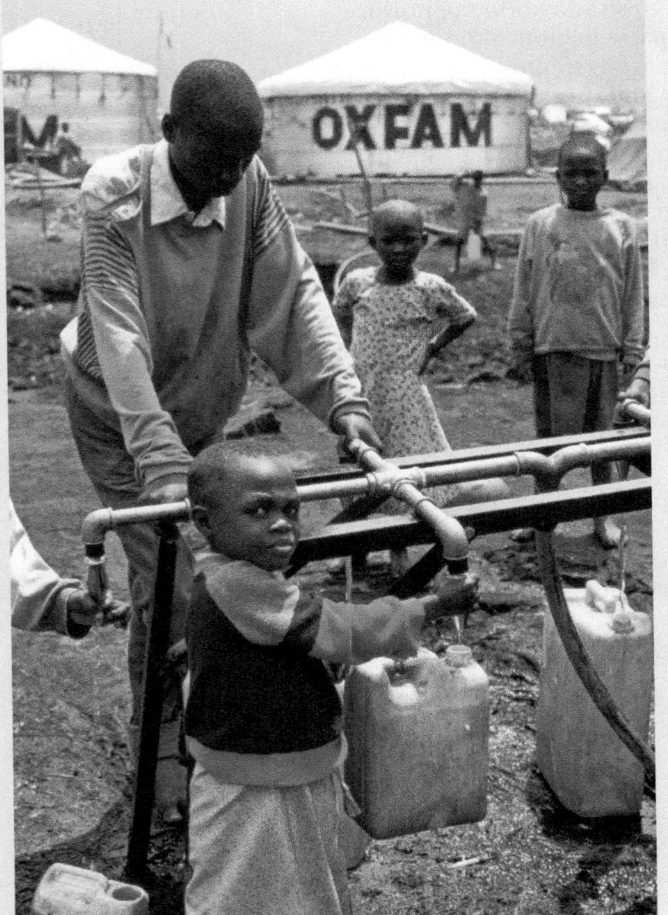

Corbis/Howard Davies/Corbis

Because of the focus on development and social justice for disadvantaged groups in poor countries, anthropologists play key roles in NGOs. They conduct research, advise organizations, protect the interests of aid recipients and their communities, and serve as liaisons or mediators (Hursey 2001). Because of their training, anthropologists know to question the cultural assumptions and power structures that restrict people's access to health care, education, housing, and so on. They also have the background to understand how NGOs, as transnational carriers of culture, act as instruments of globalization.

CRITICAL THINKING QUESTIONS

How might recipients of NGO aid find "strings attached"? How should negative impacts of globalization be balanced with the needs for help that NGOs meet?

Study and Review on myanthrolab.com

CHAPTER SUMMARY

Political Anthropology

- Political anthropology focuses on how societies select their leaders, make decisions affecting the group, provide community functions and services, and resolve conflicts. These cultural mechanisms help integrate a community and direct relations with other communities.

Types of Political Organization

- Bands are small, loosely organized groups of people. Communities in band societies are usually relatively small and dispersed throughout a wide territory. Bands are held together by informal means. Membership in a band is typically based on kinship ties. Band leadership is based on the abilities of the leader. Such leaders have influence but cannot control the actions of others. Bands are usually egalitarian societies.
- Tribal societies are more structured, organized, and cohesive than bands. Tribal societies may have more formalized procedures for making decisions and selecting leaders with limited power to enforce their decisions.
- Voluntary associations and age-grade or age-set organizations are common in tribal societies. Members of the same age grade consider themselves to have a kin-like relationship.
- Some tribal societies link themselves in confederacies. A confederacy is a formal, well-organized political structure to counteract external threats. Confederacies have formal procedures to select leaders, debate issues, make decisions, and plan and execute actions.
- Chiefdoms are stratified societies organized by kinship. Within chiefdoms, the chiefs and their families have the most prestige, authority, and privileges, but not power. Their position and influence depend on voluntary compliance of their kin groups and communities. In chiefdoms, there is no paramount leader. Chiefs owe primary allegiance to their kin groups. Although chiefly rank may be inherited, aspirants need skills and personality traits to be appropriate heirs.
- Chiefs are often the centers of redistributive networks. They redistribute by hosting feasts.

Characteristics of State Societies

- State societies are the largest, most complex, and highly centralized political systems. In every part of the world, states have replaced other types of societies.
- State governments are hierarchical. State government systems include procedures for formally selecting leaders and their assistants. States usually divide their territory into districts and have economic systems characterized by labor specialization. States are stratified societies in which some people have greater access to property and resources than others.
- State societies promulgate ideologies that legitimate the status and privileges that elites receive. States also have mechanisms of force to maintain the status quo. States have law codes and monopolize the right to control and punish wrongdoers and conduct warfare.

Internal Political Change and State Societies

- States are inherently expansionist because their elites want to increase their wealth and power. State conquest always has cultural components as basic systems of family organization, economic relationships, and religion change to conform to the practices and beliefs of the conquerors.
- States may also be transformed from within as interest groups or factions compete. Reform or revolutionary movements may develop in response to perceived inequalities and injustices or to effect more fundamental changes. Although states resist revolutions, some revolutionary movements like the wave of post–World War II decolonization have proven to be unstoppable. Global movements toward democratization have also more recently gained momentum.

REVIEW QUESTIONS

1. How might a political anthropologist study factionalism or domestic terrorism in a state society?
2. How are bands, tribes, chiefdoms, confederacies, and states different?
3. What roles do kinship and associations play in each type of political system?
4. Are bands, tribes, chiefdoms, confederacies, and states steps in the development of political systems? If so, how? What determines which form of political organization a society is likely to have?
5. Why are state societies characterized by social stratification?
6. How have colonization and globalization affected sociopolitical systems?
7. How do political systems change?

MyAnthroLab Connections

Watch. Listen. View. Explore. Read. MyAnthroLab is designed just for you. Dynamic visual activities, videos, and readings found in the multimedia library will enhance your learning experience.

Resources from this chapter:

Watch on **myanthrolab.com**
- *Living with the Darhad—Rechinlhumble*
- *Trends in Political Organization*
- *Types of Government*

Explore on **myanthrolab.com** In MySearchLab, enter the Anthropology database to find relevant and recent scholarly and popular press publications. For this chapter, enter the following keywords: primogeniture, social control, theocracies, factionalism

Read the **Document**
- *Bulgaria: Anthropological Corrections to Cold War Stereotypes* by Gerald W. Creed
- *Political Participation* by Marc Howard Cross

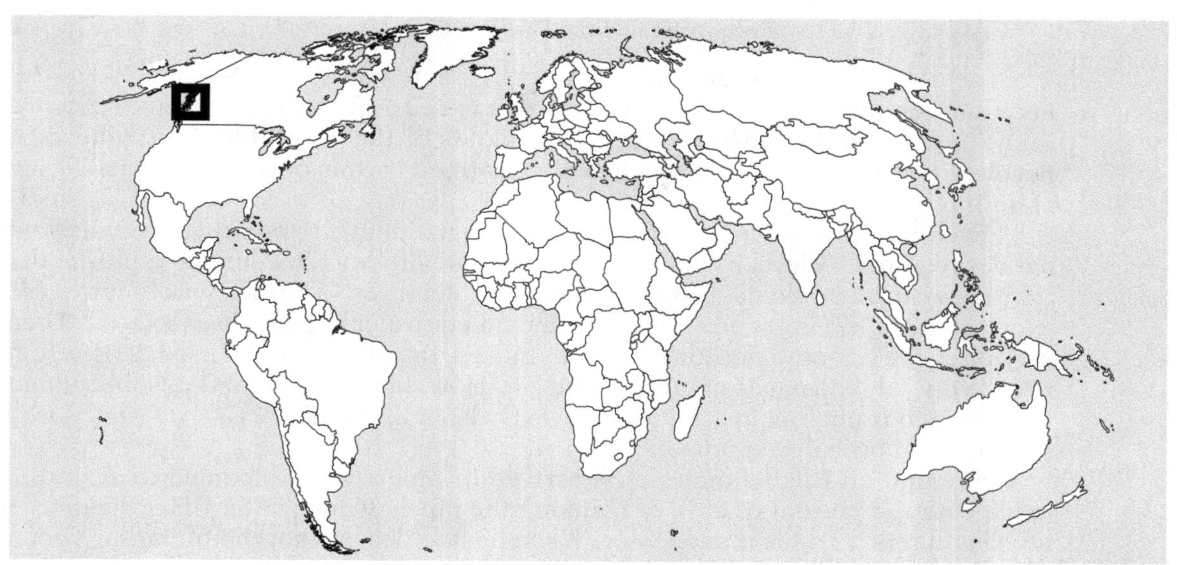

Reciprocity and the Power of Giving

Lee Cronk

Reciprocity constitutes an important exchange system in every society. At the heart of reciprocal exchange is the idea of giving. In this article, Lee Cronk explores the functions of giving using a variety of examples from societies around the world. Giving may be benevolent. It may be used to strengthen existing relationships or to form new ones. Gifts may also be used aggressively to "fight" people, to "flatten" them with generosity. Givers often gain position and prestige in this way. Gifts may also be used to place others in debt so that one can control them and require their loyalty. Cronk shows that, in every society, from !Kung hxaro *exchange to American foreign aid, there are "strings attached" to giving that affect how people and groups relate to each other.**

Listen to the **Chapter Audio** on **myanthrolab.com**

During a trek through the Rockies in the 1830s, Captain Benjamin Louis E. de Bonneville received a gift of a fine young horse from a Nez Percé chief. According to Washington Irving's account of the incident, the American explorer was aware that "a parting pledge was

*Reprinted with the permission of the New York Academy of Sciences, 7 World Trade Center, 250 Greenwich St., 40th Floor, New York, NY 10007. www.nyas.org

Reciprocity and the Power of Giving, Lee Cronk, reprinted with the permission of the New York Academy of Sciences, 7 World Trade Center, 250 Greenwich St., 40th Floor, New York, NY 10007, www.nyas.org.

From Chapter 13 of *Conformity and Conflict: Readings in Cultural Anthropology.* Fourteenth Edition. James Spradley, David W. McCurdy.

necessary on his own part, to prove that this friendship was reciprocated." Accordingly, he "placed a handsome rifle in the hands of the venerable chief; whose benevolent heart was evidently touched and gratified by this outward and visible sign of amity."

Even the earliest white settlers in New England understood that presents from natives required reciprocity, and by 1764, "Indian gift" was so common a phrase that the Massachusetts colonial historian Thomas Hutchinson identified it as "a proverbial expression, signifying a present for which an equivalent return is expected." Then, over time, the custom's meaning was lost. Indeed, the phrase now is used derisively, to refer to one who demands the return of a gift. How this cross-cultural misunderstanding occurred is unclear, but the poet Lewis Hyde, in his book *The Gift,* has imagined a scenario that probably approaches the truth.

Say that an Englishman newly arrived in America is welcomed to an Indian lodge with the present of a pipe. Thinking the pipe a wonderful artifact, he takes it home and sets it on his mantelpiece. When he later learns that the Indians expect to have the pipe back, as a gesture of goodwill, he is shocked by what he views as their short-lived generosity. The newcomer did not realize that, to the natives, the point of the gift was not to provide an interesting trinket but to inaugurate a friendly relationship that would be maintained through a series of mutual exchanges. Thus, his failure to reciprocate appeared not only rude and thoughtless but downright hostile. "White man keeping" was as offensive to native Americans as "Indian giving" was to settlers.

In fact, the Indians' tradition of gift giving is much more common than our own. Like our European ancestors, we think that presents ought to be offered freely, without strings attached. But through most of the world, the strings themselves are the main consideration. In some societies, gift giving is a tie between friends, a way of maintaining good relationships, whereas in others it has developed into an elaborate, expensive, and antagonistic ritual designed to humiliate rivals by showering them with wealth and obligating them to give more in return.

In truth, the dichotomy between the two traditions of gift giving is less behavioral than rhetorical: our generosity is not as unconditional as we would like to believe. Like European colonists, most modern Westerners are blind to the purpose of reciprocal gift giving, not only in non-Western societies but also, to some extent, in our own. Public declarations to the contrary, we, too, use gifts to nurture long-term relationships of mutual obligation, as well as to embarrass our rivals and to foster feelings of indebtedness. And this ethic touches all aspects of contemporary life, from the behavior of scientists in research networks to superpower diplomacy. Failing to acknowledge this fact, especially as we give money, machines, and technical advice to peoples around the world, we run the risk of being misinterpreted and, worse, of causing harm.

Much of what we know about the ethics of gift giving comes from the attempts of anthropologists to give things to the people they are studying. Richard Lee, of the University of Toronto, learned a difficult lesson from the !Kung hunter-gatherers, of the Kalahari desert, when, as a token of goodwill, he gave them an ox to slaughter at Christmas. Expecting gratitude, he was shocked when the !Kung complained about having to make do with such a scrawny "bag of bones." Only later did Lee learn, with relief, that the !Kung belittle all gifts. In their eyes, no act is completely generous, or free of calculation; ridiculing gifts is their way of diminishing the expected return and of enforcing humility on those who would use gifts to raise their own status within the group.

Rada Dyson-Hudson, of Cornell University, had a similar experience among the Turkana, a pastoral people of northwestern Kenya. To compensate her informants for their help, Dyson-Hudson gave away pots, maize meal, tobacco, and other items. The Turkana reaction was less than heartwarming. A typical response to a gift of a pot, for example, might be, "Where is the maize meal to go in this pot?" or, "Don't you have a bigger one to give me?" To the Turkana, these are legitimate and expected questions.

The Mukogodo, another group of Kenyan natives, responded in a similar way to gifts Beth Leech and I presented to them during our fieldwork in 1986. Clothing was never nice enough, containers never big enough, tobacco and candies never plentiful enough. Every gift horse was examined carefully, in the mouth and elsewhere. Like the !Kung, the Mukogodo believe that all gifts have an element of calculation, and they were right to think that ours were no exception. We needed their help, and their efforts to diminish our expectations and lessen their obligations to repay were as fair as our attempts to get on their good side.

The idea that gifts carry obligations is instilled early in life. When we gave Mukogodo children candies after visiting their villages, their mothers reminded them of the tie: "Remember these white people? They are the ones who gave you candy." They also reinforced the notion that gifts are meant to circulate, by asking their children to part with their precious candies, already in their mouths. Most of the youngsters reluctantly surrendered their sweets, only to have them immediately returned. A mother might take, at most, a symbolic nibble from her child's candy, just to drive home the lesson.

The way food, utensils, and other goods are received in many societies is only the first stage of the behavior surrounding gift giving. Although repayment is expected, it is crucial that it be deferred. To reciprocate at once indicates a desire to end the relationship, to cut the strings; delayed repayment makes the strings longer and stronger. This is especially clear on the Truk Islands, of Micronesia, where a special word—*niffag*—is used to designate objects moving through the island's exchange network. From the Trukese viewpoint, to return niffag on the same day it is received alters its nature from that of a gift to that of a sale, in which all that matters is material gain.

After deciding the proper time for response, a recipient must consider how to make repayment, and that is dictated largely by the motive behind the gift. Some exchange customs are designed solely to preserve a relationship. The !Kung have a system, called *hxaro*, in which little attention is paid to whether the items exchanged are equivalent. Richard Lee's informant !Xoma explained to him that "Hxaro is when I take a thing of value and give it to you. Later, much later, when you find some good thing, you give it back to me. When I find something good I will give it to you, and so we will pass the years together." When Lee tried to determine the exact exchange values of various items (Is a spear worth three strings of beads, two strings, or one?), !Xoma explained that any return would be all right: "You see, we don't trade with things, we trade with people!"

One of the most elaborate systems of reciprocal gift giving, known as *kula*, exists in a ring of islands off New Guinea. Kula gifts are limited largely to shell necklaces, called *soulava*, and armbands, called *mwali*. A necklace given at one time is answered months or years later with an armband, the necklaces usually circulating clockwise, and the armbands counterclockwise, through the archipelago. Kula shells vary in quality and value, and men gain fame and prestige by having their names associated with noteworthy necklaces or armbands. The shells also gain value from their association with famous and successful kula partners.

Although the act of giving gifts seems intrinsically benevolent, a gift's power to embarrass the recipient and to force repayment has, in some societies, made it attractive as a weapon. Such antagonistic generosity reached its most elaborate expression, during the late nineteenth century, among the Kwakiutl, of British Columbia.

The Kwakiutl were acutely conscious of status, and every tribal division, clan, and individual had a specific rank. Disputes about status were resolved by means of enormous ceremonies (which outsiders usually refer to by the Chinook Indian term *potlatch*), at which rivals competed for the honor and prestige of giving away the greatest amount of property. Although nearly everything of value was fair game—blankets, canoes, food, pots, and, until the mid-nineteenth century, even slaves—the most highly prized items were decorated sheets of beaten copper, shaped like shields and etched with designs in the distinctive style of the Northwest Coast Indians.

As with the kula necklaces and armbands, the value of a copper sheet was determined by its history—by where it had been and who had owned it—and a single sheet could be worth thousands of blankets, a fact often reflected in its name. One was called "Drawing All Property from the House," and another, "About Whose Possession All Are Quarreling." After the Kwakiutl began to acquire trade goods from the Hudson's Bay Company's Fort Rupert post, in 1849, the potlatches underwent a period of extreme inflation, and by the 1920s, when items of exchange included sewing machines and pool tables, tens of thousands of Hudson's Bay blankets might be given away during a single ceremony.

In the 1880s, after the Canadian government began to suppress warfare between tribes, potlatching also became a substitute for battle. As a Kwakiutl man once said to the anthropologist Franz Boas, "The time of fighting is past. . . . We do not fight now with weapons: we fight with property." The usual Kwakiutl word for potlatch was *p!Esa,* meaning to flatten (as when one flattens a rival under a pile of blankets), and the prospect of being given a large gift engendered real fear. Still, the Kwakiutl seemed to prefer the new "war of wealth" to the old "war of blood."

Gift giving has served as a substitute for war in other societies, as well. Among the Siuai, of the Solomon Islands, guests at feasts are referred to as attackers, while hosts are defenders, and invitations to feasts are given on short notice in the manner of "surprise attacks." And like the Kwakiutl of British Columbia, the Mount Hagen tribes of New Guinea use a system of gift giving called *moka* as a way of gaining prestige and shaming rivals. The goal is to become a tribal leader, a "big-man." One moka gift in the 1970s consisted of several hundred pigs, thousands of dollars in cash, some cows and wild birds, a truck, and a motorbike. The donor, quite pleased with himself, said to the recipient, "I have won. I have knocked you down by giving so much."

Although we tend not to recognize it as such, the ethic of reciprocal gift giving manifests itself throughout our own society, as well. We, too, often expect something, even if only gratitude and a sense of indebtedness, in exchange for gifts, and we use gifts to establish friendships and to manipulate our positions in society. As in non-Western societies, gift giving in America sometimes takes a benevolent and helpful form; at other times, the power of gifts to create obligations is used in a hostile way.

The Duke University anthropologist Carol Stack found a robust tradition of benevolent exchange in an Illinois ghetto known as the Flats, where poor blacks engage in a practice called swapping. Among residents of the Flats, wealth comes in spurts; hard times are frequent and unpredictable. Swapping, of clothes, food, furniture, and the like, is a way of guaranteeing security, of making sure that someone will be there to help out when one is in need and that one will get a share of any windfalls that come along.

Such networks of exchange are not limited to the poor, nor do they always involve objects. Just as the exchange of clothes creates a gift community in the Flats, so the swapping of knowledge may create one among scientists. Warren Hagstrom, a sociologist at the University of Wisconsin, in Madison, has pointed out that papers submitted to scientific journals often are called contributions, and, because no payment is received for them, they truly are gifts. In contrast, articles written for profit—such as this one—often are held in low esteem: scientific status can be achieved only through *giving* gifts of knowledge.

Recognition also can be traded upon, with scientists building up their gift-giving networks by paying careful attention to citations and acknowledgments. Like participants in kula exchange, they try to associate themselves with renowned and prestigious articles, books, and institutions. A desire for recognition, however, cannot be openly acknowledged as a motivation for research, and it is a rare scientist who is able to discuss such desires candidly. Hagstrom was able to find just one mathematician (whom he described as "something of a social isolate") to confirm that "junior mathematicians want recognition from big shots and, consequently, work in areas prized by them."

Hagstrom also points out that the inability of scientists to acknowledge a desire for recognition does not mean that such recognition is not expected by those who offer gifts of knowledge, any more than a kula trader believes it is all right if his trading partner does not answer his gift of a necklace with an armband. While failure to reciprocate in New Guinean society might once have meant warfare, among scientists it may cause factionalism and the creation of rivalries.

Whether in the Flats of Illinois or in the halls of academia, swapping is, for the most part, benign. But manipulative gift giving exists in modern societies, too—particularly in paternalistic government practices. The technique is to offer a present that cannot be repaid, coupled with a claim of beneficence and omniscience. The Johns Hopkins University anthropologist Grace Goodell documented one example in Iran's Khu-zesta-n Province, which, because it contains most of the country's oil fields and is next door to Iraq, is a strategically sensitive area. Goodell focused on the World Bank–funded Dez irrigation project, a showpiece of the shah's ambitious "white revolution" development plan. The scheme involved the irrigation of tens of thousands of acres and the forced relocation of people from their villages to new, model towns. According to Goodell, the purpose behind dismantling local institutions was to enhance central government control of the region. Before development, each Khu-zesta-ni village had been a miniature city-state, managing its own internal affairs and determining its own relations with outsiders. In the new settlements, decisions were made by government bureaucrats, not townsmen, whose autonomy was crushed under the weight of a large and strategically placed gift.

On a global scale, both the benevolent and aggressive dimensions of gift giving are at work in superpower diplomacy. Just as the Kwakiutl were left only with blankets with which to fight after warfare was banned, the United States and the Soviet Union now find, with war out of the question, that they are left only with gifts—called concessions—with which to do battle. Offers of military cutbacks are easy ways to score points in the public arena of international opinion and to shame rivals, and failure either to accept such offers or to respond with even more extreme proposals may be seen as cowardice or as bellicosity. Mikhail Gorbachev is a virtuoso, a master potlatcher, in this new kind of competition, and, predictably, Americans often see his offers of disarmament and openness as gifts with long strings attached. One reason U.S. officials were buoyed last December [1988], when, for the first time since the

Second World War, the Soviet Union accepted American assistance, in the aftermath of the Armenian earthquake, is that it seemed to signal a wish for reciprocity rather than dominance—an unspoken understanding of the power of gifts to bind people together.

Japan, faced with a similar desire to expand its influence, also has begun to exploit gift giving in its international relations. In 1989, it will spend more than ten billion dollars on foreign aid, putting it ahead of the United States for the second consecutive year as the world's greatest donor nation. Although this move was publicly welcomed in the United States as the sharing of a burden, fears, too, were expressed that the resultant blow to American prestige might cause a further slip in our international status. Third World leaders also have complained that too much Japanese aid is targeted at countries in which Japan has an economic stake and that too much is restricted to the purchase of Japanese goods—that Japan's generosity has less to do with addressing the problems of underdeveloped countries than with exploiting those problems to its own advantage.

The danger in all of this is that wealthy nations may be competing for the prestige that comes from giving gifts at the expense of Third World nations. With assistance sometimes being given with more regard to the donors' status than to the recipients' welfare, it is no surprise that, in recent years, development aid often has been more effective in creating relationships of dependency, as in the case of Iran's Khūzestān irrigation scheme, than in producing real development. Nor that, given the fine line between donation and domination, offers of help are sometimes met with resistance, apprehension and, in extreme cases, such as the Iranian revolution, even violence.

The Indians understood a gift's ambivalent power to unify, antagonize, or subjugate. We, too, would do well to remember that a present can be a surprisingly potent thing, as dangerous in the hands of the ignorant as it is useful in the hands of the wise.

√• **Study** and **Review** on **myanthrolab.com**

Review Questions

1. What does Cronk mean by *reciprocity*? What is the social outcome of reciprocal gift giving?
2. According to Cronk, what are some examples of benevolent gift giving?
3. How can giving be used to intimidate other people or groups? Give some examples cited by Cronk and think of some from your own experience.
4. How does Cronk classify gift-giving strategies such as government foreign aid? Can you think of other examples of the use of exchange as a political device?

Religion

Religion

PREVIEW

- What is religion?
- What perspectives do anthropologists take in studying religion?
- What types of spirit entities and powers or forces do people believe in?
- How do religious practitioners reflect their society and culture?
- What are the main types of religious practice?
- What are some psychological, social, and cultural sources and functions of religion?
- How do religions help maintain the social order? How do they both instigate and reflect culture change?

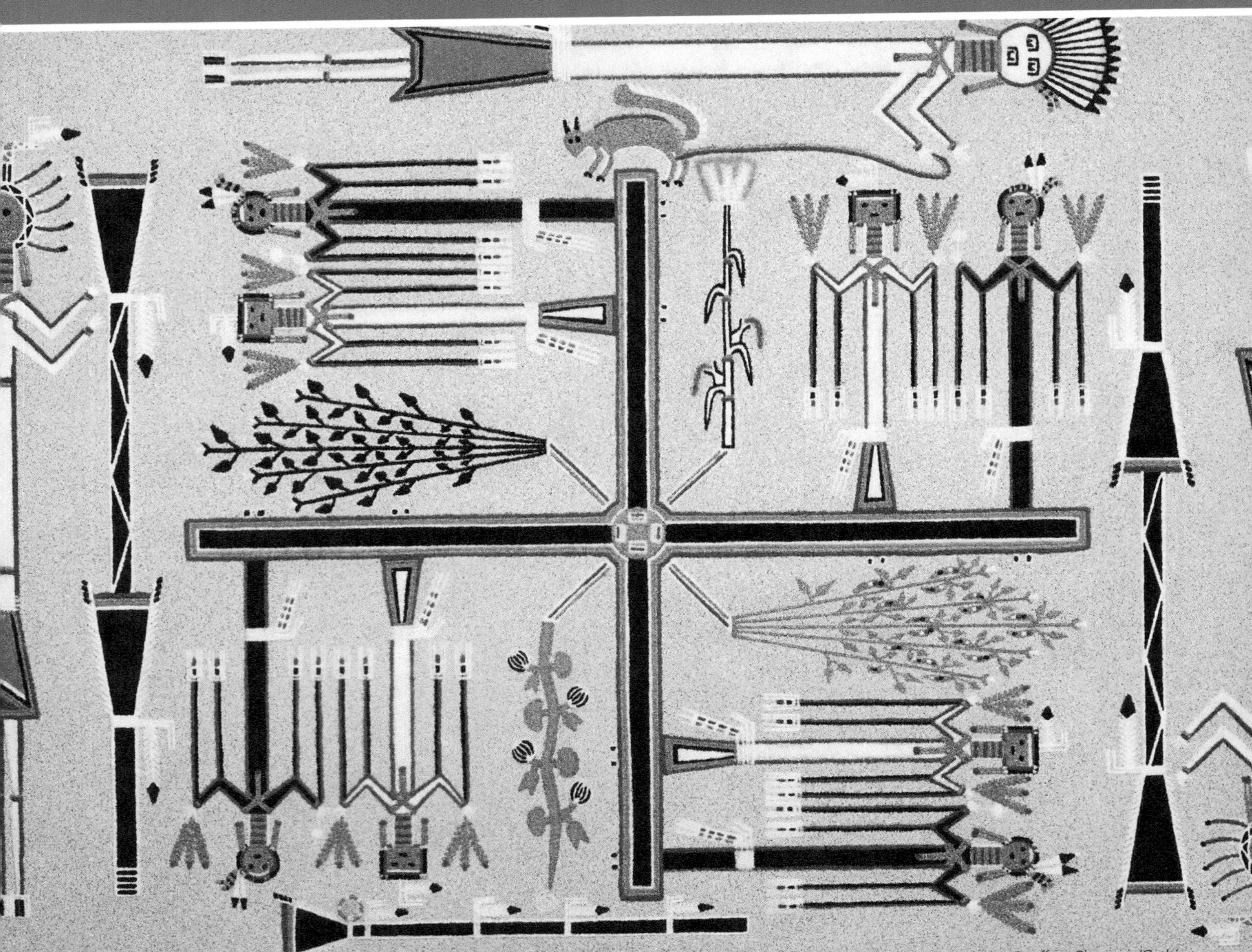

A Navajo sandpainting depicting the Whirling Logs narrative, often identified with the curing ceremony known as the Nightway chant. *Geoffrey Clements/Corbis*

The surface of the fourth world was unlike the surface of any of the lower worlds. For it was a mixture of black and white. The sky above was alternately white, blue, yellow, and black, just as it had been in the worlds below. But here the colors were of a different duration. As yet there was no sun and no moon; as yet there were no stars.

When they arrived on the surface of the fourth world, the exiles from the lower worlds saw no living thing. But they did observe four great snow-covered peaks along the horizon around them. One peak lay to the east. One peak lay to the south. One peak lay likewise to the west. And to the north there was one peak.

It was now evident to the newcomers that the fourth world was larger than any of the worlds below.

Twenty-three days came and went, and twenty-three nights passed and all was well. And on the twenty-fourth night the exiles held a council meeting. They talked quietly among themselves, and they resolved to mend their ways and to do nothing unintelligent that would create disorder. This was a good world, and the wandering people meant to stay here, it is said.

[Eventually the gods or "Holy People" gave the people instructions about how to prepare themselves to live in the fourth world. The Holy People promised to give them advice and to teach them to live properly.]

Proceeding silently the gods laid one buckskin on the ground, careful that its head faced the west. Upon its skin they placed two ears of corn, being just as careful that the tips of each pointed east. Over the corn they spread the other buckskin, making sure that its head faced east.

Under the white ear they put the feather of a white eagle. And under the yellow ear they put the feather of a yellow eagle. Then they told the onlooking people to stand at a distance.

So that the wind could enter.

Then from the east the white wind blew between the buckskins. And while the wind thus blew, each of the Holy People came and walked four times around the objects they had placed so carefully on the ground. As they walked, the eagle feathers moved slightly. Just slightly. So that only those who watched carefully were able to notice. And when the Holy People had finished walking, they lifted the topmost buckskin. And lo! The ears of corn disappeared.

In their place there lay a man and there lay a woman.

The white ear of corn had been transformed into our most ancient male ancestor [First Man] and the yellow ear of corn had been transformed into our most ancient female ancestor [First Woman].

It was the wind that had given them life: the very wind that gives us our breath as we go about our daily affairs here in the world we ourselves live in. When this wind ceases to blow inside of us, we become speechless. And we die.

In the skin at the tips of our fingers we can see the trail of that life-giving wind. Look carefully at your own fingertips. There you will see where the wind blew when it created your most ancient ancestors out of two ears of corn, it is said.

Listen to the Chapter Audio on myanthrolab.com

Read on myanthrolab.com

Creation stories from various cultures express different ideas about how people were given life and relate to their physical and social universe. The stories express different worldviews about themselves and their relationships with their environment, other people, and the spirit world. The narrative told by the Diné (or Navajo) describes the physical environment in which the people come to be. It is a world surrounded by four sacred mountains. This environment is also the fourth world in which people now live. The fact that it is the fourth world surrounded by four sacred mountains is no coincidence. Four is the sacred number for the Diné and for most Native Americans.

religion
Thoughts, actions, and feelings based on belief in the existence of spirit beings and supranormal (or superhuman) forces.

When the people emerged into this fourth world, they saw that it was beautiful and well formed. The three previous worlds had also been beautiful and well formed, but the people had made those worlds dangerous and frightening by their own behavior. Because of their lying, adultery, and greed, they had rendered their worlds uninhabitable. Through their own wrongdoings, they created worlds of disorder. Now, arriving in the fourth world, they hoped, as the narrative says, "to do nothing unintelligent," so that they could live in peace and harmony.

The gods, called the "Holy People," created First Man and First Woman out of ears of corn, the most potent and sacred of all Diné symbols of life. These sacred ears of corn, white symbolizing maleness and yellow symbolizing femaleness, came to life through the breath of wind that animates all living things. The narrative is an origin story, explaining why we breathe and why our fingertips have whorls.

The Diné story sets out a physical and moral landscape for the people to live in. They learn the importance of proper behavior, of goodness, so that the inherent harmony of the world can be maintained. Disorder comes through wrong behavior, whereas harmony, balance, and order come through ritual and right thinking. The story ties the people to a specific place, giving explanations for their surroundings and linking them to an ancient and sacred past.

WHAT IS RELIGION?

Religion is thoughts, actions, and feelings based on beliefs in the existence of spirit beings and supranormal (or superhuman) forces. It includes constellations of beliefs and practices about the spirit world and its relationship to everyday existence. Religious beliefs and practices also give people ways to contact spirit beings and forces to show them honor and respect, as well as to invoke their blessings and protection.

Spirits may be thought to inhabit a realm different from our own, or they may be ever-present, although usually unseen. People believe that the spirit world, whether visible or invisible, is connected in some ways to humans, influencing the course of human life and the outcome of human activities. To obtain the help of spirit beings and to harness spirit forces, people perform rituals that convey their desires and intentions.

Although we often speak of the spirit world as "supernatural," this term may be misleading and not fitting for all cultures. People in some cultures believe that the spirit realm is ever-present as part of their natural world and informs their daily lives in significant ways. For them, the spirit world and spirit forces are not distinct from, but rather are intertwined with, everyday life.

The "Creation of Adam" shows the bearded figure of God touching the finger of the first man. In the book of Genesis from the Judeo-Christian-Islamic tradition, the first humans are created in the image of God and instructed to "replenish the earth," so that people will live in every habitable place, not one specific locale as in the Diné story. (Michelangelo, *The Creation of Adam*, 15-08-1512. Fresco, ceiling [restored], Sistine Chapel, The Vatican, Rome. Photograph © Nippon Television Network Corporation, Tokyo.) Alamy Limited/ Michele Falzone/Alamy

Religion includes both beliefs and practices. Beliefs are a people's ideas about the spirit world, the kinds of beings and forces that have spirit power, and the ways in which the universe is created and continues to be. Religions also embody worldviews that teach people ethical values and attitudes. Sacred rituals also dramatize people's beliefs and allow them to actively express those beliefs. Through ritual action and speech, people make contact with the spirit world and manipulate spirit power for their own purposes.

Anthropologists analyze religious beliefs and rituals using etic and emic perspectives, reviewing objective conditions and subjective experiences. What do people's beliefs and practices mean for them? How do people interpret their world and their experience? How does participating in rituals affect them, and what meanings do they ascribe to the rituals? Also, how are people's religious beliefs and practices consistent with other aspects of their culture? How do people's economies and modes of subsistence influence the meanings and actions of their rituals, for example? How do their political systems or systems of social stratification frame the ways they structure their beliefs about the spirit world?

Variations in religious practices and beliefs sometimes correlate with other aspects of society. In egalitarian, stateless societies, for example, relationships between deities or spirit beings tend to be egalitarian as well. Just as all individuals have more or less equal access to economic resources and social prestige, they also have the potential to acquire spirit powers. In contrast, people in societies with hierarchical social structures are more likely to believe in the existence of a ranked pantheon of deities. The Greek and Roman gods and goddesses are a good example of such a system. Zeus (in Greece) or Jupiter (in Rome) stood at the apex of a pyramidal structure of power. Each was allied with a spouse, Hera and Juno, respectively, with whom they formed a conjugal unit, a reflection of the household structure of ancient Greece and Rome.

Monotheistic religions with their single supreme deity reflect political systems having central supreme leaders—a king or emperor. In the past, rulers of these societies were thought to be divine or to derive their authority directly from a god. Thus, many of the first state societies are referred to as theocracies—literally, governments by god. The relationships of gods and their activities are thus metaphors for ways of life on earth but on a more heroic, larger-than-life scale.

Religious behavior is both practical and symbolic. Performing rituals is doing something to achieve practical results, but these actions also have symbolic meanings. **Religious speech**— invocations, prayers, prophecies, songs of praise, curses—is a powerful means of transmitting messages about the world, and it creates the world as well. Religious speech attempts to change a state of being, to exert agency or control over people or over events or natural phenomena. Through both speech and action, people express their ideas about causality, about how things happen and how human and other powers affect the world.

Hindu worshipers carry a statue of the elephant-headed god, Ganesha, through the streets of Mumbai, India. Ganesha, the god of wisdom, prosperity, and good fortune, is celebrated in an annual festival. Alamy Limited/Dinodia Photos/Alamy

These gospel singers illustrate the concept of religious speech. Alamy Limited/imagebroker/Alamy

religious speech
Invocations, prayers, prophecies, songs of praise, and curses that are powerful means of transmitting messages about the world and also creating the world.

In what ways does your life philosophy reflect the religious and secular values of your society?

Religious beliefs are subject to change and respond to change in the social system, partly because of their underlying ambiguity and mystery. The mystery stems from the impossibility of proof, replaced instead by the certainty of faith. Ambiguity arises in religious speech, in which messages are layered with meanings. These messages must be interpreted and reinterpreted. In reinterpreting religious messages, people refer to their wants and needs to weave together a meaningful philosophy of life.

Religion is thoughts, actions, and feelings based on beliefs in the existence of god(s), spirit being(s), or supernatural force(s). Religious beliefs and practices give people ways to contact such beings or forces, to honor and respect them, and to invoke their blessings and protection. Anthropologists use comparison and cultural relativism to analyze religious beliefs and behaviors. Religions tend to reflect the structure of the societies in which they arise.

THE ORIGINS AND FUNCTIONS OF RELIGION

It is impossible to know when or where religious beliefs first appeared in human societies. Archaeologists have discovered ancient human burials and can infer ritual practices that may have had religious meaning, such as the use of red ochre, grave goods, caches of ritual objects, and reliquaries or shrines. But we cannot know what was in the minds of those ancient peoples. Did they have some feeling of community and family ties that made them want to memorialize the burial places of their kin? Or did they have some beliefs in an eternal soul that made them want to give their relatives a respectable interment? Did they include grave goods with the burial so that the deceased could use them in an afterlife? Possible evidence of religious practices also comes from ancient cave paintings and rock paintings discovered in France, Spain, southern Africa, and Australia (Peregrine 2003). Most of the paintings in these venues are of animals. Why?

Explaining the World

People often turn to their religion to seek explanations for events whose causes seem unknown or uncontrollable. Their beliefs help them gain some sense of control over what is ultimately unexplainable, unpredictable, and uncontrollable. People may wonder why their efforts are sometimes successful and sometimes not, why the same effort on different occasions may lead to a positive outcome and sometimes not. Why are some hunting expeditions successful but others fail? Why are some babies born healthy but others are sickly? Why do people die? Through ritual, people attempt to impose order and control over the outcomes of their efforts. Through ritual, they appeal to spirit forces to aid them in their endeavors and to ensure successful outcomes and to avoid misfortune.

The explanatory power of religious beliefs also helps people understand why the world is the way it is, why the earth has the shape it has, why the animals and plants have the form they have, and why people look and act the way they do. In most religions, there are thought to be creator or transformer deities who gave the world and all the creatures in it their present shape. These creator deities may also be responsible for imparting knowledge to people, teaching them how to plant, hunt, and organize their social life. They may be responsible for the origin of kinship groupings and of political structure. They may be responsible for setting out the kind of work that people do, the roles that men and women fill, and the values and ethics that people live by. In this way, religious beliefs are not only explanatory but also serve to legitimate a particular social or political system. For example, social inequality may be explained as part of a divine plan. A loved one's death may be explained as god's will.

Science and technology serve many of the same functions of explaining, predicting, and attempting to control the world. In science, however, the underlying premises about cause and effect are different. The scientific approach is based on empirical observation or modeling of effects that are believed to have physical causes. Religious interpretations of observations are based on the belief that ultimate causes are spiritual processes and forces.

Solace, Healing, and Emotional Release

Religious faith provides psychological support in times of anxiety and stress, and religious practices can be emotionally therapeutic for individuals and groups. Confession of wrongdoings enables people to express their remorse, shed their guilt, and feel rehabilitated in their own eyes, in the eyes of their community, and in the eyes of the deities who may see and judge their actions and bestow forgiveness or mercy. Psychological functions of religion may be seen, for example, in visionary experiences or spirit quests. The profound emotional catharsis that can result from prayer, participation in rituals, and contact with the spirit world may have a healing effect by comforting a sufferer, releasing tension and worry.

cosmology
Religious worldview of a people, including beliefs about the origin of the world, the pantheon of deities that exist, and their relationships to the spirit realm.

Social Cohesion

Religious beliefs and practices often function to support cohesive communities. Most rituals involve, in addition to individuals, their family, wider kinship grouping, and social networks that connect them to others. Some rituals, such as seasonal or annual celebrations, unite an entire local population or tribal group.

Religious beliefs and practices can further function to justify the existing social order. Relationships among deities may reflect the sociopolitical nature of the human society. In stratified societies, the leader (whether chief, emperor, or king) may be thought to be a descendant of the divinity, endowed with divine power, or chosen directly by the deities. In the Polynesian chiefdoms, central and southern African kingdoms, European monarchies, and the Inca Empire, the head of state was thought to rule by divine right.

Teachings conveyed by spirits, especially in stories of creation and transformation, also legitimate the existing social order. Gender roles, for example, and the relations between women and men may be mandated through divine teachings or modeled through the relationships of male and female deities. For example, in the Hindu pantheon of deities, gods and goddesses have important and powerful roles and are equally likely to be worshipped by believers. However, married and unmarried goddesses have strikingly different personalities. When married, goddesses are nurturing, benevolent, and trustworthy; when unmarried, they are aggressive, dangerous, and unpredictable.

In contrast, Diné **cosmology**—a belief system concerning the origin and nature of the universe—presents many deities as interdependent and complementary male and female pairs. First Man and First Woman are important creator and transformer deities. Twilight Man and Twilight Woman and Dawn Man and Dawn Woman are deities of the daytime cycle. Although they play different roles, male and female deities have similar powers, personalities, and effects on the lives of humans.

What do texts in a religion with which you are familiar teach about gender roles and relationships? What social order do those teachings tend to support?

Social Control

Rituals often function as formal and informal mechanisms of social control. In some stratified societies, codified criminal and civil laws, judicial processes, and punishments or penal sanctions are based on religious doctrines, customs, or texts. The function of social control can also be subtle, however. In some cultures, for example, the time of puberty is marked by role reversals in which socially disapproved behavior is permitted briefly in ritual context. Amish teenagers completing high school are permitted to drink beer and have noisy parties before settling down to a serious and devout life, for example. Similarly, central African teenagers are permitted to act in ways considered deviant—publicly speaking obscenities or acting lewd. They may also engage in gender reversals, boys dressing and acting like girls and girls mimicking the behavior and language of boys. Such ritualized permission to act inappropriately may temporarily ease tensions in societies where norms of proper behavior are strictly followed. They also serve to highlight social values through the transgression of norms.

Economic Adaptation

Another function of religion is to give people additional means to adapt to their environments and changes in their circumstances. Anthropologists using cultural materialist or ecological perspectives analyze religious practices as means of adapting to one's environment. Consider, for example, Marvin Harris's interpretation of the sacred cow in India as protection against the slaughter of cattle in light of their central importance in the economy of farmers. In another classic study, Roy Rappaport (1969; 2000) demonstrates how a complex ritual cycle relates to the economy and environment of the Tsembaga of New Guinea.

CASE STUDY

Pigs for the Ancestors

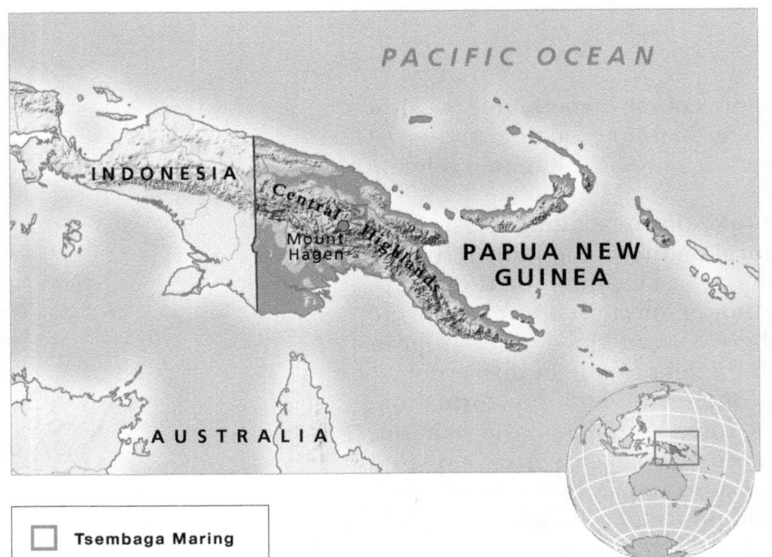

The Tsembagas of New Guinea, numbering about 200 people, participate in an interrelated system of rituals, economic production, social activity, and warfare. The Tsembagas practice horticulture and animal husbandry. Women are the principal farmers, planting and harvesting yams that feed the people and the dozens of pigs that each family maintains. Tsembagas live in balanced competition with neighboring tribes. Intergroup relations involve mutually beneficial trade and social interactions that lead to marriage alliances and military support for raids. Raids help balance the ratio of people to land and resources. Raids also create buffer zones of uninhabitable land that is left fallow to regenerate. However, too frequent raiding would disturb people's ability to farm and raise their pigs. Therefore, a complex set of practices controls the frequency of warfare, and these practices are couched in beliefs about people's obligations to their ancestors and the spirit realm.

The cycle of practices may last twenty years. At the end of a period of hostilities, Tsembagas ritually plant a shrub, called a *rumbin,* in their territory. This act communicates the group's symbolic and real connection to their territory. An elaborate feast is then held, centered around the slaughter of nearly all the group's pigs. Only juvenile pigs are spared, to ensure future supplies. The pigs are slaughtered as a sacrifice to the ancestors who assisted the group to win the warfare with its neighbors.

No matter how many pigs are sacrificed, however, the people think that the obligations to the ancestors remain partly unfulfilled. People then solemnly promise the ancestors that they will offer future sacrifices. Until that time, hostilities must cease, because renewing hostilities is considered improper until all obligations to the ancestors have been discharged. Thus, episodes of warfare are regulated by the amount of time it takes to increase the pig population to the number needed for a proper sacrifice.

Complex factors are involved in people's judgments about whether they have enough pigs to offer to the ancestors. When the pig population is relatively small, the animals can be fed without too much effort, but after a while, the women gardeners must use more land to grow food for pigs that would otherwise be used for human consumption. For instance, during Rappaport's fieldwork in the 1960s, about 36 percent of active farmland was used to feed the village's 170 pigs.

Eventually, a woman's complaints to her husband about the undue burdens on her labor reach a critical point, and he becomes willing to speak to other men. By that time, most of the men in the village are receiving similar complaints from their wives. Once people experience the burdens of maintaining a large number of pigs, they acknowledge their readiness to make sacrifices to the ancestors.

The next episode of the cycle commences with the uprooting of the *rumbin,* signaling the beginning of a yearlong festival. During the festival, they invite friendly neighboring groups to visit the village to socialize and feast on the sacrificed pigs. They may pursue social and economic goals during these festivals. They distribute pork to allies and exchange other articles of trade. In addition, young men hold dances to signal their interest in and availability for marriage. Eligible young women attend the dances and observe the qualities of eligible men. The young men's presence is also interpreted as a willingness to aid the hosts as allies in future conflicts.

The final segment of the cycle begins after the festival period has ended. Raiding one's enemies (one's competitors for land) may now resume. When the hostilities have temporarily resolved tensions, the *rumbin* is replanted, marking the end of one cycle and the beginning of the next. **Read** the **Document** on **myanthrolab.com**

Whatever their origins, religious beliefs and practices provide explanations for the world as it is, for how people are, and for major events in people's lives. Religion also provides solace in times of trouble and sorrow, allowing for emotional release and providing emotional support. Religious beliefs and practices also bind communities into cohesive networks. As ideologies, they can both support and change the existing social order and people's adaptations to their environment.

SPIRIT BEINGS AND FORCES

Spirit beings and forces have extraordinary, more-than-human powers. They typically are eternal or indestructible; they know more than an ordinary person can know; and they are able to act in ways that humans cannot. Thus, people seek contact with them to gain their protection and aid. Spirits may have the shape of animals, humans, or other unusual forms and may change their shape at will. Sometimes they imbue inanimate objects with special powers. A supernatural force may be a vague spirit essence that pervades the universe.

Animism and Animatism

One common, nearly universal form that spirit takes is the soul. Souls are the eternal aspect of living things. In some belief systems, such as Judaism, Christianity, and Islam, only human beings have souls. But in many cultures, people believe that animals and plants—all living things—have souls as well. The soul is seen as the animating aspect of living things. It gives life to the body that it inhabits. When the body dies, the soul leaves and exists eternally in some other form or in a nonmaterial state. The belief in souls and the spirit essences of all living things is called **animism.** In some belief systems, what we might think of as inanimate objects may be endowed with spirit essence as well. For example, people with animistic beliefs might ascribe consciousness and personality to a thunderstorm, a tree, or a rock. In some societies, people believe that an impersonal spiritual force exists that can manifest itself in people, animals, or inanimate objects. This belief is sometimes called **animatism.** For example, a person's success or good fortune are signs of one's access to this impersonal force just as one's failures result from the absence of spiritual force.

Gods and Heroes

Some religious traditions have many spirit beings in human form—gods—with specific attributes, powers, and functions. Belief in numerous deities, called **polytheism,** is widespread throughout the world. In Hinduism, with its hundreds of millions of followers, as well as in the belief systems of small subsistence societies numbering in the hundreds, polytheistic spirit worlds are inhabited by multitudes of beings, each with a name, identity, genealogy, history, and domain of influence. In contrast, in **monotheistic religions** people believe in one supreme deity who has powers and knowledge that affect all aspects of life. In addition, there may be other, lesser spirit beings and important mortal heroes as well.

Ancestors, Ghosts, and Demons

Other types of spirit beings include the spirit forms of deceased ancestors. Ancestral spirits have a particular connection to their living descendants, who honor them through prayer and ritual. In return, the spirits bestow blessings, health, and good fortune on their surviving kin. If people fail to perform the rituals, ancestor spirits can bring illness and misfortune.

After a death in Japan, especially of a man, the eldest son prepares a mortuary tablet that commemorates his father (Morioka 1984). These tablets are kept in a household altar for at least several generations. They are honored and given offerings from

animism
Belief in the existence of souls.

animatism
Belief that all things are endowed with some spirit form or essence.

polytheism
Belief in the existence of numerous deities that have specific attributes, powers, and functions.

monotheistic religions
Belief systems that hold to the existence of one supreme deity who has powers and knowledge that affect all aspects of life.

This Japanese woman honors a dead ancestor by presenting offerings at an altar in her home. Photo Japan/Shimizu Teruyo/Photo Japan

time to time in commemorative rituals. Eventually, the tablets of the eldest ancestor may be retired, either buried or broken and discarded. This ritual or ceremony is sometimes referred to as **ancestor worship.** In the past, reflecting Japan's patrilineal descent and patriarchal society, tablets for women usually were discarded after only one or two generations, but tablets for men were kept for a longer time. Today, however, a bilateral principle governs ancestor worship, and mothers and grandmothers are honored along with fathers and grandfathers. Any member of the family, not just the eldest son, can carry out the rituals. These changes reflect shifts in Japanese household composition from extended family to nuclear family forms.

Among the Ju/'hoansi of the Kalahari, ancestral spirits, called *gangwasi,* are thought to cause illness and misfortune. People are wary of their ancestral spirits, avoiding contact with them in the night and hoping to be spared misfortune. They periodically perform dances to prevent ancestral spirits from attacking them and causing harm. Most important is treating people right while they are alive so that their spirit will not seek out offenders to harm them after death.

The Hopis of Arizona believe that ancestral spirits join the kachinas, powerful beings that bring rain. When people die, their spirits become mist and clouds that return to the people in the form of rain, helping to sustain crops in an arid environment. Hopis view themselves as eternally linked in cycles of life and death, and they pray to and honor their ancestors so that they will be blessed with rain. Representational wooden carvings of spirits, called kachina dolls, are conduits to the spirit world.

In many cultures, people believe that deceased individuals may return or appear in the form of ghosts. Ghosts may have human shape, or they may be only shadows. Ghosts may be welcomed or feared, and they may return to the living to cause mischief or harm or to transmit messages of great importance. In some societies, ghosts are cast as demons. Among New Guinea natives, for example, village compounds must be ritually protected against wandering demons.

How are ghosts viewed in American popular culture today?

Mana, Totems, and Taboos

In addition to or instead of believing in spirit beings, many people believe in the existence of a pervasive spirit power. This power or essence endows people, animals, other living things, and possibly inanimate objects with special qualities or powers. This force has its own name in every culture, but is often referred to as **mana,** from Polynesian languages where it was first described, in the anthropological literature on religion. A belief in mana is a form of animatism. Having mana gives a person special knowledge and power or an object special properties and qualities. Perfectly grown yams may be said to have mana, for example. Spirit powers are sometimes held in talismans or fetishes to give the wearer good luck. A rabbit's foot held or worn for luck, for example, is an expression of animatism.

In some cultures of Australia and the Pacific Northwest of North America, people believe that they are the descendants of spirit beings or ancestors, a belief called **totemism.** Totemic ancestors may have human or animal form. From ancient times, they gave protection or lifesaving advice to human beings in need or in danger. Thus, they are the primordial protectors of the people. Ancestral totems may also be identified as the actual progenitors of the present-day people. In either case, people owe them gratitude and respect and perform rituals in their honor so that they will continue to receive protection and guidance.

Totemism celebrates the solidarity of social groups. Australian Aborigines believe that each clan is descended from a specific animal in the mythic past or "the Dreaming" (Hume 2000). At some time in an earlier realm of existence, the mythic animal ancestor was transformed into a human being and continues to be connected to its human descendants. The descendants honor their animal ancestor, or totem, by performing rituals in its honor and by refraining from eating its flesh. The totemic figure functioned to unite Aborigines, who, because of their nomadic lifestyle and dispersed populations,

ancestor worship
Belief in the importance of ancestors as they affect the lives of their survivors, protecting their descendants in return for rituals of honor performed to show them respect.

mana
A force, power, or essence that endows people, animals, other living things, and possibly inanimate objects with special qualities or powers.

totemism
Belief system in which people believe they are descendants of spirit beings.

The familiar totem poles of some Pacific Northwest Native American groups depict the record of a kin group and its relationship with its spirit ancestor—in the form of a mammal, bird, or other animal. This pole was carved by David Boxley, Port Gamble S'Klallam Reservation, Washington. Alamy Limited/Jean Boyle/Alamy

rarely came into sustained contact. Spirit links among people have survival value because they create bonds of mutual acknowledgment, interdependence, and obligations to extend hospitality and share resources.

Spirit forces and beings are dangerous if contacted in the wrong way, in the wrong place, or at the wrong time. Some spirits inhabit particular locales that may be dangerous if entered without spiritual protection. Objects used in rituals may also be dangerous if touched or used when a person is not prepared. Societies that believe in these dangers may have organizations, known as **secret societies,** that control the special places or the use of special objects. For example, among Australian Aborigines and Amazonian Indians, only men may touch special musical instruments or ritual objects. If women come into contact with these objects, they may be seriously harmed or even killed by the spirit forces associated with them. Even to hear the sounds of the music or the singing of the men may be dangerous to women.

Restrictions such as these are called taboos. A taboo object or place is one that can cause harm if contacted or entered. Its danger derives from its power. A dangerous person, object, or place may not be regarded as evil, however, because spirit power in itself is neither positive nor negative. Rather, the use to which the power is put renders it good or bad. Individuals may use their spirit powers to become healers, fortune-tellers, or other ritual practitioners, serving their communities in important ways. Others, however, may seek to acquire spirit powers to do harm.

An example of taboos is seen in rituals surrounding pregnancy and birth. In many cultures, expectant mothers, and sometimes their husbands as well, avoid eating certain foods or engaging in certain kinds of activities. Many of these restrictions are geared toward ensuring a safe pregnancy and easy delivery. Inuit parents were not to tie their belts tight lest the placenta strangle the baby during birth. Haida mothers refrained from eating sticky substances, such as salmon eggs, to ensure a smooth and quick delivery.

Pregnancy taboos symbolize the dangers of pregnancy and birth and the uncertainty of outcomes. Through taboos, people express their fears and their desires to control essentially unpredictable events. In addition, taboos allow people to explain both positive and negative results. If the birth goes well and the baby is healthy, parents can feel that their behavior contributed to the happy occasion. However, if the baby is sickly or dies, parents can find the reason for their misfortune by recalling taboos that they failed to observe.

secret societies
Organizations that control the use of special objects used in religious rituals.

Spirit beings and forces include gods, ancestors, ghosts, demons, totems, mana, souls, and spirit powers that may be evidenced in good or bad luck. Animism is belief in souls, and animatism is the belief that animals, plants, and inanimate objects are endowed with souls or personalities and have spiritual powers. Some religions are monotheistic (with one god), whereas others are polytheistic (with many gods). In totemism, people trace their descent from animal ancestors and observe ritual taboos to protect the ancestral spirits. Spiritual power, such as mana, may be positive or negative, depending on how it is used. Potentially dangerous or contaminating spiritual power may be managed through secret societies or taboos. Religious rituals and religious speech often are aimed at giving people agency or control over forces and events that affect their lives. Shared religious beliefs and practices also contribute to people's social solidarity.

RELIGIOUS PRACTITIONERS

Most religions have individuals or groups who function as either part-time or full-time specialists or practitioners. Sometimes people receive a calling from the spirit world to become a religious specialist. The calling could be received in a dream, a waking vision, or an omen or sign. Some societies believe that particular individuals inherit spiritual abilities from one generation to the next. In other cases, a person decides to become a religious practitioner because of interests, experiences, or wishes to benefit the community through ritual practice. Some people may be drawn to ritual practice because of its creative and aesthetic qualities that give outlet for artistic expression through music, song, dance, and drama. Religious specialists may enlist others to take the training necessary to become a practitioner. Mediums, healers, shamans, diviners, and priests are all religious practitioners.

How do mediums and diviners practice in your society or community today?

Mediums, Diviners, and Healers

Mediums are believed to have special gifts that enable them to make contact with the spirit world and with spirit beings or spirits of the dead. They usually establish a direct relationship with a particular spirit or group of spirits. Through rituals they perform, mediums become conduits or channels between ordinary people and the contacted spirit beings. They often conduct these rituals in a state of trance—an altered state of consciousness in which they are not fully conscious of their surroundings. Trance states can be achieved through various means, including meditation or mental concentration; once in a trance, mediums can pass messages between individuals and members of the spirit world.

Diviners have the power to predict the future through messages and omens they receive and interpret from the spirit world. They use various divination techniques to obtain the spirit's guidance or answers to specific questions or problems. For example, they may recognize patterns or designs that tell a story, as in reading tea leaves or tarot cards. In some African societies, diviners roll chicken bones to read a person's fortune or examine animal entrails to predict a family's best course of action. In some Central American societies, diviners tell fortunes by throwing corn kernels into a bowl and finding meaning in the pattern the kernels make. In North America, native diviners threw fruit pits to read patterns in the way they fell. Diviners may also look at the stars or gaze into water to retrieve omens and warnings.

Healers are religious practitioners who acquire spirit power to heal. They can diagnose the spirit cause of illness and effect cures through the performance of rituals. In North America, many people heed the advice of "faith healers," some of whom have large followings of enthusiastic believers. Traditional healers usually have some practical knowledge of human anatomy and physiology, pharmacology, and pharmaceutical substances in their environment. Healers may use this practical knowledge in their cures in addition to religious rituals. In some societies, healers may be suspected of sometimes using their control of spirit powers to cause harm rather than to cure illness. Beliefs and practices of sorcery or witchcraft constitute powerful sources of social control.

mediums
People having special gifts to make contact with the spirit world, often in a state of trance.

diviners
People with the power to predict the future through messages and omens from the spirit world.

healers
Religious practitioners who acquire spirit power to diagnose the spirit cause of illness and effect cures.

Ritual healers are usually called in to treat a patient when the illness is protracted or life-threatening. The following account, related in 1918 by a Fox woman, describes her experience with a healer called to assist her in the difficult birth of her first child:

> When that woman [the healer] came, she at once boiled some medicine. After she had boiled it, she said: "Let her sit up for a while. You must hold her so that she will not fall over." After I was made to sit up, she spat upon my head; and she gave me the medicine to drink. After she had given me the medicine, she began singing. She started to go out singing and went around the little lodge singing. When she danced by where I was, she knocked on the side. "Come out if you are a boy," she would say. And she would again begin singing. When she danced by she again knocked the side. "Come out if you are a girl," she would say again. After she sang four times in a circle, she entered the lodge. And she gave me medicine to drink. "Now it will be born. She may lie down." Lo, sure enough, my baby was born. (Michelson 1920, 319)

This female shaman, or *mudang,* in Korea is summoning the spirit world to promote harmony, heal, bring messages to the living, or appease the dead. Cedar Bough Photography/Cedar Bough Photography

Shamans and Priests

Shamans are part-time religious practitioners who contact the spirit world through ritual, prayer, and trance. They may use masks that represent spirit beings. Shamans are similar to mediums in many respects, except that they may not channel with a particular spirit being. Rather, they enter trance states to receive visions and messages from the spirit realm. Their work tends to be on behalf of the community as a whole. Shamans may also perform healing rituals or rituals seeking spirit protection, advice, and support. Ecstatic experience, whether through trance, visions, or dreams, is central to the way that shamans make contact with the spirit world. Shamanism may be quite ancient in the origins of religions (Goodman 1990).

Some societies have full-time religious practitioners called **priests,** who lead religious organizations and officiate at rituals but are not necessarily expected to be able to communicate directly with gods or the spirit world. The category of priest includes spiritual and ritual leaders of formally institutionalized religions with places of worship, such as churches, mosques, or congregations, including ministers, rabbis, and mullahs, in addition to Roman Catholic or Greek Orthodox priests. Priests work on behalf of their religious organization, as well as their community and its members. Priests often preside at rites of passage, such as those that mark birth, puberty, marriage, and death.

shamans
Part-time religious practitioners who make contact with the spirit world through prayer, ritual, and trance.

Religious practitioners include mediums, healers, diviners, shamans, and priests. Mediums enter trance states to communicate between individuals and the spirit world; diviners tell the future or enter trance states to receive omens or advice from the spirit world. Healers use both spiritual and practical means to treat illness. Priests are full-time specialists who work for religious organizations and lead congregations in religious ceremonies and rituals. Unlike shamans, priests are not expected to have spirit power or communicate directly with divine beings.

RELIGIOUS PRACTICE

Religious practices, or **rituals,** are demonstrations of belief, putting belief into action. Rituals may be formal and public with many well-rehearsed participants and performers. They may also be informal and private, carried out by individuals or small groups. Rituals, including those involving religious speech, play a central role in most religions. They are the means by which believers make contact with the gods or spirit world; express honor and respect for spirit beings; obtain blessings, health, prosperity, or success; and achieve particular personal or communal goals. Rituals also can have specific ends, such as purification (spiritual cleansing), sanctification (making something sacred), veneration (worshipping

priests
Full-time religious practitioners who lead a religious organization and officiate at rituals but are not expected to be able to communicate directly with the spirit world.

rituals
Activities, including religious speech, ceremonies, and behaviors, that are demonstrations of belief.

sacred rituals
Activities, places, or objects that are connected to the spirit realm and are imbued with power.

rites of renewal
Rituals performed with the goal of renewing the bounty of the earth.

The Nuna and Bwa peoples of Burkina Faso use wooden painted animal masks and dances to make the spirit world come alive, as the butterfly dancer shows here. Christopher D. Roy/Christopher D. Roy

something), or absolution (giving spiritual forgiveness). Individual rituals may be linked together in a ceremonial, a series of interconnected rituals.

Rituals usually involve the visual and performing arts. The aesthetic impact and spiritual meaning of rituals transport participants to a mental, emotional, and spiritual state of being that is different from their ordinary lives. Participants may adorn themselves with special clothing, masks, or face and body painting. They typically employ special objects made with precious metals, or such objects may be carved, painted, or decorated with jewels, feathers, or stone in designs that incorporate religious symbols. Religious art and iconography (the meaning of symbols and design) thus reveal people's aesthetic values. Rituals also involve poetic language and the arts of music, song, and dance.

Sacred and Secular Rituals

Watch the **Video:** *Woman in the Clergy Talks about Her Spiritual Self* on **myanthrolab.com**

Secular life is full of rituals or ritualized activities, but these are not the same as sacred rituals. **Sacred rituals** are dedicated to the spirit realm and the expression of religious faith. Secular rituals may also be important culturally. For example, secular holidays such as Independence Day (in the United States) and Canada Day (in Canada) are times to display national symbols such as flags, sing national songs, and hear patriotic speeches. Sporting events may also be marked by ritualized protection, such as wearing team insignia or colors and cheering. The players may practice personal rituals to bring success, such as wearing good-luck gear in the game. These behaviors and attitudes involve magical thinking not unlike practices associated with religious beliefs, but their purpose is secular rather than spiritual.

In many societies, seasonal or annual rituals with both sacred and secular elements are held to celebrate the earth's bounty. Celebrations serve both as a thanksgiving for the past year's plants and animals and as a request to the spirits for renewed generation and continued supplies. These are examples of **rites of renewal,** also called rites of intensification.

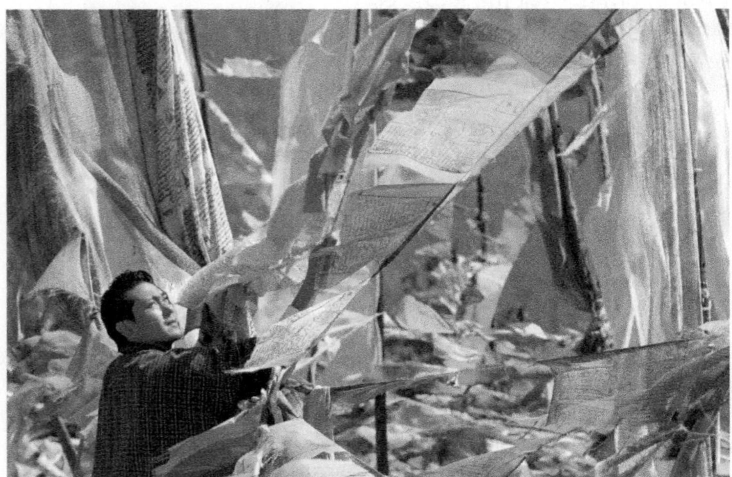

Devotee offering prayer flags in Thimphu, Bhutan. The flags carry Buddhist sacred texts and symbols. Corbis/Christophe Boisvieux/Corbis

Prayer and Sacrifice

Prayer is both a private and a public ritual. Through **prayer,** believers transmit messages to the spirit beings or to particular deities or ancestors. Prayers are meant to honor the spirits, ask favors of them, or win future blessings. Some religions emphasize the memorization and correct verbatim repetition of prayers. Without correct recitations, prayers may not be effective. Other religions permit or encourage private prayers that individuals make up as they pray.

Believers also transmit messages to the spirit realm through the **sacrifice** of offerings that honor spirit beings by giving up something important. Offerings may consist of foods that the deities are thought to prefer or valuable objects. People may also fast, refrain from sleep, or subject themselves to some kind of ordeal as a kind of sacrifice. Offerings may also include animals given in rituals of blood sacrifice in which the animals are slaughtered. Societies where people keep domesticated animals may use their stock in sacrificial offerings.

In the Sun Dance, young North American Plains Indian warriors like the one pictured here sacrificed small parts of their bodies in honor of their spirit protectors. Corbis/Edward S. Curtis/Corbis

Blood sacrifice centers on the killing of a valuable domesticated animal, but some societies practiced human sacrifice. Perhaps the best-known example was the human sacrifice performed by the Aztecs in central Mexico in the fifteenth and sixteenth centuries. Aztecs believed that the sun god (also the war god), called Huitzilopochtli, needed to be fed so that he would have the energy to travel across the sky from sunrise to sunset every day. He was nourished on human blood from daily sacrifices. This practice eventually contributed to the downfall of the Aztec Empire: As the need for more sacrificial victims increased, the priesthood demanded sacrifices from defeated groups forcibly incorporated into the expanding Aztec state. Those groups thus became even more hostile toward the Aztec state and aided the Spanish invasion of the Aztec Empire in the early sixteenth century.

prayer
Religious speech or thought through which believers transmit messages to spirit beings.

sacrifice
Offerings made to spirit beings to show gratitude and honor.

CASE STUDY

Making Contact with the Spirit World

Religious practice includes rituals that enable people to contact the spirit world. These rituals may be personal and private or public communal demonstrations of belief. Prayer is the most personal method of attempting to contact the spirit world. Through prayer, believers convey their thoughts, feelings, hopes, and worries. The purpose of prayer is both cathartic and practical. The cathartic element comes about from the relief that people feel in the act of prayer, allowing themselves to express feelings and fears. Prayer is also aimed at achieving practical goals such as healing an illness in oneself or family members, gaining prosperity, or obtaining spiritual knowledge. Prayer attempts to establish a relationship with the spirit world through words and thoughts. But how can people know if their messages have been received? In some belief systems, a spirit being might communicate directly with a believer through visual or auditory contact. In others, a person might receive a symbolic or mysterious message that would have to be interpreted. Such messages might occur in dreams, visions, signs, or omens that are so obscure or mundane that a specialist has to interpret them.

Certain religious practitioners specialize in seeking out and deciphering messages from the spirit realm. They may do this for an entire community, or they may interpret signs or omens for individuals. For example, oracles have skills that enable them to understand the hidden meanings of ordinary objects and patterns. Oracles employ their skills in response to questions. They may interpret past events or advise about future options. For example, a parent might request advice about whether a child's marriage will be favorable; a person might wonder whether a dwelling he or she wants to build is in a location that will bring health or misfortune; or someone might ask whether a visit will turn out well. Oracles are not consulted lightly. Their advice is sought when danger and disruption threaten social relations or familial or community stability.

Once consulted, oracles use their spiritual gifts to foresee the future. They might do this by entering a state of trance or altered consciousness that allows them to get in touch with another realm of existence and meaning. Oracles may also use techniques of divination, reading the signs ordinary objects make. Some oracles cut open sacrificed animals such as goats or chickens to see whether the form or color of internal organs conveys positive or negative messages.

Although divination may appear to lead to random results, successful oracles are intimately familiar with their clients' circumstances and have keen understanding of social networks and relationships. The actions people take as a result of an oracle's advice, therefore, fit well with accustomed and appropriate behavior consistent with community norms.

In some societies, ordinary people may make direct contact with the spirit world through trance or heightened awareness of the spirit realm. People may acquire this ability spontaneously and without training. Messages or visions may appear to them while awake or sleeping. They may find objects that have special meaning and can be used for protection and "good luck." These objects may appear mundane but are representations of spirit contact.

The most direct form of communication with the spirit realm is through possession, in which a spirit being invades a person's body, taking over some of that person's physical and cognitive functions. The spirit may then speak through the person's mouth, imparting messages or simply expressing a state of being in an unknown language. In some belief systems, spirit possession happens spontaneously, whereas people in other systems may consciously seek it out. However initiated, the experience can be both fearful and cathartic, from the close contact with extraordinary power. The experience is transformative, changing a person's sense of self.

In addition, people in many indigenous societies who participate in rituals are thought to be in close contact with spirit powers. They may be privileged to understand and partake of a realm of knowledge outside ordinary experience. For example, when dancers put on costumes and masks that represent spirit beings, they are not merely impersonating the spirits; they actually become transformed into those beings, even if only temporarily. Read the **Document** on **myanthrolab.com**

Rites of Passage

People in most societies perform rituals to celebrate socially significant transitions in an individual's life cycle. Such rites of passage are typically conducted to mark birth, puberty, marriage, and death. Rituals may also mark other aspects of the life cycle, such as naming or initiation into an association. According to anthropologist Arnold van Gennep (1961), rites of passage ritualize three aspects of change in life status: separation, transition, and reincorporation. That is, individuals separate from their families, learn new knowledge and skills, and return and are reincorporated into their communities as new people. Let us apply this model to two rites of passage: puberty rites and funerary rites.

As an ethnographer, how might you describe a puberty rite, funerary rite, or other rite of passage that you have observed?

Puberty Rites. Van Gennep's model can be applied to **puberty rites,** also called initiation rites, which celebrate the transition from childhood to adulthood. In some cultures, puberty rites are held for only girls or only boys; in others, both boys and girls receive ritual recognition. The Jewish and Christian faiths have rituals that mark a child's growth and maturation. The Jewish bar mitzvah (for boys) and bat mitzvah (for girls) incorporate the child into the adult community of believers. In the Christian ceremony of confirmation, children pledge themselves to their faith and join the congregation of their own volition. Children are usually around 10 or 11 years old when they are confirmed, an age associated with cognitive maturation. In some Christian denominations, christening marks religious as well as social birth, baptism consecrates the person in the faith, and confirmation welcomes the individual into the community of believers. The Western Apaches of New Mexico and the Sukus of the Congo (formerly Zaire) conduct elaborate ceremonies when girls and boys, respectively, reach puberty (see the Case Study).

puberty rites
Rituals performed to mark the passage of an individual from childhood to adulthood; also called initiation rites.

funerary rites
Rituals performed to mark a person's death and passage to the afterworld.

Funerary Rites. Funerals, or **funerary rites,** mark the final stage of life and are usually solemn. Death rituals serve purposes for both the living and the dead. According to many belief systems, the proper performance of a funeral allows the soul of the deceased to

Hindu funeral rites in India end in an above-ground cremation of the deceased on a funeral pyre.
Magnum Photos New York/Raghu Rai/Magnum Photos, Inc.

depart in peace. At death, the soul, which is the activating, invigorating, life-giving aspect of a person, leaves the body and eventually travels to the afterworld. Usually, though, the soul does not make its final journey until after the funeral. If the funeral is not properly conducted, the soul may never be fully released. It may hover near the living or wander aimlessly, possibly causing mischief and harm.

Watch the **Video:** *Rights of Passage* on **myanthrolab.com**

After a death, relatives or hired specialists usually cleanse, decorate, and dress the body in special clothes. After a set number of days, the funeral takes place. Cultures vary widely in the degree of elaboration of funerals and the amount of time spent on them. For example, foragers spend less time and resources on funerals than people in settled populations. In some cultures, funerals are a time for the display of solidarity or interdependence among kin. For example, Mohawk funerals were arranged and conducted not by members of the deceased's own clan and moiety but by people belonging to the opposite moiety. Mohawks thought that close relatives of the deceased were too overcome by grief to be bothered with funeral details; the exchange of roles also symbolized interdependence, unity, and societal balance. In some societies, the treatment of the dead depends on characteristics such as gender, age, and status. Among the Turkana pastoralists of Kenya, people have different burial sites (Broch-Due 2000, 176, 178–79). A married man is buried in his household's goat corral at the center of his homestead. This placement symbolizes his role as the head of household and emphasizes his central economic contributions. Married women are buried in their night huts, the dwelling where they conceived and gave birth to most of their children, emphasizing their roles as mothers. Children, teenagers, and unmarried adults are not buried; rather, their bodies are left outside the borders of the camp, in the bush to the west, the direction of "badness."

Watch the **Video:** *Central Kenya Burial Site* on **myanthrolab.com**

Cave art like this from Acacus National Park, Libya, may have expressed magical beliefs. The ancient painters drew pictures of animals that they wanted to hunt.
Alamy Limited/MARKA/Alamy

Finally, in stratified societies, the burials of high-status and wealthy individuals are more elaborate than those of commoners. The deaths of high-status people also are ritually commemorated for longer periods of time. And funerals marking the deaths of central political leaders such as presidents or monarchs may become occasions for the display of national unity and public mourning.

CASE STUDY

Puberty Rites among the Apache and the Suku

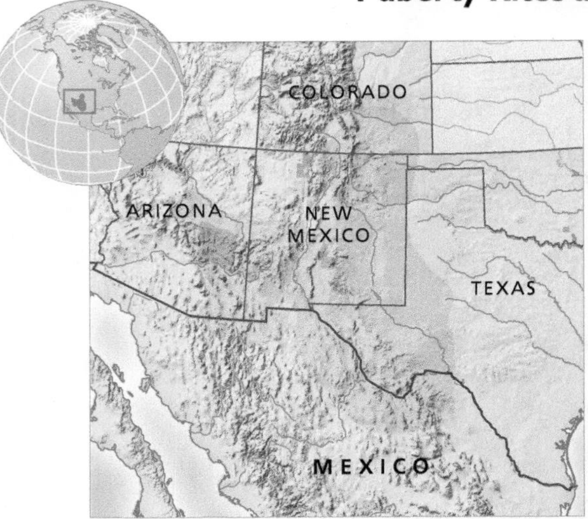

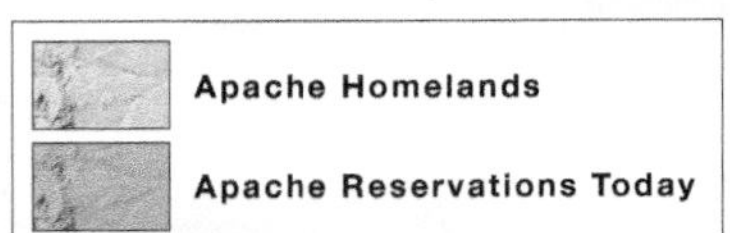

The Western Apaches associate girls' puberty with themes of fertility and power. The ritual occasioned by a girl's first menstruation, or menarche, is thought to benefit both her and her entire community (Basso 1970). The name of the ritual, *nai'es,* or "preparing her," "getting her ready," signifies one of its themes. It readies the pubescent girl for adulthood and motherhood. Preparations for the ceremony, always held in the summertime, begin immediately after menarche. The girl's parents choose a woman as sponsor for their daughter. The sponsor must not belong to the girl's matrilineal clan or that of her father. Thereafter, the sponsor and the girl's parents establish a lasting reciprocal bond, aiding one another as if they were kin.

The *nai'es* ceremony is a public event that everyone in the community attends. It begins shortly after sunrise, a time considered spiritually powerful. The rite consists of eight phases, each highlighting a different theme or activity believed to endow the girl with spiritual and material benefits. In the first phase, she dances on a public dance ground to attract supernatural powers from a deity known as Changing Woman, a symbol of fertility and benevolence. Apaches believe that the girl is transformed into Changing Woman and acquires her qualities and powers during puberty rites.

The next to last phase is one of "blessing her." The young girl and her sponsor dance in place and are blessed by each person at the ceremony. Anyone may request aid from the powers of Changing Woman that reside in the girl. Basso (1970, 68) recorded specific requests made at one rite, including:

To have a good crop of corn and beans
To make my sick wife get better
My cattle, to get fat for sale time
To cure my daughter
Rain
My son in Dallas learning to be a barber, not get into any trouble

The ritual ends when the girl shakes out the buckskin blanket on which she has been dancing and then throws it toward the east, the sacred direction of the rising sun, and then toward each of the other three cardinal directions. The spiritual powers of Changing Woman remain in the girl's body for four more days, during which time she can cure illness or bring rain.

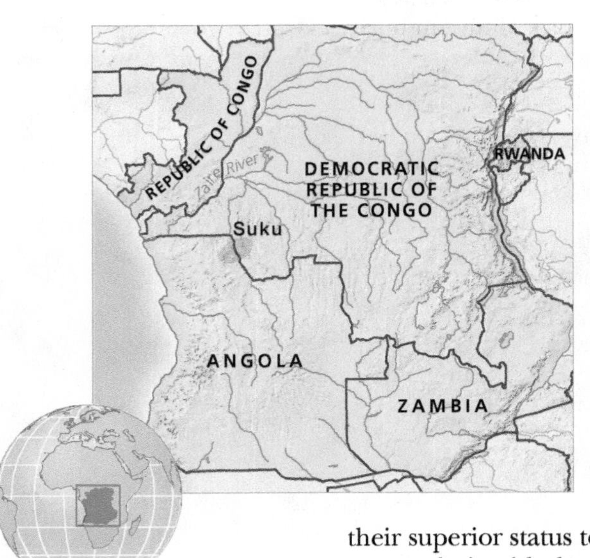

Among the Sukus, a farming people of southwestern Congo, boys traditionally undergo a circumcision rite in groups when they are between 10 years and 15 years old (Kopytoff, 1961). The ritual takes place in the summertime, the dry season. Following their circumcision, the boys are taken to a ceremonial hut outside the village, where they remain for weeks. In the past, the seclusion lasted months; today, it is shortened so that the boys can return to school in September. During the summer, the initiates are taught ritual songs and dances and receive rough physical and verbal treatment from the elder men who are charged with the boys' training. At the end of seclusion, the boys go to the river to cleanse themselves and put on new clothing. They take new names by which they will be known henceforth, and return to the village, where relatives and neighbors greet them joyously. The boys have become men. They have learned their superior status to women and uninitiated boys, and have developed ties of loyalty and camaraderie with the other initiates. **Read** the **Document** on **myanthrolab.com**

In addition to marking the departure of the deceased, funerals serve to underscore family solidarity and allow for people's expression of sorrow and loss. Funerals are usually followed by a period of mourning during which close relatives of the deceased may wear special clothing, eat or avoid eating certain foods, refrain from engaging in some activities, and act out their grief in culturally prescribed ways. The duration of the mourning period varies widely. In some patriarchal cultures, widows may be expected never to remarry.

Healing or Curing

In every culture, people have theories about health maintenance, causes of disease, and strategies for treatment. In many cultures, health is thought of as a state of harmony or balance. Health depends on the orderly functioning of a person's body, a person's relations with other people, the environment in which a person lives, and the spirit beings and forces with which a person interacts. When this balance is disturbed, illness and misfortune may follow.

Most people make a distinction between illnesses with natural causes and those caused by spirit beings or forces. Natural illnesses include minor aches and pains, accidents, and transitory ailments such as the common cold. These ailments are typically treated with natural remedies, such as medicinal plants and animal or mineral substances. If problems persist or worsen, spiritual causes may be suspected that call for ritual diagnosis and treatment. Patients then seek the aid of religious specialists who can diagnose the cause and recommend or perform the cure. Diagnosis may be achieved through divination or revelation in a dream or vision. Spirit causes can include soul loss, object intrusion, spirit possession, or the violation of taboos.

Many Hispanic and Latino people living in North, Central, and South America believe that illness may be caused by the sudden departure of a person's soul, a condition known as *susto.* Because the soul is the activating, life-giving part of a person, soul loss is obviously a serious, potentially fatal, illness. Soul loss may cause fearfulness, listlessness, loss of appetite, loss of interest in social activities, and a general lack of enthusiasm and vitality (Rubel 1977). *Susto* is usually triggered by sudden fright resulting from natural disasters, such as earthquakes or thunderstorms, car accidents, or emotional shocks, such as the sudden and unexpected death of a loved one. In treating *susto,* a specialist, with the help of spirit messages from dreams or visions, is able to locate the missing soul and coax it back into the patient, thus effecting a cure.

Object intrusion may be the diagnosis when a person experiences a sudden, localized pain in some part of the body. It is believed that a spirit, witch, or malevolent person somehow shot a foreign object into the patient's body, causing pain and distress. The object may have a specific shape, such as a pebble, grain of sand, feather, or animal tooth, or it could be an amorphous substance or liquid. The specialist ritually extracts the foreign object by "cupping" (pressing with the hands) or by sucking at the site of the pain. After the object is extracted, it is ritually disposed of to prevent further harm.

Spirit possession may be welcomed in some religions as a positive experience or spiritual gift or as evidence of faith. In other religions, it is considered a symptom of illness. In all societies with this belief, signs of spirit possession commonly include convulsions or loss of muscular control, erratic and rapid changes in mood, or insomnia. People possessed by spirits seek treatment aimed at removing the spirit or enticing it to leave the person's body. Techniques of exorcism range from cajoling, bargaining with, threatening, or punishing the spirit to make it leave.

In Korea, women are most commonly the targets of spirit possession. When such a diagnosis is made, a shaman, also usually a woman, entreats the spirit to leave the afflicted person. The shaman gives offerings and promises that the patient will, in the future, erect a shrine in the spirit's honor and furnish it periodically with food and drink. Spirits choose to possess women who experience tension in their households, usually from conflicts over their roles as dutiful daughter, wife, and mother. These women may feel burdened by excessive demands, and spirit possession may be an outlet for them to express frustration about their life circumstances, as well as a means of extracting themselves from their daily burdens (Harvey 1979; Kendall 1984). The woman is not blamed for her predicament, but other members of her household may be held responsible for her unhappiness.

In Haiti, both men and women may become possessed. Male spirits generally possess women and female spirits possess men. The spirits are attracted to their targets by physical or personality characteristics. To persuade the spirit to leave the body, the afflicted

spirit possession
Belief that spirits can enter a body and take over a person's thoughts and actions.

person may agree to establish a lifelong conjugal relationship with the spirit. In some cases, a formal marriage ceremony is performed between the patient and the possessing spirit. Thereafter, a separate bed is kept to which the patient retires for one or two nights each week for conjugal visits with the spirit spouse (Lewis 1989).

Religious beliefs, such as spirit possession, allow for emotional release. Brazilian practitioners of macumba, which combines West African, Roman Catholic, and Native American beliefs and practices, enter a trance induced by a deity or *orisha,* a Yoruba term. In large public gatherings held several times a week, spirit mediums are serially possessed by four different deities. These include the Old Black Slave, the Indian, and two trickster deities, the Child and Eshu, a Yoruba trickster figure. In the macumba belief system, spirits possess people to impart advice and protection to the mediums as well as to their clients. Clients seek help making decisions or finding solutions for problems of illness, social tension, emotional distress, or difficulties such as unemployment. But possession also provides mediums with an outlet for behavior that would otherwise be deemed inappropriate. When possessed by "the child," for example, adults may act silly, play with toys, perform pranks, giggle for no reason, and express childish exuberance in other ways. It has been suggested (Lewis 1989) that, through the ecstatic experience, people give vent to their frustrations in a socially channeled and acceptable form. They are able to air their grievances in a way that does not disrupt or undermine the social order. Lewis (1989) has suggested that spirit possession and other ecstatic experiences are more common among women and marginalized men in stratified societies because powerless people may use the messages received from the spirit world to validate their claims for recognition and autonomy. Through these experiences, they can bring attention to themselves and make their voices heard. However, their frustrations are also contained because they are expressed in a socially acceptable, albeit unusual, form.

A study of the recent emergence of spirit possession episodes among Maasai women in Tanzania analyzes these experiences as responses to fundamental changes in Maasai social and economic life, especially as it affects women's roles (Hodgson 1997). The Maasai have an economy centered on the care of large herds of cattle. In the past, both men and women had rights to cattle and participated in decisions about their care and about their disposal as gifts in marriage exchanges and other ceremonial contexts. However, with the increasing focus on individual ownership and control of resources and on the growing market potential of cattle in the modern economy, women have gradually lost their rights to contribute to economic life because colonial and postcolonial government authorities have favored men's participation. Gender roles have become more rigid, disallowing women from many of the positive contributions that they have made in the past. As a consequence of British colonial influences during the span of the twentieth century, continued and compounded after independence by the Tanzanian government, incidents of spirit possession grew steadily. The Maasai themselves see this as a relatively recent phenomenon. In their view, foreign (nonlocal) spirits invade the target, causing a variety of initial symptoms including ". . . headaches, fevers, burning sensations, general listlessness and apathy, lack of appetite and insomnia. Later symptoms include wailing, shaking, thrashing, fits, and nightmares" (Hodgson 1997, 114). Most of the victims are women of childbearing age.

Through spirit possession, Maasai women enact their critique of changes to the core of indigenous culture that adversely affect their roles in their households and villages. In addition, women who are afflicted by spirits seek cures through Christian baptism and remain healthy by participating in group meetings with other victims. Christian baptism can, in this context, also be seen as a rejection of dominant male norms because men in particular have converted to Islam in the last century. As Hodgson concludes, "Orpeko [spirit possession] has emerged and spread alongside a particular historical, political-economic conjuncture between the increasing pressures and alienation produced by the intensifying economic, political, and social disenfranchisement of women, and the alternative possibilities for female community and solidarity provided by the Christian missions" (1997, 124–25). Although Christianity is itself founded in patriarchal cultures, Maasai women can at least find refuge through its "foreignness" and voice their opposition to changes in their lives.

Illness may result when a person commits some ritual transgression. For example, people become ill if they fail to adhere to taboos, trespass on territory protected by spirit beings, or come in contact with powerful ritual objects. To be cured, the patient needs to undergo purification and ritual rebalancing. Most spirit causes of disease are metaphors for imbalance or disorder.

In Their Own VOICES

Macumba, Trance and Spirit Healing

In these excerpts from the film Macumba, Trance and Spirit Healing, documenting spiritist beliefs in Brazil, two practitioners talk about their feelings when possessed by macumba orishas. The Old Black Slave, the Indian, and the Child. Moisir, a lawyer, and his daughter Beje, a schoolteacher, have been participating in macumba ceremonies several times each week for about ten years. In these group rites, dozens of mediums become possessed by four different spirits in succession. The mediums can then receive messages from the spirit world, giving advice to people who are sick, depressed, or in need. The experiences of Moisir and Beje reflect their direct contact with the spirit world, a contact that gives them emotional release and a prestigious role as healer or adviser in their community.

MOISIR: Coming out of Senior Tupan (the Indian), my guide is annoyed, then I fall to the floor on the knees with one inside the other. He beats the floor twice with the hand opened and three times with the hand closed. They are strong blows, even violent enough to injure the hand. With this the recovery is complete.

BEJE: I feel that weight. Such a heavy weight. That once I am on my knees, as much as I want to, I can't get up. It's like I'm carrying something on my shoulders. Although the possession of the Old One is easy, coming out of it is a horrible thing. I think my head will leave my body. I begin to feel weak. Now, the Children are another story; they just say goodbye. With the Indian, the entrance and departure are equal. We feel tired to a degree but with a rested head. I have the impression of it being a little like a catharsis, you know, you get everything bad out and bring in a great deal of peace and tranquility.

MOISIR: The possession of the Old Black leaves the person very well. In spite of it being slow and difficult for the medium, it leaves the person feeling very well afterwards. Possession by the Old Black makes me feel very differently from the one by the Indian. In the possession of the Old Black, instead of feeling vibrations in the upper region, I feel it in both of my legs. My legs begin to get cold and a kind of pain comes into the knee and ends up knocking me on the floor. Upon feeling knocked down on the floor, I am nearly unconscious. I don't have the ability to reason, to talk for myself, to know people. I have a certain lack of consciousness in my work as the Old Black.

BEJE: The two possessions are totally different, not at all similar. For example, with the Indian, my hand begins to tremble, tremble, it keeps trembling, trembling, trembling until I feel the vibrations and fall to the knees. With the Old Black, I don't feel anything. Bam, bam, I'm on the floor.

MOISIR: As for coming out of the Old Black, it is very difficult. It really hurts when he leaves the medium. After, you feel a pleasant sensation as if you've come out of a sauna. You feel very tranquil, serene, without pain or preoccupations.

I don't like to call these "consultations" because we are not doctors. We simply give advice as to what people should do to better their spiritual and material lives. They look for jobs and they don't know what to do with all this desperation we are experiencing today. So we raise their morale. The Old Blacks have this objective, they are very much alive in material worlds.

CRITICAL THINKING QUESTION

What are some emotional and social benefits to Macumba practices for the participants?

Religious, ritual, and practical approaches to illness and health go hand in hand, even in societies with medical treatment models based on modern science. Spiritual and magical treatments are especially effective if people believe in them at the same time as other factors are at work, such as the use of pharmaceuticals, the therapeutic effects of receiving treatment, and the curative passage of time. A critical factor in the efficacy of ritual treatments is the patients' psychological state and beliefs. Patients become the center of attention of their family and community and benefit psychologically from the knowledge that people care about them and want them to recover. The patient's belief in the healer, whether shaman or physician, and in the treatment also affect the outcome of the cure.

How can spirit-caused illnesses give people outlets for expressing their needs for order, balance, and security in their lives? How do healers address those needs?

Magic and Witchcraft

In addition to spirit causes of illness, witchcraft (also called sorcery) may be suspected in cases of illness, death, or misfortunes such as crop failure or infertility. Witches are people who employ spirit powers to cause harm to others, the opposite of healers. They are usually thought to be motivated by anger, jealousy, or simply the desire to see

imitative magic
Magic that operates on the principle of "like causes like."

contagious magic
Magic that operates on the principle that positive and negative qualities can be transferred through proximity or contact.

calendric rituals
Ceremonies performed at specific times during the year, for example, agricultural rituals performed for planting, growing, and harvesting crops.

other people suffer. Their targets may be people with whom they have quarreled, but they may also harm someone randomly. Witchcraft is also used as a form of social control and a means of achieving social justice. It is effective partly because people believe in it. For example, the literature cites many cases of healthy young people sickening and dying upon learning that a sorcerer has placed a curse on them.

Witches employ different forms of magic to produce a specific and connected result. **Imitative magic,** for example, operates on the principle that "like causes like" or that "life imitates art." Thus, depictions and enactments of harmony may predispose a community toward harmony. Manipulating drawings or replicas of individuals may cause good or harm to come to those individuals in life. Witches may use imitative magic by cursing or damaging images or objects that represent their targets.

A practice known as *couvade* is an example of benign imitative magic. In Amazonian cultures, men leave the village when their wives are about to give birth, retiring to the forest. There they imitate the actions of women in labor. They may clutch their abdomens, writhe in pain, and scream out as though in physical distress. These actions are intended to attract evil spirits who lurk about in hopes of attacking newborns. These spirits are lured to the men, allowing the expectant mother to give birth in safety.

Contagious magic operates on the principle that positive and negative qualities can be transferred through proximity or contact, like an infection. Thus, one can become more sanctified or blessed by touching something holy. In pre-Christian Europe, contagious magic was used as a palliative for pain. The cure for a toothache, for example, was to nail a lock of one's hair to an oak tree, known for its strength, and then to pull one's head away. The pain of the toothache passed through the hair to the tree, where it remained. Gaining power or immunity by touching or wearing objects made powerful or immune through ritual, such as amulets or shrunken heads, are also examples of contagious magic. Witches use contagious magic by secretly collecting a victim's nail clippings, hair, urine, or excrement and saying a spell over it to harm their target.

In some cultures, witches are thought to sprinkle harmful substances in people's food or drink, on their bodies while they sleep, or along the thresholds of their houses. People may believe that witches are capable of extraordinary physical feats, making things appear or disappear, transforming themselves into animals to lurk near a victim's house, or transporting themselves great distances in an instant.

Witchcraft may be a vehicle for the conscious or unconscious expression of anger and envy. For example, patterns of witchcraft accusations may follow lines of social tensions. Among the Cewas of Zimbabwe, accusations of witchcraft are usually preceded by quarrels, especially among matrilineal kin (Marwick 1967). Cewa society has formal mechanisms for airing and resolving disputes between matrilineal groups but not within them. When conflict arises between members of the same matrilineal group, accusations about witchcraft may emerge as outlets.

Thus, beliefs in witchcraft are also expressions of people's fears, revulsions, and suspicions about the unusual behavior of others and about the sources or causes of misfortunes. It is also an expression of people's desires and intentions in situations over which they have no direct control. Because of the secrecy of witchcraft, very little is known about its actual frequency. However, magic is not confined to societies with witchcraft. All religions incorporate principles or practices that can be understood as magic.

Do you practice magic or magical thinking in your daily life? Are there principles or practices in a religion in your society that could be understood as magic?

REVIEW

Religious practices include ritual, prayer, and sacrifice—ways of mediating between people and their spirit world. Rituals, both sacred and secular, may include rites of renewal or intensification, **calendric rituals,** and rites of passage. Rituals are also used in curing ceremonies for illnesses with spirit causes, such as soul loss, object intrusion, spirit possession, or the violation of taboos. Imitative magic or contagious magic may be used in curing ceremonies and in other contexts, such as the couvade. Witchcraft or sorcery, which has complex social and psychological functions, also involves the use of magic.

RELIGION AND CULTURE CHANGE

Religious beliefs and practices, like every other aspect of culture, are responsive to changes in society. Social, economic, political, and historical developments have an impact on religions. Changes in other areas of their lives may cause people to think about their relationship with the spirit world in different ways, altering some practices or abandoning them altogether. People may begin to rethink the roles of religious practitioners, possibly changing the criteria for choosing them or how they are trained. Ritual practice may change as people adopt new ceremonies and modify or discard older ones. Although religion seems like a timeless tradition, it is subject to transformation like any other system of ideology and practice.

Religions are dynamic systems, incorporating new ideas either from external sources or from the innovative creativity of believers. Some religions may be inherently more receptive to change. Polytheistic religions, for example, usually do not have a single standardized doctrine. They allow for additions of new ideas or ritual elements that appear to be effective and the elimination of those that no longer achieve desired results. People might borrow new rituals from neighbors or from the religions of more distant people met in travel or trade. People observe one another's rituals, listen to religious narratives, and adopt practices that they find beautiful, compelling, or effective. New deities may be incorporated into a local pantheon as believers find them appealing or useful. This process is more common in religions that lack central texts whose interpretation can be argued or even fought over. People tend to borrow stories and mythic characters readily, often changing details to suit their own circumstances and attitudes. This process of combining and modifying elements from different religions is called *syncretism,* and is a process inherent to all religions.

What is an example of a belief or practice in a religion that you know about that has been changed or abandoned?

Syncretism is a common result of political processes, especially in situations of conquest and colonization. As state societies have expanded throughout history, conquerors have imposed their religious beliefs and practices on defeated populations.

Defeated populations, seeing the conquerors' gods as superior, may willingly adopt their religious systems, especially since the conquerors usually try to convert others to their own religions. In many situations, however, conquered people resist change and resist abandoning their own religious beliefs and practices. They may hold even more tightly to their own traditions, keeping their rituals as acts of resistance and self-empowerment. They may do this openly or in secret in order to protect themselves from retaliation or punishment. In this context, new religious traditions may arise that give former practices new meanings and interpretations.

Revitalization Movements

A source of new religious traditions is revitalization movements—religion-based responses to societal crises. Revitalization movements arise in times of social and political upheaval, often in situations of invasion, conquest, and control, when people are confronted by a loss of their rights and restrictions on their freedom. Such movements may also arise as a response to increasing social and political inequalities within a society among people who lack rights or advantages. They are aimed at restructuring power relationships within a society or between conquered peoples and their rulers.

Revitalization movements frequently begin after individuals receive direct messages from the spirit world telling them to convey divine teachings to the community. Referred to as **prophets,** such individuals become the conduits for communication between the spirit world and ordinary people. Essentially, the messages point out how people have become demoralized by straying from the right path and abandoning their traditional values and ethics. Although external forces may be causing people's suffering, the people themselves contribute to their troubles. The prophets teach that the people must return to traditional ways, stressing the values of hospitality or civility, generosity, cooperativeness, and solidarity with relatives and community members. Leaders of revitalization movements proselytize others, always seeking to enlarge the community of followers and establish a network of believers.

There are several kinds of revitalization movements. **Nativistic movements** attempt to rid the society of foreign elements, returning to what is conceived to be a prior state of cultural purity. The late nineteenth-century **Ghost Dance** cult of the Plains Indians is an example of a nativistic movement, inspired by the prophet Wovoka. **Revivalistic movements** stress the importance of reviving cultural and religious practices that express core values but have been marginalized or abandoned. **Millenarian movements** incorporate apocalyptic themes, prophesying an abrupt end to the world as we

prophets
Religious leaders who receive divine inspiration, often in a vision or trance.

nativistic movements
Revitalization movements attempting to rid society of foreign elements and return to what is conceived to be a prior state of cultural purity.

revivalistic movements
Revitalization movements focused on bringing back cultural and religious practices that express core values that have been largely abandoned.

millenarian movements
Revitalization movements incorporating apocalyptic themes, prophesying an abrupt end to the world as we know it, leading to the establishment of a new way of life or form of existence.

messianic movements Revitalization movements stressing the role of a prophet or messiah as a savior for people.

cargo cults Revitalization movements arising in Melanesia in the early twentieth century with the aim of obtaining material wealth through magical means.

know it by a specific time or date in the future, leading to the establishment of a new way of life or form of existence. **Messianic movements** stress the role of a prophet or messiah as a savior. These are not discrete types but rather are examples of various features present in revitalization practices. Many religion-based social movements combine several aspects of these revitalization themes.

Although revitalization movements are religious, they also have social and political messages. They are always at least potentially revolutionary and can develop into direct challenges to the established order with the aim of transforming or overturning social and political systems. Historical factors affect whether political movements develop. If authorities recognize the political potential of revitalization themes, for example, they may brutally suppress the movement. However, the leaders of the movement may direct people's energies away from political action to protect them from attack. Messages might call for accommodating external situations, or they might postpone the rewards for faith to some distant time in the future, even until after death. These kinds of messages also direct people away from political rebellion.

Some revitalization movements have a small number of adherents and may last only a short time before they are abandoned and forgotten. Presumably such movements have arisen in countless societies across millennia. Others, however, attract thousands, even millions, of followers and persist for many centuries. Some of the widespread religions of today, such as Buddhism, Christianity, and Islam, began many centuries ago as revitalization movements. They gained adherents through active proselytizing by the initial believers until they now have followers throughout the world.

Cargo Cults

A different kind of revitalization movement arose in Melanesia in the early twentieth century. Referred to as **cargo cults,** these movements were a response to British colonial control, the expropriation of native land, and the relegation of indigenous peoples to roles as menial laborers and second-class citizens. Cargo cults arose at various times and in various places in Melanesia, most notably in New Guinea (Worseley 1967; 1968). Prophets received spirit messages telling people to perform rituals, based on traditional principles of magical cause and effect, that were supposed to result in the arrival of material wealth ("cargo") for the native people.

Members of the John Frum cargo cult in Vanuatu blend traditional Pacific beliefs with Christian practices. The red cross may be a symbol borrowed from the United States military medical units during World War II.
Corbis/Anders Ryman/Corbis

Cargo cult followers built loading docks along the coast and, later, landing strips for airplanes in the bush, intending to make landing sites for ships and airplanes. They had seen these vehicles bringing in goods for the colonial Europeans, and they believed that if they acted as if the goods were coming, life would imitate art. On this principle of magic, the people imitated European behavior that they thought was responsible for the arrival of the cargo: They wore European-style top hats, neckties, and jackets, and sat around tables and scribbled on pieces of paper that they then put into boxes—all in imitation of having meetings and sending orders for goods.

Cargo cult activities appeared foolish to the Europeans, but these activities were consistent with the native worldview. According to Melanesian principles, wealth was obtained by a combination of hard work and ritual. Native people never saw Europeans doing what the Melanesians regarded as work, yet the foreigners received wealth from across the ocean or from the sky, so, clearly, their rituals were powerful. The preliterate Melanesians imitated what they took to be European rituals involving costumes and actions such as writing. Eventually, rituals were abandoned as they failed to attract cargo, until another prophet came with a new set of instructions on what to do. Waves of cargo rituals emerged and dissipated in the 1930s and 1940s. In contrast to the repressive responses to the Ghost Dance of the American Plains, however, the colonial government in New Guinea ignored the cargo cults because they posed no threat to colonial power. Eventually, most of the cargo movements dissolved because they failed to achieve the desired results. Note that cargo cults and the imitation of European behavior also demonstrate the political message underlying revitalization movements. In 2007, residents of the Pacific island of Vanuatu celebrated the 50th anniversary of the establishment of the John Frum Movement in their territory

(Mercer 2007). John Frum was an earlier cargo cult leader whose spirit reemerged in Vanuatu, urging his followers to reject Christianity and instead maintain their traditional beliefs and practices.

Role of Founders in Buddhist, Judeo-Christian, and Islamic Traditions

As noted, some of the most widely practiced religions in the world today began as revitalization movements. Buddhism, Christianity, and Islam originated with individuals who received divine inspiration. These founders essentially reacted against human suffering and the social and political inequalities in their societies, giving as their message the need for all people to establish freedom, equality, justice, and peace. These messages ultimately became institutionalized in formal religions under the control of ecclesiastical elites who serve as intermediaries and interpreters of divine messages. Although Moses was not a "founder" in the sense of originating a new religion, he played a pivotal role during a crucial period of Jewish history.

Siddhartha Gautama, later referred to as Buddha, or "Enlightened One," was born about 563 B.C. in India, the eldest son of a local prince, destined to inherit his father's position. But Gautama rejected the privilege to which he was entitled by birth, choosing instead to leave his parents, wife, and son to seek inner wisdom and the end to physical and spiritual suffering (Koller 1982). Buddha's message was in part a reaction against inequities in the caste system maintained through Hinduism. That system consigned people at birth to specific inherited occupations, social standing, and degrees of ritual purity. Hinduism also emphasized people's roles in an inescapable cycle of reincarnation with its inescapable cycle of suffering. The message of Buddhism is, in part, that people can escape caste duty through right thinking and right action to achieve spiritual enlightenment, equality, and oneness with the universe. Eventually people can escape the cycle of reincarnation by attaining perfect knowledge and self-control.

Jesus, whose teachings led to the founding of Christianity, was born sometime after the death of Herod around 4 B.C. Biblical scholars have different interpretations of the life of Jesus, and those interpretations reflect the social and political beliefs of the analysts (Meier 1991). Some scholars emphasize Jesus's role as a prophet of "restoration theology," predicting the divine destruction of the imperial order imposed by Rome on Israel and the establishment of a world of justice and mercy (Sanders 1985). In this view, Jesus's spiritual prophecy was central and within the tradition of Jewish law and interpretation. Other scholars emphasize his role as a teacher and somewhat subversive commentator on the life of his times (Mack 1988). Still others stress the social context of Jesus's life and see his message as relating fundamentally to sociopolitical conditions (Borg 1994; Crossan 1994). According to this view, like Buddha, Jesus was appalled by inequalities in the prevailing social system of his day. He was also angered by the cooperation of some members of the inner circles of power in the Hebrew state with their Roman invaders and conquerors. Although the common people chafed under increased control and demands for labor and tribute, the local secular and religious elites benefited from their favored positions as puppets of Roman colonial rule. This dynamic is not unique to that area but, rather, occurs in most colonized societies: Indigenous elites are co-opted by the conquerors with the offer that they can maintain some of their former wealth and power.

According to one modern interpretation (Crossan 1994), Jesus's critique of his own society focused on inequalities within the family, particularly the privileged role of the father in a patriarchal system of male dominance. Because hierarchical relations begin with lessons on dominance and subordination within the family, Jesus advocated the equality of women and men (Fiorenza 1983). Jesus used the metaphor of "open commensality"—the practice of eating at the same table—to undermine norms that segregated people according to rank and gender (Crossan 1994). The "open table," where everyone—men and women, beggars, lepers, and all types of social outcasts—were welcome and could eat together, became a powerful symbol of the egalitarian society Jesus envisioned. In addition, Jesus urged his followers to create the kingdom of God on earth through social and religious transformation.

The founder of Islam, Muhammad, was born in Mecca around A.D. 570 of a poor family. The Arabian Peninsula at the time was home to many small tribal groups who practiced polytheistic religions with an array of nature deities (Guillaume 1986). During a solitary meditation, Muhammad experienced a vision of the angel Gabriel, who told him that God is the one and only God whom people must obey. Muhammad began to

proselytism
The attempt to convert a person or group from one religion to another.

fundamentalism
A term coined in the United States in 1920 meaning a commitment to do battle to defend traditional religious beliefs.

preach his message of a monotheistic religion, initially attracting only a small following of mostly slaves and poor people. He was attacked as a sorcerer, but he continued to proclaim his message for all Arabs. His mission, then, was to unite the Arab world under the mantle of one religion with its one God. However, unity came with the price of war: If people did not join the faith on their own, they had to be compelled through force to believe, thus unleashing a holy war of proselytizing religion through conquest.

Moses shares with these founders (Buddha, Jesus, and Mohammed) participation in a belief system that allows for prophecy and divine inspiration. Moses received direct messages from the deity to instruct his followers in moral and social behavior so that they could once again obtain divine blessings, in the form of the Ten Commandments. And he rallied an oppressed population to escape their rulers and seek refuge and rebuild their communities in their own territory.

In Buddhism, Christianity, and Islam, disciples or followers began to spread the faith to others following the deaths of the founders. Over the centuries, increasingly centralized "churches" were organized to pull together a body of worship, setting out practices and doctrine. Eventually, ecclesiastical elites took control not only of priestly functions but also of standardized religious doctrines. People who had divergent interpretations of religious texts were deemed dissidents, and religious authorities have harassed and punished dissidents as heretics at various times in the history of Buddhism, Christianity, and Islam. According to some views, these authorities moved away from the original messages, replacing them with doctrines of obedience to the state, hierarchical family systems, and a controlling priesthood.

Religion and Globalization

As state societies expand their borders and influence throughout many parts of the world far from their centers of origin, they have spread their religious beliefs through proselytism. **Proselytism** is the attempt to convert a person or group from one religion to another. State societies throughout history have brought their religions to the people they have conquered. Various denominations of Buddhism, Christianity, and Islam have gained millions of converts through this process. As missionaries spread their religions to all parts of the world, some locally indigenous religious beliefs and practices have been modified and others have been abandoned and replaced by the new religions. In some cases, people have modified foreign rituals and developed different interpretations of standard beliefs.

Diffusion of beliefs and practices and their absorption by distant peoples have resulted in marked contrasts between local practices and those in the centers of origin. For example, in Africa and the Caribbean, Roman Catholic saints are identified with tribal African deities, and rituals dedicated to indigenous deities are merged with Roman Catholic practice. Spirit possession, a phenomenon marginalized in mainstream Roman Catholic doctrine, is given central importance in Haiti, Brazil, and many African indigenous churches. Similarly, Native American Christians may incorporate traditional practices, especially prayers to the Great Creator and such offerings as the burning of sage or cedar.

Buddhism, Christianity, and Islam, the major proselytizing religions, have been successful in part because their practice is not tied to a specific locale. They can be transplanted anywhere and incorporate local beliefs and practices. This characteristic contrasts with religions whose cosmologies are tied to specific places, such as those of the Diné or Australian Aborigines.

In the world today, as in the past, global economic and political processes have affected religious practices and interpretations of sacred texts. Some revitalization movements within Christianity and Islam have led to an increase in religious fundamentalism. **Fundamentalism,** a term coined in the United States in 1920, means a commitment to do battle to defend traditional religious beliefs. In the United States, members of some Christian fundamentalist movements advocate a return to both religious and social orthodoxy. They keep to a literal interpretation of the Bible and tend to believe in the divine origin of gender roles differentiating the work and family roles of women and men. They also tend to support an ideologically conservative political agenda and to place religious authority above secular authority in life matters. Fundamentalists organize against abortion rights, for example, and against gay marriage. They oppose the teaching of evolution in schools. Some fundamentalist groups have become associated with beliefs in white supremacy.

CULTURE CHANGE

THE DEVELOPMENT OF RELIGIOUS DENOMINATIONS

The major world religions have changed many times and continue to change. The development of various Hindu, Buddhist, Judaic, Christian, and Islamic denominations follows local practices and beliefs. People in different places at different times interpret central texts in their own ways, adapting them to their cultures and their circumstances. Religions also change because philosophical or ethical issues become important to their followers. As times change, as social norms are transformed, religions respond by altering emphases in their practices and beliefs.

Some current controversies demonstrate these processes. Among Jews, the distinction among Orthodox, Conservative, and Reformed branches focuses partly on issues of dietary rules and gender roles. Orthodox Jews, for example, adhere strictly to biblical dietary restrictions, principally taboos on eating pork and shellfish. Kosher rules also prescribe the separation of meat and dairy foods, necessitating separate cooking utensils, dishes, and cutlery for each type of food. In contrast, Reformed and some Conservative Jews do not adhere to kosher dietary regulations. In Orthodox synagogues, men sit on the main level of the building, while women sit in a balcony, symbolizing and enacting the segregation of the genders. Rules of ritual purity and contamination also demand that women take purifying baths, called *mikvas,* at the end of their menstrual periods. Reformed Judaism and many Conservative Jews have abandoned these practices, which highlight gender differences and the polluting effects of women. In addition, Reformed and some Conservative Jews ordain women as rabbis, whereas the Orthodox will not.

Christian churches and denominations are distinguished on the basis of doctrine and practice. One major doctrinal difference between Roman Catholics (and Eastern Orthodox churches) and many Protestants concerns the meaning of the rite of communion. Roman Catholicism and Eastern Orthodoxy teach that the bread and wine taken at communion have inner forms that become the body and blood of Jesus when blessed and consumed. Most Protestants treat the bread and wine only symbolically as representing but not actually becoming Christ's body. Protestants also tend to believe that individuals and groups are free to read and interpret the Scriptures for themselves rather than receive correct interpretations from the clergy. In addition, women may be ordained as ministers in many Protestant denominations but are barred from the Roman Catholic and Orthodox priesthood.

In Islam, the major Shi'ite and Sunni branches, among others, differ in their acceptance of religious authority, interpretation of the Qur'an, and application of religious law to secular activities. Sunnis, the majority, believe that any devout man can become a religious leader and that the Qu'ran should be taken at face value and not be subject to interpretation. Shi'ites, on the other hand, believe that religious leaders, imams, must be descended from Muhammad or divinely appointed and duly praised scholars, and that they are authorities on interpreting the Qur'an to address current events.

Strict adherence to religious doctrines is strongest in countries such as Saudi Arabia, where Islam began and is the only religion allowed by law, and among groups such as the Taliban, a militant Islamic group that took over Afghanistan from 1995 to 2001 and enforced a strict Muslim code of behavior. They are currently attempting to regain control of the country. In regions far from the centers of Islamic origins, beliefs, practices, local traditions, and worldviews temper Islamic beliefs and practices. For example, in Indonesia, the most populous Muslim country, people rarely conform to strict interpretations of Islamic law.

Fundamentalist organizations and lobbies have become a powerful influence in American politics. Other church groups, such as Americans United for Separation of Church and State, advocate separation between religious and political agendas. Some religious organizations work for progressive social and political change and are outspoken members of peace and antinuclear movements. Within the Roman Catholic Church, clergy and lay workers associated with liberation theology have been in the forefront of movements for social, economic, and political justice and equality, particularly in Central and South America.

View the **Slideshow:** *The Emergence of Fundamentalism* on **myanthrolab.com**

In 2008, the number of adherents of Christian denominations worldwide was estimated at more than 2.1 billion, about a third of the world population. European state expansion, missionism, colonialism, economic and political hegemony, and imperialism have contributed to what some observers refer to as the globalization of Christianity. Islam, another strongly proselytizing religion historically associated with state expansion and consolidation and with economic and political domination, has about 1.3 billion adherents worldwide.

Islamic fundamentalism has become increasingly popular and dangerous. In some countries of the Middle East and Africa, Islamic fundamentalists have taken over local or national governments, imposing a strict interpretation of the Qur'an on social and political policies. In Iran, for example, and in several states in Nigeria, public laws must conform to Islamic principles, and crimes and punishments are defined according to sacred texts. Religious authorities double as political leaders, whether by election or proclamation. In other Middle Eastern countries—for example, Iraq, as well as in Indonesia and the Philippines—Islamist movements have contributed to the destabilization of local and central governments and are attempting to overthrow elected or appointed authorities and institute Islamic law.

Some analysts attribute the upsurge in Islamic fundamentalism to the global spread of Western influence, chiefly from the United States. American social behaviors and social values are seen as immoral. Fundamentalist movements have gained popularity as proponents claim to resist American influence on internal affairs and foreign policies. This resistance has become increasingly violent. Al Qaeda, a terrorist network with cells in more than fifty countries, is an extreme expression of Islamic fundamentalism. Its members are both anti-Western and opposed to Arabic governments that do not espouse its own version of strict Islamic principles. On September 11, 2001, members of al Qaeda killed nearly 3,000 people by flying aircraft into the twin towers of the World Trade Center in New York City and the Pentagon across the river from Washington, DC.

The fundamentalism among Christians and Muslims that seems to be on the rise in many countries today can also be interpreted as a response to perceived social crises at home and abroad. People may feel that their ways of life and systems of belief are threatened, either by followers of other religions or by what they perceive as dangers posed by the increasing secularization of most modern nations. Rather than making an accommodation to global social and cultural changes, they turn even more staunchly to their own beliefs.

Internal and external forces change religious practices and beliefs over time. In syncretism, new religions are created by combining parts of older ones. Revitalization movements emphasize core beliefs and values as a means of adapting to undesired changes. Nativistic, revivalistic, millenarian, and messianic movements, as well as cargo cults, are all forms of religion-based adaptations to change. Major world religions such as Buddhism, Christianity, and Islam began as revitalization movements. Religions have spread through forces of globalization and the practice of proselytism. Religious fundamentalism has become a powerful force.

Study and **Review** on **myanthrolab.com**

CHAPTER SUMMARY

What Is Religion?

- Religion is actions and feelings based on beliefs in spirit beings and supranormal (or superhuman) forces. Religious beliefs and practices give people ways to contact spirit beings and forces, show them honor and respect, and invoke their protection. Anthropologists use comparison and cultural relativism to analyze religious beliefs and behaviors. They try to understand people's ideas about the spirit realm from the people's own point of view. They also focus on how religious beliefs and practices are consistent with other aspects of culture.

The Origins and Functions of Religion

- Specific origins of religious beliefs are unknown. Religions give people solace, and religious beliefs and practices bind communities together. They give ideological support for social structures, including family organization, social stratification, and political inequalities. Anthropologists using cultural materialist or ecological perspectives analyze religious practices as a means of adapting to one's environment.
- Social, economic, political, and historical developments affect religions. Changes may cause people to think about their relationship with the spirit world in different ways, altering practices or even abandoning them altogether. Religions incorporate new ideas from external sources or the innovations of believers.

Spirit Beings and Forces

- Spirit entities and forces have extraordinary powers. They are typically eternal or indestructible. They know more than a person can know and can act in ways that humans cannot. Thus, people seek to gain their protection and aid.

ANTHROPOLOGY APPLIED

Medical Anthropology and Ethnomedicine

Shutterstock/StockLite/Shutterstock

Medical anthropologists apply the holistic and cross-cultural approaches of anthropology to understand and respond to questions of human well-being, health, and disease. How are illnesses caused, experienced, and spread, and how can they be prevented and treated? What healers, healing substances, and healing processes do people use, and what beliefs and values inform those uses? How is human health related to social structure, the health of other species, and the environment?

Medical practitioners use information from medical anthropology in treating their culturally diverse patients. For example, reaching a diagnosis and prescribing effective treatment are not based strictly on the scientific model but involve understanding people's perceptions and interpretations of their bodies and bodily processes and their beliefs about illness. Those perceptions, interpretations, and beliefs are culturally constructed because what is considered pathological is culturally defined. Some diseases are even culture-specific.

At a broader level, medical anthropologists may study epidemics, endemic diseases that persist in a society, or disease vectors that cause the spread of disease. They may study the distribution of disease in the world and the disparities in health among different populations. Some focus on the relationships between people's health and health care and the political and economic factors in societies. Others focus on problem areas, such as child and maternal health, eating habits and nutrition, or sanitation in a world where 1,400 children die each day from diarrhea.

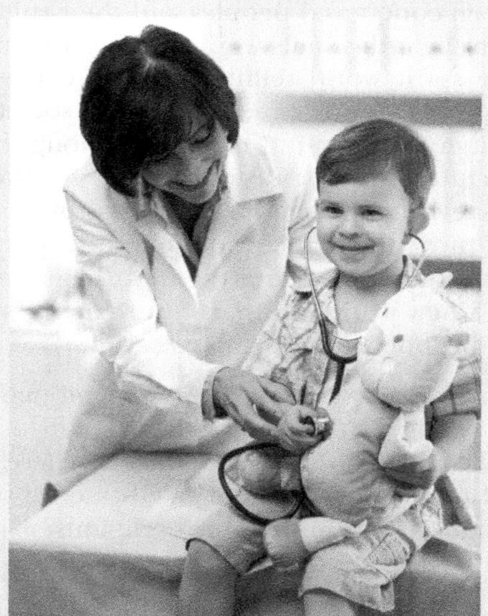
Superstock/Image Source/SuperStock

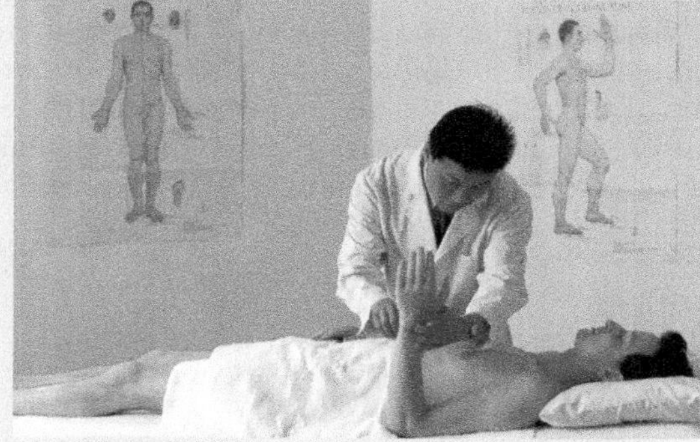
Alamy Limited/Nick Hanna/Alamy

Ethnomedicine is the study of traditional medicine in cultural groups or in preindustrial societies. Beliefs and practices in different human groups include ideas about hygiene, disease prevention, and the healing properties of objects in their environment. For example, the Maasai use an infusion of the bark from a kind of acacia tree as a digestive aid during ceremonies that call for consuming huge quantities of meat. The Maasai also use the bark from a kind of albizia tree as an emetic. The root can be boiled and mixed with milk to get rid of or prevent intestinal parasites in people and animals (Ryan 2000).

According to the World Health Organization (2004), 80 percent of Africans rely on traditional medicine for daily health. In Asia and Latin America as well, reliance on traditional medicines and practices may be more culturally acceptable and psychologically satisfying than those based on the Western scientific medical model. In addition, modern medicine, which is also the subject of ethnomedical research, may be inaccessible to most people in a developing country. Traditional medicines and practices may be just as effective. Plants that preindustrial people used to treat illness include the sources of aspirin, morphine, ephedrine, and penicillin.

CRITICAL THINKING QUESTIONS

What are some of your beliefs and values about health and illness? Where do those beliefs and values come from?

- One nearly universal form that spirit takes is the soul—the eternal aspect of living things. In some beliefs, only humans have souls. Souls are seen as the animating aspect of living things. When the body dies, souls escape and exist eternally in another form. The belief in souls is called animism; the belief that all things are endowed with some spirit essence is animatism.
- Some religious traditions have many spirit beings in human form with specific attributes, powers, and functions. Polytheism, belief in numerous deities, is widespread. In monotheistic religions, people believe in one supreme deity who affects all aspects of life, although there may also be lesser spirits and moral heroes.
- Mana is a spirit power or essence that endows people, animals, objects, or events with special qualities or powers. In some cultures of Australia and North America, people believe that they are descended from human or animal spirit beings called totems, the primordial protectors of the people.
- Spirit beings and forces are dangerous if contacted in the wrong way, in the wrong place, or at the wrong time. Restrictions on places or objects are called taboos. A tabooed object or place can cause harm because the spirit power within it can become dangerous.

Religious Practitioners and Specialists

- Most religions have individuals or groups who function as either part-time or full-time religious specialists. In some cases, a person receives a calling from the spirit world to become a religious specialist or inherits spiritual powers. In other cases, a person decides to become a religious practitioner for personal reasons.
- Mediums make contact with spirit beings or spirits of the dead. Diviners have the power to predict or shape the future through messages and omens they receive and interpret from the spirit world. Healers diagnose the spirit cause of illness and effect cures through rituals. Shamans receive visions and messages from the spirit realm and may serve as diviners and healers. Priests are full-time religious practitioners who lead religious organizations and officiate at rituals but are not expected to be able to communicate directly with the spirit world.

Religious Practice

- Rituals are a fundamental aspect of all religious practices and include prayer and offerings. Rituals mark events in religious and secular calendars.
- People also perform rituals to celebrate transitions in an individual's life cycle. Such rites of passage mark birth, puberty, marriage, and death. Rites of passage ritualize three aspects of a change in life status: separation, transition, and reincorporation. Puberty rites mark sexual maturity and the transition from childhood to adulthood. Funerals mark the departure of the deceased and reinforce family and community solidarity.
- Health is often thought of as a state of harmony or balance among a person's body, relations with others, the health of the environment, and relations with spirit beings and forces. When this balance is disturbed, illness and misfortune may follow. Serious illness is often attributed to spiritual causes needing ritual diagnosis and treatment by religious specialists. Spirit causes can include soul loss, object intrusion, spirit possession, or the violation of taboos. Curative rituals attempt to restore balance through magic, practical remedies, therapeutic effects, social validation, and the passage of time.
- Witchcraft may be suspected in cases of illness, death, or misfortune. Witches or sorcerers employ spirit powers to harm others. Witchcraft can be a form of social control and a means of achieving social justice. Witches, like healers, employ imitative and contagious magic. Magic is an expression of people's desires and intentions in situations over which they have no direct control.

Religion and Culture Change

- Revitalization movements are religion-based responses to societal crises. Revitalization movements are aimed at restructuring power relationships within a society or between conquered peoples and their rulers. They are begun by individuals who receive direct messages from the spirit world telling them to convey divine teachings. Nativism is aimed at ridding society of foreign elements, returning to what is thought to be a state of cultural purity. Revivalism stresses the importance of reviving cultural and political practices. Millenarian movements incorporate apocalyptic themes and an abrupt end to the present world and establishment of a new world. Messianic movements stress the role of a prophet or messiah as a savior.
- The major world religions have changed many times. As times change and social norms are transformed, religions alter their practices and beliefs. These changes can lead to the development of distinctive sects and denominations within the world religions.
- State societies have spread their religious beliefs through proselytism. Revitalization movements within Christianity and Islam have increased religious fundamentalism. Christian fundamentalists advocate a literal interpretation of the Bible and tend to support a conservative political agenda and to place religious authority above secular authority. Islamic fundamentalism includes terrorism and rejection of Western influences.

REVIEW QUESTIONS

1. What questions do all religions answer?
2. How are animism, animatism, and deism different? How are these belief systems expressed?
3. How do different religions define and treat spirits of the dead?
4. How is a shaman different from a priest?
5. What are other types of religious practitioners? What roles and functions do they play in their societies?
6. How do people make distinctions between the sacred and the secular? How are concepts such as mana, taboo, and blessing used to bestow sacredness?
7. How is religion expressed through symbolic culture and religious speech?
8. In what ways is religion expressed through behavior? What religious concepts do people use to explain human behavior?
9. What types of secular and sacred rituals do people everywhere perform?
10. Why do people sometimes use magical thinking?
11. What are some social and cultural functions of sorcery or witchcraft?
12. What are some examples of the relationship between religion and other social systems in a society?
13. What five basic functions does religion serve for people?
14. How do religions change in response to social and culture change?
15. How do syncretisms reveal adaptations to cultural contact and the diffusion of ideas?
16. What are the types and characteristics of revitalization movements?
17. What is the impact of globalization on world religions?

MyAnthroLab Connections

Watch. Listen. View. Explore. Read. MyAnthroLab is designed just for you. Dynamic visual activities, videos, and readings found in the multimedia library will enhance your learning experience.

Resources from this chapter:

Watch on **myanthrolab.com**
- *Woman in the Clergy Talks about Her Spiritual Self*
- *Rites of Passage*
- *Central Kenya Burial Site*

View on **myanthrolab.com**
- *The Emergence of Fundamentalism*

Explore on **myanthrolab.com** In MySearchLab, enter the Anthropology database to find relevant and recent scholarly and popular press publications. For this chapter, enter the following keywords: animism, funerary rites, messianic movements, fundamentalism

Read the **Document**
- *Iroquois: The Tree of Peace and the War Kettle* by Thomas Abler
- *Tlingit: Chiefs Past and Present* by Kenneth Tollefson

Taraka's Ghost

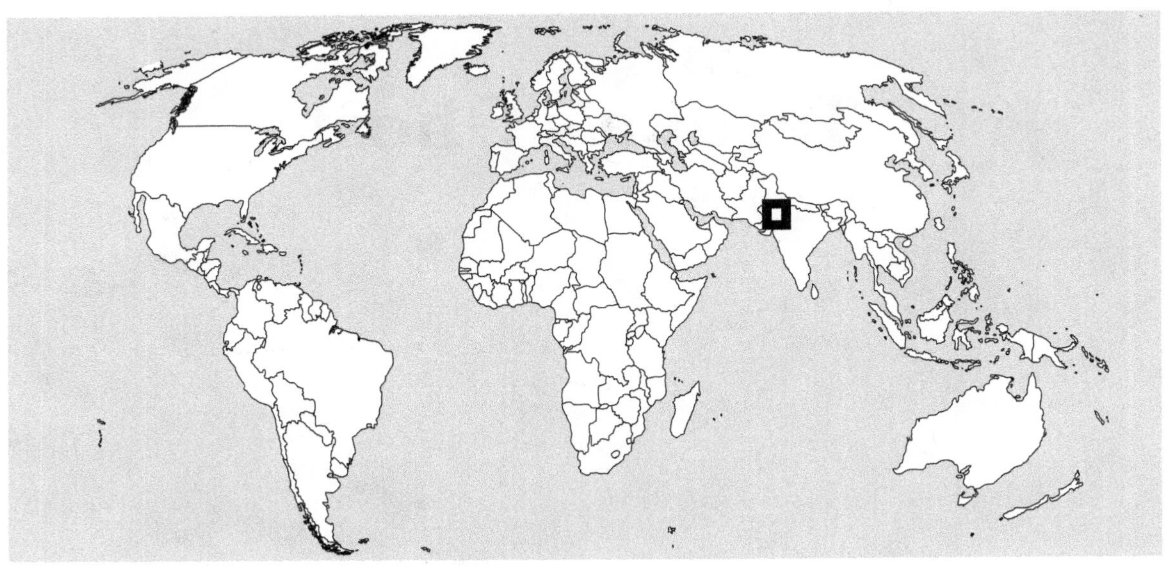

Taraka's Ghost

Stanley A. Freed and Ruth S. Freed

*Most people meet life's challenges by using an array of normal, and often effective, cultural responses. U.S. traffic is dangerous, for example, but we use driving skills we have learned to survive with confidence on the road. But some circumstances fall beyond our everyday abilities. We exercise and eat properly, but still may unexpectedly become ill. We work diligently and skillfully at our jobs, yet fail to be promoted. Many anthropologists see a relationship between religion and the anxieties that are caused by stressful and seemingly unmanageable aspects of life. In this article, Stanley Freed and Ruth Freed describe such an association. They report that a low-caste girl, Sita, is possessed by Taraka, the ghost of a childhood friend who committed suicide. Sita is stressed by the need to have sex with a new husband, the lack of support that meets a bride in her husband's household, and the deaths of three friends and several brothers and sisters. Ghost possession reduces her anxiety and gains her the support of her natal and conjugal families.**

Listen to the **Chapter Audio** on **myanthrolab.com**

When we saw our first ghost possession in a North Indian village, on a hot September day in the late 1950s, we were struck by the villagers' matter-of-fact response to what seemed an extraordinary event. We were seated with a group of low-caste villagers who were softly chatting

*From Stanley A. Freed and Ruth S. Freed, "Taraka's Ghost," *Natural History,* October 1999, pp. 84–91. Reprinted from *Natural History,* October 1999, copyright © Natural History Magazine, Inc., 1999.

in front of a mud hut. Sita, a newly married fifteen-year-old girl, was sittin ground, and, conforming to the proper behavior of a bride, she was inconspic and silent. Still wearing her bridal finery, her face veiled below the eyes, she work her sewing machine, of which she was proud.

A man of her caste, who had recently lost his job, commented that sewing on a machine was man's work (at that time, it was mainly the province of the village tailor). The remark implied that Sita was doing something inappropriate, an insinuation to which, as a new bride, she could not respond. Moreover, the criticism struck at Sita's pride and joy, her sewing machine, which was part of her dowry. To her it was a talisman, protecting her and providing her with higher status than other brides of her caste, for she was the first to possess one.

Sita's mother-in-law, who had witnessed earlier ghost possessions of the girl, realized that the criticism had distressed Sita, and anticipating that Sita would again be possessed, the older woman abruptly began to discuss the ghost attacks that plagued the teenager. We couldn't imagine why the conversation had taken such a turn until Sita began to shiver, a symptom preceding possession. Despite the heat, she complained of feeling cold, so some women covered her with quilts. She moaned, breathed with difficulty, and then collapsed in a semiconscious state.

The spectators accepted that a ghost had possessed her and tried a variety of standard curing techniques. These ranged from engaging the ghost in conversation, identifying it, and trying to satisfy its wishes or demands so that it would leave voluntarily, to attempting to drive it away with verbal abuse and, if necessary, physically painful or unpleasant measures (applied to the victim but aimed at the ghost). First, the women propped Sita up in a sitting position and wafted smoke from some smoldering cow dung under her nose. She jerked violently, so they had to restrain her. Then they shouted at the ghost: "Who are you? Are you going?" The ghost, speaking through Sita, promised to leave, and the women released the girl. But they were not deluded. They suspected that the ghost would not leave permanently and that a cure would be difficult. "Ghosts don't keep their promises," they confided to us.

Sita again fell unconscious, a sign that the ghost had returned. To revive her, the women dropped stinging hookah water in her eyes and pulled her braids. Sita returned to semiconsciousness and emitted a high-pitched wail, which announced the ghost's presence and readiness to talk. There followed a conversation between the ghost (speaking through Sita) and Sita's in-laws and a few other women, in the course of which the ghost identified herself as Sita's cousin Taraka, who had committed suicide by drowning in a well. Taraka's ghost declared that she would not leave Sita. The spectators again attempted to drive out the ghost, but Sita finally relapsed into unconsciousness.

For a fortnight thereafter, Sita experienced a series of possessions, so her father-in-law called various exorcists. They used generally similar techniques, calling on their familiars—supernatural beings who served them—to assist with the cure. Among these familiars were Hanuman, the monkey god; Kalkaji, goddess of the cremation grounds, with whom ghosts are closely linked; Jahar or Guga Pir, a Hindu-Muslim saint, who cut off his maternal cousins' heads in battle and later buried himself alive; and the ghost of a conjurer from Dacca. Each curer began a session by calling on his familiars, thus reassuring Sita and her relatives as to his curing powers.

When Sita's possessions persisted, her father was notified. He brought two exorcists to collaborate in an all-night session to drive off the ghost. They first induced possession in Sita by the power of suggestion and by the hypnotic effects of chanting mantras (hymns) believed to have supernatural power and using a fire to focus her concentration. Then they tried to exorcise Taraka's ghost by verbal abuse, hitting Sita, squeezing rock salt between her fingers (which was painful), pulling her braids, and throwing bits of her hair into the fire. During the session, Sita alternated between seeing a ghost, falling into a semiconscious state while a ghost spoke through her, unconsciousness, and intermittent returns to consciousness. Sita was not cured, however, and soon thereafter left for an extended visit with her parents, who lived in another village.

During the rest of our stay in India, we came to learn more about the villagers' beliefs in ghosts and the particular circumstances that led to Sita's afflictions. In rural North India, almost all Hindus believe that the soul goes through a cycle of rebirths. Following a person's death, it becomes a ghost, lingering for thirteen days in the village cremation grounds. Villagers who adhere to the doctrines of the Arya Samaj, a reform sect of Hinduism, believe in only one God, Bhagwan, and expect his judgment after cremation. The majority of villagers, who follow a more traditional version of Hinduism with multiple supernatural beings, believe that the soul travels to the Land of the Dead, ruled by Yama, Lord of the Dead. There Yama and his scribe review the soul's past actions before deciding on its future.

The important element in what happens to the soul at death is its karma, the sum of its good and bad actions from all its past lives. After being judged, the soul may be reborn or, if the sum of its actions is unusually good, released from the cycle of rebirths to join with many other souls and the Universal Absolute, a neuter deity known also as the Ultimate Reality, the joining of all souls in one.

Many Hindus believe in an additional possibility: a soul may become a ghost that lingers, possibly for decades, haunting the places where it lived and died. These are the souls of people who die tortured, from disease, accident, suicide, or murder; who violate village norms of behavior; who die before the years allotted to them by Yama; or who never attain the satisfactions of adult life. The ghosts of persons who are murdered or commit suicide are the most malevolent and tarry longest.

Ghosts are feared because they are believed to attack the living to seize their souls. Many villagers, but not all, believe that being seized by a ghost can cause illness or death. Ghost possession is the most vivid form of attack, in which a ghost enters and speaks through its victim, who has fallen into semiconsciousness. After recovering, the victim does not remember what took place. Because people in a state of possession may attempt to commit suicide by drowning in a well or by jumping in front of a train, they are usually watched by relatives and neighbors.

There is often a relationship between a ghost and its victim. For example, we learned that Taraka was not only a cousin but also a very close friend of Sita's. Sita had lived with Taraka's family for six months. Engaged to a man of another village, Taraka had an illicit affair with a boy of her own village. Because she became pregnant, the loss of her premarital chastity could not be long concealed.

The virtue of daughters is crucial to family honor in North India, and a daughter's sexual misbehavior, if it becomes generally known, may force a father to get rid of her by inducing suicide or even by murder. Taraka's parents learned of her pregnancy and quickly arranged her wedding to her fiancé. They handed over only a small dowry, in case Taraka's in-laws, realizing she was pregnant, returned her.

When Taraka went to her husband's family to begin her marital life, her husband's parents immediately discovered that she was pregnant. Renouncing all rights to her, they returned her to her father. Despite Taraka's pleas, her father was unforgiving and told her to commit suicide. Shortly thereafter, when Taraka, Sita, and some other girls were playing, Taraka decided to leave the group and asked Sita to accompany her. Sita refused. Taraka ran from the group, went to a nearby well, jumped in, and drowned. Sita blamed herself for the suicide.

Taraka was one of Sita's three close childhood friends, all of whom she lost during the three years before her own marriage. Prior to Taraka's indiscretions and suicide, a schoolmate had been murdered by her father. She was raped by a schoolteacher, and even though the girl was the victim and the identity of the assailant was known, her father was furious and blamed her. He flew into a rage, raped and murdered her, and threw her into a well (villagers regard such crimes as family business and rarely interfere). Another of Sita's schoolmates died of typhoid and malaria, shortly after beginning sexual relations with her husband.

The episode of the untrustworthy schoolteacher worried Sita's mother, who took her daughter out of school. The abrupt end of her education was a shock to Sita, who wanted to be a schoolteacher herself. Instead, Sita and her mother went to visit her mother's brother in her mother's natal village. This was when Sita's life became entwined with Taraka's, for Taraka was this man's daughter.

In Sita's mind, the deaths of her friends were linked with mating, marriage, childbirth, and disappointed dreams of further education. This link was reinforced by other painful memories. As her parents' first-born child, Sita had lived through the deaths of four infant brothers and five infant sisters, who had died because they could not digest their mother's milk. Mother, daughter, and other villagers believed that a ghost had taken these infants' souls. (Two brothers born subsequently had survived.) With the memory of the deaths of her friends and infant siblings, the fifteen-year-old Sita went to her husband to consummate her marriage, on her second visit to her in-laws.

On the first night, Sita told her sister-in-law that she was afraid to sleep with her husband and implored her to stay with her instead. The sister-in-law did so, but when Sita awoke in the night, she found her husband sleeping beside her. They did not have sexual relations that night. The following day, Sita went to the well for water and either jumped or accidentally slipped and fell in. Fortunately, two men who were nearby threw her a rope and pulled her out. As a result of this incident, the young couple did not have sexual relations that night either, and the next day Sita returned to her parents' home.

The marriage was finally consummated on Sita's next visit to her husband, some months later. During the fourth night of sexual relations, however, Sita was possessed by Taraka's ghost, who said that Sita's husband was her husband. The statement indicated that Taraka's ghost had been with Sita at the time of Sita's wedding, which meant that both women were married to Sita's husband.

At best, a North Indian rural woman must make an extraordinary social and psychological adjustment when she marries. At an early age, she moves from her natal family, where she is loved, cherished, and indulged, to her marital family, where she is chaperoned and required to restrict her movements. She leaves her natal village to settle in the unfamiliar surroundings of her husband's village. She must adjust to her husband and his often large family, especially his parents, sisters, and brothers' wives. And in this rural society, where marriages are arranged by parents, the bride may not have even seen her husband before the wedding day (although nowadays at least some families arrange for the young couple to meet at the time of the engagement).

A married woman and her kin are regarded as social inferiors to her husband's kin. A new bride is expected to shoulder harder and more onerous household chores and farm work than the daughters in her husband's family (they too, when they marry and go to live with their husbands, will go through a similar experience). A new bride also is generally uninformed about the relation between menarche and childbirth and is apprehensive about beginning sexual relations with her husband. The social and psychological vulnerability of a bride makes her a prime candidate for attacks by ghosts. In Sita's case, with three friends who had all died before their allotted time and without issue, the ghosts were waiting in the wings. All three possessed Sita at one time or another, but Taraka's ghost was her main tormentor.

The transition from beloved and only surviving daughter to daughter-in-law was particularly stressful for Sita. Moreover, having been raised in a one caste village, she had faced little caste discrimination, but her husband's village was multicaste, and her caste was near the bottom of the hierarchy. Her fear of mating and bearing infants whose souls might be seized by ghosts was a source of stress, as were various physical ailments. These cultural, psychological, and physical stresses were preconditions for her possessions. Research by neuroscientists during the past two decades may shed light on the underlying physiological mechanism of ghost possession. Under the stress of mental or physical pain, the body produces morphinelike substances called endorphins, which relieve the pain and may trigger mental states called alternate, altered, or dissociative. Ghost possession is one such dissociative mental state.

Stress is not confined to brides or women in North India nor is ghost possession. On a return visit to the village in 1978, we recorded the cases of three young men who were troubled by ghosts. Although some of the details of the cases were different, they all involved the stresses of modern life, especially school examinations and job hunting. Education and employment are signs of economic responsibility that a girl's parents often require before entrusting their daughter to a young husband. For example, one of the young men, a 22-year-old member of the Potter caste, was desperate for a job because his wife's parents would not let their daughter come to live with him unless he found one.

The young man was possessed, according to his mother and sister, by the ghost of his mother's first husband's first wife. The belief that the ghost of a first wife will haunt her husband's next wife and children was a strong motif in village culture. In this case, the husband had subsequently passed away too, and his next wife had remarried and the children were of this marriage; but the principle was similar. Known as the Lady, this ghost had possessed the young man's older brother twenty years before under similar circumstances and was now intermittently possessing the younger man.

The young man was treated by two village exorcists. One was a high-caste Brahman. The other was the man whose remark had disturbed Sita twenty years before: unemployed at the time and subsequently saddened by the deaths of many of his infants and by his wife's long illness, he believed that the great god Shiva visited his home. Following this experience, he became an exorcist.

During our 1978 stay, we also interviewed Sita, who recounted her medical history. Now a poised, intelligent, 35-year-old woman, she recalled her early possessions, which had lasted three years until the birth of her first child. Then the possessions had become fits, which she described as follows:

> They start from the head. I feel giddy and drowsy. Then I can't see anything and everything goes dark. My legs, hands, and veins stiffen, then a pain goes to my stomach. I don't know what happens, but I have a pain in my heart, my eyes shut, and my tongue comes out. I shriek so loud that the whole village, even the Brahmans, know that I am having a fit. I have a weak heart. Whenever there is a fight in the family or elsewhere, or if I see a dead body, I have fits.

In 1978 Sita's fits were still taking place. Well acquainted with modern medicine—she went to modern hospitals for what she recognized as biological problems—she nonetheless blamed her twenty years of possessions and fits on Taraka's ghost. According to Sita, Taraka's ghost had possessed Taraka's mother, and she herself had then been infected through contact with Taraka's mother. She continued to consult indigenous curers, mainly exorcists, who drove off the ghost or gave her amulets to control it.

In the intervening years, Sita told us, her mother had given birth to three more infants who had died. The older of Sita's surviving brothers had died at age fourteen, and her grieving mother had died soon after. Sita's remaining brother became a schoolteacher with Sita's assistance, and she accompanied him and his wife on their honeymoon.

Sita's father was still alive, retired from military service. As a small child, Sita had idolized him—a soldier who traveled to other countries but came home every year for two months. The relationship persisted through the years. When she visited him every summer, free from the stress and anxiety of life in her marital family, she never had fits.

Sita detailed her pregnancies, illnesses, and operations in the years since we first met her. Pregnant nine times, she had six children born alive (one of whom died at age three), two miscarriages, and one induced abortion, prior to being sterilized in 1972. Sita's family had a history of an inability to digest milk, and her first child, a daughter, did not take Sita's milk. Sita's father arranged for Sita and her daughter to be hospitalized while the infant was fed glucose. Because of her father's influence, Sita thereafter went to hospitals for physical problems that she considered serious. She had an operation for kidney stones. She suffered from menstrual complaints and side effects from being sterilized. A constant worrier, she was badly disturbed when one of her brothers-in-law was diagnosed as having tuberculosis, for she feared that she might have it.

Nevertheless, with regard to her appearance, the maintenance of her household, and care of her children, she managed very well and, except for her fits, was in control of her life. The treatment for ghost possession and fits by exorcists and the various amulets they gave her for protection from Taraka's ghost relieved her anxiety and helped to reduce stress. They also brought her other advantages, especially support from her natal and marital families, a reduction in her workload, and permission to visit her retired father every summer. When we last saw her, Sita was the leader of the women of her family, confidently planning the education and future of her children.

Study and **Review** on **myanthrolab.com**

Review Questions

1. What aspects of her life make Sita a prime candidate for ghost possession in Indian society?
2. What happens to the souls of dead people according to Hindu village belief? What accounts for the presence of ghosts?
3. How did ghost possession help Sita adjust to her life as a married woman?

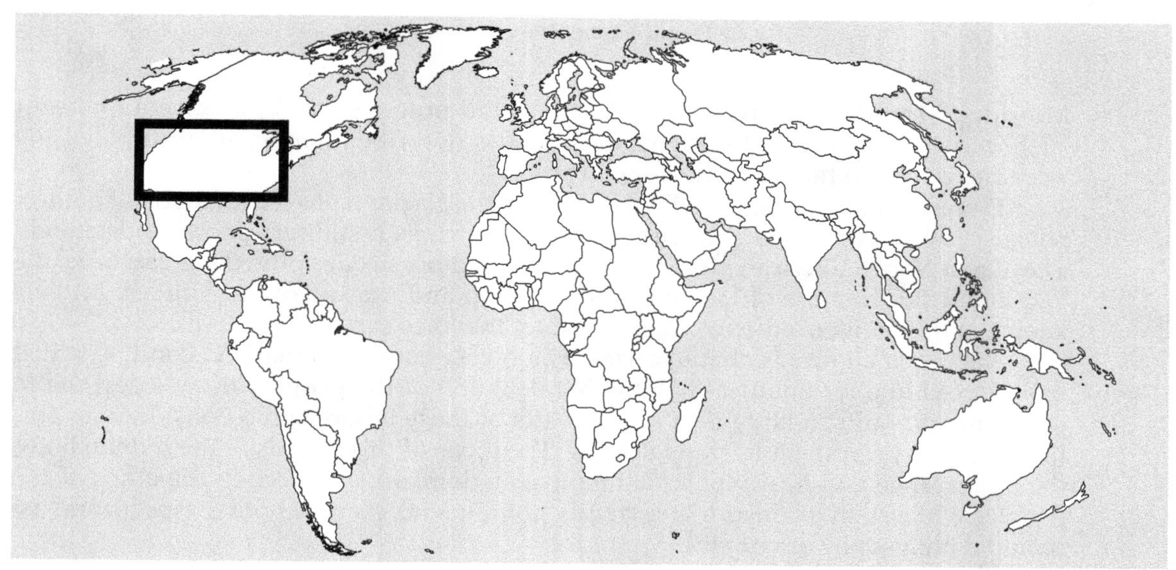

Body Ritual among the Nacirema

Horace Miner

*Ritual involving repeated symbolic acts can be about many things—the growth of crops, the response to death, movement from one social identity to another, community solidarity, and much more. It can also be about one's body, including how to care for it, how to make it socially acceptable, and how to make it impressive to others. This classic article written in 1958 by Horace Miner describes the extensive body ritual of a North American group, the Nacirema, whose houses contain special shrines in which body ritual takes place. From the article, it is clear that the society's elaborate variety of body rituals reveals important Nacirema cultural values.**

Listen to the **Chapter Audio** on **myanthrolab.com**

The anthropologist has become so familiar with the diversity of ways in which different peoples behave in similar situations that he is not apt to be surprised by even the most exotic customs. In fact, if all of the logically possible combinations of behavior have not been found somewhere in the world, he is apt to suspect that they must be present in some yet undescribed tribe. This point has, in fact, been expressed with respect to clan organization by

*From Horace Miller, "Body Ritual among the Nacirema," *The American Anthropologist,* vol. 58, June 1956. Used by permission of Blackwell Publishing.

Body Ritual Among the Nacirema, from Horace Miller, "Body Ritual among the Nacirema," The American Anthropologist, vol. 58, June 1956.

From Chapter 31 of *Conformity and Conflict: Readings in Cultural Anthropology.* Fourteenth Edition. James Spradley, David W. McCurdy.

Murdock.[1] In this light, the magical beliefs and practices of the Nacirema present such unusual aspects that it seems desirable to describe them as an example of the extremes to which human behavior can go.

Professor Linton first brought the ritual of the Nacirema to the attention of anthropologists twenty years ago, but the culture of this people is still very poorly understood.[2] They are a North American group living in the territory between the Canadian Cree, the Yaqui and Tarahumare of Mexico, and the Carib and Arawak of the Antilles. Little is known of their origin, although tradition states that they came from the east. . . .

Nacirema culture is characterized by a highly developed market economy which has evolved in a rich natural habitat. While much of the people's time is devoted to economic pursuits, a large part of the fruits of these labors and a considerable portion of the day are spent in ritual activity. The focus of this activity is the human body, the appearance and health of which loom as a dominant concern in the ethos of the people. While such a concern is certainly not unusual, its ceremonial aspects and associated philosophy are unique.

The fundamental belief underlying the whole system appears to be that the human body is ugly and that its natural tendency is to debility and disease. Incarcerated in such a body, man's only hope is to avert these characteristics through the use of the powerful influences of ritual and ceremony. Every household has one or more shrines devoted to this purpose. The more powerful individuals in the society have several shrines in their houses and, in fact, the opulence of a house is often referred to in terms of the number of such ritual centers it possesses. Most houses are of wattle and daub construction, but the shrine rooms of the more wealthy are walled with stone. Poorer families imitate the rich by applying pottery plaques to their shrine walls.

While each family has at least one such shrine, the rituals associated with it are not family ceremonies but are private and secret. The rites are normally only discussed with children, and then only during the period when they are being initiated into these mysteries. I was able, however, to establish sufficient rapport with the natives to examine these shrines and to have the rituals described to me.

The focal point of the shrine is a box or chest which is built into the wall. In this chest are kept the many charms and magical potions without which no native believes he could live. These preparations are secured from a variety of specialized practitioners. The most powerful of these are the medicine men, whose assistance must be rewarded with substantial gifts. However, the medicine men do not provide the curative potions for their clients, but decide what the ingredients should be and then write them down in an ancient and secret language. This writing is understood only by the medicine men and by the herbalists who, for another gift, provide the required charm.

The charm is not disposed of after it has served its purpose, but is placed in the charm–box of the household shrine. As these magical materials are specific for certain ills, and the real or imagined maladies of the people are many, the charm–box is usually full to overflowing. The magical packets are so numerous that people forget what their purposes were and fear to use them again. While the natives are very vague on this point, we can only assume that the idea in retaining all the old magical materials is that their presence in the charm–box, before which the body rituals are conducted, will in some way protect the worshipper.

[1]Murdock, George P. 1949. Social Structure. New york: The Macmillan Co.

[2]Linton, Ralph. 1936. The Study of man. New Yuork: D. Appleton Century co.

Beneath the charm–box is a small font. Each day every member of the family, in succession, enters the shrine room, bows his head before the charm–box, mingles different sorts of holy water in the font, and proceeds with a brief rite of ablution. The holy waters are secured from the Water Temple of the community, where the priests conduct elaborate ceremonies to make the liquid ritually pure.

In the hierarchy of magical practitioners, and below the medicine men in prestige, are specialists whose designation is best translated "holy–mouth–men." The Nacirema have an almost pathological horror of and fascination with the mouth, the condition of which is believed to have a supernatural influence on all social relationships. Were it not for the rituals of the mouth, they believe that their teeth would fall out, their gums bleed, their jaws shrink, their friends desert them, and their lovers reject them. They also believe that a strong relationship exists between oral and moral characteristics. For example, there is a ritual ablution of the mouth for children which is supposed to improve their moral fiber.

The daily body ritual performed by everyone includes a mouth–rite. Despite the fact that these people are so punctilious about care of the mouth, this rite involves a practice which strikes the uninitiated stranger as revolting. It was reported to me that the ritual consists of inserting a small bundle of hog hairs into the mouth, along with certain magical powders, and then moving the bundle in a highly formalized series of gestures.

In addition to the private mouth–rite, the people seek out a holy–mouth–man once or twice a year. These practitioners have an impressive set of paraphernalia, consisting of a variety of augers, awls, probes, and prods. The use of these objects in the exorcism of the evils of the mouth involves almost unbelievable ritual torture of the client. The holy–mouth–man opens the client's mouth and, using the above mentioned tools, enlarges any holes which decay may have created in the teeth. Magical materials are put into these holes. If there are no naturally occurring holes in the teeth, large sections of one or more teeth are gouged out so that the supernatural substance can be applied. In the client's view, the purpose of these ministrations is to arrest decay and to draw friends. The extremely sacred and traditional character of the rite is evident in the fact that the natives return to the holy–mouth–men year after year, despite the fact that their teeth continue to decay.

It is to be hoped that, when a thorough study of the Nacirema is made, there will be careful inquiry into the personality structure of these people. One has but to watch the gleam in the eye of a holy–mouth–man, as he jabs an awl into an exposed nerve, to suspect that a certain amount of sadism is involved. If this can be established, a very interesting pattern emerges, for most of the population shows definite masochistic tendencies. It was to these that Professor Linton referred in discussing a distinctive part of the daily body ritual which is performed only by men. This part of the rite involves scraping and lacerating the surface of the face with a sharp instrument. Special women's rites are performed only four times during each lunar month, but what they lack in frequency is made up in barbarity. As part of this ceremony, women bake their heads in small ovens for about an hour. The theoretically interesting point is that what seems to be a preponderantly masochistic people have developed sadistic specialists.

The medicine men have an imposing temple, or *latipso*, in every community of any size. The more elaborate ceremonies required to treat very sick patients can only be performed at this temple. These ceremonies involve not only the thaumaturge but a permanent group of vestal maidens who move sedately about the temple chambers in distinctive costume and headdress.

The *latipso* ceremonies are so harsh that it is phenomenal that a fair proportion of the really sick natives who enter the temple ever recover. Small children whose indoctrination is still incomplete have been known to resist attempts to take them to the temple because "that is where you go to die." Despite this fact, sick adults are not only willing but eager to undergo the protracted ritual purification, if they can afford to do so. No matter how ill the supplicant or how grave the emergency, the guardians of many temples will not admit a client if he cannot give a rich gift to the custodian. Even after one has gained admission and survived the ceremonies, the guardians will not permit the neophyte to leave until he makes still another gift.

The supplicant entering the temple is first stripped of all his or her clothes. In everyday life the Nacirema avoids exposure of his body and its natural functions. Bathing and excretory acts are performed only in the secrecy of the household shrine, where they are ritualized as part of the body–rites. Psychological shock results from the fact that body secrecy is suddenly lost upon entry into the *latipso*. A man, whose own wife has never seen him in an excretory act, suddenly finds himself naked and assisted by a vestal maiden while he performs his natural functions into a sacred vessel. This sort of ceremonial treatment is necessitated by the fact that the excreta are used by a diviner to ascertain the course and nature of the client's sickness. Female clients, on the other hand, find their naked bodies are subjected to the scrutiny, manipulation and prodding of the medicine men.

Few supplicants in the temple are well enough to do anything but lie on their hard beds. The daily ceremonies, like the rites of the holy–mouth–men, involve discomfort and torture. With ritual precision, the vestals awaken their miserable charges each dawn and roll them about on their beds of pain while performing ablutions, in the formal movements of which the maidens are highly trained. At other times they insert magic wands in the supplicant's mouth or force him to eat substances which are supposed to be healing. From time to time the medicine men come to their clients and jab magically treated needles into their flesh. The fact that these temple ceremonies may not cure, and may even kill the neophyte, in no way decreases the people's faith in the medicine men.

There remains one other kind of practitioner, known as a "listener." This witchdoctor has the power to exorcise the devils that lodge in the heads of people who have been bewitched. The Nacirema believe that parents bewitch their own children. Mothers are particularly suspected of putting a curse on children while teaching them the secret body rituals. The counter-magic of the witchdoctor is unusual in its lack of ritual. The patient simply tells the "listener" all his troubles and fears, beginning with the earliest difficulties he can remember. The memory displayed by the Nacirema in these exorcism sessions is truly remarkable. It is not uncommon for the patient to bemoan the rejection he felt upon being weaned as a babe, and a few individuals even see their troubles going back to the traumatic effects of their own birth.

In conclusion, mention must be made of certain practices which have their base in native esthetics but which depend upon the pervasive aversion to the natural body and its functions. There are ritual fasts to make fat people thin and ceremonial feasts to make thin people fat. Still other rites are used to make women's breasts larger if they are small, and smaller if they are large. General dissatisfaction with breast shape is symbolized in the fact that the ideal form is virtually outside the range of human variation. A few women afflicted with almost inhuman hyper-mammary development are so idolized that they make a handsome living by simply going from village to village and permitting the natives to stare at them for a fee.

Reference has already been made to the fact that excretory functions are ritualized, routinized, and relegated to secrecy. Natural reproductive functions are similarly distorted. Intercourse is taboo as a topic and scheduled as an act. Efforts are made to avoid pregnancy by the use of magical materials or by limiting intercourse to certain phases of the moon. Conception is actually very infrequent. When pregnant, women dress so as to hide their condition. Parturition takes place in secret, without friends or relatives to assist, and the majority of women do not nurse their infants.

Our review of the ritual life of the Nacirema has certainly shown them to be a magic–ridden people. It is hard to understand how they have managed to exist so long under the burdens which they have imposed upon themselves. But even such exotic customs as these take on real meaning when they are viewed with the insight provided by Malinowski when he wrote:

> Looking from far and above, from our high places of safety in the developed civilization, it is easy to see all the crudity and irrelevance of magic. But without its power and guidance early man could not have mastered his practical difficulties as he has done, nor could man have advanced to the higher stages of civilization.[3]

Study and **Review** on **myanthrolab.com**

Review Questions

1. Where are the Nacirema located?
2. Describe the main body rituals that occur in Nacireman household shrines.
3. What kinds of ritual specialists does Miner describe for the Nacirema in this article? What do they function to do for people?
4. What is the *latipso,* and for what is it used?
5. What do you think the psychological functions of Nacireman body ritual are, and how do these fit with Malinowski's theory about the functions of religion and magic described in the earlier article on baseball magic?

[3]Malinowski, Bronislaw. 1948. magic, Science, and Religion. Glencoe, IL: The Free Press, p. 70

Equality and Inequality

PREVIEW

- What is social stratification? How does inequality arise in human societies?
- What are three basic types of social organization? How do they work?
- How do caste and class systems differ as two forms of stratified societies?
- What are some determinants and indicators of social standing in stratified societies?
- How are societies stratified by gender, race, and ethnicity?
- Why is the concept of race controversial?
- How and why do people create, accept, maintain, reject, and change their ethnic identities?
- How do ideologies reinforce systems of stratification?
- What does an anthropological perspective of class, ideology, ethnicity, and race indicate about American society?

Tsar Mikhail Fyodorovich (1596-1645) with Boyars Sitting in his Room, 1893 (oil on canvas). *Tretyakov Gallery, Moscow, Russia/The Bridgeman Art Library*

Listen to the Chapter Audio on myanthrolab.com

Read on myanthrolab.com

A Rabbi was asked why it was that everything was permitted the rich but not the poor.

"Is there a separate Torah for the rich and another for the poor?"

"It's all a matter of luck," answered the Rabbi." Moses came down from Mount Sinai and found that the Jews had fashioned a golden calf. He got so angry that he went and shattered the Ten Commandments. The Tables of the Law, as you know, were made of the most precious gems. When the multitude saw Moses break them they leaped forward to pick up the valuable pieces that fell in every direction. Now who do you think had all the luck in the world? The rich, of course! They picked up all the pieces on which was written—*Thou shalt*. The poor, on the other hand, had no luck at all. All they could pick up in the scramble were little bits of the Tables on which was written the word *not*. So there!

"... But you've just got to give me some money!" insisted the poor man.

"Why so?" demanded the rich man.

"Because if you don't, I'll... I'll go into the hat business!"

"So what?"

"What do you mean, so what? If a man with my luck goes into the hat business, every baby in this country from that day on will be born without a head!"

Source: A Treasury of Jewish Folklore, 1948, edited by Nathan Ausubel, New York: Crown Publishers, p. 346, p. 347.

In these Yiddish tales, differences in wealth and status are at the center of the narratives. Poor people are generally looked down on because of their poverty and "bad luck," but these stories tell their tales with logic and humor. The stories can therefore be read as forms of resistance to the dominant ideology in Europe which granted privileges to some and disadvantages to others. In narrative style, they are subverting the prevailing system of inequality.

"Four score and seven years ago our fathers brought forth on this continent a new nation, conceived in liberty, and dedicated to the proposition that all men are created equal." This is the opening sentence of the Gettysburg Address by President Abraham Lincoln, one of the most famous and most quoted excerpts from American oratory. But the world of 1863 was not the world implied in this speech. Presumably Lincoln meant that the founders of the United States intended to establish a nation where all people were free. But the United States in its beginnings was a country with slavery and founded on land appropriated from indigenous peoples. In contrast, an ideology of equality, stated in the Declaration of Independence, in Lincoln's Gettysburg Address, and in countless political speeches ever since, has permeated American public discourse for centuries. Through this discourse, people come to believe in an equality of opportunity that did not, and does not, exist.

EQUALITY, INEQUALITY, AND SOCIAL STRATIFICATION

There are societies in which everyone has equal access to resources, livelihood, and respect. There are also societies in which access to resources, livelihood, and respect is given more to some people than to others. The first type of system, based on principles of equality among members of communities, is called egalitarian. The second type, based on social, economic, and political inequality, is called stratified. In this chapter, we are particularly concerned with systems of social and political inequality.

Before beginning, though, several important distinctions must be made clear. Although people in egalitarian societies have equal access to resources and to positions of prestige and respect, all people are not equal in ability. Individuals everywhere differ in that some have more talent, intelligence, skill, or valued personality traits than others. And, of course, those people with more desirable characteristics are more respected, appreciated, and liked than those people lacking such positive traits. Nonetheless, everyone may make use of the group's resources, secure subsistence, and live a decent life more or less comparably to other people in their community.

In contrast, some people in stratified societies achieve positions of respect, influence, and power that grant them privileges and opportunities denied to others. We will be examining the bases on which stratified societies make social distinctions and the differing rewards and benefits available to some.

Three categories of culturally valued resources are wealth, power, and prestige (Fried 1967). **Wealth** refers to economic resources, whether in land, goods, or money. **Power** refers to the ability to exert control over the actions of other people and to make decisions that affect them. **Prestige** is a social resource that is reflected in other people's good opinions, in their respect, and in their willingness to solicit and to listen voluntarily to one's advice. According to Max Weber (1968; 1981), prestige, or honor as he called it, is central to the establishment and maintenance of status. Weber related honor to the notion of personal charisma. People strive to be well thought of because they then can influence other people. In stratified societies, prestige is linked to wealth and power. Because social values emphasize the worthiness of accumulating wealth, wealthy people are considered successful and are looked to as models to emulate. Prestige, then, built on wealth, can be used to obtain and exercise power.

Another set of terms relevant to our discussion of egalitarian and stratified societies has to do with various statuses and roles. Some of these are achieved and some are ascribed. An **achieved status** is one that people attain on the basis of their own efforts and skills. An **ascribed status** is one that a person occupies simply by birth or through a culturally determined right. In our society, leadership is an achieved status; we elect our mayors, governors, and presidents, presumably because of their abilities. In monarchies, leadership is an ascribed status; a king occupies his position simply because he is the eldest son of the previous king.

Finally, the distinctions among societies are not absolute, discrete types but, rather, form a continuum from egalitarian to stratified. Many societies contain elements of both, combining principles of equality in certain contexts with principles of inequality in other contexts. Indeed, there is a type of society, called ranked, that exhibits characteristics of both. **Ranked societies** differentiate individuals or, more usually, kinship groups along a continuum from lowest to highest, based partly on achieved status and partly on ascribed status. The benefits of high rank are primarily social rather than economic or political. People of high rank have prestige and respect but they do not have a living standard significantly better than that of people of lower rank, although there may be some differences in the size or decoration of their houses or in the amount of their clothing and ornaments. Although people of high rank may have influence in their communities, they do not have the power to control the activities of others. Still, high-ranking people may be able to exert wider influence than others and therefore be able to have their voices heard in economic and political domains. However, they cannot force others to comply with their wishes.

In any stratified society, wealth, power, and prestige confer privileges. Here, King Leruo Tshekedi Molotlegi of Bafokeng in South Africa rides in a donkey cart at his coronation to symbolize his pledge not to personally profit from the mineral riches of his country.
Reuters/Thomas White/Reuters

wealth
Economic resources, whether in land, goods, or money.

power
The ability to exert control over the actions of other people and to make decisions that affect them.

prestige
A social resource reflected in others' good opinions, respect, and willingness to be influenced.

achieved status
A social position attained by a person's own efforts and skills.

ascribed status
A social position that a person attains by birth. A person is born into an ascribed status.

ranked societies
Societies in which people or, more usually, kinship groups are ordered on a continuum in relation to each other.

What is an example of one of your achieved statuses? What is an example of one of your ascribed statuses?

Have you been a member of a ranked social organization? How would your experience compare with living in a ranked society?

Egalitarian Societies

Egalitarian societies are ones in which all people have equal access to valued resources. Everyone has available land and natural resources to supply the food that they need to survive. Everyone can achieve positions of respect and influence. Although people may seek the advice of respected individuals, no one is able to exert control or dominance over other people. Egalitarian social systems are usually found in cultures with economies based on producing for subsistence and use rather than to accumulate large surpluses and wealth. Foraging societies tend to be egalitarian in their social and ethical principles. Many horticultural societies are also egalitarian. This does not mean, however, that such societies have no forms of inequality. There are the inequalities of intelligence, skill, and personality that render some people more respected and influential than others. There are also attribute inequalities, such as age and gender, which may affect one's position in the household and society. Older people may be consulted and asked for their opinions about personal or community matters because of their greater experience in life.

The importance of age may be reflected within the household as well. Some of the authority and influence of parents derives from their age as well as from their genealogical relationship to their children. In some societies, the importance of seniority among siblings may be reflected in kinship terms that distinguish older and younger siblings and in behavior where younger siblings act deferentially toward their elders.

In addition, gender may be a factor in the respect and authority that people exert. If men and women are thought of as equal, both have influential roles in family and community decision making, conflict resolution, and group action. In male-dominated societies, however, men's opinions have paramount weight in these matters, and women's voices are muted. Other kinds of inequalities derived from kinship relationships may exist as well. Heads of lineages or clans may have important, decisive roles, certainly within their families and often in wider social contexts. In some societies, lineage or clan leaders may form village or district councils to discuss matters of community concern.

Despite all of these possible forms of inequality, "status tends to be individual or situational rather than categorical" (Berreman 1989, 8). That is, people's prestige and influence are based primarily on their personal qualities and relationships. Finally, people with influence do not use their advantages for personal material gain. The reward for being respected, skilled, and charismatic is social prestige, not wealth or power.

In egalitarian societies, social ethics stress generosity, hospitality, cooperation, and loyalty. People are expected to share resources and to aid one another in household and community work. Coupled with responsibilities to kin and community members, individual autonomy and the rights of all men and women to make decisions and act independently are valued. Coercion of others, either within households or in camps, is not tolerated and, given the strong negative reactions against such behavior, it is rarely attempted. Group leadership tends to be diffuse, flexible, and dependent on personal qualities and skills. People look for advice to those who are intelligent and successful in the particular endeavor requiring assistance or consultation—for example, skilled hunters are consulted regarding hunting. However, a man's or a woman's influence is temporary, fitted to the given occasion. Advice, therefore, is sought among local "experts," but such people cannot exert authority or control. Decisions are made jointly by all involved.

Ranked Societies

In systems of rank, every person—or, more accurately, every lineage or kin group—has a different position in the social hierarchy. Each rank is ordered in relation to all others. People of higher ranks have more social prestige than people of lower ranks, but they do not have significantly greater wealth or power. Their rewards are social, manifested in the respect given to them and the influence allowed them. If people follow their advice and direction, it is only because they have earned respect by their intelligence, behavior, and sound judgment. Ranked positions are established and maintained through a complex

egalitarian societies
Societies in which all members have equal access to valued resources, including land, social prestige, wealth, and power.

interplay of economic resources, political alliances, personal demeanor, and charisma, all leading to the formation of people's opinions of others.

Ranked systems are not static. Indeed, they are inherently extremely dynamic, even potentially competitive types of social organization. People can raise their status by their behavior and achievement and by the support of their relatives. But one's status can also fall. To move up the metaphoric "ladder of success," people have to mobilize public opinion because public opinion legitimates one's place in the system. People attempt to increase their economic wealth, forge alliances and attract dependents or clients, and act in ways that convey self-respect and conform to social norms of personality and attractiveness. To be successful and achieve these results, people need the support of their kin. Because of the competitive nature of ranked systems, competition within the family might prove disruptive if family members vied with one another for access to rank. Therefore, many such systems include the rule of primogeniture, or inheritance by seniority, so that the eldest child has the privilege of representing the family by occupying a position of rank. (In some societies, only men may hold rank; in others, women or men might occupy status positions.)

stratified societies
Societies in which people have differential access to valued resources, including land and property, social prestige, wealth, and political power.

Stratified Societies

In **stratified societies,** people do not have equal access to valued resources. Because of their ability to accumulate all three elements of culturally valuable resources—wealth, power, and prestige—in stratified societies, some people have more economic resources than others. They have more land, food, and possessions, and their standard of living is superior to that of other people. Some people have more power than others, and they are able to exert control over the actions of other people by making decisions that affect them with or without their consent. As a consequence of having more wealth and power, they also have more social prestige. People respect them and regard them with envy. In stratified societies, some wealth, power, and prestige accrue to people because of their achievements, hard work, and personal characteristics. However, some of their good fortune comes to them because of their birth. They are the children of wealthy and powerful people. Prestige, wealth, and power, therefore, are both ascribed and achieved.

CASE STUDY

The Samoans: A Ranked Society

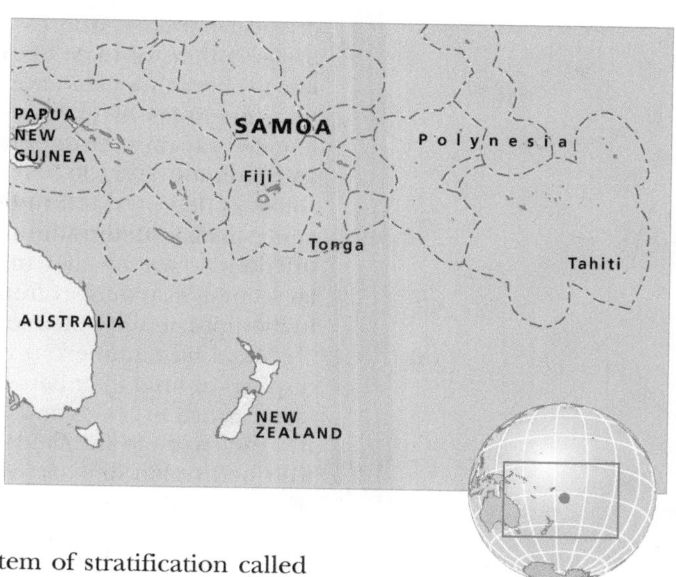

The Samoan Islands are in the Pacific Ocean about halfway between Hawaii and New Zealand. The islands are divided into two groups: Western Samoa, an independent nation since 1961, and American Samoa, a territory under United States jurisdiction since 1904. The two groups of islands share most practices and systems of organization.

Samoan subsistence centers on farming, especially coconuts, taro (a starchy tuber), and breadfruit. Both women and men participate in farming, although men do the heavy work of clearing fields. The principal source of protein comes from ocean fish and shellfish, but domesticated pigs are eaten on ceremonial occasions. Kinship groups hold land communally, under the stewardship of family leaders who allocate individual plots for each family. Farm work, however, is generally carried out collectively by the appropriate members of the household, considering age and gender roles.

Samoan social and political life is organized around a system of stratification called "rank." In ranked societies, kinship groups are ordered in terms of prestige, influence, and privilege. In Samoa, the most important units of affiliation are the household, the extended family, and the village (Holmes and Holmes 1992, 28). Households generally consist of a leading man, his wife, their children, and additional relatives possibly including elderly parents, siblings, and siblings of the parents. People have the right to claim residence with relatives by either blood or affinal ties. Such flexibility allows people to make strategic decisions about individual affiliation. A newly married couple may live with either the husband's or the wife's family, possibly depending on the number and gender of siblings already living in the household, on personal affection, or on the status of the household head. The size of households usually varies from ten to twenty individuals.

Members of extended families may live together in one household or in several different dwellings. The heads of extended families have titles, called "matai," derived from ancient or mythological times. They are ranked relative to one another depending on their association with mythical beings or venerable historical personages. There are two types of matai titles: Chief and Talking Chief. Some extended families have claim to Chief titles, whereas others claim Talking Chief titles.

The position of matai is held by a man, chosen by all the adult members of the extended family that he represents. Ordinarily, a man holds this position for life, but someone who loses favor may be demoted, or an elderly matai may retire. The successor is chosen at a public meeting at which anyone who wishes may speak in support of a candidate. Discussions may last weeks. Although present, candidates do not participate in the deliberations. Good character, generosity, intelligence, hard work, dedication to the family, and oratorical skills are favored traits. If a son of the former chief has these qualities, he is a likely, although not assured, successor, but if not, the field is open to other candidates.

Successors to the position of matai are celebrated in a family ritual involving drinking "kava," a beverage made from kava root, steeped in water. It is the Samoans' ceremonial beverage, drunk on a variety of celebrations. The new matai is given the honor of drinking "first kava," a mark of prestige and respect. Later, the matai is formally installed at a meeting of the village council of chiefs, composed of all of the matai of the extended families represented in the village. There, he also drinks first kava and gives an elaborate speech full of metaphor and imagery. Each of the other chiefs in order of their rank answers the speech. Seating arrangements at the council meetings and other official occasions also indicate relative rank.

The new matai's first obligation is to provide a feast for the community. To amass the quantities of food and gifts of bark cloth for the feast, he must mobilize his extended family to work harder to supply these goods. They are willing to do so because their own status rises and falls with that of their matai. This feature of social organization is also the essence of a ranked society.

In addition to the extended family as a unit, the Samoans recognize internal branches derived from the sons and daughters of the first founder. The sons were the originators of male branches, whereas the daughters were originators of female branches. In principle, members of male branches are more likely to be chosen as matai, but members of female branches also have claims. Furthermore, to balance their privileged social position, members of male branches have special responsibilities toward members of the female branches, owing them respect and performing services when called on (Holmes and Holmes 1992, 30). Although women are not named as matai, they have significant voices collectively and individually in choosing successors to the title. A woman's birth and marriage determine her own status. That is, daughters of titled fathers or wives of titled men have prestige in their communities. However, the respect that is due a particular woman also derives from her own character, intelligence, oratorical skills, and ability to manipulate the system of status in her favor.

Matai have numerous responsibilities, including overseeing communal land, settling disputes among members of the extended family, and representing the family on the village council of chiefs and at other public functions. Although matai have high social status, they work in the fields alongside other family members. Each matai has an assistant who helps plan daily activities and communicates the matai's decisions to the relevant people. Chiefs and Talking Chiefs have different roles. Each group (Chiefs and Talking Chiefs) is divided into three grades: High Chiefs, Chiefs, and Between-the-Posts Chiefs. The High Chiefs have titles closely associated with gods or culture heroes. They serve as heads of village councils and settle disputes arising between village residents. They receive the largest share of food and other gifts at ceremonial feasts hosted by other matai. Chiefs are heads of large extended families that have influence and stature. Between-the-Posts

Chiefs (so named because, in council houses, they sit between the end posts reserved for more distinguished members) are holders of titles that have been created recently to acknowledge special service or abilities of individual men. Chiefs within each group are also internally ranked according to their origins and accomplishments.

Talking Chiefs are skilled orators who sometimes function as speakers for High Chiefs on special occasions. They also represent their villages in intervillage meetings and rituals. When an important delegation is sent to another village, the emissaries are accompanied by a Talking Chief who makes elaborate speeches and is greeted in turn by a resident Talking Chief.

In ranked societies, as in all systems of social stratification, the privilege and status of elites depends on the existence of a large group of untitled people or commoners. In Samoa, untitled men in each village may participate in a voluntary association called "aumaga." This group has both economic and ceremonial functions. The men perform collective labor for the village, clearing fields, building houses, repairing paths, and fishing. When the village council of chiefs meets, men from the aumaga prepare and serve the food and kava. They perform the same functions on ceremonial occasions. They also carry out and enforce council decisions. The internal organization of the aumaga is similar to that of the village council of chiefs. It is an internally stratified group, with a leader (often a son or close relative of a High Chief) and members ranked according to principles similar to the ranking of chiefs.

Unmarried women may join an association called an "aualuma." In the past, these women served mainly ceremonial functions, but today they work primarily in public health, child care, and other community services (Holmes and Holmes 1992, 42). Like the men's organizations, the aualuma is headed by the wife of one of the High Chiefs or Talking Chiefs. She leads group meetings, plans activities, and assigns work to members.

Although matai have social privileges due their high rank in a stratified system, Samoan society is also based on egalitarian ethics. A matai who abuses his position or becomes arrogant and ignores the sentiments of his relatives is likely to be demoted. People who disagree with the decisions of the matai can leave and affiliate with another household in which they have rights by blood or marriage. The prestige of a matai falls if the number of people in his household declines. Therefore, untitled people have many ways to influence a matai's reputation. Just as the status of untitled people depends on the rank of their matai, his status depends on their good favor.

The Samoan system of social stratification continues today to order relations among people in village life. Changes in the system have, of course, taken place throughout Samoa, especially in larger towns. Even in the villages, however, there have been moves toward individual control over farmland. Although most land is still held communally under the stewardship of the matai, nuclear families can gain access to small plots of land. The qualities that make a man a likely successor to the title of matai have also changed. Education and/or job experience in the United States enables young men to advance more rapidly than would have been possible in the past. Untitled men with job skills are encouraged to work in the United States for brief periods so that they can send money to their families and the matai. These gifts demonstrate the donor's generosity and hard work, important assets for a future matai. The position of matai remains crucial, not only to leadership in the extended family, but also as a necessary qualification for election to the Samoan Senate, one of the two island-wide legislative bodies (the other is the House of Representatives, whose members may be either titled or untitled).

The traditional "aumaga" of untitled young men continues to have ceremonial functions, but its role in mobilizing cooperative labor has declined. Especially in rural villages, many young men migrate to the larger towns or to the United States (mostly to Hawaii or West Coast states) to find employment. The "aualuma" association of unmarried women has largely disappeared, its collective social welfare functions taken over by women's associations that include unmarried, married, and widowed women. Because of traditional gender roles and attitudes, women are less likely to migrate to the United States, but those who do send money home to their families. Although most Samoan immigrants have low incomes by American standards, the money they send back to Samoa has a significant impact both in purely financial terms and in contributing to the prestige of their families. Read the Document on myanthrolab.com

social stratification
Division of society into two or more groups, or strata, that are hierarchically ordered.

elites
Members of a social group in a stratified society who have privileges denied to the majority of the population.

Social stratification refers to a division of society into two or more groups, or strata, that are hierarchically ordered in relation to each other. Within each stratum, members are all more or less of equal social standing. Although there are differences among individuals in stratified systems, people in the same stratum have equivalent opportunities, privileges, and similar standards of living, at least when compared to people in other strata.

One of the significant features of all systems of stratification is that the highest group is usually, if not always, a numerical minority. Why, then, are the majority of people willing to accept a system that does not benefit them? There are many and complex explanations. One reason is that the elite group controls the means of forcing compliance with their wishes. Because the **elites** control social, economic, and political resources, they are in a position to use political (and often military) power against those who resist their control. However, the use of force is costly, not just in economic terms. When force is used against people, especially if they constitute the majority of the population, they will likely sooner or later rebel against a system that disadvantages them. So, instead, social attitudes and beliefs are developed to induce conformity. People are taught to believe that the system they live in is just. If not entirely just, it is at least seen as legitimate.

There are many ways of creating and transmitting such attitudes or ideologies. Religious teaching, for example, is an effective means of instilling obedience to the rulers. People may be taught that the deities chose their leaders or that the system they live in has divine approval. Or they may be pacified by the hope that divine beings favor them, an idea conveyed by the biblical dictum "The meek shall inherit the Earth." In addition, social ideologies transmit the notion that elites are more capable, more intelligent, and in other ways superior to common people. Common people absorb these ideologies through their socialization and through exposure to public discourse that elites control.

Thus, for example, many fail to see that poverty and wealth are part of the structure of our society. They fail to see that our capitalist economic system depends as much on the existence of poverty as it does on the existence of wealth. The wealth of some people depends on the labor of other people, many of whom work for low wages. In addition, the existence of a group of unemployed and underemployed people exerts a downward pressure on all wages because more people are wanting work than there are jobs available. This situation leads to competition among workers for jobs and creates a situation where even low-paying jobs become attractive.

Systems of stratification based on the control of capital and the concept of social mobility have spread throughout the world as a consequence of globalization. Stratification based on class membership is rapidly replacing other forms of stratification, as well as ranked and egalitarian societies.

Explaining Social Stratification

Social stratification is a characteristic of complex state societies. Among other traits, states have economies based on intensive agricultural production, resulting in a large surplus. This surplus can be used to support ever-growing populations and to free some people from agricultural work. Labor specialization develops so that some people work as farmers, others as artisans, traders, soldiers, or government officials. States are also characterized by unequal access to resources. Some people accumulate more goods, land, and other property than others. Rather than distributing their wealth to community members in need, they use their property for themselves, raising their standard of living and living better than people with fewer resources. Over time, inequalities in standards of living become entrenched as children of wealthy parents are born with advantages and opportunities lacking to the children of poor people.

This woman is one of many working poor who earn minimum wages in the United States. The Image Works/Rachel Epstein/The Image Works

Several types of explanations are offered to explain the existence of stratification. Functional analyses emphasize the fact that different sectors of the population perform different roles in society. Rewards are given to those people who are more capable and hardworking than others. In functionalism, people who are leaders, traders, and officials, performing important functions for the community as a whole, are acknowledged and permitted to accumulate wealth, social prestige, and power. These benefits are believed to be just compensation for their societal contributions.

Although there is merit in this argument, because it points out the various roles of different people in systems of economic specialization, it fails to take into account several important factors. People with wealth are not necessarily more capable than others. Some people inherit their wealth without any effort or achievement of their own. Also, some leaders are incompetent. In monarchies where the eldest son of the king automatically becomes the next ruler, there is no guarantee that the person so promoted is the most capable. Hard work does not necessarily translate into wealth, prestige, and power. As an extreme example, African slaves in the United States and the Caribbean certainly contributed great effort and often gave their lives in the production of wealth, but received no benefit at all from their work. The value of their labor was extracted and used by their owners. In modern societies as well, the hard work and long hours of, for example, factory workers, secretaries, and nurses are not reflected in luxurious standards of living.

Karl Marx explained social stratification as an outgrowth of class conflict over the control of resources and wealth. Corbis/ Alfredo Dagli Orti/The Art Archive/ Corbis

A second set of explanations for social stratification emphasizes the conflicts between members of different strata or classes. These analyses, following Karl Marx, focus on the processes that create groups in opposition to each other. Members of different classes have different class interests. They develop a consciousness of their class and strive to protect and expand their interests. Members of elite classes try to influence economic and political policies that will benefit themselves. Although members of lower classes may also try to influence leaders to implement policies that will aid them, they are generally less successful, in part because the leaders tend to come from or identify with the elites.

These explanations focus on societies as dynamic systems. They emphasize the processes of struggle between members of opposing groups. Through these struggles, societies can be transformed. Then new types of group formation and new types of opposition and conflict lead to further series of changes and adaptations. Of course, although complex societies are composed of groups with different, often conflicting, interests and goals, societies also attempt to build consensus and foster cooperation among groups. Therefore, functional and Marxist explanations for social stratification both offer insights that can be useful in analyzing societal structures and processes.

How might a functionalist or a Marxist explain homelessness in a stratified society such as the United States? Alamy Limited/Pegaz/Alamy

Societies become stratified through the unequal distribution of wealth, power, and prestige, which attach to the different ascribed statuses (inherited) and achieved statuses (acquired) in a society. In ranked societies, different groups are ranked hierarchically on the basis of both ascribed and achieved statuses. Egalitarian societies provide equal access to resources, whereas some individuals and groups in stratified societies have more resources and others less. Structuralism, functionalism, Marxism, and other theoretical perspectives offer alternative explanations for social stratification.

CASTE AND CLASS

A caste is a social group whose membership is hereditary. Castes are endogamous. That is, people must marry within their caste, and their children are also members of the same group. Thus, caste is an ascribed status with automatic, involuntary, and unchanging membership and identity. Separation on the basis of caste may be manifested by restrictions on living spaces, occupation, style of dress, and demeanor. In caste systems, each group is assigned a particular order of prestige relative to the others on a scale from lowest to highest. Unlike rank, caste order cannot change.

Determinants of Class

Systems of class are also ways of grouping people in a hierarchical order. Whereas castes are differentiated according to the sole criterion of ancestry, class may be defined in various ways. One way to talk about class is to talk about economic factors, primarily income,

CULTURE CHANGE

CASTE IN INDIA

In India, there are hundreds of discrete castes (called *jati*), all ranked in relation to one another (Koller 1982). The caste system unifies constituent groups into four large groupings (called *varna*), each containing numerous castes that are perceived to be similar in their origin, function, and especially in their ritual purity. Members of the highest varna, called the Brahmins, were traditionally the priests and scholars. The second-highest category is the Kshatriyas, who were the warriors. The merchants and traders constitute the third varna, called Vaishyas. The fourth varna are the Shudras, or artisans, carpenters, blacksmiths, barbers, farmers, and menial workers. Finally, a fifth group ranks below all the others: the untouchables. Untouchables are considered ritually impure, fit to do only the most menial work, such as cleaning toilets. According to Hindu beliefs, a member of one of the higher castes can become ritually polluted by touching or being touched by an untouchable.

Caste in India is an example of a comparatively closed system of stratification. Although some social mobility is possible, people are traditionally born into a particular caste and remain in it throughout their lives. Rural villages are often divided into caste neighborhoods, and occupations are determined by caste. In the most traditional contexts, people can do little, if anything, to change their circumstances. Even if people move to another community and do not reveal their heredity, their ways of talking and behaving would probably be telltale signs of their ancestry and, by implication, caste identity.

The behavior of people in different castes is a barrier to social interactions, acting as boundary markers. People belonging to different castes should not eat together or have sexual relations with one another. Members of higher castes may avoid taking food offered by members of lower castes. Higher-caste people are more likely to be vegetarians and not drink alcohol. Members of different castes may have different ways of speaking, including pronunciation and choice of words. The most stringent restrictions concern untouchables. In villages, untouchables must reside in their own section and cannot drink from wells used by the higher castes.

The most prestigious group, the Brahmins, are considered ritually pure. They need to maintain their purity through social distance. But Brahmins are not necessarily wealthy. For example, they may work as cooks in restaurants because members of all castes may eat food touched by the highest group.

Indian castes also have economic functions. High-caste people cannot perform important subsistence and productive functions for themselves because of the polluting nature of these activities, such as working with wood or making pottery. Lower-caste people provide these goods and services in return for food, clothing, and money. Over the years, a permanent and stable relationship between patron and client may provide for an exchange of goods and services between the two parties. This relationship may pass to the descendants of the originators, continuing important economic exchanges through the generations. Both groups thus receive significant benefits.

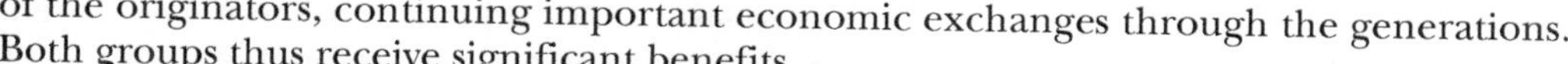

Hindus revere many deities, including the god Shiva, here represented at Shiva Temple in Gangaikonda Cholapuram, India. Corbis/Atlantide Phototravel/Corbis

Caste economic relationships are both divisive and integrating. They are divisive because people are restricted to performing caste-specific economic roles, but they are integrating because they create necessary interdependence among people of different castes. However, despite the advantages of stability and security lower-caste people obtain from their patrons, the system as a whole stigmatizes them and takes more from them than it gives. As in any system of social stratification, higher-ranked people benefit most.

Finally, Indian castes were intimately associated and intertwined with political power. The structures of caste functioned in villages and regional territories to both segment and articulate various kinship groups and residential communities. They formed the basic structure of political alliances and control. British colonial administrators ignored and obliterated much of the political significance of caste. By reinventing caste significance as primarily ritual, the British pretended that India lacked "genuine politics," in effect providing a rationale for British control (Dirks 2001).

The system of caste in India is less static than it is often described, however. Since India's independence in 1947, laws have loosened restrictions on caste behavior. People belonging to different castes can now legally marry and cannot be prosecuted for engaging in sexual relations. Family and community opinion, however, still often frowns on such unions. It is illegal to discriminate against untouchables. Indeed, a variable percentage of public sector jobs and services and some 27 percent of openings in both public and private universities must be reserved for members of the lower castes. Each state may adopt higher percentages if they choose to do so. And all people have the right to vote, a right that carries with it the potential, if exercised, to improve the economic and social position of the lower castes.

View the **Slideshow:** *The Varnas of India* on **myanthrolab.com**

In modern India, especially in the cities, caste ranking is not immutable. Upward mobility for the caste as a group is possible if members have achieved wealth and prestige. Upward mobility pertains to the group; it is not a narrowly individual process. However, striving for upward mobility does not necessarily undermine the system of stratification. It merely changes the ordering of groups rather than challenging the legitimacy of the social principles on which the system is based. Over time, fluidity in caste may fundamentally challenge the system. Indeed, in urban areas, people are less aware of or concerned about other people's caste membership. These social divisions are more apparent and significant in rural areas, where the majority of Indians reside. Untouchables, now called "Dalits," are especially vocal opponents of the system, calling for laws that ban discrimination. Thousands have converted from Hinduism to Buddhism or Christianity to protest the injustices of caste hierarchies. In northwest India, a group called the Guijars, traditionally nomadic shepherds, wants the government to classify them as a "lower-caste group" to enable them to qualify for government benefits and job opportunities (Johnston 2008).

These Saudi royals experience privilege in their living standards, health, and the control they have over other people. SIPA Press/Abd Rabbo-Niviere/SIPA Presss

education, and occupation. These factors tend to go together, so that people with the highest incomes usually have the most advanced education and the most prestigious jobs. However, cases can easily be cited that contradict this general tendency, such as occupations requiring advanced education but earning lower incomes than other occupations with lower educational requirements. In this economic meaning of class, the groups are not closed, discrete units but, rather, are categories differentiated along a continuum. These categories form social layers or strata that are ranked in relation to one another. There are no absolute boundary markers between them; they differ only in relative terms.

Unlike caste, class is an achieved status because the criteria for determining class membership are subject to achievement by individuals as well as to change. Also, unlike caste, where a person's identity is rigidly determined, the factors used to determine class membership are less easily and less consistently specified. Also unlike the fixed and closed nature of caste, systems of class are open and allow for mobility from one group to another. Class **mobility** may be either upward or downward.

How does your social class influence your life experiences? How does your culture reinforce the class system of which you are a part?

Another way of talking about class is to talk about relations of production. In this Marxian sense of class, there are two contrasting groups—the group that owns the means of economic production and controls the distribution of products and the group that does not own the means of production. These two groups, or classes, can be simplified as owners and workers. Owners control production, distribution, and profit from the productive labor of others, and workers sell their labor to the owners for a wage. In modern corporate capitalism, the distinction between owners and workers is more complicated than was true in the late nineteenth century, when Karl Marx developed his insights about the European capitalist economic system.

In North American discourse on class, there are strong pressures against public discussion of class interests and underlying class conflicts. Rather, we are led to believe that anyone can grow up to be president. Nevertheless, members of different classes, however defined, occupy different places in society, and their life experiences are fundamentally different.

Social Class and Language

Class differences are revealed and reinforced by patterns of language use. When we speak, we consciously and unconsciously use forms (pronunciations, words, grammar) that identify who we are. People can immediately tell something about us—where we come from, how old we are, what gender we are, and what social group we belong to. Our class, race, and ethnicity are some of the social factors that we reveal when we speak. When we hear other people speak, we make judgments about them based on their language use.

One of the significant markers of social class in language is the differential use of "standard" and "nonstandard" forms in pronunciation and in grammar. Although all speakers may employ both the standard and nonstandard forms at various times in their speech, middle-class speakers tend to use standard forms more frequently, and lower-class speakers tend to more often use nonstandard forms. For example, in the United States and Great Britain, instead of the standard pronunciation of "thing" and "the," lower-class speakers might say "ting" and "de," replacing the "th" sound with "t" or "d" (Labov 1966; 1972b; Trudgill 1974; 1983). Class-related variations in these sounds have been documented in the English language in both Great Britain and the United States since as early as the seventeenth century.

Research in Belgium conducted by Jef van den Broeck (1977) also showed differences in the speech styles of working-class and middle-class speakers, focusing on length and complexity of sentence constructions. Van den Broeck discovered that middle-class and working-class speakers showed no significant differences in sentence complexity

mobility
A principle that people can move from membership in one social group to another.

in informal situations, but a marked distinction in formal contexts. In formal situations, middle-class speakers used more complex constructions than in informal situations, but working-class formal grammar was less complex than working-class informal style. Van den Broeck suggested that, in formal situations, middle-class speakers want to distinguish their style from that of the working class. They use linguistic mechanisms as an "act of conspicuous ostentation, a marker of social distance." Working-class speakers, on the other hand, may reflect through their speech their feelings of relative powerlessness in formal situations when they feel "on display" and avoid using complex constructions because of their uncertainty with this style of speaking.

A group of slaves gather under a tree as they wait for freedom in Southern Sudan.
Corbis/David Orr/Sygma/Corbis

Studies of class-based language use lead to explanations for the behavior of speakers of different classes. For example, why do lower-class speakers continue to use styles of speech that are nonstandard and therefore stigmatized? Possible explanations involve theories of social network, solidarity, and "covert prestige" (the latter term introduced by Peter Trudgill in a study of language and gender 1974). The term covert prestige refers to the fact that, although the use of nonstandard forms is generally criticized, their use may have prestige among some speakers as a sign of rejection of standard, formal norms associated with the middle class. In addition, these speech styles become markers of class membership, transmitted through networks of family, neighborhood, and coworkers. And in this process, they become vehicles for expressing group identity and solidarity.

Slavery

Slavery, the most extreme form of stratification, is an ascribed status. People become slaves either by being born into slavery or by being captured in warfare or slaving raids. Slavery is thus forced upon a person, either through accident of birth or through the deliberate actions of others. The slave group, like castes and classes, is endogamous. Slaves usually marry other slaves, not necessarily because of their preferences but because nonslaves are unwilling to marry them. Slavery generally entails the loss of a person's independence and autonomy. At the least, slaves work at the direction and the behest of their owners. They cannot control their own labor, and they do not benefit materially from the goods that they produce. In addition, slaves cannot leave and find homes and work elsewhere. With low social status, slaves cannot hope to achieve any position of prestige or influence in their society, except within the community of other slaves. Social attitudes attribute negative qualities to slaves. They are thought to be inferior and incapable of valued achievements.

The quality of a slave's life varies across cultures. We are familiar from the history of the United States with a form of slavery in which slaves had no rights of any kind. They could be bought and sold without any concern for their feelings, safety, or family relationships. And they had no political rights, no way to seek redress for any wrongs done to them.

In other societies with slavery, the life of a slave was not necessarily much different from that of ordinary people. For example, among the Kwakwaka'wakw and other indigenous societies of the Pacific Northwest, slaves lived in the homes of their owners, ate the same kind of food, and wore the same kind of clothing. They usually performed menial tasks and suffered the indignity of low social status, but they could be ransomed by their relatives and returned to their own communities. In some African states, people might become slaves as the result of their capture in warfare or as a means of repaying a debt that they owed. Once the debt was considered to have been paid, the slave could be released from bondage and could return to their home. Although not usually called slavery, the European and American practice of indentured servitude was in practice a form of slavery.

slavery
An ascribed status forced on a person upon birth or through involuntary servitude.

Some people became indentured servants in order to pay off debts; others voluntarily contracted to work for a master for a set period of time, usually about five years, in exchange for transportation and expenses from England to the American colonies.

REVIEW

Societies may be stratified by caste—a hierarchical, hereditary, endogamous, closed system of social strata defined by occupation and concepts of religious purity. Societies may also be stratified by class—a hierarchy of social strata based mainly on achieved economic status, in which people may be upwardly or downwardly mobile but tend to marry within their own group. Class membership typically is identified by lifestyle and the use of language. Slavery is an extreme form of social stratification, based on ascribed status, in which people are defined and treated as commodities.

RACE AND ETHNICITY

Like caste and class, **race** is a social, not a biological, category. There are no absolute biological differences among people that would allow for an objective categorization of human beings into discrete, nonoverlapping groups. Rather, so-called racial distinctions focus on particular sets of external physical traits that are then used to identify different "races." In the United States and elsewhere, these traits most especially include skin color, hair color and texture, and facial features. However, it is obvious that all of these characteristics appear in human populations on a continuum. Indeed, we are all the descendents of humans who originated in Africa. Our skin color, for example, differs depending on whether and when our ancestors left Africa and where they settled, adapting to local environmental and climatic conditions. The classification, labeling, and valuing of superficial physical differences as races are entirely arbitrary. Race, then, like gender, is a cultural construction, based in societies that order social categories and that use "race" as one such ordering criterion.

Watch the **Video:** *It's an Illusion That There Are Races* on **myanthrolab.com**

In the process of constructing race as a cultural category, people are identified as belonging to different "races" based on supposed biological differences. Social ideologies are then developed to justify the system. The next step associates certain constellations of behavior with each group. So, for example, members of one race are said to be more intelligent, more honest, more capable than members of another race. These associations and the social foundation on which they are based privilege some groups and disadvantage others. The group that controls the social, economic, and political structures of the society thinks of itself as superior and of different others as inferior. Whether a majority or minority of the population, the group in power has the ability to control the ideological grounds on which the social order rests.

Race as Caste

In its artificiality, race is very much like caste. In both systems, particular groups are said to have separate ancestral origins, thus explaining their appearance, behavioral characteristics, and place in society. Both caste and race are ascribed statuses, and both are closed systems. Like castes, racial groups tend to be endogamous because people usually marry members of their own race for a number of social and emotional reasons. People are more likely to live near, work with, and socialize with members of their own group. In addition, one's race, although a culturally derived construct, becomes a feature of one's personal and emotional identity. In some racialist societies, marriage between members of different races is legally forbidden, but, even where there are no legal boundaries to intermarriage, people generally choose to marry members of their own group. In the United States in 2009, for example, only 4.01 percent of married couples were of different racial backgrounds. The U.S. Census Bureau reports that 0.9 percent of married couples consisted of a white partner and an African American partner, 2.89 percent consisted of a white partner and a partner who was neither white nor African American, 0.21 percent of married couples consisted of an African American partner married to someone of a race other than white or African American, 3.98 percent of marriages consisted of one Hispanic/Latino spouse and

race
A cultural category that groups people according to so-called racial distinctions.

someone not Hispanic, and, finally, 0.48 percent of married couples consisted of a Native American spouse and a white spouse (U.S. Census Bureau, *Statistical Abstract of the United States, 2011,* Table 60).

Finally, race is like caste in the attribution of purity to superior groups and impurity to inferior groups who are often thought of as "unclean" in some ways. Contact between the races is thought to pollute those of higher status. For example, in some southern American states until the 1950s and 1960s, African Americans were legally barred from drinking from the same public water fountains as whites, from using the same restrooms, and from sitting in the same sections on buses and trains. Although these laws were repealed in the 1950s and 1960s, their underlying symbolism has not been entirely eradicated in some communities.

These Amerasian children of mixed descent would be regarded as outcasts in their home countries in Southeast Asia. Alamy Limited/Francisco Villaflor/Alamy

Race in the United States

In the United States, the races are ordered in a hierarchy that is arbitrary and culturally derived. Attitudes toward members of the different races are learned and transmitted without any basis in fact, although holders of these attitudes believe that they are factually true. In addition, racial groupings tend to be endogamous, partly because of lingering attitudes about racial separation.

Although it is true that many workplaces are racially mixed, occupational stratification often contributes to boundaries between the races. Attitudes toward members of the disadvantaged groups are fraught with negative stereotypes and prejudice. These attitudes are no doubt changing, but members of disadvantaged races are still burdened by unfair treatment, lack of equal opportunity, and a marginalized role in public life.

CASE STUDY

Out-Groups of Japan

The Japanese believe they belong to a homogeneous racial and cultural group. They believe that they are physically similar to each other and look different from other Asians. They also believe that "Japanese" is an identity that is ascribed and cannot be acquired. As George De Vos and Hiroshi Wagatsuma state, "In the Japanese mind only those born of Japanese parents are genetically Japanese—nobody can become a Japanese" (1995, 268). People who are not defined as "Japanese" face overt and covert discrimination even though their ancestors may have lived in Japan for thousands of years.

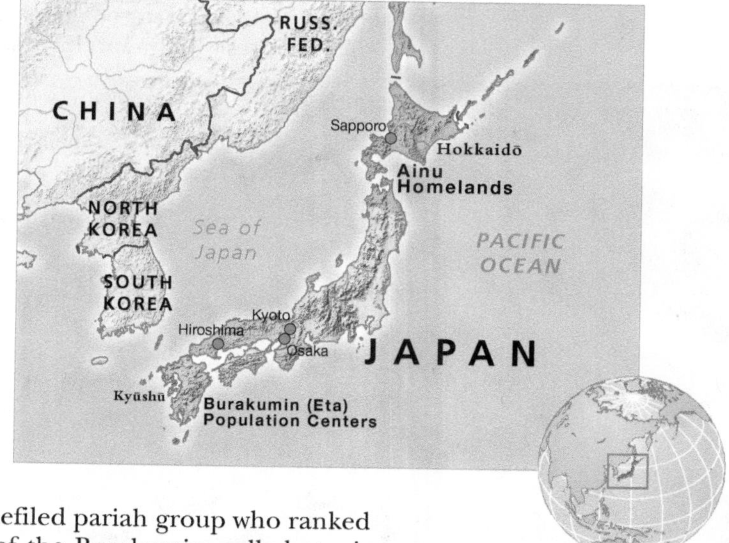

According to De Vos and Wagatsuma, about 4.5 percent of the population in Japan belongs to "minority" groups. Some are Japanese citizens, but others are denied citizenship. The largest minority group socially defined as "not Japanese" are the 3 million Burakumin, descendants of an ancient group of outcasts. In the traditional stratified social system, the Burakumin were a defiled pariah group who ranked below the four classes of Japanese. The official name of the Burakumin, called eta, is written with characters meaning "full of filth." Their traditional occupations included work considered ritually polluting, such as slaughtering animals, disposing of the dead, and making musical instruments (containing leather and other animal products). The Burakumin, literally "village people," originally lived in separate villages, but now they may also live in certain urban neighborhoods. Despite no supporting evidence, most Japanese believe that the Burakumin are racially distinct.

The Buraku community is as heterogeneous as any other in a modern state. Class distinctions exist, based principally on occupation and income. Some Burakumin work in their traditional occupations, but others own land and property. Some members accept their minority status and identify as Burakumin, but others attempt to "pass," principally by learning new occupations and changing their residence. However, changing one's residential identity is not simple in Japan because official records list all past addresses, and teachers and employers, among others, can investigate them.

In the past, the Burakumin were the only Japanese to eat meat, in violation of Buddhist principles, but now many Japanese eat meat. As a self-conscious marker of identity, some Burakumin wear a distinctive sandal called *setta zari*. Otherwise, Japanese consider Buraku dress to be "careless," a negative characteristic in Japan. Finally, Buraku speech is generally more "informal" and "less refined" than that of the general population. Most Burakumin work in their own communities, employed by or working with relatives or people familiar to them. But many are unemployed or underemployed and rely on government assistance. A high rate of endogamy exists within the Buraku community because of both their own preferences and the prejudices among other Japanese.

Because the Burakumin physically look just like ordinary Japanese, they can "pass" in public simply by avoiding the dress styles and speech patterns considered identity markers. Middle-class Burakumin have stronger pressures to pass than do poor people because they hope to give their children educational and financial advantages that would allow them to become white-collar and professional workers. The major impediment to "passing" is the record of residence that betrays one's origin.

Japanese have negative stereotypes about the Burakumin. They are considered impulsive, volatile, hostile, and aggressive. Because polite behavior and an even-tempered demeanor is so highly regarded in Japan, the behavior attributed to the Burakumin is especially disvalued. The Burakumin also demonstrate less conformity and deference to authority than ordinary Japanese. The Burakumin tolerate and may even reward deviant behavior, especially toward authority figures, as a reaction to the discrimination they experience. Finally, the Burakumin are more open about engaging in and talking about sexual activity than is acceptable in Japan. That some Burakumin behave in ways that they know most Japanese criticize may be an example of a subversive challenge to dominant ideologies.

Interviews with officials in the city of Kobe revealed that the small Buraku minority contributed disproportionately to the number of cases brought before the courts because of family problems and delinquency. Partly because of real criminal problems and partly because of negative stereotypes, ordinary Japanese claim to be fearful of the Burakumin. Other cultures with hierarchical social systems often have similar attitudes. Disadvantaged groups frequently bear the brunt of derogatory suspicions and fears that undermine their own self-esteem and serve to justify the majority's discrimination against them.

The Ainu, descendants of the indigenous people of ancient Japan (pictured here at a Thanksgiving festival), live in a few small villages on the northern island of Hokkaido, where they were driven when Japan invaded their territory. The Image Works/Hideo Haga/HAGA/The Image Works

Other groups, supposedly distinguished racially from the Japanese, also face discrimination. Okinawans, Taiwanese, and Koreans are considered foreigners even though they have lived in Japan for generations. The ancestors of some of these groups were forced to come to Japan by the Japanese army. Most are not Japanese citizens and live in urban ghettos. Koreans in particular are thought to be "inherently uncouth and uncivilized." Because of the discrimination they face, many Koreans in Japan are poor. Rather than being considered victims of discrimination, they are seen as deserving the negative attitudes toward them. To become citizens, some people of Korean or Taiwanese ancestry have hidden their origins by taking Japanese names. As in other cultures with racial or ethnic discrimination, children of mixed marriages are considered tainted and impure.

The 200,000 Ainu are an indigenous people, native to the northern Japanese island of Hokkaido. Until 2008, the Japanese government refused to recognize them as a separate ethnic group (Makino 2008). As a result of discrimination, Ainu are more than three times more likely to live on welfare than other Japanese. They also have low educational levels and substandard housing.

Another group of people who face negative attitudes are the *hibakusha,* survivors of the atomic bombs that the United States dropped on Japan in 1945 during World War II. These victims are considered "irrevocably contaminated" because of their illnesses and deformities. Children of marriages or sexual relationships between Japanese women and American soldiers stationed in Japan during the U.S. occupation also face discrimination. According to De Vos and Wagatsuma, "More than any other minority group in Japan, offspring of Japanese and non-Asian foreigners are maliciously stereotyped in mass media, including popular literature, films, and comic books."

Attitudes about race in Japan are similar to those in the United States. So-called minority groups are thought to be physically different from the majority population no matter how erroneous this assumption and no matter how little evidence supports it. Negative personality traits and behavior are attributed to them, again with little supporting evidence. The poverty in which disadvantaged and stigmatized groups live actually results from discrimination but is used to prove their lack of merit and justify the negative stereotypes about them. **Read** the **Document** on **myanthrolab.com**

White Privilege

It is apparent to most North Americans that racial groups in the United States are ordered hierarchically with "white" as the privileged group. Stating that whites are privileged does not mean that all white people live well and have power. Clearly, this is not the case. Many white people are poor, unemployed, undereducated, and endure many kinds of hardships. Most white people lack social and political power because they, like members of the minority groups, do not control the means of producing wealth and influence. However, although individual whites suffer from poverty and lack of opportunity, their suffering is based on class, not race. Poor whites are marginalized in a class system that disadvantages them, but poor African Americans, Native Americans, and Hispanics are marginalized by both class and race, compounding their structural powerlessness.

Despite the economic and social differences among whites, "white privilege" grants them all certain benefits that together obscure issues of race and the racialized structure of U.S. society. They can be unaware of the fact that they receive bank loans, mortgages, preferential treatment in stores and restaurants, and are generally accorded respect in daily interactions with others because they are "white." According to Tim Wise, white people's privileged place in a racial hierarchy is "... the flipside of discrimination against persons of color" (Wise 2005, xi).

Among the many benefits resulting from white privilege is that most white people think of themselves in non-racial terms. To them, "race" applies to people of color while "whiteness" is a normative, unmentioned trait. They can remain unaware of the fact that they too are racialized and that they receive daily privileges because of the racial hierarchy that they participate in.

The antagonism that pervades and obscures issues of class and race surfaces in attitudes toward affirmative action programs, for example. Working-class and middle-class whites who oppose affirmative action are expressing an anger that stems from competitive relations underlying capitalist economies, turned instead toward people who are even more disadvantaged than they.

Despite the successes of social movements, there are still barriers between racial groups. One reason is the reluctance of North Americans to acknowledge issues of class. Of course, although most members of the highest classes are white, there are wealthy African Americans, Hispanics, and Native Americans. Focusing attention on race helps hide distinctions of class that account for much of the disadvantage experienced by many members of minority groups. In addition, racial antagonisms are used to create barriers to the formation of multiracial interest groups based on class. Members of privileged

In Their Own VOICES

The Souls of Black Folk

W. E. B. DuBois was born in Great Barrington, Massachusetts, in 1868. He received his undergraduate degree from Fisk College and his PhD in sociology from Harvard University. Having grown up in western Massachusetts, DuBois was shocked at the overt racism that he experienced when he went to college in the South. He taught school for several years in Georgia, where he again confronted bigotry. In this excerpt from his book, The Souls of Black Folk *(1903), DuBois writes about the lives and destinies of two men, one black and one white.*

The white folk of Altamaha, Georgia voted John a good boy,—fine plough-hand, good in the rice-fields, handy everywhere, and always good-natured and respectful. But they shook their heads when his mother wanted to send him off to school. "It'll spoil him,—ruin him," they said. But full half the black folk followed him proudly to the train station.

Up at the Judge's they too had a John—a fair-haired, smooth-faced boy, who had played many a long summer's day to its close with his darker namesake. "Yes, sir! John is at Princeton, sir," said the Judge every morning as he marched down to the post-office. "Showing the Yankees what a Southern gentleman can do," he added.

Thus in the far-away Southern village the world lay waiting for the coming of two young men, and dreamed in an inarticulate way of new things that would be done and new thoughts that all would think. And yet it was singular that few thought of two Johns,—for the black folk thought of one John, and he was black; and the white folk thought of another John, and he was white. And neither world thought the other world's thought, save with a vague unrest.

John grew slowly to feel almost for the first time the Veil that lay between him and the white world; he first noticed now the oppression that had not seemed oppression before, differences that erstwhile seemed natural, restraints and slights that in his boyhood days had gone unnoticed or been greeted with a laugh. He felt angry now when men did not call him "Mister," he clenched his hands at the "Jim Crow" cars, and chafed at the color-line that hemmed in him and his.

It left John sitting so silent and rapt that he did not for some time notice the usher tapping him lightly on the shoulder and saying politely, "Will you step this way, please, sir?" A little surprised, he arose quickly at the last tap, and, turning to leave his seat, looked full into the face of the fair-haired young man. For the first time the young man recognized his dark boyhood playmate, and John knew that it was the Judge's son. The White John started, lifted his hand, and then froze into his chair; the black John smiled lightly, then grimly, and followed the usher down the aisle.

[When John arrived back in his segregated hometown, he applied for a job teaching at a school for Black children.]

The Judge plunged squarely into the business. "You've come for the school, I suppose. You know I'm a friend to your people. I've helped you and your family. Now I like the colored people,

groups benefit from a system that pits poor people against one another based on race, each group believing that its problems are caused by members of other racial groups rather than by members of other classes, even within their own racial group.

Although racial categorization springs from and is connected to issues of control and oppression, "race" identity can also be a means of mobilizing and countering oppression. In the words of Manning Marable:

> "Race" for the oppressed has come to mean an identity of survival, victimization and opposition to those racial groups or elites which exercise power and privilege. What we are looking at here is not an ethnic identification or culture, but an awareness of shared experience, suffering and struggles against the barriers of racial division. These collective experiences, survival tales and grievances form the basis of an historical consciousness...this sense of racial identity is both imposed on the oppressed and yet represents a reconstructed critical memory of the character of the group's collective ordeals. Definitions of "race" and "racial identity" give character and substance to the movements for power and influence among people of color. (1995, 365)

Race in Brazil

In Brazil, there is the same mix of races as in the United States, with people whose ancestry stems from indigenous groups, Africa, and Europe. However, there is not the same rigidity of categories, and there is much greater public recognition of multiracial ancestry. Brazilians employ some 500 different labels to identify a person's race, many more than the dual division of black/white that dominates U.S. racial discourse (Harris 1970).

and sympathize with all their reasonable aspirations; but you and I both know, John, that in this country the Negro must remain subordinate, and can never expect to be the equal of white men. In their place, your people can be honest and respectful; and God knows, I'll do what I can to help them. But when they want to reverse nature, and rule white men, and marry white women, and sit in my parlor, then, by God! We'll hold them under if we have to lynch every Nigger in the land. Now, John, the question is, are you, . . . going to accept the situation and teach the darkies to be faithful servants and laborers as your fathers were?"

"I am going to accept the situation, Judge Henderson," answered John, with a brevity that did not escape the keen old man. He hesitated a moment, and then said shortly, "Very well,—we'll try you awhile. Good-morning."

[As a teacher, John instructed his students well, teaching them to read and write but also teaching them to think about their lives and the world in which they lived.]

"John, this school is closed. You children can go home and get to work. The white people of Altamaha are not spending their money on black folks to have their heads crammed with impudence and lies. Clear out! I'll lock the door myself."

The great brown sea lay silent. The air scarce breathed. The dying day bathed the twisted oaks and mighty pines in black and gold. There came from the wind no warning, not a whisper from the cloudless sky. There was only a black man hurrying on with an ache in his heart, seeing neither sun nor sea, but starting as from a dream at the frightened cry that woke the pines, to see his dark sister struggling in the arms of a tall and fair-haired man.

He said not a word, but, seizing a fallen limb, struck him with all the pent-up hatred of his great black arm; and the body lay white and still beneath the pines, all bathed in sunshine and in blood. John looked at it dreamily, then walked back to the house briskly, and said in a soft voice, "Mammy, I'm going away—I'm going to be free."

He leaned back and smiled toward the sea, whence rose the strange melody, away from the dark shadows where lay the noise of horses galloping, galloping on. With an effort he roused himself, bent forward, and looked steadily down the pathway.

Amid the trees and in the dim morning twilight he watched their shadows dancing and heard their horses thundering toward him, until at last they came sweeping like a storm, and he saw in front that haggard white-haired man, whose eyes flashed red with fury. Oh, how he pitied him,—pitied him,—and wondered if he had the coiling twisted rope. Then, as the storm burst round him, he rose slowly to his feet and turned his closed eyes toward the Sea.

And the world whistled in his ears.

From W. E. B. DuBois, *The Souls of Black Folk*, pp. 246–63.

CRITICAL THINKING QUESTIONS

What contrasts does DuBois draw here? What does he conclude about race relations in the United States?

Not everyone knows and uses all of these labels, but in a study of a small village in northeastern Brazil, about forty different racial terms are used (Kottak 1999). Most of these terms make fine distinctions about skin color, hair color and texture, eye color, eye shape, shape of the nose, and shape of the lips. The same person might describe himself or someone else using different labels in different contexts. The terms selected are based on comparisons with other people present—for example, whether someone were lighter or darker, had lighter, darker, or redder hair, and so on. People in the village also disagree about the proper labels to use for specific individuals.

Although the Brazilian system might appear to be more flexible, a hierarchy of race-based privilege exists nonetheless. This system is more flexible than that in the United States, but the wealthiest and most powerful elites, whether measured in economic or political terms, tend to be light-skinned and/or of European ancestry. In fact, the distribution of wealth in Brazil is even more unequal than that in the United States. The gap between rich and poor in income, education, standard of living, and social and political power is enormous (Andrews, 1992). In general, the ranks of the poor are made up largely of nonwhites.

Listen to the **Audio:** *Racial Democracy in Brazil* on **myanthrolab.com**

Ethnic Identity

Like race, **ethnicity** is a social category. Its definition includes a complex mix of ancestry, culture, and self-identification. Ethnicity is largely based on a "shared cultural heritage" (Berreman 1989). This heritage may include language, religion, family and household structure, preferences for foods and clothing, and a general perspective and worldview.

ethnicity
Social category based on a complex mix of ancestry, culture, and self-identification.

In homogeneous societies of the type that anthropologists formerly studied, all members of the group shared their basic cultural heritage. But in complex societies where people of many different backgrounds are united within the same nation, cultural differences can be significant. Ethnicity, as a social category, is a feature of such societies. In many nations, ethnic groups are ranked relative to one another. Some groups have higher status, and therefore greater privilege and power, than others.

Ethnicity, unlike race and caste, is not an entirely closed or ascribed status. Although ethnicity is based on ancestry, it is also based on identification with a cultural group. For example, if a person is a recent immigrant in another country, his or her ethnic identity is automatically assigned, but if that person is the child or descendant of immigrants, there may be more flexibility in that person's identity. Under most circumstances, people who are not themselves immigrants may choose to either retain or abandon the cultural traits that identify them as members of a particular ethnic group. The process of relinquishing one's cultural heritage is called assimilation. Immigrants may want to positively identify with their new country, but they may also want to distance themselves from the social stigma attached to their immigrant status. Contrasting ethnicity and race in the United States, Gerald Berreman points out that "the American 'melting pot' works for ambitious ethnic groups because they can assimilate by relinquishing their heritage; it does not work for race groups because their status is an unalterable consequence of birth that they cannot relinquish (i.e., are not allowed to relinquish), and hence they cannot assimilate (this is the very essence of racism)" (1989, 16).

Pan-Africanism refers to various movements in Africa that have sought to define African ethnic, racial, and transnational identity at the continental level. Starting in 1900, these movements had the common goal of unifying Africans against colonialism and colonial influences. The great diversity of peoples and interests prevented that unity. In 1963, the Organization of African Unity (OAU) was founded as a forum for discussing problems in Africa and achieving shared goals. In 2002, the OAU was replaced by the African Union (AU), modeled on the European Union (EU).

In some contexts, ethnic identification is irrelevant and not thought about; in other situations, ethnicity may be a key feature of one's personal identity. In multiethnic nations undergoing rapid social change, identifying with and asserting one's ethnicity may be an important means of group formation. In Africa, for example, the search for identity has complex meanings attached to different ethnic symbols, depending on the contexts and frames of reference used. According to Victor Uchendu (1995), the search for an African identity takes place on four contrasting planes: continental, racial, national, and tribal. A continental-wide identity as "African" contrasts Africa with other continents. As Uchendu observed, "Continental identity became an instrument for decolonization and a weapon for post independence international diplomacy" (p. 129). Racial identity contrasts black Africans with other groups living on the continent, that is, Arabs and whites. National identity refers to the quest for the formation of a cohesive identity within a given country. This goal is often problematic in Africa because of the artificial national boundaries created by colonial European powers for their own interests. Finally, the search for tribal identity takes place within the newly independent and emerging multiethnic African nations.

CASE STUDY

Ethnic Identity in the United States

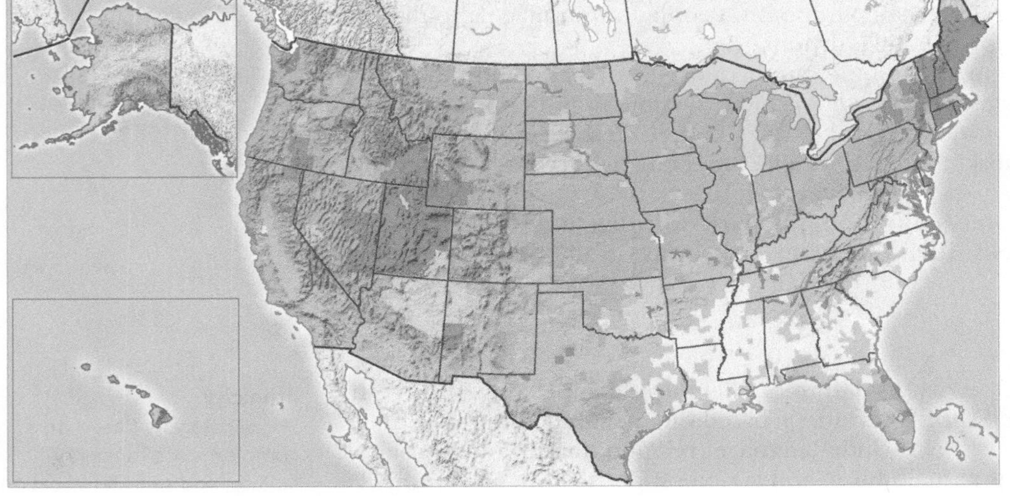

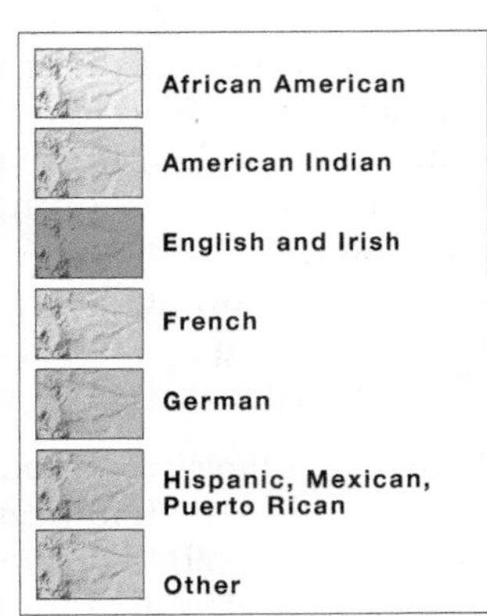

Because of their growing numbers, particularly since the mid-twentieth century, people of Spanish origin or ancestry, variously referred to (and self-referred) as Hispanic or Latino, have received prominent attention (Fears 2003). Some members of this group, especially in the Southwest, are the descendants of Spaniards who settled in North America in the 1600s, but most are immigrants or descendants of recent immigrants from Mexico, the Caribbean, and Central and South America rather than from Spain. However, "Hispanic" is clearly an ethnic, not racial, label because Hispanic people may be white, black, or Native American.

Recent federal census questionnaires reflect the complexity of categories of race and ethnicity. For the first time, in the 2000 census respondents were asked to identify their "race" and were given the option of choosing "one or more" of these identifications: White; Black, African-American, or Negro; American Indian or Alaska Native; Asian Indian; Chinese; Filipino; Japanese; Korean; Vietnamese; Native Hawaiian; Guamanian or Chamorro; Samoan; Other Asian; Other Pacific Islander; Some Other Race. People were also asked to state whether they were "Spanish/Hispanic/Latino." If they responded affirmatively, they were then asked to identify their "group" from among the following: (1) Mexican, Mexican-American, Chicano; (2) Puerto Rican; (3) Cuban; (4) Other.

Census Bureau statistics, reported for the 2010 national census, revealed the following percentage makeup of the U.S. population: white: 72.4 percent; Hispanic: 16.3 percent; African American: 12.6 percent; Asian: 4.8 percent; Native American: 0.9 percent; Native Hawaiians and Pacific Islanders: 0.2 percent. Since 2000, Hispanics have outnumbered African Americans. The Hispanic population experienced the fastest growth, increasing at a rate of nearly 5 percent since the 2000 census. This growth is a result of high fertility rates and increased immigration. Both the absolute numbers and percentage of Hispanics are projected to continue to rise.

Similar counting procedures are not used for Native Americans. In fact, the government's practice of categorizing many respondents with mixed Indian ancestry as whites, African Americans, or Hispanics undercounts native peoples. According to Jack Forbes (1990), a more accurate assessment of the number of people with Indian ancestry should include people with "Hispanic" identification, as well as the 30 percent to 70 percent of African Americans who report themselves to be part Indian. In the 1990 census, the official native population stood at 1.9 million and by 2010 it had risen to 2.9 million. In addition, the U.S. census reported nearly 8 million people with Native American ancestry. The large growth in the reported number can be accounted for by changes in census questionnaires and counting people who claimed either Native American identity or ancestry.

In 2010, 2.9 percent of the total population chose two or more racial/ethnic identities. The number of biracial and multiracial individuals will continue to grow. According to the census reports for 2008, 41 percent of people identifying as mixed race were under 18 years of age (Navarro 2008). Read the Document on myanthrolab.com

---

Until the 1960s and 1970s, when African nations won their independence from their European colonizers, African peoples did not identify as "African," even though Europeans identified them as such. Self-identifications were tribal and ethnic. Today, people choose from among numerous possibilities for self-identification based on circumstances. For example, "Nigerian students in London or New York are more likely to identify themselves as African than as Nigerian unless the situation clearly indicates that identification of country is expected or required. To another Nigerian, they are most likely to identify themselves with state or region; if they are speaking to a co-ethnic, they are likely to name the provincial or administrative headquarters to which they belong. Thus, identity is likely to change as the frame of reference changes" (Uchendu 1995, 131).

Ethnic allegiance also has different meanings in rural and urban settings. According to Uchendu, tribal identity is paramount in rural Africa because "the tie to the tribal, communal, or lineage land, often phrased in the idiom of filial loyalty to ancestors, is still an important social and economic asset" (p. 129). Although such ties are not significant in urban areas, ethnic loyalty may be advantageous in the context of "the competition for jobs, the uneven distribution of government patronage, and the insecurity of urban employment" (p. 129). Through ethnic identification, a person can claim membership in a cohesive community that provides economic, social, and emotional support.

In many countries, the inherent stratification of ethnic groups in relation to each other can come to crisis in times of economic and political stress. In these situations, ethnic groups can be pitted against one another in struggles for prestige and power. Loyalty to one's ethnic group then becomes a paramount factor in taking sides, only exacerbating underlying tensions and furthering the processes of ethnic identification and conflict.

Just such a crisis developed in the 1980s and 1990s in the former Yugoslavia. Although the causes of the breakup of Yugoslavia need much more study and reflection, political leaders on all sides used long-standing ethnic animosities to gain support in their own identifiable ethnic enclaves. According to Mary Kay Galliland (1995), most of the people residing in a "midsize town" in eastern Croatia on the border with Bosnia were "relatively unconcerned about ethno-national identity" during the 1980s (p. 201), thinking of themselves primarily as citizens of the unified country of Yugoslavia. Their primary concerns were economic: food shortages, inflation, and lack of jobs and housing. After the death of the longtime Yugoslav president, Josip Broz (known as Tito), in 1982, the government instituted an austerity program aimed at limiting imports and increasing exports to gain hard currency needed to repay Yugoslavia's large debts to Western nations. The government also rationed domestic products, such as gasoline, coffee, and laundry detergent (p. 206). The basic Yugoslav currency, the dinar, was devalued, resulting in a precipitous decline in real wages as prices soared. Shortages of many foods and domestic products also became widespread. All of these conditions contributed to feelings of uncertainty and instability.

Each group saw itself as victims of economic and political policies promulgated by other groups. According to Galliland, "Serbs [a minority in Croatia] blamed Croats for their own lack of economic development; the Western portion of the former Yugoslavia, they said, had gained at Serbian expense. Croats turned the argument around; they had been supporting the less-developed regions with the products of their own hard work. Worse, they had also been paying for a growing military and corrupt [federal Yugoslav] government bureaucracy heavily dominated by Serbs" (1995, 203).

As tensions mounted and incidents of interethnic violence occurred, nationalist politicians and the media contributed to the "production of fear" that characterized much of Yugoslav discourse. Although the causes of the violence are complex, ethnic nationalism clearly played a role in solidifying group identity and creating rigid boundaries among the various ethnic groups. By culturally constructing groups in opposition to each other, people came to see themselves and their group as distinct from all others. In addition, people began to speak more openly about the past, redefining the past as they talked about it. No longer did they remember Yugoslavian unity but instead recalled incidents that provided reasons for distrust and animosity. Although throughout much of the postwar period these memories were not considered important, they were lying beneath the surface, "waiting to be called into action, if the times were right, if someone wanted to make use of them, and if the means of communication were available" (Galliland 1995, 216). Nationalist Serbian and Croatian political leaders tapped into this reservoir of memory, exploiting it to mobilize followers and gain power. But, by intensifying people's fears, political leaders unleashed a wave of hatred and violence that ended by destroying a nation and creating new reasons for people to distrust one another.

REVIEW

Race is a social, not a biological classification. Race and ethnic identity are culturally constructed and are stratified differently in different societies. Racial or ethnic minorities may be viewed negatively and experience discrimination. Ethnicity is based on identification with a cultural or ethnic group.

CLASS, RACE, ETHNICITY, AND IDEOLOGY IN AMERICAN SOCIETY

As in other stratified societies, the system of inequality in the United States that grants privilege to members of some groups and denies opportunities to others is supported by ideological beliefs that members of high-status groups, whether based on class, race, or ethnicity, deserve their advantages. In contrast, it is believed that members of low-status groups are responsible for their plight because of their lack of motivation and initiative. However, some hope of achievement and advance is held out to less privileged people in order to diminish their anger and resistance. Many people are nurtured by the "American Dream," convinced that if they work hard enough and are sensible and practical, they can achieve a better standard of living for themselves and their children.

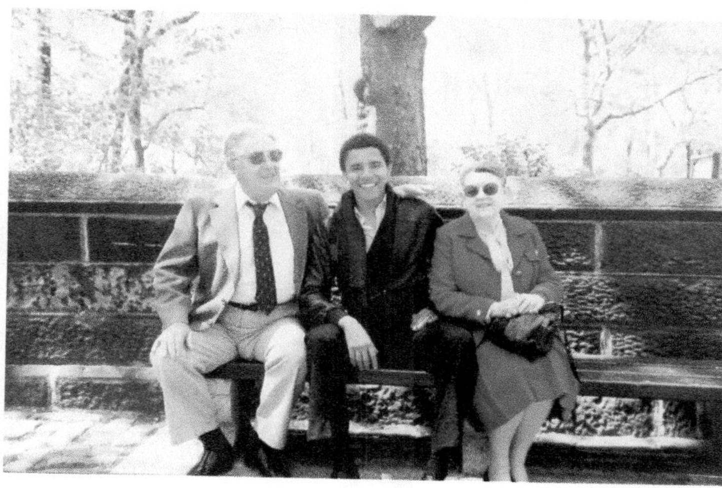

The election of Barack Obama to the presidency of the United States in 2008 generated discussion of biracial identity. In this photo, Obama is shown with his maternal grandparents, Madelyn and Stanley Dunham. Newscom/OBAMA PRESS OFFICE/New/Newscom

The dream of the rewards of hard work, elusive though it may be for most people, is based on the fact that class, at least theoretically, is a social ordering that allows for mobility. The hope of upward class mobility helps alleviate the burdens of class disadvantage and blunts potential anger on the part of lower-class people who might otherwise challenge the legitimacy of the system. Issues of class and class interests are also masked behind an ideology of equality. Even to talk about class may be considered disruptive and antagonistic, especially in political campaigns and media rhetoric. And the language that we use to talk about social strata reveals an ideological stance. For example, we can talk about poor people as "underprivileged" but we don't talk about rich people as "overprivileged." Indeed, the word does not exist in the English language. Does this imply that we don't think a person can have too much wealth or too much "privilege"?

To what extent and in what ways are you upwardly mobile? In what circumstances could you become downwardly mobile, and what are your chances of this?

However, it is clear that members of the upper classes act in their class interests. They may not talk about their identity as a class, at least not publicly, because to do so would violate the ideology of classlessness that makes up the American Dream. However, their actions in formulating economic and political policies do indicate their awareness of class solidarity. Even the trend toward living in gated communities translates class segregation into architecture. In contrast, members of the middle and lower classes generally do not understand their social position as part of the structure of a hierarchical social order. Those who do perceive it as temporary, amenable to change if they persist.

There are, in addition, other difficulties in uniting as a class. Among these are antagonisms that develop between members of groups defined in ways other than by class, such as race, ethnicity, and gender. These three factors are employed as part of the hierarchical structure to divide members of nonelite classes to keep them from recognizing and acting on their common interests.

Talking about race is also perceived as divisive. Much of the popular discourse on race focuses on the partial successes of the civil rights movement of the 1950s and 1960s that led to passage of legislation mandating equal treatment and recognition of the civil rights of all Americans. One can point to vigorous programs to end segregation in schools, to bar the most overt forms of racial discrimination, and to redress underrepresentation of nonwhites in many occupations through affirmative action policies. Nonetheless, these programs and policies have not created full racial equality. Members of nonwhite groups remain disadvantaged in terms of income, employment, quality of education and health care services, and political representation. However, race was supposed to be eliminated in the vocabulary of a "color-blind" society, proven so by the fact that some African Americans could achieve wealth and status (Baker 1998).

Despite the hope of upward class mobility, most people do not experience improvements in their class standing. Indeed, some members of the middle and upper classes experience downward mobility. As the work of Katherine Newman (1989) has documented, since the 1980s in the United States, a large but largely unpublicized number of Americans have been catapulted from comfortable and rewarding lifestyles after they lost their jobs. Newman found that people "fall from grace" for a variety of reasons. Some lose jobs as well-paid executives or managers in large corporations when the firms "downsize." Others lose jobs in factories when the plants move to "more profitable and business-friendly" regions of the United States or to foreign countries in a trend toward outsourcing that is becoming increasingly frequent, with dire economic consequences

Listen to the **Audio:** *Does Wealth Imbalance Threaten Society's Fabric?* on **myanthrolab.com**

The apartheid policies of South Africa created a caste-like hierarchy of whites and blacks. After the collapse of the regime in 1992, schools, such as this one in Cape Town, were desegregated. Corbis/David Turnley/Corbis

for many North American workers. Still others are fired when they participate in strikes. When plants close down or workers in small communities go out on strike, the economic effects can be disastrous to more than just the people immediately involved. Whole communities may suffer when residents no longer have money to spend in stores, restaurants, and on local entertainment.

The extent of downward mobility is much greater than most Americans realize. The true picture certainly does not square with the mythology of the American Dream that many people adhere to. And it doesn't square with media coverage of the U.S. economy. Newman uses several indices to measure downward mobility. People who experience a decline in income or are employed in a job having less prestige or status than their previous jobs can be victims of downward mobility. In a national survey taken every year by the National Opinion Research Center, approximately 25 percent of respondents claimed that their financial situation in the 1980s had worsened during the year they were questioned (Newman 1989, 21). Federal statistics indicate that individual real income (adjusted for inflation) declined 14 percent between 1972 and 1982. The rate of decline accelerated so that between 1978 and 1982, 56 percent of the population was falling behind inflation, a clear indicator that their standard of living declined. Economic decline affects families in all socioeconomic groups. Many families experiencing downward mobility are not just "sliding" but are actually "plunging." In the 1970s, studies indicated that nearly one-third of the American population experienced a drop in family income of 50 percent or more (p. 23).

Job loss affects all economic sectors but is most severe in manufacturing and heavy industry. Plant closings often occur to save money by relocating to areas of the country that are less heavily unionized (especially the South) or to foreign countries where wages are lower and job protection is nearly absent. The plight of displaced industrial workers is compounded by general economic trends resulting in the decline of manufacturing in the United States. In addition, managers and professional, technical, and administrative workers have also been displaced in high numbers. Women have a harder time finding new jobs than do men. African Americans and Hispanics have longer periods of unemployment than do whites. Using government statistics, Newman concluded that job displacement in the 1980s caused nearly 6 million people to become downwardly mobile (p. 27).

Divorce has a deleterious effect on women's income and is often the catalyst that propels them into a downward economic spiral. Divorced women with children, particularly when they have little or no continued financial support from their husbands, usually experience downward mobility. Many divorced women who were not working at the time of their divorce have great difficulty finding employment. Even those who work do not earn as much money as their husbands and therefore cannot support themselves and their children at their previous standard of living.

The global economic recession that began officially in 2008 has had a continuing impact on American individuals and families, as elsewhere in the world. The economic crisis has deep and complex roots in banking, insurance, and financial policies in the United States as well as in international lending agencies and private banks. The financial failure of banks and insurance companies meant the loss of savings of millions of people, limiting their ability to maintain their standard of living and to purchase new goods. As a result, production of goods worldwide experienced a steep decline, with the further consequence that millions of people lost their jobs in production downturns. Unemployment rates in most countries of the world have risen dramatically. These rates of course have led to declines in income and increases in the numbers of people living below poverty levels. In the United States, for example, the official unemployment rate reported for February 2011 stood at 8.9 percent, counting 13.7

million unemployed Americans (U.S. Department of Labor, Bureau of Labor Statistics, www.bls.gov/news.release/pdf; accessed March 19, 2011). The rate varied by race and gender: The unemployment rate for whites was 8.0 percent; for African Americans, 15.3 percent; for Hispanics, 11.6 percent; and for Asians, 6.8 percent. Of adult men, 8.7 percent were unemployed, while 8.0 percent of women were unemployed. In addition to the 13.7 million unemployed Americans, 2.7 million people were considered "marginally attached" to the labor force. These people are able and willing to work but had not looked for jobs in the four weeks prior to the survey. Among marginally attached workers, a total of 1.0 million were "discouraged workers," that is, those people who have given up looking for work because they do not believe that there are jobs available for them. Both categories of marginally attached workers are not counted in the official "unemployment" rate.

As unemployment rates rise, the numbers of people living below the poverty level have also increased. For 2009, the Census Bureau estimates that 13.5 percent of all Americans lived below the poverty level. However, the rates varied considerably based on race: 10.8 percent of whites, 10.9 percent of Asians, 21.9 percent of Hispanics, 25.1 percent of African Americans, and 25.9 percent of Native Americans lived below the poverty level. From the perspective of families, 15.3 percent of families with children under the age of 18 were poor. Married couples fared better than single parent households: 6.7 percent lived below the poverty level, while 37.1 percent of families headed by women with no husband present were poor (U.S. Census Bureau, American Community Survey, 2010, Table S1702). In terms of income, 7.4 percent of American households had annual incomes below $10,000, while 4.0 percent had incomes of more than $200,000 (Table S1091).

One of the most highly publicized indicators of the economic crisis in the United States has been the rate of foreclosures on home mortgages, with the consequent loss of people's dwellings. According to a real estate tracking company, one out of every 136 housing units received foreclosure notices in the final financial quarter of 2009, a rate that was nearly 23 percent higher than in the previous year (RealtyTrac.com). This rate amounted to a total of just under one million homes (937,840). In 2010, foreclosures on home properties continued to increase. States with the highest foreclosure rates include Nevada, Arizona, California, and Florida. The first cause of rising foreclosures was increases in mortgage rates when loans to low-income people were renegotiated by banks and lending companies, but the ongoing problem is at least as much caused by people's loss of income due to forced unemployment or underemployment and their lack of funds to pay their mortgages.

A dark side of globalization today is widespread trafficking of women and children for the sex trade and illicit trade in human body parts for transplants. These and other transborder crimes feed on a global service economy.

People who experience downward mobility suffer socially and psychologically in addition to their economic losses. They may have to give up spacious houses and a comfortable lifestyle. They may lose their friends because they can no longer afford to socialize in the ways they had in the past. Economic problems may put strains on marriages, resulting in separation and divorce. People also feel ashamed because of what they perceive to be their lack of success. They feel that they have not lived up to their own and others' expectations.

Although people who experience downward mobility are actually disadvantaged by a hierarchical social system, there are many ways that social ideologies about the American Dream blunt people's awareness of class as a major determinant of their lives and their opportunities. Rather than becoming angry at a system that not only tolerates inequality but is in fact built on necessary inequality, they feel disappointed and ashamed. Rather than understanding their predicament as part of the integral structure of capitalist economies, they make a judgment about their personal deficiencies.

Social, political, economic, educational, and religious ideologies serve to justify and maintain a society's system of social stratification. Thus, people learn to believe that social inequalities are normal or necessary. Furthermore, ideologies influence people's sentiments and behaviors, so that people readily believe in things that are not true and act on those beliefs.

ANTHROPOLOGY APPLIED

Working against Human Trafficking

In both government and nongovernment organizations, anthropologists are among those combating international human trafficking. Human trafficking includes buying and selling women and children into indentured servitude or slavery, illegally transporting migrants, and marketing body parts. The United Nations and national governments publish reports on the effectiveness of measures against human trafficking. In the summer of 2004, the U.S. State Department's report on human trafficking named ten countries—including Sudan, Myanmar, and North Korea—as being among the world's most negligent in protecting human rights. Forty-two other nations, including Japan, had inadequate measures

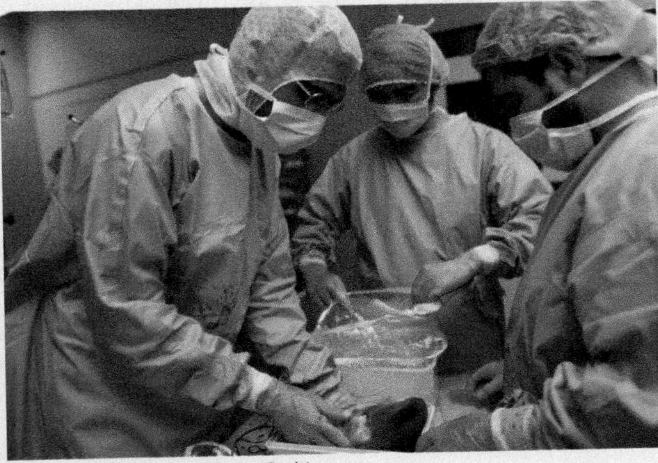

Corbis/Frederic Pitchal/Sygma/Corbis

Shutterstock/my-summit/Shutterstock

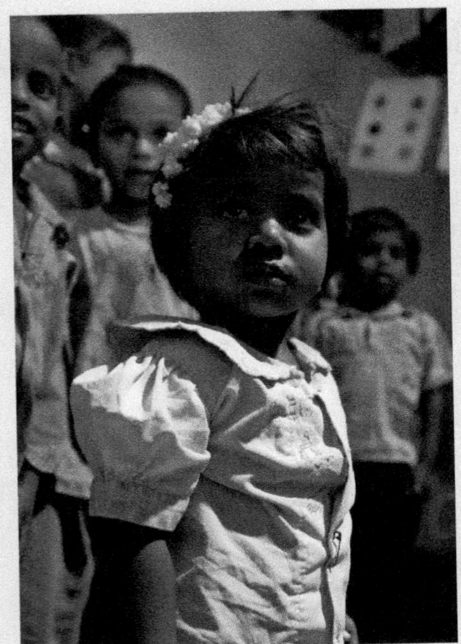

Alamy Limited/Barry Vincent/Alamy

against human trafficking. Japan is a destination for Asian, Latin American, and East European women and children trafficked for forced labor and sexual exploitation by the *yakuza*, Japan's organized crime groups. Other countries in this group include Russia, Thailand, Vietnam, the Philippines, Pakistan, India, Zimbabwe, Greece, Mexico, and Peru (Sakajiri 2004).

Anthropologists may combat human trafficking in different ways. For example, anthropologists working for HimRights (International Institute for Human Rights, Environment and Development), a watchdog organization, in Nepal conduct preventive educational campaigns and help monitor border crossings to detect and report suspected trafficking and protect Bhutanese and Tibetan refugees. They may help rescue and repatriate trafficked people. They also provide data for the region to the United Nations Commission on Human Rights.

In addition, human rights work often involves surveillance (or observation) and documentation, which are the skills of an ethnographer. The underworld trafficking of human organs for transplants was exposed largely through "undercover ethnography." This kind of work, which raises ethical issues for anthropologists and the medical profession, led to the discovery of an extensive network of "outlaw surgeons, kidney hunters, and transplant tourists" buying and selling human body parts (Scheper-Hughes 2004).

CRITICAL THINKING QUESTIONS

Why is anthropologist involvement in human rights work controversial? What are arguments for and against undercover ethnography?

Study and Review on myanthrolab.com

CHAPTER SUMMARY

Equality, Inequality, and Social Stratification

- Societies differ in respect to people's access to resources, livelihood, respect, and prestige. In egalitarian societies, all individuals have equal access to resources and equal likelihood of achieving respect and prestige. Although people's different skills and talents are rewarded, no one is denied opportunities for achievement. Foraging societies and some horticultural societies are likely to be egalitarian.
- In social systems based on rank, individuals and kinship groups occupy different positions in the social hierarchy. Each position is ranked in relation to all others. High rank confers advantages. In some ranked systems, high-ranking individuals are freed from subsistence activities and are supported by the productive work of others. High-ranking individuals are awarded prestige and influence and wield political influence as leaders of kinship groups and territorial units. Despite the privileges of rank, no one is denied a basically decent standard of living. In fact, high-ranking people have the responsibility of distributing goods to members of their kin groups.
- In stratified societies, people are differentiated on the basis of attributes they have at birth. These differences allow some people to have greater access to resources, wealth, and positions of prestige, influence, and power than other people. Granting privileges and opportunities to some people effectively denies them to others. Many traditional agrarian societies and all modern industrial states are highly stratified. Unlike systems of rank, some people in stratified societies may go hungry and be poorly clothed and housed. The gap in the standard of living between rich and poor may be wide.

Caste and Class

- A caste is a closed social group whose membership is hereditary; that is, people are born into a particular caste and remain so for life. Caste membership is an ascribed status. The various castes are ordered hierarchically from highest to lowest in a fixed order. Mobility is impossible. Members of higher castes have rights and privileges denied to members of lower castes. They have better standards of living, greater opportunities for achievement, and are more likely to occupy positions of influence and power.
- Some stratified systems are organized into classes rather than castes. Class systems are, at least theoretically, based on achievement, including education, occupation, and income. However, in practice, people whose parents are wealthier and are in higher classes have greater access to education and thus to higher incomes and occupations. In addition, although mobility is theoretically a characteristic of class systems, most people remain more or less constant in their social position. Downward mobility is as likely as upward mobility.

Race and Ethnicity

- Race is a social construct, focusing on a particular set of external physical traits but having no biological basis as separate, discrete categories. Physical traits that are used to demarcate the races, including skin color, hair color and texture, and facial features, appear in human populations on a continuum, not as consistent markers of groups. But race, once identified on the basis of physical characteristics, becomes projected onto social and personal behavior. The races are then ranked hierarchically. The dominant social group ascribes negative qualities to groups it considers inferior.
- Ethnicity is a feature of cultural identification. Cultural traits that often define group membership include language, residence, food, dress, and body ornamentation. Ethnicity is an ascribed status in that people are born into a cultural group. It is also an achieved status because people can choose either to identify with their ethnic group of origin or assimilate into the mainstream society.

Class, Race, Ethnicity, and Ideology in American Society

- In the United States, an ideology coalescing around the American Dream obscures the actual facts of the structure of class and class privilege. Although elites who control government policies act in the interests of their class, barriers hinder class consciousness among disadvantaged groups. People blame themselves for their disadvantages instead of recognizing that a hierarchical system imposes a position on them. People also feel that their low position in the socioeconomic system is temporary, amenable to change if they try harder to achieve. Other barriers that divide people include racial, ethnic, and gender differences.

REVIEW QUESTIONS

1. What core concepts are used to analyze systems of social stratification?
2. How are egalitarian, ranked, and stratified societies different?
3. What are three basic theoretical explanations for systems of social stratification?
4. How is caste different from class? What role does social mobility play in caste and class societies?
5. How can ideologies be used to socialize conformity to the social order, to reinforce the system of social stratification, and to challenge the system?
6. How does language reveal class membership? What else indicates social class?
7. How are race and ethnicity social constructs? How are race and ethnicity a form of caste?

MyAnthroLab Connections

Watch. Listen. View. Explore. Read. MyAnthroLab is designed just for you. Dynamic visual activities, videos, and readings found in the multimedia library will enhance your learning experience.

Resources from this chapter:

Watch on **myanthrolab.com**
- *It's an Illusion That There Are Races*

Listen on **myanthrolab.com**
- *Racial Democracy in Brazil*
- *Does Wealth Imbalance Threaten Society's Fabric?*

View on **myanthrolab.com**
- *The Varnas of India*

Explore on **myanthrolab.com** In MySearchLab, enter the Anthropology database to find relevant and recent scholarly and popular press publications. For this chapter, enter the following keywords: social stratification, mobility, ascribed status

Read the **Document**
- *Origins of Social Inequality* by Elizabeth M. Brumfiel
- *Is There Caste Outside of India?* by Morton Klass

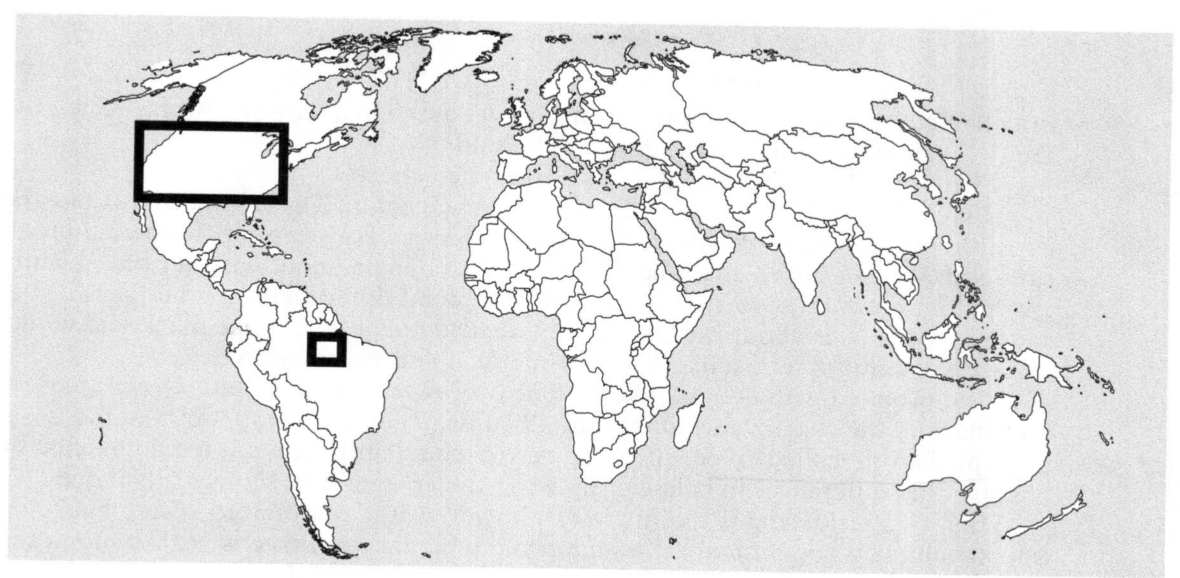

Mixed Blood

Jefferson M. Fish

*Many Americans believe that people can be divided into races. For them, races are biologically defined groups. Anthropologists, on the other hand, have long argued that U.S. racial groups are American cultural constructions; they represent the way Americans classify people rather than a genetically determined reality. In this article, Jeffrey Fish demonstrates the cultural basis of race by comparing how races are defined in the United States and Brazil. In America, a person's race is determined not by how he or she looks, but by his or her heritage. A person will be classified as black, for example, if one of his or her parents is classified that way no matter what the person looks like. In Brazil, on the other hand, people are classified into a series of tipos on the basis of how they look. The same couple may have children classified into three or four different tipos based on a number of physical markers such as skin color and nose shape. As a result, Fish's daughter, who has brown skin and whose mother is black, can change her race from black in the United States to moreno (brunette), a category just behind branca (blond) in Brazil, by simply taking a plane there.**

Last year my daughter, who had been living in Rio de Janeiro, and her Brazilian boyfriend paid a visit to my cross-cultural psychology class. They had agreed to be interviewed about

Brazilian culture. At one point in the interview I asked her, "Are you black?" She said, "Yes." I then asked him the question, and he said "No."

"How can that be?" I asked. "He's darker than she is."

Psychologists have begun talking about race again. They think that it may be useful in explaining the biological bases of behavior. For example, following publication of *The Bell Curve,* there has been renewed debate about whether black–white group differences in scores on IQ tests reflect racial differences in intelligence. (Because this article is about race, it will mainly use racial terms, like black and white, rather than cultural terms, like African-American and European-American.)

The problem with debates like the one over race and IQ is that psychologists on both sides of the controversy make a totally unwarranted assumption: that there is a biological entity called "race." If there were such an entity, then it would at least be possible that differences in behavior between "races" might be biologically based.

Before considering the controversy, however, it is reasonable to step back and ask ourselves "What is race?" If, as happens to be the case, race is not a biologically meaningful concept, then looking for biologically based racial differences in behavior is simply a waste of time.

The question "What is race?" can be divided into two more limited ones. The answers to both questions have long been known by anthropologists, but seem not to have reached other social or behavioral scientists, let alone the public at large. And both answers differ strikingly from what we Americans think of as race.

The first question is "How can we understand the variation in physical appearance among human beings?" It is interesting to discover that Americans (including researchers, who should know better) view only a part of the variation as "racial," while other equally evident variability is not so viewed.

The second question is "How can we understand the kinds of racial classifications applied to differences in physical appearance among human beings?" Surprisingly, different cultures label these physical differences in different ways. Far from describing biological entities, American racial categories are merely one of numerous, very culture-specific schemes for reducing uncertainty about how people should respond to other people. The fact that Americans believe that Asians, blacks, Hispanics, and whites constitute biological entities called races is a matter of cultural interest rather than scientific substance. It tells us something about American culture—but nothing at all about the human species.

The short answer to the question "What is race?" is: There is no such thing. Race is a myth. And our racial classification scheme is loaded with pure fantasy.

Let's start with human physical variation. Human beings are a species, which means that people from anywhere on the planet can mate with others from anywhere else and produce fertile offspring. (Horses and donkeys are two different species because, even though they can mate with each other, their offspring—mules—are sterile.)

Our species evolved in Africa from earlier forms and eventually spread out around the planet. Over time, human populations that were geographically separated from one another came to differ in physical appearance. They came by these differences through three major pathways: mutation, natural selection, and genetic drift. Since genetic mutations occur randomly, different mutations occur and accumulate over time in geographically separated populations. Also, as we have known since Darwin, different geographical environments select for different physical traits that confer a survival advantage. But the largest proportion of variability among populations may well result from purely random factors; this random change in the frequencies of already existing genes is known as genetic drift.

If an earthquake or disease kills off a large segment of a population, those who survive to reproduce are likely to differ from the original population in many ways. Similarly, if a group divides and a subgroup moves away, the two groups will, by chance, differ in the frequency of various genes. Even the mere fact of physical separation will, over time, lead two equivalent populations to differ in the frequency of genes. These randomly acquired population differences will accumulate over successive generations along with any others due to mutation or natural selection.

A number of differences in physical appearance among populations around the globe appear to have adaptive value. For example, people in the tropics of Africa and South America came to have dark skins, presumably, through natural selection, as protection against the sun. In cold areas, like northern Europe or northern North America, which are dark for long periods of time, and where people covered their bodies for warmth, people came to have light skins—light skins make maximum use of sunlight to produce vitamin D.

The indigenous peoples of the New World arrived about 15,000 years ago, during the last ice age, following game across the Bering Strait. (The sea level was low enough to create a land bridge because so much water was in the form of ice.) Thus, the dark-skinned Indians of the South American tropics are descended from light-skinned ancestors, similar in appearance to the Eskimo. In other words, even though skin color is the most salient feature thought by Americans to be an indicator of race—and race is assumed to have great time depth—it is subject to relatively rapid evolutionary change.

Meanwhile, the extra ("epicanthic") fold of eyelid skin, which Americans also view as racial, and which evolved in Asian populations to protect the eye against the cold, continues to exist among South American native peoples because its presence (unlike a light skin) offers no reproductive disadvantage. Hence, skin color and eyelid form, which Americans think of as traits of different races, occur together or separately in different populations.

Like skin color, there are other physical differences that also appear to have evolved through natural selection—but which Americans do not think of as racial. Take, for example, body shape. Some populations in very cold climates, like the Eskimo, developed rounded bodies. This is because the more spherical an object is, the less surface area it has to radiate heat. In contrast, some populations in very hot climates, like the Masai, developed lanky bodies. Like the tubular pipes of an old-fashioned radiator, the high ratio of surface area to volume allows people to radiate a lot of heat.

In terms of American's way of thinking about race, lanky people and rounded people are simply two kinds of whites or blacks. But it is equally reasonable to view light-skinned people and dark-skinned people as two kinds of "lankys" or "roundeds." In other words, our categories for racial classification of people arbitrarily include certain dimensions (light versus dark skin) and exclude others (rounded versus elongated bodies).

There is no biological basis for classifying race according to skin color instead of body form—or according to any other variable, for that matter. All that exists is variability in what people look like—and the arbitrary and culturally specific ways different societies classify that variability. There is nothing left over that can be called race. This is why race is a myth.

Skin color and body form do not vary together: Not all dark-skinned people are lanky; similarly, light-skinned people may be lanky or rounded. The same can be said of the facial features Americans think of as racial—eye color, nose width (actually, the ratio of width to length), lip thickness ("evertedness"), hair form, and hair color. They do not vary together either. If they did, then a "totally white" person would have very light skin color, straight blond hair, blue eyes, a narrow nose, and thin lips; a "totally black" person would have very dark skin color, black tight curly hair, dark brown eyes, a broad nose, and thick lips; those in between would have—to a correlated degree—wavy light brown hair, light brown eyes, and intermediate nose and lip forms.

While people of mixed European and African ancestry who look like this do exist, they are the exception rather than the rule. Anyone who wants to can make up a chart of facial features (choose a location with a diverse population, say, the New York City subway) and verify that there are people with all possible admixtures of facial features. One might see someone with tight curly blond hair, light skin, blue eyes, broad nose, and thick lips—whose features are half "black" and half "white." That is, each of the person's facial features occupies one end or the other of a supposedly racial continuum, with no intermediary forms (like wavy light brown hair). Such people are living proof that supposedly racial features do not vary together.

Since the human species has spent most of its existence in Africa, different populations in Africa have been separated from each other longer than East Asians or Northern Europeans have been separated from each other or from Africans. As a result, there is remarkable physical variation among the peoples of Africa, which goes unrecognized by Americans who view them all as belonging to the same race.

In contrast to the very tall Masai, the diminutive stature of the very short Pygmies may have evolved as an advantage in moving rapidly through tangled forest vegetation. The Bushmen of the Kalahari desert have very large ("steatopygous") buttocks, presumably to store body fat in one place for times of food scarcity, while leaving the rest of the body uninsulated to radiate heat. They also have "peppercorn" hair. Hair in separated tufts, like tight curly hair, leaves space to radiate the heat that rises through the body to the scalp; straight hair lies flat and holds in body heat, like a cap. By viewing Africans as constituting a single race, Americans ignore their greater physical variability, while assigning racial significance to lesser differences between them.

Although it is true that most inhabitants of northern Europe, east Asia, and central Africa look like Americans' conceptions of one or another of the three purported races, most inhabitants of south Asia, southwest Asia, north Africa, and the Pacific islands do not. Thus, the 19th century view of the human species as comprised of Caucasoid, Mongoloid, and Negroid races, still held by many Americans, is based on a partial and unrepresentative view of human variability. In other words, what is now known about human physical variation does not correspond to what Americans think of as race.

In contrast to the question of the actual physical variation among human beings, there is the question of how people classify that variation. Scientists classify things in scientific taxonomies—chemists' periodic table of the elements, biologists' classification of life forms into kingdoms, phyla, and so forth.

In every culture, people also classify things along culture-specific dimensions of meaning. For example, paper clips and staples are understood by Americans as paper fasteners, and nails are not, even though, in terms of their physical properties, all three consist of differently shaped pieces of metal wire. The physical variation in pieces of metal wire can be seen as analogous to human physical variation; and the categories of cultural meaning, like paper fasteners versus wood fasteners, can be seen as analogous to races. Anthropologists refer to these kinds of classifications as folk taxonomies.

Consider the avocado—is it a fruit or a vegetable? Americans insist it is a vegetable. We eat it in salads with oil and vinegar. Brazilians, on the other hand, would say it is a fruit. They eat it for dessert with lemon juice and sugar.

How can we explain this difference in classification?

The avocado is an edible plant, and the American and Brazilian folk taxonomies, while containing cognate terms, classify some edible plants differently. The avocado does not change. It is the same biological entity, but its folk classification changes, depending on who's doing the classifying.

Human beings are also biological entities. Just as we can ask if an avocado is a fruit or a vegetable, we can ask if a person is white or black. And when we ask race questions, the answers we get come from folk taxonomies, not scientific ones. Terms like "white" or "black" applied to people—or "vegetable" or "fruit" applied to avocados—do not give us biological information about people or avocados. Rather, they exemplify how cultural groups (Brazilians or Americans) classify people and avocados.

Americans believe in "blood," a folk term for the quality presumed to be carried by members of so-called races. And the way offspring—regardless of their physical appearance—always inherit the less prestigious racial category of mixed parentage is called "hypo-descent" by anthropologists. A sentence thoroughly intelligible to most Americans might be, "Since Mary's father is white and her mother is black, Mary is black because she has black 'blood.'" American researchers who think they are studying racial differences in behavior would, like other Americans, classify Mary as black—although she has just as much white "blood."

According to hypo-descent, the various purported racial categories are arranged in a hierarchy along a single dimension, from the most prestigious ("white"), through intermediary forms ("Asian"), to the least prestigious ("black"). And when a couple come from two different categories, all their children (the "descent" in "hypo-descent") are classified as belonging to the less prestigious category (thus, the "hypo"). Hence, all the offspring of one "white" parent and one "black" parent—regardless of the children's physical appearance—are called "black" in the United States.

The American folk concept of "blood" does not behave like genes. Genes are units which cannot be subdivided. When several genes jointly determine a trait, chance decides which ones come from each parent. For example, if eight genes determine a trait, a child gets four from each parent. If a mother and a father each have the hypothetical genes BBBBWWWW, then a child could be born with any combination of B and W genes, from BBBBBBBB to WWWWWWWW. In contrast, the folk concept "blood" behaves like a uniform and continuous entity. It can be divided in two indefinitely—for example, quadroons and octoroons are said to be people who have one-quarter and one-eighth black "blood," respectively. Oddly, because of hypo-descent, Americans consider people with one-eighth black "blood" to be black rather than white, despite their having seven-eighths white "blood."

Hypo-descent, or "blood," is not informative about the physical appearance of people. For example, when two parents called black in the United States have a number of children, the children are likely to vary in physical appearance. In the case of skin color, they might vary from lighter than the lighter parent to darker than the darker parent. However, they would all receive the same racial classification—black—regardless of their skin color.

All that hypo-descent tells you is that, when someone is classified as something other than white (e.g., Asian), at least one of his or her parents is classified in the same way, and that neither parent has a less prestigious classification (e.g., black). That is, hypo-descent is informative about ancestry—specifically, parental classification—rather than physical appearance.

There are many strange consequences of our folk taxonomy. For example, someone who inherited no genes that produce "African"-appearing physical features would still be considered black if he or she has a parent classified as black. The category "passing for white" includes many such people. Americans have the curious belief that people who look white but have a parent classified as black are "really" black in some biological sense, and are being deceptive if they present themselves as white. Such examples make it clear that race is a social rather than a physical classification.

From infancy, human beings learn to recognize very subtle differences in the faces of those around them. Black babies see a wider variety of black faces than white faces, and white babies see a wider variety of white faces than black faces. Because they are exposed only to a limited range of human variation, adult members of each "race" come to see their own group as containing much wider variation than others. Thus, because of this perceptual learning, blacks see greater physical variation among themselves than among whites, while whites see the opposite. In this case, however, there is a clear answer to the question of which group contains greater physical variability. Blacks are correct.

Why is this the case?

Take a moment. Think of yourself as an amateur anthropologist and try to step out of American culture, however briefly.

It is often difficult to get white people to accept what at first appears to contradict the evidence they can see clearly with their own eyes—but which is really the result of a history of perceptual learning. However, the reason that blacks view themselves as more varied is not that their vision is more accurate. Rather, it is that blacks too have a long—but different—history of perceptual learning from that of whites (and also that they have been observers of a larger range of human variation).

The fact of greater physical variation among blacks than whites in America goes back to the principle of hypo-descent, which classifies all people with one black parent and one white parent as black. If they were all considered white, then there would be more physical variation among whites. Someone with one-eighth white "blood" and seven-eighths black "blood" would be considered white; anyone with any white ancestry would be considered white. In other words, what appears to be a difference in biological variability is really a difference in cultural classification.

Perhaps the clearest way to understand that the American folk taxonomy of race is merely one of many—arbitrary and unscientific like all the others—is to contrast it with a very different one, that of Brazil. The Portuguese word that in the Brazilian folk taxonomy corresponds to the American "race" is *"tipo." Tipo,* a cognate of the English word "type," is a descriptive term that serves as a kind of shorthand for a series of physical features. Because people's physical features vary separately from one another, there are an awful lot of tipos in Brazil.

Since tipos are descriptive terms, they vary regionally in Brazil—in part reflecting regional differences in the development of colloquial Portuguese, but in part because the physical variation they describe is different in different regions. The Brazilian situation is so complex I will limit my delineation of tipos to some of the main ones used in the city of Salvador, Bahia, to describe people whose physical appearance is understood to be made up of African and European features. (I will use the female terms throughout; in nearly all cases the male term simply changes the last letter from *a* to *o*.)

Proceeding along a dimension from the "whitest" to the "blackest" tipos, a *loura* is whiter-than-white, with straight blond hair, blue or green eyes, light skin color, narrow nose, and thin lips. Brazilians who come to the United States think that a *loura* means a "blond" and are surprised to find that the American term refers to hair color only. A *branca* has light skin color, eyes of any color, hair of any color or form except tight curly, a nose that is not broad, and lips that are not thick. *Branca* translates as "white," though Brazilians of this tipo who come to the United States—especially those from elite families—are often dismayed to find that they are not considered white here, and, even worse, are viewed as Hispanic despite the fact that they speak Portuguese.

A *morena* has brown or black hair that is wavy or curly but not tight curly, tan skin, a nose that is not narrow, and lips that are not thin. Brazilians who come to the United States think that a *morena* is a "brunette," and are surprised to find that brunettes are considered white but *morenas* are not. Americans have difficulty classifying *morenas,* many of whom are of Latin American origin: Are they black or Hispanic? (One might also observe that *morenas* have trouble with Americans, for not just accepting their appearance as a given, but asking instead "Where do you come from?" "What language did you speak at home?" "What was your maiden name?" or even, more crudely, "What *are* you?")

A *mulata* looks like a *morena,* except with tight curly hair and a slightly darker range of hair colors and skin colors. A *preta* looks like a *mulata,* except with dark brown skin, broad nose, and thick lips. To Americans, *mulatas* and *pretas* are both black, and if forced to distinguish between them would refer to them as light-skinned blacks and dark-skinned blacks, respectively.

If Brazilians were forced to divide the range of tipos, from *loura* to *preta,* into "kinds of whites" and "kinds of blacks" (a distinction they do not ordinarily make), they would draw the line between *morenas* and *mulatas;* whereas Americans, if offered only visual information, would draw the line between *brancas* and *morenas.*

The proliferation of tipos, and the difference in the white–black dividing line, do not, however, exhaust the differences between Brazilian and American folk taxonomies. There are tipos in the Afro-European domain that are considered to be neither black nor white—an idea that is difficult for Americans visiting Brazil to comprehend. A person with tight curly blond (or red) hair, light skin, blue (or green) eyes, broad nose, and thick lips, is a *sarará.* The opposite features—straight black hair, dark skin, brown eyes, narrow nose, and thin lips—are those of a *cabo verde. Sarará* and *cabo verde* are both tipos that are considered by Brazilians in Salvador, Bahia, to be neither black nor white.

When I interviewed my American daughter and her Brazilian boyfriend, she said she was black because her mother is black (even though I am white). That is, from her American perspective, she has "black blood"—though she is a *morena* in Brazil. Her boyfriend said that he was not black because, viewing himself in terms of Brazilian tipos, he is a *mulato* (not a *preto*).

There are many differences between the Brazilian and American folk taxonomies of race. The American system tells you about how people's parents are classified but not what they look like. The Brazilian system tells you what they look like but not about their parents. When two parents of intermediate appearance have many children in the United States, the children are all of one race; in Brazil they are of many tipos.

Americans believe that race is an immutable biological given, but people (like my daughter and her boyfriend) can change their race by getting on a plane and going from the United States to Brazil—just as, if they take an avocado with them, it changes from a vegetable into a fruit. In both cases, what changes is not the physical appearance of the person or avocado, but the way they are classified.

I have focused on the Brazilian system to make clear how profoundly folk taxonomies of race vary from one place to another. But the Brazilian system is just one of many. Haiti's folk taxonomy, for example, includes elements of both ancestry and physical appearance, and even includes the amazing term (for foreigners of African appearance) *un blanc noir*—literally, "a black white." In the classic study *Patterns of Race in the Americas,* anthropologist Marvin Harris gives a good introduction to the ways in which the conquests by differing European powers of differing New World peoples and ecologies combined with differing patterns of slavery to produce a variety of folk taxonomies. Folk taxonomies of race can be found in many—though by no means all—cultures in other parts of the world as well.

The American concept of race does not correspond to the ways in which human physical appearance varies. Further, the American view of race ("hypo-descent") is just one among many folk taxonomies, [none] of which correspond to the facts of human physical variation. This is why race is a myth and why races as conceived by Americans (and others) do not exist. It is also why differences in behavior between "races" cannot be explained by biological differences between them.

When examining the origins of IQ scores (or other behavior), psychologists sometimes use the term "heritability"—a statistical concept that is not based on observations of genes or chromosomes. It is important to understand that questions about heritability of IQ have nothing to do with racial differences in IQ. "Heritability" refers only to the relative ranking of individuals *within* a population, under given environmental conditions, and not to differences *between* populations. Thus, among the population of American whites, it may be that those with high IQs tend to have higher-IQ children than do those with low IQs. Similarly, among American blacks, it may be that those with high IQs also tend to have higher-IQ children.

In both cases, it is possible that the link between the IQs of parents and children may exist for reasons that are not entirely environmental. This heritability of IQ *within* the two populations, even if it exists, would in no way contradict the average social advantages of American whites as a group compared to the average social disadvantages of American blacks as a group. Such differences in social environments can easily account for any differences in the average test scores *between* the two groups. Thus, the heritability of IQ *within* each group is irrelevant to understanding differences *between* the groups.

Beyond this, though, studies of differences in behavior between "populations" of whites and blacks, which seek to find biological causes rather than only social ones, make a serious logical error. They assume that blacks and whites are populations in some biological sense, as sub-units of the human species. (Most likely, the researchers make this assumption because they are American and approach race in terms of the American folk taxonomy.)

In fact, though, the groups are sorted by a purely social rule for statistical purposes. This can easily be demonstrated by asking researchers how they know that the white subjects are really white and the black subjects are really black. There is no biological answer to this question, because race as a biological category does not exist. All that researchers can say is, "The tester classified them based on their physical appearance," or "Their school records listed their race," or otherwise give a social rather than biological answer.

So when American researchers study racial differences in behavior, in search of biological rather than social causes for differences between socially defined groups, they are wasting their time. Computers are wonderful machines, but we have learned about "garbage in/garbage out." Applying complex computations to bad data yields worthless results. In the same way, the most elegant experimental designs and statistical analyses, applied flawlessly to biologically meaningless racial categories, can only produce a very expensive waste of time.

As immigrants of varied physical appearance come to the United States from countries with racial folk taxonomies different from our own, they are often perplexed and dismayed to find that the ways they classify themselves and others are irrelevant to the American reality. Brazilians, Haitians, and others may find themselves labeled by strange, apparently inappropriate, even pejorative terms, and grouped together with people who are different from and unreceptive to them. This can cause psychological complications (a Brazilian immigrant—who views himself as white—being treated by an American therapist who assumes that he is not).

Immigration has increased, especially from geographical regions whose people do not resemble American images of blacks, whites, or Asians. Intermarriage is also increasing, as the stigma associated with it diminishes. These two trends are augmenting the physical diversity among those who marry each other—and, as a result, among their children. The American folk taxonomy of race (purportedly comprised of stable biological entities) is beginning to change to accommodate this new reality. After all, what race is someone whose four grandparents are black, white, Asian, and Hispanic?

Currently, the most rapidly growing census category is "Other," as increasing numbers of people fail to fit available options. Changes in the census categories every 10 years reflect the government's attempts to grapple with the changing self-identifications of Americans—even as statisticians try to maintain the same categories over time in order to make demographic comparisons. Perhaps they will invent one or more "multiracial" categories, to accommodate the wide range of people whose existence defies current classification. Perhaps they will drop the term "race" altogether. Already some institutions are including an option to "check as many as apply," when asking individuals to classify themselves on a list of racial and ethnic terms.

Thinking in terms of physical appearance and folk taxonomies helps to clarify the emotionally charged but confused topics of race. Understanding that different cultures have different folk taxonomies suggests that we respond to the question "What race is that person?" not by "Black" or "White," but by "Where?" and "When?"

Study and **Review** on **myanthrolab.com**

Review Questions

1. What is Jeffrey Fish's main point about the way Americans define race?
2. What is the difference between the way race is defined in the United States and in Brazil? List the Brazilian folk taxonomy of *tipos* and how to translate *tipos* into U.S. racial categories.
3. What evidence challenges the view that races are biologically defined types? What evidence would have to exist to prove that the human species is genetically divided into races?
4. Why does Fish feel it is important to understand that race as Americans define it does not represent a biological reality?

Living in a Global World

Living in a Global World

PREVIEW

- How is migration changing national and world demographics?
- How does migration affect local, national, and global economies?
- How have new nations re-created themselves in the postcolonial era, and how have they adapted to their own cultural diversity?
- Why can ethnogenesis reflect both a colonial past and a globalized future?
- What is transnationalism and the emerging "global identity"?
- What is the status of cultural minorities in the world today? How are they threatened, and how can they protect themselves?

Myanmar refugee women along with their children rest by their completely destroyed huts after troops loyal to the Rangoon government attacked Maw Ker refugee camp in Tak province, northwestern Thailand province bordering Myanmar. *Vichira/AP Images*
AP Photos/Vichira/AP Images

Maran Kai Ra
Female, age 28.
From: Sumprabum, Kachin State.
Occupation: family grocery store and distributing medicine.
Education: BA, Myitkyina University.
Ethnicity: Kachin.
Religion: Baptist.
Left Burma: September 2000.

Listen to the Chapter Audio on myanthrolab.com

Read on myanthrolab.com

Q: Why did you leave Burma?

A: Because of the political movement. Since 1988, I started to be involved in the student movement, and after that, when Aung San Suu Kyi came to Myitkyina, I welcomed her with flowers. After she left, I was asked to come to the MI for interrogation, and after that I had a record. I was also involved with the 1996 student movement and continuously I was involved in the political movements and organizing and distributing political pamphlets. Most recently they suspected me of involvement with Aung San Suu Kyi's party and the underground student movement. My name was on their list.

Q: What was political organizing like as a student?

A: We had to do it as an underground movement, through the religious groups and the Kachin literature and the cultural organizations. We don't have formal organizations like student unions.

Q: How did you get information?

A: News from abroad we get from BBC, VOA and AIR, but within Burma, within the student organization we have a kind of representative or student leader from Myitkyina or Rangoon and they travel and give information to each other.

Q: Were many university students involved in politics?

A: About 60% of the students were interested in politics.

Q: What education was available in Sumprabum?

A: There's only up to 8th grade [standard] in Sumprabum. So mostly they have to go to Myitkyina or Rangoon for higher education.

Q: What were the health conditions in Sumprabum?

A: There's no proper clinic or hospital, there's not a single doctor. And there's plenty of health problems, especially malaria. The local people in Sumprabum are taught by the nurses, not by the doctors, how to avoid the diseases. As far as I know, there's no HIV positive in the area, but some TB. The people who have TB have to go to Myitkyina for treatment, there's no clinic.

Q: Are there traveling doctors in the area?

A: There's a kind of doctor who goes around checking villagers, almost once a year.

Q: What is the food situation in the Sumprabum area?

A: Mostly everything is locally grown. But salt and oil ... they bring from Myitkyina. There's not enough rice. Because of the hill cultivation we cannot produce enough rice for the local people.

Q: Is there much government army in the area?

A: Yes, they have an army base there.

Q: Do they ever ask people to work for them?

A: Yes, many times. In the past, there's plenty of portering. People were forced to work as porters. But now, there's almost no more portering. But still people are forced to do forced labor to build their army camp or to build roads or such things. There's no payment. Every household has to do it one by one. If this week it's this household, next week it will be the other to help the military.

Q: Is there logging in that area?

A: Yes, the government gives the permit to businessmen, mostly Chinese, to cut the wood, and taking the gold and cane for trading. They hire the local people and people who come from Myitkyina, not just Kachin, everyone. Because of that permission to cut the tree and do the gold mining and other stuff, most of the mountains and the hillsides have been emptied of forests. And the way of the streams, they also changed it to dig the gold. So everything's changed, and also the wildlife. In the past we heard the sound of the wildlife. But no more. They all ran away.

Q: What about fishing?

A: In the past the villagers, the local people only used nets for fishing. But the people from the city, when they arrived, they used the mines [explosives] for the fishing. That's why now there is almost no more fish at all.

Q: How is the water for drinking?

A: The water's very good.

Q: In Sumprabum, in the last two years before you left, was life for the local people getting better?

A: There's not much change, but I would say slightly better because of the cease-fire between the KIA [Kachin Independence Army] and the government, since there is no fighting. So it's a little bit safer than before.

Q: Is the gold mining or logging improving people's economic status?

A: Slightly better, but I believe that for the long term it won't be good.

Q: Are people able to freely practice their religion there?

A: They are allowed to, if they get the permission from the military authorities. In advance they have to ask for permission. How many days the Christian festival or religious festival will take place, how many people will come to the festival.

Maran Kai Ra was interviewed in Guam, where she was seeking political asylum in the United States. In this interview, she discusses some of the conditions that led her to leave her country, Burma, also called Myanmar. Her experiences are fairly typical of political refugees. Although refugees account for many people who move from one country to another, many more voluntarily enter new countries to obtain education or employment. This pattern is not unique to our times, but global processes of change and interaction have accelerated migration throughout the twentieth and into the twenty-first century. The present-day global economy, although initiated centuries ago, has accelerated the transfer of goods, services, and peoples around the world. International migration has brought people far from their homes. As they settle into their new countries, they adopt new cultural practices, often blending them with their own values and perspectives. They contribute their labor and spend their money in their new countries. They also add cultural diversity and richness to their immigrant communities.

Political processes have also strengthened ties among countries. International organizations such as the United Nations, the World Health Organization, and many regional groups coordinate activities; set economic, social, and environmental policies; and resolve conflicts. The success of these organizations varies. Although, in principle, countries are equals, in practice, the voices of larger, richer, and more powerful countries drown out those of smaller and poorer ones. The rich and powerful countries exert greater influence because they can promise economic rewards, political support, and military aid to those who follow their lead, while they threaten to withdraw aid or retaliate against those who defy them.

The Nenets, Samoyeds of western Siberia, are nomadic foragers, fishers, and reindeer herders. They inadvertently consume deadly heavy metals from pollution when they eat mosses and reindeer meat.
Corbis/Staffan Widstrand/Corbis

cultural minorities
Members of ethnic or cultural groups who have become minorities in their native lands due to migrations of other peoples into their territories or due to the historical configuration of a nation-state made up of diverse groups.

labor migration
Migration of people from one area of a country to another or across national borders in search of jobs.

All of these factors are part of the process of globalization. Globalization includes the movement of people and the exchange of cultural practices, goods and services, and attitudes worldwide. Through global exchanges, people learn from one another, obtain goods made elsewhere, and share information through media outlets and technological advances such as the Internet. This chapter explores some of the characteristics and consequences of these processes.

The ways of life of **cultural minorities** have come under increasing threat. Their lands and resources are vulnerable to encroachment and exploitation by the governments of the countries in which they live and by multinational corporations that covet their minerals, forests, and other natural products. In the last quarter of the twentieth century, however, indigenous peoples began to protect their lands and their cultures. This trend has continued and, indeed, has become more visible and vocal.

As a result of present-day globalization, international organizations and multinational corporations have tremendous impacts on nations and on cultural minorities living in those nations, as well as on global interrelationships among nations.

MIGRATION

Temporary travel and permanent migration have been features of human life for millennia, but the last several centuries have witnessed an acceleration of these processes both in the numbers of people who leave their native countries and in the distances they travel. In addition to voluntary migrants, some people become refugees because of war and other turmoil. Indeed, wars in the Middle East and Africa have created the largest number of refugees in the world. In 2006, for example, 2.1 million Afghans, who made up 21 percent of the world's refugee population, were refugees in more than 70 asylum countries, mainly Pakistan, Iran, and Saudi Arabia. Iraqis accounted for the second-largest group, with 1.5 million people leaving to find shelter in neighboring countries. Many people from the African countries of Sudan, Somalia, the Democratic Republic of the Congo, and Burundi also fled (see Tables 1 and 2).

Rural-to-Urban Migration

Migration takes place within a country as well. Urban centers attract people from rural areas who seek better employment and income. In Europe and the United States, rural-to-urban migration intensified after the Industrial Revolution of the early nineteenth century, but it also accelerated in the last century. Industrial development led to the creation of jobs in manufacturing and service occupations, attracting people from the countryside. In addition, advances in agricultural technology meant that fewer people were needed to grow the food sustaining larger urban populations. The spread of industrial agriculture, particularly in the United States, led to wealthy and efficient corporations buying out small family farmers. After World War II, many thousands of African Americans left the predominantly rural South, heading north for work and a less overtly racist social and political environment. These are all patterns of **labor migration.**

Similar trends in labor migration take place in Asia and Africa. In Malaysia, for example, rural peasant families send some of their children to work in electronics and

Do you know anyone who has come to this country to work? What circumstances made them come?

TABLE 1 MAIN ORIGIN OF REFUGEES, 2009

Origin	End of 2009
Afghanistan	2,887,100
Iraq	1,785,200
Somalia	678,300
Democratic Republic of the Congo	455,900
Myanmar (Burma)	406,700
Colombia (internally displaced)	389,800
Sudan	368,200
Vietnam	339,300
Eritrea	209,200
Serbia	195,600

Source: 2010 UNHCR Statistical Yearbook, Figure 11.4.

TABLE 2 MAIN COUNTRIES OF ASYLUM, 2009

Country of Asylum	Number of Refugees
Pakistan	1,740,700
Iran	1,070,500
Syria	1,054,500
Germany	593,800
Jordan	450,800
Kenya	358,900
Chad	338,500
China	301,000
United States	275,500
United Kingdom	269,400

Source: 2010 UNHCR Statistical Yearbook, Figure 11.2.

other factories owned by multinational corporations, especially from Japan and Korea (Ong 1983). As in Mexico, Malaysian peasants adapt to poverty by sending their daughters to work in factories (see the Case Study).

Industrial work is divided by class and world region. The high-tech skilled jobs in research and development are centered in developed countries, whereas the low-skilled assembly-line tasks are performed in peripheral areas. The Malaysian government grants tax benefits and reduces tariffs for multinationals because jobs are needed for people who are displaced from their lands, especially in a country experiencing high population growth. Lack of health and safety regulations, no minimum wage, and restrictions on union membership also attract companies. For example, to join a union, a worker must be employed in the same job for a minimum of three years, but most of the workers in multinational industries are hired on six-month contracts, resulting in high turnover and little job security. The Malaysian government's goals are both economic (providing jobs) and political (forestalling political unrest) (Ong 1983).

CASE STUDY

Labor Migration in Mexico

Patterns of labor migration reveal the complex causes of people's relocations and dislocations as a consequence of globalization. A significant trend in Latin America and Asia is the migration of workers from rural areas to factories owned by multinational corporations in development or free trade zones. Companies are attracted to the zones because they receive tax exemptions for capital investment and find a large labor pool. Moreover, these zones have low wages, weak or nonexistent unions, and few environmental or health and safety regulations (Fuentes and Ehrenreich 1983).

The young women who make up most of the work force are relatively unskilled. They are literate but are rarely graduates of secondary schools and, therefore, tend to lack higher aspirations. For example, Mexico has seen an enormous growth in manufacturing jobs since the 1960s, when its government embarked on a policy of industrial development in conjunction with multinational corporations, principally based in the United States. Mexico hoped the program would attract investment, create jobs, and alleviate its soaring rates of unemployment and poverty.

Before the North American Free Trade Agreement (NAFTA) eliminated tariffs on products traded among the United States, Mexico, and Canada, foreign companies established what was known as the maquiladora system in Mexico. Maquiladoras assembled electronics parts and precut garment pieces made in the United States or in other foreign factories that then entered the United States at low tariff rates. The companies leased or acquired land near the U.S. border at low prices and paid little or no local taxes. They had access to a constant supply of workers willing to work for low wages with few, if any, job benefits (Fernandez-Kelly 1983).

By the 1990s, over 500 maquiladora companies were employing more than half a million people. About 85 percent of those workers were young women with some, but low, education. About one-third of the workers were single parents and heads of households (Fernandez-Kelly 1997, 526). Women were favored as employees because of their willingness to do monotonous work, accept low wages, and follow orders. Men, in contrast, were not recruited as assembly-line workers because, quoting an electronics plant manager, "The man in Mexico is still the man. This kind of job is not doing much for his macho image. It's just a little quirk of a different culture. They'd rather run a factory" (Fuentes and Ehrenreich 1983, 30).

Since the beginning of the twenty-first century, economic changes due to NAFTA have eliminated many maquiladora jobs. Although the maquiladoras still employed more than 200,000 people in 2008, the economic downturn that began that year has resulted in the loss of more than 90,000 factory jobs in the Mexican city of Juárez alone, and even larger numbers of people are unemployed or underemployed because businesses that catered to the workers have also suffered (Kolenc 2008).

Because of widespread poverty in Mexico, young women, like the one shown here, have left their villages to work in maquiladora plants.
The Image Works/Jack Kurtz/The Image Works

The Mexican experience is just one example of a familiar pattern. Because of the prevailing landholding tradition in Latin America, young men tend to work on and inherit family lands. Peasant women whose families own little or no land may migrate to urban centers to seek jobs and relieve their families of the burdens of supporting them. Many of these young women initially work in domestic service, later leaving for other kinds of jobs or to marry and become housewives. In addition, both male and female migrants often work in the "informal sector," selling food, crafts, and other goods on the streets. Although most would prefer factory work, there are not enough jobs, which creates a marginal population who try to earn a living as best they can. Read the Document on myanthrolab.com

TABLE 3 U.S. FOREIGN-BORN POPULATION BY WORLD REGION, 2008	
Total	36, 961,000
Europe	4,919,000
Asia	10,356,000
Africa	1,436,000
Oceania	223,000
Latin America and Caribbean	20,150,000

Source: 2008 American Community Survey, U.S. Census Bureau, Place of Birth for the Foreign-Born Population, Table 42.

Transnational Migration

Watch the **Video:** *Migration: A Profile of the U.S.* on **myanthrolab.com**

International migration has had a profound effect on people in both the countries of origin and of settlement. Poor countries lose citizens to wealthier countries with better job opportunities. Although population loss might relieve economic burdens within a poor country in theory, many of the people who leave are among the better educated and more skilled in practice. Thus, the possibilities of economic recovery are undermined in their home countries. However, today's migrants often send a portion of their earnings back to their families, money that makes its way into the local and national economies. Still, the loss of people's skills, experience, and knowledge is more significant and has greater long-term effects than the loss of money alone. Table 3 tallies the foreign-born population in the United States in 2008 by region of origin. In addition to the foreign-born population, in 2009 the United States accepted 74,602 refugees and granted asylum to 22,119 people (U.S. Department of Homeland Security 2009, Refugees and Asylees, Table 44).

Listen to the **Audio:** *Iraq refugees Find Michigan is no Land of Plenty* on **myanthrolab.com**

Until the middle of the twentieth century, the vast majority of migrants were people leaving poor countries that had few jobs, particularly in the industrial sector, when manufacturing and service industries were concentrated in Europe, North America, and Japan. Many initially thought of themselves as temporary residents of their new countries, hoping to save enough money to return home and use their savings to live better. This goal was usually unfulfilled, however. Although the wages that they received were higher than what they could have expected at home, their cost of living was also greater

A call center in India. Alamy Limited/Fredrik Renander/Alamy

and far exceeded their ability to save. Although some eventually abandon their desire to return, they may face difficulties adjusting to the countries where they settle.

Some of these difficulties result from the marginalization of migrants within their new countries. They are often segregated in poor neighborhoods, a spatial division that dramatizes and reinforces their separation from the dominant society. Cultural differences of language, religion, and values also set them apart. Eventually, immigrants form "ethnic groups" based on markers of cultural identity, a process called ethnogenesis. Ethnic groups are also formed because of rejection from members of the dominant culture, creating "a generalized culture of ethnic inequality in which immigrants are perceived in stereotypical terms by the indigenous population, whatever their actual attributes, as a race apart, as primitives" (Worsley 1984, 239).

tribalization
A process of identification with one's tribal origins.

REVIEW

Migration patterns include international or transnational migration to escape persecution, war, or poverty; rural-to-urban migration in developing countries; and labor migration to take advantage of new economic opportunities. Refugee and immigrant groups affect the communities or countries they leave, as well as the ones they join. Often, they become tolerated but isolated ethnic minorities.

ETHNOGENESIS AND ETHNIC IDENTITIES

Ethnic identity is context-bound but changeable, an adaptation to circumstances. Although we may think of an ethnic identity as a single, stable concept, in fact, people can have various identities, depending on the way they see themselves in relation to others. Ethnic groups are formed and transformed in response to interactions with other people. As with other social identities, ethnic labels are applied as conditions arise that favor their use. People may think of themselves as members of groups based on one set of criteria but may find themselves categorized as members of other groups based on different criteria.

Group identity based on a political stance as well as an ethnic or tribal identity complicates social relations, even in comparatively homogeneous societies. An example is Papua New Guinea. Its colonial history began in the nineteenth century, when the British and the Germans divided the eastern portion of the island of New Guinea between themselves. (The western portion was formerly a Dutch colony, invaded and annexed by Indonesia in 1975.) At the end of World War I, the two colonial regions were united under Australian administration as Papua New Guinea, becoming an independent country in 1975. Although independence has led to some detribalization as the central government attempts to form a national identity, other factors led to **tribalization,** or the formation of tribal identities. One of the consequences of the competition for access to political power and economic benefits has been a resurgence of "tribal" warfare, especially in the highlands. Such warfare "has defined and redefined groups in such a way as to re-create, in part, an earlier tribal structure—a structure uncomfortably at odds with its own national government" (Strathern 1992, 232).

Even though government agencies have attempted to quell the fighting, people's respect for state authority has declined. Instead, local businessmen vie for economic advantages and political power, very much in the traditional model of the Melanesian "big men." These men attract armed fighters who support them and are in return protected by them. The central government occasionally sends in police and military patrols to keep order, but they are largely unsuccessful in eliminating violence.

Pakistani Brahmin immigrants to the United Kingdom who may think of themselves as white and as superior to dark-skinned South Indians are shocked to find out that the British may think of them as "black" or "coloured," in the same category as immigrants from the West Indies. Corbis/Michael Nicholson/ Corbis

CASE STUDY

Ethnic Identity in Sudan

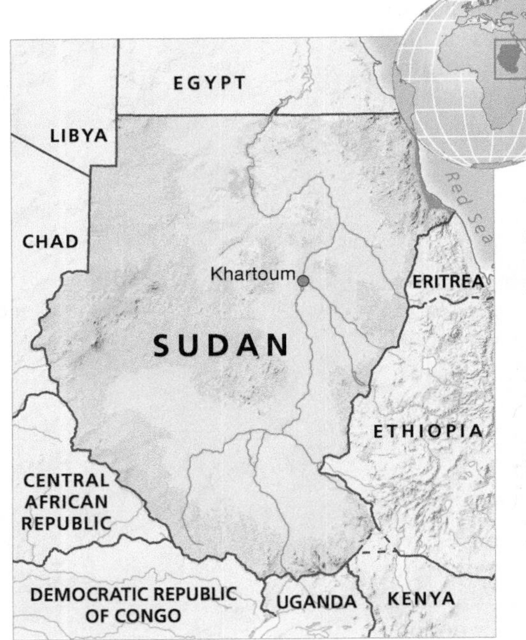

In a study of Sudanese agricultural production, Jay O'Brien (1986) details how ethnic identities were formed as different groups of people were incorporated into the work force. Their roles in production became linked to their ethnic identity. In the early 1900s, farmers and pastoralists began to work on plantations that produced cotton for export. These plantations were in what came to be known as the Gezira Scheme, a large area of irrigated fields. As elsewhere in the British Empire, indigenous people had to pay taxes in cash, but their sources for obtaining money were limited because they had few markets for their subsistence crops, and the importation of cheap manufactured goods undermined home craft production.

Sudanese farmers and pastoralists continued to maintain their traditional productive strategies but were available for seasonal work on the plantations when needed. They received wages but remained marginal actors in the new economy. Then, as the plantation system expanded, workers from other countries were recruited, especially Muslim Hausa from West Africa. These landless immigrants were a ready pool of cheap wage labor. Other West African Muslims also provided seasonal labor. They came from several ethnic groups and spoke different languages, although many learned Hausa as a second language (O'Brien 1986, 901).

Almost as soon as the immigrants arrived, distinctions developed between them and their indigenous coworkers. The immigrants came to be known as *Fellata,* a term with negative connotations that obliterated their own, separate tribal distinctions. In response to their new cultural environment, the West Africans adopted some outward traits of their Sudanese neighbors, especially styles of dress and housing. However, to differentiate themselves from the Sudanese, they also intensified some of their own cultural practices, emphasizing fundamentalist Islamic practices in contrast to the animistic beliefs in spirit possession and trance found among Arabs in North Africa. They began to apply the word *Takari* to themselves, a respectful term signifying "pilgrims." Although they replaced a negative term (Fellata) with a positive one, they essentially accepted the view of themselves as members of an ethnic group different from their hosts. Thus, they participated in the formation of an ethnic identity, initially imposed on them but then adopted as part of their self-definition.

A third group, the Joamas, were also incorporated into plantation production. The Joamas of central Sudan became known as efficient and hardworking cotton pickers. They earned a high reputation and a relatively stable income. Gradually, migrants from West Africa settled on the outskirts of Joama communities and were also hired as seasonal cotton pickers. By their own hard work and commitment to the region, they came to refer to themselves and to be referred to as *Joama.* They thus adopted an ethnic identity that was theirs only by assertion and lifestyle. It was an identity that they had to earn. **Read** the **Document** on **myanthrolab.com**

Transnationalism

transnationalism
Processes by which immigrants maintain social, economic, religious, and political ties to both their immigrant communities and their communities back home.

Although migrants adjust and adapt to their country of settlement, they all do not necessarily focus solely on developing their lives in their new environment. Rather, they also maintain emotional and cultural ties with their homeland. Because of increased ease of communication and travel, a new phenomenon of transnationalism is developing. **Transnationalism** is the constellation of "processes by which immigrants build social fields that link together their country of origin and their country of settlement, connecting them to two or more societies simultaneously" (Schiller, Basch, and Blanc-Szanton 1992, 1–2). Transmigrants maintain complex social, economic, religious, and political ties linking them to their immigrant communities and to their communities back home.

The Internet features many transnational sites like this one, which embraces all people with roots in India living anywhere in the world, including those who have become citizens of other countries.
HT Media Limited/HT Media Ltd.

Transnationalism has developed in the context of the spread of global capitalism that has shifted capital and labor across borders. As capital investments flow from high-wage countries to low-wage regions, labor shifts take place in both developed and developing countries. A transnational identity based on transnational commitments is a sensible and appropriate response to economic vulnerability and possible job displacement. In addition, transmigrants are important players in the creation of ethnic identities in their countries of settlement, forming connections among people who identify as a group on the basis of shared activities, values, beliefs, and goals.

Transnationalism is a phenomenon in which migrants create new sociocultural networks and identities for themselves that link their country of origin and their country of settlement. Although not new, transnationalism has redeveloped in the context of the spread of global capitalism, which has shifted populations across borders.

Nationalism and Pluralism

In addition to analyzing the ways that people create themselves as ethnic groups, anthropologists also look at the ways that ethnic groups are formed as structural features that support social, economic, and political systems. Ethnic groupings are especially significant in state societies composed of peoples of disparate origins and traditions. They are also "inherently political, shaped by and shaping the politics of 'us versus them' in political systems" (Ferguson and Whitehead 1992, 15).

At the same time, states also generate nationalistic views of themselves as overriding ethnic differences in the formation of a national identity. Peter Worsley describes nationalism as a form of ethnicity that is the "institutionalization of one particular ethnic identity by attaching it to the State" (1984, 247). Nationalism, though, is more than identifying with a state as a political institution. It is also an allegiance to the nation as a symbolic identity, as a people associated with a particular way of life and sets of values. As members of a state develop a national identity, they ignore their differences and concentrate on achieving commonly shared goals and interests. Nationalism also involves the process of selective memory and the construction of a fictive past, as the past is formulated according to contemporary values and goals. As Worsley points out, "They project the values of the present onto a past which does not always sustain them" (p. 274).

States utilize various processes to resolve relationships between a central identity and disparate ethnic groups. A dominant ethnic group may assert itself as the only legitimate identity, equating the national culture with its own. Also, a state may assert a uniformity of culture, subsuming and homogenizing differences. Finally, a state may maintain a pluralistic attitude toward cultural differences, allowing secondary identities to coexist along with a national one (Worsley 1984, 252).

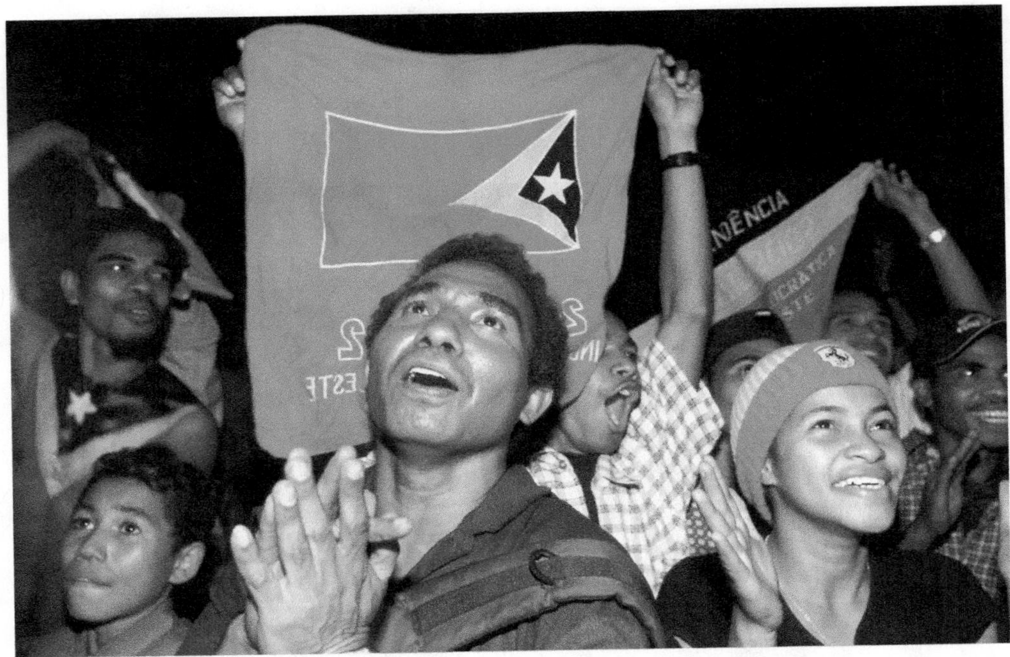

On May 20, 2002, these East Timorese celebrated their independence after twenty-four years of Indonesian rule and centuries of Portuguese colonization. Corbis/Reuters/Corbis

A state's strategies may change over time. A state often chooses a dominant identity as it embarks on consolidation and expansion, exerting control over its constituent populations. An emphasis on uniformity then becomes prominent as states become secure and attempt to eliminate ethnic boundaries. Recognition of cultural pluralism often emerges with the formation of ethnically diverse nation-states as older colonial empires crumble. The rise of ethnic pluralism, therefore, was often a product of decolonization, giving legitimacy to the strivings of disparate groups within a country for recognition and some degree of social and political autonomy. As in the past, however, newly independent states vary in the approaches that they take to ethnic diversity.

Islamization
The process of imposing the Islamic religion and associated cultural values within a nation to foster cultural uniformity.

CULTURE CHANGE

IMPACTS OF INDONESIAN STATE EXPANSION

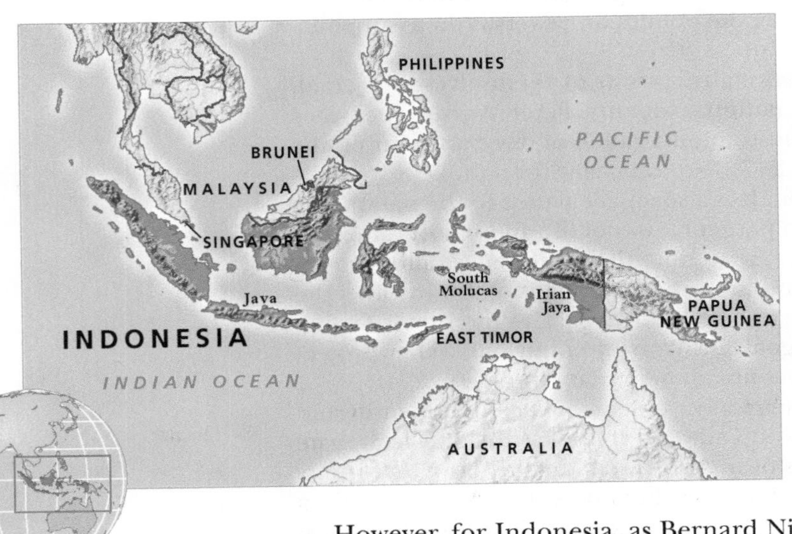

Indonesia is an instructive example of a central government's attempts to create a national identity that privileges one ethnic group, the Javanese, as the national norm (Perry 1996). Javanese cultural traditions are exported to other Indonesians through formal education, the media, and public discourse. Following a process of **Islamization,** Islam is imposed on others, either obliterating or subsuming local beliefs. A national language called Indonesian (based on a dialect of Malay) is taught throughout the country and is used in all public contexts. The Indonesian government has embarked on an aggressive policy of creating and imposing cultural uniformity while giving some recognition to ethnic diversity.

However, for Indonesia, as Bernard Nietschmann (1988) puts it, "nation-building" sometimes is state expansion by "nation-destroying." Authorities developed a program of forced internal migration, sending Javanese to outlying regions inhabited by tribal groups who, in turn, were sent to live elsewhere. The program of intense directed culture change is in the service of national unity. But it is also an attempt to wrest lands rich in resources from indigenous peoples. Multinational corporations allied with the state can then exploit the resources. The Indonesian policy is also aimed at dissipating indigenous resistance movements. The army is often deployed to indigenous territories, ostensibly to fight terrorism and insurgencies.

Just one year after Indonesia gained its independence from the Netherlands in 1949, the central government embarked on policies of state expansion by invading and annexing independent islands. In 1950, the army took over the South Moluccas, followed by the annexation of West Papua (renamed Irian Jaya) in 1962 and the invasion of East Timor in 1975.

In West Papua, the Indonesian government implemented its program of transmigration to "redistribute overpopulation" by importing 5 million people from Java (Nietschmann 1988). Indigenous peoples were displaced, and their lands and resources were appropriated to accelerate economic development and national unity. The region is especially rich in timber, minerals, and offshore oil. The World Bank, the United Nations, the Islamic Development Bank, and several countries, including the United States, Germany, France, and the Netherlands, helped finance the program. The government also established "assimilation camps," in which cultural minorities were taught the official national Indonesian language and Islam. These were also called "centers for social development," with the aim of "cultivating national pride and defending the state." People who resisted Indonesian political control and cultural hegemony were branded "terrorists," justifying military action against them.

The eastern half of the island of Timor became a battleground where the struggles of the indigenous East Timorese erupted in violence after decades of clandestine resistance. The Indonesian government had forced many East Timorese from their homes, transporting them to Sumatra and other majority Javanese islands while importing Javanese to East Timor. Between 1975 (when the Indonesian army invaded and unilaterally annexed East Timor) and 1990, an estimated 200,000 East Timorese (about one-third of the population) were killed. The international community ignored the situation until the 1990s, when world public opinion shifted to support independence for East Timor. In 2002, a referendum monitored by the United Nations resulted in independence, but East Timor still struggles with poverty, poor infrastructure, and political upheaval, all legacies of Indonesian colonial rule. Read the Document on myanthrolab.com

Genocide? The Case of Rwanda

Some postcolonial conflicts have centered on internal competition for power rather than independence from expanding new states. Conflicts in many countries in Africa, for example, are often portrayed as ethnic or tribal genocide, but they are more appropriately seen as struggles for power between groups with different interests and loyalties. The 1994 civil war in Rwanda that took the lives of some 800,000 people at first glance looks like a conflict between the majority Hutus (about four-fifths of the population) and the minority Tutsis (about one-fifth). In addition, about 1 percent or 2 percent of the population belongs to a tribal group called Twa, who are considered aboriginal and marginal to Rwandan society (Maybury-Lewis 1997, 100).

Although the Tutsis and Hutus are now thought of as ethnic groups, they represented political strata before Belgian colonial rule was established in 1916. The name *Tutsi* was applied to lineages that controlled wealth and chiefly power, whereas Hutu were lineages without wealth whose members formed a majority peasantry. Although the hierarchical system was relatively stable, particular individuals could rise or fall in status. If members of Tutsi lineages lost wealth and prestige, they would be considered Hutus, and Hutus who acquired wealth could become Tutsis. Hutus allied themselves as clients of particular Tutsi chiefs, giving political support and gaining protection.

During the colonial period, lasting until 1962, the Belgian government administered the territory through indirect rule, essentially using Tutsi chiefs as their surrogates. The chiefs who cooperated enhanced their power. Belgian policies led to an increased rigidity in the system of status and power, fomenting hostility between the Tutsi and Hutu "ethnic groups."

After independence, in 1962, the former Belgian colony split into two countries, Rwanda and Burundi. Civil wars in both countries ensued out of struggles for power. In Burundi, the Tutsi minority persevered and were able to hold on to their positions of power, but Hutu rebels maintained pressure on the Tutsi minority, and between 100,000 and 200,000 were killed in 1972. In Rwanda, the Hutu majority took control. Many Tutsis fled the country, forming a resistance movement with the aim of returning to Rwanda and regaining power. In 1993, after many years of conflict, the two sides agreed to form a coalition government in Rwanda. Then, a few months later, members of the Tutsi-dominated army assassinated the newly elected Hutu president of Burundi. As civil war erupted there, about 200,000 Hutus fled into Rwanda, where they joined anti-Tutsi militias that were trying to undermine the peace accords.

In 1994, on their way back from Tanzania to attend a United Nations–sponsored meeting discussing implementation of the agreements, the airplane carrying the presidents of both Rwanda and Burundi was shot down by still unknown assailants. At the news, Hutu militias in Rwanda began genocidal campaigns against Tutsis and moderate Hutus who advocated peace and accommodation, including the moderate Hutu prime minister and many other government officials. Estimates put the number of deaths at about 800,000. The Tutsi-controlled army finally defeated the Hutus, many of whom then fled into neighboring Zaire, where most still remain in refugee camps. These tragic events show the influence of policies that rigidify "collective identities ... [that are] reactivated, mythologized and manipulated for political advantage" (Lemarchand 1994, 31).

Although Rwandans directly caused the violence in the country, the historical roots of the conflict can be traced to the period of Belgian colonization. Belgian policies had and continue to have their legacy in creating and/or exacerbating tensions among different segments of the population.

In an attempt to avoid any future "ethnic" conflicts, the Rwandan constitution of 2002 forbids the description of people according to ethnic categories. While this seems like a progressive and conciliatory move, it leaves some marginalized groups without any public or legal means to self-identify and to seek redress for grievances. For example, the Batwa (a grouping of peoples, sometimes referred to as "Pygmies," living in several central African countries) face discrimination and a loss of traditional forest territories but, by law, cannot mobilize as a distinctive cultural group and their claims for land cannot be heard (Van Uitert 2009).

Reactions against Pluralism

Listen to the Audio: *Nicole Bacharan on Integration* on myanthrolab.com

In many Western countries, ethnic identities have become significant vehicles for the development, channeling, and recruitment of individuals for social and political action. This rise in cultural identities is coincident with large increases in immigration throughout the twentieth century. Perhaps the worldwide movement toward decolonization since the end of World War II is a contributing factor because it champions political and cultural independence and autonomy.

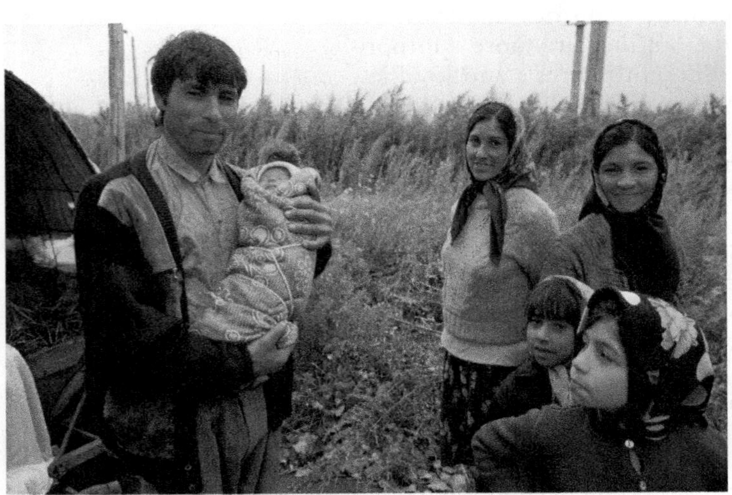

Ancestors of these nomadic Rom ("Gypsies") originated in northern India and were victims of xenophobia in every country they entered on their long-distance treks. Corbis/Barry Lewis/Corbis

In addition, large numbers of people immigrating from the same country or region are more likely to maintain ties among themselves. These bonds can create cohesion and solidarity that can be used to achieve social and political goals. They also allow immigrants to resist social and political pressures toward assimilation. For instance, the influx into the United States of people from Central and South America since the 1970s has led to the development of a strong power base wielding political influence both regionally and nationally. In Europe, the rise in immigration from the Caribbean, Africa, and South Asia has brought to the foreground issues of nationality and national identity. For example, the multiracial and multicultural makeup of the populations of the United Kingdom or France must redefine what it means to be "British" or "French."

Cultural pluralism is usually tolerated as long as members of disparate ethnic groups do not attempt to build political power blocs. However, at the same time as the complexion (both literally and figuratively) of American and European countries is changing, internal political movements opposing immigration have strengthened. Members of some anti-immigration movements claim that immigrants threaten national unity because they do not share prevailing heritage, values, and attitudes. These claims are based on a view of a nation that has been "mythologized and manipulated" for political purposes. In addition, a rise of xenophobic sentiments—the fear and hatred of out-groups—is stimulated by economic shifts and the perceived downward mobility of members of the middle and lower classes who then blame their misfortunes on the newcomers. Thus, xenophobia and anti-immigration movements are two common reactions to cultural pluralism. The contentious debates in the United States about federal and state immigration policies are reflections of these reactions. Although Congress has failed to act decisively to shape federal policy, in 2010, the state of Arizona passed legislation that allows law enforcement agencies greater latitude in questioning people about their immigration status and restricts the kinds of services permitted to people who are undocumented. Several other states passed similar laws in 2011.

Malaysia, Singapore, and Indonesia are examples of countries with complex histories that, in postcolonial times, have led to the establishment of multicultural societies (Hefner 2001). Prior to the European presence in Southeast Asia, these countries had a long history of maritime trade that brought in people from elsewhere, particularly from China and India. Ethnic differences were recognized, but people cooperated in the formation of pluralistic societies. However, the Dutch and the British treated the inhabitants as segregated groups to assert control and foster competition for access to influence and rewards. When the countries became independent in the mid-twentieth century, their constituent ethnic groups then vied for control of the newly emerging states. Competition for the benefits of economic development programs contributed to intergroup tensions.

In Malaysia and Indonesia, social and political distinctions were maintained between indigenous peoples and the ethnic Chinese, descended from merchants who prospered from trade even before European colonial powers came to dominate the region. However, treatment of the Chinese differs in Malaysia and Indonesia. In Malaysia, the Chinese have been permitted to send their children to Chinese-language schools if they wish to maintain their culture. Still, Malaysian political parties are organized along ethnic lines and, although pluralism is part of the social and political fabric of society, ethnic Malays have ascendancy over people of Chinese, Indian, and other origin. Also, although religious differences are protected, Islam is the state religion of Malaysia. In Indonesia, however, the Chinese have faced discrimination despite official statements of ethnic inclusion and pluralism. Cultural and religious distinctions are used to promote Javanese interests and claims to power over those of the Chinese and other groups.

Globalization and Cultural Identities

Anthropologists and other social scientists have been studying the global marketplace as a kind of borderless society. The shared beliefs, values, expectations, and behaviors of members of this society constitute a global culture. This culture has emerged as a result of rapid changes in technology and the political and economic process known as globalization. Researchers seek to make sense of what may be called a global culture of consumerism.

Globalization is popularly thought of as an economic and cultural process that spreads wealth and investment throughout the world. However, as in the past, wealth and investment are concentrated regionally and in the hands of elites. Today, much of the world's wealth comes from Europe and the United States, but investment increasingly goes elsewhere, such as Asia and the Pacific Rim. European companies account for twenty-one of the world's fifty largest corporations; the rest are Asian (Friedman 1999). Since the 1960s, the centers of manufacturing have shifted to Japan and other Asian countries, particularly Hong Kong, Taiwan, Korea, and China. The United States has been a major importer of goods from these and other countries (Friedman 1999, 187–88).

A Global Identity?

These economic shifts have contributed to what some theorists see as the re-creation of an international or **global identity** based on social class. That is, in North America and Europe, regions that Jonathan Friedman (1999) calls "declining hegemonies," members of elite classes have a global identity that links them to elites in other countries on the basis of class. Characteristics include sharing privileges, interests, leisure activities, locations, and tastes. This global identity is different from the global popular culture in which the world's middle classes increasingly participate, in which they eat food from

global identity
An identity of shared interests, practices, and values across international borders, uniting people worldwide.

McDonald's, watch the same movies, listen to the same music, discuss the same topics on the Internet, and buy the same books and other consumer goods.

A global identity has developed as middle and lower classes have tended to fragment along ethnic lines, with groups asserting their own interests. In addition, the power of the state to "manufacture consent" (to use the term from Herman and Chomsky [1988]) and to create and transmit a national identity tends to decline as the nation's economic and political elites focus their activities elsewhere. At the same time, immigrants tend to remain identified with their countries of origin or with emigrants residing in other countries. Thus, some theorists see both a rise in ethnic pluralism and an increasing gap between the classes as major factors in the process of globalization and the invention of a global identity.

The mass media contribute to, and reflect, a growing global identity. People throughout the world watch many of the same movies and television programs, listen to much of the same music, and read the same magazines translated into dozens of languages. These sources of information and entertainment disseminate people's activities, attitudes, and tastes, contributing to shared experiences and frames of reference. Although there are and will continue to be local variations, the media provide outlets for creating global identities. The Internet is also a powerful and increasingly utilized forum through which people in many countries can communicate, learn from one another, and share ideas. The global spread of the English language, now the most common second language of the world, facilitates this exchange. Although English will presumably continue to be the world's dominant international language for some time to come, other languages have begun to challenge its role in personal communication. For example, in 1990, an estimated 75 percent of all mail and 80 percent of computer data sent worldwide were written in English (Baron 1990). However, by 2008, the dominance of English on the Internet was being challenged by that of Chinese: English was employed by 29.4 percent of all Internet users, whereas 18.9 percent used Chinese (Internet World Statistics 2008). Rounding out the top five Internet languages are Spanish, Japanese, and French, although these three combined for slightly less than 20 percent. In all, the top ten Internet languages accounted for 84.9 percent of all Internet users, leaving all of the other thousands of languages spoken in the world with only 15.1 percent of user share.

REVIEW

Ethnogenesis involves a group's creation of a new ethnic identity through both self-definition and definition by other groups. Proliferating identities can lead to tribalization rather than national unity. In transnationalism, however, groups identify across nationalities, based on their shared country or culture of origin. Nationalism calls for minimizing differences to achieve national rather than group unity and loyalty. In pluralistic or culturally diverse societies, ethnic minorities may become marginalized or forced to conform to majority culture. Ethnic minorities, like immigrant groups, are also often victims of xenophobic reactions against outsiders, and conflicts between groups based on their cultural identities can lead to genocide. A global identity may be developing, based on social class.

CULTURAL MINORITIES IN A GLOBAL WORLD

Are you or any of your friends members of cultural minorities or indigenous peoples?

The mid- and late twentieth century saw a revitalization of indigenous communities in many countries and a new energy and focus in their struggles for self-determination. An estimated half of the world's conflicts are now fought over lands and resources of foragers, horticulturalists, and pastoralists (Nietschmann 1988). The term *indigenous* refers to peoples who self-identify as members of a defined group, who share the same culture, and are "native" to their territory or have occupied it for a long time. Defining who is indigenous is a complex matter, however, and depends also on historical and cultural contexts. In countries with a history as a settler colony (the United States, Canada, Australia, New Zealand, and Mexico, and all the countries of modern Central and South America), the term *indigenous* refers to the peoples who lived in these regions prior to the arrival of Europeans, beginning in the late fifteenth century. In these countries, descendants of the original settlers and later immigrants now dominate.

Watch the **Video:** *American Indian Testimony about Assimilation* on **myanthrolab.com**

State policies toward indigenous peoples vary considerably in the Western Hemisphere. In the United States and Canada, treaties were negotiated between colonial powers and indigenous peoples, guaranteeing some rights to land and certain rights to limited forms of sovereignty. However, in both countries, federal governments are empowered to override treaty rights in some circumstances, despite the fact that the treaties were legally ratified agreements backed by the force of international law. It should be noted that the U.S. and Canadian governments are "empowered" by their own laws or constitutions. That is, they unilaterally grant themselves the power to break treaties without the consent of the peoples affected. The following sections survey the state of indigenous peoples in the Americas and Africa.

United States and Canada

In the United States and Canada, the federal governments recognize the sovereignty of native tribes (or First Nations, as they are called in Canada), although the people's exercise of sovereignty is limited either by federal law or by judicial rulings. In each country, the specific history of treaty signing and of legislation affecting native peoples varies, but the general trends are similar. Since the 1960s, native peoples in both countries have won important advances in their quest for sovereign powers.

The U.S. Congress passed the Indian Self-Determination and Education Assistance Act in 1975, establishing principles of self-government for native reservations. Indian tribes have used these principles to broaden their claims of sovereignty and to extend tribal jurisdiction in planning and implementing educational, medical, and social services, as well as to gain control over their territories, economic development plans, and tax immunity.

Do you think native people living and working on reservations should not have to pay taxes? Why or why not?

Tax immunity is a critical issue for native peoples in both Canada and the United States. The concept refers to the fact that Indian lands are immune, not exempt, from all forms of state, provincial, or federal taxation. This means that Indians living on reservations do not pay property taxes, sales taxes on goods purchased on the reservation, or income tax on wages earned on reservations. The tax-immune status of reservations has become especially contentious in New York State since 1997, when the state government first attempted to collect sales taxes on gasoline and cigarettes sold to nonnative people by Native Americans at reservation stores. Because of objections by the native governments, the state delayed its move until 2003, two years after the terrorist attacks of September 11, 2001, in New York City caused a sharp decline in state revenues. Then, New York Governor George Pataki again announced his plan to impose sales taxes on goods purchased by nonnative people from stores on reservations. In 2004, the state legislature authorized collection of those taxes, but in a reversal, Pataki vetoed the bill. Subsequent administrations and legislatures again reinstated the plan to collect taxes, but the actual implementation has now been postponed until sometime in 2011.

Congress has dealt several times with the issue of Native American religious practices. In 1978, it passed the American Indian Religious Freedom Act, extending protection for Native Americans to "believe, express, and exercise" their traditional religions, granting access to sacred sites and objects, and guaranteeing rights to perform ceremonies. Subsequently, the Native American Religious Freedom Restoration Act of 1993 furthered these protections, with an added amendment in 1994 that specifically protects the use of peyote in religious services. The Restoration Act itself has been declared unconstitutional by the U.S. Supreme Court, but the Court has not ruled on the amendments.

Although most economic activities of native tribes are not specifically addressed by legislation, Congress has enacted laws dealing with casino gambling on Native American reservations. The Indian Gaming Regulatory Act of 1988 sets standards for gambling on reservations and requires agreements between tribes and their state governments that stipulate the kinds of gaming permitted and the percentage of revenues that the tribes agree to give to the states.

Some thirty years after the Florida Seminoles opened the first tribal bingo hall in 1981, there are currently 442 casinos operated by 237 tribal governments in 28 states (some governments operate more than one casino). Native people in Canada operate other casinos. In 2009, the total U.S. tribal government gross revenue from gaming amounted to $26.2 billion (National Indian Gaming Association 2010). Although casinos run by Native Americans account for a mere 5 percent of gambling revenue in the United States, one of the most lucrative is Foxwoods, owned by the Pequots in eastern Connecticut (*American Indian Report* 1999). With more than 11,000 employees, they are one of the ten largest employers in the state. Their profits, amounting to about $1 billion a year, have been invested in reinvigorating their community and the surrounding area. They have built new housing and roads and provide job training, scholarships, and health services to tribal members. The casino and its accompanying resort generate additional income for nearby hotels, restaurants, and stores (Harvey 1996). This pattern holds true for casinos throughout the country. In the rest of the United States, approximately 628,000 jobs have been created through Indian gaming both in the casinos and in support services and businesses that provide goods, meals, and other amenities to casino workers and patrons. Nationwide, Native Americans held 25 percent of these jobs, whereas people of other races and ethnicities held 75 percent (National Indian Gaming Association 2010). Therefore, nonnative people, both as workers and as owners of businesses catering to casino customers, profit as much or more from Indian gaming as do Native Americans.

In addition, Native American casinos generate $9.4 billion in federal taxes and government revenue savings as well as $2.4 billion in state taxes and revenue sharing profits agreed upon by compacts between tribes and the states in which they are located.

Most of the net profits realized by casino gambling is spent on projects and services in Native communities and also in nearby locations. According to the National Indian Gaming Association report in 2010, revenues were expended in the following categories: 20 percent for education, child care, elder care, cultural endeavors, and charity gifts; 19 percent for economic developments; 17 percent for health care; 17 percent for police and fire protection; 16 percent for infrastructure improvements; and 11 percent for housing.

The presence of a casino can boost income for all residents of an area, but it can also bring changes to the community that not all residents desire. The work that casinos create tends to be low-wage jobs with little future. Some people do not approve of gambling on moral grounds or because of its historical connection with organized crime.

The courts have been the major site of contestation between Native American tribes and federal and state governments over issues of sovereignty and jurisdiction. Since the statutes do not specify the exact scope of Native American sovereignty, tribes use the courts to expand their jurisdictions while federal and state governments attempt to limit Native American sovereignty. The courts have also been asked to deal with specific issues resulting from the historical relationships between tribes and the federal government. A major victory for Native American litigants came in December 2010 with settlement of the landmark *Cobell v. Salazar* trust fund case, originally filed in 1996 by Elouise Cobell, a member of the Blackfeet Nation in Montana, as a class-action suit. The suit charged that royalty payments due to some 300,000 individual Indians for their lands that were leased to non-Indians for farming, ranching, and mining had been mismanaged since the 1800s. According to the settlement, ratified by Congress and signed by President Barak Obama as the Claims Resolution Act of 2010, a total of $1.5 billion will be divided among the plaintiff class, with many probably receiving about $2,000 each (*Indian Country Today* 2010).

Despite some legal victories and economic improvements, native peoples still lag behind other Americans in employment, income, and educational attainment. For example, data from the federal American Community Survey of Selected Population Profiles for 2004 (released in 2007) revealed that the median household income for American Indians was $31,605, as compared to the figure for white Americans, which was $48,784. Poverty rates also indicate the comparative disadvantage of native peoples. Some 24.6 percent of American Indians live below the poverty level, nearly three times the poverty rate of white Americans (8.8 percent). Finally, 23.4 percent of native people aged 25 or older do not complete high school, compared to 11.4 percent of whites; and only 14.2 percent of American Indians completed college, less than half the rate for white Americans (29.7 percent).

In the state of Hawaii, some Native Hawaiians are asking for recognition of their claims to ancestral territories and their desire to have a legal status somewhat comparable to that of Native Americans living in the other forty-nine states. In 1978, the state created an Office of Hawaiian Affairs with responsibility for administering 1.8 million acres of royal land held in trust for Native Hawaiians. This land was exempt from annexation when Hawaii became a state. The office collects revenues generated by the natural resources, minerals, and use of these lands for the benefit of Native Hawaiians. It also formulates policies regarding social, economic, and health services applicable to native people.

In Canada, the Constitution Act of 1982 included a short section that affirmed the existing rights of the country's aboriginal peoples. Subsequently, both the federal and provincial governments concluded numerous government-to-government agreements with native reserves covering and expanding indigenous control over health, education, and social services, as well as economic development. By calling these "government-to-government agreements," the Canadian government implicitly recognizes sovereign rights of First Nations (the term used in Canada to refer to indigenous peoples). However, as in the United States, residents of native reserves lag far behind the general population in every social, health, and economic statistic. Indicators of living conditions, such as the quality of housing, electricity, sewage systems, and roads, are generally poor or nonexistent. The quality of schools and the level of educational attainment for reserve children are much below national averages. Life expectancy, poverty rates, employment rates, and income statistics all indicate the comparative disadvantage of indigenous peoples.

For example, data from the 2006 Canadian census document an employment rate for aboriginal people of 53.8 percent compared to the non-aboriginal population of 62.7 percent. The aboriginal unemployment rate stood at more than double the rate for non-aboriginal people (14.8 percent compared to 6.3 percent). High levels of unemployment among First Nations result in low incomes. Divided into income groups, the percentage of aboriginal families with relatively low annual income averages exceeds that of the non-aboriginal family population, whereas at the higher income levels, aboriginal families are underrepresented. Specifically, 1.44 percent of aboriginal families had annual incomes of less than $2,000, while a smaller percentage (0.89%) of non-aboriginal families had such low incomes. The figures for additional groupings are: $2,000 to $9,999: 24.29 percent of aboriginal families and 10.01 percent of non-aboriginal families; $10,000 to $49,999: 66.59 percent of aboriginal families and 63.82 percent of non-aboriginal families; $50,000 to $74,999: 5.82 percent of aboriginal families and 16.40 percent of non-aboriginal families; $75,000 and higher: 1.86 percent of aboriginal families and 8.88 percent of non-aboriginal families. Finally, levels of educational attainment differ in the two Canadian populations. In the following list of educational attainment, the first number represents the percentage of the aboriginal population, while the second number represents the percentage of the non-aboriginal population: less than high school graduation (42.7 percent; 30.8 percent); high school graduation only (11.1 percent; 14.2 percent); trades diploma (12.2 percent; 10.8 percent); college diploma (13.6 percent; 15.1 percent); university degree (6.4 percent; 15.8 percent); master's degree (0.9 percent; 2.8 percent); and doctorate (0.2 percent; 0.6 percent).

Recently in Canada, attention has been drawn to the poor quality of education and of living conditions in boarding schools operated from the 1880s until the 1980s under the auspices of the federal government by church groups, especially Anglican, Presbyterian, and Roman Catholic churches. At first, attendance at the schools was voluntary, but in 1920 it became mandatory. Tens of thousands of children were forcibly removed from their home communities and sent hundreds, sometimes thousands of miles to be kept in the boarding schools all year long until they reached 18 years of age. Testimonies from former students of many of these schools document not only the inadequate education that they received, but also the physical and psychological abuses to which they were exposed. Children were punished with beatings for any supposedly bad behavior or even for speaking their own native languages. And many were subjected to sexual abuse ranging from molestation to rape.

After many years of advocacy by First Nations and their supporters, the Canadian government agreed to a settlement of reparations for survivors of the boarding schools, currently estimated to number about 80,000 out of the 150,000 children who attended the schools (*Indian Country Today* 2011, vol. 1, no. 5, 17). This settlement includes $1.9 billion Canadian to be awarded to students, $60 million to establish a truth and reconciliation commission to collect testimony and educate the public about the schools, $20 million for a program of commemoration, and $125 million for an Aboriginal Healing Foundation to provide psychological services for survivors. Each former student is scheduled to receive $10,000 for the first year that they spent in the schools and $3,000 for each subsequent year, with average estimated payments of $30,000 (Cherrington 2007, 18).

Finally, land claims cases in both the U.S. and Canada continue to be of paramount importance, enlarging reservation territory and establishing indigenous rights to self-government. Recent settlements in both Canada and the United States usually stipulate some degree of sovereign native control over economic, social, and cultural policies. Hundreds of cases are pending, with outcomes most likely to be decided in the first few decades of the twenty-first century. Some analysts expect large amounts of land and monies to be transferred to native sovereignty, especially in Canada. According to Canadian government estimates, settlements of more than 210 claims may give First Nations control over about 10 percent of the country, an increase from the current native land base of 0.3 percent (Brooke 1999). In the United States, native peoples now control about 2 percent

CONTROVERSIES

Who "Owns" the Past? NAGPRA and American Anthropology

In the past century, anthropologists and archaeologists have contributed to the "cultural dispossession" of Native Americans. Archaeologists could excavate sites without permission on the grounds of scientific interest alone. Some collected artifacts and human remains for study without much concern for their relationship to present-day native peoples in the region, and a few looted those sites for sales to collectors. Despite successive migrations, artifacts and remains found in an area could belong to ancestors of living people. This is especially true for finds from recent eras.

Native Americans have spoken out against the desecration of Indian burial grounds. According to Walter and Roger Echohawk, Native Americans have had to witness the destruction of their burial grounds and removal of the remains of their ancestors (Echohawk and Echohawk 1994). In 1989, for example, an "Indian burial pit" was opened in Salina, Kansas, displaying skeletons as a tourist attraction.

In 1979, Congress passed the Archaeological Resources and Protection Act of 1979, which required the consent of a Native American tribe before archaeologists could get a federal permit to excavate on or remove material from tribal lands. In 1990, Congress passed the Native American Graves Protection and Repatriation Act (NAGPRA), which requires that skeletal remains and certain cultural items uncovered on federal or tribal land must be returned to the nation concerned upon request, including materials uncovered at construction sites. In addition, human remains, sacred objects, and other artifacts of "cultural patrimony" held in museums receiving federal funds must be returned to the appropriate tribal group, if requested.

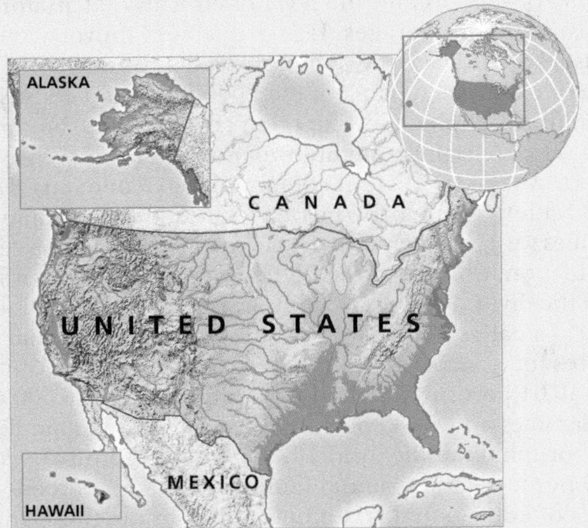

NAGPRA also requires that any group or individual making a claim first satisfy federal officials that they are part of a recognized Native American group. Then they must demonstrate "cultural affiliation" with the people whose objects or remains they are claiming. The law defines cultural affiliation as "a relationship of shared group identity that can be reasonably traced historically or prehistorically between a present-day Indian tribe and an identifiable earlier group." Thus, the older the objects or remains are, the harder it is to establish an unambiguous affiliation between them and a present-day group.

Some of the fiercest controversies generated by the law involve objects thousands of years old. In 2004, courts upheld

of the country's territory. The increase in their land base is not expected to be very great because monetary compensation settlements are more the norm in the United States.

Mexico and *Indigenismo*

The Mexican government, like several others in South America, has vacillated in its policies toward indigenous peoples throughout its history since independence from Spain in 1821. At times, some indigenous peoples had recognized rights to land that they held communally, but these rights were often ignored and the state appropriated indigenous land at other times. At various periods in the last century, Mexican intellectuals and officials embraced the concept of *mestizaje,* or the construction of a mestizo population. This concept was championed especially by Jose Vasconcelos, an educator and government official in the early twentieth century. Vasconselos' treatise on the subject, *The Cosmic Race* (1997/1925), discussed the development of the mestizo from a mixture of indigenous and Spanish roots. This mixture was championed as the proud foundation of the Mexican identity. However, it was to the ancient Aztec Empire that Mexican officials looked for their Indian roots, thus excluding the many indigenous peoples who were members of farming or foraging societies lacking the dramatic history and power of the Aztecs. And the twentieth-century descendents of all indigenous groups, whether they had Aztecan or other ancestries, continued to be ignored because of their poverty and supposed backwardness.

the right of scientists to study skeletal remains excavated from a riverbed in Kennewick, Washington. These remains are nearly 10,000 years old, far too early in the history of occupation of North America for any present-day native group to be able to claim them.

The desire of Native American groups to reclaim masks, figurines, and other ritual paraphernalia is an expression of their sense of the sacred. Under NAGPRA's provisions, once a tribe gains possession, it may keep or dispose of the item as it sees fit. Between 1978 and 1992, the Zunis repatriated sixty-nine wooden sacred figures from museums, art galleries, and collectors (Merrill, Ladd, and Ferguson 1993), including two of their most sacred wooden sculptures, Twin War Gods, from the Smithsonian Institution in Washington, DC. The War Gods have subsequently been used in ceremonies that expose them to the elements. As a result, they will eventually decompose, a natural process in keeping with Zuni practices.

NAGPRA is a federal statute and therefore sets guidelines for federal actions. Many states have their own regulations describing the kinds of archaeological excavations allowed and the processes that archaeologists must follow in order to gain permission to excavate any area under state jurisdiction. In addition, many Native tribal governments have their own procedures for determining and supervising the kinds of research activities permitted on their lands. Some have archaeologists working directly for the tribe involved in research projects.

The archaeological community has not been uniformly in favor of NAGPRA. Although most archaeological associations support the moral principles underlying the act, many argue about the law's effects on research and the discovery of knowledge. The clash between the native and archaeological communities reveals underlying tensions and differences in perspectives on science and the past. By letting their War Gods deteriorate through use and exposure, for example, the Zunis are asserting the precedence of their ethical and religious claims on the sculptures over the scientific and aesthetic claims of scholars who want them preserved as art objects and objects of study. Similarly, groups that rebury remains of their ancestors assert the priority of their beliefs over whatever knowledge further study of those remains might have revealed. Even when impoverished groups sell repatriated objects, they are disposing of them as they see fit (Killhefer 1995).

Many archaeologists and anthropologists have begun to confront their own status as privileged experts who, until recently, framed the discourse about the past and ownership of cultural artifacts in terms that suited their needs for research. Many welcome the opportunity to rethink their assumptions. As archaeologist Tamara Bray noted, "We must acknowledge that archeology, like all other social and natural sciences, is legitimately subject to criticism on the level of 'values,' not just 'facts'" (1996, 444). According to anthropologist T. J. Ferguson, despite restrictions and loss of research materials, archeologists may find "new opportunities available . . . if they work in partnership with Native Americans" (1996, 64).

CRITICAL THINKING QUESTIONS

Should archaeologists be able to examine cultural, even skeletal, remains from Native American archaeological sites? Why or why not? What "new opportunities" do you think researchers may find in working with Native Americans?

Whenever new governments took control and Mexican constitutions were rewritten, changes in policies toward indigenous peoples were included. Finally, the constitution of 1993 acknowledged rights of indigenous peoples in a policy known as *indigenismo,* which guarantees protection of native customs. However, the actual living conditions of native peoples have not improved, particularly in the southernmost state of Chiapas with its majority Mayan population. There, some indigenous people maintain their traditional land-use patterns, holding their land communally in *ejidos.* Others had been forced off their land by intruding settlers and multinational companies. Some retreated farther into the highlands, where they cleared new farmland, many growing coffee for sale and export.

In the early 1990s, the Mexican government embarked on policies to exploit its vast oil deposits. As an adjunct to this strategy, the government abandoned its stated intentions to grant additional indigenous groups the right to their communal *ejidos.* The government also eliminated price supports to small farmers, another policy that harmed the Mayan farmers of Chiapas. As well, the government allowed wealthy ranchers to expand their holdings, buying up the land of poor farmers. In addition, public projects to develop and generate electricity from hydropower led to the flooding of indigenous lands. Finally, the Mexican government has begun to develop biodiversity projects, concluding agreements with pharmaceutical companies for the exploitation of forests and plants for research into the manufacture of drugs. As a result of these policies,

After decades of conflict, Zapatistas have gained international support for their struggle to gain autonomy in their region of Mexico. The Image Works/ Josh Reynolds/The Image Works

Mayans often become landless wage workers, but their wages are so low that they need to maintain links to strong family networks in traditional communities to survive (Barreda and Cecena 1998).

Mayans suffer discrimination because they have become a cultural minority within their traditional territories. They are outnumbered by Ladino settlers whose incomes and levels of education far exceed those of the Mayans. The Ladinos—an ethnic term for Mexicans with an appearance, language, and identity that are more Spanish than Indian—feel justified in their negative attitudes toward the Mayans, because the indigenous people are poor and lack the education or job skills that would suit them for the modern sector. But the Indians' poverty is a result, not a cause, of their marginalization.

The issue of indigenous rights in Mexico became nationally and internationally visible because of the efforts of a group of Mayans in Chiapas to mobilize for their collective rights in land and resources. Their organization, called the Zapatista Army for National Liberation (named after the Mexican revolutionary leader Emiliano Zapata), burst upon the world scene on January 1, 1994. On this date, they took up arms against the Mexican military, a move that was timed to coincide with the implementation of the North American Free Trade Agreement (NAFTA) signed by the United States, Canada, and Mexico.

During the crisis that followed the insurrection of January 1994, the army entered their territory and attempted to arrest their leaders and squelch the resistance. However, the government softened its approach because of the media publicity that drew attention to the conflict, generating generally positive support from the international community. The government then agreed to enter into negotiations with the Zapatistas to settle some of these issues without further violence. However, the government has not yet agreed to anything other than minor concessions.

The Zapatistas have been particularly effective in utilizing sophisticated communication technologies, especially the Internet, to publicize their movement and to forge alliances with other indigenous and marginalized groups striving for social, economic, and political justice. They have used these communication channels to gain international support.

Brazil and the "Indian Problem"

Due to the establishment of plantations by the Portuguese in the seventeenth century, the immigration of many Portuguese and Spanish settlers, and the importation of millions of African slaves, the indigenous population of Brazil is relatively small, currently about 300,000 people, only 0.2 percent of the total population. Estimates of the number of inhabitants in 1500 range from 1 million to 6 million. Although enormous population losses occurred in the early centuries of European colonization, about one hundred indigenous nations disappeared in the first seventy years of the twentieth century (Ribeiro 1971). Most remaining indigenous communities are located in isolated regions in the Amazon. They are generally small settlements, each consisting of a few hundred residents.

Brazil's policies toward its indigenous peoples have wavered between protecting native lands and cultures and allowing intrusions into native territories by ranchers, settlers, and multinational corporations exploiting their resources. Earlier in the twentieth century, the Brazilian government had established a federal agency to protect Indian rights to maintain their lands and their cultures. The agency was to be guided by the motto of "Die if need be, but never kill" (quoted in Maybury-Lewis 1997, 22). In the 1960s, however, the government changed course and instituted aggressive efforts to develop remote regions. Settlers and ranchers took this as permission to go into indigenous territories and either push out or kill the residents. Although the government did not officially condone their actions, it did little to stop them. In fact, it permitted cattle ranchers in particular to invade the region in large numbers and clear the forests for their herds.

Guarani Indians in Paraguay and Brazil today focus on establishing strong communities based on village life. This Guarani Indian family rides a horse-drawn cart on one of the ranches they reclaimed as ancestral land.
Corbis/Andrew Hay/Reuters/Corbis

Operation Amazonia. In a program called Operation Amazonia, the Brazilian government granted tax credits and exempted companies from paying import or export duties. By 1980, more than $1 billion had been invested in cattle ranching in the Brazilian Amazon (Schmink 1988, 168). Forest timber and minerals, especially tin, copper, uranium, iron, gold, and diamonds, are found in rich deposits as well. Finally, Brazil and the other countries that share the Amazon have recently attracted investment in biodiversity projects. Of the estimated 500,000 species of plants currently existing in the world, about 16 percent (35,000 to 50,000 species) are located in the Amazon (Tyler 1996, 7). Brazil in particular is home to about 22 percent of the world's "higher" plant species, as well as about 24 percent of primate species and between 10 million and 15 million species of insects (Elisabetsky 1996, 405).

To develop these resources, the Brazilian government has set aside some fourteen "extractive reserves," together containing more than 49 million acres of land (Barrionuevo 2008, 14). These reserves are defined as "forest areas inhabited by extractive populations granted long-term usufruct rights to forest resources which they collectively manage" (Elisabetsky 1996, 403). The term *extractive populations* refers to rubber tappers, miners, timber workers, and settlers, but the territories set aside are often also claimed by indigenous peoples, groups whose use of the land is not protected. Instead of protecting Indians' interests in their resources, officials drew up policies aimed at "civilizing" them, attempting to solve the "Indian problem" through assimilation, with the hope of eventually phasing out the government's national Indian Service, which oversees native land.

Brazil's "Operation Amazonia" was a direct response to the global economy and the globalization of industries that exploit natural resources. To encourage economic development, this government program granted tax credits to foreign companies and exempted them from paying import or export duties.

However, despite the efforts of the Brazilian government to assimilate Indian nations, formerly unknown communities of indigenous peoples are "discovered" from time to time. In 1999, a group known as the Korubu was found deep in the Amazonian region of northwestern Brazil, near the borders with Colombia and Peru. Brazilian officials have documented at least fifty sites of Indian habitation that were previously unknown (Schemo 1999). When new groups are found, authorities working for the National Indian Foundation (FUNAI) attempt to have further contact by placing tools, utensils, and clothing in forest clearings. This is done on the assumption that the Indians will continue to return to the clearings to obtain more goods and can eventually be convinced to leave the region or settle in supervised communities. Lands claimed by indigenous peoples can then be opened for development of their timber, mineral, and pharmaceutical resources.

Yanomami at Risk. Because of pressure exerted on the Brazilian government by indigenous peoples and their advocates, a number of reservations have been set aside where lands are under indigenous control and given government protection. The largest of these, and, indeed, the largest indigenous reservation in the world, is an area of 20.5 million square acres inhabited by some 23,000 Yanomamis, the largest indigenous nation in the Amazon (Schemo 1999, 72).

Traditional Yanomami territory had been made vulnerable in the early 1980s, when the Brazilian government permitted road construction cutting through their lands. Although the road was never completed, the initial projects brought a number of deadly diseases to the people, including measles, influenza, and malaria. These diseases killed many hundreds of Yanomamis, decimating 90 percent of some communities (Gorman 1991). The government also conducted aerial surveys that revealed valuable deposits of gold, tin, and radioactive materials.

As an anthropologist, to what extent do you think you would get involved in the political, economic, or medical problems or struggles of the people you were studying? What ethical dilemmas would you face in deciding this question?

In particular, gold has brought about 50,000 miners to the region. They have illegally built some 120 airstrips hidden in the jungle and dammed dozens of rivers to obtain water pressure to make prospecting easier. In addition, the use of mercury in gold prospecting has polluted many of the rivers, contaminating the fish that Yanomamis eat, in turn leading to birth defects and nerve disorders (ibid.). New waves of epidemic diseases have stricken the communities. In addition, the miners killed hundreds of people, burned their houses, and destroyed forestland (Wiessner 1999, 77).

Infringements on their lands, the spread of diseases, and competition over resources had the further effect of creating or exacerbating internal conflicts between neighboring Yanomami settlements and within the communities as well (Ferguson 1992). Therefore, what might look to an outsider like endemic warfare was actually, at least in part, a response to turmoil caused by external forces.

The plight of the Yanomamis came to international public awareness in 1987, when four Yanomamis and one miner were killed in a clash (Gorman 1991). Brazilian authorities then drew up plans to reduce the size of Yanomami lands, giving the Indians nineteen separate "islands of habitation" and creating state parks and national forests in which gold mining was permitted. However, an indigenous advocacy group called Survival International brought a lawsuit to the Brazilian High Court, which ruled the government's plan to be unconstitutional and instead ordered the expulsion of the gold miners. In the following year, the government reached a compromise that would return most of the confiscated land to the Yanomamis, keeping about 3,000 square miles for mining operations.

The establishment of reservations throughout Brazil grants the Indians their rights to control their own destinies, living according to their own cultural norms and absorbing as much external influences as they choose. However, despite the intentions of FUNAI, ranchers and resource developers continue to encroach on Indian lands. They often operate in remote regions far from contact with government officials. In addition, although reservation lands are formally protected, most have unclear and unmarked boundaries, making it difficult for Indians to assert claims over particular acreage. So far, about 80 percent of the lands in Brazil officially defined as indigenous territory have been mapped, although even their boundaries are vulnerable to encroachment by settlers, miners, and resource companies (Wiessner 1999, 79). These territories amount to approximately 12 percent of Brazil's total land and about 21 percent of the Amazonian region (Barrionuevo 2008, 14).

Indians of the Brazilian Savanna

Not as widely known as the Amazon, Brazil has another vast region that is home to many indigenous peoples. This is the Cerrado, or savanna, an area encompassing some 800,000 square miles (about one-third of Brazil's land mass) of rolling hills and grasslands that was until recently little exploited by Brazilian or international companies but has now attracted economic, particularly agricultural, investment. As elsewhere, the search for arable land has disturbed the territories and lives of many peoples, numbering an estimated 53,000 people belonging to 42 different groups (Graham 2009, 28). Some groups, such as the Xavante, live in lands that have been formally demarcated and legally allotted to them, while others live in territories not officially designated. For all peoples, though, the spread of agricultural plantations, especially for soy, sugarcane, and eucalyptus, has destabilized the region. In addition to land under cultivation, numerous roads have been constructed through native lands, hydroelectric dams have been built, and rivers have been transformed, altering the very landscape and resources that indigenous peoples have depended on for centuries. In addition, illegal operations of ranchers and loggers further destroy the environment.

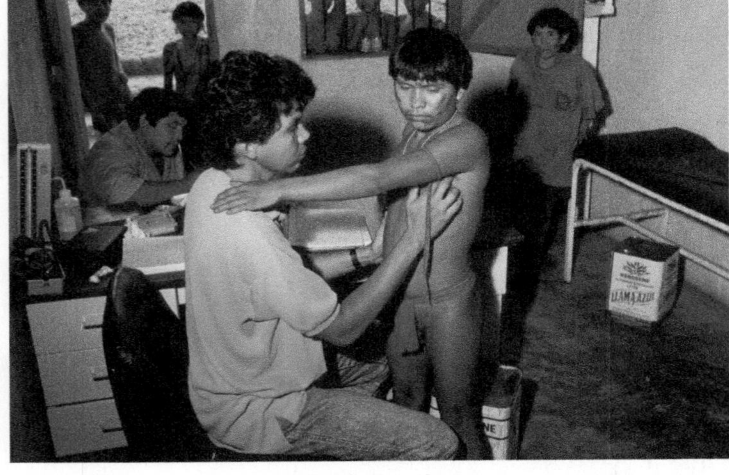

In 1991, Brazil established a protected reservation in Yanomami territory. Here, a Brazilian doctor aids the Yanomami. Getty Images/Eco Images/Getty Images

Brazil's "Urban Indians." In addition to the indigenous communities officially recognized by the Brazilian government, many more self-identified Indian people live in small villages, towns, and cities throughout the country, even in the densely settled northeast. Some estimates suggest that urban Indians account for about one-quarter of Brazil's Indian population (Warren 2001, 16). And their numbers are increasing. In Brazil, as in the United States and Canada, the number of people who self-identify as Indian has steadily risen in the last several decades. Part of the increase can be explained on the basis of natural growth, but the numbers far exceed that process. Most of the increase results from the easing of people's reluctance to identify themselves as indigenous because of prevailing racism and social stigma.

Many Indians living in rural or urban settings are oriented toward indigenous traditions that have been transformed or destroyed over the past five centuries. Still, they "define indigenous ancestral roots as essential to [their] identity, to make them the anchor of [their] dreams and future, and to work toward their recovery" (Warren 2001, 21). They have an orientation that is "post-traditional" in the sense that they look to traditions but also mold and adapt these traditions in a way that is meaningful today. And many face negative attitudes held in Brazilian society toward Indians and Indianness. Some are denied social recognition as Indians because they are the products of racial mixtures, and their appearance, therefore, does not conform to stereotypical images of Indians. Their behavior similarly combines practices and attitudes of their multiple ancestries. However, although they recognize their complex past, they gravitate most toward their Indian identity. They feel most comfortable associating with other Indians, living in Indian communities or neighborhoods, and decorating their homes with symbols of their indigenous heritage (Warren 2001, 254–59).

Brazilian Indians and their supporters are active in forming organizations that advocate for their lands and their rights. Some of these organizations are backed and funded by members of the Catholic clergy, espousing "liberation theology," which looks to the church to ally itself with the struggles of indigenous and other poor people who are fighting for social, economic, and political justice (Ramos 1997). Although they do not represent the dominant or mainstream church, they do constitute a vocal and active faction. In addition, Brazilian Indians forge alliances among themselves, as well as with other indigenous peoples in South, Central, and North America, learning from one another's experiences and working together to accomplish their common goals.

"Uncontacted Tribes" in the Amazon

According to some estimates, there are between 80 to 90 indigenous tribes living in the Amazon region that have had very limited, if any, direct contact with outsiders, including government authorities, loggers, or other resource extraction workers (Dudenhoefer 2011, 27). These peoples live in small autonomous villages in Brazil, Peru, and Ecuador. Some are horticulturalists, while others are foragers. The largest concentration of such groups is in Brazil near the border with Peru, where an estimated eight tribes, numbering approximately 4,000 people, reside. Some of the groups previously did have contact with non-natives but then subsequently moved deeper into the forests in order to avoid any more interactions. The several countries involved have differing policies regarding these groups. In Brazil, the government's official stance is to prevent unwanted contact and to respect the people's rights to their lands, resources, and voluntary isolation. However, logging companies and independent farmers and settlers continue to encroach on indigenous territory.

In Ecuador and Peru, isolated tribes face similar threats to their lands and lives. While officially issuing policies that respect indigenous claims, in accordance with international agreements, the governments do little or nothing to stop mining, logging, and oil extraction companies from entering native territories and exploiting their resources. These inroads sometimes lead to violent clashes, with injuries and deaths on both sides. But as Eduardo Pichilingue, a former employee of the Ecuadorian Environment Ministry, remarked, "When somebody from the outside dies, the media cover it, and we know their name. When an isolated Indian dies, there is nobody to protest or go to the media. The jungle swallows those dead" (quoted in Dudenhoefer 2011, 29).

In addition to these dangers, isolated indigenous peoples in the Amazon are threatened by the spread of newly introduced diseases, especially measles and influenza, to which they have no resistance or immunity. As has happened elsewhere in the Americas since the beginning of European contact, many natives have succumbed. For example, the Harakmbut, a tribe living in Peru, experienced a sharp population decline since the 1950s, when their numbers were estimated by missionaries to be about 10,000, falling to approximately 3,000 currently as the result of several waves of epidemics in their communities.

Costs of Economic Development in Ecuador and Bolivia

Do you think the indigenous people of Ecuador have the right to block oil drilling on their property? How would you resolve the conflict of interest in this situation?

Indigenous peoples in Ecuador and Bolivia are in the forefront of movements to organize opposition to government policies that encroach on their lands, harm their environments, and destroy their cultures. Both countries have a majority population of indigenous people; some are the descendants of powerful and complex societies, while others are horticultural or foraging peoples. Today, indigenous territories are the targets of oil exploration and extraction. In Ecuador, for example, the government is focusing on oil as the basis of its projected economic development. Ecuador has the largest petroleum reserves in Latin America, equal to those of Mexico and Nigeria (Forero 2003). Most of the oil is located in remote areas of the Amazon inhabited primarily by indigenous communities. Many of these communities oppose the oil companies because of the environmental pollution and destruction that follow oil drilling and pipelines, interfering with the people's ability to maintain traditional economies that rely on horticulture and foraging. In addition, the people do not receive monetary benefits from the resources because profits from the oil are rarely reinvested in their communities. Instead, the resources benefit wealthy investors and consumers elsewhere in Ecuador, as well as in foreign countries.

Indians have organized protests against government policy and have also occasionally sabotaged the drilling equipment and pipelines. The Ecuadorian government responded by sending military patrols to protect oil company gear and personnel. In addition, representatives of the indigenous Kichwa, Achuar, and Shuar have sent delegations to the capital at Quito and to meetings of the Organization of American States and of petroleum company shareholders. They have also forged coalitions with environmental groups. They have filed lawsuits against giant petroleum companies such as Texaco, suing for compensation for damages to the environment, especially leakage of black sludge into rivers, destroying the waterways (Taxin 2003). The government of Ecuador has promised aid to those communities that permit oil development. However, although some indigenous people favor the development, hoping that they will reap economic benefits, the majority opposes petroleum extraction. As a result of the instability in the Amazon, major foreign companies have been reluctant to invest in the region.

In Bolivia, indigenous peoples led protests against government policies in 2003, which eventually led to the resignation of the president, Gonzalo Sanchez de Lozada (Rohter 2003). In 2005, they organized protests calling for nationalizing oil and gas resources. The proportion of indigenous peoples in Bolivia is the highest in all of South America, constituting about 60 percent of the total population. Since the 1980s, Indians in Bolivia have gained recognition of their rights to land, obtaining ownership of 1 million hectares of territory in the Andes. In 1994, an addendum to the Bolivian constitution officially designated the country as a "multiethnic, pluricultural society" (p. 84). However, despite favorable political and legal status, indigenous peoples occupy the lowest stratum economically and socially.

Indigenous activism in Bolivia continued to affect national and international policies. Then, in December 2005, an indigenous socialist candidate, Evo Morales, was elected president in a landslide victory. He is an Aymara Indian, with close ties to native communities. Coming to office with a reformist agenda, Morales embarked on policies to nationalize some gas and oil industries and to redistribute wealth to aid the overwhelmingly poor indigenous and nonindigenous sectors of society in a country where 60 percent of the residents are indigenous and 70 percent are living in poverty (Chavez 2006). Morales promised not to interfere with property rights of land under production but pledged to redistribute nonproductive land to landless farmers. By 2011, his government had moved to implement these promises by redistributing publicly owned land and confiscating some acreage from large plantations that was not being used, most of which lies in the eastern lowlands of Bolivia. In addition, landless people in the Andean western highlands are being encouraged to resettle in the east on the newly available acreage (Shariari 2011). Although controversial both in Bolivia and abroad, many of Morales's policies have galvanized political participation among the poor and indigenous populations.

Developments in Africa

The situation for indigenous peoples in Africa shares some similarities with, and yet differences from, that of peoples in North and South America. Most European colonial efforts in Africa did not include large numbers of settlers. Therefore, in contemporary Africa, the delineation of who is "indigenous" or "tribal" is more complex than in the settler colonies of the Americas and Australia. After former colonies gained their independence, the new countries developed policies that affected various groups within their borders. In general, members of large and powerful groups came to dominate the governments and benefited from political, economic, and social policies, whereas members of small, isolated groups received far fewer advantages. In many cases, they remain marginalized in their own countries and face various forms of discrimination and control. These factors are reflected in various definitions of "indigenous" proposed by scholars of international law. However, a consensus summary states the following:

> Indigenous communities are best conceived of as peoples traditionally regarded, and self-defined, as descendants of the original inhabitants of lands with which they share a strong, often spiritual bond. These peoples are, and desire to be, culturally, socially and/or economically distinct from the dominant groups in society, at the hands of which they have suffered, in past or present, a pervasive pattern of subjugation, marginalization, dispossession, exclusion and discrimination. (Wiessner 1999, 115)

Central governments in the East African countries of Sudan, Kenya, and Tanzania have continued colonial policies aimed at encouraging or forcing nomadic pastoral societies to become sedentary farmers or wage workers. Colonial and postcolonial governments prefer sedentary citizens because they are more easily supervised and controlled. In addition, nomadic pastoralists rely on large tracts of land to graze their animals. Gaining access to these lands allows national governments to proceed with economic development projects. Also, the governments often phrase their policies in terms of building national unity through cultural uniformity. In some cases, pastoralists are forced to change their economic systems by the unilateral confiscation of their territory. For example, in the 1970s, the Sudanese government undertook the construction of canals on the Nile River that would control flooding but disrupted the traditional economies of the Dinkas, cattle pastoralists of southern Sudan (Lako 1988).

Sudan and the Dinka. The Dinkas rely on floodwaters to irrigate pastureland for their cattle, but the Sudanese authorities claim that such use of water is wasteful. Instead, the government diverts floodwaters for the use of farmers and urban dwellers in the populous northern Sudan. These choices have political implications as well because Sudanese society is split between the predominantly Muslim north and the predominantly Christian south. The two regions are frequently at odds, a conflict that periodically erupts in sectarian violence. The government's plan was to build the Jonglei Canal at a part of the Nile that is in the heart of Dinka territory. They claimed that the Dinkas would benefit from the changes as the people became incorporated into the modern economy. The authorities tried to convince the Dinkas that they would be able to maintain their cattle as sedentary ranchers rather than as nomadic pastoralists. They held out the promise of health care, educational services, and agricultural training as incentives to living in stable villages. In response to Dinkas' complaints that the canal would disrupt animal migration routes, the government established crossing points on the canal. However, the crossing points created a further problem because animals would be concentrated in these areas, leading to depletion of resources through heavy use. In addition, the amount of fish available to the Dinkas would be diminished, curtailing an important source of food.

Given their awareness of the potential negative effects, most Dinkas feared the loss of their traditional way of life. Although they objected to the presence of the canal in their territory, opposition was relatively weak, and a minority of canal supporters consisting mainly of traders, businessmen, and civil servants proved to be more vocal. The Jonglei

Canal project uncovered latent class distinctions and contrasts in class interests in Dinka society. Many Dinkas were forced to move, although they did receive some financial compensation.

Sudan and Darfur. Since 2003, a civil war in the southern Sudan has resulted in what the United Nations has termed "violations of international humanitarian and human rights law." After many years of economic and political neglect, factions from several African tribes in the Darfur region, especially the Zaghawa, Massalit, and Fur, took up arms against the central Sudanese government in an attempt to establish autonomy or independence. In response, the government has fought on two fronts, first by sending military units against the rebels, especially using air campaigns, and second by supporting Arab-dominated militias, called the Janjaweed (from an Arabic term meaning "horse and gun") to terrorize civilians. Hundreds of villages have been destroyed and the residents either killed or forced to flee. In 2004, the United Nations Security Council demanded that the Sudanese government disarm the Janjaweed militias and allow humanitarian aid to reach the civilian population. However, the Sudanese government has not heeded the United Nations demands and continues to deny the severity of the conflict and its own support of the Janjaweed militias. According to United Nations data, corroborated by other international sources, at least 200,000 people had been killed in Darfur by the end of 2007, and at least 2.5 million (out of a total Darfur population of 6 million) were made homeless (CNN 2008). Many of these victims have fled, often seeking shelter in refugee camps in neighboring Chad. People unable to leave Darfur are victims of attacks, rapes, and destruction of their meager subsistence base.

The media and public discourse have tended to portray the conflict in Darfur as the result of ethnic divisions, but economic inequalities and social discrimination have also led to policies by the Sudanese government that are more complex than ethnic tensions. Disputes over valuable resources have also contributed to these conflicts.

In 2005, the United Nations brokered a peace treaty between the Sudanese government based in the north and leaders of the Sudan People's Liberation Movement (SPLM) in the south, ending nearly 40 years of civil war that took the lives of an estimated 2.5 million people. This treaty led to a referendum in the south on January 9, 2011, to decide the region's status. Some 98.8 percent of the voters (with a voter turnout rate of 97.6 percent) chose to secede and establish an independent nation, South Sudan, that came into being in July 2011 (http://southernsudan2011.com). There are many difficult economic and political issues to be resolved. For example, 80 percent of the oil in Sudanese territory is located in the south but the pipeline delivering this oil to international markets runs through the north to Port Sudan on the Red Sea, leading to the Suez Canal and the Mediterranean to the north and the Indian Ocean to the south. Currently, despite the fact that the majority of the oil is located in the south, 52 percent of oil revenues go to the north while 48 percent remains in the south. This imbalance in revenues is one of the major economic issues to be renegotiated. Leaders of SPLM assert that they will no longer agree to revenue sharing but instead will pay a fee to use the pipeline to Port Sudan. In addition, compared to the north, South Sudan lacks adequate infrastructure, schools, and health clinics. There are only fifty miles of paved roads in the region.

Kenya and Tanzania: The Maasai and the Barabaig. The Maasai, a group of fourteen independent tribal entities of about 375,000 people, have seen their grazing lands in Kenya and Tanzania decreased, first by actions of British and German colonial authorities and then by postcolonial governments. In the early nineteenth century, European settlers encroached on Maasai lands, taking about half of their acreage (Fratkin and Wu 1997). Then, in the mid-twentieth century, the Kenyan and Tanzanian governments took additional land to create wildlife parks and reserves. In addition, the Maasai have lost grazing territories to small-scale independent farmers and large-scale corporate estates. Governments and international funding sources claim that the Maasai and other pastoralists are inefficient utilizers of the land, which could be better used for producing cash crops and commercial beef (ibid.). In Tanzania, Maasai grazing lands have been confiscated to make way for commercial rice farms and irrigation projects.

However, the Maasai are no longer willing to see their way of life deteriorate. In Kenya, the Loita Maasai have organized the Loita Naimina Enkiyio Conservation Trust

In Their Own VOICES

Viktor Kaisiepo on the International Decade of the World's Indigenous People

In this excerpt, Viktor Kaisiepo, a Papuan activist and member of the Presidium Dewan Papua (an organization of indigenous people in Papua), reflects on some of the goals and accomplishments of indigenous people involved in activities related to the International Decade of the World's Indigenous People (1994–2004), declared by the United Nations. Kaisiepo assesses the gains indigenous peoples made during that decade.

Sometimes I wish I were a carpenter, because if I were a carpenter, at the end of two or three days I could say, "Here's a chair." But in the field of human rights how do you measure success? Some people feel empowered by being part of the U.N. process, and others say, well I've been here 10 years but still nothing has changed. So there has been a huge progress when you look back over the years. Let me put it this way: If I am a member of the liberation movement, 22 years down the road I'm still occupied. Is that success? Is that failure? According to my own objectives it is a failure because I am still occupied, but in terms of building international networks and support I've gained a lot. Like I said, when you throw the stone in the Pacific Ocean, one day down the road the waves will come to the shore. So, I think, the people that are here, they will gain a lot of experience, a lot of knowledge.

I don't think this first International Decade of the World's Indigenous People will be a clear indicator of the success of the indigenous movement, but during this decade we will have accumulated a lot of information, and generated a lot of interaction. The best way to see whether there are big results or not is to wait for the second decade. Whether it's declared a second International Decade by the United Nations or not, the results of the first International Decade will be seen in the next 10 years. Some people become involved in the beginning, some a quarter of the way down the road, some halfway down the road, some three quarters down the road.

You need capacity-building processes for indigenous peoples. Do I understand my rights properly; do I understand the mechanisms made available to me? How do I utilize them, when am I supposed to utilize them, and whom do I have to address? When people come to the United Nations, they think, well, when I address them, that's the end of the story. No, it's the beginning of the story. Things are changing for the better and you must appreciate that. When you meet moments like we did, in 1993, when we asked for the establishment of the Permanent Forum, and in 2002 it was established—within 10 years—then that is a great success. And you have to celebrate it.

The United Nations has declared a Second International Decade of the World's Indigenous People (2005–2015).

From: Viktor Kaisiepo, "We've Gained a Lot," *Cultural Survival Quarterly* 28(3) (Fall 2004), pp. 19–20.

CRITICAL THINKING QUESTIONS

According to Kaisiepo, what gains have indigenous peoples made? What still needs to be done?

to help protect their legal rights to lands in Narok County against a plan to turn some of their acreage into a wildlife reserve that would include the construction of roads and a hotel for tourists.

In Tanzania, the Barabaigs, a group of cattle pastoralists numbering about 30,000, are fighting government and private projects that will turn much of their land into commercial wheat farms. In an important decision, the Tanzanian High Court supported the Barabaigs' suit on the basis of customary use rights. However, the decision was overturned in 1986, after the government filed an appeal on the grounds that not all of the plaintiffs in the case were "native" according to official definitions, because some were not indigenous Barabaigs but instead were descendants of Somali immigrants.

The Kenyan and Tanzanian governments took thousands of square miles of land from the Maasai when they created one of the world's largest and most visited wildlife reserves and national parks. When the British originally established the Serengeti National Park in 1929, the Maasai lost resource-rich grazing and farming territory. In response to protests, the British granted the tribes access to the nearby Ngorongoro Conservation Area (NCA). However, by 1975, the Kenyan government prohibited farming in the NCA, even though Maasais had come to rely on maize as a necessary supplement to their shrinking herds. Malnutrition is becoming an increasingly serious problem. Restrictions on access to lands now turned into game parks have also created and exacerbated intertribal tensions as various groups compete for scarcer territories and resources.

What do you predict for the future of pastoralism as a mode of human subsistence?

Nigeria and the Ogoni. Indigenous lands are confiscated elsewhere in Africa so that economic development can proceed apace. For example, the Nigerian government has granted licenses to the Shell Oil Company for drilling on land claimed by the Ogonis, a group of about 500,000 people (Beveridge 2003, 9). Most of the oil drilled in Nigeria is located in Ogoni territory, land that has been harmed by toxic emissions and oil leakages from ruptured pipelines. A group of eight Ogoni activists and one of their supporters, the internationally known writer Ken Saro-Wiwa, were arrested, charged with murder, and executed in 1995, despite vigorous protests from the United Nations and from many countries in the world.

Biodiversity prospecting is becoming big business in parts of Africa, as in Asia and the Pacific (Reid et al. 1996). However, the issue of ownership is a contentious problem in many countries (Iwu 1996). Africa, for example, is rich in plants and animals containing medicinal properties that could be used to treat many ailments. A research project in Nigeria identified several plants that could be used for the treatment of viral infections, and other agents that have antiparasitic, antiplaque, and antifungal properties, as well as a greaseless body oil (Iwu 1996, 243). Management of these and other resources is complicated by competing needs. Conservation of biodiversity resources is critical to their continuation but, at the same time, the intense poverty many Africans suffer drives the governments to allow rapid harvesting even though this policy threatens future supplies.

REVIEW

In the United States, issues have centered on indigenous peoples' control of land and resources and gaming, while in Canada, efforts have also focused on achieving sovereignty. In Mexico, the policy of *indigenismo* has granted rights to natives, but cultural minorities continue to struggle for independence. South American governments vacillate between protecting indigenous peoples and exploiting the natural resources in their homelands. In Africa, pastoralists struggle to retain grazing land, while people try to keep commercial oil interests at bay.

LEGAL RIGHTS AND INTERNATIONAL RECOGNITION

To protect themselves and their lands, indigenous peoples have formed coalitions to place their concerns on the agendas of international organizations. In the international forum, the question of who is "indigenous" becomes politically and legally significant. Self-identification and community cohesiveness are some of the relevant factors. However, historical changes, migrations of individuals and groups, and intermarriage with members of other communities blur identities and social cohesion. In 1993, a United Nations working group proposed a Draft Declaration on the Rights of Indigenous Peoples that contains forty-five articles outlining international recognition of their rights. Among these are the right to self-determination (to determine their political status and identity), to maintain their cultures, and to be protected from genocide, ethnocide (cultural genocide), or forced relocation. In addition, the document recognizes indigenous peoples' right to practice, develop, and teach their traditions, histories, languages, and religions. They have the right of access to all forms of media, and they are protected in their rights to fully participate in the development of policies and decisions that affect them through their own chosen representatives. Fourteen years after it was first introduced, the Declaration on the Rights of Indigenous Peoples was finally passed by the United Nations General Assembly in 2007. The resolution to accept the Declaration won overwhelming international support. However, four countries voted against the Declaration: the United States, Canada, Australia, and New Zealand. There were eleven abstentions. Significantly, the four countries voting in opposition are all the historical descendants of settler colonies, each having a history of violence toward its indigenous peoples and of policies aimed at eradicating these peoples and their cultures. Then in 2009, the Australian government reversed its initial position and endorsed the UN Declaration, followed shortly by New Zealand. In 2010, the government of Canada issued a statement "in support" of the Declaration and the United States similarly stated that it "lends its support to" the Declaration, but neither government has yet to formally register its vote in favor of the international document.

CASE STUDY

Papua New Guinea's Customary Law

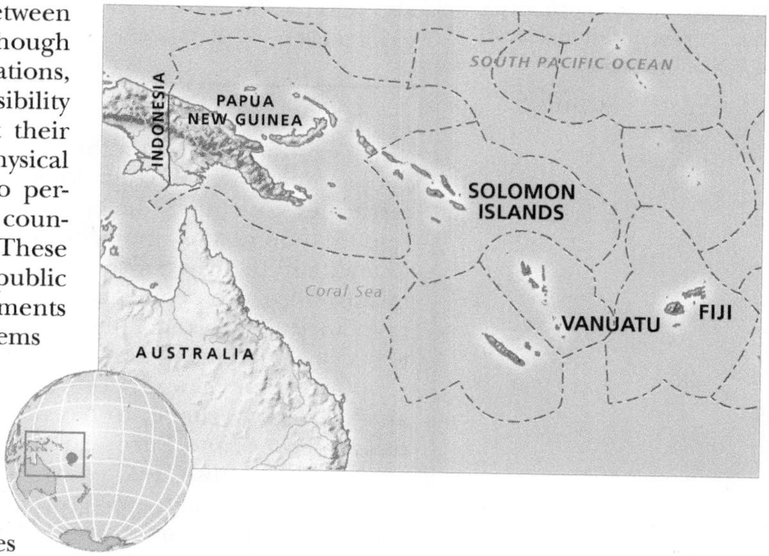

Legal practice in Papua New Guinea has vacillated between formal jurisprudence and customary procedures. Although the country consists of numerous and diverse populations, the traditions of most communities stress the responsibility of kin groups to redress wrongs committed against their members, either by demanding compensation or by physical retaliation against the perpetrators. People resort to personal redress with or without the approval of informal councils who hear complaints and attempt reconciliation. These councils have no coercive authority, only the force of public opinion. Kinship groups may try to facilitate agreements through negotiation and compromise to resolve problems and reconstitute social harmony.

SOUTH PACIFIC OCEAN
INDONESIA
PAPUA NEW GUINEA
SOLOMON ISLANDS
Coral Sea
VANUATU
FIJI
AUSTRALIA

During most of the colonial period, British and, later, Australian authorities did not recognize customary practices in state legal settings. The adversarial system of due process was imposed through the courts and the laws. In the villages, away from official view, people continued seeking to resolve disputes through traditional means, either by consulting village councils or by calling on their kinship groups to act as mediators. In the 1960s, colonial jurisprudence began to accept defenses or reduce sentences based on customary practices and attitudes.

The courts nevertheless regarded customary law as illegitimate, a product of the "primitive culture and environment of the accused, which made it impossible for the accused to understand and accept Australian values" (Ottley and Zorn 1983, 265). For example, people accused of assault, manslaughter, or murder might claim that cultural expectations led them to commit the offense after the victim had provoked them. If the accused were members of a remote community where traditional practices and attitudes prevailed, they might be acquitted or receive light sentences. However, if the accused were, in the court's judgment, sufficiently assimilated, cultural defenses might not be accepted.

In addition, the Australian Supreme Court denied defenses based on retaliation for sorcery, even though beliefs in sorcery are widespread in Papua New Guinea. The court did not acknowledge that Papuans consider a belief in sorcery to be "reasonable" but imposed its own cultural and legal standards. The court would allow Australian defendants, but not Papuans, to plead insanity for killing someone they believed was a sorcerer. In the court's opinion, "In Papua New Guinea, although most people believe in sorcery, and most sane people do so, no reasonable person would" (Ottley and Zorn 1983, 276).

Following independence in 1975, the Papua New Guinea Law Reform Commission formulated a system of law emphasizing customary law consistent with traditional principles of conflict resolution (Ottley and Zorn 1983). These principles were based on provisions of the new constitution that aimed to legitimate customary practices where possible. However, customary principles and procedures have only been marginally and inconsistently incorporated into the country's legal system. The Supreme Court has relied heavily on colonial statutes in cases involving customary practices. For example, the court ruled unconstitutional a statute called the Inter-Group Fighting Act, passed in 1973, in response to a perceived escalation of fighting in tribal areas. That statute was consistent with customary attitudes that hold each member of a group responsible for the actions of the group as a whole. The act was aimed at limiting fighting by permitting the legal system to punish all members of a group engaged in fighting, even though each person may not have been involved in a particular incident. In declaring the act to be unconstitutional, the Supreme Court referred to the Western tradition of individual responsibility rather than the Papuan tradition of collective responsibility for criminal acts. The court also continues to base its judgments on rulings made before independence, again impeding the establishment of customary law.

The actions of the Papua New Guinea courts highlight resistance to custom as a legitimate source of judicial and political processes. This resistance suggests the desire of the

customary international law Traditional practices of dispute and conflict resolution, involving mechanisms for mediation and negotiation and principles for punishment or restoration of community relations.

state to retain control over competing local interests. Central control and consistency are impossible if communities have their own mechanisms of solving disputes and punishing wrongdoers. The post-independence government is also concerned with establishing a national identity distinct from its colonial past and with attracting foreign investment. It also sees customary law not as an aspect of society that is uniquely Papuan but as a threat to its power. Read the Document on myanthrolab.com

In economic spheres, the United Nations Declaration on the Rights of Indigenous Peoples guarantees the right to own and control "the total environment of their traditional territories," including the conservation, development, and protection of their lands and resources. In politics, indigenous peoples have the right to autonomy or self-government, to maintain their own systems of justice and conflict resolution, to maintain "traditional relationships with peoples across international borders," and to protect their rights agreed in treaties. Finally, the United Nations is charged with creating a special indigenous body to oversee implementation of the Declaration of the Rights of Indigenous Peoples.

International law supports the claims of indigenous peoples to their lands, resources, and cultural heritage. In North America, treaties signed between representatives of native peoples and European or American colonial powers have the force of international law. Because treaties are documents signed by sovereign countries, they either explicitly or implicitly recognize the basic sovereignty of native nations. The fact that subsequent governments in the United States and Canada have unilaterally abrogated provisions of these treaties does not alter the underlying principles of international law.

However, in most countries, treaties were never signed between governments and native populations. Therefore, the rights of indigenous peoples rest on other principles, especially on the principle of **customary international law.** Customary rights include the right to respect traditional lands; to maintain languages and cultural practices; to obtain welfare, health, educational, and social services; and the right to self-determination (Wiessner 1999, 98–99). Indigenous peoples, therefore, have both individual rights and collective rights that need to be protected by international organizations as well as by domestic laws. However, domestic laws often fail to capture the spirit and intent of native customs.

Recognizing their relatively low numbers worldwide and the low priority that their interests have within their own countries, indigenous peoples are increasingly seeking to establish alliances among themselves to exert more pressure on national and international policies. For example, representatives of hundreds of indigenous groups from eleven countries of Latin America met in 2008, to establish the International Alliance of Forest Peoples, aimed at having a voice in international climate change policy. Their meeting, also attended by representatives from Indonesia and Africa, proposed the establishment of a fund donated by wealthy countries (principally the United States and Europe) that would pay developing countries for not cutting down trees in forestlands such as the Amazon (Barrionuevo 2008, 14.).

REVIEW

To protect themselves and their lands, indigenous peoples have formed transnational coalitions to place their concerns on the agendas of international agencies and nongovernmental organizations. International law supports the claims of indigenous peoples to their lands, resources, and cultural heritage, as well as to basic human rights. The legal systems of newly independent countries, however, tend to be based on colonial rather than customary law.

CLIMATE CHANGE AND INDIGENOUS PEOPLES

Climate change affects and will affect all people living on this planet. Rising temperatures, fluctuating rain and drought cycles, and alterations in food growth patterns will force adaptations on a global scale. The United Nations predicts that some 575 million people worldwide will lose their homes due to the effects of climate change. Furthermore, the United Nations and other international agencies also predict that climate change will have an especially rapid and harmful impact on indigenous societies. First, indigenous peoples often have subsistence adaptations that make them vulnerable to changes in weather patterns affecting the growth of plants and the migratory movements of animals that the people depend on for survival. Second, indigenous societies are often located in territories that are likely to be negatively affected by changes in temperature, rainfall, deforestation, and rising sea levels. These territories include the Arctic, forest regions, desert or semi-desert lands, and coastal areas. Indeed, these are the very regions that have remained available for indigenous peoples because they either lack resources or present particular difficulties for permanent habitation or intensive subsistence activities. And third, because of the political and social marginalization of indigenous peoples in the countries in which they live, their needs are not likely to be seriously considered and their predicament is not likely to be ameliorated quickly.

But members of indigenous societies are not simply waiting to be affected by climate change. They are suggesting solutions on a local level based on their intimate knowledge of environmental conditions developed over centuries of their experiences in their ancestral territories.

In 2008, the United Nations Permanent Forum on Indigenous Issues held a conference on "Indigenous Peoples and Climate Change" in Copenhagen, Denmark, to explore the particular effects that climate change is having and will have on indigenous societies and to formulate policies to help alleviate future crises. As their report points out, indigenous peoples "... inhabit diverse but fragile ecosystems ... [and they] are among the world's most marginalized, impoverished and vulnerable peoples. Hence, while they bear the brunt of the catastrophe of climate change, they have minimal access to resources to cope with the changes" (UNPFII E/C.19/2008/CRP.3). The effects of climate change are likely to erode indigenous peoples' adaptive strategies, leaving them with few options in their desire to maintain traditional subsistence practices and territories. National governments tend to overlook the basic human rights of indigenous peoples and as conditions worsen, they are even more likely to claim that "national" needs for land and resources override the specific rights of people to their homelands, despite international declarations safeguarding those rights.

In the Arctic, rising temperatures are resulting in the thinning of ice cover year round and the erosion and disappearance of glaciers. Temperatures are increasing in the Arctic at faster rates than elsewhere on the planet, as much as five degrees Celsius through the twentieth century (Macchi 2008, 32). According to an Inuit observer, "When I was born 60 years ago the ice was 3.5 miles thick, on average. Now, 60 years later, it's 1.5 miles. In just 60 years" (Angaangaq 2009, 8). Another sign of global warming is the receding of ice caps. In one area, the ice receded thirty miles in one year. As the ice caps melt, the sea level rises and waves become stronger, leading to erosion of coastal areas. In addition, weather patterns are becoming increasingly unstable, affecting the migratory cycles of both marine and terrestrial animals that Inuit subsistence is still dependent on. With warmer temperatures and melting of the sea ice, hunting becomes increasingly dangerous, lessening the food supply. Malnutrition is a serious risk in Arctic communities.

Deforestation in tropical regions is an additional symptom of climate change. Indeed, loss of forest cover is both a symptom and a cause of further change, because as the forests disappear, increased levels of carbon are released into the atmosphere, exacerbating environmental alterations. Globally, deforestation is ranked as the third largest contributor of greenhouse gas emissions (energy and industry-related emissions are first and second) (Tauli-Corpuz and Lynge 2008, 14). Between 1990 and 2005, about 3 percent of the world's total forest area was lost. The major cause of deforestation is excessive cutting of timber for export to be made into furniture and other wood products. Indigenous peoples living in these regions see a loss of their traditional territories

Shoreline of the Arctic Ocean Shutterstock/George Burba/Shutterstock

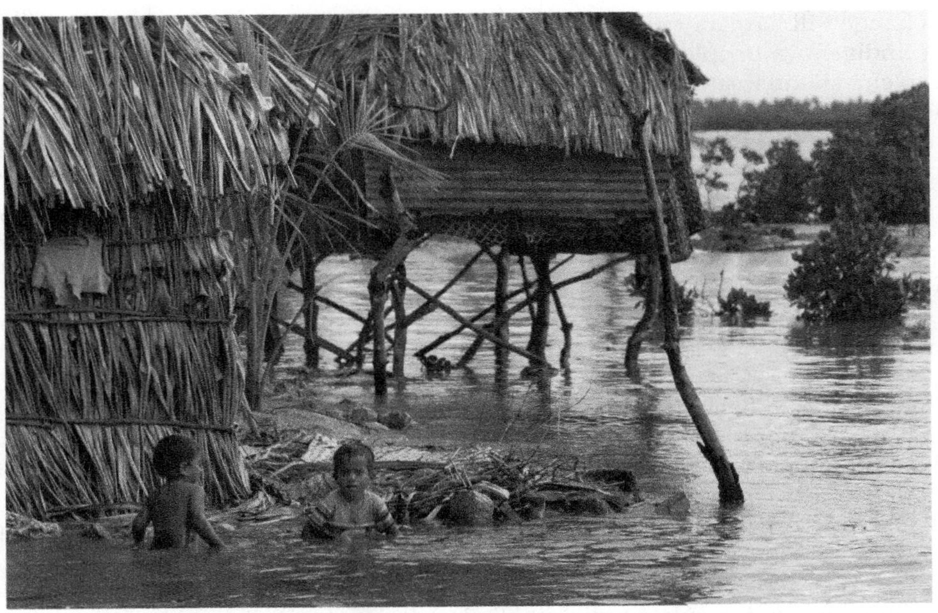

Rising waters surrounding Kiribati Islands in the Pacific Ocean Alamy Limited/Jeremy Sutton-Hibbert/Alamy

and livelihoods. A United Nations report estimates that about one million people, members of some four hundred indigenous groups in the Amazon, are vulnerable to the loss of their forests, with at worst a complete collapse of the Amazonian rain forest (Macchi 2008, 13). Worldwide there are some 2,500 indigenous societies living in forest regions whose livelihoods may be threatened (ibid., 39).

Pastoral peoples living in eastern and central Africa face the problems that warming temperatures cause for their lands and cattle. As temperatures rise, the deserts spread, affecting the growth of plants that the cattle eat, leading to declines in the herds. Fluctuating and both excessive rainfall and drought further diminish the grasslands, limiting food supplies for animals and for people.

Some people whose homes are on small islands in the Pacific Ocean have already become "climate change refugees." For example, in 2006, villagers in Lateu on one of the eighty-three islands making up the Pacific country of Vanuatu had to leave their coastal homes and move to higher ground. Their traditional economy based on farming and the domestication of pigs was disrupted. And in the island nation of Kiribati, people are facing their imminent removal to nearby Australia. Because of warming temperatures of the water, ocean levels are rising and sea water often inundates people's fields, damaging crops. The sea water also seeps into freshwater pools and springs that the people use as their primary drinking water supply. In addition, some fish and marine species are disappearing. Many people have already left some of the smaller islands making up Kiribati, resulting in overcrowding on the capital island of South Tarawa and straining resources and infrastructural supports. The president of Kiribati, Anote Tong, fears the day when the island nation will become uninhabitable. This will mean not only a loss of territory but a loss of cultural identity. In his words, "Can we remain nationals of Kiribati when we are living in Australia? What would be our citizenship? Do we still have sovereignty of Kiribati when there is no longer the country of Kiribati?" (Blair 2008, 25–27).

In many regions, a projected decline in food supplies, especially in grains and other staples, will continue and in fact intensify. According to a United Nations survey in 2011, rising prices for food are caused by shortages due to fluctuations in temperature, rainfall and drought, and severe weather conditions. Food shortages and rising prices led, in 2008, to food riots and demonstrations in more than a dozen countries, particularly in Africa and the Middle East. The United Nations Food and Agricultural Organization reported a worldwide 3.4 percent rise in the prices of basic commodities in January 2011 (the highest level since they began tracking prices in 1990), with a prediction of further future increases (McFarquhar 2011).

In addition to the environmental impacts of climate change, the health status of indigenous peoples is predicted to suffer. Rising temperatures and exposure to the sun can cause damage to the skin, leading to higher incidence of skin cancer. Exposure to droughts, floods, and storms also results in deaths. Infectious diseases, such as malaria and dengue fever, carried by mosquitoes and other insects are expected to rise. Waterborne diseases, prompted by deterioration in the availability and cleanliness of water sources, are also expected to increase (Macchi 2008, 16). Malnutrition is an added danger in the context of declining resources and food supplies.

Compounding the problems that indigenous peoples face from the direct effects of climate change, many groups may also be negatively affected by proposed solutions to energy policies that release greenhouse gases. Principal among these is the development of biofuels, especially extraction of oil palm and soy products as alternatives to petroleum. Oil palm is a plant native to West Africa, grown there for centuries as part of subsistence strategies but now becoming a lucrative plantation crop in tropical countries, especially in Indonesia, Malaysia, and the Amazon region of South America. Oil is extracted from the fruit and seeds of the trees and processed into a product usable for fuel. In order to accelerate production for global markets, natural forests are cut down for the expansion of plantations. In Indonesia alone, palm oil production increases at an estimated 12 percent per year. In 1960, only 261,000 acres of land were devoted to oil palm trees, but by 2000 nearly 15 million acres were under production, with a government estimate that an additional 44.5 million acres were cleared for the market (Tauli-Corpuz and Tamang 2008, 31). In order to reach these levels of production, forests are cut down and their indigenous inhabitants are displaced. The people's claims to traditional territories are ignored, in part because the government has never agreed to official demarcation of their lands to grant them legal title. Worldwide, the United Nations' report on the global food crisis cites "crops diverted to biofuels" as one of four major causes, along with weather, higher demand, and smaller yields (McFarquhar 2011).

Despite the ecological and economic ramifications of climate change for indigenous peoples, some groups are not waiting idly for their situation to worsen but rather are suggesting and implementing innovative strategies that allow them to maintain their traditional lands and obtain adequate supplies of foods and other resources. For example, Quechua farmers living in the Peruvian Andes, whose subsistence base has for centuries centered on a wide variety of potatoes, are dealing with changes in the growing cycle and in planting locations. Since potatoes are usually a cold-weather crop, the warming temperatures mean that people need to delay planting for at least a month and also need to plant at higher altitudes where temperatures remain cooler, as much as 600 feet higher than usual. However, if this trend continues indefinitely, the crops will not be harvestable at such high mountain summits. In addition, rainfall at these high altitudes is unpredictable, alternating between downpours, hail, and drought. In order to deal with these problems, in 1998 a group of Quechua villages banded together and received official registration and recognition as a "Potato Park," thus banning mining, logging, and other commercial development encroaching on their remaining lands (Townsend and Murphy 2010, 21). One of their arguments is the protection of biodiversity, safeguarding the large inventory of native potato varieties, now estimated to number about 3,800 (Macchi 2008, 18). Their project is supported by the Andes Association, allied with the United Nations Food and Agriculture Organization. In the words of its director, Cesar Argumedo, "The struggle to preserve the potato is connected to the struggle of communities all over the globe to protect their agricultural biodiversity and continue feeding themselves, in spite of climate change" (Townsend and Murphy 2010, 23).

Fields of potatoes grown by Quechua Indians near Cusco, Peru Alamy Limited/ Mo Fini/Alamy

In 2010, a delegation from indigenous villages in Ethiopia visited the Peruvian Potato Park and are planning to use this model to protect their staple crop, called "enset" (a plant similar to bananas). Enset is used for food and for the manufacture of fences and numerous types of household goods. In their country as well, climate change is causing warmer temperatures and erratic rainfall patterns, leading to crop failures. Proposals for an "enset park" are supported by scientists hoping to preserve traditional varieties of native foods.

In North America, several native peoples are proposing and constructing new energy projects to replace their reliance on fossil fuels such as coal and oil. The Navajos located in the southwestern states of Arizona and New Mexico and the Rosebud Lakota in South Dakota are harnessing two sources of energy abundantly available in their territories, wind and sun. The Navajos are developing a wind farm near Flagstaff, Arizona, that is projected to provide power to some 20,000 homes in the area (Navarro 2010). And the Rosebud Lakota began using wind energy at their commercial wind turbine in 2003, generating power for utility companies on and off their reservation.

Elsewhere in the world, numerous groups of indigenous peoples are utilizing traditional practices that have sustained their economies for centuries (Macchi 2008). For example, the Aymara in Bolivia are expanding their construction of small dams to collect rainwater in mountainous regions to protect their supply of water in times of drought, providing enough for themselves and for their animals. In Honduras, indigenous villagers living in mountainous regions have developed several techniques to limit the erosion of soil for their planting cycles. They plant their crops in places close to trees so that the trees' roots help protect against the loss of soil, especially during rainstorms. They also use a system of terracing their plots to curtail the effects of soil erosion. And in the Bara province of western Sudan, where the hotter and drier climate is damaging the land and causing desertification, people are organizing rangeland rehabilitation projects that are community based and controlled. Local committees are in charge of coordinating resource management and development. Their projects include stabilizing sand dunes to stop desert expansion, constructing windbreaks to protect farmland from the possibility of soil erosion during sandstorms, managing wells, and encouraging people to replace their goat herds with sheep because sheep do less damage to grasslands.

All of these various efforts share several features. First, they are based on traditional knowledge of local ecological conditions gained through direct experience and transmitted through the centuries. Second, they are planned and managed by members of the communities involved, not by outside "experts" attached to international agencies. And finally, they are projects of scale, adapted to local circumstances and the needs of people to sustain their communities and ways of living.

CONSERVATION, ECOTOURISM, AND INDIGENOUS LANDS

In addition to projects aimed at economic development, increasing numbers of countries in Africa, Asia, and Latin America are infringing on indigenous lands to set up national parks and wildlife reserves (Colchester 2004; Dowie 2010). Initiatives aimed at conservation have created great demand for these areas worldwide. Today, more than 110,000 conservation areas are officially recognized. This amounts to approximately 20 percent of the earth's landmass (11.75 million square miles), a percentage that doubles the recommendation made by the World Parks Commission in 1990, setting a goal of 10 percent. About half of the lands set aside for conservation over the past century were either inhabited or exploited for resources by indigenous peoples. An unlikely coalition has formed between government agencies and conservation organizations that often oppose the people's attempts to secure the resources that they and their ancestors have depended on for generations.

In an international meeting of the World Parks Congress, held in South Africa in 2003, representatives of indigenous groups issued an appeal protesting their "dispossession and resettlement, the violation of rights, the displacement of peoples, the loss of sacred sites, and the slow but continuous loss of cultures, as well as impoverishment. First we were dispossessed in the name of kings and emperors, later in the name of State development and now in the name of conservation" (MacKay and Caruso 2004, 14). Their position brings them into conflict with conservation groups who favor preserving "wilderness areas" kept "primitive and natural," that is, uninhabited (Colchester 2004, 18). Although firm statistics are unavailable, some estimates suggest that indigenous peoples actually inhabit 85 percent of reserved and protected lands in Latin America and some 600,000 "tribal peoples" living in India have been forced to relocate in order to establish protected areas. Hundreds of thousands of "conservation refugees" have also been evicted from their territories in Africa, although most governments do not keep accurate figures on such populations.

Walter Pukitiwara walks near Uluru (Ayers Rock) in Australia, which is a sacred site to Aborigines. Photo Researchers/Tom Hollyman/Photo Researchers, Inc.

The desire of people to remain in their traditional territories and to pursue sustainable economies is sometimes at odds with international funding agencies, including the World Bank and the Global Environmental Fund, that support conservation projects. The argument sometimes put forward is that human occupation and activities disturb the natural balance of the environment and may lead to a decline in biodiversity. However, studies of indigenous practices indicate just the opposite. For example, the grazing patterns that Maasai cattle herders in Tanzania utilize are similar to those of wild animals and in fact work in concord with natural cycles to maintain the land (Dowie 2010, 32). Similarly, the horticultural practices of indigenous farmers in Central and South America benefit the resilience and fertility of the land by using periodic slash-and-burn techniques to clear small areas of land and allow other areas to lie fallow in order to regenerate. The farmers also rotate crops and intermingle specific plants in order to enhance their growth and return nutrients to the soil.

Some countries are attempting to reconcile the needs of indigenous peoples and the desire to conserve natural resources. For example, the Peruvian government has established what it calls "communal reserves" to be managed jointly by indigenous communities and conservation agencies (Newing and Wahl 2004, 38). Indigenous peoples maintain legal title to the land and are guaranteed protection against encroachment by loggers, miners, and settlers. However, government agencies also monitor activities of indigenous people to ensure that their land use does not conflict with the goals of "biodiversity conservation."

In South Africa, government commissions staffed by representatives from indigenous groups and conservation agencies work out equitable management policies that recognize the people's rights to their lands. The San, an indigenous people whose traditional lands are located in the Kalahari Desert spanning Namibia and Botswana, have concluded agreements with the Namibian government that establishes the Nyae Nyae Conservancy to oversee the people's communal lands, with control over management and utilization of natural resources (Hitchcock and Biesele 2002, 9). Other groups of San have won recognition of their rights to land and, importantly, to water, the most critical resource in the desert.

And in Australia, Aborigines have established "Indigenous Protected Areas" under agreement between local communities and the central government. In accord with these agreements, Aborigines have returned to rural territories that they once inhabited and over which they now have all legal rights. The community members are responsible for drawing up plans for resource management that maintain or enhance the natural biodiversity of the region. Similar projects, negotiating agreements between federal governments and indigenous peoples aimed at resource management in conservation areas or national parks, have been established in other countries on other continents, including in Laos, Colombia, and the United States.

ecotourism
Visiting wildlife sanctuaries and national parks to enjoy a more pristine environment than found in urban life.

In addition to maintaining traditional economic utilization of lands, some indigenous groups in many parts of the world have embarked on initiatives that promote tourism in their territories. Called **"ecotourism"** or "ethnotourism," these projects have the potential to generate income that supports people, public parks, and animal and plant species, an attractive prospect for many governments and for many indigenous groups. However, the projects are not without controversy. First, revenues obtained often go to governments and commercial interests who organize tourist visits rather than directly benefiting the people. Second, in order to attract tourists, indigenous people may have to "dress up" and put on cultural displays that are consistent with outsiders' views of who they are. Still, ecotourism may have the positive educational effect of promoting the social and political rights of indigenous peoples to a wider audience. And it may promote a sense of cultural and group identity within the community.

REVIEW

The conflicts between conservation groups and indigenous peoples pose challenges for safeguarding the people's economic and human rights as well as preserving environmental biodiversity. Ecotourism offers a means of protecting native populations and lands but also encroaches on those lands and the people. The double-edged sword of ecotourism is a metaphor for the complexity of human problems in our postcolonial and increasingly postmodern and globalized world.

ANTHROPOLOGY APPLIED

FUNAI Anthropologists

Anthropologists work both for the Brazilian government and for indigenous communities to protect or extend Indian rights while furthering government policies and national goals—a balancing act that is often difficult. Anthropologists have played crucial roles in (1) mapping aboriginal lands to support Indian claims to ancestral territories; (2) contacting new groups deep in the Amazon to help them prepare for contact with the outside world; (3) reporting abuses of Indians; (4) representing Indians in disputes with settlers, prospectors, and government agents; (5) educating indigenous communities about their political and economic rights and interests; and (6) advocating on behalf of indigenous Amazon peoples.

In March 2003, for example, indigenous leaders from across Brazil, politicians, anthropologists, and officials from the National Indian Foundation (FUNAI) met in Brasília to discuss indigenous rights. Topics included proposals to improve the quality of life of indigenous populations and strategies to prevent the invasion of indigenous lands. They also discussed the corruption of FUNAI officials and the murder of indigenous leaders (Radiobras 2003).

In 2004, anthropologists helped prevent bloodshed when 3,000 Guarani Indians invaded fourteen ranches near the Paraguayan border that they claim as part of their ancestral land. In negotiations through FUNAI, the Guaranis agreed to leave eleven of the farms, but continued to occupy the three largest ranches to press FUNAI to expand their tribal reserve by incorporating the land on which the ranches are located.

Landov Media/REUTERS/STR/Landov

Reuters/Rickey Rogers/Reuters

Anthropologists say that the indigenous community has a legitimate ancestral claim to this property. Rubem Almeida, one of the two anthropologists who wrote the report that will serve as the basis for FUNAI's demarcation of the Guarani territory, said the Guaranis are legally entitled to the land. Almeida presented testimony and material evidence that the Guaranis traditionally lived on the property, as well as "specific documents from 1927" that confirm their legal claim to the land. Despite the ranchers' protests, the local indigenous community has a right to that land under the Brazilian constitution, which cancels out the land titles held by the ranchers. Although a law the Brazilian government passed in 2005 guaranteed the Guarani territory, called Nanderu Marangatu, ranchers still occupy most of the land. This continuing conflict was the subject of a Great Assembly called by the Guarani in 2008, demanding an end to the illegal occupation of their territory (Survival International 2008).

CRITICAL THINKING QUESTIONS

Why is being a government anthropologist a balancing act in Brazil? How might this compare with being an anthropologist in the Bureau of Indian Affairs in the United States?

Study and Review on myanthrolab.com

CHAPTER SUMMARY

Migration

- The global economy accelerates the transfer of goods, services, and peoples from one part of the world to others. International migration has increased cultural diversity. Political processes have strengthened ties among countries.
- Processes of internal migration, particularly from rural to urban areas, have also accelerated, often because people seek job opportunities. Factories run by multinational corporations in development or free trade zones in Asia and Latin America have increased internal migration. Young women make up most of the work force in labor-intensive factories.
- International migration has shifted populations to wealthier countries with better job opportunities. As transnational migrants, people are increasingly maintaining ties with their native countries and communities. The ease of transportation and communication makes a transnational identity more likely.
- Although many international migrants assimilate into their new countries, others develop an identity based on their origin and ethnicity. However, ethnic identities are context-bound and adaptable to circumstances. People may think of themselves as members of groups based on one set of criteria but may find themselves categorized as members of other groups based on different criteria. Ethnic groups may develop strong political influence on the basis of their relative numbers and cohesiveness as a social and political community.

Ethnogenesis and Ethnic Identity

- Multiethnic states may employ various strategies to resolve relationships between central identities and disparate ethnic groups. One ethnic group may equate national culture with its own. A state may seek to assert cultural uniformity. A state may allow secondary identities to coexist along with a national identity. Ethnic strife may lead to tension and conflict within a multiethnic country. As well, cultural pluralism may spawn xenophobic sentiments.
- An international or global identity based on social class has developed among elites. A popular global culture has also developed as people throughout the world eat the same foods, watch the same movies, listen to the same music, and purchase the same consumer goods.

Cultural Minorities in a Global World

- Policies toward indigenous peoples vary considerably. In the United States and Canada, treaties and court rulings support limited sovereignty for native communities. In Mexico, federal policies have vacillated between recognizing and ignoring the land rights of indigenous peoples. In South America, although indigenous communities have gained some recognition of their rights to land, resources, and their cultural practices, their lands have also been the target of resource extraction.
- In many African states, indigenous peoples remain marginalized and face discrimination and control. In Sudan, Kenya, and Tanzania, governments have attempted to force nomadic pastoralists to adopt a sedentary lifestyle.

Legal Rights and International Recognition

- To protect themselves and their land, indigenous peoples have formed coalitions to assert their rights under international law. The United Nations has formulated a Declaration on the Rights of Indigenous Peoples.

Ecotourism and Indigenous Lands

- In addition to projects aimed at economic development, many countries are infringing on indigenous lands to create national parks and wildlife reserves for ecotourism. However, in some countries, indigenous residents have gained protections.

REVIEW QUESTIONS

1. What are the distinguishing features and effects of forced migration, urban migration, and labor migration?
2. What difficulties can transnational migration cause for cultural minorities? How might they participate in a culture of transnationalism?
3. What are some examples of ethnogenesis?
4. How have postcolonial states treated cultural minorities in the process of nation building?
5. How has globalization affected cultural identities and consumerism?
6. What challenges do cultural minorities face around the world? How do situations in Canada, Brazil, Nigeria, and other countries show how those challenges play out?
7. How has the law worked both against and for cultural minorities?
8. What role could ecotourism play for cultural minorities?

MyAnthroLab Connections

Watch. Listen. View. Explore. Read. MyAnthroLab is designed just for you. Dynamic visual activities, videos, and readings found in the multimedia library will enhance your learning experience.

Resources from this chapter:

Watch on **myanthrolab.com**

- *Migration: A Profile of the U.S.*
- *American Indian Testimony about Assimilation*

Listen on **myanthrolab.com**

- *Iraqi Refugees Find Michigan Is No Land of Plenty*
- *Nicole Bacharan on Integration*

Explore on **myanthrolab.com** In MySearchLab, enter the Anthropology database to find relevant and recent scholarly and popular press publications. For this chapter, enter the following keywords: transnationalism, cultural minorities, global identity, ecotourism

Read the **Document** on **myanthrolab.com**

- *Badagas: Sometime Refugees in a New Land* by Paul Hockings
- *Gaining Ground? Evenkis, Land and Reform in Southeastern Siberia* by Gail A. Fondahl

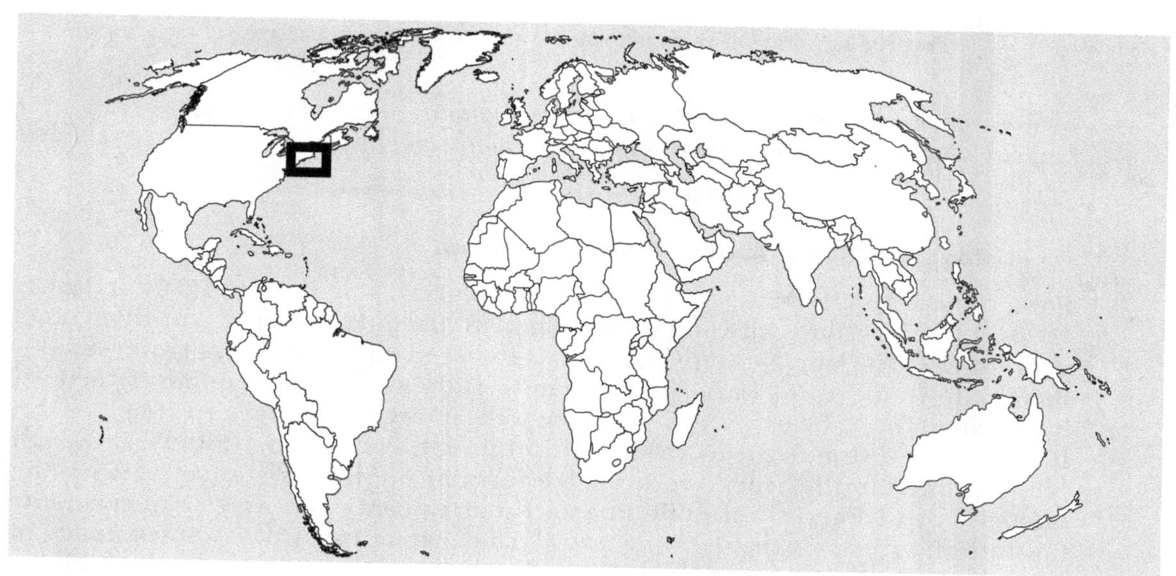

Poverty at Work: Office Employment and the Crack Alternative

Philippe Bourgois

There was a time in the United States when people with little education and money could find work in manufacturing plants or other settings requiring manual labor. Many of the skills they needed could be learned on the job and they could make a modest but decent living and support a family. And despite their working-class identity, their jobs gave them dignity and a place in society. But in today's America, manufacturing jobs have often disappeared, leaving thousands of poorly educated people without equivalent work.

In this article, Philippe Bourgois illustrates how this problem has affected unskilled and largely uneducated Puerto Rican men and women in New York City's Spanish Harlem. Manufacturing jobs once provided dignified and stable employment for Puerto Rican men and women. As factories closed during the 1960s, 1970s, and 1980s, the unemployed could find work only in service industries such as security corporations, law firms, and insurance companies. Because they were uneducated and culturally different, they could hold only minimum-wage jobs in such worlds, as they are usually controlled by educated, largely Anglo people who openly look down on them. In the end, they could achieve higher status and often higher income in their own ethnic community by dealing drugs. The result has been a destructive spiral into addiction, murder, and prison. Bourgois concludes the article with an addendum noting that high employment in the late 1990s provided more work *opportunities for Puerto Ricans in the formal economy and that crack dealing has largely given way to the less visible sale of marijuana and heroin.**

Listen to the **Chapter Audio** on **myanthrolab.com**

For a total of approximately three and a half years during the late 1980s and early 1990s, I lived with my wife and young son in an irregularly heated, rat-filled tenement in East Harlem, New York. This two-hundred-square-block neighborhood—better known locally as *El Barrio* or Spanish Harlem—is visibly impoverished yet it is located in the heart of New York, the richest city in the Western Hemisphere. It is literally a stone's throw from multimillion-dollar condominiums. Although one in three families survived on some form of public assistance in 1990, the majority of El Barrio's 110,600 Puerto Rican and African-American residents fall into the ranks of the working poor.[1] They eke out an uneasy subsistence in entry-level service and manufacturing jobs in one of the most expensive cities in the world.

The public sector (e.g., the police, social welfare agencies, the Sanitation Department) has broken down in El Barrio and does not function effectively. This has caused the legally employed residents of the neighborhood to lose control of their streets and public spaces to the drug economy. My tenement's block was not atypical and within a few hundred yards' radius I could obtain heroin, crack, powder cocaine, hypodermic needles, methadone, Valium, angel dust, marijuana, mescaline, bootleg alcohol, and tobacco. Within two hundred feet of my stoop there were three competing crack houses selling vials at two, three, and five dollars. Several doctors operated "pill mills" on the blocks around me, writing prescriptions for opiates and barbiturates upon demand. In the projects within view of my living-room window, the Housing Authority police arrested a fifty-five-year-old mother and her twenty-two-year-old daughter while they were "bagging" twenty-two pounds of cocaine into ten-dollar quarter-gram "Jumbo" vials of adulterated product worth over a million dollars on the streets. The police found twenty-five thousand dollars in cash in small-denomination bills in this same apartment.[2] In other words, there are millions of dollars' worth of business going on directly in front of the youths growing up in East Harlem tenements and housing projects. Why should these young men and women take the subway downtown to work minimum-wage jobs—or even double minimum-wage jobs—in downtown offices when they can usually earn more, at least in the short run, by selling drugs on the street corner in front of their apartment or schoolyard?

*Reprinted by permission of Waveland Press, Inc. from Philippe Bourgois, "Office Work and the Crack Alternative among Puerto Rican Drug Dealers in East Harlem," from *Urban Life: Readings in the Anthropology of the City*, 4th edition, George Gmelch and Walter P. Zenner, eds. (Long Grove, IL: Waveland Press, Inc., 2002).

[1]According to the 1990 Census, in East Harlem 48.3 percent of males and 35.2 percent of females over sixteen were officially reported as employed—compared to a citywide average of 64.3 percent for men and 49 percent for women. Another 10.4 percent of the men and 5.7 percent of the women in East Harlem were actively looking for legal work. . . . In El Barrio as a whole, 60 percent of all households reported legally earned incomes. Twenty-six percent received Public Assistance, 6.3 percent received Supplemental Security Income, and 5 percent received Medicaid benefits.

[2]Both of these police actions were reported in the local print and television media, but I am withholding the cities to protect the anonymity of my street address.

This dynamic underground economy is predicated on violence and substance abuse. It has spawned what I call a "street culture" of resistance and self-destruction. The central concern of my study is the relationship of street culture to the worlds of work accessible to street dealers—that is, the legal and illegal labor markets that employ them and give meaning to their lives. I hope to show the local-level implications of the global-level restructuring of the U.S. economy away from factory production and toward services. In the process, I have recorded the words and experiences of some unrepentant victims who are part of a network of some twenty-five street-level crack dealers operating on and around my block. To summarize, I am arguing that the transformation from manufacturing to service employment—especially in the professional office work setting—is much more culturally disruptive than the already revealing statistics on reductions in income, employment, unionization, and worker's benefits would indicate. Low-level service sector employment engenders a humiliating ideological—or cultural—confrontation between a powerful corps of white office executives and their assistants versus a younger generation of poorly educated, alienated, "colored" workers. It also often takes the form of a sharply polarized confrontation over gender roles.

Shattered Working-Class Dreams

All the crack dealers and addicts whom I have interviewed had worked at one or more legal jobs in their early youth. In fact, most entered the labor market at a younger age than the typical American. Before they were twelve years old they were bagging groceries at the supermarket for tips, stocking beers off-the-books in local *bodegas*, or shining shoes. For example, Primo, the night manager at a video game arcade that sells five-dollar vials of crack on the block where I lived, pursued a traditional working-class dream in his early adolescence. With the support of his extended kin who were all immersed in a working-class "common sense," he dropped out of junior high school to work in a local garment factory:

> I was like fourteen or fifteen playing hooky and pressing dresses and whatever they were making on the steamer. They was cheap, cheap clothes.
>
> My mother's sister was working there first and then her son, my cousin Willie—the one who's in jail now—was the one they hired first, because his mother agreed: "If you don't want to go to school, you gotta work."
>
> So I started hanging out with him. I wasn't planning on working in the factory. I was supposed to be in school; but it just sort of happened.

Ironically, young Primo actually became the agent who physically moved the factory out of the inner city. In the process, he became merely one more of the 445,900 manufacturing workers in New York City who lost their jobs as factory employment dropped 50 percent from 1963 to 1983. . . .

Almost all the crack dealers had similar tales of former factory jobs. For poor adolescents, the decision to drop out of school and become a marginal factory worker is attractive. It provides the employed youth with access to the childhood "necessities"—sneakers, basketballs, store-bought snacks—that sixteen-year-olds who stay in school cannot afford. In the descriptions of their first forays into legal factory-based employment, one hears clearly the extent to which they, and their families, subscribed to mainstream working-class ideologies about the dignity of engaging in "hard work" rather than education.

Had these enterprising, early-adolescent workers from El Barrio not been confined to the weakest sector of manufacturing in a period of rapid job loss, their teenage working-class dreams might have stabilized. Instead, upon reaching their mid-twenties, they discovered themselves to be unemployable high school dropouts. This painful realization of social marginalization expresses itself across a generational divide. The parents and grandparents of the dealers continue to maintain working-class values of honesty and hard work which conflict violently with the reality of their children's immersion in street culture. They are constantly accused of slothfulness by their mothers and even by friends who have managed to maintain legal jobs. They do not have a regional perspective on the dearth of adequate entry-level jobs available to "functional illiterates" in New York, and they begin to suspect that they might indeed be *"vago bons"* [lazy bums] who do not *want* to work hard and cannot help themselves. Confused, they take refuge in an alternative search for career, meaning, and ecstasy in substance abuse.

Formerly, when most entry-level jobs were found in factories, the contradiction between an oppositional street culture and traditional working-class, masculine, shop-floor culture was less pronounced—especially when the work site was protected by a union. Factories are inevitably rife with confrontational hierarchies. Nevertheless, on the shop-floor, surrounded by older union workers, high school dropouts who are well versed in the latest and toughest street culture styles function effectively. In the factory, being tough and violently macho has high cultural value; a certain degree of opposition to the foreman and the "bossman" is expected and is considered appropriate.

In contrast, this same oppositional street-identity is nonfunctional in the professional office worker service sector that has burgeoned in New York's high-finance-driven economy. It does not allow for the humble, obedient, social interaction—often across gender lines—that professional office workers routinely impose on their subordinates. A qualitative change has occurred, therefore, in the tenor of social interaction in office-based employment. Workers in a mail room or behind a photocopy machine cannot publicly maintain their cultural autonomy. Most concretely, they have no union; more subtly, there are few fellow workers surrounding them to insulate them and to provide them with a culturally based sense of class solidarity.[3] Instead they are besieged by supervisors and bosses from an alien, hostile, and obviously dominant culture who ridicule street culture. Workers like Primo appear inarticulate to their professional supervisors when they try to imitate the language of power in the workplace and instead stumble pathetically over the enunciation of unfamiliar words. They cannot decipher the hastily scribbled instructions—rife with mysterious abbreviations—that are left for them by harried office managers. The "common sense" of white-collar work is foreign to them; they do not, for example, understand the logic for filing triplicate copies of memos or for post-dating invoices. When they attempt to improvise or show initiative they fail miserably and instead appear inefficient, or even hostile, for failing to follow "clearly specified" instructions.

Their "social skills" are even more inadequate than their limited professional capacities. They do not know how to look at their fellow co-service workers, let alone their supervisors, without intimidating them. They cannot walk down the hallway to the water fountain without unconsciously swaying their shoulders

[3]Significantly, there are subsectors of the service industry that are relatively unionized—such as hospital and custodial work—where there is a limited autonomous space for street culture and working-class resistance.

aggressively as if patrolling their home turf. Gender barriers are an even more culturally charged realm. They are repeatedly reprimanded for harassing female co-workers.

The cultural clash between white "yuppie" power and inner-city "scrambling jive" in the service sector is much more than a superficial question of style. It is about access to power. Service workers who are incapable of obeying the rules of interpersonal interaction dictated by professional office culture will never be upwardly mobile. Their supervisors will think they are dumb or have a "bad attitude." Once again, a gender dynamic exacerbates the confusion and sense of insult experienced by young, male inner-city employees because most supervisors in the lowest reaches of the service sector are women. Street culture does not allow males to be subordinate across gender lines.

"Gettin' Dissed"

On the street, the trauma of experiencing a threat to one's personal dignity has been frozen linguistically in the commonly used phrase "to diss," which is short for "to disrespect." Significantly, one generation ago ethnographers working in rural Puerto Rico specifically noted the importance of the traditional Puerto Rican concept of *respeto* in mediating labor relations:

> The good owner "respects" (*respeta*) the laborer. . . . It is probably to the interest of the landowner to make concessions to his best workers, to deal with them on a respect basis, and to enmesh them in a network of mutual obligations.[4]

Puerto Rican street-dealers do not find respect in the entry-level service sector jobs that have increased two-fold in New York's economy since the 1950s. On the contrary, they "get dissed" in the new jobs that are available to them. Primo, for example, remembers the humiliation of his former work experiences as an "office boy," and he speaks of them in a race- and gender-charged idiom:

> I had a prejudiced boss. She was a fucking "ho'," Gloria. She was white. Her name was Christian. No, not Christian, Kirschman. I don't know if she was Jewish or not. When she was talking to people she would say, "He's illiterate."
>
> So what I did one day was, I just looked up the word, "illiterate," in the dictionary and I saw that she's saying to her associates that I'm stupid or something!
>
> Well, I am illiterate anyway.

The most profound dimension of Primo's humiliation was being obliged to look up in the dictionary the word used to insult him. In contrast, in the underground economy, he is sheltered from this kind of threat:

> Rocky [the crack house franchise owner] he would never disrespect me that way. He wouldn't tell me that because he's illiterate too. Plus I've got more education than him. I got a GED. . . .

[4]Eric Wolf, "San Jose: Subcultures of a 'Traditional' Coffee Municipality," in Julian Stewart (ed.), *The People of Puerto Rico* (Chicago: University of Chicago Press, 1956), p. 235.

Primo excels in the street's underground economy. His very persona inspires fear and respect. In contrast, in order to succeed in his former office job, Primo would have had to self-consciously alter his street identity and mimic the professional cultural style that office managers require of their subordinates and colleagues. Primo refused to accept his boss's insults and he was unable to imitate her interactional styles. He was doomed, consequently, to a marginal position behind a photocopy machine or at the mail meter. Behavior considered appropriate in street culture is considered dysfunctional in office settings. In other words, job requirements in the service sector are largely cultural style and this conjugates powerfully with racism.

> I wouldn't have mind that she said I was illiterate. What bothered me was that when she called on the telephone, she wouldn't want me to answer even if my supervisor who was the receptionist was not there. [Note how Primo is so low in the office hierarchy that his immediate supervisor is a receptionist.]
>
> When she hears my voice it sounds like she's going to get a heart attack. She'd go, "Why are you answering the phones?"
>
> That bitch just didn't like my Puerto Rican accent.

Primo's manner of resisting this insult to his cultural dignity exacerbated his marginal position in the labor hierarchy:

> And then, when I did pick up the phone, I used to just sound *Porta'rrrican* on purpose.

In contrast to the old factory sweatshop positions, these just-above-minimum-wage office jobs require intense interpersonal contact with the middle and upper-middle classes. Close contact across class lines and the absence of a working-class autonomous space for eight hours a day in the office can be a claustrophobic experience for an otherwise ambitious, energetic, young, inner-city worker.

Caesar, who worked for Primo as lookout and bodyguard at the crack house, interpreted this requirement to obey white, middle-class norms as an affront to his dignity that specifically challenged his definition of masculinity:

> I had a few jobs like that [referring to Primo's "telephone diss"] where you gotta take a lot of shit from bitches and be a wimp.
>
> I didn't like it but I kept on working, because "Fuck it!" you don't want to fuck up the relationship. So you just be a punk [shrugging his shoulders dejectedly].

One alternative for surviving at a workplace that does not tolerate a street-based cultural identity is to become bicultural: to play politely by "the white woman's" rules downtown only to come home and revert to street culture within the safety of one's tenement or housing project at night. Tens of thousands of East Harlem residents manage this tightrope, but it often engenders accusations of betrayal and internalized racism on the part of neighbors and childhood friends who do not have—or do not want—bicultural skills.

This is the case, for example, of Ray, a rival crack dealer whose tough street demeanor conflates with his black skin to "disqualify" him from legal office work. He quit a "nickel-and-dime messenger job downtown" in order to sell crack full time in his project stairway shortly after a white woman fled from him shrieking down the hallway of a high-rise office building. Ray and the terrified woman had ridden the elevator together, and, coincidentally, Ray had stepped off on the same floor as her to make a delivery. Worse yet, Ray had been trying to act like a "debonair male" and suspected the contradiction between his inadequate appearance and his chivalric intentions was responsible for the woman's terror:

> You know how you let a woman go off the elevator first? Well that's what I did to her but I may have looked a little shabby on the ends. Sometime my hair not combed. You know. So I could look a little sloppy to her maybe when I let her off first.

What Ray did not quite admit until I probed further is that he too had been intimidated by the lone white woman. He had been so disoriented by her taboo, unsupervised proximity that he had forgotten to press the elevator button when he originally stepped on after her:

> She went in the elevator first but then she just waits there to see what floor I press. She's playing like she don't know what floor she wants to go to because she wants to wait for me to press my floor. And I'm standing there and I forgot to press the button. I'm thinking about something else—I don't know what was the matter with me. And she's thinking like, "He's not pressing the button; I guess he's following me!"

As a crack dealer, Ray no longer has to confront this kind of confusing humiliation. Instead, he can righteously condemn his "successful" neighbors who work downtown for being ashamed of who they were born to be:

> When you see someone go downtown and get a good job, if they be Puerto Rican, you see them fix up their hair and put some contact lens in their eyes. Then they fit in. And they do it! I seen it.
>
> They turn-overs. They people who want to be white. Man, if you call them in Spanish, it wind up a problem.
>
> When they get nice jobs like that, all of a sudden, you know, they start talking proper.

Self-Destructive Resistance

During the 1980s, the real value of the minimum wage for legally employed workers declined by one-third. At the same time, social services were cut. The federal government, for example, decreased the proportion of its contribution to New York City's budget by over 50 percent. . . . The breakdown of the inner city's public sector is no longer an economic threat to the expansion of New York's economy because the native-born labor force it shelters is increasingly irrelevant.

New immigrants arrive every day, and they are fully prepared to work hard for low wages under unsavory conditions. Like the parents and grandparents of Primo and Caesar, many of New York's newest immigrants are from isolated rural communities or squalid shanty towns where meat is eaten only once a week and there is no running water or electricity. Half a century ago Primo's mother fled precisely the same living conditions these new immigrants are only just struggling to escape. Her reminiscences about childhood in her natal village reveal the time warp of improved material conditions, cultural dislocation, and crushed working-class dreams that is propelling her second-generation son into a destructive street culture:

> I loved that life in Puerto Rico, because it was a healthy, healthy, healthy life.
>
> We always ate because my father always had work, and in those days the custom was to have a garden in your patio to grow food and everything that you ate.
>
> We only ate meat on Sundays because everything was cultivated on the same little parcel of land. We didn't have a refrigerator, so we ate *bacalao* [salted codfish], which can stay outside and a meat that they call *carne de vieja* [shredded beef], and sardines from a can. But thanks to God, we never felt hunger. My mother made a lot of cornflour.
>
> Some people have done better by coming here, but many people haven't. Even people from my barrio, who came trying to find a better life [*buen ambiente*] just found disaster. Married couples right from my neighborhood came only to have the husband run off with another woman.
>
> In those days in Puerto Rico, when we were in poverty, life was better. Everyone will tell you life was healthier and you could trust people. Now you can't trust anybody.
>
> What I like best was that we kept all our traditions . . . our feasts. In my village, everyone was either an Uncle or an Aunt. And when you walked by someone older, you had to ask for their blessing. It was respect. There was a lot of respect in those days [original quote in Spanish].

The Jewish and Italian-American white workers that Primo's mother replaced a generation ago when she came to New York City in hope of building a better future for her children were largely absorbed into an expanding economy that allowed them to be upwardly mobile. New York's economy always suffered periodic fluctuations, such as during the Great Depression, but those difficult periods were always temporary. The overall trend was one of economic growth. Primo's generation has not been so lucky. The contemporary economy does not particularly need them, and ethnic discrimination and cultural barriers overwhelm them whenever they attempt to work legally and seek service-sector jobs. Worse yet, an extraordinarily dynamic underground drug economy beckons them.

Rather than bemoaning the structural adjustment which is destroying their capacity to survive on legal wages, streetbound Puerto Rican youths celebrate their "decision" to bank on the underground economy and to cultivate their street identities. Caesar and Primo repeatedly assert their pride in their street careers. For example, one Saturday night after they finished their midnight shift at the crack house, I accompanied them on their way to purchase "*El Sapo Verde*" [The Green Toad], a twenty-dollar bag of powder cocaine sold by a new company three blocks away. While waiting for Primo and Caesar to be "served" by the coke seller a few yards away, I engaged three undocumented Mexican men drinking beer on a neighboring stoop in a conversation about finding work in New York. One of the new immigrants was already earning five hundred dollars a week fixing deep-fat-fry machines. He had a straightforward racist explanation for why Caesar—who was standing next to me—was "unemployed":

> OK, OK, I'll explain it to you in one word: Because the Puerto Ricans are brutes! [Pointing at Caesar] Brutes! Do you understand?
>
> Puerto Ricans like to make easy money. They like to leech off of other people. But not us Mexicans! No way! We like to work for our money. We don't steal. We came here to work and that's all [original quote in Spanish].

Instead of physically assaulting the employed immigrant for insulting him, Caesar embraced the racist tirade, ironically turning it into the basis for a new, generational-based, "American-born," urban cultural pride. In fact, in his response, he ridicules what he interprets to be the hillbilly naiveté of the Mexicans who still believe in the "American Dream." He spoke slowly in street-English as if to mark sarcastically the contrast between his "savvy" Nuyorican (New York-born Puerto Rican) identity versus the limited English proficiency of his detractor:

> That's right, m'a man! We is real vermin lunatics that sell drugs. We don't want no part of society. "Fight the Power!"[5]
>
> What do we wanna be working for? We rather live off the system. Gain weight, lay women.
>
> When we was younger, we used to break our asses too [gesturing towards the Mexican men who were straining to understand his English]. I had all kinds of stupid jobs too . . . advertising agencies . . . computers.
>
> But not no more! Now we're in a rebellious stage. We rather evade taxes, make quick money, and just survive. But we're not satisfied with that either. Ha!

Conclusion: Ethnography and Oppression

The underground economy and the social relations thriving off of it are best understood as modes of resistance to subordination in the service sector of the new U.S. economy. This resistance, however, results in individual self destruction and wider community devastation through substance abuse and violence. This complex and contradictory dynamic whereby resistance leads to self-destruction in the inner city is difficult to convey to readers in a clear and responsible manner. Mainstream society's "common sense" understanding of social stratification around ethnicity and class assumes the existence of racial hierarchies and blames individual victims for their failures. This makes it difficult to present ethnographic data from inner-city streets without falling prey to a "pornography of violence" or a racist voyeurism.

The public is not persuaded by a structural economic understanding of Caesar and Primo's "self-destruction." Even the victims themselves psychologize their unsatisfactory lives. Similarly, politicians and, more broadly, public policy ignore the fundamental structural economic facts of marginalization in America. Instead the first priority of federal and local social "welfare" agencies is to change the psychological—or at best the "cultural"—orientations of misguided individuals . . . U.S. politicians furiously debate family values while multinational corporations establish global free-trade zones and unionized factory employment in the U.S. continues to disappear as overseas sweatshops multiply. Social science researchers, meanwhile, have remained silent for the most part. They politely ignore the urgent social problems engulfing the urban United States. The few marginal academic publications that do address issues of poverty and racism are easily ignored by the media and mainstream society. . . .

Epilogue

In the six years since this article was first published, four major dynamics have altered the tenor of daily life on the streets of East Harlem and have deeply affected the

[5]"Fight the Power" is a rap song composed in 1990 by the African-American group, Public Enemy.

lives of the crack dealers and their families depicted in these pages: (1) the U.S. economy entered the most prolonged period of sustained growth in its recorded history, (2) the size of the Mexican immigrant population in New York City and especially in East Harlem increased dramatically, (3) the War on Drugs escalated into a quasi-official public policy of criminalizing and incarcerating the poor and the socially marginal, and (4) drug fashion trends among inner-city youth rendered marijuana even more popular and crack and heroin even less popular among Latinos and African Americans.

Crack, cocaine, and heroin are still all sold on the block where I lived, but they are sold less visibly by a smaller number of people. It is still easy to purchase narcotics throughout East Harlem, but much of the drug dealing has moved indoors, out of sight, dealers no longer shouting out the brand names of their drugs. Most importantly, heroin and crack continue to be spurned by Latino and African-American youth who have seen the ravages those drugs committed on the older generations in their community. Nevertheless, in the U.S. inner city there remains an aging hardcore cohort of addicts. In most large cities crack is most visibly ensconced in predominantly African-American neighborhoods on the poorest blocks, often surrounding large public housing projects. In New York City, Puerto Rican households also continue to be at the epicenter of this ongoing, but now more self-contained, stationary cyclone of crack consumption.

In contrast to crack, heroin consumption has increased. Throughout most of the United States, heroin is cheaper and purer than in the early 1990s, belying any claims that the War on Drugs is winnable. Heroin's new appeal, however, is primarily among younger whites outside the ghetto for whom crack was never a drug of choice. It is not a drug of choice among Latino and African-American youth.

To summarize, both heroin and crack continue to be part of a multi-billion-dollar business that ravages inner-city families with special virulence. The younger generations of East Harlem residents, however, are more involved as sellers rather than consumers. Those Latino and African-American youth who do use crack or heroin generally try to hide the fact from their friends.

More important than changing drug-consumption fashions or the posturing of politicians over drug war campaigns has been the dramatic long-term improvement in the U.S. economy resulting in record low rates of unemployment. Somewhat to my surprise, some of the crack dealers and their families have benefited from this sustained economic growth. Slightly less than half have been allowed to enter the lower echelons of the legal labor market. For example, during the summer of 2000: one dealer was a unionized doorman, another was a home health care attendant, another was a plumber's assistant, three others were construction workers for small-time unlicensed contractors, and one was a cashier in a discount tourist souvenir store. Three or four of the dealers were still selling drugs, but most of them tended to be selling marijuana instead of crack or heroin. Three other dealers were in prison with long-term sentences and ironically were probably employed at well below minimum wage in the United States' burgeoning prison-based manufacturing sector. In short, the dramatic improvement in the U.S. economy has forced employers and unions to integrate more formally marginalized Puerto Ricans and African Americans into the labor market than was the case in the late 1980s and early 1990s when the research for this [article] was conducted. Nevertheless, even at the height of the growth in the U.S. economy in the year 2000, a large sector of street youth found themselves excluded. These marginals have become almost completely superfluous to the legal economy; they remain enmeshed in a still-lucrative drug economy, a burgeoning prison system, and a quagmire of chronic substance abuse.

From a long-term political and economic perspective, the future does not bode well for inner-city poor of New York. In the year 2000, the United States had the largest disparity between rich and poor of any industrialized nation in the world—and this gap was not decreasing.

Study and **Review** on **myanthrolab.com**

Review Questions

1. What kinds of jobs in the formal economy could Puerto Ricans living in East Harlem hold forty years ago? How did these jobs enable the men to preserve respect as it was defined in their culture?
2. What kinds of jobs are currently available to Puerto Rican men in New York's service economy? How do these jobs challenge the men's self-respect?
3. What structural changes in New York's formal economy have changed over the past forty years? How have these changes affected the lives of young men living in Spanish Harlem?
4. Why do Puerto Rican men take pride in their street identities?
5. Why does Bourgois claim that the Puerto Rican men's resistance to work in the legal economy leads to "self-destruction" and "wider community devastation"?

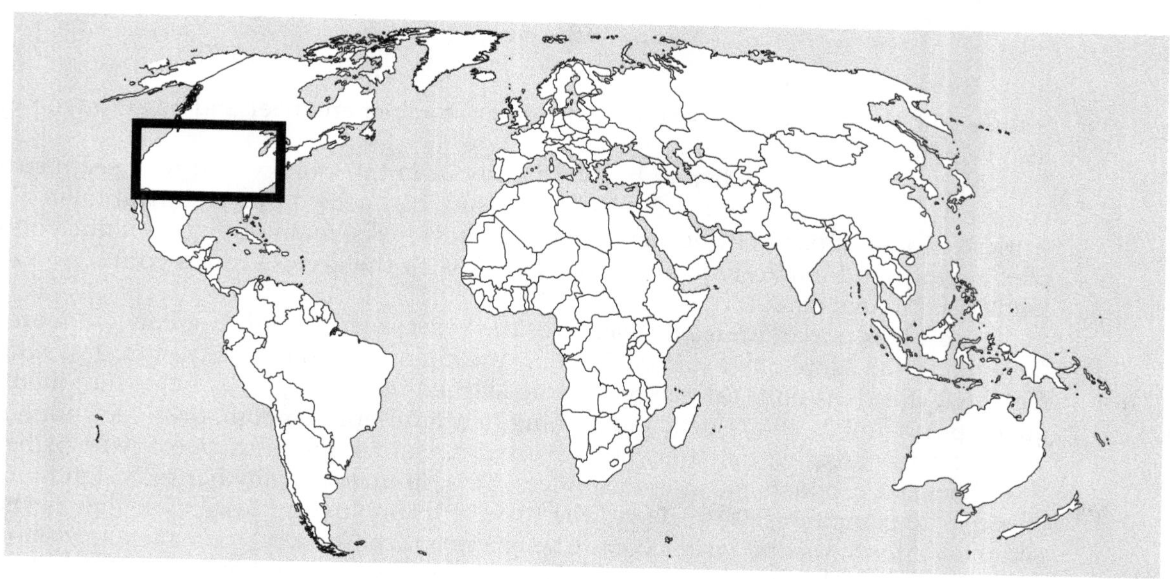

Using Anthropology

David W. McCurdy

*Some disciplines, such as economics, have an obvious relationship to the nonacademic world. Economic theory, although generated as part of basic research, may often prove useful for understanding the "real" economy. Anthropology, on the other hand, does not seem so applicable. In this article, David McCurdy discusses some of the professional applications of anthropology and argues that there is a basic anthropological perspective that can help anyone cope with the everyday world. He uses the case of a company manager to illustrate this point, asserting that ethnographic "qualitative" research is an important tool for use in the nonacademic world.**

Listen to the **Chapter Audio** on **myanthrolab.com**

In 1990 a student whom I had not seen for fifteen years stopped by my office. He had returned for his college reunion and thought it would be interesting to catch up on news about his (and my) major department, anthropology. The conversation, however, soon shifted from college events to his own life. Following graduation and a stint in the Peace Corps, he noted, he had begun to study for his license as a ship's engineer. He had attended the Maritime Academy and worked for years on freighters. He was finally granted his license, he continued, and currently held the engineer's position on a container ship that made regular trips between

Seattle and Alaska. He soon would be promoted to chief engineer and be at the top of his profession.

As he talked, he made an observation about anthropology that may seem surprising. His background in the discipline, he said, had helped him significantly in his work. He found it useful as he went about his daily tasks, maintaining his ship's complex engines and machinery, his relationships with the crew, and his contacts with land-based management.

And his is not an unusual case. Over the years, several anthropology graduates have made the same observation. One, for example, is a community organizer who feels that the cross-cultural perspective he learned in anthropology helps him mediate disputes and facilitate decision making in a multiethnic neighborhood. Another, who works as an advertising account executive, claims that anthropology helps her discover what products mean to customers. This, in turn, permits her to design more effective ad campaigns. A third says she finds anthropology an invaluable tool as she arranges interviews and writes copy. She is a producer for a metropolitan television news program. I have heard the same opinion expressed by many others, including the executive editor of a magazine for home weavers, the founder of a fencing school, a housewife, a physician, several lawyers, the kitchen manager for a catering firm, and a high school teacher.

The idea that anthropology can be useful is also supported by the experience of many new Ph.D.s. A recent survey has shown, for the first time, that more new doctorates in anthropology find employment in professional settings than in college teaching or scholarly research, and the list of nonacademic work settings revealed by the survey is remarkably broad. There is a biological anthropologist, for example, who conducts research on nutrition for a company that manufactures infant formula. A cultural anthropologist works for a major car manufacturer, researching such questions as how employees adapt to working overseas, and how they relate to conditions on domestic production lines. Others formulate government policy; plan patient care in hospitals; design overseas development projects; run famine relief programs; consult on tropical forest management; and advise on product development, advertising campaigns, and marketing strategy for corporations.

This new-found application of cultural anthropology comes as a surprise to many Americans. Unlike political science, for example, which has a name that logically connects it with practical political and legal professions, there is nothing in the term *anthropology* that tells most Americans how it might be useful.

The research subject of anthropology also makes it more difficult to comprehend. Political scientists investigate political processes, structures, and motivations. Economists look at the production and exchange of goods and services. Psychologists study differences and similarities among individuals. The research of cultural anthropologists, on the other hand, is more difficult to characterize. Instead of a focus on particular human institutions, such as politics, law, and economics, anthropologists are interested in cross-cultural differences and similarities among the world's many groups.

This interest produces a broad view of human behavior that gives anthropology its special cross-cultural flavor. It also produces a unique research strategy, called *ethnography,* that tends to be qualitative rather than quantitative. Whereas other social sciences moved toward *quantitative methods* of research designed to test theory by using survey questionnaires and structured, repetitive observations, most anthropologists conduct *qualitative research* designed to elicit the cultural knowledge of the people they seek to understand. To do this, anthropologists often live and work with their subjects, called *informants* within the discipline. The result is a highly detailed ethnographic description of the categories and rules people consult when they behave, and the meanings that things and actions have for them.

It is this ethnographic approach, or cultural perspective, that I think makes anthropology useful in such a broad range of everyday settings. I particularly find important the special anthropological understanding of the culture concept, ethnographic field methods, and social analysis. To illustrate these assertions, let us take a single case in detail, that of a manager working for a large corporation who consciously used the ethnographic approach to solve a persistent company problem.

The Problem

The manager, whom we will name Susan Stanton, works for a large multinational corporation called UTC (not the company's real name). UTC is divided into a number of parts, including divisions, subdivisions, departments, and other units designed to facilitate its highly varied business enterprises. The company is well-diversified, engaging in research, manufacturing, and customer services. In addition to serving a wide cross-section of public and private customers, it also works on a variety of government contracts for both military and nonmilitary agencies.

One of its divisions is educational. UTC has established a large number of customer outlets in cities throughout the United States, forming what it calls its "customer outlet network." They are staffed by educational personnel who are trained to offer a variety of special courses and enrichment programs. These courses and programs are marketed mainly to other businesses or to individuals who desire special training or practical information. For example, a small company might have UTC provide its employees with computer training, including instruction on hardware, programming, computer languages, and computer program applications. Another company might ask for instruction on effective management or accounting procedures. The outlets' courses for individuals include such topics as how to get a job, writing a résumé, or enlarging your own business.

To organize and manage its customer outlet network, UTC has created a special division. The division office is located at the corporate headquarters and is responsible for developing new courses, improving old ones, training customer outlet personnel, and marketing customer outlet courses, or "products" as they are called inside the company. The division also has departments that develop, produce, and distribute the special learning materials used in customer outlet courses. These include books, pamphlets, video and audio tapes and cassettes, slides, overlays, and films. These materials are stored in a warehouse and are shipped, as they are ordered, to customer outlets around the country.

It is with this division that Susan Stanton first worked as a manager. She had started her career with the company in a small section of the division that designed various program materials. She had worked her way into management, holding a series of increasingly important positions. She was then asked to take over the management of a part of the division that had the manufacture, storage, and shipment of learning materials as one of its responsibilities.

But there was a catch. She was given this new management position with instructions to solve a persistent, although vaguely defined, problem. "Improve the service," they had told her, and "get control of the warehouse inventory." In this case, "service" meant the process of filling orders sent in by customer outlets for various materials stored in the warehouse. The admonition to improve the service seemed to indicate that service was poor, but all she was told about the situation was that customer outlet personnel complained about the service; she did not know exactly why or what "poor" meant.

In addition, inventory was "out of control." Later she was to discover the extent of the difficulty.

> We had a problem with inventory. The computer would say we had two hundred of some kind of book in stock, yet it was back ordered because there was nothing on the shelf. We were supposed to have the book but physically there was nothing there. I'm going, "Uh, we have a small problem. The computer never lies, like your bank statement, so why don't we have the books?"

If inventory was difficult to manage, so were the warehouse employees. They were described by another manager as "a bunch of knuckle draggers. All they care about is getting their money. They are lazy and don't last long at the job." Strangely, the company did not view the actions of the warehouse workers as a major problem. Only later did Susan Stanton tie in poor morale in the warehouse with the other problems she had been given to solve.

Management by Defense

Although Stanton would take the ethnographic approach to management problems, that was not what many other managers did. They took a defensive stance, a position opposite to the discovery procedures of ethnography. Their major concern—like that of many people in positions of leadership and responsibility—was to protect their authority and their ability to manage and to get things done. Indeed, Stanton also shared this need. But their solution to maintaining their position was different from hers. For them, claiming ignorance and asking questions—the hallmark of the ethnographic approach—is a sign of weakness. Instead of discovering what is going on when they take on a new management assignment, they often impose new work rules and procedures. Employees learn to fear the arrival of new managers because their appearance usually means a host of new, unrealistic demands. They respond by hiding what they actually do, withholding information that would be useful to the manager. Usually, everyone's performance suffers.

Poor performance leads to elaborate excuses as managers attempt to blame the troubles on others. Stanton described this tendency.

> When I came into the new job, this other manager said, "Guess what? You have got a warehouse. You are now the proud owner of a forklift and a bunch of knuckle draggers." And I thought, management's perception of those people is very low. They are treating them as dispensable, that you can't do anything with them. They say the workers don't have any career motives. They don't care if they do a good job. You have to force them to do anything. You can't motivate them. It's only a warehouse, other managers were saying. You can't really do that much about the problems there so why don't you just sort of try to keep it under control.

Other managers diminished the importance of the problem itself. It was not "poor service" that was the trouble. The warehouse was doing the best it could with what it had. It was just that the customers—the staff at the customer outlets—were complainers. As Susan Stanton noted:

> The people providing the service thought that outlet staff were complainers. They said, "Staff complain about everything. But it can't be that way. We have checked it all out and it isn't that bad."

Making excuses and blaming others lead to low morale and a depressed self-image. Problems essentially are pushed aside in favor of a "let's just get by" philosophy.

Ethnographic Management

By contrast, managers take the offensive when they use ethnographic techniques. That is what Stanton did when she assumed her new managerial assignment over the learning materials manufacturing and distribution system. To understand what the ethnographic approach means, however, we must first look briefly at what anthropologists do when they conduct ethnographic field research. Our discussion necessarily involves a look at the concepts of culture and microculture as well as ethnography. For as we will shortly point out, companies have cultures of their own, a point that has recently received national attention; but more important for the problem we are describing here, companies are normally divided into subgroups, each with its own microculture. It is these cultures and microcultures that anthropologically trained managers can study ethnographically, just as fieldworkers might investigate the culture of a !Kung band living in the Kalahari Desert of West Africa or the Gypsies living in San Francisco.

Ethnography refers to the process of discovering and describing culture, so it is important to discuss this general and often elusive concept. There are numerous definitions of culture, each stressing particular sets of attributes. The definition we employ here is especially appropriate for ethnographic fieldwork. We may define culture as the acquired knowledge that people use to generate behavior and interpret experience. In growing up, one learns a system of cultural knowledge appropriate to the group. For example, an American child learns to chew with a closed mouth because that is the cultural rule. The child's parents interpret open-mouthed chewing as an infraction and tell the child to chew "properly." A person uses such cultural knowledge throughout life to guide actions and to give meaning to surroundings.

Because culture is learned, and because people can easily generate new cultural knowledge as they adapt to other people and things, human behavior and perceptions can vary dramatically from one group to another. In parts of India, for example, children learn to chew "properly" with their mouths open. Their cultural worlds are quite different from the ones found in the United States.

Cultures are associated with groups of people. Traditionally, anthropologists associated culture with relatively distinctive ethnic groups. *Culture* referred to the whole life-way of a society, and particular cultures could be named. Anthropologists talked of German culture, Ibo culture, and Bhil culture. Culture was everything that was distinctive about the group.

Culture is still applied in this manner today, but with the advent of complex societies and a growing interest among anthropologists in understanding them, the culture concept has also been used in a more limited way. Complex societies such as our own are composed of thousands of groups. Members of these groups usually share the national culture, including a language and a huge inventory of knowledge for doing things, but the groups themselves have specific cultures of their own. For example, if you were to walk into the regional office of a stock brokerage firm, you would hear the people there talking an apparently foreign language. You might stand in the "bull pen," listen to brokers make "cold calls," "sell short," "negotiate a waffle," or get ready to go to a "dog and pony show." The fact that an event such as this feels strange when you first encounter them is strong evidence to support the notion that you don't yet know the culture that organizes them. We call such specialized groups *microcultures*.

We are surrounded by microcultures, participating in a few, encountering many others. Our family has a microculture. So may our neighborhood, our college, and even our dormitory floor. The waitress who serves us lunch at the corner restaurant shares a culture with her co-workers. So do bank tellers at our local savings and loan. Kin, occupational groups, and recreational associations each tend to display special microcultures. Such cultures can be, and now often are, studied by anthropologists interested in understanding life in complex American society.

The concept of microculture is essential to Susan Stanton as she begins to attack management problems at UTC because she assumes that conflict between different microcultural groups is most likely at the bottom of the difficulty. One microculture she could focus on is UTC company culture. She knows, for example, that there are a variety of rules and expectations—written and unwritten—for how things should be done at the company. She must dress in her "corporates," for example, consisting of a neutral-colored suit, stockings, and conservative shoes. UTC also espouses values about the way employees should be treated, how people are supposed to feel about company products, and a variety of other things that set that particular organization apart from other businesses.

But the specific problems that afflicted the departments under Stanton's jurisdiction had little to do with UTC's corporate culture. They seemed rather to be the result of misunderstanding and misconnection between two units, the warehouse and the customer outlets. Each had its own microculture. Each could be investigated to discover any information that might lead to a solution of the problems she had been given.

Such investigation would depend on the extent of Stanton's ethnographic training. As an undergraduate in college, she had learned how to conduct ethnographic interviews, observe behavior, and analyze and interpret data. She was not a professional anthropologist, but she felt she was a good enough ethnographer to discover some relevant aspects of microcultures at UTC.

Ethnography is the process of discovering and describing a culture. For example, an anthropologist who travels to India to conduct a study of village culture will use ethnographic techniques. The anthropologist will move into a community, occupy a house, watch people's daily routines, attend rituals, and spend hours interviewing informants. The goal is to discover a detailed picture of what is going on by seeing village culture through the eyes of informants. The anthropologist wants the insider's perspective. Villagers become teachers, patiently explaining different aspects of their culture, praising the anthropologist for acting correctly and appearing to understand, laughing when the anthropologist makes mistakes or seems confused. When the anthropologist knows what to do and can explain in local terms what is going on or what is likely to happen, real progress has been made. The clearest evidence of such progress is when informants say, "You are almost human now," or "You are beginning to talk just like us."

The greatest enemy of good ethnography is the preconceived notion. Anthropologists do not conduct ethnographic research by telling informants what they are like based on earlier views of them. They teach the anthropologist how to see their world: the anthropologist does not tell them what their world should really be like. All too often in business, a new manager will take over a department and begin to impose changes on its personnel to fit a preconceived perception of them. The fact that the manager's efforts are likely to fail makes sense in light of this ignorance. The manager doesn't know the microculture. Nor has he or she asked employees about it.

But can a corporate manager really do ethnography? After all, managers have positions of authority to maintain, as we noted earlier. It is all right for professional anthropologists to enter the field and act ignorant; they don't have a position to maintain and they don't have to continue to live with their informants. The key to the problem appears to be the "grace period." Most managers are given one by their employees when they are new on the job. A new manager cannot be expected to know everything. It is permissible to ask basic questions. The grace period may last only a month or two, but it is usually long enough to find out valuable information.

This is the opportunity that Susan Stanton saw as she assumed direction of the warehouse distribution system. As she described it:

> I could use the first month, actually the first six weeks, to find out what was going on, to act dumb and find out what people actually did and why. I talked to end customers. I talked to salespeople, people who were trying to sell things to help customer outlets with their needs. I talked to coordinators at headquarters staff who were trying to help all these customer outlets do their jobs and listened to what kinds of complaints they had heard. I talked to the customer outlet people and the guys in the warehouse. I had this six-week grace period where I could go in and say, "I don't know anything about this. If you were in my position, what would you do, or what would make the biggest difference, and why would it make a difference?" You want to find out what the world they are operating in is like. What do they value? And people were excited because I was asking and listening and, by God, intending to do something about it instead of just disappearing again.

As we shall see shortly, Stanton's approach to the problem worked. But it also resulted in an unexpected bonus. Her ethnographic approach symbolized unexpected interest and concern to her employees. That, combined with realistic management, gave her a position of respect and authority. Their feelings for her were expressed by one warehouse worker when he said:

> When she [Susan] was going to be transferred to another job, we gave her a party. We took her to this country-and-western place and we all got to dance with the boss. We told her that she was the first manager who ever tried to understand what it was like to work in the warehouse. We thought she would come in like the other managers and make a lot of changes that didn't make sense. But she didn't. She made it work better for us.

Problems and Causes

An immediate benefit of her ethnographic inquiry was a much clearer view of what poor service meant to customer outlet personnel. Stanton discovered that learning materials, such as books and cassettes, took too long to arrive after they were ordered.

Worse, material did not arrive in the correct quantities. Sometimes there would be too many items, but more often there were too few, a particularly galling discrepancy since customer outlets were charged for what they ordered, not what they received. Books also arrived in poor condition, their covers ripped or scratched, edges frayed, and ends gouged and dented. This, too, bothered customer outlet staff because they were often visited by potential customers who were not impressed by the poor condition of their supplies. Shortages and scruffy books did nothing to retain regular customers either.

The causes of these problems and the difficulties with warehouse inventory also emerged from ethnographic inquiry. Stanton discovered, for example, that most customer outlets operated in large cities, where often they were housed in tall buildings. Materials shipped to their office address often ended up sitting in ground-level lobbies, because few of the buildings had receiving docks or facilities. Books and other items also arrived in large boxes, weighing up to a hundred pounds. Outlet staff, most of whom were women, had to go down to the lobby, open those boxes that were too heavy for them to carry, and haul armloads of supplies up the elevator to the office. Not only was this time-consuming, but customer outlet staff felt it was beneath their dignity to do such work. They were educated specialists, after all.

The poor condition of the books was also readily explained. By packing items loosely in such large boxes, warehouse workers ensured trouble in transit. Books rattled around with ease, smashing into each other and the side of the box. The result was torn covers and frayed edges. Clearly no one had designed the packing and shipping process with customer outlet staff in mind.

The process, of course, originated in the central warehouse, and here as well, ethnographic data yielded interesting information about the causes of the problem. Stanton learned, for example, how materials were stored in loose stacks on the warehouse shelves. When orders arrived at the warehouse, usually through the mail, they were placed in a pile and filled in turn (although there were times when special preference was given to some customer outlets). A warehouse employee filled an order by first checking it against the stock recorded by the computer, then going to the appropriate shelves and picking the items by hand. Items were packed in the large boxes and addressed to customer outlets. With the order complete, the employee was supposed to enter the number of items picked and shipped in the computer so that inventory would be up to date.

But, Stanton discovered, workers in the warehouse were under pressure to work quickly. They often fell behind because materials the computer said were in stock were not there, and because picking by hand took so long. Their solution to the problem of speed resulted in a procedure that even further confused company records.

> Most of the people in the warehouse didn't try to count well. People were looking at the books on the shelves and were going, "Eh, that looks like the right number. You want ten? Gee, that looks like about ten." Most of the time the numbers they shipped were wrong.

The causes of inaccurate amounts in shipping were thus revealed. Later, Stanton discovered that books also disappeared in customer outlet building lobbies. While staff members carried some of the materials upstairs, people passing by the open boxes helped themselves.

Other problems with inventory also became clear. UTC employees, who sometimes walked through the warehouse, would often pick up interesting materials from the loosely stacked shelves. More important, rushed workers often neglected to update records in the computer.

The Shrink-Wrap Solution

The detailed discovery of the nature and causes of service and inventory problems suggested a relatively painless solution to Stanton. If she had taken a defensive management position and failed to learn the insider's point of view, she might have resorted to more usual remedies that were impractical and unworkable. Worker retraining is a common answer to corporate difficulties, but it is difficult to accomplish and often fails. Pay incentives, punishments, and motivation enhancements such as prizes and quotas are also frequently tried. But they tend not to work because they don't address fundamental causes.

Shrink-wrapping books and other materials did. Shrink-wrapping is a packaging method in which clear plastic sheeting is placed around items to be packaged, then through a rapid heating and cooling process, shrunk into a tight covering. The plastic molds itself like a tight skin around the things it contains, preventing any internal movement or external contamination. Stanton described her decision.

> I decided to have the books shrink-wrapped. For a few cents more, before the books ever arrived in the warehouse, I had them shrink-wrapped in quantities of five and ten. I made it part of the contract with the people who produced the books for us.

On the first day that shrink-wrapped books arrived at the warehouse, Stanton discovered that they were immediately unwrapped by workers who thought a new impediment had been placed in their way. But the positive effect of shrink-wrapping soon became apparent. For example, most customer outlets ordered books in units of fives and tens. Warehouse personnel could now easily count out orders in fives and tens, instead of having to count each book or estimate numbers in piles. Suddenly, orders filled at the warehouse contained the correct number of items.

Employees were also able to work more quickly, since they no longer had to count each book. Orders were filled faster, the customer outlet staff was pleased, and warehouse employees no longer felt the pressure of time so intensely. Shrink-wrapped materials also traveled more securely. Books, protected by their plastic covering, arrived in good condition, again delighting the personnel at customer outlets.

Stanton also changed the way materials were shipped, based on what she had learned from talking to employees. She limited the maximum size of shipments to twenty-five pounds by using smaller boxes. She also had packages marked "inside delivery" so that deliverymen would carry the materials directly to the customer outlet offices. If they failed to do so, boxes were light enough to carry upstairs. No longer would items be lost in skyscraper lobbies.

Inventory control became more effective. Because they could package and ship materials more quickly, the workers in the warehouse had enough time to enter the size and nature of shipments in the computer. Other UTC employees no longer walked off with books from the warehouse, because the shrink-wrapped bundles were larger and more conspicuous, and because taking five or ten books is more like stealing than "borrowing" one.

Finally, the improved service dramatically changed morale in the division. Customer outlet staff members, with their new and improved service, felt that finally someone had cared about them. They were more positive and they let people at corporate headquarters know about their feelings. "What's happening down there?" they asked. "The guys in the warehouse must be taking vitamins."

Morale soared in the warehouse. For the first time, other people liked the service workers there provided. Turnover decreased as pride in their work rose. They began to care more about the job, working faster with greater care. Managers who had previously given up on the "knuckle draggers" now asked openly about what had got into them.

Stanton believes the ethnographic approach is the key. She has managers who work for her read anthropology, especially books on ethnography, and she insists that they "find out what is going on."

Conclusion

Anthropology is, before all, an academic discipline with a strong emphasis on scholarship and basic research. But, as we have also seen, anthropology is a discipline that contains several intellectual tools—the concept of culture, the ethnographic approach to fieldwork, a cross-cultural perspective, a holistic view of human behavior—that make it useful in a broad range of nonacademic settings. In particular, it is the ability to do qualitative research that makes anthropologists successful in the professional world.

A few years ago an anthropologist consultant was asked by a utility company to answer a puzzling question: Why were its suburban customers, whose questionnaire responses indicated an attempt at conservation, failing to reduce their consumption of natural gas? To answer the question, the anthropologist conducted ethnographic interviews with members of several families, listening as they told him about how warm they liked their houses and how they set the heat throughout the day. He also received permission to install several video cameras aimed at thermostats in private houses. When the results were in, the answer to the question was deceptively simple: Fathers fill out questionnaires and turn down thermostats; wives, children, and cleaning workers, all of whom, in this case, spent time in the houses when fathers were absent, turn them up. Conservation, the anthropologist concluded, would have to involve family decisions, not just admonitions to save gas.

Over the past two or three years, anthropology's usefulness in the world of work has been discovered by the United States press. For example, *U.S. News and World Report* carried a story in 1998 entitled "Into the Wild Unknown of Workplace Culture: Anthropologists Revitalize Their Discipline," which traced changing trends in academic anthropology and highlighted the growth of the discipline's penetration of the business world.[1] Included in the article were examples of useful ethnography, such as the discovery by one anthropologist consultant that rank-and-file union members were upset with shop stewards because the latter spent more time recruiting new members than responding to grievances. In another instance, the article reported on the work of anthropologist Ken Erickson. Hired to find out why immigrant meatpackers had launched a wildcat strike, he was able to show that the workers struck because they felt their supervisors treated them as unskilled laborers, not because there was a language problem, as proposed by management. The workers had developed elaborate strategies to work quickly, effectively, and safely that were ignored or unknown to their supervisors.

[1]Brendan I. Koerner, "Into the Wild Unknown of Workplace Culture: Anthropologists Revitalize Their Discipline," *U.S. News & World Report*, August 10, 1998, p. 56.

In 1999, *USA Today* carried a story that further emphasized anthropology's usefulness. Entitled "Hot Asset in Corporate: Anthropology Degrees," the article began with, "Don't throw away the MBA degree yet. But as companies go global and crave leaders for a diverse workforce, a new hot degree is emerging for aspiring executives: anthropology."[2] The piece carried numerous examples—the hiring of anthropologist Steve Barnett as a vice president at Citicorp following his discovery of the early warning signs that identify people who do not pay credit card bills; the case of Hallmark, which sent anthropologists into immigrant homes to discover how holidays and birthdays are celebrated so that the company could design appropriate cards for such occasions; the example of a marketing consultant firm that sent anthropologists into bathrooms to watch how women shave their legs, and in the process, to discover what women want in a razor.

The article also listed executives who stressed how important their anthropology degree has been for their business successes. Motorola corporate lawyer Robert Faulkner says that the anthropology degree he received before going to law school has become increasingly valuable in his management job. Warned by his father that most problems are people problems, Michael Koss, CEO of the Koss headphone company, is another example. He received his anthropology degree from Beloit College. Katherine Burr, CEO of The Hanseatic Group, has an MA in anthropology and was quoted as saying, "My competitive edge came completely out of anthropology. The world is so unknown, changes so rapidly. Preconceptions can kill you." The article concluded with the observations of Ken Erickson of the Center for Ethnographic Research. "It takes trained observation. Observation is what anthropologists are trained to do."

In short, cultural anthropology has entered the world of business over the past twenty years. I argue that the key to its special utility and value in the commercial world is the ethnographic approach. Anthropologists have this ethnographic field experience and a sense of how social systems work and how people use their cultural knowledge. They have the special background, originally developed to discover and describe the cultural knowledge and behavior of unknown societies, needed to, in the words of Susan Stanton, "find out what is going on."

Study and **Review** on **myanthrolab.com**

Review Questions

1. What kinds of jobs do professional anthropologists do?
2. What is special about anthropology that makes fundamental knowledge of it valuable to some jobs?
3. What is meant by *qualitative research?* Why is such research valuable to business and government?
4. What difficulties did the company manager described in this article face? What solutions did she invent to deal with them? How did her knowledge of anthropology help her with this problem?
5. Why is ethnography useful in everyday life? Can you think of situations in which you could use ethnographic research?

[2]Del Jones, "Hot Asset in Corporate: Anthropology Degrees," *USA Today,* February 18, 1999, section B, p. 1.

Index